COUNTER-TERRORISM for EMERGENCY RESPONDERS

Second Edition

Robert Burke

COUNTER-TERRORISM for EMERGENCY RESPONDERS

Second Edition

Taylor & Francis
Taylor & Francis Group
Boca Raton London New York

CRC is an imprint of the Taylor & Francis Group,
an informa business

Published in 2007 by
CRC Press
Taylor & Francis Group
6000 Broken Sound Parkway NW, Suite 300
Boca Raton, FL 33487-2742

International Standard Book Number-10: 0-8493-9923-8 (Hardcover)
International Standard Book Number-13: 978-0-8493-9923-7 (Hardcover)
Library of Congress Card Number 2006002466

Library of Congress Cataloging-in-Publication Data

Burke, Robert (Robert A.)
    Counter-terrorism for emergency responders / Robert Burke.-- 2nd ed.
        p. cm.
    Includes bibliographical references and index.
    ISBN-13: 978-0-8493-9923-7 (hardcover : alk. paper)
    ISBN-10: 0-8493-9923-8 (hardcover : alk. paper)
    1. Terrorism--Prevention. 2. Emergencies. I. Title.

HV6431.B866 2006
363.325'7--dc22   2006002466

Taylor & Francis Group
is the Academic Division of Informa plc.

Visit the Taylor & Francis Web site at
http://www.taylorandfrancis.com

and the CRC Press Web site at
http://www.crcpress.com

Dedication

To Kimberly, My Daughter

It seems like only yesterday that I was at the hospital with your mother, watching as you were born into a new world. Watching you grow from a baby into a young woman. Getting married, having children of your own, becoming the wonderful mother you are to my grandchildren. While I was not always there in person, you have always been and will always be in my mind and in my heart. It is with great pride in you for all that you have accomplished in life and my great love for you that I dedicate this book to you.

Preface

Terrorism has been a fact of life in many countries around the world, such as Northern Ireland, England, Israel, and Japan. It is, however, no longer a problem that just happens somewhere else. Bombings at the World Trade Center, the Oklahoma City Federal Building, the 1996 Atlanta Olympics, and in many other locations throughout the U.S. brought the idea of terrorism home. Since September 11, 2001, we know that the U.S. is a high priority target on the radar of terrorist organizations worldwide. It is not just foreign countries and factions that sponsor terrorism, but domestic groups as well, including militia, antigovernment, antiabortion, and animal rights organizations, to mention a few. While bombings have been the terrorist weapons of choice in the past, chemical and biological agents will likely be the weapons of choice in the future. Biological agents, in particular, are cheap and easy to make without detection. They have often been referred to as the "poor man's atom bomb." A very small amount of a chemical or biological agent has the potential to kill thousands of people if disseminated in an effective manner, and there may be little we can do to prevent its rapid spread. The outcome of a terrorist attack may well depend on how thoroughly emergency responders at all levels plan and train to deal with terrorist events.

The underlying mission of this book is to present the idea to emergency responders that chemical, biological, nuclear, explosive, and incendiary agents are hazardous materials. Responding to terrorist incidents is not unlike responding to hazardous materials releases. In fact, a terrorist response is a combination of a mass casualty incident, technical rescue incident, hazardous materials incident, and crime scene rolled into one. Many warfare and terrorist agents are common industrial chemicals and explosives. Acts of terrorism are hazardous materials incidents. To quote Chicago Fire Department deputy commissioner and former hazardous materials team commander Gene Ryan, chemical and biological terrorist agents are "hazmats with an attitude." Responders will still need to exercise recognition and identification procedures, enforce scene security, establish isolation zones and perimeters, wear proper protective equipment, and implement decontamination procedures. When dealing with acts of terrorism, there are new recognition and identification tools, advanced equipment technologies, and additional players involved on the scene of an incident. However, it is still a hazardous materials response at the local level. If emergency responders are prepared to deal with releases of hazardous materials, they can also deal effectively with chemical and biological agents. What will be required is additional planning, procedures, equipment, and training.

Sadly, however, some emergency response organizations and individual personnel are not ready to deal with "ordinary" hazardous materials, let alone chemical and biological agents. Response personnel, in some cases, will take the same passive attitude they did with hazardous materials in the beginning. A turning point occurred when the Emergency Planning and Community Right-To-Know Act (EPCRA) was passed by Congress in 1986. The legislation led to training competencies and response procedures for hazardous materials incidents. Some response organizations still said "it can't happen here" and did not prepare.

Chances are that chemical and biological agent attacks, bombings, nuclear devices, and incendiary device threats will not happen in every community across the country; however, no one knows where the attack might occur. The numbers of attacks, when and if they occur, are likely to be small. But the potential loss of life and disruption of lifestyle as we now know it is too great to put our heads in the sand and pretend it cannot happen to us. We must all prepare for the worst and hope for the best.

Every person in this country who responds to emergencies, whether he or she is a fire, EMS, police, or other emergency professional, should be aware of the basic tools needed to recognize and safely respond to acts of terrorism. This book is written to provide concise information for emergency responders who might be called upon to confront explosive, chemical, nuclear, biological, or incendiary acts of terrorism. Specific procedures are necessary to properly respond to acts of terrorism.

Terrorism is another type of hazardous materials incident — with some special circumstances. How well prepared are you to deal with terrorism?

Acknowledgments

Not long ago, while I was teaching at the National Fire Academy in Emmitsburg, Maryland, I happened to run into Jan Kuczma — an old friend and respected mentor, who has since retired as the chief of the Technical Programs Branch at the Academy. He was there in various positions since its inception. Over the years, he has provided me with guidance, friendship, and fatherly advice, getting me over many "bumps" in my personal life and career. He doesn't always say a lot, but he is a good listener, always equipped with wisdom, and gets right to the point. This time, he said he had the opportunity to "view" my first book, *Hazardous Materials Chemistry for Emergency Responders*. His advice was to be sure and followup with another book, perhaps one dealing with terrorism. Frankly, I had thought of the idea prior to that but had not been motivated to act any further. By this time, I had pretty much abandoned the thought. Well, once again, Jan lit the fire that motivated me to take action on a book concerning terrorism. This is the second edition of that first finished project. Its content should not reflect on Jan in any way, shape, or form, but once again, without Jan's guidance, it very likely would not have happened. For that reason and all of the other help and friendship over the years in my times of need, Jan, I thank you. Jan Kuczma is one of the most caring and genuine persons I have ever had the pleasure to know. He cares about people, he cares about the National Fire Academy and its programs, and he is one of the best friends the American fire service has had at the Emmitsburg facility.

About the Author

Robert A. Burke was born in Beatrice, Nebraska, and raised in Lincoln, Nebraska, and Dundee, Illinois. He currently lives in Glen Burnie, Maryland, and is the fire marshal at the University of Maryland in Baltimore. He is married to his lovely wife, Clare, and has 10 children, 14 grandchildren, and 1 great grandchild. Burke earned an A.A. in fire protection technology from Catonsville Community College and a B.S. in fire science from the University of Maryland. He also completed graduate work in public administration at the University of Baltimore. He is a graduate of numerous classes at the National Fire Academy (NFA) in Emmitsburg, Maryland; the Emergency Management Institute (EMI), also in Emmitsburg; the Center for Domestic Preparedness (CDP) in Anniston, Alabama; Oklahoma State University Fire Service Training; and Maryland Fire and Rescue Institute (MFRI). Burke is a certified fire protection specialist (CFPS), certified fire investigator, certified fire inspector, certified hazardous materials technician, certified fire instructor III, and a certified hazardous materials incident commander.

Burke has over 26 years of experience in emergency services as a career and volunteer firefighter and has served as an assistant fire chief for the Verdigris Fire Protection District in Claremore, Oklahoma; deputy state fire marshal in the State of Nebraska; a private fire protection and hazardous materials consultant in Maryland; and exercise and training officer for the Chemical Stockpile Emergency Preparedness Program (CSEPP) at the Maryland Emergency Management Agency. He is currently the fire marshal for the University of Maryland, Baltimore campus.

Burke is an adjunct instructor at the National Fire Academy, where he teaches Emergency Response to Terrorism: Basic Concepts, Tactical Considerations: Hazardous Materials, Tactical Considerations Company Officer, and other hazardous materials courses. He is also an adjunct instructor for the Community College of Baltimore County Catonsville campus. Burke is a contributing editor for *Firehouse* magazine and has had numerous articles published in *Firehouse*, *Fire Chief*, and *Fire Engineering* magazines. He has developed several training programs, including the *2004 Emergency Response Guidebook,* Dispatcher and 911 Operator Hazmat and Terrorism Awareness, Hazardous Materials Operations, Hazardous Materials and Terrorism Awareness for Law Enforcement, WMD Emergency Response Guide Book, Physical and Chemical Characteristics of Chemical and Biological Terrorist Agents, Understanding Anhydrous Ammonia, Understanding Liquified Petroleum Gases, Understanding Cryogenic Liquids, Chemistry of Hazardous Materials and Chemistry of Hazardous Materials Refresher and Bloodborne Pathogens for Emergency Services and Law Enforcement. He has conducted training classes for Louisiana State University Firemen's Training School in Baton Rouge; the New York State Academy of Fire Science in Montour Falls; the Michigan State Police Academy in East Lansing; the Delaware County Emergency Services Training Center outside Philadelphia; the Pennsylvania State Fire Academy in Lewistown; the Motorola Corporation in Buffalo, New York; the Massachusetts Regional Hazardous Materials Team outside Boston; the Honolulu Fire Department Training Academy; the Anchorage, Alaska, Fire Department Training Academy; the National Fire Academy in Emmitsburg, Maryland; and the Maryland Fire and Rescue Institute. Burke is also the author of the book *Hazardous Materials Chemistry for Emergency Responders* published by CRC/Lewis Publishers in 1997, with a second edition published in 2003. He has given presentations at the Firehouse Expo in Baltimore; the International Hazardous Materials Spills Conference in New Orleans; the Illinois State Association of Fire Protection Districts in Springfield; Region III EPA Conference in Norfolk, Virginia; HazMat 2000 in Las Vegas; and at various other state and local functions.

In 1997, Burke was commissioned as a Kentucky Colonel by the Governor of Kentucky, the highest honor given by the state, for his Train-the-Trainer program about the *1996 North American Emergency Response Guidebook.* Using the program he developed, he trained over 100 instructors in two courses held in Louisville and Lexington, Kentucky. The Governor of Maryland awarded Burke a "Governor's Citation" in 1997 for his work with the Chemical Stockpile Preparedness Program (CSEPP) in Maryland. Once again, in 1998, Burke received a "Governor's Citation" for fire prevention work at the University of Maryland, improving life safety for the staff, students, and faculty. He is also an Honorary Citizen of the State of Oklahoma and an admiral in the Great Navy of the State of Nebraska.

Contents

8   Monitoring and Detection Equipment for Terrorist Agents   265

9   Personal Protective Equipment (PPE) and Decontamination for Terrorist Agents   299

10   Response Tactics for Terrorism: "The Rules Have Changed"   335

11   Terrorism Resources and Response Training   397

Introduction: It's Just Another Hazardous Materials Incident!

1

Several tragic events in the mid-1990s caused emergency responders to stop, pause, and consider both their luck and preparedness. Multiple terrorist attacks using the nerve agent sarin in Tokyo/Yokohama, Japan; explosions at the World Trade Center in New York City; the bombing of the Alfred Murrah Federal Building in Oklahoma City, Oklahoma; bombings at the Olympics, an abortion clinic, and at a gay night club in Atlanta, Georgia; and an attack on a family planning clinic in Birmingham, Alabama made the threat all too clear. Terrorism was not just something that occurred somewhere else, it was happening right here in the U.S. We as emergency responders were not prepared to deal with acts of terrorism. Federal agencies such as the Federal Emergency Management Agency (FEMA), the National Fire Academy (NFA), and the U.S. Justice Department developed training programs for emergency responders to prepare them for response to acts of terrorism. But, as with any new preparedness concept, there were those who thought it couldn't happen in their communities and felt that preparing for something that was unlikely to occur was not necessary (ostrich syndrome). Then came the terrorist attacks of September 11, 2001 — another "day that will live in infamy." Al Qaeda-backed terrorists hijacked four commercial aircrafts (Boeing 757s and 767s) and crashed two of them into the World Trade Center in New York City, killing 157 aboard the aircraft and hundreds on the ground, including 343 firefighters, 21 police officers, and 37 Port Authority police officers. Another flight was crashed into the Pentagon in Washington, D.C., killing 64 on board and 125 on the ground at the Pentagon. A fourth plane destined for the U.S. Capitol Building in Washington, D.C. crashed into a field in Pennsylvania after passengers tried to take back the plane, killing all 45 on board. The crashes into the World Trade Center led to the total collapse of both buildings and several surrounding buildings. The crash into the Pentagon resulted in a partial collapse of that building. Total fatalities as of

September 2005 include: confirmed dead — 2,948, reported dead — 24, reported missing — 24, total — 2,996. Terrorists had declared war on America. While the first battles of the war were fought in big cities, we need to be careful not to think that it only happens in some other city, not our own — or it happens in the big cities, not in rural America. Terrorism can happen anywhere at anytime, and there is little we can do to prevent it. No place is immune. As security increases in major population areas, the terrorists will likely turn to soft targets in other places they feel are vulnerable, like smaller cities and rural America.

Remember the mailbox bombings in the Midwest in 2002 where John Helder planted 18 pipe bombs in mailboxes in five states? That event, even though a criminal act, created terror in rural America. Think about it, the mailbox is a very important part of daily life in most parts of America. But in rural America it is the lifeline to the outside world. What if people were afraid to go to the mailbox and get their mail? After all, the goal of the terrorist is to cause fear among the population and distrust in government's ability to protect its citizens. Then there were the snipers in Maryland, Virginia, and Ohio, whose actions resulted in fear among people living in the affected areas. Those events were also criminal acts and not terrorism, but what if terrorists used those tactics? What if it happened in dozens of states or cities? What if it happened during major events such as the Super Bowl, NCAA Basketball Tournament, state fairs, NASCAR races? While we may not be able to do anything to stop terrorism, we can certainly prepare to handle the aftermath in a safe and appropriate manner. We are all at the mercy of radical groups or individuals who have extreme political or religious agendas, personal grievances, or psychological disturbances. Terrorists strongly believe in their causes. Many believe they are patriots. Not unlike Paul Revere, Ben Franklin, George Washington, and others in the American Revolution. Wasn't the Boston Tea Party really an act of terrorism? It really depends on your mindset at the time you commit the act. To some you are a patriot or a religious or political hero; to others you are a terrorist.

Philip Stern, a terrorism expert with The Fairfax Group, a New York-based corporate security firm, said, "As an open society and a democracy, this country is particularly vulnerable. We have free passage coast to coast, anyone can apply for a visa to visit, and the population is both enormous and diversified." Our borders are virtually unprotected, with Canada and Mexico offering potential routes for terrorists who might want to cross over. After all, thousands of illegal immigrants cross over the virtually unprotected borders each year. According to Stern, "Such factors provide cover to anyone who may wish to commit an act of violence against this country. Those kinds of people may be resentful economic 'have-nots' or even religious fundamentalist extremists who see Western culture, values, and power as oppression.

At the same time, we have the Montana Freemen, the Branch Davidians, and the people who bomb our churches — all symptomatic of disenchantment with society among people who are willing to use violence." Abortion clinics, family planning clinics, fur stores, research facilities that use animals, and farms that raise them for their fur have been targets for terrorists in this country. Thousands of bombings occur in this country every year, though on a fairly small scale compared to the bombings in Oklahoma City and at the World Trade Center in New York City.

No one could have ever imagined the events that took place on September 11, 2001. Most people thought hijackings on U.S. soil had ended in the 1970s with the resulting increase in security measures at airports. For the first time ever America was attacked from the air at home. Terrorists executed a well-planned attack against the Twin Towers of New York City's World Trade Center and the Pentagon with our own commercial airliners. In fact the terrorists were taught to fly those planes at our own training facilities in this country! This attack created the largest single loss-of-life event for emergency responders that has ever occurred in this country. I am sure no one ever dreamed we could lose so many emergency responders in one incident. In addition, 2749 civilians were killed. I will never forget the report on the radio of a plane crashing into the World Trade Center in New York City. Terrorism was not my first thought; to me it was an accident, and I wanted to get more information. It was not the first time planes had flown into buildings by accident. I never considered the possibility of a hijacking, as I thought our airports were secure; after all, there hadn't been any hijackings in the U.S. since the 1970s. My first move was to turn on the television in the training room at work. There it was, the image of the North Tower of the World Trade Center burning and a huge cloud of smoke rising above the Twin Towers. The sight was almost beyond belief. No one knew exactly what had happened at that point. As I stood watching the events unfold for several minutes, I saw, live, the second plane crash into the South Tower. I could not believe what I was seeing; it was like something out of a Hollywood movie, not something happening live in New York City. It was surreal, yet I knew then it was no accident. The events of September 11, 2001, were mind boggling as they unfolded. Many things were so hard to understand or comprehend. I had not felt such uncertainty since growing up as a child during the Cold War and, in particular, the Cuban Missile Crisis in 1962. Could this really be happening here? People (approximately 200) were jumping from the burning towers on live television; the enormity of the emergency response efforts was even taxing the resources of the largest fire department in the U.S. Once again I watched, live, as the South Tower collapsed, followed by the North Tower a short time later. This could not be happening, I thought. Not even al Qaeda could have hoped for more. There had to be hundreds of victims and emer-

Figure 1.1 **(See color insert following page 236.)** Smoke billows from one of the towers of the World Trade Center, and flames and debris explode from the second tower. (Source: AP/Worldwide Photos. Used with permission.)

gency responders inside the building when it collapsed, and many were going to be killed. The events were becoming too much to comprehend. Huge clouds of smoke and debris rolling through the streets, people running, seeking what shelter they could find. It all happened so fast. As bad as the crashes and fires were, the thought of collapse had never entered my mind. There had never been collapses of buildings that size, or even close. What a horrible twist to an already enormous tragedy. Reports started coming in from Washington of a crash at the Pentagon. That was pretty close to home — would Baltimore be next? Rumors were rampant: car bombings in Washington, D.C., more planes headed for Washington. Where was the government? How could they let this happen? Where was the military? All of these questions were going through my mind as the events unfolded. It turns out there were no antiaircraft capabilities in Washington, D.C. — not even to defend our nation's capital. Fighter jets had to be dispatched from southeast Virginia. Then there were the thoughts of rescue efforts. Surely there were victims alive in the rubble. We had to get them out — firefighters, police officers, civilians — someone had to rescue them. But as it turned out there wasn't anyone alive to be rescued; ambulances waited to transport victims and triage areas were set up, but none were needed. The force of the collapse, the weight of the debris, everyone was gone. Rescue turned into months of body recovery and years of body identification, 1,161 bodies were never found or identified, including those of emergency responders. Life as we knew it had changed forever. Funerals, memorial services — hundreds of them — our worst nightmares about terrorism had come true.

Figure 1.2   For a successful outcome, police and fire department personnel will need to work closely together during a terrorist attack.

It has been my strong personal belief since we began planning and training personnel for terrorism response back in the early 1990s that terrorism is "just another hazardous materials incident" with some special circumstances. If emergency responders are trained and equipped to deal with hazardous materials incidents, they can handle the aftermath of terrorist incidents with some additional training and equipment. Responders who are not prepared for hazmat response will not do well at terrorist incidents either. One of the biggest lessons learned from the September 11 attacks was that all levels of government must support each other to maximize response effectiveness to acts of terrorism. There needs to be planning, security improvements, training, and exercises to validate the planning and security. Fire departments, law enforcement agencies, EMS systems, hospitals, military agencies, as well as all levels of local, state, and federal government, need to come together to plan and prepare. Such an event could happen anywhere in the U.S. If agencies and organizations do not develop plans, train and equip personnel, and conduct exercises in preparation for acts of terrorism, emergency scenes will be chaos.

During the 2005 hurricane disasters on the Gulf Coast of the U.S., it became painfully apparent that we had not learned much about responding to major catastrophic events. That was a natural disaster just four years after September 11, oddly enough also in the month of September, but what if it had been an act of terrorism instead? There was time to prepare, we had notice that the hurricanes were coming, and yet the response from government at all levels was severely lacking. People had been talking about the vulnerability of New Orleans in the path of a major hurricane for years. Terrorist acts are unlikely to come with any warning at all. If we are so unprepared to respond to a major natural disaster, how can we hope to deal with the results of an act of terrorism? During training classes since the early 1990s, I have told responders that the federal assets, no matter what they might be, will not be available at best during the first hours and likely the first days of a major terrorist attack. Response personnel might be left on their own for extended periods of time. Look at New Orleans during Hurricane Katrina. Emergency responders and their equipment were victims of the hurricane as well. Yet many of them remained on the job fighting crime, fighting fires with enormous obstacles, without relief, without much sleep or rest, without the basic needs of food and water, and in some cases adequate shelter, yet they still did their job. Where was the federal response? Where was the state response? There was chaos in New Orleans, lack of communication, no electricity, lawlessness, much of the city was under water and inaccessible except by boat. The disaster was well beyond the capability of the local resources and state resources. Yet it took days for help to come from the federal government. There were days of warning before this disaster occurred, yet the response was a total failure of government at all levels. How could this happen in the United States of America, the richest country in the world? I fully expected that if any terrorist organizations had any resources or plans to attack the U.S., it would occur as the disaster on the Gulf Coast was unfolding. What better time; government resources were stretched thin. What happened on the Gulf Coast is just the type of thing the terrorist is looking for: disruption of life as we know it. What have the terrorists learned about our capability from the hurricane disasters? What will they do to capitalize on that information? What would the attacks on September 11 have been like if emergency response from the local area was not available or severely hampered as in New Orleans? What would September 11 have been like if we needed to rely on state and federal resources? It was the heroic efforts of the local emergency responders that kept September 11 from becoming a bigger disaster than it already was. What if the acts of terrorism on September 11 had happened in a smaller community with fewer local resources than those available in New York City? We saw how long it took for significant state and federal resources to respond when we knew a disaster was going to happen and resources were staged near the disaster zones. Terrorist events will likely be unannounced. We need to be ready at the local level to deal with acts of terrorism. By coming together for planning and training before an incident occurs, and working together in the aftermath, we can greatly reduce the impact on the community during the event and following recovery efforts. It is time to put aside our petty differences, drop our jurisdictional boundaries, and work together for the common good. Only by doing this can we mount an effective counter-terrorism strategy.

During the mid 1980s, the buzzwords in emergency response were SARA (Superfund Amendments and Reauthorization Act) Title III, EPCRA (also known as the Emergency Planning and Community Right-To-Know Act of 1986), and hazardous materials. Definitions of hazardous materials usually revolve around the U.S. Department of Transportation (DOT) definition, "A substance or material which has been determined by the Secretary of Transportation to be capable of posing an unreasonable risk to health, safety, and property when transported." While some hazardous materials that may be used by terrorists are not generally transported legally, they certainly do "pose an unreasonable risk to health, safety, and property." Materials used in weapons of mass destruction (WMD) can be placed into DOT hazard classes and NFPA (National Fire Protection Association) 704 numbers can also be assigned to them, indicating flammability, health, and reactivity hazards. Hazardous materials used in acts of terrorism can be included in the following hazard classes: poison gases, explosives, oxidizers, flammable liquids, combustible liquids, poisons, and radioactive materials. With the passage of EPCRA, for the first time, the federal government, through the Environmental Protection Agency (EPA) and the Occupational Safety and Health Administration (OSHA), mandated Standard Operating Procedures (SOPs) and specific training competencies for emergency personnel who respond to hazardous materials incidents.

While there are currently no training mandates for response to acts of terrorism, all emergency responders should have a minimum of terrorism awareness training. NFPA Standard 472 covers competencies required for various levels of hazardous materials responders to a terrorist incident, but it is not mandatory. Responders need to be able to identify when an act of terrorism may have occurred. They need to know what protective measures should be taken for themselves and the public. Training courses are available for responders like hazmat team members who conduct more advanced operational functions at a terrorist incident scene. These will be discussed further in Chapter 11 Terrorism Training Opportunities.

Initially funding for hazmat training was limited, and some departments resisted compliance with the federal hazmat training requirements. There were fire chiefs who said, "We do not respond to hazardous materials incidents" or "We won't respond to hazardous materials incidents" (once again, the ostrich syndrome). How many times do calls come in as something other than a hazmat incident and turn out to be one? All responders must be able to recognize hazardous materials incidents and take appropriate actions. Responders should not be responding to emergency scenes without hazmat and terrorism awareness training. In the beginning of regulatory requirements, most departments did comply with the EPA and OSHA hazardous materials regulations. As a result of the federal requirements, hazardous materials teams were formed and trained along with first responders. Training competencies were established by NFPA 472 and OSHA 1910.120 for hazardous materials awareness and operations that applied to first responders across the country. Hazardous materials team members were trained as technicians and specialists to deal with the mitigation of incident hazards. Those same first responders and technicians will be called upon to deal with WMD used by terrorist organizations. OSHA established minimum contact hours for some training courses; awareness had no hourly requirement, while operations required 8 hours, and technician and specialist 24 hours each. Some jurisdictions expanded their programs far beyond those minimum requirements because they did not allow enough time for the type of training that was really needed. Hazardous materials training can serve as a solid base on which to build the competencies for response to terrorist incidents. NFPA 472 has been revised to include competencies for emergency response to acts of terrorism, while there have not been any training standards or requirements created at the federal level.

Hazardous materials incidents occur on a frequent basis in many parts of the U.S. Emergency responders, in general, have the training, experience, and motivation to handle the incidents properly. However, there are locations in the country that might experience only several small or perhaps just one major incident in a lifetime. Acts of terrorism might not occur at all. Responders in these locations are unable to gain experience dealing with hazardous materials. It is difficult to maintain interest among response personnel for hazardous materials or acts of terrorism when they do not occur on a regular basis. In fact, in many areas responders do not look for or expect to find hazardous materials when responding to daily emergencies, and they certainly do not look for potential acts of terrorism. Personnel may become complacent about the potential for finding hazardous materials or terrorist incidents in their communities. It is those types of situations where the greatest danger lies. If responders do not maintain an awareness of the potential presence and dangers of hazardous materials and terrorist agents, they will face a great potential to be injured or die at an incident scene. Incidents might not happen frequently, but there is no way of knowing when or where they will happen, and therefore we must always be prepared. Without awareness of hazardous materials it is also likely that we will fail to identify potential terrorist incidents.

Over the years, firefighters have lost their lives responding to releases of hazardous materials in places like Kingman, Arizona, and Waverly, Tennessee. Most of the materials involved in typical hazmat incidents, such as propane, anhydrous ammonia, and chlorine, are very common. By now, responders should be familiar with the characteristics and dangers of common hazardous materials such as propane. Yet on June 27, 1993, three Warwick, Quebec, Canada, volunteer firefighters were killed by a propane tank explosion during a barn fire. Another incident occurred October 7, 1997, when two volunteer firefighters were killed in Carthage, Illinois, as a propane tank exploded on a farm during a grain dryer fire. As recently as April 9, 1998, two more firefighters were killed in Albert City, Iowa, due to another propane tank explosion on a farm. An all-terrain vehicle (ATV) struck two pipelines carrying liquid propane from an 18,000 gallon (68,220 L) capacity tank to two vaporizer units. The ensuing cloud of vapor was ignited by a nearby ignition source. The fact remains that hazardous materials are everywhere in the U.S. — in transportation, fixed facilities, and manufacturing operations. They can be found in large cities and small towns alike. No responder can escape the potential for hazardous materials. Both career and volunteer firefighters are at risk. They must have a keen awareness of the dangers and potential locations of hazardous materials in every community and be prepared to deal with them, whether the incidents occur frequently or once in a lifetime.

Terrorists may choose to use everyday hazardous materials in fixed storage, hijacked shipments of highway containers, or even strategically derail trains to cause the release of the materials over populated areas. The Baltimore Tunnel train fire that paralyzed the city for days is a prime example of the effects that could be expected if a terrorist group were to cause a train derailment in a major city. At 3:04 PM on July 18, 2001, a 60-car CSX freight train entered the Howard Street Tunnel, pulled by three engines and manned by two engineers. The load included 31 full cars and 29 empty cars with a mix of freight that included paper products, plywood, soy oil, and several tank cars containing hazardous materials. At 3:07 PM, the engineers heard a grinding noise, saw the air pressure in the brake line drop, felt a lurch, and then noted that the train came to an abrupt stop. Their radio did not work as they were in a dead zone in the tunnel, but at 3:15 PM, one of the engineers used his cell phone to reach the train master to report the problem that the train was stopped in the tunnel. The fumes were getting worse, so the engineers cleared the tunnel with their three engines decoupled from the rest of the train at 3:27 PM. The fumes and smoke continued to worsen, which suggested to the engineers that the train cars remaining inside the tunnel were on fire. They reviewed the bill of lading, which listed the train's contents. Hazardous materials were listed on the bill, so the engineers contacted the Baltimore City firefighters "somewhere between 3:35 PM and 4:15 PM" (the time is disputed). From the time the Baltimore City Fire Department (BCFD) arrived at 4:15 PM (1 hour, 8 minutes after the train unexpectedly stopped in the tunnel, time zero) and assumed incident command responsibilities, the management of the disaster moved quickly. At 4:15 PM, CSX Transportation notified the Maryland Department of the Environment (MDE)-Emergency Response Division of the derailment of train cars carrying hazardous materials, whose staff arrived at the scene in 5 minutes. CSX contacted the National Transportation Safety Board (NTSB), the BCFD Battalion Chief 6, and the BCFD's hazardous materials coordinator. Light rail and rail freight movement were disrupted, so the Maryland Transit Authority initiated a bus bridge to bring light-rail passengers around the tunnel. Freight trains were rerouted as far west as Ohio. At 4:20 PM, the chief of the BCFD requested that all major roads (I-395, I-83, US-40) into Baltimore City be closed. Baltimore City Police Department and Department of Public Works worked quickly to bring this about. Still, no one was really sure about the identity or harmfulness of the hazardous materials that were presumed to be burning in the tunnel, which was so hot by this time (1474°F) that firefighters could not enter. MDE requested a chemist from the private sector mutual aid plan known as the South Baltimore Industrial Mutual Aid Plan (SBIMAP), which produced two chemists immediately. At 4:35 PM (1 hour, 28 minutes after time zero) the chemists declared that there was a potential for hydrogen fluoride vapor from one of the tanker cars containing fluorosilicic acid. This type of exposure requires special medical treatment.

Baltimore City emergency managers decided (and MDE concurred) at 4:45 PM to sound the sirens to notify nearby residents to shelter in place (the actual sounding occurred at 5:45 PM, 2 hours, 38 minutes after time zero). At 4:53 PM the MDE contacted the U.S. Coast Guard, which 7 minutes later closed Inner Harbor to boat traffic. Meanwhile, Orioles' office workers were told to leave the B & O Warehouse. The MDE and SBIMAP began monitoring air quality at 4:53 PM As a result of that incident, which was an accident, several Orioles' baseball games had to be postponed, the city was in a lock-down mode for hours, and transportation systems and businesses were interrupted. This incident went on for several days. Had a terrorist targeted a specific train that had a toxic chemical, such as chlorine, on it, the outcome would have been much worse. Until that incident occurred, many people didn't even know the tunnel existed.

During the 1990s, a new buzzword appeared along with new challenges for the emergency responders: terrorism. Many definitions exist to specifically define an act of terrorism. Every federal agency involved in terrorism training, response, or investigation usually has one of their own. Generally, terrorism is defined as the use or threatened use of force to intimidate persons, or a society, for political or social goals. The U.S. Department of Justice defines terrorism as "a violent act or an act dangerous to human life, in violation of the criminal laws of the U.S. or any segment to intimidate or coerce a government, the civilian population or any segment thereof, in furtherance of political or social objectives." Goals of terrorists include causing fear among the people and creating mistrust between a government and its citizens. They may also try to change public perceptions and attitudes toward a government, its policies, or its anticipated actions. In the U.S., the right to advocate change in the government is guaranteed under the Constitution; however, the Constitution provides for an organized peaceful process, where terrorists choose to influence the change through acts of violence.

The Federal Bureau of Investigation (FBI) categorizes terrorism as either domestic or international. Domestic terrorism involves groups or individuals who are U.S. citizens. Their acts are targeted toward the government or populations, without direction from foreign countries. The bombings in Oklahoma City, Atlanta, and Birmingham were acts of domestic terrorism. International terrorism involves groups or individuals whose activities are foreign-based or directed by countries outside the U.S. The World Trade Center bombing in 1993 was an act of international terrorism carried out by Islamic fundamentalists. The events of September 11, 2001, were acts of international terrorism carried out by members of the al Qaeda terrorist network.

As previously mentioned, terrorist incidents are not unlike hazardous materials incidents when it comes to response operations. However, they can also become a combination of mass casualty incident, hazardous materials incident, and technical rescue incident — in addition to being a crime scene. Terrorist incidents are even less likely to happen than hazardous materials incidents, but following threats of chemical and biological attacks in Washington, D.C., and at Disneyland in California and the events of September 11, 2001, we know terrorist attacks happen here.

Just as with hazardous materials regulation mentioned earlier, the federal government is actively involved in preparation for acts of terrorism. Congress passed the Nunn-Lugar-Domenici Act and the Nunn-Lugar Cooperative Threat Reduction Act, both aimed at reducing the threat and effects of terrorists using WMD. The Nunn-Lugar-Domenici Act has led to the development of domestic programs to prepare for terrorism. This act is also designed to aid the republics of the former Soviet Union in reduction of their nuclear arsenals to help keep nuclear materials out of the hands of terrorists. Senator Richard Lugar has said many times that "the threat of terrorism is real and we must be prepared. Preparation must take the form of help to local 'first responders,' the firefighters, police, emergency medical and emergency management teams who will be on the front lines if deterrence and prevention of such incidents fail." Emergency responders must be properly trained and equipped to deal with nuclear, chemical, biological, and explosive terrorist incidents. This time, though, it is not mandates that the legislation has provided but rather preparedness issues and money to conduct training and purchase equipment. Early in 1998, the Justice Department awarded nearly $12 million to 41 jurisdictions in the U.S. to acquire personal protective, detection, decontamination, and communications equipment. Since that time, millions of dollars in grants have been awarded to emergency response organizations nationwide for training and equipment to deal with acts of terrorism from the Department of Justice, the Department of Homeland Security, and the Department of Defense. Several different federal agencies continue to develop and provide training for state and local personnel who may be asked to respond to terrorism. However, it appears that there is still little coordination between each administrative level. The Department of Defense (DOD) personnel have limited experience in dealing with emergency responders at the local level. From a military standpoint, the DOD feels there is a level of "acceptable casualties" during a terrorist attack. Emergency response leaders feel there is no level of acceptable civilian casualties or acceptable casualties for response personnel. Following the attacks of September 11, Congress passed the Patriot Act. The purpose of the act as stated by Congress was to "deter and punish terrorist acts in the United States and around the world, to enhance law enforcement investigatory tools, and for other purposes." Major sections of the act were to enhance domestic security and give law enforcement more power when investigating and gathering intelligence for acts of terrorism. In addition to the Patriot Act, Congress passed the Homeland Security Act, which created the Department of Homeland Security. Pennsylvania Governor Tom Ridge was appointed by President George W. Bush as the first Secretary of Homeland Security in November 2001. On February 15, 2005, Judge Michael Chertoff was sworn in as the second Secretary of the Department of Homeland Security.

During the late 1990s, the army's Chemical and Biological Defense Command (CBDCOM) was merged with the U.S. Army Soldier Systems Command (SSCOM) to become the U.S. Army Soldier and Biological Chemical Command (SBCCOM). SBCCOM developed training aimed at response personnel in the 120 largest cities in the U.S., which was mandated by the Nunn-Lugar Act. There are those in the fire service and Congress who feel the SBCCOM training should be made available to smaller departments and volunteers who may respond to terrorist incidents through mutual-aid agreements. On October 9, 2003, SBCCOM was redesignated into the following organizations: RDECOM (Research, Development and Engineering Command); CMA (Chemical Materials Agency); GUARDIAN BRIGADE; PM NBC (PM Nuclear, Biological and Chemical Defense); and SSC (Soldiers System Center). Texas A&M University, in cooperation with Science Applications International, provides training for emergency responders at A&M's Emergency Response Training Field in College Station, Texas. Training is conducted in virtual reality simulators to convey the effects of chemical and biological weapons. Texas A&M University has also been designated as the National Training Center for Urban Search and Rescue (US&R). The facility includes a "disaster city" to prepare responders to handle earthquakes and bombings in addition to chemical and biological agents. These training programs, like many others, only provide training; responders will also need equipment and supplies to respond safely and effectively to terrorist incidents.

Competencies for responders to terrorist incidents have also been developed by the NFPA and incorporated into the competency sections for Awareness, Operations, Technician, Incident Commander and Safety Officer in the 2002 edition of NFPA 472. NFPA 472 will be discussed in detail in Chapter 11 Terrorist Resources and Response Training. A complete text of NFPA 472 and NFPA 471, Recommended Practice for Responding to Hazardous Materials Incidents, provides specific operational and equipment information on responding to hazardous materials incidents, including acts of terrorism; NFPA 473, Competencies for EMS Personnel Responding to Hazardous Materials Incidents; NFPA 1951, Protective Ensembles for USAR Operations; and NFPA 1994 are available free of charge from the NFPA at nfpa.org.

There is a "cultural" difference between firefighters and law enforcement personnel. Training for firefighters emphasizes work as a team player and using the incident command system, with personal safety and accountability the number one priority. Law enforcement training emphasizes being self-sufficient, retaining control of the situation, and performing investigative functions. Given these varied traits, law enforcement and firefighting personnel need to learn more about each other and to strive to cross the boundaries. They should train together, participate in exercises, and get to know each other personally, which should provide for a smoother unified command during actual incidents.

The common thread among all terrorist incidents is their cultivation of new groups of buzz words and catch phrases, especially "weapons of mass destruction" (WMD), which are actually hazardous materials in a quantity, form, or hazard class that, when they are successfully dispersed as the result of a terrorist act, threaten large numbers of people. WMD generally include explosives and nuclear, biological, and chemical (NBC) agents. Other terrorist weapons may also include dirty bombs and nuclear materials, incendiary devices, and irritants such as tear gas and pepper spray. Bombing has been the terrorist weapon of choice in the past, which may continue into the future. However, tomorrow might bring even more devastating weapons. The use of the nerve agent sarin by members of the Aum Shinri Kyo Millennialist Sect in the streets of Matsumoto and the subway systems of Tokyo, Japan, resulted in a major pattern shift in terrorist activity. Overall, incidents of terrorism are decreasing in number, while larger bombs and more lethal weapons are presenting a threat to larger numbers of civilians. Bombings of Spanish trains in May 2005, English subways and buses in July 2005, and almost daily bombings on the streets of Iraq continue to target, injure, and kill hundreds of civilians as terrorists seek to advance their cause through the use of terror.

Literally hundreds of distinct types of chemical and biological warfare agents are known to exist. Only a few have actually been used in military battle. Terrorist acts in Japan and other locations demonstrate the need for appreciation of the characteristics that chemical and biological weapons present and the need to prepare for a potential attack. Agents used by terrorists will likely be those materials most capable of causing injury, incapacitation, and, in sufficient quantity, a large body count. Military nerve agents are close relatives of organophosphate pesticides. Many have been discovered while scientists were trying to develop a better pesticide. Nerve agents were first developed in the 1930s by Germans. Symptoms from exposure to nerve agents are similar to those experienced by organophosphate pesticide poisoning. Nerve agents are no longer the sole property of military forces and a threat to be expected only on the battlefield. Use of chemical weapons by terrorists now supports the premise that civilians are susceptible to attack, and the entire world is now the battlefield. Other types of chemical warfare agents are common industrial chemicals such as chlorine, hydrogen cyanide, cyanogen chloride, and phosgene, which are all DOT Hazard Class 2.3 and 6.1 poisons. Nerve agents and blister agents are less volatile and listed as Class 6.1 poisons. Riot-control agents are not highly toxic, but are irritants classified as Class 6.1 poisons. Biological agents are actually infectious substances — disease-causing organisms — which are classified as DOT Hazard Class 6.2. Radioactive isotopes and other materials are classified as Radioactive Class 7. Remember that regardless of the primary hazard indicated by a hazard class, almost all hazardous materials have more than one hazard.

The decline and dismantling of the former Soviet Union produced an unprecedented uncertainty as to the safety of chemical and biological agents and nuclear devices. For the first time in history, a country that was a dominant "superpower" with a large stockpile of nuclear materials and weapons, as well as chemical and biological warfare agents, has experienced a radical reformation. This change has left the safety, and of course the location, of these agents and their nuclear stockpile in question. Threats of nuclear terrorism are therefore more credible than ever. However, the reality of a thermal nuclear device being used by terrorists is relatively small compared to other options available. Weapons that might be purchased on the "black market" probably won't have the necessary codes with them to activate the device. Radioactive materials could, however, be disseminated by a conventional explosive device and create a serious public health threat. Building a nuclear device requires a high level of technical expertise that might not be available to most terrorist groups. Assembling a device also requires large quantities of weapons-grade plutonium, which is not readily available.

Firefighters are accustomed to fighting fires set by arsonists. They have been taught over the years to watch for signs of arson and to preserve the incident scene as a crime scene. Incendiary devices may also be chosen by terrorists. Terrorist attacks involving explosives and other materials could also result in fires. The rash of church burnings in the south in the late 1990s could very well be classified as a form of domestic terrorism, targeted at specific ethnic or religious groups. It will be difficult, at best, to determine if an arson fire was actually a terrorist event. The real difference between arson and terrorism is the motive of the perpetrator. Without catching those who set the fire, the motive may never be known. Only the target and circumstances of a suspicious fire may provide clues to possible terrorism.

Biological agents are living organisms or their toxins, also known as infectious substances or disease-causing organisms. Biological organisms have a delayed period of time between infection and the actual onset of symptoms, which may vary from days to weeks. Toxins, however, are actually chemical poisons and may act quickly. Biological weapons are usually odorless, colorless, and are generally not a skin absorption hazard, except for mycotoxins. When dispersed, these agents are more difficult to distinguish than chemical weapons, and can be much more toxic. Some biological toxins are more lethal than the strongest nerve agent, VX. Biological agents have sometimes been referred to as the "poor man's atom bomb." Making or obtaining them can be easily done with little outside detection of the operations. All biological agents occur naturally and can be found harvested from nature and cultivated in a laboratory setting.

Handling incidents of terrorism safely and effectively means remembering what we should already know about hazardous materials response and learning some new skills specific to terrorist activities. Most responders have limited knowledge of chemical, biological, explosive, and radiological agents and materials. Responders need to have knowledge of chemical and biological agent symptoms. Rapid assessment of the incident situation and technical consultation are essential. Integrated response is a necessity to acquire the technical resources to assist with special tasks such as agent monitoring, identification, personnel protective equipment, and decontamination. Responding to terrorist activities also means personnel should anticipate dealing with some new players who may be unfamiliar. New participants include the DOD; FBI; FEMA; the Department of Homeland Security; the Secret Service; the Bureau of Alcohol, Tobacco and Firearms (ATF); and various other local, state, and federal government and military agencies. The FBI has been designated as the lead federal agency in charge of terrorist incident investigation. FEMA is the lead agency for consequence management during the recovery phase of the incident. Terrorist incident scenes are also large crime scenes. Response personnel need to preserve the integrity of evidence and maintain the chain of custody at the scene, just as they do with arson fires. They must also perform the necessary functions to rescue and treat victims, mitigate the incident, and return the scene to normal. Terrorist incidents may have rescue and law enforcement concerns that necessitate an integrated command involving fire, police, and federal law enforcement agen-

Figure 1.3 Terrorist incidents will require multiple agencies and a Unified Incident Command System patterned after the National Incident Command System.

cies as well as others. Terrorist incidents will require multiple agencies and a Unified Incident Command System to successfully manage the outcomes.

Identification of hazardous materials used in conjunction with acts of terrorism will not be easy to accomplish. It is unlikely the terrorist will hand you a material safety data sheet (MSDS) before departing or leave one behind. There will not likely be placards or labels available or shipping papers for identification. Symptoms presented by victims may be the only indications that a terrorist incident has taken place. Once the material is identified or suspected, there is information available concerning the physical and chemical characteristics. The army has developed MSDS for military nerve and blister agents. MSDS can help response personnel in determining hazards, symptoms, protective clothing, and decontamination protocols. Health Canada Office of Biosafety has developed MSDS for 178 biological materials, which are referred to by the DOT as infectious substances. These can also benefit responders when trying to identify biological agents and symptoms. MSDS are also available for common industrial chemicals that might be used by terrorists. The chemicals would, however, have to be identified at an incident scene before the MSDS would be of any great benefit. A search for MSDS on the Internet will reveal a number of sites where common industrial chemicals, such as chlorine and hydrogen cyanide, can be found. These are chemicals that have been used as chemical warfare agents in the past and could be used by terrorists. Some of these sites are listed in Appendix A.

When responders approach the scene of an emergency, they are taught to recognize when hazardous materials might be present. This is accomplished by looking for such clues as placards and labels; types of occupancies and locations; markings and colors; container/vehicle shapes; shipping papers; MSDS sheets; and the use of human senses. First of all, do not expect that terrorists will take the time to provide any useful information to responders about the materials used in the attack. In fact, it is quite possible that information placed with potential terrorist agents might be designed to mislead responders about the materials that are present. On the other hand, labels might indicate if biological or chemical materials are present when, in fact, the materials are harmless. In April 1997, a hoax occurred in Washington, D.C. where a package marked "anthrax and plague" was sent to the B'nai B'rith headquarters, a Jewish organization. This incident turned out to involve harmless bacteria found in the atmosphere, not anthrax or plague. Because of the potential, however, the incident had to be handled just as if the biological agents were real. The implications are that mere suspicions or threats that a biological or chemical material might be present would accomplish some of the goals of the terrorist. Washington, D.C. traffic was tied up for hours, right through rush hour, as a result of the anthrax hoax. The fire department, police department, and various federal agencies were also committed to the scene, keeping them from other emergencies. Many resources were used just as they would be during an actual dispersion of a chemical or biological material. This incident certainly caused fear among the people of the building in question. It might have also caused concern for people living in the area, the citizens of Washington, D.C., and others who might have thought this incident involved real materials.

Responders should be able to recognize occupancies and locations that might become targets of terrorism, in much the same way as they should recognize potential locations of other hazardous materials. Terrorist targets might include government buildings, such as court houses, office buildings, military installations, historical buildings or monuments, and other symbolic targets. Terrorist targets might include places where large numbers of people congregate, such as convention centers, concert halls, shopping malls, and subway systems. Large outdoor events, such as sporting events, fairs, festivals, amusement parks, and tourist attractions might also become targets. Historically significant anniversary dates, days of the week, and times of day might also be important to the terrorist. Terrorists and radical groups could target controversial businesses, such as abortion clinics, nuclear facilities and power plants, and animal research facilities. Animal rights groups and activists might target a college or university that uses laboratory animals to conduct research. Anti-abortion groups might target abortion clinics, family planning clinics, or doctors who perform abortions. People who oppose nuclear power or the transportation of nuclear waste through their communities could target nuclear power plants, power company offices, railroads, or rail facilities. Infrastructure might also be a target of the terrorist to disrupt normal life and erode confidence in the government. Targets might include infrastructure such as conventional power plants, mass transit systems, phone companies, water treatment plants, and hospitals. When responders are called to reports of explosions, mass casualty incidents, or reports of strange odors involving these types of locations, they should recognize this situation might be a terrorist event. Terrorist attacks can also be carried out in an attempt to damage our economic system. Threats were made against the financial district in New York City in the early 2000s. Following September 11, U.S. airlines suffered financial loss as a result of people's reluctance to fly. This had a ripple effect on hotels, restaurants, tourist attractions, and entertainment venues.

Though the use of the human senses as a tool for recognition and identification of hazardous materials and terrorist agents could be dangerous, there are some senses that can be used safely. These include sight, hearing, and, though not normally considered one of the human senses, common sense. All can be important when dealing with hazardous materials and terrorist incidents. Responders should be aware of the potential for hazardous materials and acts of terrorism and size up the incident scene thoroughly from a safe distance. Responders should recognize the signs and symptoms of chemical and biological agents that victims may be experiencing, or a lack of symptoms. This may be the only method that can be effectively used to identify a terrorist attack or the type of potential agent used. Personnel should also be aware of the forms and methods of dissemination of chemical and biological agents and the time of day that would be most effective. Chemical nerve agents, if used in proper concentrations during acts of terrorism, would produce instant victims. There are similarities between light exposure to nerve agents and exposure to irritants. Looking at the eyes is the only way to tell the difference. Irritants can also cause blisters or vesicants like blister agents if the victim is exposed for a long period in a confined area. Blister agents like mustard would not produce symptoms for 2 to 24 hours in most people who are exposed. Because of long incubation periods, biological agents used in a terrorist attack would not produce symptoms for several days or longer. Symptoms may be the only thing that responders have available to determine that a terrorist incident has occurred. A large number of victims, or several victims experiencing the same symptoms without evidence of trauma, is a good indication of a terrorist attack. It is rare that emergency personnel respond to an incident where there are multiple casualties experiencing the same types of symptoms. Arriving on a scene with mass casualties and no visible trauma should trigger a caution sign in the minds of responders. Explosions that occur with little, if any, physical damage are unusual. An explosion might have been used to disseminate a chemical or biological agent. Serious thought should be given as to what might have happened when responding to locations that might be terrorist targets. Become aware of the potential for secondary devices when responding to explosions. Responders themselves might be the target of secondary explosive devices. Secondary devices were used in the abortion clinic and lounge bombings in Atlanta, as well as the clinic in Birmingham. Taking the time to do a good size-up and understand the clues that indicate a possible terrorist attack might save your life and the lives of your fellow responders.

We often plan and train for mass casualty incidents from airplane crashes, school bus accidents, and train wrecks. These types of incidents could produce hundreds of victims. Hospitals have disaster plans in place to deal with multiple casualties. Depending on the size of the community, hospitals could be overwhelmed by just a few seriously injured patients. The fact is most of us in the emergency response community have little actual experience dealing with mass casualty incidents. During May 1996, Philadelphia hospitals were overwhelmed by more than 100 heroin addicts who had used a lethal mixture of heroin containing cocaine, dextromethorphan, thiamin, and scopolamine. Emergency room facilities quickly became overburdened by the influx of casualties, some of whom had to be turned away. An attack involving the use of nerve agents could easily overshadow the problems these hospitals experienced trying to treat the "heroin cocktail" casualties. Also in the spring of 1996, the Community Hospital of Monterey, California treated a patient that had ingested a large amount of an organophosphate pesticide. The patient vomited, and the fumes being given off by the pesticide in the vomitus caused the ER staff to become victims. Emergency facilities at the hospital were shut down until the area could be decontaminated by a local hazardous materials team, which took several hours.

Bhopal, India, witnessed the only hazardous materials incident to produce anything close to the casualties that might result from an effective terrorist attack. Theirs was the world's worst chemical disaster. In Bhopal on December 3, 1984, methyl isocyanate was accidentally released from the Union Carbide chemical plant, killing over 3,800 and injuring over 200,000 others, with several thousand permanently disabled. In the beginning, medical personnel did not know what the chemical was because the chemical company would not tell anyone. Medical personnel could not determine what caused the illness and did not know how to treat it. The Bhopal incident aftermath is much the same type of situation that might result from a chemical or biological agent terrorist attack. There would likely be thousands of deaths and injuries. Little may be known initially about what caused the incident or what the potential hazards are. The medical system could be overwhelmed by the potential number of dead and injured. Studying the Bhopal incident can help us learn how to prepare our emergency response organizations and our medical community for such a large-scale mass-casualty incident.

On November 8, 2005, a suitcase was found in front of a building at the University of Maryland in Baltimore. It had been strategically located near a structural support next to an overhead door. Several major streets were shut down. Baltimore City Police, University of Maryland Police, and the Baltimore City Bomb Squad responded. Bomb squad members x-rayed the suitcase, found nothing suspicious looking, and opened the suitcase. It was full of clothes! This incident disrupted activities at a major research university for several hours. All of the proper procedures were used, and it turned out to be a good exercise.

Clues and factors associated with terrorist attacks require a look beyond common assumptions. There are no specific types of automotive vehicles that could be tied to a potential terrorist attack, although several incidents have involved rented vehicles. Response personnel should watch for vehicles that might appear to be out of place. Appearances of rental trucks or vans, and tractor-trailer box trucks with the tractor gone, parked in front of a public building or at a public festival should be investigated. It is better to be safe than sorry. Personnel should also watch out for packages of all types and shapes that appear to have been abandoned in places that you would not expect to find them. Use your gut feelings, be suspicious, ask yourself questions, use the "what if" approach, and do not take things for granted. It is up to emergency responders to consider that there may be hazardous materials present in any given situation. It is also up to responders to recognize when the hazardous materials might be terrorist WMD. There might be multiple targets or devices that could put a strain on emergency response resources. Booby traps might also be used to kill or injure responders. Minimal resources should be used at an incident to protect responders so that others are not assembled in harm's way or are available to respond to additional incidents as needed. False alarms might be called in or arson fires set to delay response to a terrorist incident. Keep the number of personnel operating at an incident scene to the absolute minimum necessary in case a secondary device has been set. In an explosive event, do not rush into the immediate vicinity of the explosion. Law enforcement or military bomb squad personnel should first sweep the area for additional devices and unexploded ordinance. The terrorist might know how long it takes responders to reach the scene and appropriately set a timing device to catch responders off guard. No police officer responding to a report of a burglar alarm sounding would do so without expecting that there might actually be a burglary in progress, with potential for a dangerous confrontation. Medics responding to a severe laceration of a patient at an AIDS clinic would be foolish not to take universal precautions and wear disposable gloves and other protective clothing. No firefighter would walk into a house with smoke banked down to the floor without wearing full structural firefighting equipment. Responders need to think about the situation they are walking into. Watch for the

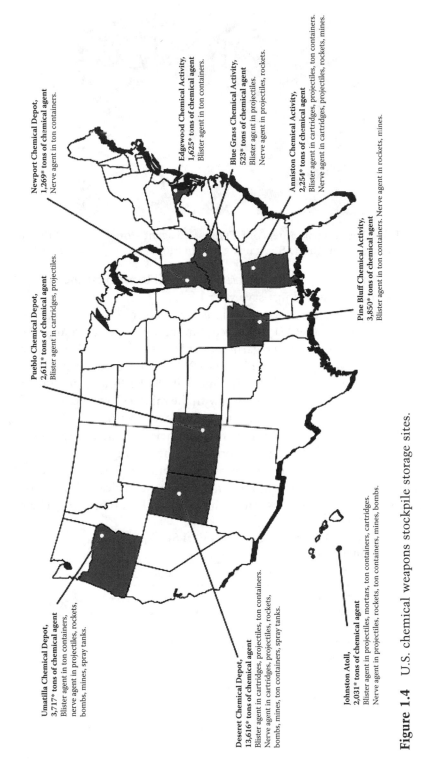

Newport Chemical Depot,
1,269* tons of chemical agent
Nerve agent in ton containers.

Edgewood Chemical Activity,
1,625* tons of chemical agent
Blister agent in ton containers.

Blue Grass Chemical Activity,
523* tons of chemical agent
Blister agent in projectiles.
Nerve agent in projectiles, rockets.

Anniston Chemical Activity,
2,254* tons of chemical agent
Blister agent in cartridges, projectiles, ton containers.
Nerve agent in cartridges, projectiles, rockets, mines.

Pueblo Chemical Depot,
2,611* tons of chemical agent
Blister agent in cartridges, projectiles.

Pine Bluff Chemical Activity,
3,850* tons of chemical agent
Blister agent in ton containers. Nerve agent in rockets, mines.

Umatilla Chemical Depot,
3,717* tons of chemical agent
Blister agent in ton containers,
nerve agent in projectiles, rockets,
bombs, mines, spray tanks.

Deseret Chemical Depot,
13,616* tons of chemical agent
Blister agent in cartridges, projectiles, ton containers.
Nerve agent in cartridges, projectiles, rockets,
bombs, mines, ton containers, spray tanks.

Johnston Atoll,
2,031* tons of chemical agent
Blister agent in projectiles, mortars, ton containers, cartridges.
Nerve agent in projectiles, rockets, ton containers, mines, bombs.

Figure 1.4   U.S. chemical weapons stockpile storage sites.

Figure 1.5 One-ton containers of HD mustard agent stored at one of the chemical stockpile sites in the U.S. awaiting destruction. (Source: U.S. Army.)

clues that indicate hazardous materials or possible terrorist incidents. The extra time you take could just save your life.

Terrorist agents, like other hazardous materials, require special personal protective equipment (PPE) and decontamination. Special charcoal-lined suits called Battle Dress Over garments (BDOs) and cartridge respirators called positive air purifying respirators (PAPRs) are used by the military. FEMA and DOD established the Chemical Stockpile Emergency Preparedness Program (CSEPP) in conjunction with the military's stockpile of unitary chemical agents that were scheduled to be destroyed by the year 2004 through a treaty signed by the U.S. and many other countries. (United States stockpiles have not been destroyed at all locations as of the writing of this book.) (See Figure 1.4.) Stockpiles are located in nine communities around the country. Emergency responders were trained and equipped to deal with releases of blister agents and nerve agents from these stockpiles (Table 1.1). There are

Table 1.1   U.S. Army Chemical Stockpile Inventory

Location	GA	GB	VX	Mustard	Lewisite
Aberdeen, MD				X	
Anniston, AL		X	X	X	
Hermiston, OR		X	X	X	
Newport, IN			X		
Pine Bluff, AR		X	X	X	
Pueblo, CO				X	
Richmond, KY		X	X	X	
Tooele, UT	X	X	X	X	X

Source: CSEPP ACT FAST Student Manual.

Figure 1.6 New York, NY, September 25, 2001 — Fragments of the World Trade Center facade are all that remain of the 110-story structures that once dominated the skyline of lower Manhattan. (Source: Photo by Mike Rieger/ FEMA News Photo.)

several chemical suits that have been tested against chemical agents and approved for use by responders. Usually, cartridge respirators are not considered protection for emergency response personnel. The Self-Contained Breathing Apparatus (SCBA) carried by many responders only provides air for a limited time before the tank has to be changed. Because of the potential for mass casualties, and extended decontamination and treatment involving chemical or biological agents, terrorist incidents may require a longer supply of air or filtered air than other incidents. PAPRs provide breathable filtered air for up to 16 hours, depending on the concentration of the agent. In addition to emergency responders, large numbers of victims might have to be decontaminated when a chemical or biological attack occurs. Ordinary decontamination procedures might not be adequate. Decontamination might require more than just soap and water, like most hazardous materials incidents. Solutions of bleach or disinfectant chemicals might be required for decontamination of equipment, depending on the type of agent used by the terrorist.

Terrorist incidents, if they occur, will be far more challenging than any other type of incident responders are called upon to resolve. Knowledge, training, equipment, and planning will be necessary to ensure responders and civilians are properly protected and the impact on the community will be kept to a minimum. It is up to you. This book is written to provide emergency responders of all types, including firefighters, law enforcement officers, emergency medical personnel, and others, with information to assist them in planning and responding to acts of terrorism. Support personnel such as dispatchers, 911 operators, advanced EMS professionals at hospitals, and others may also benefit from the information presented here.

History of Terrorism

2

The threat of terrorism impacts all communities, large and small, in the U.S. and at U.S. facilities throughout the world. Events of the past have shown that no place is immune from the potential of a terrorist attack. Incidents have occurred in cities of all sizes, as well as in rural America. Both domestic and international terrorists have demonstrated their ability to strike almost at will. While the weapons of choice in the past have been explosives and explosive devices, chemical and biological agents have also been used. In the future, terrorists will almost certainly resort to weapons of mass destruction (WMD) including nuclear, biological, and chemical materials. Technology is improving, and terrorists are learning to use materials that are much deadlier than any bomb of the past. Materials such as biological agents are cheap and easy to produce without detection. Case studies of several acts of terrorism will be presented in this chapter. Most of the incidents mentioned occurred in the U.S. Some additional foreign incidents are mentioned to illustrate the ability of terrorist groups to use chemical and biological agents in addition to explosive devices used in previous incidents. It is also likely that these materials could be used in the U.S. by domestic and international terrorist organizations.

Headlines throughout 1997 and 1998 were filled with Iraq's attempts to keep United Nations (U.N.) weapons inspectors from investigating all suspected weapons of mass destruction sites in Iraq. Following the terrorist attacks on the U.S. in 2001, President George W. Bush carried out two attacks in foreign countries in an attempt to wipe out terrorist organizations in Afghanistan and WMD in Iraq. As it turns out, WMD materials have yet to be found during the war in Iraq as of the winter of 2005. Iraq is only one of the international countries suspected of having chemical and biological agents that could be used against U.S. troops or civilian populations here and abroad. In his State of the Union Address on January 29, 2002, President Bush referred to "regimes that sponsor terror," naming North Korea, Iran, Iraq, and Syria as an "axis of evil." The countries of the former Soviet Union have nuclear materials and devices that could reach the black market and fall into the hands of terrorists. Iran and North Korea are suspected of having nuclear weapons programs, which could result in nuclear materials or devices falling into the hands of terrorists. Russia has continued to pursue its biological weapons research program at Vector, a top-secret facility for biological research in Siberia. Because the Russian economy fell into decline after the breakup of the former Soviet Union, scientists have gone unpaid for months at a time. Some scientists have left, possibly taking biological materials with them — or at the very least, the knowledge to make them. There is the strong possibility of theft, because of few police officers and antiquated security at the Vector facility. Russia is believed to have over 52 biological agents, including 140 strains of smallpox, 3 kinds of ebola virus, and a stockpile of over 10,000 other viruses — one of the largest in the world. It is believed they have been successful in developing a genetic "marriage" between smallpox and Venezuelan Equine Encephalitis (VEE). Smallpox and ebola virus combinations have also been engineered, which would produce a projected mortality rate of 90 to 100%. Russia is thought to have developed a vaccine-proof strain of anthrax. Dr. Ken Alibek defected to the U.S. from the Soviet Union in 1992, after serving in their biological weapons program for more than 20 years. He has since served as a consultant to numerous U.S. government agencies dealing with medical microbiology, biological weapons defense, and biological weapons nonproliferation. He has given the U.S. government much insight into the bio weapons program of the former Soviet Union. North Korea, Libya, Iran, and other countries support acts of terrorism around the world and could access nuclear, biological, or chemical weapons for terrorist attacks. More than 25 countries have or are developing nuclear, biological, and chemical weapons. There are also domestic antigovernment groups that pose a threat to the government and general population of the U.S. Chemical and biological weapons could become their weapons of choice for the future.

On the domestic front, the bombing of the Alfred Murrah Federal Building in Oklahoma City, an antigovernment attack, was thought to be in retaliation for the federal government's actions in Waco, Texas, and Ruby Ridge, Idaho. On August 12, 1992, federal marshals attempted to arrest Randy Weaver, an alleged white supremacist, in Ruby Ridge, Idaho, for agreeing to buy sawed-off shotguns from an undercover agent for the Bureau of Alcohol, Tobacco and Firearms (ATF). Weaver's 13-year-old son and wife were killed in the confrontation, along with a U.S. marshal. Weaver was later cleared of the charges. ATF agents were trying to infiltrate the Aryan Nations, a group of white supremacists based at nearby Hayden Lake. It remains hotly debated whether Weaver, a local farmer, was a sympathizer, but he had visited the Aryan Nation church on more than one occasion. He seemed well placed to act as an infiltrator, but refused to when asked. Perhaps intending to elicit his cooperation, the ATF used an undercover operation in which they told Weaver to saw off the barrels of two shotguns an inch below the legal limit. It is disputed between the ATF and Weaver as to who exactly shortened the barrels to below the minimum legal length of 18 inches. He failed to appear in court to answer the charges, citing an incorrect date on his summons. However, the U.S. Marshals Service attempted to negotiate Weaver's surrender for more than a year after the scheduled court date. At one point in the negotiations, Weaver sent a letter to the Boundary County Sheriff stating he refused to leave his property. After several months of unsuccessfully attempting to negotiate Weaver's surrender for the arrest warrant issued for his failure to appear in court, the U.S. Marshals Service began surveillance of the Weavers in preparation for an arrest. At one point, Randy Weaver, his 14-year-old son, Sam, and his friend and house guest, Kevin Harris, went hunting on the property, along with several of the family's dogs. The three split up in the hopes of flushing out a deer. Harris and Sam were together, while Weaver went in a different direction. Harris and Sam unknowingly stumbled upon a group of Deputy U.S. Marshalls (DUSM), when one of their dogs scented the agent. The canine approached the agent, who opened fire on the dog, killing it. Sam, upon seeing the camo-clad agent shoot the dog, returned fire. In the ensuing exchange of gunfire, Sam was shot and wounded. As Sam ran away, he was fatally shot in the back. At that point, Harris, who had seen the dog and child die, fired back, killing one of the agents.

The next day, an FBI sniper named Lon Horiuchi wounded Weaver while Weaver, Harris, and Weaver's daughter were outside. As the three ran back to the house, Horiuchi fired again in an attempt to shoot Kevin Harris, but the shot went through the open door of the cabin, killing Weaver's wife, Vicki, and only wounding Harris. Vicki Weaver was holding a baby in her hands when shot. Much controversy was later generated by the fact that, after the first day's events, the FBI had changed the rules of engagement. Specifically, they decided that "deadly force could be used against any armed adult male if the shot could be taken without a child being injured." A standoff ensued for 10 days as several hundred federal agents surrounded the house, in which Weaver and his three surviving children remained with Harris. The area was surrounded by protesters angered at the heavy-handed nature of the authorities' actions. James "Bo" Gritz, then a third-party presidential candidate who had formerly been Weaver's commanding officer during the Vietnam War, served as a mediator between Weaver and the government. Eventually, Weaver elected to abandon the standoff and trust his case to the judicial system. At his trial in 1993, Weaver faced an array of charges, including the original weapons violations as well as murder. He was represented by noted trial lawyer Gerry Spence. Spence successfully argued that Weaver acted in self defense, winning Weaver's acquittal on all charges except missing his original court date, for which he was sentenced to 18 months and fined $10,000. He was credited with time served and spent an additional 3 months in prison.

From February 28 to April 19, 1993, a standoff between the Branch Davidians and the Justice Department took place near Waco, Texas. On February 28, 1993, at approximately 9:30 AM, agents from the Federal Bureau of Alcohol, Tobacco, and Firearms (ATF) attempted to serve an arrest warrant to David Koresh and the Branch Davidian residents. They were met with armed resistance, and gunfire erupted. In the aftermath, four ATF agents were killed and 16 were wounded. An undetermined number of Davidians were killed and injured. The FBI entered the case and took charge of the scene. Fifty-one days later, the siege ended on April 19, 1993. At 5:51 AM, the Davidians were notified that a gas attack by federal agents was imminent. A short time later, CS gas (a type of tear gas) was put into the compound through spray nozzles attached to a boom on a combat engineering vehicle (CEV). The Davidians responded with gunfire. The FBI responded by firing CS gas canisters mixed with methylene chloride into the windows of the compound; within moments, the entire compound had been gassed. More rounds of CS were propelled into the windows over the next several hours. Final rounds of tear gas were propelled into the building around 11:45 AM. At 12:07 PM, the Davidians started simultaneous fires in several parts of the compound. Nine Davidians fled the building around 12:12 PM and were arrested by FBI agents. Shortly after, gunfire was heard inside the compound. It is not known whether the Davidians were killing each other or themselves. Around 12:41 PM, firefighting efforts began and agents entered the compound to search for survivors, especially children. Eighty people perished that day from gunshot wounds and from the fire, including several children. While the incident at Waco may not be considered a terrorist event by some, it is presented here because, along with the Ruby Ridge incident, it may have contributed to the motive for bombing the Murrah Federal Building in Oklahoma City on April 19, 1995, just two years later to the day.

Incidents at Waco and Ruby Ridge have become rallying points for many domestic militia and radical antigovernment terrorist groups around the country. Criminal events have occurred in the U.S. that, while not acts of terrorism, certainly caused fear among the population. Bombing of rural mailboxes in the Midwest and sniper attacks on the East Coast and in Ohio challenged law enforcement organizations. Had terrorists used such tactics on a larger scale it certainly would have had the potential to be effective.

Terrorism is not just something that developed during the 1990s. Throughout modern history, terrorist attacks have occurred around the world. During the 18th century, Russia catapulted corpses infected with the plague into positions held by Sweden. This was one of the earliest uses of biological agents as a weapon of terrorism. Smallpox has been used on several occasions as a biological weapon. During the French and Indian War of 1754, British troops provided blankets that had been contaminated with smallpox to the American Indians. Native Americans defending Fort Carillon sustained epidemic casualties of smallpox, which directly contributed to the loss of the fort to the English. During the 19th century, President Lincoln and 12 other public officials were assassinated. These were acts of terrorism connected to the Civil War. Ku Klux Klan (KKK) groups began acts of terrorism against African Americans that included the use of incendiary devices, arson, bombings, and murder. Acts of terrorism continued into the 20th century when five members of Congress were wounded by gunfire during an attack by Puerto Rican nationalists in 1954. LaGuardia Airport in New York City was bombed by Croatian nationalists in 1975, killing 11 and injuring 75. Terrorist incidents have been going on in the U.S. for many years. However, the incidence and severity increased during the 1990s.

For 17 years, the Unabomber baffled law enforcement officials and spread terror throughout the U.S. Some of the bombs were sent through the mail in packages, while others were planted at target facilities. Eight of the bombings occurred on the West Coast, five in the Chicago area, two each on the East Coast and Salt Lake City areas, and one in Nashville, Tennessee (Figure 2.1; a complete chronological listing of the sites can be found in Appendix F). Primary bombing targets were universities, corporate and government facilities, and their personnel. Devices constructed by the Unabomber were carefully crafted pipe bombs. Pipe bombs can be very unsophisticated devices. There are any number of books and Internet sources that give step-by-step instructions for making these and other terrorist bombs. Component parts for pipe bombs can be purchased at local hardware stores.

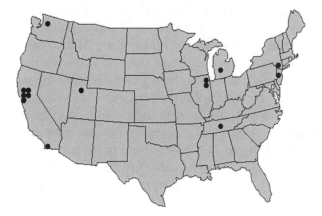

Figure 2.1   Unabomber target locations.

The 1990s brought a wave of terrorist attacks to many parts of the world and at home to the U.S. Domestic terrorism targeting organizations that do research on animals or raise them for their fur and stores that sell products from animals have become commonplace. Most people in this country love animals; so, it should not be a shock to anyone that the animal rights movement, which hardly existed just 10 years before, is emerging as a menacing force. Outspoken Hollywood celebrities including Doris Day, Bob Barker, Paul McCartney, and Liza Minnelli raise millions of dollars annually to support peaceful animal rights actions. However, there is also a dangerous side of the campaign for animal rights. A mink research center was attacked at Washington State University on August 13, 1991, when 18 animals were set free and the facility was extensively damaged. In September 1992, Animal Liberation Front (ALF) supporters set fire to a research facility at Michigan State University. A researcher's office was set ablaze and a laboratory where mink are kept was vandalized. Damage to the offices and lab was estimated at $50,000 to $100,000. An additional $20,000 to $25,000 worth of damage occurred to the research facility. Years of data research were lost. Attacks were carried out against Utah State University on October 24, 1992, where an arson fire caused $110,000 in damage; at the University of Edmonton, Canada, 29 cats were stolen on June 1, 1992 with over $50,000 in damage caused to the facility. Other similar incidents occurred at the University of Buffalo, University of Pennsylvania, Texas Tech University, University of Arizona, University of California, Davis, and Oregon State University. The FBI classifies these attacks as "acts of domestic terrorism." Information taken from the Animal Rights Resource Web site provides some background material concerning the Animal Rights Movement: "The Animal Liberation Front (ALF) carries out direct action against animal abuse in the form of rescuing animals and causing financial loss to animal exploiters, usually through the damage and destruction of property." Actions of the ALF are against the law, "activists work anonymously, in small groups or individually, and do not have any centralized organization or coordination." The FBI has listed the ALF as a domestic terrorist group. Justice Department documents indicate over 300 incidents of break-ins, vandalism, arson, and theft involving medical research facilities and university labs by animal extremists in the U.S. Any facility that conducts animal research or business in animal furs or other animal body parts may become a target of this domestic terrorist group.

On February 26, 1993, at 12:18 PM, international terrorism struck the U.S. The World Trade Center in New York City was bombed by Islamic fundamentalists (Figure 2.2) under suspected mastermind Ramzi Yousef. The World Trade Center was comprised of two high-rise towers. Each tower was 110 stories tall, reaching a height of 1,368 and 1,362 feet, with several other buildings completing the complex. Ground breaking took place August 5,

Figure 2.2 World Trade Center bombing scene 1993. (Source: The New York City Fire Department, Firefighter John Strandberg, FDNY Photo Unit. Used with permission.)

1966, and the complex opened 1970–1973 with a ribbon cutting taking place on April 4, 1973. When fully occupied, there were over 150,000 people in the buildings. Noontime is the busiest period of day at the complex and was the ideal time to launch a terrorist attack to produce a large number of deaths and injuries. At the time, the World Trade Center bombing was considered the worst terrorist attack conducted on American soil. The apparent motive was to weaken U.S. support of Israel. This bombing was intended to send a message to all Americans that terrorism could happen at anytime and anywhere in the U.S.

Components of the World Trade Center bomb included urea pellets, nitroglycerin, sulfuric acid, aluminum azide, magnesium azide, and bottled hydrogen. Ramzi Yousef added sodium cyanide to the mix so the vapors could go through the ventilation shafts and elevators of the towers. A rented truck was used to transport the bomb into the parking garage. The bomb in the van that Yousef used had four 20-foot (6 m) long fuses, all covered in surgical tubing. He calculated that the fuse would trigger the bomb in 12 minutes after he used a cheap cigarette lighter to light the fuse. Yousef wanted to prevent smoke from escaping the towers, therefore, catching the public eye by poisoning people inside. He foresaw Tower One collapsing onto Tower Two following the blast. However, the sodium cyanide burned up in the explosion. Materials used to build the bomb cost some U.S. $300 dollars. Explosive effects from the 1,300-pound bomb carved a crater 180 feet deep, 100 feet long, and 200 feet wide in the underground parking garage. The crater was six levels deep.

Following the bombing at the World Trade Center, the Clinton Administration called upon Congress to strengthen U.S. counter-terrorism policies. On February 7, 1995, Ramzi Yousef, the suspected mastermind of the World Trade Center bombing, was arrested in Pakistan. In January 1995, Yousef and his associates also plotted to blow up 11 U.S. commercial aircraft in one spectacular day of terrorist rage. The bombs were to be made of a liquid explosive designed to pass through airport metal detectors. But while mixing his chemical brew in a Manila apartment, Yousef started a fire. He was forced to flee, leaving behind a computer that contained the information that led to his arrest a month later. During the trial of the bombing suspects, testimony revealed that 12 locations in the U.S. had been targeted for sarin nerve agent attacks. Bombing of the World Trade Center was thought to be a part of a larger terror campaign being carried out by several groups of Islamic fundamentalists from several countries. The same group(s) had also been planning the New York City landmark bomb plot as a "sequel" to the February 1993 World Trade Center bombing. Additional attacks would have potentially inflicted hundreds of American casualties on American soil. The landmark bomb plot was concocted by blind Sheikh Omar Abdel-Rahman, a radical Muslim cleric in New York City, and by some of his followers. The attacks were to take place on July 4, Independence Day, in the U.S. The first target was the U.N. Building; it was to be destroyed by a suicide bomber driving a truck bomb. Also to be destroyed by car bombs were the Lincoln Tunnel and the Holland Tunnel, two busy underground roadways in the city. The George Washington Bridge would be bombed next, as well as the FBI's main office in New York. There was also some talk of bombing Jewish targets in the city as well as assassinating U.S. Sen. Al D'Amato and Egyptian President Hosni Mubarak. Perpetrators of these plots were arrested in June 24, 1993, putting an end to the threats. At the time they were arrested, the conspirators were mixing fertilizer and diesel fuel to create an ammonium nitrate fuel oil (ANFO) bomb like the one used on the World Trade Center. Rahman and nine others were convicted on October 1, 1995; Rahman was sentenced to life in prison.

Since the 1993 World Trade Center bombing, several additional plots have been discovered and stopped. In August 1997, a letter was found written by two men who were plotting to bomb a Brooklyn subway station. The letter was found in a Brooklyn apartment, demanding that six jailed Islamic or Arab militants be released, including Ramzi Yousef and Omar Abdel–Rahman. The letter threatened the bombing of a Brooklyn subway station and subsequent attacks at other locations. On October 15, 1995, a bomb damaged an unmanned weather station used by air traffic controllers at LaGuardia Airport. Damage was sustained by a windshear alert system, designed to notify air traffic controllers about dangerous, abrupt changes in wind speed and direction that can affect planes during takeoffs and landings.

During the evening of June 27, 1994, authorities in Matsumoto, Japan, received calls from terrified residents in Kaichi Heights, a normally quiet neighborhood near the old heart of the city. Matsumoto is located 100 miles west of Tokyo on the Japanese main island of Honshu. Emergency response personnel were sent to the scene and transported dozens of persons to area hospitals where they were treated for acute exposure to toxic chemicals. Doctors were surprised to find significantly reduced cholinesterase levels in practically all victims, and followed a course of treatment for organophosphate pesticide poisoning. Organophosphate pesticides and chemical nerve agents act to inhibit cholinesterase enzymes throughout the body. Cholinesterase normally acts to hydrolyze acetylcholine wherever it is released in the body. The process is the body's method of controlling nerve impulses that cause the muscles to function normally. When cholinesterase is reduced or absent, the muscles spasm uncontrollably. This whole process will be covered in more detail in Chapter 3. Seven people died, and over 200 were injured from nerve agent exposure. Sampling and analysis identified the presence of the super-toxic nerve agent sarin, a true chemical weapon, at several sites in the Kaichi Heights neighborhood. The sarin appeared to have been generated from a vacant lot, near a fish pond. No containers or related equipment were found; however, significant damage occurred to plant life, possibly caused by another gas, hydrogen fluoride, which might have been released at the same time as the sarin. Dead fish found in the pond, along with water and soil samples from the area, showed traces of sarin. It was identified through gas chromatography from the samples taken in the neighborhood. Trees around the fish pond and the darkness of night might have prevented anyone from observing the exact source of the deadly vapors. There were, however, several reports of odd, sharp smells reported by citizens. Two witnesses noted a white, mistlike cloud coming from the area of the vacant lot. The Matsumoto incident received media coverage in Japan but was not covered to any extent in the world media. Japanese national authorities deemed the event a matter for local authorities.

As it turns out, the Matsumoto sarin attack was a trial run for the Tokyo incident that followed almost a year later. It is also believed that the attack was an act of revenge against three justices trying an Aum Shinri Kyo religious sect case in court. The possibility that the Matsumoto incident may have been a terrorist attack was supported by several details in the case. Sarin is the product of a specific and rather complex series of chemical processes. While well within the capabilities of a technically skilled chemist, the production of sarin is simply not something that can be done by accident. Chemicals used in the manufacture of sarin are very toxic and difficult to obtain. They must be combined in an exact formulation, usually at high temperatures, to produce the nerve agent. The sarin at Matsumoto had to be purposely formulated. Weather conditions play a significant role in the deadliness of sarin. Rain both cleans the air of vapors and neutralizes the nerve agent through hydrolysis. Sarin, a volatile liquid when compared to other nerve agents, produces more vapor when the ambient temperatures are warm. June in Matsumoto is the rainy season, with steady showers and temperatures hovering around 67°F. On June 26, the weather changed unexpectedly. Skies cleared and temperatures climbed to around 87°F. Forecasters predicted the dry, warm conditions would last until June 28. The sarin poisonings took place on the evening of June 27, the second day of the weather break. Someone apparently anticipated the weather break and took advantage of it. No individual or group came forward to claim credit for the attack, which on the surface might seem a bit unusual. It is still not improbable to believe that a small group of persons might be carefully testing and evaluating the effectiveness of a weapon such as sarin. Such testing would be sensible prior to planning a major strike using a weapon which might be new to its users. Testing might be warranted both to prevent accidents and to assure maximum effectiveness. It might be that the responsible party did not want it known that they possessed such a weapon. This tactic could play a part in the group's overall strategy, or perhaps satisfy a desire for optimum surprise and shock. In any case, the person(s) responsible for the incident in Matsumoto certainly understood that a significant quantity of nerve agent, delivered into a warm crowded urban site, such as a department store or subway station, could have catastrophic consequences. The Matsumoto attack has generally been referred to by Japanese authorities and the media as "the incident." There was powerful evidence that whatever the complete story of the fatal June night turned out to be, the events in that quiet city were anything but accidental. This case deserves further attention as the potential forerunner of the next phase of terrorist horror, which occurred in the subway system of Tokyo.

On March 20, 1995, nearly nine months after the Matsumoto incident, sarin was released into the Tokyo subway system (it might have just as easily been the subway system in London or New York City). Aum Shinri Kyo claimed responsibility, and a new era of terrorism began. This cult had set up offices in New York City in 1987, and sought to purchase high-technology equipment, including computers, software, air filtration media, a laser measuring system, and gas masks. Two cult members earned helicopter flying licenses in Florida, and the cult obtained a Soviet-made helicopter from Russia. Russian government reports indicate that the Aum cult has more than 35,000 followers in Russia. Cult members were in Australia in 1993 and purchased a 500,000-acre sheep farm in western Australia. They also bought eight mining leases for the purpose of exporting uranium ore. Although sarin is highly toxic, the Tokyo subway incident did not produce the numbers of deaths and injuries that might have been expected by the terrorists. Had the terrorists been able to effectively disseminate the sarin, the death rate might well have been in the thousands. Methods used in the dispersion of the sarin nerve agent were very inefficient and ineffective. On the other hand, the level of proper training and preparation of emergency responders contributed to a higher level of casualties than could be expected from the ineffective dispersion of the agent. Makeshift chemical devices were placed at 15 stations on three subway lines scheduled to converge from the north and west on Kasumigaseki (the government district of Tokyo) between 8:09 and 8:13 AM local time. Only two of the devices actually released their toxic agent at the government station. The other three were either found before or after the trains had reached the target area. It is believed that the sarin vapors were intended for the government employees who worked in the Kasumigaseki area, and the release was scheduled to affect the peak point of rush hour, just before the usual 8:30 AM starting time of the employees.

Only very small amounts of sarin are needed to kill. A single milligram of sarin coming into contact with the skin is sufficient to produce death in most people. In the vapor form, it takes a concentration of 100 mg/m^3 in air to be fatal. Passengers on the subway trains reported seeing persons leaving packages, or noticed unaccompanied packages spilling oily substances on the floor. Some passengers moved away from the packages and continued on to their stops, while others took part in mass evacuations from subway cars at the next station. One woman remained on the subway in spite of the onset of symptoms, which included headache and miosis, until it was announced that the subway was closed. Symptoms of those mildly to moderately affected varied from headaches and miosis to vomiting and convulsions. The first call for help came from the Kayabacho Station at 8:09 AM for a passenger who was experiencing convulsions. This was followed in short order by a flood of requests for ambulances from other stations. Initial calls also reported an explosion, which created confusion for responders, along with the reports of several subway stations attacked simultaneously, creating additional confusion. Response routes were not cleared, making the response to the scene difficult. Many people took themselves to hospitals or used taxicabs, which further blocked response routes. The Tokyo Fire Department dispatched 340 units, including hazmat vehicles, engine companies, and EMS units, along with 1,364 emergency response personnel. Almost 10%, or 135, of the response personnel would be exposed to the sarin gas and become victims themselves. In a typical year, the Tokyo Fire Department experiences around 100 injuries to personnel during the entire year. Responders who wore a self-contained breathing apparatus (SCBA) and did not contact the sarin were not injured. Most of the injuries to personnel took place down in the subway stations. Approximately 25% of the injuries took place above ground while treating victims. All of the injured eventually returned to duty over the following year.

Firefighters were the first emergency responders to arrive on the scene. They were not only unauthorized to give antidotes, they were also completely unaware of what substance they were dealing with. The colorless, odorless sarin was not detected, and consequently the hazard at each scene was not identified. During treatment, victims' conditions worsened suddenly. Most of the responders injured were contaminated by contact with the patients. Attempts were made to triage victims, but many of the less severely affected hailed passing cars and taxicabs for transportation to hospitals.

Hospitals became overwhelmed by over 5,500 people who sought treatment. As it turns out, thousands of those who jammed into hospitals were not even exposed to the sarin. The people were afraid of the unknown and wanted to be reassured that they were not poisoned. There was little consistency in the decontamination and treatment of patients. Initially, hospital personnel had no idea what the people had been exposed to. Approximately 1,000 persons had experienced symptoms from mild to moderate. Eight people died during the first two days, and four more in the next few months. Others are expected to die in following years. While the actual casualties of the incident were low, the amount of fear the attack generated increased triage time due to the large numbers of victims reporting for medical treatment even though they had not been exposed to the nerve agent. Responsibility for the sarin attack was attributed to the Aum Shinri Kyo cult, a religious terrorist group headed by Shoko Asahara. It is reported that the police were the first to determine that sarin was the agent responsible for the casualties. Hazardous materials personnel first detected acetyl nitrate while monitoring the air during the incident. Acetyl nitrate is a solvent used during the production of sarin. Doctors who treated patients at the Matsumoto incident are reported to have contacted Tokyo doctors, suggesting the symptoms were similar to those experienced in Matsumoto and further suggesting it might be sarin.

Less well known is the incident that happened on May 5, 1995, at the Shinjuke station, when a cleaning lady found an unexploded hydrogen-cyanide gas bomb. The device was removed and destroyed before it went off. It had been placed near a ventilation duct that would have spread the gas. Police estimate that as many as 10,000 people could have died if the bomb had gone off.

April 19, 1995, was the second anniversary of the end of the siege of the Branch Davidian compound in Waco, Texas. At approximately 9:02 AM, an explosion ripped through the Murrah Federal Building in Oklahoma City, Oklahoma (Figure 2.3), killing 168 people, including 19 children and 1 rescue worker and injuring another 850. Eighty-five rescue workers also suffered injuries during the rescue and body recovery operations. This incident

Figure 2.3 Car fires first greeted response personnel at the Oklahoma City blast scene, obscuring some of the views of the explosion damage. (Source: City of Oklahoma City, Public Information and Marketing. Used with permission.)

became the worst act of terrorism ever carried out on American soil to date. It took rescue workers over two weeks to remove all of the bodies from the damaged building. Over 300 buildings sustained some type of damage from ground shock and blast pressure. Of the buildings damaged, 50 would have to be demolished. Windows were broken as far as 2 miles from the blast site and the blast was heard 50 miles away. It registered 3.5 on the open-ended Richter scale in Denver, Colorado. Across the street in a parking lot, 60 cars were completely destroyed. Property loss was estimated to be over $250 million. A 4,000-pound bomb made up of an ammonium nitrate and fuel oil mixture detonated inside a Ryder rental truck that was parked in front of the Murrah Federal Building. This was the same type of explosive material used in the bombing of the World Trade Center in New York City, but a much larger amount. Timothy McVeigh, a radical antigovernment "militia" member, was arrested by the Oklahoma Highway Patrol just 90 minutes after the bombing for driving without a license plate.

The Alfred P. Murrah Federal Building was a nine-story high-rise constructed of reinforced concrete built in 1977 at a cost of $14.5 million. It was named after Alfred P. Murrah, a federal judge who was an Oklahoma native. The front of the building was ripped off by the blast (Figure 2.4), leaving it open on all nine floors. A pile of debris three stories high was left in front of the building as a result of the explosion, which ripped away 80% of the building front. The Federal Building housed 19 government agencies, including the ATF, the Secret Service, and the Drug Enforcement Agency (DEA). Because of the magnitude of the disaster, President Clinton invoked the resources of the Stafford Act and declared a presidential disaster. Generally, under the Stafford Act a state must first declare a disaster and then make a formal request to the President for a federal disaster declaration. However,

Figure 2.4 Oklahoma City Federal Building, following explosion. (Source: City of Oklahoma City, Public Information and Marketing. Used with permission.)

the blast involved federal property, and the Stafford Act allows the President to act without a state request. The presidential declaration was made within an hour after the blast, providing unlimited federal resources to assist with the emergency. The Federal Emergency Management Agency (FEMA) activated the Urban Search and Rescue (US&R) portion of the National Disaster Response System. Eleven of the 23 teams established at the time of the bombing worked on the search and rescue process at the Murrah Federal Building. Phoenix was the first team activated, and they were in Oklahoma City searching the rubble by 6:00 PM the day of the explosion. In all, over 12,384 volunteers and rescue personnel took part in rescue, recovery, and support activities. Following the investigation and final removal of bodies, the remaining building was demolished with explosives on May 23, 1995. Seven thousand people were left without a workplace as a result of the explosion, 462 people were left homeless, 30 children were orphaned, 219 children lost at least one parent, and more than 1,000 people survived the attack.

Along with Timothy McVeigh, another suspect discovered he was wanted by the FBI for questioning concerning the bombing, and surrendered to police in Herington, Kansas. Both Timothy McVeigh and Terry Nichols were arrested and charged with the bombing. It is believed that the explosion was in retaliation for the government actions during the Waco siege, although the exact target of the bomb is unknown. The federal courthouse where the Waco trial took place is on the next street over from the Federal Building. It was reported to me by one of the first arriving battalion chiefs from the Oklahoma City Fire Department that the Murrah Federal Building was not the first choice of targets for Timothy McVeigh, the convicted bomber. McVeigh had planned on blowing up the federal courthouse across the street to the south of the Federal Building. Road construction narrowing the street and blocking direct access to the courthouse the day of the bombing caused a change of plan and the destruction of the Murrah Federal Building. Timothy McVeigh was indicted on terrorism, murder, and conspiracy charges, convicted in Denver, Colorado, of the bombing of the Federal Building, and sentenced to death. McVeigh was executed on June 11, 2001, at 8:14 am EDT at the federal prison in Terre Haute, Indiana. He was given a lethal injection after telling a federal judge six months earlier he did not want to go through the appeals process. McVeigh's execution was the first federal execution since 1963. Several of the victims' families witnessed the execution live, while others viewed with closed circuit hook-ups arranged in Oklahoma City. Also charged in the bombing was Terry Nichols. He received life sentences in both his state and federal trials, which started in 1997. The FBI announced on April 1, 2005, that they had found additional bombing materials buried in a crawl space at Nichols' home in Kansas, just three weeks short of the 10th anniversary of the Oklahoma City bombing. Materials included blasting caps and other materials believed to be a part of the original bombing plot. During many previous searches prior to the trials, the items were not discovered. Everything found was sent to the FBI laboratory for analysis.

In July 1997, plans were announced for the design of a memorial to be built on the site of the former Murrah Federal Building in Oklahoma City (Figure 2.5 through Figure 2.7). This memorial would "honor the victims, survivors, rescuers, and those whose lives were forever changed on April 19, 1995." Ground was broken during September 1998 for the Oklahoma City National Memorial, and it was dedicated on April 19, 2000, by President Bill Clinton. I personally had the opportunity to visit the site of the memorial in November 2000, and it was quite a moving experience. While teaching a one-week class for the National Fire Academy, primarily for the National Guard Civil Support Team, I met a battalion chief from the Oklahoma City Fire

Figure 2.5   One of the gates to the memorial overlooking the reflecting pond, the time 9:01 representing the last moments of peace before the explosion.

Figure 2.6 **(See color insert following page 236.)** To the side of the reflecting pond are 168 bronze colored chairs each engraved with the name of one of the 168 victims of the terrorist attack.

Figure 2.7 This tree is a 70-year-old American elm tilted by the force of the explosion but still standing and living on in spite of the explosion.

Department who was one of the first chief officers on the scene. He was kind enough to take me on a walking tour of the memorial and provide an overview of his and his department's actions during the response to the bombing. That personal touch made my tour of the site much more meaningful. Two of the most outstanding features of the memorial are the "Gates of Time." One gate is located on each end of the memorial. The concrete gates are covered with a "naval" and "yellow" bronze. On one of the gates is the time 9:01, representing the last moments of peace and on the other gate is the time 9:03, representing the first moments of recovery. For me the most moving part of the memorial was the 168 bronze colored chairs, each engraved with the name of one of the 168 victims of the terrorist attack. Also on the site is the "Survivor Tree." This tree is a 70-year-old American elm tilted by the force of the explosion, but still standing and living on in spite of the explosion. Portions of the lower level of the building wall were left in place and incorporated into the memorial site as well. Through the center of the site between the Gates of Time is a reflecting pool in front of the 168 chairs. It is truly a well-designed and well-built memorial, fitting for all those who were affected by the April 19 terrorist attack on the now-demolished Murrah Federal Building. Anyone who gets a chance to visit the site should certainly take the opportunity, as I am sure it is something they will never forget. I know I won't.

On October 10, 1995, it appears that domestic terrorists may have struck again, this time in Arizona. The Amtrak Sunset Limited, carrying 248 passengers and a crew of 20, was derailed, killing 1, and seriously injuring 12, with another 100 receiving minor injuries in a remote area near Hyder, Arizona, 59 miles southwest of Phoenix. It took rescuers over an hour to reach the victims because the site is accessible only by air or with four-wheel drive vehicles. A group calling themselves the "Sons of Gestapo" claimed to have pulled 29 spikes holding the rails in place, sending the train over a bridge into a dry stream bed. The warning device designed to alert train crews of dangerous tracks had been tampered with. A note found outside the train, and signed Sons of Gestapo, made references to the federal sieges at Waco and Ruby Ridge, both of which have become rallying points for right-wing, antigovernment extremists. The FBI reported that it is unaware of the existence of the Sons of Gestapo and did not know if it was a real group or not. Acting on a tip, FBI agents found another derailing device on a set of tracks in downtown Phoenix. It was unknown if the two incidents are connected. It was noted that whoever was responsible for the accident knew something about rail service, and the rails removed were designed to send the train into the creek bed.

The 1996 Olympics in Atlanta, Georgia, became the next site of domestic terrorism in the U.S. on July 27, 1996, at 1:25 AM (Figure 2.8 and Figure 2.9). In spite of heavy security and enormous preparations for the possibility of a terrorist attack, a pipe bomb exploded in Olympic Park, killing two and injuring 111, including 10 emergency responders. It was the worst attack at the Olympics since the Munich games in 1972, where 11 Israeli athletes were killed by Palestinian guerrillas. Atlanta police were warned of the device from a pay phone near the scene of the blast at 12:58:34 AM. The caller, believed to be a "white male with an indistinguishable accent" and American, stated that "a bomb was in Centennial Park, you have 30 minutes" (the bomb actually exploded 10 minutes earlier than the time given by the caller). A partial evacuation of the park occurred, but only because police already on duty in the park happened upon the unattended knapsack that held the bomb. The device was an unsophisticated pipe bomb placed in a satchel near the concert stage in Olympic Park. Nails and screws were loaded into the

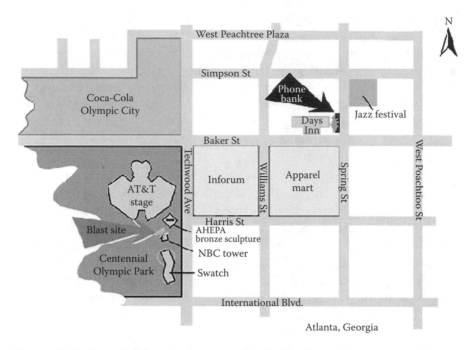

Figure 2.8   Map of Olympic Centennial Park bomb site. (Source: FBI.)

bomb to create shrapnel to harm people. Police indicated they saw three pipes but did not know if they were three separate bombs or were all hooked together. Experts do not think international terrorists were involved because of the primitive type of explosive device used in the attack.

Prior to the games, three members of a Georgia militia group were arrested in April 1996 for plotting to attack the Olympics. They allegedly belonged to a militia group called the 112th Regiment, Militia-at-Large for the Republic of Georgia. The members arrested were charged with conspiracy to make pipe bombs. They were planning to stockpile explosives, ammunition, weapons, and other military equipment for a terror campaign.

On January 12, 1997, in the Atlanta, Georgia, suburb of Sandy Springs, two bombs went off at the Northside Family Planning Services. The first bomb did not cause any injuries. However, the second bomb apparently was planted and timed to kill or injure emergency responders. Thirteen emergency responders including three federal agents were injured, though not seriously, by the second blast. A little over a month later, another pair of bombs went off at an Atlanta nightclub called the Otherside Lounge, which caters to gay clientele. Five people were injured, one seriously by the first blast. Police found a third bomb outside by the curb that was, again, set to target emergency responders. The bomb exploded while a robot tried to disarm it. However, precautions were taken and no one was injured by the

Figure 2.9 Investigators inspect the scene of the explosion at the Olympic Centennial Park in Atlanta. Two people were killed and more than 100 others injured in the explosion. (Source: AP/Wide World Photos. Used with permission.)

blast. The day after the second attack, letters were sent claiming responsibility for both of the bombing incidents. A group calling itself "The Army of God" indicated it had declared and would wage a total war against agents of the federal government. The author(s) of the letter indicated they were violent opponents of abortion, homosexuality, and the federal government.

On January 30, 1998, a bomb exploded at an abortion clinic in Birmingham, Alabama (Figure 2.10). The blast killed an off-duty police officer who was moonlighting as a security guard at the facility and critically injured a clinic counselor. From January to May 1997, additional acts of violence, including the use of incendiary devices and bombs, occurred against abortion clinics in Tulsa, Oklahoma; Falls Church, Virginia; North Hollywood, California; Bozeman, Montana; Yakima, Washington; and Portland, Oregon. During May 1998, attacks involving butyric acid occurred at eight abortion clinics in Florida. This was the first report of the use of butyric acid against abortion clinics in over four years. From 1992 through May 1998 (Figure 2.11), there had been 99 reports of "noxious" chemical attacks on abortion clinics. Butyric acid is a colorless organic acid with a penetrating, obnoxious odor. It is a strong irritant to skin and tissue and

Figure 2.10   An unidentified man looks down on damage to the New Woman All Women Health Care clinic in Birmingham, Alabama, caused by a bomb blast that killed an off-duty police officer and severely injured a nurse. (Source: AP/Wide World Photos. Used with permission.)

can cause severe burns. The most significant problem with butyric acid is removing the odor. With little exception, anything the acid comes into contact with will have to be replaced. As a result, the attacks have caused over $800,000 in damage since 1992.

Federal investigators have determined that the bombings in Olympic Park, the Sandy Springs abortion clinic, the Otherside Lounge, and the abortion clinic in Birmingham were all connected and may have been carried out by the same person(s). Tests performed by ATF and FBI laboratories in Washington, D.C. have discovered that some of the bomb components from the clinic and nightclub in Atlanta are identical. Nails used as shrapnel found at all three bombing sites came from the same foundry. Federal agents feel that the bombings were carried out by a single person or a small group. During February 1998, Eric Rudolph, a 32-year-old resident of Murphy, North Carolina, was charged with the bombing of the New Woman All Women Health Care clinic in Birmingham. On October 14, 1998, Rudolph was also charged with the bombings in Olympic Park and the abortion clinic and nightclub in Atlanta. A $1 million reward was offered for his arrest. He

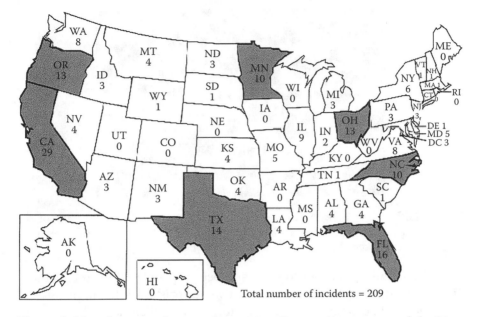

Figure 2.11 Abortion Clinic Violence Map. (Source: Department of the Treasury, Bureau of Alcohol, Tobacco and Firearms.)

was on the FBI's 10 most wanted list of fugitives since 1998. Rudolph was captured without incident on May 31, 2003, by a Murphy, North Carolina, sheriff's deputy. The mountain town of Murphy had long been a focus of the FBI, who formed the Southeast Bomb Task Force and at one point had 200 agents scouring the mountainous terrain in western North Carolina for any sign of Rudolph. He will be put on trial in Birmingham for the killing of Birmingham Police Officer Robert "Sande" Sanderson and the wounding of Emily Lyons, a nurse who was severely injured by the blast.

Explosive devices in the past have been the weapons of choice for both domestic and international terrorists. Their use has increased over the past few years. Bombings almost doubled from 1989 to 1994. During May, June, and July 1996, ATF agents made many high-profile raids on antigovernment militia groups in Georgia, Arizona, and Washington State. For every incident that occurs like the World Trade Center or the abortion clinic in Atlanta, officials report dozens of attempts where death and destruction are narrowly averted. Some of the increase in the use of explosive devices can be attributed to the readily available information to make bombs that is on the Internet, and other sources such as videos and how-to books. Chemical and biological weapons are thought to become the weapon of choice in the future. Chemical and biological weapons are cheaper and easier to produce than nuclear weapons and are extremely deadly. The two incidents in Japan confirm that these types of weapons are available to terrorists and, when released effectively,

Figure 2.12 New York, New York, October 4, 2001 — An aerial view of the recovery operation underway in lower Manhattan at the site of the collapsed World Trade Center. (Photo by Andrea Booher/ FEMA News Photo.)

present a significant danger to large numbers of people. While the methods of dissemination in Japan were ineffective, terrorists will learn, in time, to do a better job, creating more death and injury by their acts. The threat of chemical and biological weapons is neither far-fetched nor far off. There is, in fact, a clear and present danger today, one that is only going to increase with time. Emergency responders need to be trained to recognize the signs and symptoms of chemical and biological agents, explosive and incendiary devices, as well as the other signs of acts of terrorism. They also need to be equipped and to develop plans for dealing with terrorist attacks with WMD.

September 11, 2001 — "the day the world changed" — terrorists used a new WMD to attack the U.S., commercial aircraft (Table 2.1). Four commercial airliners were hijacked, two following departures from Boston's Logan International Airport, one from Newark, New Jersey International Airport, and one from Washington, D.C.'s Dulles International Airport. United Airlines Flight 175, a Boeing 767, was the first to depart Boston at 7:58 AM. The plane had on board 56 passengers, 2 pilots, and 7 crew members bound for Los Angeles. At 7:59 AM American Airlines Flight 11, a Boeing 767, departed Boston also bound for Los Angeles, with 81 passengers, 2 pilots, and 9 crew members. At 8:01 AM United Airlines Flight 93, a Boeing 757 with 38 passengers, 2 pilots, and 5 crew members departed Newark International Airport headed for San Francisco. Finally, at 8:10 AM an American Airlines Boeing 757, Flight 77 took off from Washington bound for Los Angeles, carrying 58 passengers, 2 pilots, and 4 crew members. All four aircraft were hijacked shortly after takeoff. There were 22 hijackers in all, 5 on Flight 11, 6 on Flight 175, 6 on Flight 77, and 4 on Flight 93. Following the attacks there were some reports in the media that not all of the hijackers knew the flights were suicide missions. American Airlines Flight 11 from Boston crashed into the South

Figure 2.13   New York, New York, September 29, 2001 — Firefighters continue to battle smoldering fires at the World Trade Center. (Photo by Andrea Booher/ FEMA News Photo)

Tower of the World Trade Center at 8:46 AM. Seventeen minutes later Flight 175 crashed into the North Tower of the World Trade Center. At that point the Federal Aviation Administration (FAA) shut down all New York area airports. At 9:21 AM all bridges and tunnels to New York were shut down. The FAA ordered all aircraft in the skies over the U.S. to immediately land at the closest airport. American Airlines Flight 77 from Dulles crashed into the Pentagon at 9:45 AM (Figure 2.15). At 10:05 AM the South Tower of the World Trade Center collapsed and the White House was evacuated. A portion of the Pentagon collapsed at 10:10 AM, and Flight 93 crashed into a wooded area of Pennsylvania. It is believed that passengers had tried to regain control of the aircraft. Finally, the North Tower of the World Trade Center collapsed at 10:28 AM (Figure 2.12). All passengers and crew, including the hijackers, perished in the crashes. September 11, 2001, will be remembered always and will go down with December 7, 1941, as a date that will "live in infamy."

Much discussion has taken place concerning the collapse of the Twin Towers of the World Trade Center. Initial impact of the aircraft did not cause enough structural damage to cause an immediate collapse of the buildings. It will likely never be known just how much the crashes contributed to the eventual collapse of the buildings. Certainly the resulting fires caused by the large amounts of jet fuel would have weakened the steel structure. Steel does not hold up well to flame impingement. Since there was never any fire suppression mounted on the fires, they burned unabated until the eventual collapse. The buildings had been constructed so that if a collapse were ever to occur, there would be a pancake effect and the buildings would not just fall over, reducing the structural impact on surrounding buildings. There is no question that the design for collapse worked very well. Floors below the impact and resulting fire areas were not damaged, but when the buildings

Table 2.1 Details of Four Airline Flights on September 11, 2001

Flight	Departed From	Crash	Time	People on Board
UA 175	Boston 7:58 AM	South Tower	9:05 AM	65
AA 11	Boston 7:59 AM	North Tower	8:45 AM	92
UA 93	Boston 8:01 AM	Pennsylvania	10:10 AM	45
AA 77	Dulles 8:10 AM	Pentagon	9:40 AM	64

Source: Washington Post.

Figure 2.14   New York, New York, September 21, 2001 — New York firefighters and Salt Lake City Urban Search and Rescue crews gather at the site of the cleanup operations underway at the site of the World Trade Center. (Photo by Michael Rieger/ FEMA News Photo.)

Figure 2.15   Arlington, Virginia, September 12, 2001 — Exterior of the crash site following the attack on the Pentagon. (Photo by Jocelyn Augustino/ FEMA News Photo.)

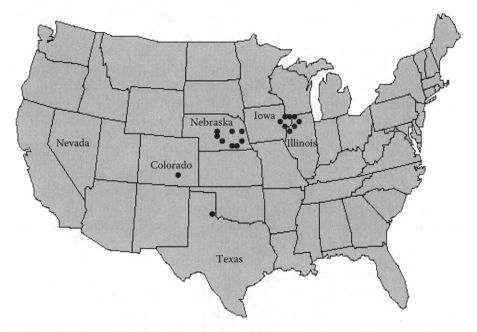

Figure 2.16 Mailbox bomber Lucas Helder told authorities he was planting pipe bombs in a pattern to show a happy face during his five-state weekend spree.

began to collapse the lower floors could not withstand the tremendous weight of the floors above collapsing on top of them. There has never before been such a catastrophic failure of a high-rise building. Much can be learned from the collapse of the World Trade Center towers that will help in future high-rise construction. Hopefully no one will ever have to experience the horror of September 11, 2001, again.

During May 2002, Lucas Helder, 21, of Pine Island, Minnesota, planted 18 pipe bombs in rural mailboxes in five states (Figure 2.16). He told authorities he was planting pipe bombs in a pattern to show a happy face during his five-state weekend spree. Helder admitted "manufacturing eight pipe bombs in his apartment in Wisconsin" and 16 more at a hotel near Omaha. Eight pipe bombs were left at locations in Illinois and Iowa, where six people were injured. Another eight bombs were placed in Nebraska and one each in Colorado and Texas. Helder was captured in Reno, Nevada, heading to California with six more pipe bombs in his trunk. During October 2004, Helder was ordered by a U.S. federal magistrate to be committed to a mental institution. U.S. Magistrate Judge Franklin Noel wrote that Helder was mentally ill and "there is no evidence that any treatment has worked to diminish the risk" that Helder would commit similar crimes again.

Following the September 11, 2001, terrorist attacks on the U.S. in mid-to-late September and continuing into October, letters with anthrax were delivered on the East Coast. Certainly in the minds of almost everyone initially was, is this a continuation or sequel to the September 11 attacks? This theory was strengthened by allegations that the "skin lesion," for which Ahmed al-Haznawit, one of the alleged September 11 hijackers, sought treatment at Holy Cross Hospital in Fort Lauderdale, Florida, was in fact caused by cutaneous anthrax. The FBI now claims that they are concentrating on a domestic terrorist. They believe that the anthrax attacks were not related to the September 11, 2001, attacks after all. Anthrax, which was sent to news media sources and members of Congress, was weapons grade and alleged to have been traced to a secret U.S. anthrax program at Dugway Proving Ground in Utah, approximately 80 miles south of Salt Lake City, which had been operating for over a decade. The first attack surfaced on September 18 at American Media in Boca Raton, Florida, and resulted in an employee checking into a hospital very ill but with no diagnosis. It was later confirmed that he had inhalation anthrax and later died. Inhalation anthrax is very rare and usually does not occur accidentally. Anytime a case of inhalation anthrax is diagnosed, it should be suspected that an incident of some kind has occurred. Two additional employees of American Media who worked in the mailroom tested positive for anthrax. Spores were found on the dead employee's computer keyboard. The source of the anthrax at American Media remains unknown at this time. Letters containing anthrax were mailed to Senator Tom Daschle and Senator Patrick Leahy in Washington, D.C. News organizations in New York City were targeted next with anthrax letters. News anchor Tom Brokaw's assistant tested positive for cutaneous anthrax. Brokaw's assistant recalled seeing a letter, weeks earlier, containing a brown, granular substance, most of which was discarded but the letter was kept. Cutaneous anthrax occurs when anthrax spores penetrate an opening in the skin. This form of anthrax is very treatable and is rarely fatal. Next, two New Jersey postal workers reported possible anthrax symptoms, and both were diagnosed with inhalation anthrax. Several Washington, D.C. postal workers were suspected of having anthrax. By October 25, two D.C. postal workers were dead and two more ill. A U.S. State Department mail processor was also diagnosed with inhalation anthrax. There were numerous exposures, 19 infections, and five fatalities. Thousands were tested. Ten thousand people in the U.S. took a two-month course of antibiotics after possible exposure. Hundreds or thousands of unexposed persons acquired the antibiotic Cipro through their doctors or over the Internet. Approximately five deaths and 25 nonfatal cases of anthrax were prevented by prompt antibiotic use.

As a result of the anthrax attacks, affected postal facilities and Senate office buildings were closed. Many government buildings were also closed as a precaution for testing during that same time period. U.S. mail was ordered to undergo irradiation to prevent other infections. Irradiation is a process of exposing mail to radiation in order to inactivate the anthrax. Five people eventually died of exposure to the anthrax through inhalation. In several of the cases the disease was not recognized when victims first sought medical attention. Once symptoms are present it is very difficult to treat victims, and they usually die. As of March 1, 2006, those responsible for the mailing of the anthrax have not been identified. Washington D.C. postal facilities that were contaminated by the anthrax remained closed until they were completely decontaminated and were reopened in 2003. Beyond the actual anthrax letters and effects were the thousands of hoax anthrax incidents that occurred across the country as a result. Emergency response agencies, including the FBI, were overwhelmed by the volume of incidents, and response to individual locations were greatly curtailed.

On October 2, 2002, "Beltway Snipers" John Allen Muhammad and Lee Boyd Malvo began their killing spree, shooting five people in 15 hours in Montgomery County, Maryland. Montgomery County is a suburban county north of Washington, D.C. The attacks continued for the next three weeks in the Washington metropolitan area, filling residents of the region with fear. Police received messages left at the murder locations and believed, correctly, that the killer worked in concert with another person. The shootings occurred at gas stations and in parking lots outside supermarkets, restaurants, and schools in a rough circular pattern around Washington. The victims were apparently selected at random, crossing racial, gender, and socioeconomic categories. The locations of the attacks always had close freeway access. It is believed the sniper used the circular Capital Beltway (also resulting in the Beltway Sniper name) to get from place to place, although several of the attacks occurred along Interstate 95, south of the Beltway in Virginia. The attacks were carried out with a Bushmaster XM-15 semiautomatic .223 caliber rifle, the civilian equivalent of the U.S. military's selective fire M-16 assault rifle, at a range of 50 to over 100 yards. The rifle came from Bull's Eye Shooter Supply in Tacoma, Washington, which had an extensive history of firearms violations and had not reported the rifle as missing, as required by federal law. The sniper attacks finally ended on October 24, when police arrested Muhammad and Malvo at a highway rest area on Interstate 270 near Hagerstown, Maryland. Two separate tips to police from alert citizens who saw a parked occupied car that matched the description distributed by the media led to the arrests. The former police car had been especially configured with a firing port so that a sniper could shoot from inside the closed trunk. Police called it a "killing machine." They had shot 13 people, including a 13-year-old boy at a school, and 10 of the victims died. During their respective trials in the fall of 2003, involving two of the victims in Virginia, Muhammad and Malvo were each found guilty of murder and weapons charges. The jury in Muhammad's case recommended that he be sentenced to death, while Malvo received a sentence of life in prison without parole. The judges concurred in both cases. Alabama law enforcement authorities allege that the snipers engaged in a series of previously unconnected attacks prior to October 2 in Montgomery, Alabama. Other charges are also pending in Maryland and other communities in Virginia. After the initial convictions and sentencing, one Virginia prosecutor (in Prince William County) stated he would wait to decide whether to try Malvo on capital charges in his jurisdiction until the U.S. Supreme Court ruled on whether juveniles may be subject to the penalty of execution. While that decision in an unrelated case was still pending before the high court, in October 2004, under a plea agreement, Malvo pleaded guilty in another case in Spotsylvania County, Virginia, for another murder to avoid a possible death penalty sentence, and agreed to additional sentencing of life imprisonment without parole. Malvo had yet to face trial in Prince William County, Virginia. In March 2005, the U.S. Supreme Court ruled in *Roper v. Simmons* that the Eighth Amendment prohibits execution for crimes committed when under the age of 18. In light of this Supreme Court decision, the prosecutors in Prince William County decided not to pursue the charges against Malvo after all. Prosecutors in Maryland, Louisiana, and Alabama are still interested in putting both Malvo and Muhammad on trial. Since Malvo was 17 when he committed the crimes, he will no longer face the death penalty, but still might be extradited to Alabama, Louisiana, and other states for prosecution. At the time of the *Roper v. Simmons* ruling, Malvo was 20 years old and was held at Virginia's maximum security Red Onion State Prison in Pound in Wise County, Virginia.

Over the course of several days in August 2003, sniper-style attacks left three people dead in the state of West Virginia. Police said that they were looking for a dark-colored full-size pickup truck. Eyewitnesses believed that the driver was a large white male, but couldn't identify the suspect further due to the darkness. A man was eventually arrested who matched the profile and who had implied to witnesses that he was the sniper, but no charges related to the shootings were ever brought against him. The police considered the possibility that the shootings were drug related. The second two victims had drug connections, but the police were not aware of any drug connections for the first victim. In October 2003, a joint task force investigating the shootings announced a $50,000 reward for information leading to the killer. As of August 2004, a year after the shootings, the case remained unsolved.

The suspect in the Ohio highway shootings was arrested after a man recognized him in a Las Vegas sports bar. Charles McCoy Jr., the suspect in two dozen Ohio shootings, which included one fatality, was captured without incident. The 24 shootings around several highways on the southern outskirts of Columbus pierced homes and a school, dented school buses, flattened tires, and shattered windshields. The shootings began in May. The shootings prompted commuters to take back roads and schools to cancel classes and hold recess indoors. Police increased patrols and offered a $60,000 reward. The state installed cameras on poles along Interstate 270. The only person struck, Gail Knisley, 62, was killed as a friend drove her to a doctor's appointment on November 25. Lab tests showed that bullets from nine of the shootings, including Knisley's death, were fired from the same gun. Until January 2004, the gunfire was scattered along or near Interstate 270, the busy highway that encircles Columbus. The last four shootings had moved toward the southwest on I-71. McCoy's trial began in April 2005, and he was convicted and sentenced on August 9, 2005, to 27 years in prison as part of a plea agreement for the sniper shootings.

During February 2003, the Lower Manhattan Development Corporation, which was established by New York Governor Pataki to coordinate the various agencies and advisory committees involved in the rebuilding efforts, chose architect Daniel Libeskind's design for rebuilding the 16-acre site of the former World Trade Center. The design includes a hanging garden, a memorial, a cultural center, and Freedom Tower, which will be a symbolic 1,776 feet tall from the ground to the top of its spire. This will make it taller than any building currently standing in the world. (The Burj Dubai skyscraper currently under construction in the United Arab Emirates is expected to surpass it, however.) This design is from a second set of plans shown to the public; the first group was criticized for its overemphasis on office space. In July 2003, David Childs was brought in as the new lead architect of the Freedom Tower, although Libeskind remained in charge of designing the site in general. A tower design combining the approaches of both architects was unveiled in December 2003. It will include wind turbines in its spire, which may generate as much as 20% of the building's power. On July 4, 2004, New York Governor Pataki, New Jersey Governor McGreevey, and New York City Mayor Bloomberg laid the cornerstone for Freedom Tower. The skyscraper, estimated to cost $1.5 billion, is expected to be ready for its first occupants by late 2008, while construction on the site in general is expected to last through 2015.

The Lower Manhattan Development Corporation announced in January 2004 that architects Michael Arad and Peter Walker had won a competition to design the memorial to the people who died at the World Trade Center. The memorial, Reflecting Absence, will honor those who died at the World Trade Center in two terrorist attacks — on September 11, 2001, and February 26, 1993. In the 1993 tragedy, a truck bomb exploded in a garage in the North Tower, killing six people and injuring more than a thousand. Reflecting Absence, which will be built where the Twin Towers once stood, includes two shallow pools surrounded by leafy trees. The names of the victims will be etched in walls around the pools. "In its powerful, yet simple articulation of the footprints of the Twin Towers, Reflecting Absence has made the gaping voids left by the towers' destruction the primary symbol of loss," said Vartan Gregorian, who chaired the jury that chose the winner. There were more than 5000 entries in the competition. Construction of the memorial is scheduled to begin in 2006.

Since the terror attacks on September 11, 2001, awareness and intelligence has improved a great deal. On October 7, 2005, the White House released a list of 10 serious terror plots that have been foiled by the U.S. and its allies over the past four years.

- West Coast Airliner Plot:
  In mid-2002 the U.S. disrupted a plot to use hijacked airplanes to attack targets on the West Coast of the U.S. The plotters included at least one major operational planner behind the September 11, 2001, attacks.
- East Coast Airliner Plot:
  In mid-2003 the U.S. and a partner disrupted a plot to use hijacked commercial airplanes to attack targets on the East Coast of the U.S.
- The Jose Padila Plot:
  In May 2002 the U.S. disrupted a plot that involved the blowing up of apartment buildings in the U.S. One of the alleged plotters, Jose Padila, allegedly discussed the possibility of using a "dirty bomb" inside the U.S. President Bush designated him as an "enemy combatant."
- 2004 British Urban Targets Plot:
  In mid-2004 the U.S. and partners disrupted a plot to bomb urban targets in Britain.
- 2003 Karachi Plot:
  In spring 2003 the U.S. and a partner disrupted a plot to attack Westerners at several targets in Karachi, Pakistan.
- Heathrow Airport Plot:
  In 2003 the U.S. and several partners disrupted a plot to attack London's Heathrow Airport using hijacked commercial airliners. The planning for this alleged attack was undertaken by a major operational figure in the September 11, 2001, attacks.
- 2004 Britain Plot:
  In the spring of 2004 the U.S. and partners, using a combination of law enforcement and intelligence resources, disrupted a plot to conduct large-scale bombings in Britain.

- 2002 Arabian Gulf Shipping Plot:
  In late 2002 and 2003 the U.S. and a partner nation disrupted a plot by al Qaeda operatives to attack ships in the Arabian Gulf.
- 2002 Strait of Hormuz Plot:
  In 2002 the U.S. and partners disrupted a plot to attack ships in the Strait of Hormuz, the entrance to the Persian Gulf from the Indian Ocean.
- 2003 Tourist Site Plot:
  In 2003 the U.S. and a partner nation disrupted a plot to attack a tourist site outside the U.S. The White House did not list what that site was.

Chemical Terrorist Agents

3

Dating from 431–404 B.C. during the Peloponnesian War, the first chemical weapons were used on the battlefield. Spartans deployed wood that had been saturated with pitch and sulfur to produce sulfur dioxide gas (a highly toxic gas with a threshold limit value (TLV) of 2 ppm in air). During World War I, the French introduced chemical warfare using 26 mm gas grenades containing ethyl bromacetate (a strong irritant that is toxic by inhalation, ingestion, and skin absorption). The weapons were not very effective, and were soon discarded. Four months later, the Germans introduced T-shells containing xylyl-e bromide (a strong irritant to skin, eyes, and tissue, toxic by inhalation and ingestion), and used them against the French. During April 1915, the first large-scale use of chemicals occurred during World War I, when the Germans released 265 tons of chlorine. Over 5,000 casualties resulted from the chlorine attack at Ypres, France. Later, in 1915, 8,000 Russians were killed by chlorine released on the battlefield. Gas masks were developed by the Allies to protect soldiers from the German gas attacks. The Germans then resorted to using mustard agents. While seldom lethal, mustard incapacitated allied troops and was the highest casualty producer among chemical agents. By the 1930s, several chemical nerve agents were discovered by German scientists trying to develop new insecticides.

During World War II, the Germans had large stockpiles of nerve agents but chose not to use them. Allied forces had no protection against the agents, and if those had been used, troops would have been at a huge disadvantage. Surprisingly, the reason they were not used was Adolf Hitler. He was a German soldier during World War I and witnessed the effects of chemical agents used against troops. Because of this, he refused to use them offensively during World War II.

Use of chemical weapons has until recently been confined to the battlefield. However, with the introduction of the nerve agent sarin during terrorist attacks in Matsumoto and Tokyo, Japan, and chemical agent incidents in several other cities (Table 3.1), chemical agents have become a weapon of

Figure 3.1 Chlorine tank cars on rail siding in Baltimore, Maryland — potential terrorist target.

Table 3.1 Chemical Agent Incidents in Japan

June 21, 1995, Matsumoto; 7 killed and 200 injured by sarin nerve agent attack.

July 1994, Karnikuishiki; citizens experience nausea and eye irritation caused by unidentified fumes.

September 1, 1994, Nara; 231 citizens injured in seven towns from unidentified fumes.

March 5, 1995, Yokohama; 19 injured after inhaling fumes on a subway car.

March 20, 1995, Tokyo; 12 dead and 5000 injured in sarin attack during the morning rush.

April 19, 1995, Yokohama; 400 citizens injured during a chemical attack on the subway.

May 6, 1995, Tokyo; plastic bags of cyanide found in subway station by guards.

July 5, 1995, Tokyo; plastic bags of cyanide soda and sulfuric acid found in subway.

July 6, 1995, Tokyo; cyanide gas emission device found in subway. Unknown fumes are reported at another station an hour later, overcoming commuters.

terrorism. There are no reported incidents in the U.S. involving the use of chemical nerve agents by terrorists. Because of the attacks in Japan, however, the threat of nerve agent use is very real. When an individual or group decides to make a threat to use chemical agents at a target in the U.S., it must be taken seriously. On April 14, 1995, less than a month after the sarin attacks in Tokyo's subway systems, a threat was made against Disneyland in Anaheim, California. U.S. Army Chemical Warfare personnel, the FBI, the Department of Defense, and other federal agencies took the threat seriously. Federal resources assembled in Anaheim to prepare for the worst. Officials at Disneyland refused to close the theme park despite the seriousness of the threat. They did, however, provide support to the response personnel by providing food, sleeping facilities, and other supplies. Security at the theme park was increased, and everyone entering the park was searched as they passed through the gates. Local emergency response officials were not notified of the threat until five days after it was made. Once notified, the Anaheim Fire Department, under the direction of Chief Jim Cox, established an incident command post and began to plan for the release, which was threatened for 7 PM on April 15, 1995. Preparations were made to treat 30,000 to 40,000 victims. Stockpiles of atropine were assembled. After waiting for three days past the threat date, on April 18, 1995, personnel on the scene were debriefed. FBI representatives cautioned those present that this would happen again. This incident, or nonincident if you prefer, points out the disruption to the system that can occur just by making a threat of a chemical or biological attack. On April 22, 1995, the Baltimore Sun reported that federal authorities had foiled an apparent terrorist gas attack at Disneyland. Acting on a tip from Tokyo police, federal agents arrested two Japanese citizens, reported to have been associated with the Aum Shinri Kyo Cult, at the Los Angles International Airport. A federal official reported to the Sun that cult members brought with them written instructions on how to make sarin and a videotape revealing details of the attack plans. Disney executives reported a threatening letter was received at Disneyland, which was investigated by federal authorities and dismissed as a hoax.

Chemical agents can be divided into several groups, which include nerve agents, vesicants (blister agents), blood agents, choking agents, and riot control agents.

Nerve agents function by inhibiting the enzyme acetylcholinesterase, resulting in an excess of acetylcholine in the body. This results in the characteristic uncontrolled muscle movements associated with exposures to nerve agents (Table 3.2). Nerve agents presented in this section will include GA (tabun), GB (sarin), GD (soman), GF, and VX. Vesicants include mustard agents, sulfur mustard (H), (HD) (agent "T"); nitrogen mustards (HN), (HN-2), and (HN-3); lewisite (L); and phosgene oxime (CX). Vesicants produce vesicles (blisters) when in contact with the human body and thus their name, blister agents. Mustard agents also cause damage to the eyes and respiratory system by direct contact and inhalation.

Table 3.2 Nerve Agent Relative Data

Comparative Data	GA	GB	VX
Rate of action	Very rapid	Very rapid	Rapid
State at 68°F	Colorless liquid	Colorless liquid	Colorless or pale amber liquid
Odor	Faint fruity; none when pure	Almost none when pure	Odorless when pure
Volatility (mg/mp^{3p} at 77°F)	610	22,000	10.5
LCtb$_{50b}$ (mg-min/mp^{3p})	135	70	30
Vapor density	5.6	2.9	9.2
Vapor pressure (mm Hg at 77°F)	0.07	2.9	0.0007

Source: CSEPP ACT FAST Student Manual.

Blood agents (cyanide compounds) have an undeserved reputation as an effective chemical warfare agent. Because they are so volatile, it is difficult to maintain effective concentrations for extended periods of time. However, at high concentrations cyanide does kill very quickly. Common forms of cyanide chemical agents include hydrocyanic acid (AC) and cyanogen chloride (CK).

Choking agents (lung-damaging agents) include the World War I agents phosgene and chlorine. Other choking agents are by-products of conventional warfare rather than chemical agents. They present themselves as products of combustion such as perfluroisobutylene (PFIB), which comes from the burning of Teflon-7®, which lines the inside of many military vehicles. HC smoke (a smoke that contains zinc) and oxides of nitrogen (from burning munitions) also produce lung hazards when exposed.

Riot control agents have been used on the battlefield; however, they are more likely to be used by police officers and National Guard troops during a civil disturbance rather than as a battlefield agent. CS, which is used by the law enforcement agents and the military, and CN (Mace 7), which is sold in devices for self-protection, are the primary types of riot control agents. Several other agents will also be presented.

Like all hazardous materials, chemical agents can exist as solids, liquids, or gases, depending on the existing temperatures and pressures. The only exception is riot control agents, which exist as aerosolized solids at normal temperatures and pressures. When chemical agents are weaponized, they are in the liquid state within the weapon. When the container (weapon shell) is exploded, the agent is expelled as a liquid or aerosol, which is a group of small solid particles or liquid droplets suspended in gas. Tear gas isn't really a gas; it is actually a solid that is aerosolized. Mustard and nerve agents likewise are not gases at normal temperatures and pressures. Therefore, to be an effective terrorist agent, they must be heated to produce vapor and the vapor has to be disseminated in order for people to breathe it.

Not all chemical agents are just military weapons materials. Chlorine, hydrogen cyanide, and phosgene are common industrial chemicals. Nerve and mustard agents are liquids under the same conditions in which chlorine, hydrogen cyanide, and phosgene are gases. Some mustard agents are frozen solid at 57°F. When in the liquid state, they evaporate at a rate similar to that of water. Chemical agent evaporation occurs not only because of its chemical makeup but because of the temperature and air pressure, wind velocity, and nature of the surface the agent comes in contact with. Water, for example, evaporates at a slower rate than gasoline, but at a faster rate than motor oil at a given temperature and pressure. Mustard is less volatile than the nerve agent sarin, but more volatile than the nerve agent VX. Volatility is the liquid's ability to produce a vapor at normal temperatures and pressures. So a liquid that is said to be volatile is producing a lot of vapor; one that is not volatile will be producing vapor at a much lower rate. Evaporation rates of all chemicals mentioned are accelerated by increases in temperature and wind speed or when they are resting on a smooth surface rather than a porous one. Volatility has an inverse relationship to persistence. The more volatile a substance is, the more quickly it evaporates, and the less it tends to stay or persist as a liquid. Because of the relatively low volatility of persistent liquid chemical agents, the liquid hazard is generally more significant than the danger from the small amounts of vapor that may be generated. The reverse is true of the nonpersistent agents. They evaporate quickly enough so as not to present a liquid hazard for an extended period of time. However, nonpersistence makes them more dangerous because more vapor will be present during an incident. Generally, the division between persistence and nonpersistence is related to the amount of the material left after 24 hours. The nonpersistent agents are usually gone after 24 hours. Nonpersistent materials remain for a period of minutes, semipersistent for hours, and persistent for days or longer.

Toxicity, or the poisonous effect of a hazardous material — the primary hazard of chemical agents — depends upon the concentration or amount of material present; the way in which the body is exposed to the material; the route by which the material enters the body; the target organ within the body that is affected by the material; and health variables such as age, general health and physical fitness, sex, and body chemistry. Those who are very young or very old may be more affected by a toxic material at a lower concentration than other persons. Toxic materials can affect the reproductive systems of men and women and cause birth defects. The amount of biological effect that will occur as the result of chemical exposure is based upon the concentration of the agent and the length of time over which the exposure occurs. Chlorine is a common industrial chemical used throughout the U.S. It has an IDLH of 10 ppm, is placarded as a 2.3 Poison Gas by the Department of Transportation (DOT), and is considered quite toxic. By comparison, military agent cyanogen chloride is twice as toxic; phosgene is 6 times more toxic; hydrogen cyanide is 7 times more toxic; mustard is 13 times more toxic; sarin is 200 times more toxic; and VX is 600 times more toxic.

Terminology and measures of toxicity that are commonly used with hazardous materials may in some cases be appropriate for chemical agents and biological toxins. They are presented here for review purposes. These terms include dose/response, immediate vs. delayed reactions, MLD, LDB_{50b}, LCB_{50b}, TLV-TWA, TLV-STEL, PEL, IDLH, and TLV-C. Dose represents the concentration of the toxic material and the length of time a person is exposed to it. Response is the biological effect that occurs from the given dose. Response can range from no effect at all to rapid death or anything in between. Some hazardous materials are medicines when given at low doses, while larger doses may prove to be fatal. Immediate effects are responses that occur instantly upon exposure to a toxic material. Exposure to chemical nerve agents, blood agents, choking agents, and riot control agents could have immediate effects. Delayed effects might range from 24 to 72 hours after the exposure. Toxic materials have to enter the body and reach a target organ or body system to cause damage. This process may take hours or days to occur. Mustard agents are examples of chemical agents that cause a delayed response. Other delayed effects may be cancer or some other disease, which may take years to develop. Teratogenic and mutagenic birth defects may also be caused by chemical exposure. Teratogens are one-time birth defects resulting from exposure to a particular chemical during pregnancy. If no future exposures occur, it is possible to have normal children again. Fetal Alcohol Syndrome is an example of a teratogenic affect. A fetus exposed to alcohol during the pregnancy may cause the child to be born with the syndrome. Mutagens, on the other hand, damage the DNA and genes, which prevents normal reproduction from occurring ever again. This can be caused by excessive exposure to radiation or other chemicals.

When discussing measures of toxicity, it is important to understand that the data available is primarily obtained from tests conducted on laboratory animals. Toxicity is based upon the physical amount, usually expressed in milligrams (mg) of the toxic material that it takes per kilogram (kg) of weight of the test animal to cause toxic effects. These test procedure results are then related to the amount it would take to cause effects on a human. For example, if 1 milligram of a given toxic material caused adverse effects on a 10-kilogram test animal, then it is estimated that it would take 10 milligrams to cause adverse effects on a 100-kilogram person, and so on. Some battlefield data is available on the effects of mustard agents, chlorine, and phosgene used on Allied troops during World War I. In addition to their primary symptoms, mustard agents are also known to cause cancer. MLD is the median lethal dose of a given material. Scientists conduct studies using laboratory animals, exposing them to a predetermined amount of a toxic substance, such as 5 mg/kg of body weight of the animal. If 50% of the test animals die, the MLD would be 5 mg/kg of body weight. LDB_{50B} is the dose determined by either ingestion or skin absorption that would be lethal to 50% of the laboratory animals exposed. LCB_{50B} is the dose determined by inhalation that would be lethal to 50% of the laboratory animals exposed. TLV-TWA is the threshold limit value, which is a time-weighted average concentration for 8 hours a day 40 hours a week exposure. This amount of material is what workers can be safely exposed to over and over, without experiencing adverse health effects. It should be noted, however, that this is not an absolute science. Benzene once was given a TLV-TWA of 1,000 parts per million. Because of workplace exposures over the years, many people started developing cancer and other illnesses from benzene exposure. For this reason, the TLV-TWA for benzene today has been lowered to 10 ppm! TLV-STEL is the threshold limit value short-term exposure limit. This is the concentration to which workers can be exposed continuously for a short period of time without suffering from irritation, chronic or irreversible tissue damage, or impairment of mental capacities which might cause accident or injury. STEL is a 15-minute exposure limit that should not be exceeded at any time during a workday. PEL is the permissible exposure limit, which is the amount of a given material that a person can be exposed to without toxic effect, over a given period of time. IDLH is immediately dangerous to life and health. This term is a measure of toxicity of a substance; the concentration of a toxin that is capable of causing irreparable injury or death. The TLV-C is the threshold limit value-ceiling, which is a concentration that should not be exceeded during any part of the work day. Emergency responders should be most concerned with determining the IDLH of a potential toxic material, because when a spill occurs, it is likely that the concentrations encountered will be much higher than any acceptable workplace exposure.

Concentrations of hazardous materials can be expressed using a number of terms, including percentages, mg/kg of body weight, parts per million (ppm) or parts per billion (ppb), or as mg/mp^{3p} in air. Terms are also associated with frequency of exposure, which we know as acute and chronic. Acute exposure is a short duration exposure, which can be seconds, minutes, or days. Acute may also indicate a single event without any further exposures. Effects may range from none at all to rapid death. Chronic exposure occurs over a prolonged period of time and may be hours, days, months, or years. Effects can be cancer or other illnesses that may lead to death. Chronic exposure is often thought of as workplace exposure.

Toxic materials can enter the body through four primary routes: inhalation, ingestion, skin or tissue absorption (direct contact), or injection. When a toxic material contacts the body, it may cause damage at the point of contact, or it may enter the body and affect some organ or system. When a system is affected, it is called a systemic effect. Not all parts of the body are affected in the same way by all chemicals. For example, if a pesticide or chemical nerve agent enters the body through inhalation (lungs and respiratory system) it may not cause damage there (Table 3.3). The pesticide or chemical agent would proceed to the central nervous system, where the actual damage occurs. Organs affected by specific chemicals are referred to as the susceptible target organs. Knowing the target organ is important so that medical personnel can be aware of what types of symptoms to watch for.

Specialized toxicology terms have been developed by the military for exposures to chemical agents in addition to the LDb_{50b} and LCb_{50b} already discussed. They are the EDb_{50b} and IDb_{50b}. EDb_{50b} is the dose (D) of liquid

Table 3.3 Inhalation Exposures to Nerve Agent Vapor by Degree of Severity

Degree of Severity	Body Part Affected	Symptom(s)
Mild	Eyes	Miosis, pain (deep in eye or head); dim or blurred vision
	Nose	Runny
	Lungs	"Tightness in chest," bronchoconstriction, secretions in airways, cough, moderate difficulty in breathing
Moderate	Eyes	Miosis, pain, dim or blurred vision
	Nose	Runny (severe), nasal congestion
	Lungs	"Tightness in chest", breathing is more difficult, secretions more copious
	Muscles	Feeling of generalized weakness, generalized twitching of large muscle groups
	GI	Nausea, vomiting, diarrhea, cramps
Severe	Muscles	Convulsions, weakness with eventual flaccid paralysis
	Lungs	Cessation of respiration
	(All)	Loss of consciousness, coma, death

Source: CSEPP ACT FAST Student Manual.

agent that will predictably cause effects (E) to anyone exposed. IDb_{50b} is the dose (D) that will cause the person exposed to become incapacitated (I). When applying the LDb_{50b} to military agents, the lower the LDb_{50b} value, the less the amount of agent that is required to cause harm and the more potent is the agent. There is a difference in absorption rates for chemical agents and, therefore, the EDb_{50b} and LDb_{50b} for a particular agent are specific to the site of entry into the body. For example, the LDb_{50b} for mustard absorbed through dry intact skin is much higher than agent absorbed through the eyes.

The military uses a term called the concentration-time product, or Ct, which is the concentration of the agent present (usually expressed in terms of milligrams per cubic meter in air [mg/mp^{3p}]) multiplied by the time (usually expressed in minutes) of exposure to the agent. For example, exposure to a 4 mg/mp^{3p} concentration of soman (GD) vapor for 10 minutes results in a Ct of 40 mg-min/mp^{3p}. Exposures of 8 mg/mp^{3p} for 5 minutes results in the same Ct (40 mg-min/mp^{3p}). This result is true for most of the chemical agents except for cyanide. The Ct associated with a biological effect remains relatively constant even though the concentration and length of time of exposure may vary within certain limits. For example, a 10-minute exposure to 4 mg/mp^{3p} of soman causes the same effects as a 5-minute exposure to 8 mg/mp^{3p} of the agent or to a 1-minute exposure to 40 mg/mp^{3p}. When the exposure threat is in the form of a vapor or gas, the "E" for effect is attached to the "Ct," which is the agent concentration and time of exposure. The result is the effect that will occur from the given time/concentration ($ECtb_{50b}$) exposure by inhalation of the vapor or gas to 50% of those exposed.

The same concept holds true for the "I" indicating incapacitation. Of those exposed to a certain concentration/time by inhalation, 50% will be incapacitated by the exposure, which is expressed by the value $ICtb_{50b}$. Lethal concentrations over a given time to 50% of those exposed by inhalation are represented by $LCtb_{50b}$. When the exposure involves a liquid agent, the terms used to identify the exposure are EDb_{50b} for the effects dose by ingestion or skin absorption, IDb_{50b} for the incapacitation effect by ingestion or skin absorption, and LDb_{50b} for the lethal dose by ingestion or skin absorption.

Chemical Agent Development History

GB is a "first generation" nerve agent, identified in 1938 as a potential chemical agent by German researchers examining toxic organophosphates as a result of the discovery of GA (tabun). Chemical agents with a G in the military designation were developed by the Germans. During the research, GB was identified by the code number T-144. After its toxic properties made it a candidate for weaponization, it was given the name sarin, which is derived from the names of the researchers involved in the project (Schrader, Ambros, Ritter, and Linde). GB was the most expensive (in terms of raw materials) nerve agent selected for mass production by the Germans, requiring 1,058 tons of raw materials to produce 100 tons of agent. A more efficient production method was subsequently identified, requiring only 893 tons of raw materials to produce 100 tons of GB. But this is still large in comparison to the 356 tons of raw materials required to produce 100 tons of tabun. Total wartime production was 61 tons, with 38 tons produced in 1944 and 23 in 1945. After the war ended, the victors became aware of the German research into, and weaponization of, nerve agents. They immediately began their own investigations into these materials.

The Soviet Union would divide their attention between sarin and soman. Full-scale production is said not to have gotten underway until 1959 at the S.M. Kirov plant in what was then named Stalingrad. The Russian Federation would declare that about 12,900 tons (11,700 metric tons) of stockpiled sarin were under its control on signing the Chemical Weapons Convention.

The U.S. and other NATO countries would decide to make sarin their major nerve agent (later supplementing it with VX). The U.S. built a production plant at the Rocky Mountain Arsenal in Colorado that was capable of producing an estimated (the actual figures remain classified) 10 tons a day of the agent. Construction of the plant extended over the period 1951–1953, and GB was produced there from February 1953 until August 1957. The site was also used to fill weapons with GB from bulk stocks, with the last such filling operation being completed in 1969. Destruction ("demilitarization") of weapons that were obsolete was, of course, a part of the routine of the army. The Rocky Mountain Arsenal was the facility that was usually given the responsibility for demilitarizing chemical weapons, the chemical agents from the weapons being either recycled or chemically destroyed. Considerable experience was acquired at the arsenal over the years; in the period 1955–1970, more than 204,000 GB-filled munitions were reported to have been demilitarized there. The experience gained from these routing disposal operations led to the decision to assign responsibility to the Rocky Mountain Arsenal for disposing of GB from both obsolete weapons and from some bulk storage containers when the U.S. Army decided on a major cleanup of its chemical weapons inventory in 1969. The disposal operation, known as Project Eagle Phase 2 (Phase 1 was the destruction of sulfur mustard) began on October 29, 1973. A chemical neutralization process in which alkaline hydrolysis of the agent was induced using a sodium hydroxide solution was employed. Some 4,188 tons of GB had been destroyed when the project ended in November of 1976. The disposal process did not proceed totally smoothly, however. More than 100 incidents in which workers were exposed to sarin occurred during the demilitarization operations, in part because the existing M-3 rubber protective suits were not up to the job of protecting the workers. In 1974, the Colorado Health Department complained about finding DIMP (diisopropylmethylphosphonate, a by-product of the GB destruction product) in drinking water. And the tests for residual GB seemed to indicate that sometimes the process did not completely eliminate the sarin (although it was subsequently concluded that this was an artifact of the testing process). A consequence of these difficulties would be that, when faced with the need to completely destroy the nerve agent stockpiles after the U.S. signed the Chemical Weapons Convention, the chemical neutralization process would initially be rejected.

In large part in response to concerns over the safety of the nerve agent stockpile, the U.S. Army had also undertaken development of a binary 155 mm shell. The first successful test firing of a binary shell took place on September 16, 1969 at the Dugway Proving Ground. Seven years later the design of the shell was finally standardized as the M687 Binary GB2 155 mm projectile. This shell did not enter production immediately, as the U.S. Congress elected to restrict the production of binary weapons unless the President certified that such production was essential. The M687 would finally enter production on December 16, 1987 after President Reagan certified the need for the weapons. The life of the shells would be short, however, as the U.S. and the Soviet Union would sign a bilateral agreement to destroy chemical weapons on June 1, 1990. The destruction of the 258,548 M687 shells (and the associated OPA canisters) was completed in July 1999.

The production of sarin was not limited solely to superpowers. Chemical weapons were seen as relatively simple and cheap (especially in contrast to nuclear weapons) WMD, and nerve agents were the stars of the chemical warfare world. While it is impossible to be sure about what countries have actually mass produced sarin, there is much speculation that it has been investigated by countries such as North Korea and most of the countries in the Middle East, including Israel, as indicated by the consequences of the crash, on October 4, 1992, of an El Al cargo plane in Amsterdam. Subsequently, health problems among those living near the crash site prompted an investigation, which revealed that the cargo included the sarin precursor's dimethyl methylphosphanate, hydrogen fluoride, and isopropyl alcohol consigned to the Israeli CBW research facility at Nes Ziona. The most notorious possessor of sarin was, of course, Iraq, which not only produced this agent but which also used it in substantial quantities against both its enemies in the Iran-Iraq war and against its own citizens.

During its war with Iran, Iraq initiated the use of chemical weapons, beginning with sulfur mustard in 1983, progressing to tabun in 1984, and then to sarin (and eventually VX) beginning in 1987. Sarin was also used in attacks on Iraqi civilians, most notably in the March 1988 destruction of the Halabja, where civilian deaths caused by a cocktail of different agents have been estimated at 5,000.

Iraq mass produced sarin during the Iran-Iraq war with the expectation that it would be used quickly, and they therefore skipped several purification steps. Fresh agent was about 60% pure and heavily contaminated with hydrogen fluoride (which, of course, also causes health problems in exposed individuals). When production caught up with demand, the Iraqis started storing their sarin in refrigerated "igloos" to prolong its storage life. However, even when stored in the igloos, the material rapidly degraded, becoming less than 10% pure within two years.

This was one of the factors that led the Iraqis to investigate binary weapons, for which sarin is particularly well suited. A project (described in the revised "Full, Final, and Complete" disclosures issued by Iraq after the defection of Hussein al Kamal) was established, which achieved some success in the design and construction of binary munitions using 122 mm rockets and 155 mm artillery shells, although the project does not seem to have progressed to full-scale manufacture. This is not so surprising; as can be inferred from the seven-year gap between the first successful U.S. binary shell test firing and the standardization of a design, the actual implementation of the binary concept is somewhat complex. There is no evidence that more than a few hundred binary shells were produced — more than were needed as prototypes, perhaps, but nowhere near what would have been needed for use against the Iranians had the war continued.

But, while they still had not mastered the art of manufacturing binary munitions in which the mixing of the precursors occurred after firing ("mix-in-flight") at the time of the invasion of Kuwait, they had developed a simple process for generating the agent immediately before use: a warhead or bomb would be given a partial fill of isopropanal (and often cyclohexanol, a precursor for the related nerve agent GF, sometimes known as cyclosarin) and stored along with plastic containers of methylphosphonic difluoride (DF). Shortly before the munition was to be used, an Iraqi soldier would be provided with a gas mask and would pour an appropriate amount of the DF into the munition. This reduced storage issues. While sarin does not appear to have been intentionally released during the Gulf War, a link between Gulf War Syndrome and the possible release of sarin during bombing raids and during the destruction of weapons depots following the war has been suggested.

Nerve Agents

Nerve agents are the most lethal of all chemical agents. All declared military nerve agents belong to the organophosphate family of compounds. The carbamates have not, at least according to the open literature, been militarized. In the open, 6 pounds of sarin, disseminated by a 3-pound burster charge at a height of 15 feet, would create a dosage of 3,500 mg min/mp^{3p}, 20 yards from the burst site within 10 seconds (the airborne exposure limit [AEL] for sarin is 0.0001 mg min-mp^{3p}). Within 25 seconds, the plume would increase to a 50-yard radius, with a minimum dosage of 100 mg min/mp^{3p}. In less than a minute of the blast, anyone within an area of over 70,000 square feet around the burst will have received at the very least a medial lethal dose and likely much more than that. If the blast were to occur indoors, the effect would be much greater. Nerve agent VX is 10 times more toxic than sarin, and would result in even more lethality. As was previously mentioned, terrorist organizations already have this capability!

Nerve agents at normal temperatures and pressures are all liquids, although they are often incorrectly referred to as gases. The most common nerve agents are tabun (GA), sarin (GB), soman (GD), GF, and VX. Other agents that exist include GF, GE, VE, VG, and VM. "G" agents are volatile, and penetrate the skin well in terms of seconds or minutes. "V" agents are less volatile, and penetrate the skin well in terms of minutes and hours. All nerve agents are related to organophosphate pesticides. Common chemical nerve agents are sometimes referred to as unitary agents because they do not have to be mixed with any other chemical in order to function. Modern nerve agents that involve more than one chemical are called binary chemical agents. Binary agents are also a part of the U.S. military arsenal. Binary agents are composed of two separate chemicals that are relatively nontoxic until they are mixed together. The weapons are designed to mix the chemicals together as the shell is fired.

All nerve agents in pure form are colorless. However, nerve agents may also be light brown in color when contaminated and vary in their degree of volatility. Some agents have the volatility of motor oil, while others have volatility similar to water. Compared to liquids that are considered to be volatile, such as gasoline, none of the nerve agents are significantly volatile. When comparing the nerve agents as a group, sarin would be considered the most volatile. VX, on the other hand, is the least volatile of the nerve agents but it is also the most toxic. G-agents such as sarin are considered to be nonpersistent, while mustard and V-agents like VX are considered persistent agents. Thickened nonpersistent agents may present a hazard for a longer period of time such as TGB, which is thickened sarin. Most nerve agents are odorless; however, some may have a faint fruity odor like Juicy Fruit gum or geraniums when contaminated. Nerve agents are highly toxic and quick-acting. Initial effects of organophosphorus agents occur within 1–10 minutes of exposure. Death occurs within 15 minutes for tabun, sarin, and soman and from 4–42 hours for VX. Nerve agents enter the body through inhalation or skin absorption. Poisoning can occur also with ingestion of the agents placed in food or drink. Nerve agents work the quickest if inhaled. Inhalation of high concentrations can cause death within minutes. The LCb_{50b} for sarin is 100 mg/min/mp^{3p} while VX is 50 mg/min/mp^{3p}. Primary target organs for nerve agents are the respiratory and central nervous systems. Entry into the body through skin absorption requires a longer period of time for symptoms to develop. First symptoms from skin contact may not appear for 20–30 minutes after exposure (Table 3.4). However, if the dose of nerve agent is high, the poisoning process may be rapid. Eye exposure is extremely dangerous, and eyes should be flushed immediately with copious amounts of water if exposed. Liquid nerve agent splashed into the eyes is absorbed faster into the body than through skin contact.

Acetylcholine is an important neurotransmitter that is essential to complete the transmission of neural impulses from one neuron (fibers that convey impulses to the nerve cell) to another. Without acetylcholine, the body cannot

Table 3.4 Skin Exposures to Nerve Agent by Degree of Severity

Degree of Severity	Body Part Affected	Symptom(s)
Mild	Skin	Sweating at exposure site
	Muscle	Localized, unorganized fasciculation at exposure site
Moderate	Muscle	Generalized fasciculation and twitching; generalized weakness that increases with any form of activity
	GI	Nausea, vomiting, diarrhea
Severe	Muscles	Extremely weak; convulsions (seizures) with eventual flaccid paralysis
	Lungs	Cessation of respiration
	All	Sudden loss of consciousness and collapse, death

function normally. When a message is sent from the brain for a muscle to move or some other bodily function to activate, acetylcholine is released. It then binds to the post-synaptic membrane, which starts and continues the movement or action. When it is time for the movement or action to stop, acetylcholinesterase is released to remove the acetylcholine from the synapse, so it can be used again. Nerve agents are acetylcholinesterase enzyme inhibitors and can affect the entire body. Acetylcholinesterase enzymes normally act upon acetylcholine when it is released. Nerve agents inhibit this action, and an accumulation of acetylcholine occurs. Initially, it results in an over-stimulation of the nervous system. The system then becomes fatigued and paralysis results. Paralysis of the diaphragm muscle, resulting in the cessation of breathing, is the primary cause of death from nerve agent poisoning. Accumulation of acetylcholine causes increased nerve and muscle activity, with overfunctioning of the salivary glands, secretory glands, and sweat glands. Muscular twitching, easy fatigue, mild weakness, cramps, and flaccid paralysis, accompanied by dyspnea and cyanosis, result from the excess acetylcholine present. Accumulation of excess acetylcholine in the brain and spinal cord results in the occurrence of central nervous system symptoms. Unless the accumulation of acetylcholine is reversed by the use of antidotes, atropine and 2-Pam Chloride, the effects become irreversible and death will occur. CDC has begun a program to have nerve agent antidote stocks in every state within two years. New York City and Boston were among the first cities to get the "chem packs." Each chem pack contains atropine and some auto injectors. Each pack will treat approximately 1,000 patients.

U.S. Army researchers are getting closer to perfecting a way to protect soldiers from nerve agents, which may ultimately extend to emergency responders and others. Butyrylcholinestease is an enzyme found in the body that appears to be an effective pretreatment for nerve agent exposure. Butyrylcholinesterase naturally detoxifies a variety of toxins in the body. When administered in an appropriate dose, it protects people from nerve agent exposure for up to two weeks. If a person is exposed to a nerve agent poison, they are not affected. So far tests have shown there are no serious side effects from elevated levels of butyrylcholinesterase in the body. Human clinical trials will be the next step.

Time Course: Onset time: minutes to several hours. The greater the concentration of the chemical agent, the shorter the onset time in which symptoms will occur. After a high concentration exposure (lethal amount or greater), the effects may occur within minutes; after an asymptomatic period, the first effect may be loss of consciousness. Onset time may be as long as 18 hours after exposure; however, in such cases the effects are usually not lethal.

Symptoms of nerve agent poisoning, resulting from a low dose, include:

- Increased saliva production
- Runny nose and a feeling of pressure on the chest
- Pupils of the eyes exhibit pinpoint constriction (miosis)
- Short-range vision is impaired and the victim feels pain when trying to focus on a nearby object
- Headache may follow with tiredness, slurred speech and hallucinations

Exposures to higher doses present more dramatic symptoms.

- Bronchoconstriction
- Secretion of mucous in the respiratory system
- Difficulty in breathing and coughing
- Discomfort in the gastrointestinal tract
- Cramps and vomiting
- Involuntary discharge of urine and defecation

The military uses the term SLUDGEM to describe symptoms of nerve agent exposure. SLUDGEM stands for salivation, lacrimation, urination, defecation, gastrointestinal, emesis, and miosis. Saliva discharge is powerful and may be accompanied by running eyes and sweating. Muscular weakness, local tremors, or convulsions might follow in cases of moderate poisoning. Exposure to a high dose of nerve agent might lead to more pronounced muscular symptoms. Convulsions and loss of consciousness might occur. Those individuals most sensitive to nerve agents will experience a lethal dose at about 70 mg/min/mp^{3P}. More resistant persons require about 140 mg/min/mP^{3P}. Dermal exposure from nerve agent liquid that would result in lethal effects is a very small amount. In fact, if you were to look at the back of a Lincoln penny and notice the Lincoln Memorial, the amount of liquid that it would take to cover one of its columns would be a toxic dermal exposure! Toxic effects depend on both the concentration of nerve agent in the air and the length of time the person is exposed. For example, inhalation of sarin vapor with a concentration of 100 mg/mp^{3P} for one minute gives the same result as inhalation of 50 mg/mp^{3P} for two minutes. Lower concentrations require longer periods of exposure because the body has some ability to detoxify itself.

Sarin (GB) is a fluorinated organophosphorous compound with the chemical name of phosphonofluoridic acid, methyl-isopropyl ester. GB is an organophosphate nerve agent with low persistence (evaporation rate about the same as water). It has a faintly fruity odor (which is absent for the pure material). The chemical formula is CHb$_{3b}$PO(F)OCH(CHb$_{3b}$)b$_{2b}$. The structure of the compound is shown in Figure 3.2.

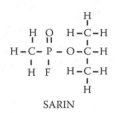

Figure 3.2 Structure of sarin.

Synonyms
- EA1208
- IMPF
- Isopropoxymethylphosphoryl fluoride
- Isopropyl methylfluorophosphonate
- Isopropyl methylphosphonofluoridate
- Methylfluorophosphoric acid isopropyl ester
- Methylphosphonofluoridic acid isopropyl ester
- O-Isopropyl methylfluorophosphonate
- O-Isopropyl methylphosphonofluoridate
- T-144
- Zarin

Sarin would be classified as a Class 6.1 poison by the DOT and have a National Fire Protection Association (NFPA) 704 designation of Health-4, Flammability-1, Reactivity-1, and Special-0. The United Nations (U.N.) 4-digit identification number for sarin is 2810. Chemical Abstract Service (CAS) numbers have been issued for some of the chemical agents. The CAS number for sarin (GB) is 107-44-8. Binary weapons in which GB is formed at the time of use have been developed by several countries. The agent from the binary weapons is sometimes designated GB2 to distinguish it from that dispersed by unitary weapons. One component in the U.S. binary is methylphosphonyldifluoride (Code DF; CAS Registry Number 676-99-3) and the other is either isopropanol (CAS Registry Number 67-63-0) alone or OPA, where OPA is a mixture of isopropanol 72% with isopropylamine (CAS Registry Number 75-31-0) 28%.

Iraq fielded munitions filled with mixtures of GB and cyclosarin (TGFT). Tests on mice have indicated that GB-GF mixtures have a toxicity intermediate between the toxicities of GB and GF; thus, there appear to be no synergistic effects producing enhanced or unexpected toxic effects that would require any special treatment protocols in those exposed to a mixture.

When researching the physical characteristics of chemical agents or any other type of hazardous material in reference books or other data sources, make sure the use of temperature scales is consistent. Fahrenheit temperatures have larger numerical values than do centigrade temperatures (also known as Celsius). Confusion can develop and wrong values applied if Fahrenheit temperatures are expected, and centigrade is given or vise versa. Responders should also have a basic knowledge of the metric system of measurement. Many values of physical characteristics, toxicology terms, physical amounts of materials, evacuation, and isolation distances are expressed in terms of the metric system. The metric system also differs in numerical value when compared to the normal U.S. system of weights and measures.

SARIN

Physical Characteristics	Toxic Characteristics
Molecular Weight: 140.10	Airborne Exposure Limit: 0.0001 mg/mp^{3p}
Boiling Point: 158°C (316°F)	LCt50 Inhalation: 70 mg-min/mp^{3p}
Vapor Pressure: 2.9 mm/Hg at 25°C	LD50 Skin: 1700 mg/70kg man
Vapor Density: 4.86	ECt50 Eyes: <2 mg/mp^{3p}
Volatility: 22,000 mg/mp^{3p} at 25°C	ECt50 Inhalation: <2 mg-min/mp^{3p}
Specific Gravity: 1.0887 at 25°C	ICt50 Inhalation: 35 mg-min/mp^{3p}
Melting/Freezing Point: −56°C	Median Lethal Dose: 100 mg-min/mp^{3p} for a
Viscosity: 22,000 at 25°C	resting person
Flashpoint: Did not flash to 280°F	Median Incapacitating Dose: 75 mg-
Flammable Limits: Unavailable	min/mp^{3p} for a resting person
Decomposition Temperature: 150°C	TLV-TWA: 0.0001 mg/mp^{3p}
Water Solubility: Miscible	Population Exposure Limits: 0.000003
Polymerization: No	mg/mp^{3p}
Stability: Stable	Carcinogen: Unknown
Incompatibility: Steam, tin, magnesium,	
cadmium plated steel, and aluminum	
Persistency*: Non-persistent	

* Depends on Weather and Dispersion Type.

GB is miscible with water and readily soluble in common organic solvents. Sarin hydrolyzes readily in water, with a pH-dependent rate (half-life at pH=7 and 25° is 5.4 hours). Hydrolysis occurs more rapidly in alkaline solutions. Hydrolysis under acid conditions will produce hydrofluoric acid and should be avoided.

Sarin has a vapor density that is about five times heavier than air and about the same specific gravity as water. It is a colorless and odorless liquid in the pure form. To date, the Occupational Safety and Health Administration (OSHA) has not identified a permissible exposure concentration for sarin. Sarin is listed by the American Conference of Governmental Industrial Hygienists (ACGIH) and OSHA as a carcinogen. Sarin is stable when in the pure state. While sarin will burn, it has a very high flashpoint and would be difficult to ignite under normal circumstances. Sarin will react with steam or water to produce toxic and corrosive vapors. It reacts with tin, magnesium, cadmium-plated steel, and some aluminum. To a lesser degree it attacks copper, brass, and lead. There is no danger of polymerization with sarin.

Detection: Nerve agent sensitive chemical agent detectors (e.g., CAM, M18A2, M256, etc.) and papers (e.g., M8, M9) may be used for detection. In addition to direct analysis, it may be identified based on degradation products, of which the most prominent in soil samples are likely to be methylphosphonic acid and monoisopropyl methylphosphonate. Isopropyl-methylphosphonic acid has also been found in soil samples. Lowered acetyl-cholinesterase levels are indicators of nerve agent intoxication in victims. Depending on the degree of intoxication, symptoms can include:

- Nervousness/Restlessness
- Miosis
- Rhinorrhea (runny nose), excessive salivation
- Dyspnea (difficulty in breathing due to bronchoconstriction/secretions)
- Sweating
- Bradycardia (slow heartbeat)
- Loss of consciousness
- Convulsions
- Flacid paralysis
- Loss of bladder and bowel control
- Flaccid paralysis
- Apnea (breathing stopped)

Onset of symptoms is usually rapid, occurring within minutes of exposure. Masks, including self-contained breathing apparatus (SCBA) masks, alone do not provide adequate protection against this agent. Protective equipment (self-contained breathing equipment or gas mask with appropriate filter and barrier suit) must be used. Agent absorbed by cloth (clothing, blankets, etc.) can be released as a vapor by the cloth for 30 minutes or more after exposure. Remove victims from exposure as rapidly as possible. Remove the victims' clothing at least down to underwear and place in disposal bags. Victims must not be moved into clean treatment areas where unmasked/ungloved personnel are working until decontamination is complete. Medical treatment should include decontamination of victims at as early a stage as possible. Medical personnel treating casualties should avoid direct (skin-to-skin) contact; protective gear, including breathing protection, should be worn when treating casualties prior to decontamination. Latex gloves are not adequate protection. Chemical protective (butyl rubber) gloves must be worn. If breathing has stopped, a mechanical respirator should be used to ventilate the patient. While exhaled air is not ordinarily a hazard, DO NOT ATTEMPT MOUTH-TO-MOUTH RESUCITATION without proper shields owing to the possible presence of residual agent on the face. If possible, oxygen or oxygen-enriched air should be used for ventilation. If possible, monitor cardiac activity. Pralidoxime salts are effective in restoring acetylcholinesterase activity after exposure to sarin. Thus, as a supplement to treatment with atropine, treatment with pralidoxime salts should be initiated as soon as possible after exposure, with a slow intravenous infusion of 500 mg to 1 g being given initially. Atropine eye drops reportedly gave some symptomatic relief for eye problems following the use of sarin by terrorists in the Tokyo subway system. Diazepam should be administered to control convulsions. It also has value in controlling fear on the part of the patient. An initial dose of 5 mg may be followed by additional doses at 15 minute intervals up to a total of 15 mg.

Selected Precursors

The following chemicals are precursors to the production of sarin. When any of them are found in an occupancy, and their legitimate use cannot be established, law enforcement should be notified.

- Ammonium bifluoride
- Dimethyl methylphosphonate
- Diethylphosphite
- Dimethylphosphite
- Hydrogen fluoride
- Methylphosphonous difluoride
- Methylphosphonyl dichloride
- Methylphosphonyl difluoride
- Potassium bifluoride
- Potassium fluoride
- Phosphorus trichloride
- Sodium bifluoride
- Sodium fluoride
- Thionyl chloride
- Trimethyl phosphite

Tabun (GA) is an organophosphorus compound with a chemical name of ethyl N, N-dimethylphosphoramidocyanidate. The chemical formula is $Cb_{2b}Hb_{5b}OPO(CN)N(CHb_{3b})b_{2b}$. The structure of the compound is shown in Figure 3.4.

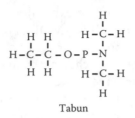

Tabun

Figure 3.3   Structure of tabun.

Synonyms
- Dimethylamidoethoxyphosphoryl cyanide
- EA1205
- Ethyl dimethylamidocyanophosphate
- Ethyl dimethylphosphoroamidocyanidate
- Ethyl N,N-dimethylphosphoroamidocyanidate
- Le-100

Tabun, like sarin, would be a Class 6.1 poison, with an NFPA 704 designation of Health-4, Flammability-2, Reactivity-1, and Special-0. The U.N. four-digit identification number used for tabun is 2810, which is the same for all of the nerve agents. The CAS number for tabun is 77-81-6.

TABUN

Physical Characteristics	Toxic Characteristics
Molecular Weight: 162.13	TLV-TWA: 0.0001 mg/mp^{3p}
Boiling Point: 247.5°C (475°F)	Population Exposure Limits: 0.000003
Vapor Pressure: 0.037 mm/Hg at 20°C	mg/mp^{3p}
Vapor Density: 5.63	Carcinogen: Unknown animal (monkey)
Volatility: 610 mg/m^3 at 25°C	LDb$_{50b}$ Percutaneous: 9.3 mg/kg
Specific Gravity: 1.073 at 25°C	LCtb$_{50\,b}$ Inhalation: 187 mg/minp^{3p} (t = 10)
Melting/Freezing Point: −50°C	
Flashpoint: 78°C (173°F)	
Flammable Limits: Unavailable	
Decomposition Temperature: 150°C	
Airborne Exposure Limit: 0.0001 mg/mp^{3p}	
LCtb$_{50b}$ Inhalation: 135 mg-min/mp^{3p} (t = 0.5–2 min) at RMV* of 15 1/min; 200 mg-min/mp^{3p} at RMV of 10 1/min.	
LDb$_{50b}$ Skin: 14–15 mg/kg	
Median Lethal Dose: 400 mg-min/mP$^{3\,p}$ for a resting person	
Median Incapacitating Dose: 300 mg-min/mp^{3p} for a resting person	

Continued.

TABUN (Continued)

Physical Characteristics	Toxic Characteristics
Water Solubility: Slight Polymerization: No Stability: Stable Incompatibility: Unavailable Persistency**: 1–2 days	

* Respiratory Minute Volume.
** Depends on weather and dispersion type.

Historical Notes

GA was the first organophosphate compound to be identified as a potential chemical agent. It was first synthesized shortly before Christmas 1936 as a part of research directed at identifying insecticides (specifically, for the control of wooly aphis, a form of aphid) under the direction of Dr. Gerhard Schrader at the Bayer facility at Elberfield, Germany. It was quickly recognized that tabun was quite toxic. In initial experiments, a concentration of 5 ppm killed all the insects in the test chambers. But when, in the course of the tests on insects, Schrader and a laboratory assistant were exposed to the vapors and strongly affected, it quickly became apparent that the material might have military applications. This was duly reported to the German government under a law requiring that the government be advised of any discovery with potential military applications. Research was continued, and a "secret" patent was issued for the material, now known as tabun, on July 22, 1937. Research was carried out on production methods, and a process which produced tabun in good yield (approximately 83%) was developed. In 1940, construction began on a plant to manufacture tabun, now also known by the code name T-83 (the number is said to be a reference to the yield; the material was also designated Trilon 83). After some initial teething problems, production began in 1942, with 675 tons being produced that year. Production rose to 4,555 tons in 1943, with a high of 7519 tons in 1944, and in the final months of the war, 120 tons in 1945, for a total of 12,869 tons. That was by far the largest quantity of any of the German nerve agents produced. It was a dangerous process, however, with at least 10 workers dying as a result of accidental exposures. A number of types of munitions were filled with tabun. Two fill mixtures were used — tabun-A, which consisted of a mixture of 95% GA with 5% chlorobenzene as a stabilizer, and tabun-B, a mixture of 80% GA with 20% chlorobenzene. Rumors of the new agents reached the Allies throughout the war but were largely ignored as propaganda. In 1943, when British intelligence interviewed a chemist who had worked on the project and who provided a description of the agent and its production, the report was simply ignored.

The Soviets presumably became aware of the nerve agents and their properties when they over ran Dyhernfurth. But the first certain knowledge that the Western Allies had of the existence of the nerve agents came when British troops investigated some 105 mm howitzer shells found at a captured ammunition dump in the spring of 1945. The shells had unusual markings — a green ring and the letters GA — and a liquid fill, and were quickly recognized as chemical munitions, but what sort was not immediately understood. The initial report described them as containing: "...a new type of filling containing 20 per cent chlorobenzene and an arsenic derivative which is under investigation." Of course, further investigation revealed that the agent was not an arsenic derivative, that it had rather startling toxic properties, and that it was only one of a family of agents.

Tabun was destined to recede from its initial prominence, however. The Western Allies, after investigating the range of German nerve agents, decided that they preferred sarin (GB) because of its greater lethality, while the Russians, after moving a large part of the Dyhernfurth facility to the Soviet Union and reportedly resuming production, decided to go with both sarin and soman (which is even more lethal than sarin). A large portion of the captured tabun was disposed of by simply dumping it at sea. GA has not completely disappeared. The relative simplicity of its manufacture coupled with the wide dissemination of information about its production has made it attractive as a "starter" nerve agent for states interested in acquiring a chemical weapons capability. Thus, when Iraq wanted to quickly produce a nerve agent for use in the war with Iran, they used tabun, apparently following the German path (a sample obtained from a dud bomb showed a composition comparable for that seen by the Germans when they were starting up). (The Iraqis also compromised to an extent in purification — the agents they used appear to have been only 30–40% pure in some cases.) Although eventually the Iraqis too abandoned tabun in favor of more lethal agents, it was certainly not chance that lead them to start with GA. It must also be noted that the Iraqi use of tabun against Iranian Troops near Basra on March 17, 1984 marked a milestone of sorts in the history of chemical warfare: it was the first confirmed use of a nerve agent on a battlefield by one state against another. While it is generally estimated that fewer than 100 casualties resulted from this attack, the use of a nerve agent meant there had been a significant change in the way the use of this most modern form of "frightfulness" was viewed.

Tabun is a colorless-to-brown liquid, with a faint fruity odor. In its pure form, it has no odor. The boiling point of tabun is approximately 159°, which is higher than sarin. Tabun has a vapor density higher than sarin, about 5.5 times heavier than air. Its specific gravity is slightly heavier than water. Tabun has a flashpoint lower than sarin. There are no explosive limits available. Contact with the agent liquid or vapor can be fatal. GA is not listed by the

ACGIH, or OSHA as a carcinogen. Tabun is a lethal cholinesterase inhibitor similar to sarin in the way it affects the human body. It is only about half as toxic by inhalation as sarin, but in low concentrations is more irritating to the eyes. Symptoms presented by GA depend on the concentration and rate of entry into the body. Very small dermal exposures may cause local sweating and tremors with few other effects. Symptoms for larger doses are much the same as for sarin, regardless of the route of exposure to the body. They include, in order of appearance:

- Runny nose
- Tightness of the chest
- Dimness of vision and pinpoint pupils (miosis)
- Difficulty breathing
- Drooling and excessive sweating
- Nausea
- Vomiting
- Cramps and involuntary defecation and urination
- Twitching, jerking, staggering; headache
- Confusion
- Drowsiness
- Coma and convulsion

These symptoms are followed by cessation of breathing and death. First symptoms appear more slowly from skin contact than through inhalation. Skin absorption of a dose great enough to cause death can occur in 1 to 2 minutes; however, death may be delayed for 1 to 2 hours. The inhalation lethal dose can kill in 1 to 10 minutes and liquid splashed in the eyes is almost as fast. Polymerization potential for tabun is not available. It is stable, and compatibility information is not known.

Detection: Nerve agent sensitive chemical agent detectors (e.g., CAM, M18A2, M256, etc.) and papers (e.g., M8, M9) may be used for detection. The presence of the dimethylamine and cyanide groups on the phosphorus makes this agent easy to distinguish from other nerve agents using NMR. Depending on the degree of intoxication, symptoms may include:

- Nervousness/restlessness
- Miosis (contraction of the pupil)
- Rhinorrhea (runny nose), excessive salivation
- Dyspnea (difficulty in breathing due to bronchoconstriction/secretions)
- Sweating
- Bradycardia (slow heartbeat)
- Loss of consciousness
- Convulsions

- Flaccid paralysis
- Loss of bladder and bowel control
- Apnea (breathing stopped)

Onset of symptoms is usually rapid, occurring within minutes of exposure. Remove casualties from exposure as rapidly as possible. Casualties must not be moved into clean treatment areas where unmasked/ungloved personnel are working until decontamination is complete. Medical treatment should include decontamination of casualties at as early a stage as possible. Medical personnel treating casualties should avoid direct (skin-to-skin) contact; protective gear, including breathing protection, should be worn when treating casualties prior to decontamination. Latex gloves are not adequate protection. Chemical protective (butyl rubber) gloves must be worn. If breathing has stopped, a mechanical respirator should be used to ventilate the patient. While exhaled air is not ordinarily a hazard, DO NOT ATTEMPT MOUTH-TO-MOUTH RESUCITATION without proper shields owing to the possible presence of residual agent on the face. If possible, oxygen or oxygen-enriched air should be used for ventilation. If possible, monitor cardiac activity. Pralidoxime salts are somewhat ineffective in restoring acetylcholinesterase activity after exposure to tabun; however, they do not interfere with treatment, and so there is no reason to refrain from their use if the agent is unidentified. Obidoxime has demonstrated effectiveness in animals. Thus, as a supplement to treatment with atropine, treatment with obidoxime (250 mg by slow intravenous infusion) should be considered, bearing in mind possible hepatotoxic effects. Diazepam should be administered to control convulsions. It also has value in controlling fear on the part of the patient. An initial dose of 5 mg may be followed by additional doses at 15 minute intervals up to a total of 15 mg.

Masks, including self-contained breathing apparatus (SCBA) masks, alone do not provide adequate protection against this agent. Evacuate uphill and upwind without moving through the agent cloud. The combustion products produced by burning GA are less toxic than the agent. If GA is burning and other considerations permit it, the fire should not be extinguished. GA is of intermediate solubility in water (9.8% at 20°F). It hydrolyzes with a half-life of 8.5 hours at pH 7 and 20°F, and with a half-life of 7 hours at pH 4–5. Phosphates increase the hydrolysis rate. Note that one of the hydrolysis products is cyanide, and that hydrogen cyanide may be evolved under certain conditions.

Selected Precursors

The following chemicals are precursors to the production of tabun. When any of them are found in an occupancy and their legitimate use cannot be established, law enforcement should be notified.

- Diethyl N,N-dimethylphosphoramidate
- Dimethylamine
- Dimethylamine hydrochloride
- Phosphorus oxychloride
- Phosphorus pentachloride
- Phosphorus trichloride
- Potassium cyanide
- Sodium cyanide

Soman (GD), like sarin, is a fluorinated organophosphorus compound with a chemical name of pinacolyl methyl phosphonofluoridate, and it is a lethal nerve agent. The chemical formula is $CHb_{3b}PO(F)OCH(CHb_{3b})C(CHb_{3b})b_{3b}$. The structure of the compound is shown in Figure 3.4.

Soman would be classified as a Class 6.1 poison by the DOT and have an NFPA 704 designation of Health-4, Flammability-1, Reactivity-1, Special-0. The U.N. four-digit identification number is 2810. The CAS number is 96-64-0. GA is a colorless-to-brown (depending on purity) liquid organophosphate nerve agent with an intermediate persistence (evaporation rate about 1/20th of water). It has a faint fruity odor or an oil of camphor odor when impure (which is absent for the pure material).

Synonyms
- 3,3-dimethyl-*n*-but-2-yl methylphosphonofluoridate
- EA1210
- Methyl pinacolyl phosphonofluoridate
- Methyl pinacolyloxy phosphorylfluoride
- Pinacoloxymethylphosphoryl fluoride
- Pinacolyl methylfluorophosphonate
- Pinacolyl methylphosphonofluoridate
- PMFP
- 1,2,2-Trimethylpropoxyfluorophosphine oxide
- 1,2,2-Trimethylpropyl methylphosphonofluoridate

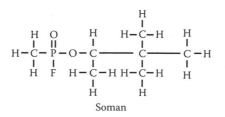

Soman

Figure 3.4   Structure of soman.

Soman was first synthesized in 1944 as a result of the investigations into organophosphate nerve agents triggered by the discovery of GA (tabun), and it was the most toxic agent of its time. Known initially by its code number, T-300, it was the last of the nerve agents that the Germans attempted to move to production during World War II. The production process settled on by the Germans for soman was a four-step process in which highly corrosive intermediates were used. The corrosive compounds required the use of special silver apparatus, and production in 1944 was only about one ton, with perhaps two more tons being produced in 1945 before the end of the war. The Soviets acquired the production facility and also recovered the documents related to soman's synthesis from an underground storage facility near Berlin. In the 1950s, several methods of producing the agent were developed by researchers in the Soviet Union and in Great Britain and the U.S., which avoided many of the production problems the Germans had encountered. This led to considerable interest in the mass production of GD for military use. The U.S. seriously considered making soman its primary nerve agent, but economics finally swung the decision against it (there was no industrial use, and thus no industrial source, for pinacolyl alcohol, and the large scale production of soman would have required the creation of such a production capability from scratch). The Soviet Union saw sufficient advantages to the material that they commenced industrial-scale production of soman in 1967. Significant amounts were produced — the Russian Federation declared some 4,800 metric tons of GD to the Organization for the Prohibition of Chemical Weapons (OPCW). In 1973, the Israelis discovered that Egyptian prisoners of war captured during the "Yom Kippur War" were carrying personal chemical protective equipment that included decontamination kits containing an antidote that comprised an unusual combination of ingredients: atropine, benactyzine, and the oxime TMB4. The Israelis were worried by the personal protective gear, since it implied the Egyptians were planning for operations in a chemical environment. It was the components of the antidote that drew the most attention in other countries, since they seemed to be intended for use against soman as well as the better-known nerve agents. As a result, several Western countries embarked on crash programs to develop countermeasures specific for this agent. No other country is known to have seen enough utility in soman (relative to the other nerve agents) to enter into mass production of it, although most countries with an interest in chemical weapons have produced it on a laboratory scale. It has been suggested that North Korea (the Democratic People's Republic of Korea) might have produced significant quantities of this agent. However, the evidence for this is somewhat vague.

SOMAN

Physical Characteristics	Toxic Characteristics
Boiling Point: 198°C (388°F)	Airborne Exposure Limit: 0.00003 mg/mp³ᵖ
Vapor Pressure: 0.40 mm/Hg at 25°C	LCtb$_{50b}$ Inhalation: 70 mg-min/mp³ᵖ (15
Vapor Density: 6.33	1/min)
Volatility: 3900 mg/mP³ ᵖ at 25°C	LDb$_{50b}$ Skin: 350 mg/70kg man
Specific Gravity: 1.022 at 25°C	ECtb$_{50b}$ Eyes: 2 mg/mp³ᵖ
Melting/Freezing Point: –42°C	ECtb$_{50b}$ Inhalation: < 2 mg-min/mp³ᵖ
Viscosity: 22,000 at 25°C	ICtb$_{50b}$ Inhalation: 35 mg-min/mp³ᵖ (15
Flashpoint: 121°C (475°F)	1/min)
Flammable Limits: Unavailable	Median Lethal Dose: GB, GA range
Decomposition Temperature: 130°C	Median Incapacitating Dose: Unavailable
Hydrolyzes to form HF	TLV-TWA: 0.0001 mg/mp³ᵖ
Water Solubility: 2.1% at 20°C	Population Exposure Limits: 0.000003
Polymerization: No	mg/mp³ᵖ
Stability: Stable	Carcinogen: No
Incompatibility: Corrodes steel	
Persistency*: 1–2 days	

* Depends on weather and dispersion type.

Lowered acetylcholinesterase levels are indicators of nerve agent intoxication in victims.

Depending on the degree of intoxication, symptoms can include:

- Nervousness/restlessness
- Miosis (contraction of the pupil)
- Rhinorrhea (runny nose), excessive salivation
- Dyspnea (difficulty in breathing due to bronchoconstriction/secretions)
- Sweating
- Bradycardia (slow heartbeat)
- Loss of consciousness
- Convulsions
- Flaccid paralysis
- Loss of bladder and bowel control
- Apnea (breathing stopped)

Onset of symptoms is usually rapid, occurring within minutes of exposure. If breathing has stopped, a mechanical respirator should be used to ventilate the patient. While exhaled air is not ordinarily a hazard, DO NOT ATTEMPT MOUTH-TO-MOUTH RESUCITATION without proper shields owing to the possible presence of residual agent on the face. If possible, oxygen or oxygen-enriched air should be used for ventilation. If possible, monitor cardiac activity. Both pralidoxime salts and obidoxime are somewhat ineffective in restoring acetylcholinesterase activity after exposure to soman (presumably due to the aging process for the soman-inhibited cholinesterase); however, they do not interfere with treatment, and so there is no reason to refrain from their use if the agent is unidentified, and some benefit may accrue from very early administration. HL-7 (a bispyridinium dioxime) may be useful if available. Diazepam should be administered to control convulsions. It also has value in controlling fear on the part of the patient. Diazepam may also help to protect against soman-induced neuropathies. An initial dose of 5 mg may be followed by additional doses at 15-minute intervals up to a total of 15 mg. Protective equipment (self-contained breathing equipment or gas mask, barrier suit) must be used. Medical personnel treating casualties should avoid direct (skin-to-skin) contact; protective gear including breathing protection should be worn when treating casualties prior to decontamination. Latex gloves are not adequate protection. Casualties should be decontaminated as rapidly as possible (see the section on decontamination). Remove casualties from exposure as rapidly as possible. Casualties must not be moved into clean treatment areas where unmasked/ungloved personnel are working until decontamination is complete.

GD is an organophosphate nerve agent with an intermediate persistence (evaporation rate about 1/4 that of water; volatility similar to that of engine oil). When pure, it has a faint fruity odor that might not be detected; impurities that are commonly present might produce a smell of camphor, nutmeg, or orange peel. Soman has a vapor density that is over six times heavier than air. Doses of soman that can cause death may be only slightly larger than those that produce symptoms. The median incapacitation dose for soman is unknown. It will not undergo polymerization and is stable after storage in steel for three months at 65°C. GD corrodes steel at a rate of 1×10.5 inch/month. In contact with water, it will hydrolyze to form hydrogen fluoride (HF). Binary weapons in which GD is formed at the time of use have been developed. One component in the binary is methylphosphonyldifluoride (Code DF; CAS Registry Number 676-99-3), and the other is pinacolyl alcohol (CAS Registry Number 464-07-3) and an amine. These weapons may be identified by the code GD-2 in some documents. Thickened forms of soman, sometimes identified by the code TGD, have also been produced. In the U.S. the thickener selected was an essentially nontoxic butyl acrylate-ethyl acrylate-methyl methacrylate copolymer with the trade name Acryloid K-125, which was added to GD to form a 5% thickener/95% GD mixture. Thickened forms of soman were also produced in the Soviet Union. In fact, only thickened soman was identified as a "standard agent" in the information released by the Soviets in 1987 about their chemical arsenal. Soviet thickened soman is sometimes identified by the code VR-55 in Western documents. This code might have been derived from the viscosity of the thickened soman — Viscous URUussian — with the 55 arising from the designation of GD by the Soviets by a code name usually translated as Substance 55. However, caution should be used in interpreting documents that contain this designation, because it might also have been applied to Soviet second-generation (V) nerve agents. Masks, including SCBA masks, alone do not provide adequate protection against this agent.

Detection: Nerve agent sensitive chemical agent detectors (e.g., CAM, M18A2, M256, etc.) and papers (e.g., M8, M9) may be used for detection.

Selected Precursors

The following chemicals are precursors to the production of soman. When any of them are found in an occupancy, and their legitimate use cannot be established, law enforcement should be notified.

- Ammonium bifluoride
- Dimethyl methylphosphonate
- Diethylphosphite
- Dimethylphosphite
- Hydrogen fluoride
- Methylphosphonous difluoride
- Methylphosphonyl dichloride
- Methylphosphonyl difluoride
- Pinacolone
- Pinacolyl alcohol
- Potassium bifluoride
- Potassium fluoride
- Phosphorus trichloride
- Sodium bifluoride
- Sodium fluoride
- Thionyl chloride
- Trimethyl phosphite

Lethal nerve agent (VX) is a sulfonated organophosphorous compound with a chemical name of O-ethyl-S-(2-iisopropylaminoethyl) methyl phosphonothiolate. The chemical formula is $(Cb_{2b}Hb_{5b}O)(CHb_{3b}O)P(O)S(Cb_{2b}Hb_{4b})N$ $[(Cb_{2b}Hb_{2b})(CHb_{3b})b_{2b}]b_{2b}$. The structure of the compound is shown in Figure 3.5.

VX would be classified as a Class 6.1 poison by the DOT and have a NFPA 704 designation of Health-4, Flammability-1, Reactivity-1, and Spe-

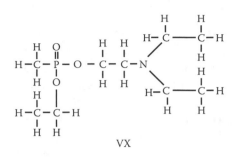

Figure 3.5 Structure of VX.

cial-0. The U.N. four-digit identification number for VX is 2810. The CAS number is 50782-69-9. VX is an amber-colored viscous liquid similar in appearance to motor oil. It is an organophosphate nerve agent with an extended persistence (evaporation rate about 1/1,500 that of water). It has been reported that it has an odor of "rotten fish," but most sources indicate no detectable odor for the purified agent.

Synonyms
- EA1701
- O-Ethyl S-(2-diisopropylaminoethyl) methylphosphonothioate
- O-Ethyl S-(2-diisopropylaminoethyl) methylthiophosphonate
- O-Ethyl S-diisopropylaminoethyl methylphosphonothioate
- S-2-Diisopropylaminoethyl O-ethyl methylphosphonothioate
- S-[2-(Diisopropylamino)ethyl] O-ethyl methylphosphonothiolate
- TX60

Binary weapons in which VX is formed at the time of use have been developed. One component in the binary is *O*-ethyl *O*-2-diisopropylamino-ethyl methylphosphonite (Code QL; CAS Registry Number 57856-11-8) and the other is a source of sulfur. Sulfur sources used include materials identified by the codes NE, which is sulfur (CAS Registry Number 10544-50-0) to which an anticaking material (a silica aerogel) has been added, and NM, a mixture of dimethylpolysulfides and sulfur. VX is one of a family of organophosphates, known as phosphonothiolates, which were investigated as possible pesticides, as well as for possible military uses, beginning in the late 1940s. Details regarding the sequence of investigations that led specifically to VX remain shrouded in secrecy. It has been suggested that the development parallels that of the G agents, beginning with the investigations into pesticides. ICI brought one of these, Amiton (also known as VG), to market, but problems with its toxic effects in people caused it to be withdrawn. It has been suggested that the toxic effects attracted the attention of the British chemical warfare establishment, which initiated more systematic studies of the class. At some point, the British researchers began to share information with the American chemical warfare establishment at Edgewood, where additional studies were conducted, which eventually led to VX being selected by the U.S. for mass production as its second-generation nerve agent in 1958. Outside awareness that a new agent was entering the U.S. Army's arsenal began in 1959, when the FMC Corporation of New York City was awarded a contract to construct a VX production plant in Newport, Indiana. The construction included conversion of a plant used in the nuclear program, the Dana Heavy Water Production Plant. The plant began operation in 1961 and produced its last batch in 1968, over which time about 4,400 tons of VX-filled munitions were produced. Exactly what was being produced, however, was intended to be a closely held secret. The structural formula for VX was not declassified until the mid-1970s (although it had been correctly speculated on by many researchers). The secrecy might have backfired, however, as it simply seems to have encouraged attempts to figure out just what it was. When the decision to declassify was finally reached, it might have gone too far — several patents dealing with methods for producing the agents were declassified at the same time by the British and American governments, and these are said to have been used for guidance by Aum Shinri Kyo and Iraq in their programs for producing VX. Interestingly, the patents demonstrate a continuing link between insecticides and nerve agents — quoting from the preamble to the claims of one of the British patents: "Basic esters of the type hereinbefore described are usually highly toxic compounds, as is now known. When mixed with suitable inert carrier material, they may be used as insecticidal compounds."

VX

Physical Characteristics	Toxic Characteristics
Boiling Point: 298°C (568°F)	Airborne Exposure Limit: 0.0001 mg/mp^{3p}
Vapor Pressure: 0.0007 mm/Hg at 25°C	$LCtb_{50b}$ Inhalation: 30 mg-min/mp^{3p} (15
Vapor Density: 9.2	1/min)
Volatility: 10.5 mg/mp^{3p} at 25°C	LDb_{50b} Skin: 10 mg/70kg man
Specific Gravity: 1.0083 at 25°C	$ECtb_{50b}$ Inhalation: < 2 mg-min/mp^{3p}
Melting/Freezing Point: −51°C	$ECtB_{50\,B}$ Eyes: < 0.9 mg/mP^{3P}
Flashpoint: 159°C (317°F)	$ICtb_{50b}$ Inhalation: 25 mg-min/mp^{3p} (15
Flammable Limits: Unavailable	1/min)
Decomposition Temperature: half-life 36	Median Lethal Dose: 100 mg-min/mp^{3p}
hours at 150°C	Median Incapacitating Dose: 50 mg-min/m^3
Water Solubility: Slight	TLV-TWA: 0.0001 mg/mp^{3p}
Polymerization: No	Population Exposure Limits: 0.000003
Stability: Stable	mg/mp^{3p}

Continued.

VX (Continued)

Physical Characteristics	Toxic Characteristics
Incompatibility: Not available	Carcinogen: No
Persistency*: Long	

* Depends on weather and dispersion type.

VX has low solubility in water (3% at 20°F). It hydrolyzes with a half-life of 350 days at pH 7 and 25°F and 100 days at pH 2–3; basic condition accelerate hydrolysis (half-life 16 minutes at pH13 and 1.3 minutes at pH 14). A number of toxic hydrolysis products form at pH 7–10, notably EA 2192 (CAS Registry Number 73207-98-4). Lowered acetylcholinesterase levels are indicators of nerve agent intoxication in victims.

Depending on the degree of intoxication, symptoms can include:

- Nervousness/restlessness
- Miosis (contraction of the pupil)
- Rhinorrhea (runny nose), excessive salivation
- Dyspnea (difficulty in breathing due to bronchoconstriction/secretions)
- Sweating
- Bradycardia (slow heartbeat)
- Loss of consciousness
- Convulsions
- Flaccid paralysis
- Loss of bladder and bowel control
- Apnea (breathing stopped)

Onset of symptoms is usually rapid, occurring within minutes of exposure. If breathing has stopped, a mechanical respirator should be used to ventilate the patient. While exhaled air is not ordinarily a hazard, DO NOT ATTEMPT MOUTH-TO-MOUTH RESUCITATION without proper shields owing to the possible presence of residual agent on the face. If possible, oxygen or oxygen-enriched air should be used for ventilation. If possible, monitor cardiac activity. Pralidoxime salts are effective in restoring acetylcholinesterase activity after exposure to VX. Thus, as a supplement to treatment with atropine, treatment with pralidoxime salts should be initiated as soon as possible after exposure, with a slow intravenous infusion of 500 mg to 1 g being given initially. Diazepam should be administered to control convulsions. It also has value in controlling fear on the part of the patient. An initial dose of 5 mg may be followed by additional doses at 15 minute intervals up to a total of 15 mg.

VX has a vapor density that is over nine times heavier than air. VX is a colorless-to-straw-colored liquid with little if any odor. It has the consistency and appearance of motor oil. Hazardous polymerization will not occur with this nerve agent. VX has not been identified as a carcinogen. It is a lethal cholinesterase inhibitor, much more toxic than sarin or any of the other nerve agents. Life-threatening doses may be only slightly larger than those producing symptoms. A drop of VX the size of a pinhead on the skin will kill in 5 to 15 minutes. Masks, including SCBA masks, alone do not provide adequate protection against this agent. Protective equipment (self-contained breathing equipment or gas mask, barrier suit) must be used. Medical personnel treating casualties should avoid direct (skin-to-skin) contact; protective gear, including breathing protection, should be worn when treating casualties prior to decontamination. Latex gloves are not adequate protection. Casualties should be decontaminated as rapidly as possible (Chapter 9). Remove casualties from exposure as rapidly as possible. Casualties must not be moved into clean treatment areas where unmasked/ungloved personnel are working until decontamination is complete.

Detection: Nerve agent sensitive chemical agent detectors (e.g., CAM, M18A2, M256, etc.) and papers (e.g., M8, M9) may be used for detection.

Selected Precursors

- Diethyl methylphosphonite
- Diisopropylamine
- Diisopropylaminoethyl chloride
- O-Ethyl O-2-diisopropylaminoethyl methylphosphonite (code designation QL)
- O-Ethyl methylphosphonothioic acid (also known as EMPTA)
- Ethyl hydrogen methylphosphonite
- Methylphosphonous dichloride (also known as SW)
- Methylphosphonous difluoride
- Methylphosphonothioic dichloride (also known as SWS)
- Phosphorus pentasulfide
- Phosphorus trichloride
- Sulfur

Iraq investigated VX beginning in the mid-1980s, in part, apparently, because of its lower volatility and greater persistence. As with all things about the Iraqi chemical program, there is much confusion about details. UNSCOM inspectors were presented with a claim that less than 260 kg of VX had been produced in an exploratory program begun in September 1987 that was subsequently abandoned in September 1988. As the U.N. inspectors uncovered more evidence of Iraq's VX program, the Iraqi government raised the amount of the agent they admitted producing, claiming in 1996 to have produced only 3.9 tons of the agent. UNSCOM found this total incompatible with the large quantities of precursor produced, estimating that at least 50 tons of VX had been produced, with several hundred tons of precursors being unaccounted for. The period over which the program ran also expanded, with a start date in 1985 and a final production run in 1990 becoming the new accepted period. Similarly, Iraq claimed to have never weaponized the agent, a claim that was considered suspect after UNSCOM found VX contamination on fragments from missile warheads. Iraq appears to have settled on a production method that involved preparing EMPTA as a precursor. This process is not considered the optimal route for VX manufacture, but it is thought that the Iraqis settled on it because the EMPTA route allows for production and isolation of VX in a simple final stage, which could be carried out in the field if necessary. Iraq may have used VX in the battle of Fao on April 17 and 18, 1988. Iraq might also have used VX in its chemical cocktail attacks on Iraqi Kurds.

On March 13, 1968, at the Dugway Proving Grounds in Utah, a malfunction in a spray tank used in a test of aerial spraying with VX coupled with unfortunate winds resulted in the contamination of a significant amount of grazing land in the vicinity of Skull Valley outside the boundaries of the test site. Over the course of the following week more than 6,000 sheep grazing in the area died. After initially denying any connection to the deaths of the sheep, the army paid damages — without, however, accepting blame. The official estimate of the amount of VX that was disseminated outside the test site was 9 kg; unofficial estimates have suggested that this is low. However, many of the larger unofficial estimates fail to take into account the fact that a primary route of exposure for the sheep seems to have been ingestion of grass contaminated with VX. This route of exposure makes the official estimate more credible.

In July 1969, a VX leak from weapons at a storage facility on Okinawa led to the hospitalization of 24 people (23 U.S. military and 1 civilian) and caused considerable consternation to the Japanese government, which had apparently been unaware that chemical weapons were present. The Japanese government, and the government of the Ryuku island chain, asked the U.S. to remove all chemical weapons from Okinawa. In 1971, in Operation Red Hat, the weapons were moved to storage on Johnston Island. (They could not be taken back to the U.S., since Public Law 91-672, passed in 1971, known as the Foreign Military Sales Act Amendment, specifically prohibited the transport of chemical weapons from the island of Okinawa to the U.S. This was in part a response to the tremendous public opposition to the army's initial plan to move the weapons to the Umatilla Army Depot in Oregon.) The weapons were eventually destroyed on the island (the final M23 VX-containing land mine in the Johnston Island stocks was destroyed on November 29, 2000). It must be noted that the program of destroying VX at mainland U.S. sites, required under the Chemical Weapons Convention, has not gone as well as that at Johnston Island. There have been frequent delays to respond to safety and environmental concerns, and the project is currently behind schedule.

Lethal nerve agent (GF) is a fluorinated organophosphate compound. The chemical formula is $CHb_{3b}PO(F)OCb_{6b}Hb_{11b}$. GF has a sweet, musty odor of peaches or shellac. GF would be classified as a Class 6.1 poison by the DOT and have a NFPA 704 designation of Health-4, Flammability-1, Reactivity-1, and Special-0. The U.N. four-digit identification number for GF is 2810. GF has a boiling point of 239°C (463°F); a vapor pressure of 0.044 mm Hg at 20°C; a vapor density of 6.2, which is over six times heavier than air; a volatility of 438 mg/m³ at 20°C; a specific gravity of 1.1327 at 20°C; and a freezing/melting point of –30°C. The flashpoint of GF is approximately 94°C (200°F), and the flammable limits are not available. GF has a $MCtb_{50\,b}$ of less than 1 mg-min/mb$_{3b}$, and a LDb_{50b} on the skin of 30 mg.

Synonyms
- CMPF
- Cyclosarin
- Cyclosin
- O-Cyclohexyl methylphosphonofluoridate
- Cyclohexyl methylphosphonofluoridate
- Methyl cyclohexylfluorophosphonate

Cyclosarin was probably first synthesized during World War II as part of the systematic study of organophosphates undertaken by the Germans after their potential military utility was identified. It was again looked at in the early 1950s by both the U.S. and Great Britain as they undertook a systematic study of potential nerve agents (some U.S. sources suggest that interest in GF was stimulated by work undertaken in "another country"). However, the higher cost of the precursors for GF relative to those for GB along with its lower toxicity prevented it from being chosen for manufacture. Iraq is the only country in which large amounts of cyclosarin have ever been produced for use as a chemical warfare agent. As with most issues surrounding the Iraqi chemical weapons programs, the basis for their decision to produce GF is somewhat unclear. However, it seems likely that the choice was driven by a combination of a desire for a more persistent agent combined with problems with obtaining alcohol precursors for sarin (due to an embargo). As noted above, Iraq also fielded weapons filled with mixtures of sarin and cyclosarin. These mixtures appear to have been produced in part for purposes of increasing persistence and in part because of raw material issues. Iraq reportedly developed a binary system in which GF was formed at the time of use. The open literature does not offer detail, but this most likely involves the use of methylphosphonyldifluoride (Code DF; CAS Registry Number 676-99-3) as one component with the other being cyclohexanol (CAS Registry Number 108-93-0) or a mixture of cyclohexylamine (CAS Registry Number 108-91-8) and cyclohexanol. Iraq fielded munitions filled with mixtures of GB (sarin) and GF. Tests on mice indicated that GB-GF mixtures have a toxicity intermediate between the toxicities of GB and GF; thus, there appear to be no synergistic effects producing enhanced or unexpected toxic effects that would require any change in treatment protocols for those exposed to a mixture.

Symptoms and Effects

Lowered acetylcholinesterase levels are indicators of nerve agent intoxication in victims.

Depending on the degree of intoxication, symptoms can include:

- Nervousness/restlessness
- Miosis (contraction of the pupil)
- Rhinorrhea (runny nose), excessive salivation
- Dyspnea (difficulty in breathing due to bronchoconstriction/secretions)
- Sweating
- Bradycardia (slow heartbeat)
- Loss of consciousness
- Convulsions
- Flaccid paralysis
- Loss of bladder and bowel control
- Apnea (breathing stopped)

Onset of symptoms is usually rapid, occurring within minutes of exposure. If breathing has stopped, a mechanical respirator should be used to ventilate the patient. DO NOT ATTEMPT MOUTH-TO-MOUTH RESUCITATION. If possible, oxygen or oxygen-enriched air should be used for ventilation. If possible, monitor cardiac activity. Oximes (pralidoxime salts, obidoxime) may be of use in restoring acetylcholinesterase activity. Obidoxime may be used to treat GF intoxication; however, it may cause liver damage. Animal studies indicate that the oxime Hi-6 may be significantly superior to other oximes in the treatment of GF intoxication, but it is not widely available. Therefore pralidoxime salts should be used, with a slow intravenous infusion of 500 mg to 1 g being given initially. Diazepam should be administered to control convulsions. It also has value in controlling fear on the part of the patient. An initial dose of 5 mg may be followed by additional doses at 15 minute intervals up to a total of 15 mg. Protective equipment (self-contained breathing equipment or gas mask, barrier suit) must be used. Medical personnel treating casualties should avoid direct (skin-to-skin) contact; protective gear, including breathing protection, should be worn when treating casualties prior to decontamination. Latex gloves are not adequate protection. Casualties should be decontaminated as rapidly as possible (see the section on decontamination in Chapter 9). Remove casualties from exposure as rapidly as possible. Casualties must not be moved into clean treatment areas where unmasked/ungloved personnel are working until decontamination is complete.

Detection: Nerve agent sensitive chemical agent detectors (e.g., CAM, M18A2, M256, etc.) and papers (e.g., M8, M9) may be used for detection. Masks, including SCBA masks, alone do not provide adequate protection against this agent.

Selected Precursors

- Ammonium bifluoride
- Cyclohexylamine
- Cyclohexanol
- Diethyl phosphite
- Dimethyl methylphosphonate
- Dimethylphosphite
- Hydrogen fluoride
- Methylphosphonous difluoride
- Methylphosphonyl dichloride
- Methylphosphonyl difluoride (DF)
- Phosphorus trichloride
- Potassium bifluoride
- Potassium fluoride
- Sodium bifluoride
- Sodium fluoride
- Thionyl chloride
- Trimethyl phosphite

Lethal nerve agent (GE) (TPhosphonofluoridic acid, ethyl-, isopropyl ester) The chemical formula is $TCb_{5b}Hb_{12b}FOb_{2b}PT$ Thas a $LDb_{50\,b}$ of 690 mg/kg.

Lethal nerve agent (VE) Phosphonothioic acid, ethyl-, S-[2-(diethylamino)ethyl] O-ethyl ester

Lethal nerve agent (VG) Phosphorothioic acid, S-[2-(diethylamino)ethyl] O,O-diethyl ester. Amiton (sold as pesticide)

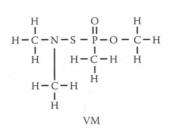

Figure 3.6   Structure of VM.

Lethal nerve agent (VM) VM (Phosphonothioic acid, methyl-, S-(2-(diethylamino)ethyl) O-ethyl ester) is a "V-series" nerve agent closely related to the better-known VX nerve agent. Like most of the agents in the V-series (with the exception of VX), VM has not been extensively studied outside of military science. Little is known about this chemical compound other than its chemical formula. It is commonly theorized that the "second-generation" V series agents came from a Cold War era Russian chemical weapons development program. They might have been developed sometime between 1950 and 1990. They have similar lethal dose levels to VX (between 10 and 50 mg) and have similar symptoms and methods of action to other nerve agents that act on cholinesterase. The treatment remains the same, but the window for effectively treating second generation V series seizures is shorter. In addition to the standard seizures, some of the second generation V series agents are known to cause coma. The structure is shown in Figure 3.6.

Lethal nerve agent (VR) Phosphonothioic acid, methyl-, S-[2 (diethylamino)ethyl] O-(2-methylpropyl) ester. VR is a liquid organophosphate nerve agent with an "oily" consistency that is colorless when pure. Chemical formula $Cb_{11b}Hb_{26b}NOb_{2b}PS$. Molecular weight 267.38. Boiling point 323°F at 760 torr (1 atm.) may decompose (86° at 1 mtorr). Vapor density heavier than air. Vapor pressure 0.00062 mm Hg at 25°F. Volatility 8.9 mg/mp^{3p}.p^{P} Specific gravity (liquid density) 1.003. Freezing point <0°F. LDb$_{50b}$ 11.3 micrograms/kg.

Synonyms

- O-isobutyl S-(2-diethylaminoethyl)methyl phosphothioate
- O-isobutyl S-(2-diethylaminoethyl)methyl thiophosphonate
- O-isobutyl S-(N,N-diethylaminoethyl)methylphosphonothioate
- Russian V-gas
- Russian VX
- RVX

VR was investigated and developed by the Soviet Union during the 1950s, in a manner that the open literature suggests roughly paralleled the development of VX in the West. It has been suggested that the Soviet investigations were partly guided by knowledge of the molecular formula of VX but lacked information about the structural formula, and so settled on the on VR, which is a structural isomer of VX. The greater difficulty of treatment and the possibility that detection might be more difficult could have served as incentives for the choice of VR even if the Soviets were aware of the structural formula for VX. This is supported by sources that suggest that a pilot production facility for VR was constructed at a facility in Stalingrad (now Volgograd) by the Soviets as early as 1956, two years before VX was selected for production by the U.S. As research on the agent continued for an extended period. Despite the early experimentation, large-scale production of VR might not have commenced until 1972. On at least one occasion, an accidental release apparently occurred at the Novocheboksarsk facility. A fire caused by a wiring fault on April 28, 1974, apparently damaged the seals on bombs filled with the agent, resulting in a "loss of control" of the agent they contained. Despite their difficulties, the Soviets produced 15,557 tons of VR according to their declaration to the OPCW. There were two major variants weaponized, a polymethyl methacrylate-thickened VR and plain VR. There are reports that a binary version was also developed.

Detection: Nerve agent sensitive chemical agent detectors (e.g., CAM, M18A2, M256, etc.) and papers (e.g., M8, M9) may be used for detection. Of VR, however, detection limits have not been determined for this agent. Some reports suggest that this agent may be misidentified by automated detectors. Lowered acetylcholinesterase levels are indicators of nerve agent intoxication in victims. Depending on the degree of intoxication, symptoms can include:

- Nervousness/restlessness
- Miosis (contraction of the pupil)
- Rhinorrhea (runny nose), excessive salivation
- Dyspnea (difficulty in breathing due to bronchoconstriction/secretions)
- Sweating
- Bradycardia (slow heartbeat)
- Loss of consciousness
- Convulsions
- Flaccid paralysis
- Loss of bladder and bowel control
- Apnea (breathing stopped)

Onset of symptoms is usually rapid, occurring within minutes of exposure. Patients exposed to VR might require higher doses of atropine than is needed for treatment of equivalent exposures to other organophosphate nerve agents. The most effective oxime for use in post-treatment of VR exposure is HI-6, based on animal studies. However, it is not widely available. Despite their lesser efficacy, pralidoxime salts are known to be of use in restoring acetylcholinesterase activity after VR exposure. Use of pralidoxime salts should be initiated in cases where VR intoxication is suspected, with a slow intravenous infusion of 500 mg to 1 g being given initially. Diazepam should be administered to control convulsions. VR has been reported to be particularly capable of inducing seizures; however, the experiments in guinea pigs suggest that diazepam should be effective in controlling them. Diazepam also has value in controlling fear on the part of the patient. An initial dose of 5 mg may be followed by additional doses at 15 minute intervals up to a total of 15 mg. Protective equipment (self-contained breathing equipment or gas mask, barrier suit) must be used. Medical personnel treating casualties should avoid direct (skin-to-skin) contact; protective gear, including breathing protection, should be worn when treating casualties prior to decontamination. Latex gloves are not adequate protection. Casualties should be decontaminated as rapidly as possible (see the section on decontamination in Chapter 9). Remove casualties from exposure as rapidly as possible. Casualties must not be moved into clean treatment areas where unmasked/ungloved personnel are working until decontamination is complete.

Lethal nerve agent (VS) Phosphonothioic acid, ethyl-, S-[2-[bis(1 methylethyl)amino]ethyl] O-ethyl ester.

The most important thing emergency responders can do when responding to terrorist incidents or dealing with patients exposed to chemical agents is to protect themselves. This protection involves wearing the proper protective clothing and making sure that patients are decontaminated before treatment is begun. Local standard operating procedures and plans dictate what protective clothing is available at the local level. MSDS sheets and other publications, including those available from the military, provide guidance on what types of protective equipment are appropriate for individual chemical agents. Information on chemical protective equipment is provided in Chapter 9. Personnel protection usually includes a mask and gloves, as a minimum, when treating patients that are decontaminated and can include respiratory protection and chemical protective clothing in cases where decon has not been done, or exposure and type of agent are unknown. During the sarin incident in Tokyo, emergency responders were injured because they did not have proper respiratory and body protection, and they did not decontaminate victims. However, they did not know what the victims had been exposed to or how toxic the material really was. Initially, the incidents were occurring at several locations and were not perceived to be connected in the early stages. Decontamination of patients involves cutting away and removing all clothing. It is important to remove all agent from contact with the victim. After the clothing is removed, the underlying skin is decontaminated using soap and water. Hypochlorite, usually a 0.5% solution, is used for equipment. When bleach solutions are not readily available, water, or soap and water, should be used on equipment until bleach becomes available. If a victim is not breathing or is having difficulty breathing, mouth-to-mouth breathing should not be used. A bag mask or other protective device should be used, with supplemental oxygen administered, to prevent contamination of EMS personnel.

No chemical warfare agent is useful without an antidote to protect your own troops. Atropine is the universal antidote for chemical nerve agent exposures. It functions by binding to the acetylcholine receptors without causing excitement. This keeps the excess of acetylcholine from reaching the receptors. Atropine treats the symptoms of nerve agent exposure rather than the cause. This is why atropine is administered in conjunction with a group of chemicals called oximes. They treat the cause of the problem by restoring the acetylcholinesterase to operation, by breaking the enzyme-nerve agent bond. The oxime that is most commonly used for nerve agent exposure is pralidoxime chloride (protopam chloride; 2-PAMCl). Preventive treatments are also available for nerve agent exposures. Some warning would have to be given before the release, because it takes up to 30 minutes for the preventative antidote to be effective. Preventative effects last for approximately two hours. One pre-exposure therapy involves the use of carbamate pyrdostigmine, which impedes the production of acetylcholine and guards the enzyme against nerve agents. Control of the acetylcholine production is approximately 25% effective, which does not result in any side effects, since the body can function on 5% of the usual levels. Diazepam tablets may also be administered as a preventative agent. Diazepam functions by strengthening the effects of other nerve agent antidotes, thus increasing the survival rate and reducing injury.

Atropine can have serious side effects and should not be given frivolously. Taking atropine before an anticipated exposure occurs is ill advised. It can cause a moderate heart rate increase, dilation of pupils, and blurred vision, along with inhibition of sweating which can cause the body to overheat. But, not giving atropine, or not giving enough atropine to a patient who has a severe agent exposure, can also cause serious consequences or result in the death of the patient. For victims with mild or moderate exposure, the recommended dose is 2 mg injected into the smooth muscles or glands. Symptoms should subside within 5 to 10 minutes. However, if there is no significant

improvement within 10 minutes, a second dose of 2 mg is usually administered (5 minutes if they are in serious distress). In another 5 to 10 minutes
the patient is reevaluated and another dose of 2 mg might be administered
if no improvement is noted. With a mild or moderate first dose, if a patient
does not get better after the second dose of 2 mg, or they worsen, the third
dose could be increased to 4 mg. Lack of improvement is usually caused by
continued contact with agent on the skin. Additional decontamination might
be considered if the victim does not improve after administration of the
second or third doses. Patients exhibiting symptoms of severe exposure may
be unconscious, experience cessation of breathing, or exhibit other airway,
gastrointestinal, or muscular distress. If breathing has stopped, a mechanical
respirator should be used to ventilate the patient. DO NOT ATTEMPT
MOUTH-TO-MOUTH RESUCITATION. If possible, oxygen or oxygen-
enriched air should be used for ventilation. If possible, monitor cardiac
activity. For such patients, atropine should be administered initially in a 6
mg dose, followed by 2 mg at 5-minute intervals until improvement occurs.
It should be administered until the victim feels improved, breathing is better,
and secretions have discontinued. Protopam® chloride; 2-PAMCl (2-PAM-
Chloride) may also be used in conjunction with atropine. Its effect is on the
skeletal muscles and causes an increase in muscle strength. Protopam® chloride should be administered in all cases of nerve agent poisoning unless the
agent is GD, which is highly unlikely. The U.S. military does not have any
GD in its stockpile. 2-PAMCl is administered intravenously at the rate of 1
gm in 250 ml of 5% D/W (dextrose and water) or saline over a 20-minute
period. **NOTE: Use of succinylcholine to assist intubation is contraindi-
cated due to possible interactions with nerve agents.** Atropine and 2-PAMCl
are used in auto injectors by the military. Some emergency responders located
near chemical agent stockpiles in this country have also been issued auto
injectors in case of an accidental release from the stockpiles. Numerous Fire
Departments have decided to place auto injectors containing atropine and
2-PAMCl on every department vehicle for the crews in case of chemical nerve
agent exposure. Material presented on the administration of atropine and
other antidotes for nerve agents is provided only for informational purposes.
Administration of atropine or any other medication should be undertaken
only upon the advice and guidance of a physician and should be based upon
local medical protocols.

Blister Agents or Vesicants

Blister agents, or vesicants as they are known, include four basic types: sulfur
mustard, nitrogen mustard, lewisite, and phosgene oxime. Like the nerve

Table 3.5 Blister Agent Relative Data

Comparative Data	H	HD	HT	L
Rate of Action	Moderately rapid	Moderately rapid	Moderately rapid	Rapid
State at 68°F	Amber to dark brown	Oily, pale yellow to black liquid; water-clear if pure	Viscous, clear to pale yellow liquid	Amber to dark brown liquid color less oily liquid when pure
Odor	Garlic-like	Garlic-like	Garlic-like	Geranium-like; little odor when pure
Volatility (mg/m^3 at 77°F)	920	920	831	6.5×10^3
LCt_{50} (mg-min/m^3)	Similar to HD	1500	Not established	1200–1500
Vapor density	5.5	5.5	6.9	7.2
Vapor pressure (mm Hg at 77°F) (Depends on purity)	0.11	0.11	0.10	0.58

Source: CSEPP ACT FAST Student Manual.

agents, mustard agents are sometimes incorrectly referred to as gases, when in fact they are not. All of the blister agents have the same basic characteristics and will be referred to as mustard, blister agents, or vesicants interchangeably (Table 3.5). Mustard agents are persistent by nature. There are locations in Europe where mustard is still evident from its use in World War I. It can be found on some bridges, in farmers' fields, and in other portions of the landscape. Mustard agents are made in varying formulations including distilled, nitrogen, sulfur, and thickened mustards. Military designations for mustard agents are as follows: mustard (H), distilled mustard (HD), (HS), and thickened mustard (HT). Nitrogen mustards have the military designation of (HNB_{1B}), (HNB_{2B}), and (HNB_{3B}). Unlike the nerve agents, mustard agent exposure is rarely fatal. Symptoms for mustard agents do not appear for several hours after exposure (Table 3.6 and Table 3.7). Developed in 1854, mustard was first used in 1917 by the Germans during World War I. There were 20,000 casualties as a result of the first battlefield attack. Mustard is designed to incapacitate troops, not to kill. It can, however, be fatal if a large enough dose is administered or a person has other health problems that will be compounded by mustard exposure.

Table 3.6   Exposures through Inhalation/Ingestion of Blister Agent by Degree of Severity

Degree of Severity	Body Part Affected	Symptom(s)
Mild	Nose, throat, and windpipe	Burning sensation, sinus pain, cough
	GI	Nausea and vomiting
Moderate	Nose, throat, and windpipe	Burning sensation
	Lungs	Chest tightness, severe cough
	GI	Nausea and vomiting, stomach pains
Severe	Nose, throat, and windpipe	Severe burning
	Lungs	Difficulty breathing due to airway damage
	GI	Nausea, vomiting, bloody diarrhea, stomach pains
	Muscles	Large amounts may affect nerve endings

Source: CSEPP ACT FAST Student Manual.

Table 3.7   Exposures through Direct Contact with Blister Agent by Degree of Severity

Degree of Severity	Body Part Affected	Symptom(s)
Mild	Skin	No immediate clinical effects (no burning, stinging, or redness); becomes "fixed" to the tissue within minutes, blisters appear about 2 to 36 hours later
	Eyes	Within 4 to 12 hours after exposure, itching, tearing, conjunctivitis (reddening of tissues surrounding the eyeball), sensation of grit in the eye, burning and photophobia (sensitivity to light), some swelling of eyelids
Moderate	Skin	No immediate clinical effects; blisters appear sooner and are more severe than in cases of "mild" dose
	Eyes	Within 3 to 6 hours after exposure, increased intensity from "mild" symptoms, edema (swelling) of lids to the point of near closure; spasms of the muscles surrounding the eye; increased photophobia; blurred vision; possible discharge; miosis may also occur; severe inflammation of conjunctiva and cornea
Severe	Skin	No immediate clinical effects; blisters appear sooner and are large; necrosis; skin charring may be evident
	Eyes	Severe pain, increased swelling lids to point of closure, discharge; possible damage to cornea (e.g., ulceration, perforation, etc.)
	Muscles	Large amounts may affect nerve endings

Source: CSEPP ACT FAST Student Manual.

Sulfur mustard (H) or **distilled mustard (HD)** is a liquid that has a consistency of motor oil and appears in colors from light yellow to brown and black, based upon the number and type of impurities that are present. Pure mustard is clear like water. The odor of mustard ranges from onions or garlic to horseradish or mustard, hence its name. It is a chlorinated sulfur compound. H or HD mustard has a chemical name of Bis-(2-chloroethyl)sulfide.

MUSTARD

Physical Characteristics	Toxic Characteristics
Boiling Point: 217°C (422°F)	Airborne Exposure Limit: 0.003 mg/mp³P
Vapor Pressure: 0.072 mm/Hg at 20°C	LCtb$_{50b}$ Inhalation: 1500 mg-min/mP³P
Vapor Density: 5.5	LDb$_{50b}$ Skin: 100 mg/70kg man
Volatility: 610 mg/mp³P at 20°C	LDb$_{50 b}$ Oral: 0.7 mg/kg
Specific Gravity: 1.268 at 25°C	ECtb$_{50b}$ Eyes: Unavailable
Melting/Freezing Point: 14.5°C	ECtb$_{50 b}$ Inhalation: Unavailable
Flashpoint: 105°C (221°F)	ICtb$_{50b}$ Inhalation: 1500 mg-min/mp³P
Flammable Limits: Unavailable	Median Lethal Dose: 1500 mg-min/mp³P
Decomposition Temperature: 149°C to	Inhalation and 10,000 skin
177°C hydrolyzes to form HCL and	Median Incapacitating Dose: 200 mg-
thiodiglycol	min/mp³P eye, 2000 skin, 150, inhalation
Water Solubility: Immiscible	TLV-TWA: 0.003 mg/mp³P
Polymerization: No	Population Exposure Limits: 0.0001 mg/mp³P
Stability: Stable	Carcinogen: No
Incompatibility: Brass, corrodes steel	
Persistency*: Many years/even decades	

* Depends on weather and dispersion type.

Mustard is only slightly soluble in water and is miscible with organophosphate nerve agents. It has a freezing point of approximately 57°F, and if it were stored outside, it would remain frozen for a large part of the year. Mustard has a specific gravity that is heavier than water. The vapor density of mustard is about 5.5 times heavier than air. While mustard is flammable, it has a fairly high flashpoint. Explosive charges may be used to ignite mustard agents. Flammable limits or explosive ranges for mustards have not been identified. The chemical formula for sulfur/distilled mustard is $(ClHb_{2b}CHb_{2b})b_{2b}S$ and its structural formula is shown in Figure 3.7.

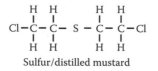
Sulfur/distilled mustard

Figure 3.7 Structure for sulfur/distilled mustard.

Time Course: Onset of symptoms may be delayed 2 to 36 hours; initial signs/symptoms are those of acute tracheobronchitis. Approximate time course for moderate exposure: 2 to 4 hrs, chest tightness, hacking cough, hoarseness, sneezing; 4 to 16 hrs, sinus pain, increased respiration rate; 16 to 48 hrs, severe cough, unable to speak, very rapid breathing; 24 to 48 hrs, severe dyspnea, lung tissue hemorrhage, bronchopneumonia.

Sulfur mustard (HT) or **Agent T** has a chemical name of Bis-(2-(2-chloroethylthio)ethyl)ether. It has a yellow color with a garlic-like odor, similar to other mustard agents.

SULFUR HT

Physical Characteristics	Toxic Characteristics
Boiling Point: 228°C (442°F)	Airborne Exposure Limit: 0.003 mg/mp^{3p}
Vapor Pressure: 2.9 × E-5 at 25°C	LCtb$_{50b}$ Inhalation: Unavailable
Vapor Density: 9.08	LDb$_{50b}$ Skin: Unavailable
Volatility: 4.1 × E-4 at 25°C	LDb$_{50b}$ Oral: Unavailable
Specific Gravity: 1.2361 at 25°C	ECtb$_{50b}$ Eyes: Unavailable
Melting/Freezing Point: 9.6 to 9.9°C	ECtb$_{50\,b}$ Inhalation: Unavailable
Viscosity: 14.7	ICtb$_{50\,b}$ Inhalation: Unavailable
Flashpoint: Unknown	Median Lethal Dose: Unavailable
Flammable Limits: Unknown	Median Incapacitating Dose: Unavailable
Decomposition Temperature: Unknown	TLV-TWA: 0.003 mg/mp^{3p}
Water Solubility: Immiscible	Population Exposure Limits: 0.0001 mg/mp^{3p}
Polymerization: Unknown	Carcinogen: No
Stability: Stable	
Incompatibility: Unknown	
Persistency*: Many years, even decades	

* Depends on weather and dispersion type.

The specific gravity of HT is heavier than air and very similar to distilled mustard. It has a vapor density over nine times heavier than air and four times heavier than distilled mustard. No airborne exposure limits have been identified for sulfur mustard. No flashpoint or flammable limits have been established, and it has a boiling point slightly lower than distilled mustard. Specific health hazard data, such as Airborne Exposure Limits, have not been established for Agent T. However, it has toxicity very similar to that of distilled mustard and under no circumstances should anyone be allowed to be exposed to any direct vapor, skin, or eye contact. HT is not listed as a carcinogenic agent; however, because of its similarity to HD it might be suspected as one. The median lethal dose (LCtb$_{50b}$) of Agent T in laboratory animals has been identified as 1,650 to 2,250 mg-min/m^3 based on 10 minutes of exposure. The chemical formula for Agent T sulfur mustard is $Cb_{2b}Hb_{4b}Sb_{2b}Cb_{2b}Hb_{4b}OCb_{2b}Hb_{4b}Cb_{2b}Hb_{4b}Clb_{2b}$ and the structural formula is shown in Figure 3.8.

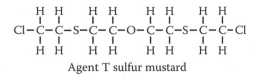

Agent T sulfur mustard

Figure 3.8   Structure for Agent T sulfur mustard.

Mustard agents (H), (HD), (HS), and (HT), like nerve agents, would be classified as Class 6.1 poisons by the DOT and would have NFPA 704 designations of Health-4, Flammability-1, Reactivity-1, and Special-0. The U.N. four-digit identification number for mustard agents would be 2,810 as it also is for all of the mustard and nerve agents.

Nitrogen mustard (HN) was developed in three formulations: HN-1, HN-2, and HN-3. HN-1 was the first to be produced in the late 1920s and early 1930s. It was originally developed as a pharmaceutical used to remove warts, before it became a military agent. Agent H-2 was developed as a military agent and became a pharmaceutical. HN-3 was designed as a military mustard agent and is the only one that remains in military use. Therefore, this section will cover only the characteristics of HN-3 mustard agent. HN-3 is colorless, to pale yellow, with a butter-almond odor.

HN-3

Physical Characteristics	Toxic Characteristics
Boiling Point: 256°C (495°F)	Airborne Exposure Limit: Unknown
Vapor Pressure: 0.0109 at 25°C	LCtb$_{50b}$ Inhalation: 1500 mg-min/mp^{3p}
Vapor Density: 7.1	LCtb$_{50b}$ Skin: 10,000 mg-min/mp^{3p}
Volatility: 121 at 25°C	LDb$_{50b}$ Skin: Unavailable
Specific Gravity: 1.2361 at 25°C	LDb$_{50b}$ Oral: Unavailable
Melting/Freezing Point: −3.7°C	ECtb$_{50 b}$ Eyes: Unavailable
Viscosity: Unknown	ECtb$_{50b}$ Inhalation: Unavailable
Flashpoint: Unknown	ICtb$_{50b}$ Inhalation: 1500 mg-min/mp^{3p}
Flammable Limits: Unknown	ICtb$_{50b}$ Eyes: 200 mg-min/mp^{3p}
Decomposition Temperature: Unknown	Median Lethal Dose: Unknown
Water Solubility: Immiscible	Median Incapacitating Dose: Unknown
Polymerization: Unknown	TLV-TWA: Unknown
Stability: Stable	Population Exposure Limits: Unknown
Incompatibility: Unknown	Carcinogen: Unknown
Persistency*: About 3 times longer than HD mustards	

* Depends on weather and dispersion type.

The chemical formula for nitrogen mustard agent HN-3 is $N(CHb_{2b}CHb_{2b}Cl)b_{3 b}$ and the structural formula is shown in Figure 3.9.

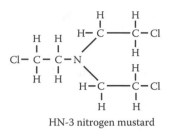

HN-3 nitrogen mustard

Figure 3.9   Structure for nitrogen mustard.

Nitrogen mustard HN-3, would be classified as a Class 6.1 poison by the DOT and would have NFPA 704 designations of Health-4, Flammability-1, Reactivity-1, and Special-0. The U.N. four-digit identification number for Agent HN-3 would be 2810, also designated for all of the mustard and nerve agents.

Mustard is effective in small doses and affects the lungs, skin, and eyes. Symptoms are likely to appear first on delicate tissues, such as the soft membranes surrounding the eyes and eyeball (Figure 3.10). This will be followed by tissues of the throat, lungs, nose, and mouth. Mustard agents have the greatest effects on warm, moist areas of the body, such as eyes, respiratory tract, armpits, groin, buttocks, and other skin folds. Because of the delayed onset of symptoms, soldiers did not know they were exposed to mustard. Once symptoms did appear during World War I, the army medical systems became overwhelmed by the sheer numbers of casualties. Recovery time from mustard exposures meant an average time of 6 weeks before soldiers could return to duty.

Mustard agents can be an inhalation or skin absorption hazard. The symptoms of the agents do not appear for 2 to 24 hours after the exposure, and the usual onset in most people is between 4 to 8 hours. Liquid exposures to the skin and eyes produce an earlier onset of symptoms than do vapor exposures. When mustard agent contacts the skin, it does not produce pain or sensation. Those exposed would not likely be aware of the contact. Once

Figure 3.10   Mustard agent vapor exposure to eyes. (Source: U.S. Army.)

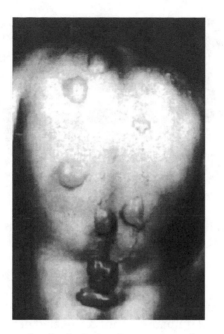

Figure 3.11 Blisters on back of victim from mustard agent exposure. (Source: U.S. Army.)

mustard contacts the skin, the damage has already occurred (Figure 3.11). If the exposure is known at that point, decontamination will at best only reduce the amount of material still on the skin. It will otherwise be ineffective against stopping the damage to the body. Because mustard is a persistent agent, it will remain on clothing of victims and anything else that it touches for a long period of time. While decontamination will not provide much help to the victim, it is important to prevent secondary contamination of responders and others. Hypochlorite solution or flooding amounts of water are necessary to remove mustard agents. Because of dormant effects, mustard would probably not be used by a terrorist who wanted an immediate impact. It would, however, be an excellent choice if the terrorist wanted to expose large numbers of people, who might disperse over a wide area within a few hours. Once symptoms begin and people start seeking medical attention, there would be a great deal of confusion about the source of the illness. For example, at major outdoor events around the country, aircraft fly around with advertising banners. Terrorists could use such an aircraft to disperse mustard over the crowd. Because mustard does not produce immediate effects, people would return to their homes after the event — some to different cities, counties, and states! Contamination could be spread from a victim's clothing to others. When people started experiencing symptoms, hospitals would be hard-pressed to determine what the source of the illness was or what the common

Figure 3.12 Agricultural spray planes and devices can be used to disseminate chemical or biological agents.

place of exposure might have been. People coming into contact with a victim's clothing or perhaps those attending events at the same location on a later date may also become contaminated because of the persistence of mustard agents if proper decontamination is not completed before contact is allowed.

Unlike nerve agents, there is no known antidote for mustard exposure. It enters the body through the skin or mucous membrane and triggers biochemical damage within seconds to minutes, and no known medical procedures can stop or minimize the damage. Once mustard enters the body through the skin, eyes, or respiratory system, it will travel to the target organs which are the bone marrow, the gastrointestinal tract, and the central nervous system. After mustard enters the body and reacts with other substances, intact mustard cannot be detected in the blister fluid, blood, tissue, or urine. Therefore, contact with these fluids will not cause exposure to mustard agent.

No laboratory tests are available that will precisely identify mustard exposure. First symptoms from mustard exposure involve erythema, which is a redness of the skin similar to a sunburn, followed by itching, burning, or stinging pain. The time between exposure and onset of symptoms may be affected by the dose of mustard, the air temperature, the amount of moisture on the skin, and area of exposure on the skin. Within the vicinity of the reddened skin, vesicles form and eventually become blisters filled with a yellowish, translucent fluid. Eyes are very sensitive to mustard agent and exposure will produce the most rapid onset of symptoms. Irritation accompanied by a "gritty" sensation of something in the eye is followed in some cases by inflammation of the eyes (conjunctivitis) (Figure 3.13). Larger doses in the eyes produce edema of the eyelids (fluid buildup), which might be followed by damage to the cornea. The eyelids might become swollen accompanied by pain in the eye, causing contraction of the muscles surrounding the eye, and finally complete closure of the eyelids. Liquid mustard causes the most severe

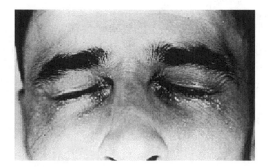

Figure 3.13   Mustard agent effects of mustard conjunctivitis. (Source: U.S. Army.)

eye damage; however, blisters do not form in the eyes. Almost all of the eye exposure symptoms are self-reversing. During World War I, only about 0.1% of all mustard exposures actually resulted in permanent eye damage.

Respiratory exposure results in damage to the mucosa or cell lining, followed by cellular damage and cellular death. The extent of the damage is dependent on the amount of the dose during exposure. Mustard enters the respiratory system through inhalation, and the greater the amount inhaled, the more severe the symptoms and damage. Small amounts of mustard result in nasal irritation and possible bleeding. Sinus passages may be irritated along with the throat, which will produce a scratchy sore throat type of pain. Laryngitis may result from larger exposures that can include complete loss of voice for a period of time. Large doses may result in shortness of breath, and productive coughs might be present in the respiratory system. When respiratory symptoms begin within 4 hours of the exposure, it is usually an indication of a large dose through inhalation.

When a large dose of mustard agent has entered the body, it may be carried to the bone marrow. Damage occurs there to the precursor cells, which is followed by a decrease in the white blood cell count. Over a period of days, red blood cells and platelets are also diminished. When the Iraqi Army used mustard on the Iranians during the Iraq-Iran War, white cell counts of under 200 cells/mm^3 were identified. Reduced white blood cell counts severely inhibit the body's ability to fight off infection. Most of those patients did not survive. The gastrointestinal (GI) tract is also a target organ for mustard agent. Nausea and vomiting are not unusual within 12 to 24 hours after exposure. Symptoms do not, however, indicate that tissue damage has occurred. Mucosa damage to the GI tract results from ingestion of mustard, or through transfer by means of blood coming from another high dose location. Vomiting may last for several days and may be accompanied by diarrhea (not usually bloody). Less severe cases produce constipation as often as diarrhea. Late diarrhea and vomiting can lead to large amounts of fluid and electrolyte loss and may indicate multiple organ involvement. Patients who have these types of symptoms retain a poor prognosis. Lastly, the central nervous system may be affected by exposure to mustard agents. Generally, the symptoms are not well recognized and may involve sluggish, apathetic behaviors. Symptoms have been recorded for as much as a year after exposure. While death from mustard exposure is rare, lethal doses will produce convulsions and severe pulmonary damage that is usually associated with infections. In large-dose exposures, death can occur within 24 to 36 hours.

Lewisite (L) is a vesicant from the arsenical chemical family. Lewisite causes many of the same types of damage to skin, eyes, and the respiratory system as do the mustard agents. It was developed at the end of World War I but never used in battle. The chemical name is dichloro-(2-chlorovinyl) arsine. It has not knowingly been used on the battlefield, and human exposure data is very limited. The major difference between lewisite and mustard is that lewisite causes pain immediately upon exposure, whereas the mustards have a delayed onset. It has been reported that the pain associated with lewisite contact is extreme. Visible tissue damage will occur very quickly in the form of a grayish-appearing area of dead skin. Blisters also develop more quickly than with mustard, but it may take up to 12 hours for full blistering effects to develop. Lewisite is also a systemic poison that can result in pulmonary edema, diarrhea, restlessness, weakness, subnormal temperature, and low blood pressure. Severity of symptoms in order of appearance is as blister agent, toxic lung irritant, tissue absorption, and systemic poison. If inhaled in high enough concentrations, lewisite can cause death in as little as 10 minutes. Common routes of exposure into the body are through the eyes, skin, and inhalation.

LEWISITE

Physical Characteristics	Toxic Characteristics
Boiling Point: 190°C (375°F)	Airborne Exposure Limit: 0.003 mg/mp^{3p}
Vapor Pressure: 0.394 at 20°C	LDb$_{50b}$ (skin): 20 mg/kg
Vapor Density: 7.1	1% Lethality: 150 mg-min/mp^{3p}
Volatility: 4,480 at 20°C	No Deaths Level: 100 mg-min/mp^{3p}
Specific Gravity: 1.89 at 20°C	NOAEL (oral): 0.5 to 1.0 mg/kg
Melting/Freezing Point: −18°C	LCtb$_{50\,b}$Skin: 100,000 mg-min/mp^{3p}
Viscosity: Unavailable	ICtb$_{50b}$ Inhalation: 1200 to 1500 mg-min/mp^{3p}
Flashpoint: None	
Flammable Limits: None	ICtb$_{50\,b}$Eyes: < 300 mg-min/mp^{3p}
Decomposition Temperature: Unavailable	TLV-TWA: 0.003 mg/mp^{3p}
Water Solubility: Immiscible	Population Exposure Limits: Unknown
Polymerization: Unknown	Carcinogen: Unknown
Stability: Stable	
Incompatibility: Unknown	
Persistency*: Shorter than HD mustards	

* Depends on weather and dispersion type.

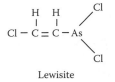

Lewisite

Figure 3.14   Structure of lewisite.

Lewisite is an oily, colorless liquid when pure. "War gas" is an amber-to-dark brown color with a geraniumlike odor; pure lewisite has little if any odor. It is much more volatile than mustard agents. Often lewisite is mixed with mustard to lower the boiling point of the mixture. The military designation for the mustard/lewisite mixture is (HL). Lewisite is insoluble in water and has a specific gravity, which makes it heavier than water. It has a vapor density that is about seven times heavier than air. Lewisite has a very low level of flammability, with no flashpoint or flammable range identified. The molecular formula for lewisite is C2H2AsCl3 and the structural formula is shown in Figure 3.14.

Lewisite would be classified as a Class 6.1 poison by the DOT and have a NFPA 704 designation of Health-4, Flammability-1, Reactivity-1 and Special-0. The U.N. four-digit identification number would be 2810. Lewisite is a vesicant and toxic lung irritant that is absorbed into tissues. The body is unable to detoxify itself from lewisite exposure. Eye contact results in pain, inflammation, and blepharospasm (spasms of the eyelid muscles), which leads to closure of the eyelids, corneal scarring, and iritis (inflammation of the iris). If decontamination of the eyes occurs quickly after exposure, damage may be reversible: however, permanent injury or blindness can occur within 1 minute of exposure. Lewisite is irritating to the respiratory tract, producing burning, profuse nasal discharge, and violent sneezing. Prolonged exposure results in coughing and large amounts of froth mucus. Vapor exposure to the respiratory tract produces much the same symptoms as mustard. The main difference is that edema of the lungs is more exceptional and may be accompanied by pleural fluid. Lewisite does not affect the bone marrow, but does cause an increase in capillary permeability, with ensuing plasma leakage into tissues. This results in sufficient fluid loss to cause hemoconcentration, shock and death. Exposures that do not result in death can cause chronic conditions such as sensitization and lung impairment. Lewisite is a suspected carcinogen.

Decontamination should occur as quickly as possible after the exposure to reduce the effects of lewisite. Eyes should be given the first attention, followed by other locations of contact. Eyes should be flushed for a minimum of 15 minutes with plain water. Eyes should not be covered with bandages; if coverage is necessary, use dark or opaque goggles. For skin contact, remove

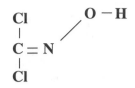

Figure 3.15 Phosgene oxime.

the victim from the source and remove contaminated clothing. Flush affected areas with a 10% sodium carbonate solution or liquid household bleach within one minute. After 3 to 4 minutes, wash affected areas with soap and water to protect against erythema. If ingested, do not induce vomiting. Give the victim milk to drink. In all instances, seek medical attention immediately. An antidote is available for lewisite exposure. BAL (British-anti-lewisite; dimercaprol) was developed by the British during World War II. The antidote is produced in an oil diluent for intramuscular administration to counter the systemic effects of lewisite. There is no effect, however, on the skin lesions, (eyes, skin, and respiratory system) from the antidote.

Phosgene oxime (CX) is also a vesicant or blister agent, but it should not be confused with phosgene, which is a lung-damaging agent. Phosgene oxime causes urticaria (eruptions on the skin) rather than the fluid-filled blisters that occur with other vesicants. CX is a solid (powder) at temperatures below 95°F, but can be considered a flashpoint solid, because of the high vapor pressure of 11.2 at 25°C. The boiling point is 53 to 54°C and it is not considered flammable. Not much is known about the mechanical action or biological activity of phosgene oxime. It is absorbed through the skin, and contact with the material causes extreme pain immediately, much like lewisite, and tissue effects occur very quickly. Irritation begins to occur in about 12 seconds at a dose of 0.2 mg-min/mp[3p]. When the agent has been in contact with the skin for 1 minute or more, the irritation becomes unbearable at a dose of 3 mg-min/mp[3p]. It is also irritating to the respiratory system and causes the same types of eye damage as lewisite. Phosgene oxime remains persistent in the soil for about 2 hours and is considered nonpersistent on other surfaces. The agent is known to be corrosive to most metals. There is no known antidote for phosgene oxime and exposures should be treated symptomatically after decontamination, which should occur immediately.

Blood Agents (Cyanogens)

Blood agents are common industrial chemicals that have been used on the battlefield to produce casualties. Two primary types of blood agents used by the military are hydrogen cyanide (AC) and cyanogen chloride (CK).

Poisonous effects of cyanide have been well known since ancient times. It has been used in assassinations and as the chemical in gas chamber executions for quite some time. Cyanide was also the substance used in Tylenol capsules to poison people in the early 1980s. It was also used by the Reverend Jim Jones in Guyana to kill his followers, when it was placed in Kool-Aid. On August 24, 1998, a 50-year-old woman in Los Angeles was arrested for planning to commit mass murder by mailing about 100 envelopes filled with deadly cyanide disguised as a nutritional supplement. Envelopes were addressed to locations as far away as Albany, New York. She was seen in the post office filling the envelopes with a powder from bottles marked poison, and authorities were notified. Cyanide was the first blood agent used as a chemical warfare agent. Cyanides are salts with the metals potassium, sodium, and calcium most commonly used to form the compounds. Cyanide salts were used during World War I; however, because the amount needed to cause death is rather high, it was difficult to weaponize and deliver in the appropriate dose. The term "blood agent" was used because at the time cyanide was introduced as a warfare agent, it was thought to be the only agent that was transported in blood to the target organ. It is now known that other agents such as nerve and vesicants are also carried by the blood. Therefore, realistically, the term has become obsolete.

Cyanide is found naturally in many foods such as lima beans, cherries, apple seeds, and the pits of peaches and similar fruits. It is reported to have an odor of burnt almonds or peach pits. However, 40% of the population cannot detect the odor of cyanide. Over 300,000 tons of cyanide are manufactured in the U.S. each year. These chemicals can be found shipped and stored in many parts of the country and could become targets of theft or sabotage for terrorist purposes. Blood agents function by interfering with the body's ability to use oxygen at the cellular level. They are considered chemical asphyxiants, because death occurs from a lack of oxygen in the body. Simple asphyxiation results from a lack of oxygen in the air to breathe, which causes the person to die. This usually results from some other gas displacing the oxygen. Inhalation is the primary route of exposure for blood agents. Unlike nerve agents and vesicants, blood agents are gases or very volatile liquids. They produce vapors easily, which dissipate quickly in air and are therefore considered nonpersistent agents. Antidotes are available for cyanide poisoning but must be administered quickly after exposure to be effective.

Hydrogen cyanide (HCN), (AC), also known as hydrocyanic acid or prussic acid, is a colorless to water-white or pale blue liquid at temperatures below 80°F. It has an odor of peach kernels or bitter almonds at 1 to 5 ppm. HCN may not have a detectable odor in lethal concentrations (Table 3.8). The acute toxicity of hydrogen cyanide is very high. There is rarely a reported chronic exposure to HCN because you either get better quickly from an

Table 3.8   Concentrations and Effects Inhalation of
Hydrogen Cyanide

Concentration (mg/mP^{3P})	Effect
300	Immediately lethal
200	Lethal after 10 minutes
150	Lethal after 30 minutes
120 to 150	Highly dangerous (fatal) after 30 minutes
50 to 60	Endurable for 20 min. to 1 hour without effect
20 to 40	Light symptoms after several hours

exposure or you die. It is toxic by inhalation, skin absorption, and ingestion with a TLV of 10 ppm in air. The LDb$_{50b}$ through ingestion is 10 mg/kg of body weight. Skin absorption LDb$_{50b}$ is estimated to be 1,500 mg/kg of body weight. Inhalation of HCN has a LCb$_{50b}$ of 63 ppm for 40 minutes. OHSA has established a permissible exposure limit (PEL) of 10 ppm (11 mg/mp^{3p}) for skin contact. TLV-TWA values are listed by ACGIH at 10 ppm (11 mg/mp^{3p}) for skin absorption. Inhalation of 18 to 36 ppm over a period of several hours can produce weakness, headache, confusion, nausea, and vomiting. Inhalation of 270 ppm can cause immediate death, and 100 to 200 ppm over a period of 30 to 60 minutes can also be fatal. Absorption of 50 mg through the skin can be fatal. Ingestion of 50 to 100 mg of HCN can also be fatal. HCN is highly soluble and stable in water. It is extremely flammable with a flashpoint of 0°F and an explosive range of 6 to 41% in air. Hydrogen cyanide has a boiling point of 25.7°C (78°F). Its vapor density is 0.990, which is slightly lighter than air, and a liquid density of 0.687, which is lighter than water. The autoignition temperature for HCN is 1000°F. Liquid HCN contains a stabilizer (usually phosphoric acid) and as it ages, may explode if the acid stabilizer is not maintained in the solution at a sufficient concentration. HCN can polymerize explosively if heated above 120°F or if contaminated with any alkali materials. Hydrogen cyanide has a molecular formula of HCN and the structural formula is shown in Figure 3.16.

Hydrogen cyanide is quite volatile, and is listed by the DOT as a Class 6.1 poisonous liquid with an inhalation hazard from the vapor. The NFPA 704 designation for AC is Health-4, Flammability-4, Reactivity-2, and Special-0. Vapors from hydrogen cyanide are highly toxic. The four-digit U.N. identification number is 1613 for less than 20% hydrogen cyanide and 1051 for greater than 20% hydrogen cyanide. The CAS number is 74-90-8. Hydrogen

$$H - C \equiv N$$

Figure 3.16   Structure of hydrogen cyanide.

cyanide is thought to act on the body by blending with cytochrome oxidase (an enzyme essential for oxidative processes of the tissues) and blocking the electron carrier system. This results in loss of cellular oxygen use. The central nervous system (CNS) and, particularly, the respiratory system are notably sensitive to this effect, and respiratory failure is the usual cause of death.

Cyanogen chloride (CK) is a colorless compressed gas or liquefied gas with a pungent odor and is slightly soluble in water. It is not flammable; however, containers exposed to radiant heat or fire may explode and give off toxic or irritating fumes. CK is highly toxic by ingestion or inhalation and is an eye and skin irritant. The TLV is 0.3 ppm and the ceiling is 0.75 mg/m^3 in air. Because it is a gas, it is considered a nonpersistent agent. The vapor density is 2.16, which is heavier than air, and the specific gravity is 1.186, which is heavier than water. It has a boiling point of approximately 58°F and rapid evaporation can cause frostbite. Cyanogen chloride has a freezing/melting point of −6.9°C. CK may polymerize violently if contaminated with hydrogen chloride or ammonium chloride. Upon heating it decomposes, producing toxic and corrosive fumes of hydrogen cyanide, hydrochloric acid, and nitrogen oxides. Hazardous polymerization can occur. Cyanogen chloride will react slowly with water to form hydrogen chloride gas. It is corrosive and will attack copper and brass metals. It acts on the body in two ways. Systemic effects of CK are very much like those of hydrogen cyanide. Additionally, it causes irritation of the eyes, upper respiratory tract, and lungs. Eye irritation results in tearing. CK, like AC, stimulates the respiratory system and rapidly paralyzes it. Exposure is followed by immediate intense irritation of the nose, throat, and eyes, with coughing, tightness in the chest, and lacrimation. This is followed by dizziness and increasingly difficult breathing. Unconsciousness comes next, with failing respiration and death within a few minutes. Convulsions, retching, and involuntary urination and defecation may occur. If these effects are not fatal, the signs and symptoms of pulmonary edema may develop. There may be repeated coughing with profuse foamy sputum, rales in the chest, severe dyspnea, and distinct cyanosis. Recovery from the systemic effects is usually as prompt as in AC poisoning. However, a higher incidence of residual damage to the CNS should be expected. Based upon the concentration of the cyanogen chloride to which the victim has been exposed, the pulmonary effects may evolve instantly or may be delayed until the systemic effects have subsided. Consequently, early prognosis must be cautious. The molecular formula for cyanogen chloride is ClCN and the structural formula is shown in Figure 3.17.

$$Cl-C \equiv N$$

Figure 3.17 Cyanogen chloride.

Cyanogen chloride becomes very volatile as temperatures increase and is listed by the DOT as a 2.3 poison gas. The NFPA 704 designation for CK is estimated to be Health-4, Flammability-0, Reactivity-2, and Special-0. Cyanogen chloride vapors are highly toxic. Its four-digit U.N. identification number is 1589 (inhibited). The CAS number is 506-77-4. Treatment for either AC or CK poisoning is to follow the treatment protocols for airway, breathing, and circulation (ABCs) and administration of oxygen to assist breathing. Sodium nitrate and sodium thiosulfate antidotes should be administered IV ONLY. Instructions for administration and dosage should be based on local protocols and with the advice of a physician. Sodium nitrate is administered to produce methemoglobin, thus seizing the cyanide on the methemoglobin. The sodium thiosulfate combines with the confiscated cyanide to form thiocyanate, which is then excreted from the body.

Choking Agents (Lung Damaging Agents)

Choking agents are known to cause pulmonary edema, which is the accumulation of fluid in the lungs. Examples of lung-damaging agents include phosgene (CG), diphosgene (DP), chlorine, and chloropicrin (PS). Lung damage can also be caused by other common materials such as perfluoroisobutylene, a product of burning Teflon; oxides of nitrogen; and HC smoke (a military agent). Phosgene is the best known of the choking agents. Phosgene was used during World War I and is now a common industrial chemical. Phosgene is produced by heating carbon tetrachloride, which was once used as a fire extinguishing agent. Carbon tetrachloride was discontinued as a fire extinguishing agent because when it came in contact with hot surfaces, it released phosgene gas. Choking agents irritate the bronchi, trachea, larynx, pharynx, and nose, which may result in pulmonary edema and contribute to a choking sensation.

Phosgene (CG) (carbonyl chloride) is produced as a liquid or liquefied gas which is colorless to light yellow. At ordinary temperatures and pressures CG is a colorless gas. Odors range from strong and stifling when

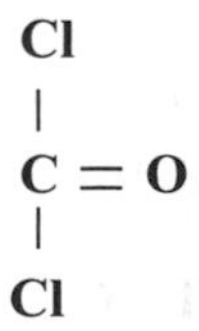

$$
\begin{array}{c}
\text{Cl} \\
| \\
\text{C} = \text{O} \\
| \\
\text{Cl}
\end{array}
$$

Figure 3.18   Structure for phosgene.

concentrated, to the smell of freshly mowed hay in lower concentrations. Phosgene has a boiling point of 8.2°C (45.6°F) and is noncombustible. The vapor density is 3.4, which is heavier than air, and the specific gravity is 1.37 at 20°C, which is heavier than water. Phosgene will not undergo polymerization, but reacts with water, ammonia, and amines. When exposed to temperatures above 572°F, it decomposes to form carbon monoxide (CO) and chlorine. The primary route of exposure is through inhalation, by which it is very toxic. It is also a strong eye irritant and has a TLV of 0.1 ppm or 0.40 mg/mp³ᵖ in air. General population limits are 0.0025 mg/m³. In addition to mild conjunctival irritation, direct effects of exposure to phosgene result in damage to the lungs. The primary effect of exposure is pulmonary edema (fluid in the lungs). Death can occur in several hours after an exposure to a high concentration. Most fatalities, however, reach a maximum effect from the pulmonary edema in about 12 hours, and death occurs from 24 to 48 hours after exposure. Symptoms include coughing, choking (thus the term choking agent), tightness in the chest, nausea, and possibly vomiting, headache, and lacrimation. There is no real relationship between the symptoms and the prognosis. Treatment involves rest and warmth, oxygen therapy, systemic steroids (prednisone IV), and steroid inhalers such as dexamethasone-sodium phosphate. Treatment protocols depend on the seriousness of exposure and the symptoms presented. Antibiotics may be administered if exposure results in bacterial bronchitis or pneumonitis. Phosgene reacts violently when in contact with strong oxidizers and attacks metals, plastic, and rubber. The molecular formula for phosgene is COClb2b and the structural formula is shown in Figure 3.18.

Phosgene is listed by the DOT as a 2.3 poison gas. The NFPA 704 designation for CG is Health-4, Flammability-0, Reactivity-1, and Special-0. Vapors of phosgene are highly toxic. Its four-digit U.N. identification number is 1076. The CAS number is 75-44-5.

Diphosgene (DP), trichloromethyl chloroformate, is a clear, colorless liquid with an odor similar to phosgene. It is noncombustible, a strong irritant to the eyes and tissue, and is toxic by inhalation and ingestion. DP has a boiling point of 127 to 128°C (263°F) and a vapor pressure of 4.2 at 20°C. There are no reported polymerization problems with DP. The liquid

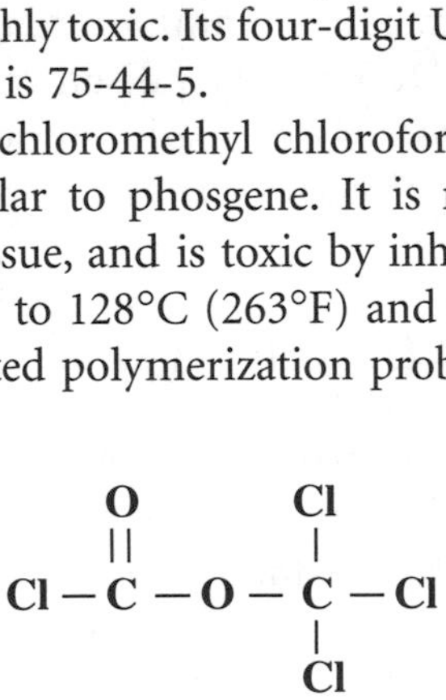

$$
\begin{array}{ccc}
\text{O} & & \text{Cl} \\
\parallel & & \mid \\
\text{Cl} - \text{C} - \text{O} - & \text{C} & - \text{Cl} \\
& \mid & \\
& \text{Cl} &
\end{array}
$$

Figure 3.19   Structure for diphosgene.

density is 1.65, which is heavier than water. The melting/freezing point is 157°C. Inhalation LCB_{50B} is 3,600 mg/mp^{3p} for 10 minutes. Effects of exposure are quite similar to phosgene gas. Its molecular formula is $ClCOOCClB_{3B}$, and the structure is shown in Figure 3.19.

Diphosgene is listed by the DOT as a 6.1 poison liquid. The NFPA 704 designation for CG is estimated to be Health-4, Flammability-0, Reactivity-1, and Special-0. Its four-digit U.N. identification number is 2972. The CAS number is 503-38-8.

Chlorine (ClB_{2B}) is a greenish-colored diatomic gas and a pure element that does not occur naturally. Chlorine is produced from naturally occurring sodium chloride (table salt), much of which comes from mining and the oceans. The boiling point is −34°C. While it is noncombustible, chlorine is a strong oxidizer and will support combustion just like oxygen. Chlorine has a pungent irritating bleachlike odor that is detectable at 0.02 to 3.4 ppm. It is slightly soluble in cold water and has a vapor density of 2.4, which is about 2.5 times heavier than air. Chlorine is irritating and corrosive to the eyes, skin, and respiratory tract. The TLV-TWA (ACGIH) is 0.5 ppm (1.5 mg/m³) in air. OSHA lists the PEL at 1.0 ppm (3 mg/m³). Its LC50 through inhalation is 293 ppm (879 mg/m³ for 1 hour) and the STEL (ACGIH) is 1 ppm (2.9 mg/m³). Chlorine is a severe irritant of the eyes, skin, and mucous membranes. Inhalation may cause coughing, choking, nausea, vomiting, headache, dizziness, difficulty breathing, and delayed pulmonary edema, which can be fatal. Exposure to 500 ppm for 30 minutes can cause death, and 1,000 ppm can be fatal after a few breaths. Contact with 3 to 8 ppm can cause stinging and burning of the eyes. Contact with liquid chlorine or high concentrations of the gas can cause severe burns. While chlorine does not burn, it reacts violently or explosively with a wide range of substances including hydrogen, acetylene, hydrocarbons, ammonia, reactive metals, and metal hydrides. It is listed by the DOT as a 2.3 poison gas with a U.N. identification number of 1017. The NFPA 704 designation for chlorine is Flammability-0, Health-4, Reactivity-0, and Special-Oxy. The CAS number is 503-38-8.

Riot Control Agents (Irritant Agents)

Riot control agents are also referred to as tear gas, irritants, and lacrimators. They are local irritants, which in very low concentrations act essentially on the eyes, resulting in intense pain and profuse tearing. Higher concentrations irritate the upper respiratory tract and skin, and sometimes cause nausea and vomiting. Exposure to these materials is rarely serious and might not require medical attention. Riot control agents are often referred to as tear gas. This is really an inaccurate naming of the compounds. Tear gases are not really gases at all. They are fine particulate smoke or aerosolized solid materials that can cause contamination of those exposed. Riot control agents are commonly used by law enforcement officers and may be present on military installations. (CS) and (CN) are the primary agents used by law enforcement agencies today. However, it may be possible to encounter an older riot control agent (DM), which is a "vomiting gas." Riot control agents were used in minor battles during World War I. They may be used by the military today only with the authorization of the President of the U.S. CN, chloroacetophenone, also known as mace, was the primary agent used in World War I. It has been replaced today by CS, O-chlorobenzylidenemalono-nitrile, which was developed in the 1950s and has become the agent of choice of law enforcement and the military (in training). Other irritant agents include (CNC), chloroacetophenone in chloroform (CA), bromobenzylcya-nide, and (CR), dibenz-(b,f)-1,4-oxazepine. OC is the designation for pepper spray. CK and PS are also considered to be lacrimators. The biological mech-anism by which riot control agents work has not been well studied or doc-umented compared to the other types of chemical agents. Generally, riot control agents cause pain, tearing, and conjunctivitis in the eyes, which can be accompanied by spasms of the muscles around the eyes. A burning sen-sation occurs in the nose and respiratory tract. This is followed by sneezing and a large volume of nasal discharge. The chest may feel tight, and there may be shortness of breath accompanied by coughing and secretions from the bronchial tubes when inhaled. Contact with the skin produces tingling, a burning feeling, and redness similar to sunburn. If conditions of high temperature and humidity are present along with a high concentration of agent, blisters may occur within 8 to 12 hours, which are similar to those produced by vesicants. Blisters have been reported by firefighters resulting from exposure when entering buildings where law enforcement personnel have discharged CS. Death may occur from riot control agents when exposure occurs in confined areas for an extended period of time. However, there are no reported deaths from open-air use.

Agent CS, O-chlorobenzylidenemalononitrile, is a white crystalline solid with a boiling point of 310° to 315°C, a flashpoint of 197°C, and a melting

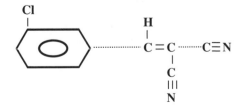

Figure 3.20   Structure for CS.

point of 194°F. CS is quite stable under ordinary storage conditions. It has a vapor pressure of 3.4×10–5 at 20°C, and a vapor density several times heavier than air. CS is immiscible in water. Volatility is 0.71 mg/mP^{3P} at 25°C. It has an odor that is biting and similar to pepper spray. CS is incompatible with strong oxidizers and, when heated to decomposition, emits very toxic fumes. Clouds produced by CS are white near the source for several seconds following the release. Usually CS is disseminated by burning, exploding, or by forming an aerosol. It may also be used in liquid form if dissolved into a solvent and aerosolized. CS acts very rapidly compared to CN, and it is 10 times more potent, while it is also much less toxic. The LDb$_{50b}$ for CS is approximately 200 mg/kg of body weight or 14 grams for a 70 kg person. CS has a TLV-TWA of 0.4 mg/mp^{3P}, an ICtb$_{50b}$ of 10 to 20 mg-min/mp^{3P}, and an LCtb$_{50b}$ of 61,000 mg-min/mp^{3P}. The chemical formula for CS is Cb$_{10b}$Hb$_{5b}$ClNb$_{2b}$, and the structural formula is shown in Figure 3.20.

Agent CR, dibenz-(b,f)-1,4-oxazepine, is a pale yellow crystalline solid that has a melting point of 163°F. It has a pepperlike odor and is only used in solution for dissemination in liquid dispensers. Solutions consist of 0.1% of CR in 80 parts of propylene glycol and 20 parts water. CR is an eye irritant in organic solutions at concentrations of 0.0025% or lower. Agent CR is less toxic when inhaled but has more profound skin effects that are longer lasting. It is a persistent agent when released in the environment and deposited on clothing.

Agents CN, chloroacetophenone, and **CA**, bromobenzylcyanide, are both white crystalline solids with boiling points of 478°F and 468°F, respectively, and freezing points of 129°F and 77°F. Vapor density for CN is 5.3 and for CA 4.0, both of which are heavier than air by four and five times. CN has an odor similar to apple blossoms, and CA smells like sour fruit. Agent CA

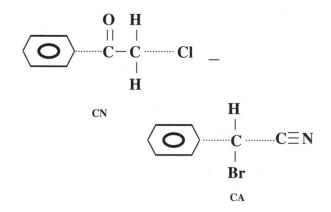

Figure 3.21   Structure for CA and CN.

is normally found as a liquid and CN can also be used as a liquid in suitable solvents. When released, these agents produce a bluish-white cloud at the time of release. Riot control agents CA and CN are dispersed as minute particulate smoke and as a vapor resulting from burning munitions, such as lacrimator candles and grenades. Liquid agents may be dispersed from aircraft spray or exploding munitions. The OSHA PEL for agent CN is 15 mg/mp^{3p} and the TLV is 10 mg/mp^{3p}. ICtb$_{50b}$ for CN is 30 mg-min/mp^{3p} and the LCtb$_{50b}$ is estimated to be 8,000 to 11,000 mg-min/mp^{3p}. For CA the ICtb$_{50b}$ is 80 mg-min/mp^{3p} and the LCtb$_{50b}$ is 7,000 mg-min/mp^{3p} from a solvent and 14,000 mg-min/mp^{3p} from a grenade. CN has a chemical formula of Cb$_{6b}$Hb$_{5b}$COCHb$_{2b}$Cl, and CA has a chemical formula of Cb$_{8b}$Hb$_{6b}$BrN. The structural formula for both CA and CN are shown in Figure 3.21.

Chloropicrin (PS), nitrotrichloromethane, trichloronitromethane, nitrochloroform, is a slightly oily, colorless, pale-to-transparent liquid that is nearly stable. It is nonflammable with a boiling point of approximately 235°F and slight water solubility. The vapor density is 5.7, which is heavier than air. PS is a strong irritant, highly toxic by inhalation and ingestion, with a TLV of 0.1 ppm (0.7 mg/mp^{3p}) in air. When heated, it decomposes to form hydrogen chloride, phosgene, carbon monoxide, and oxides of nitrogen. Decomposition can be explosive and can become shock sensitive. The LCb$_{50b}$ for inhalation is 66 mg/mp^{3p} over 4 hours and the oral dose LDb$_{50b}$ is 250 mg/kg of body weight. Chloropicrin is incompatible with strong oxidizers, alcohols, sodium hydroxide, and aniline. The DOT lists chloropicrin as a 6.1 poison liquid, and it has a U.N. identification number of 1580. The NFPA 704 designation for chloropicrin is Flammability-0, Health-4, Reactivity-3, and Special-0. The CAS number is 76-06-2.

Vomiting Agents

Vomiting agents create a strong pepperlike irritation of the upper respiratory tract along with irritation of the eyes and profuse tearing. This may be accompanied by intense uncontrollable sneezing, coughing, nausea, vomiting, and an overall feeling of malaise (nonspecific feeling of illness). Agents primarily associated with this group include (DA) diphenylchloroarsine, (DM) diphenylaminochloroarsine (Adamsite), and (DC) diphenylcyanoarsine. Inhalation of the fine aerosol mist is the principal route of entry into the body, along with irritation and symptoms resulting from direct eye contact. Unlike other riot control agents, vomiting agents generally do not produce any discomfort when in contact with skin. These agents are all crystalline solids that are released as smoke when heated. Smoke produced by DM is a light or canary yellow, while DA and DC produce a white smoke.

Table 3.9   Triage Groups for Individuals Exposed to Nerve Agents

IMMEDIATE
   Circulation intact, talking, but unable to walk
   Circulation intact, but unable to talk or walk
   Circulation not intact, unable to talk or walk — classification depends on available facilities
      — if facilities unavailable, classify as expectant
DELAYED
   Has been given or used antidotes (e.g., autoinjector); is showing signs of recovery
MINIMAL
   Capable of walking, capable of talking, capable of self-care
EXPECTANT
   Not talking, circulation failed (may be classified as IMMEDIATE if treatment resources
   are adequate)

These agents are very effective in low concentrations, which may not be detectable during exposure.

Symptoms produced include a feeling of pain and sense of fullness in the nose and sinuses, accompanied by a severe headache, intense burning in the throat, and tightness and pain in the chest. Coughing is uncontrollable, and sneezing is violent and persistent. Nasal secretion is greatly increased, and quantities of ropy saliva flow from the mouth. Nausea and vomiting are prominent. Mental depression may occur during the progression of symptoms. There are usually no long-term effects of vomiting agent exposures and symptoms generally disappear within 20 minutes to 2 hours. Like other riot control agents, deaths have occurred from exposure to high concentrations in enclosed areas. Most riot control agents would be classified as irritants under DOT/U.N. hazard Class 6.1. No information is available on NFPA 704 designations for riot control agents. U.N. four-digit identification numbers are listed for several types of tear gas and containers. Grenades and tear gas candles are poison 6.1 and flammable solids. Tear gas devices are assigned the number 1700, devices and the remaining types of tear gas are listed as 1693. Because riot control agents are particulate in nature, exposures will require decontamination of victims and responders. Bleach solutions should not be used for decontamination, because they will make the symptoms and effects of the agents worse. Plain soap and water are the best decontamination solutions. Emergency decon can be performed using the water from hose lines. Clothing must be removed. This process will remove the majority of the agent particles from the person.

Miscellaneous Chemical Agents

Psychedelic agent 3 (BZ), 3-quinuclidinyl benzilate, also known as "agent buzz," is a very potent psychoactive chemical that affects the central nervous

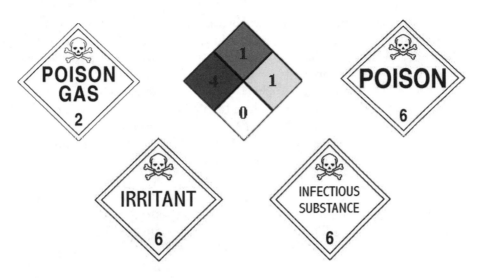

Figure 3.22

system as well as the circulatory system, digestion, salivation, sweating, and vision. It is no longer used by the U.S. because its effects on troops are unpredictable. Those exposed experience hallucinations, and the agent acts as a sedative. The experience is much the same as that encountered by the narcotics amphetamine and cocaine. Three to four days after exposure, full recovery is expected from BZ intoxication. The TLV-TWA for BZ is 0.004 mg/mp^{3p} and the general population limits are 0.0001 mg/mp^{3p}. BZ has an ICtb$_{50b}$ value of 101 mg-min/mp^{3p} (15 1/min), and an estimated LCtb$_{50b}$ of 200,000 mg-min/mp^{3p}.

White phosphorus (WP) is an element in its pure form, with a white or pale yellow, translucent, crystalline solid appearance with a waxy consistency. It is also known as yellow phosphorus. It is insoluble in water and is stored and shipped under water in its pure elemental form. WP freezes at 44°C and ignites spontaneously in air at or above 30°C (approximately 86°F). Phosphorus pentoxide vapors produced by burning white phosphorus are extremely toxic. The TLV-TWA is 0.1 mg/mp^{3p}.

Terrorist Use

Aum Shinri Kyo

GB was the first agent to be employed to cause mass casualties by nonstate actors when it was used for attacks by the Aum Shinri Kyo cult in Japan during 1994 and 1995.

Aum Shinri Kyo had first attempted to buy sarin, placing an order in 1988 with what they thought was a weapons smuggler (but which was actually a sting operation underwritten by the U.S. Customs service) for some 250 tons of sarin-containing bombs. For obvious reasons, the bombs were never delivered. Efforts were also made to obtain ex-Soviet agents after the demise of the Soviet Union, but these also failed. As a result, Aum's leadership decided to develop an internal capability for chemical agent production. The program was coordinated by Masami Tsuchiya, who started small — only 20 grams of sarin were in the first batch produced in October 1993. This was ramped up quickly to 1 kilogram in November, then 5 kilograms in December, all produced using laboratory scale equipment. The agent was tested on sheep on a ranch owned by the sect in Australia. Once it was clear that they were able to produce a lethal agent, they began to consider how to produce it and use it. The head of the cult, Shoko Asahara, wanted more, however, and a facility, "Satyan 7," for mass production of sarin was constructed. Satyan 7 reportedly cost $10 million to build, and an associated analytical facility is said to have cost the cult a further $1 million. The facility included computer-controlled reactors and industrial packaging equipment that automatically bagged specified amounts of the sarin and sealed the bags. The production target for the facility was 2 tons of sarin per day. This level of expenditure makes it clear why Tsuchiya would subsequently attempt to explain his involvement with the cult, in part because Aum's laboratories were better than those at the university where he had studied.

The first attempt to employ sarin was undertaken at the direction of the cult's leader, who wanted Daisaku Ikeda, leader of the Soka Gakkai Buddhists, killed. The attempts were made in March 1994, but the spray apparatus failed (either spraying backward or catching fire — published accounts are contradictory; in some accounts, it is stated that Tomomitsu Niimi, Aum's chief of security, was exposed to the agent but survived due to rapid administration of atropine). Three months later, they tried again, successfully releasing sarin in Matsumoto, Japan, on June 27, 1994, killing 7 people and injuring at least 500. The apparatus used to dispense the sarin was very simple — reduced to its essentials, it consisted of a container of liquid sarin from which perhaps as much as 20 kilograms of sarin was dropped onto a heated surface to produce sarin vapor; the sarin vapor was then blown into the air by fan. The dispersal took about 20 minutes.

Emergency response after the first calls was rapid, and the chief fire officer at the scene seems to have quickly recognized what had happened, although he did not identify the agent, describing the incident as a mass disaster caused by an unknown toxic gas. Victims were dispersed to six area hospitals, where the doctors recognized the symptoms as those of organophosphate poisoning, and treated the patients as they would have those exposed to pesticides.

The goal of the attack had been the death of three judges who were hearing a lawsuit over a real estate dispute involving Aum. The judges were affected, but all eventually recovered, although the suit had largely been rendered moot by the time they were all again available. However, 7 people died, and more than 500 were affected (58 were admitted to hospitals, including the 7 fatalities; 253 received outpatient care, and a subsequent survey identified 277 people who experienced symptoms but did not seek medical care). In the aftermath of the attack, the investigation was initially misdirected. Like the physicians who thought they might be dealing with a pesticide released by accident, the police could not imagine anyone doing this on purpose, even when the agent was identified as sarin. As a result, they focused their attentions initially on a former chemical company employee who they believed had accidentally made the sarin while trying to compound garden chemicals. But the focus began to change. The first problem was that sarin could not be produced the way the police thought it had. At the same time, complaints came in from neighbors of Aum Shinri Kyo's Kamikuishiki compound, where the Satyan 7 production facility was located, about strange odors (the cult attempted to explain the odors with statements about innocuous manufacturing activities and wild claims about an attack on the cult with chemical agents by the U.S. Navy).

More information began to come in pointing to the cult as the originators of the sarin, but the Japanese police had their hands tied because, without direct evidence, they had to avoid actions that might look like persecution of a religion owing to the very strong restrictions designed to maintain freedom of religion contained in the Japanese Constitution. These restrictions were so strong that, even though the police obtained soil samples from just outside the Kamikuishiki compound containing sarin precursor degradation products, the police could not act — there was, after all, no law in Japan at the time that said you could not make nerve gas, and making it did not mean Aum had used it.

Nevertheless, the police gathered enough evidence to act, although not about the use of sarin in Matsumoto. Members of Aum had carried out a kidnapping (and had murdered the kidnapee, Kiyoshi Kariya, a relative of an Aum member who had decided to leave the cult, although the police did not know this at the time), and the police had managed to find a link between the crime and Aum (fingerprints of an Aum member on papers for a rental car used in the kidnapping). They used this to get a warrant to enter the Kamikuishiki compound, planning a massive raid, which they hoped would also allow them to shut down the nerve agent production facility. The police made a mistake, however; they sent the policemen who were to make the raid to a Japanese Self Defense Force (JSDF) facility to undergo training in chemical protective measures. Members of Aum inside the JSDF sent word of the planned raid to the cult. The cult had known it was under suspicion since an article suggesting they were at fault for Matsumoto had appeared in the Yomiuri Shimbun newspaper on January 1, 1995, but they had convinced themselves they had not left a trail that the police could legally follow. The leadership decided they had to take drastic action to protect the cult. The way to dissuade the police that the cult's leadership decided on was to stage a major attack with sarin. An attack on the subway at 8:00 AM (timed to cause maximum casualties among police arriving for the 8:30 shift change) was felt to be the best option.

There was one problem — the Satyan 7 production facility had so many accidents that its use had been suspended, and the cult did not have any sarin on hand. So on March 18, a batch was made up by hand using an existing stock of precursors, and the resulting sarin was then poured into eleven plastic bags that were sealed, placed in larger bags, and covered with newspapers. (The purpose of the newspapers was to make the actions of the cult members when they were piercing the bags seem a little less odd — poking at a pile of newspapers with an umbrella was seen as less likely to attract attention than poking at a liquid-filled bag.)

The bags were assigned to five men for the attack, with four of the men getting two bags each and a fifth getting three bags. The men were to drop their bags on the floor of a train while in or just before reaching a subway station, puncture the bags, and leave the train and the station. Each man was paired with a second cult member who would drive a getaway car positioned outside the station. Each man was provided with an antidote kit (atropine-filled hypodermics) to be used in case of accidental exposure, and they were also provided with a pill (probably pyridostigmine bromide) to be taken before the action, which they were told would reduce their susceptibility to the sarin. Each of the attackers was assigned to a different subway train, on one of three lines, which converged at the Kasumigaseki station. The plan was for the attackers to pierce the bags and leave at a station before Kasumigaseki; it was expected that the trains would proceed on, poisoning stops along the line to Kasumigaseki and delivering a massive concentration where they converged.

On March 20, 1995, beginning shortly before 8:00 AM the attackers began poking holes in their bags of sarin. The attack left 12 people dead, 54 critically/severely injured, and affected 6,000. On March 22, 1995, the police moved in force against Aum Shinri Kyo, and in the ensuing days brought all those involved in the attack to justice. As bad as the attack was, several factors combined to keep it from being worse. Owing to its rushed "by hand" production, the sarin was very impure, with a purity lower than 30%. Indeed, before the bags were filled, when Seiicho Endo, a chemist involved with its production, went to Asahara to announce that production had been completed, he felt it necessary to mention that the mixture was not pure sarin. Asahara indicated that the attack should go ahead anyway. During the attack, not all of the sarin-filled bags were punctured, with one remaining completely intact and another apparently bursting when stepped on by passengers leaving the car. A passenger kicked the bags out of one of the cars at the stop after they were punctured; that probably saved many people in the car, although there were deaths at the station. At Kasumigaseki Station, assistant stationmasters Kazumasa Takahashi and Tsuneo Hishinuma soaked up the loose liquid with newspapers and picked up the bags, still wrapped in newspaper, put the material in a plastic bag, and carried it into the station office. Both lost their lives, but they prevented further dissemination of the agent.

Then, too, the Matsumoto release had served as an alert. Matsumoto certainly improved both the probability of recognition and awareness of proper responses. Many physicians had, at least informally, brushed up on the effects of and treatment for sarin intoxication. Emergency officials had, at least in the back of their minds, the thought that another attack might occur. And the experience in Matsumoto meant that there were people in Japan who had a good idea of what was happening when Japanese television stations started broadcasting reports. At least one physician, Dr. Hiroshi Morita, who had treated patients in Matsumoto, called hospitals in Tokyo to alert them to the fact that the symptoms he was seeing on television matched those he had seen in the sarin exposure, helping to direct the medical staff to a correct diagnosis. The Shinsu University Hospital faxed information about sarin treatment to the hospitals in Tokyo. Within 2 hours of the attack, JSDF experts arrived at the hospitals in the Tokyo area to advise on treatment. A plan to stockpile the nerve agent treatment drugs 2-PAM and atropine in hospitals had not been implemented, but when officers of Sumitomo Kagaku (a manufacturer of 2-PAM) in Osaka saw the news reports, they took the initiative and sent a supply of 2-PAM to Tokyo without waiting for a government request. There were many rough spots, however. The first emergency response was initiated at 8:09, roughly 20 minutes after the first bag of sarin had been punctured. It would be another 40 minutes before an advisory recommending the use of protective masks would be issued. Emergency responders had received no special training and had no idea what they were approaching; many thought that tear gas had been disseminated, despite the fact that deaths had already occurred (8 deaths occurred initially, with 4 more victims succumbing after reaching the hospital). No decontamination would be undertaken at the scene, and the conditions of victims being transported would continue to worsen as they were taken to the hospital. Emergency responders would also suffer the effects of secondary exposure, especially while transporting patients (instructions were issued to drive with the windows open, which seemed to help). No decontamination was initially undertaken at hospitals, either, and some hospital employees also suffered the effects of secondary exposure, especially when overflow patients were moved out of the emergency rooms (whose doors were constantly opening to admit fresh air) into areas with poorer air circulation. At 9:40 AM, the Tokyo fire department, equipped with IR spectrometers for gas analysis, misidentified the agent as acetonitrile, because the database used to identify gases did not include nerve agents (fortunately, this misidentification was largely ignored because the hospitals had already been advised that the agent was probably sarin by physicians with experience with chemical agents). At 11:00 AM, the police informed the press that they had identified the agent as sarin from GC-MS data, but they did not bother to inform the hospitals, who learned of the definitive identification of the agent from television news reports. The absence of a disaster plan resulted in the majority of the victims being taken to a single hospital, St. Luke's, which was nearly overwhelmed.

The use of sarin by Aum Shinri Kyo at Matsumoto and in the Tokyo subway did provide some valuable lessons. In the area of protection, Matsumoto showed that the idea of sheltering in place might well be valuable, even with materials as toxic as nerve agents. For instance, those who had gone to sleep with their windows open on that nice spring night (including many who died) were much more likely to be strongly affected than those who had gone to sleep with their windows shut. The importance of decontamination of victims was also shown — a significant number of emergency responders and emergency room personnel showed the effects of secondary exposure. The need for greater preplanning for such incidents and for training in reacting to them, was also shown — things went much more smoothly in Tokyo than they might have otherwise, because some lessons had already been learned from Matsumoto, although there was still much room for improvement. And finally, and perhaps most importantly, the Aum Shinri Kyo attacks showed that the threat of a terrorist chemical attack was real, ensuring that future investigations will not be hampered by the idea that "nobody would actually do it." Since Aum, no other terrorist group has actually used sarin, although threats of its use have escalated, presumably as a result of the publicity surrounding the Tokyo attack.

al Qaeda

The al Qaeda terrorist group has displayed a strong interest in obtaining weapons of mass destruction. In November 2001, Osama bin Laden stated that al Qaeda has a chemical capability ("I wish to declare that if America used chemical and nuclear weapons against us, then we may retort with chemical and nuclear weapons. We have the weapons as a deterrent." —interview with Hamid Mir for Dawn), but did not specify the agents. Julio Fuentes, a correspondent for the Spanish publication *El Mundo*, reported on November 19, 2001, that he had discovered at least 300 ampules (7 cm in length) containing a yellow-to-clear liquid packaged in boxes labeled "SARIN/V-GAS" in Cyrillic script at Farm Hada, an al Qaeda base south of Jalalabad in Afghanistan. Other labels indicated that atropine was antidotal. A similar report was published in the Italian daily *Corriere della Sera* by the reporter Maria Grazia Cutuli.

On August 20, 1998, the al-Shifa pharmaceutical factory in Khartoum, Sudan, was destroyed by U.S. cruise missiles. The reason cited for the destruction was the belief that the factory was producing VX precursors for the al Qaeda terrorist organization. Cited reasons for this belief included the presence of a VX precursor (EMPTA) in a soil sample taken from the vicinity of the factory and evidence that Osama bin Laden, the leader of al Qaeda, had financial interests in the plant. However, questions were raised regarding the reliability of the information, and it must currently be considered that the allegations that the plant was involved in precursor production are unproven.

Iraqi Insurgents

On May 17, 2004, it was announced that "a couple of days ago" an improvised explosive device produced using a sarin-containing 155 mm artillery round had detonated, apparently while U.S. troops were attempting to disarm it. The announcement indicated that two individuals were exposed and successfully treated. The shell was described as a binary weapon in which precursors are combined to produce the agent after firing. It is presumed that the shell was an Iraqi weapon of the type the Iraqi government claimed to have destroyed in accordance with the settlement of the 1991 Gulf War. The use of the shell as an improvised explosive device would have minimized the amount of sarin produced. Since such devices are detonated while in fixed positions rather than after having been fired from an artillery piece, little mixing of the precursors would occur.

Terrorist Use

Aum Shinri Kyo

VX was synthesized and used to commit murder and assault by the Aum Shinri Kyo organization. According to testimony at the trials of the Aum leadership, VX was used within Aum Shinri Kyo facilities to kill at least 10 members of the cult who were seen as dissidents, in at least some cases reportedly by direct injection of the agent. The bodies of the murdered individuals were disposed of, and the incidents did not come to the attention of any outside agency. VX was also used in attacks on individuals outside the cult.

- On December 12, 1994, in Osaka, Japan, Tadahiro Hamaguchi was sprayed with VX from a syringe while walking to work. He died in the hospital 10 days later. It would subsequently emerge that he was thought to be spying on the cult, and "interfering" with the cult's "practice of the truth."

- In Tokyo, in the fall of 1994, cult members made several attempts to kill the attorney Taro Takamoto, who had been assisting former Aum members. A number of these involved the use of VX, including one in which the agent was painted on the door of his car and another in which a VX-containing mixture was squirted into a keyhole. All failed.
- On November 28 and again on December 2, 1994, Noboru Mizuno, who had helped former cult members find shelter, had VX sprayed at him. The second attempt resulted in his hospitalization for 45 days.
- Hiroyuki Nagaoka, who had been helping members of the cult to leave, was sprayed with VX in front of his home in Tokyo on January 4, 1995. He was unconscious for an extended period but survived.
- Cult members injected VX into the air conditioning system of a car belonging to Ryuho Okawa in February 1995. Okawa was the head of the Institute for Research into Human Happiness, viewed as a rival group by Aum's leadership.

Asbat al-Ansar/Ansar al-Islam

Published reports claim that U.S. intelligence agencies have evidence that a quantity of VX gas had been smuggled to either the Asbat al-Ansar or Ansar al-Islam terrorist groups in October or November 2002. However, there has been no use of those agents.

Biological Terrorist Agents

4

Biological terrorist agents are microorganisms or toxins derived from living organisms to produce death or disease in humans, animals, or plants. They are odorless, tasteless, and colorless if released in a biological cloud by terrorists. All biological agents have an incubation period, which will allow the terrorist time to escape before the onset of symptoms. Anthrax, plague, and other biological agents are readily available in biological supply houses around the world outside the U.S. There are both good and bad bacteria naturally present in the environment and in living organisms. The bad bacteria are referred to as pathogens, because they can cause death to a living organism. Disease-causing microorganisms (pathogens) are classified as 6.2 infectious substances under the U.N./DOT hazard class system. Toxins that are chemical poisons produced by microorganisms or plants are classified under the U.N./DOT hazard class system as 6.1 poisons.

During medieval times, bodies diseased with plague were catapulted over walls protecting enemy forts and castles. Once inside, the disease would spread throughout the enclosed walls. Diseased bodies were also placed upstream from compounds, and residents would drink the water full of deadly microorganisms. In the American Civil War, Confederate troops placed corpses of livestock into ponds and lakes, contaminating the water supply, which delayed the advance of Union troops. By World War II, Japan had a complex of laboratories code-named "Unit 731" where biological research was conducted on prisoners of war. Prisoners were exposed to aerosolized anthrax and died. Their bodies were dissected to determine the effects of anthrax. Reports indicate that as many as 3,000 prisoners might have died in biological warfare research. It is believed that the Japanese used biological agents on Chinese soldiers and civilians during World War II. Bubonic plague, cholera, anthrax, and other diseases were released, killing tens of thousands of Chinese. By the end of World War II, the Japanese had stockpiled 400 kilograms of anthrax to be used in specially designed fragmentation bombs. The U.S. began its biological warfare (BW) program in 1943. Surprisingly, this program was created because of the anticipated German biological warfare threat rather than the Japanese. Camp Detrick, Maryland, (now Fort Detrick) was the site of the American research efforts and continues today.

Biological materials were produced at several sites in the U.S. until 1969, when President Nixon ordered a stop to all offensive biological and toxin agent research. Between May 1971 and May 1972, the U.S. offensive stockpiles of biological weapons and agents were destroyed. Agents in the stockpiles included Bacillus anthracis (anthrax); botulinum toxin (botulism); Francisella tularensis (tularemia, rabbit fever, deerfly fever); Coxiella burnetii rickettsia Q fever Venezuelan equine encephalitis (VEE); Brucella suis brucellosis undulant fever Bang's disease; and Staphylococcal enterotoxin B. The medical defensive biological agent program in the U.S., which was started in 1953, continues today at the U.S. Army Medical Research Institute of Infectious Diseases (USAMRIID). During 1972, the U.S. along with many other countries around the world signed the Convention on the Prohibition of the Development, Production, and Stockpiling of Bacteriological (Biological) and Toxin Weapons. This treaty forbids the stockpiling of biological agents for offensive military use and also forbids research into such offensive agents. All existing stockpiles had to be destroyed under the terms of the treaty.

Despite the Biological Weapons Convention, many countries hostile to the U.S. continue to conduct biological research. Additionally, there are several alleged instances where biological agents were used or accidental releases occurred, because the agents were still being stockpiled. During the 1970s, it is reported that Laos and Kampuchea experienced attacks by planes and helicopters disseminating multicolored aerosolized materials. People and animals exposed to the clouds became ill, and a small number of them died. It is thought that T2 mycotoxin was the agent used. During April and May 1979 in the city of Sverdlovsk in the former Soviet Union, an epidemic of anthrax occurred among city residents. Soviet government officials listed the cause of the outbreak as contaminated meat. However, the U.S. Government believes the epidemic was due to a release from VECTOR, a top secret biological weapons facility. Reports are conflicting, but it was originally estimated that 66 people died from the outbreak. After the fall of the Soviet Union, more accurate information was received from inside, and it is reported that as many as 259 people may have died. In 1978, a Bulgarian exile was assassinated in London when injected with a small amount of ricin, a plant toxin derived from the castor bean plant. A gun fashioned into the tip of an umbrella, loaded with a tiny pellet filled with ricin toxin, was used to subcutaneously inject the pellet into George Markov's leg. He died several days later from the effects of the ricin for which there is no known antidote. While it was later discovered that the communist government of Bulgaria

Figure 4.1 A member of a cleanup crew comprised of U.S. Coast Guard and U.S. Environmental Protection Agency agents walks from the American Media Inc., offices in Boca Raton, FL, October 25, 2001. Investigators collected samples Thursday to begin decontaminating the headquarters of the tabloid publishing company shuttered by anthrax. (AP Photo/The U.S. Coast Guard, Robert Wachal. Used with permission.)

carried out the assassination, the technology is believed to have been supplied by the former Soviet Union.

During the mid 1990s, the Aum Shinri Kyo Cult terrorist organization in Japan reportedly dispersed aerosols of anthrax and botulism throughout Tokyo on at least eight occasions. It is unclear why the attacks failed to produce illness. The Johns Hopkins Center for Civilian Biodefense Studies says that given the right weather and wind conditions, about 110 pounds of anthrax released from an aircraft could spread nearly 12 miles downwind. The cloud would be colorless, odorless, and invisible. There are currently no warning systems to detect an aerosol cloud of anthrax spores. The attack would most likely not be discovered until patients showed up at hospitals. During the fall of 2001, biological terrorism struck the U.S. Letters were sent September 18 and were postmarked Trenton, New Jersey, to ABC News, NBC News, CBS News, and the New York Post, all in New York City, and to American Media in Boca Raton, Florida (Figure 4.1). Only the letters to the New York Post and NBC News were actually found. The other three letters are suspected to exist because of the pattern of infection. Two additional letters bearing the Trenton, New Jersey, postmark were mailed on October 9. Those letters were sent to Senator Tom Daschle of South Dakota and Senator Patrick Leahy of Vermont. More potent than the first anthrax letters, the material in the Senate letters was a highly refined dry powder consisting of approximately 1 gram of nearly pure anthrax spores. Some reports described the material in the Senate letters as "weaponized" or "weapons grade" anthrax. Twenty-two people developed anthrax infections from contact with the letters, 11 of the life-threatening inhalation variety. Five died of inhalation anthrax. Of the deaths, one occurred in Florida from exposure at American Media, one in New York City, and one in Oxford, Connecticut. The two remaining deaths were employees of the Brentwood mail facility in Washington, D.C. Several thousand people potentially exposed took a two-month course of the antibiotic Cipro in an effort to prevent anthrax infections. The letters addressed to Senator Daschle and Senator Leahy had the return address 4th Grade, Greendale School, Franklin Park, NJ, 08852. The address is fictitious. Franklin Park, New Jersey, exists, but the zip code 08852 is for nearby Monmouth Junction, New Jersey. No Greendale School exists in New Jersey. Even in the absence of an arrest in the case, several conclusions can be drawn based upon the facts of the case. First, the strain and properties of the weaponized anthrax found in the letters show that it originated within the U.S. biodefense program. It can also be concluded that, given the origin of the anthrax and the warnings contained in the letters, it appears the perpetrator's motive was not to kill but rather to raise public fear and thereby spur Congress to increase spending on biodefense. According to a story appearing in the *Baltimore Sun Newspaper* December 12, 2001,

> "The anthrax spores enclosed in envelopes mailed to two leading Senate Democrats in October are biologically identical to bacteria secretly manufactured at a U.S. germ warfare facility during the last decade, according to press reports and an analysis by a leading microbiologist. The army biological and chemical warfare unit at the Dugway Proving Ground, about 80 miles southwest of Salt Lake City, Utah, may well be the source of the weapons-grade anthrax sent to Senators Daschle and Leahy. Scientists at Dugway grew and processed spores deriving from the Ames strain — the strain that appeared in all the letters sent to media outlets and Congress. The United States is the only country that is known to have produced weapons-grade anthrax in the past 25 years. While the Dugway facility produced the dried anthrax spores, they were sometimes sent to another germ warfare unit at Fort Detrick, near Frederick, Maryland, only 30 miles from Washington, D.C. Fort Detrick has equipment for killing bacteria with radiation, and received shipments of the anthrax to be sterilized so it would be safer to work on. The most recent shipment from Dugway to Fort Detrick was last June 27. The spores were returned to Dugway on September 4, one week before the terrorist attacks in New York City and Washington, and four weeks before the first anthrax cases were detected in south Florida. Spores were also sent in 1997 to

Figure 4.2   Helicopters could be used to disseminate chemical or biological agents.

the Armed Forces Institute of Pathology in Washington, according to a spokesman for that agency."

Up to the time of printing of this book no one has been charged with the anthrax crimes.

Biological warfare agents have often been referred to as the "poor man's atom bomb." This is because these agents are cheap, easy to obtain, and in many cases can be manufactured without detection. Countries that lack the technology or financial resources to assemble an atomic bomb can easily produce biological agents. Use of biological weapons produces a dramatic impact: they can penetrate fortifications, have delayed effects, and produce a large number of sick and dead. Biological agents are the ideal terrorist agent: they are highly infectious, viable and stable, easy to conceal and transport, and can withstand dissemination. Potential areas affected by biological agent dissemination may be large, due to the migration of infected individuals. Countries suspected of having biological agents or development programs include China, Taiwan, North Korea, Iraq, Syria, Egypt, Iran, Cuba, Israel, former Soviet States, the U.S., and Japan. While many of these countries are U.S. allies, others are not and actively support terrorism around the world. Biological agents are among the deadliest substances known to man. If properly disseminated, they can kill hundreds or even thousands of people (Figure 4.2).

Biological agents can be subdivided into several related groups (Table 4.1). These include bacteria and rickettsia, viruses, and toxins. Bacteria and rickettsia are single-celled microscopic organisms that can cause disease in plants, animals, and humans. Some of the bacteria that cause disease include anthrax, plague, cholera, diphtheria, tuberculosis, typhoid fever, typhus,

Table 4.1   Comparison of Biological Agent Characteristics

Disease	Likely Method of Dissemination	Infectious Man to Man	Infective Dose	Incubation Period	Duration of Illness	Lethality	Persistence
Anthrax	Spores in aerosol	No except cutaneous	8 to 10,000 spores	1 to 5 days	3 to 5 days usually fatal	High	Very stable for years
Cholera	Sabotage (food and water) Aerosol	Rare	> 106 organisms	12 hours to 6 days	> 1 week	Low when treated, high without	Unstable
Plague	Aerosol	High	< 100 organisms	1 to 3 days	1 to 6 days usually fatal	High if not treated within 12 to 24 hours	Up to a year
Tularemia	Aerosol	No	1 to 50 organisms	1 to 10 days	> 2 weeks	Moderate	For months
Q Fever	Aerosol Sabotage (food supply) (aerosol)	Rare	10 organisms	14 to 26 days	Weeks	Very low	For months
Ebola	Direct contact Aerosol	Moderate	1 to 10 plaque units	4 to 16 days	Death between 7 to 16 days	High, Zaire strain, moderate Sudan	Unstable
Smallpox	Aerosol	High	Assumed low	10 to 12 days	4 weeks	High to moderate	Very stable
VEE	Aerosol	Low	Assumed low	1 to 6 days	Days to weeks	Low	Unstable
Botulinum toxin	Aerosol	No	0.001 g/kg is LD_{50}	Variable (hours 24 to days)	Death in 72 hours; lasts months if not fatal	High without respiratory support	For weeks

Source: USAMRIID.

Legionnaire's disease, Lyme disease, and strep infections. Other bacteria produce toxins that are chemical poisons, such as botulinum. More bacteria exist in a handful of soil or in a person's mouth than all the people who have ever lived on Earth. When someone sneezes, over a million bacteria can be disseminated. Over 90% of all feces is made up of bacteria. More bacterial cells than human cells exist in your body. From 300,000 to 1,000,000 different types of bacteria exist on Earth. The majority of common bacteria is not pathogenic nor parasitic. Nearly all live and thrive in nature. Some have, however, mutated and learned to invade other cells and cause disease. Bacterial organisms have a nucleus, intracellular nonmembrane bound organelles (a specialized cellular part that resembles an organ), and a cell wall.

Rickettsia are pleomorphic (come in many varying sizes) parasitic microorganisms that live in the cells of the intestines of arthropods (invertebrate animals) such as insects, spiders, and crabs, which have segmented bodies and jointed limbs. Some are pathogenic to mammals and man, where they are known to cause the typhus group of fevers. Rickettsia are smaller than bacteria but larger than viruses. Like the viruses, rickettsia are obligate (they cannot exist on their own or in any other form); they are considered intracellular parasites.

Viruses are very small submicroscopic organisms, smaller than bacteria and unable to live on their own. They must invade the host cell and make use of its reproductive mechanism to multiply. Toxins are poisons produced by living organisms including plants, bacteria, and animals. They would be classified as 6.1 poisons rather than 6.2 infectious substances because they are toxic materials rather than disease-causing agents. Many of the biological toxins are much more toxic than any of the chemical agents discussed in Chapter 3 (Table 4.2).

Biological incidents, because of the delayed onset of symptoms, may become more of a public health emergency than an emergency response concern. Biological agents do not produce symptoms for several days, and victims would likely migrate from the source of exposure. Victims would be inclined to report to a doctor's office or multiple hospital emergency rooms on their own. Determination that a problem exists might not be realized until health officials note an unusual increase in hospital census. EMS responders might get calls to transport sick persons, but might not tie the response to biological terrorism, at least in the beginning. It might be quite some time before the impact of a biological terrorist attack is fully realized by health officials and the emergency medical system, including first responders. Dispatchers should be trained to watch for multiple incident responses with similar symptoms. The Health Department should be notified if this were to occur.

Table 4.2   Lethality of Selected Toxins and Chemical Agents in Laboratory Mice

Agent	LD_{50} (g/kg)	Source
Botulinum toxin	0.001	Bacterium
Shiga toxin	0.002	Bacterium
Tetanus toxin	0.002	Bacterium
Abrin	0.04	Plant (Rosary Pea)
Diphtheria toxin	0.10	Bacterium
Maitotoxin	0.10	Marine Dinoflagellate
Palytoxin	0.15	Marine Soft Coral
Cigualtoxin	0.40	Marine Dinoflagellate
Texilotoxin	0.60	Elapid Snake
C.perfringes toxins	0.1 to 5.0	Bacterium
Batrachotoxin	2.0	Arrow-Poison Frog
Ricin	3.0	Plant (Castor Bean)
alpha-Conotoxin	5.0	Cone Snail
Tiapoxin	5.0	Elapid Snake
Tetrodotoxin	8.0	Puffer Fish
alpha-Tityustoxin	9.0	Scorpion
Saxitoxin	10.0	Marine Dinoflagellate
	(Inhalation 2.0)	
VX	15.0	Chemical Agent
SEB	27.0	Bacterium
Anatoxin-A	50.0	Blue-Green Algae
Microcystin	50.0	Blue-Green Algae
Soman (GD)	64.0	Chemcial Agent
Sarin (GB)	100.0	Chemical Agent
Aconitine	100.0	Plant (Monkshood)
T-2 Toxin	1200.0	Fungal Mycotoxin

Bacterial Agents

Bacteria are single-celled organisms that range in shape and size from cocci (spherical cells) with a diameter of 0.5–1.0 m (micrometer), to long rod-shaped organisms — bacilli — which can be from 1–5 m in size. Chains of bacilli have been known to exceed 60 m in size. Some bacteria have the ability to turn into spores. In this form, the bacteria are more resistant to cold, heat, drying, chemicals, and radiation than the bacterial form. When in the spore form, the bacteria are inactive, or dormant, much like the seeds of a plant. When conditions are favorable, the spores will germinate just like seeds.

Bacteria have two methods by which they can cause disease in humans and animals. The first is by attacking the tissues of the host living thing. Secondly, all living organisms produce waste. Bacteria may produce a toxic or poisonous waste material that causes disease in the host. Some bacteria may attack using both methods. When selecting a biological agent, the terrorist wants an organism that will survive under varied conditions and produce certain desired results from the dissemination into a population. For example, the terrorist might just want to cause panic and might select an agent that makes people ill but does not kill them. Other terrorists might want to make an impact and will select an agent that might kill thousands of people. Genetic engineering may be used to create biological agents from otherwise harmless bacteria. Bacteria can also be created that are resistant to known antibiotics. Organisms may also be created that could withstand environmental extremes or aerosol dissemination, without alteration of their hazardous effects. For a biological agent to be effective, it must produce a specific effect: illness, disability, death, or damage to food chains. The agent must also be producible in large amounts, and stable while being manufactured, during storage, when weaponized, and during transportation. An effective biological agent must be easy and effective to disperse and remain stable once it is disseminated. Effective biological agents should also have a brief but reliable gestation period and should be persistent. According to the Centers for Disease Control (CDC), there are three biological agents likely to be used as terrorist agents. This is based upon the fact that the materials are easy to disseminate or are easily transmitted from person to person, present a major public health impact (high mortality), and present the potential for public panic and social disruption. These biological agents are anthrax, plague, and smallpox. USAMRID suggests that the list is a bit longer, including anthrax, smallpox, plague, botulism, and ricin.

Anthrax (Bacillus anthracis), also known as woolsorters' disease, is a zoonotic disease that can be naturally transmitted to humans by three methods. First, and most common, is through cutaneous contact with infected animals or animal products. Contact can also occur with the ingestion of undercooked meat from infected animals, although this is quite rare. Inhalation of anthrax may also occur from spores remaining on contaminated animal products, such as wool from sheep (Figure 4.3). In modern times, inhalation anthrax exposure is very rare and is unlikely to occur naturally. It is much more likely that inhalation anthrax will occur through the intentional release of spores during a bioterrorist attack such as the one that occurred during September 2001 on the East Coast of the U.S.. Anthrax is a rod-patterned, gram-positive, sporulating organism. It is a significant health concern when in the spore form and can remain dormant for hundreds of years as a spore until a proper host comes along for it to invade. Anthrax spores are virtually indestructible. Anthrax is highly lethal. It is estimated that 100 million lethal doses are present per gram of anthrax materials. That is 100,000 times deadlier than the deadliest chemical warfare agent. During World War II, the British started their bioweapons program to counter suspected Japanese and German biological threats. Research centered around anthrax and

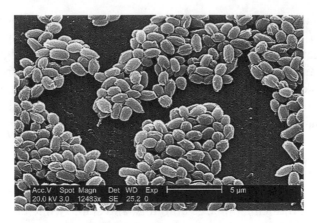

Figure 4.3 Microscopic picture of anthrax spores. (Courtesy Centers for Disease Control [CDC].)

involved an island off the Scottish coast, known as Gruinard Island. This particular island was chosen because it was believed to be far enough off the coast to prevent migration of the anthrax to the mainland during dissemination tests, which later proved to be incorrect. Testing revolved around the use of conventional bombs and the viability and "range of spread" of anthrax when disseminated. Information generated from the tests on Gruinard Island was used by the U.S. and Britain to develop bombs that could effectively disseminate the anthrax spores. In 1943, there was an outbreak of anthrax on the coast of Scotland facing Gruinard Island, which prompted the British to stop the testing. Contamination of the island as a result of the testing rendered the island uninhabitable for an extended period of time. Decontamination of the island was attempted by starting a brush fire to kill the spores on the surface of the ground. This effort proved ineffective when the spores burrowed themselves into the soil. In 1986, tons of topsoil were removed from the island, and the remaining soil was soaked with sea water spiked with large amounts of formaldehyde for decontamination purposes. Anthrax spores are very persistent, resist adverse environmental elements, and remain viable for hundreds of years in soil and dried or processed hides. Spores are very resistant to drying, heat, and sunlight. Spores have been known to survive in milk for up to 10 years, on dried filter paper for 41 years, on dried silk threads for up to 71 years, and in pond water for 2 years.

Little is known about the actual affects of inhalation anthrax on people after the onset of symptoms. This is because there have not been many cases of inhalation anthrax, and when they do occur the dose that caused the illness is unknown. Between 1955 and 1978, there were 12 cases of inhalation anthrax. There is treatment information on 10 of the 12 victims in which all were treated with single or combination doses of antibiotics. Of those 10

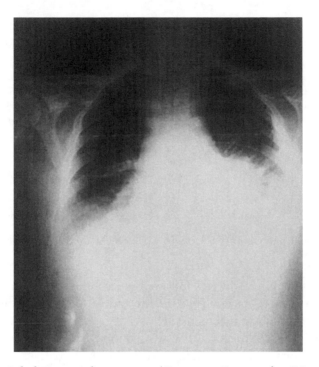

Figure 4.4   Inhalation anthrax x-ray. (Courtesy Centers for Disease Control [CDC].)

originally exposed to inhalation anthrax, eight died and two lived. Of the two that lived, one became very sick before antibiotics were administered. The cases of infection that occurred in September 2001 have not provided any new information because the dose and circumstances of exposure are unknown and several of those victims died despite state-of-the-art treatment.

Anthrax is present in the soil, and the disease occurs naturally in livestock, including pigs, horses, goats, cattle, and sheep. These animals usually become infected while grazing on contaminated land, eating contaminated feed, or drinking from contaminated water holes. In the U.S., animal infections are most often reported in Texas, Louisiana, Mississippi, Oklahoma, and South Dakota. Farmers who work with farm animals have been known to contract anthrax. Human-to-human contact has not been documented and is thought to be unlikely. Infection occurs from skin contact with infected animal tissue and possibly from biting fleas who have fed on the animals. The bacterium enters a cut or abrasion on the skin while handling contaminated products from infected animals. Items that may be contaminated include wool, hides, leather, or hair products (especially goat hair). Most commonly, the disease appears on the hands and forearms of people working with infected animals. Symptoms as a result of cutaneous exposure include:

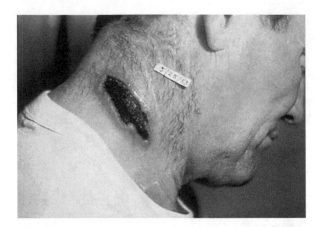

Figure 4.5 Cutaneous anthrax on the neck of a man. (Courtesy Centers for Disease Control [CDC].)

- Intense itching, which is followed by carbuncle formation
- Formation of carbuncles (inflammation of hair follicles and surrounding subcutaneous tissue)
- Swelling at the location of the infection
- Scabs form over the lesion and turn black as coal

Anthrax is the Greek term for coal, and so the name is derived from the coal-black scabs on the lesions (Figure 4.5). This localized infection can also become systemic and transformed to the inhalation form of the disease. The mortality rate for untreated cutaneous anthrax is approximately 20%. This occurs because either the infection becomes systemic or because of respiratory distress caused by edema in the cervical and upper thoracic regions. Deaths are rare with the administration of appropriate antibiotic therapy.

Inhalation exposure occurs from airborne spores in contaminated soil areas and from fried or processed skins and hides of infected animals. For successful treatment to occur, antibiotics must be started before symptoms appear. Ideally antibiotics should be administered within 24 hours of exposure. The quicker therapy is begun the more positive the potential outcome for the victim. Symptoms from inhalation exposure, depending on the concentration and length of time, will present in two distinct phases. First, spores are carried to the lungs, specifically the aveoli within the lungs. This is followed by a pus-producing infection with edema (fluid buildup) and hemorrhage in the lungs (Figure 4.4). Symptoms as a result of inhalation exposure are flulike in the beginning and include:

- Chills and mild fever
- Malaise (overall nonspecific not feeling well)

- Nausea and swelling of the lymph nodes
- Fatigue
- Myalgia (muscle pain)
- Dry cough
- Feeling of pressure in the chest

Victims will begin to feel better, which is known as the "anthrax eclipse". Following this period of feeling better, in a few days the victim will get worse with major pulmonary involvement. Mortality is near 100% despite aggressive treatment if symptoms have begun. If large numbers of people seeking medical treatment present these types of symptoms, anthrax should be suspected. Depending on the dose, the first phase can last for several days or as little as 24 hours. Onset of the second phase can be sudden, with the evolution of shortness of breath and cyanosis. Ingestion of contaminated meat can also cause infection, although that is rare. Symptoms resulting from ingestion exposure to anthrax include the following:

- Abdominal pain
- Acute inflammation of the intestinal tract
- Nausea
- Loss of appetite
- Vomiting
- Fever
- Abdominal pain
- Vomiting of blood
- Severe diarrhea

Approximately 25–60% of those victims who ingest anthrax will die. The primary cause of human outbreaks occurs from skin contact with contaminated hides, leather, and animals. Natural infection from inhalation or ingestion is very rare. Documentation of actual cases of inhalation anthrax should be considered very suspicious. To be used as an effective terrorist agent, anthrax spores would need to be aerosolized. Aerosol dissemination could be accomplished using spray devices or conventional explosives. People would then breathe in the aerosolized spores, which would get into the lungs, where the damage would occur. Anthrax that is in a gel medium or liquid solution would not be an inhalation hazard because the spores would have to be dry in order to be inhaled. The Canadian Center for Disease Control reports that the infectious dose in humans is 1,300 organisms through inhalation. This equates to one billionth of a gram (about the size of a speck of dust) which would be lethal to a single person. The U.S. Army reports 8,000–10,000 spores would be lethal if inhaled. After infection, the incubation period for inhalation anthrax is from 1–6 days, up to 6 weeks. Absorption through a break in the skin has an incubation period of 1–12 days. Ingestion anthrax has an incubation period of 1–7 days. Anthrax toxin is comprised of three proteins: protective antigen (PA), lethal factor (LF), and edema factor (EF). To gain entry into host cells, PA must recognize a receptor on the surface of the target cell. Once PA has bound to the cell, it then enables EF and LF to bind and form a pore through which PA forces EF and LF into the cell in a syringe-like action. When inhaled at the proper dose, the disease runs a swift sequence of events, and death can occur within 24–48 hours. Spore size is also an important factor in determining their effectiveness. Particles from 2–5 microns (1 millionth of a meter, 25,400th of 1 inch) in size are considered to be the most efficient in causing infection through inhalation. Particles larger than 5 microns would tend to be filtered out by the upper airway. It is expected that heavy smokers might be more susceptible to large particles. A lethal-size spore can be present in significant doses up to 20 km downwind of any dissemination. Diagnosis of infection is accomplished by isolating the bacteria from the blood, skin lesions, or from respiratory secretions. Antibodies can be measured in the blood of those suspected to have been infected.

Skin exposure and ingestion cases have been successfully treated when antibiotic therapy begins quickly. Penicillin, tetracycline, ciprofloxacin, doxycycline, or other broad-spectrum antibiotics have proven effective, although inhalation exposure is almost always fatal, even with treatment. Penicillin is the antibiotic of choice, and dosage is usually 2 million units given intravenously every 2 hours. Naturally occurring strains of anthrax may be resistant to penicillin. Terrorists might also develop strains of anthrax that are resistant to the usual antibiotic treatments. Victims who do recover from the cutaneous form of the disease may develop an immunity. Sterilization or destruction of anthrax spores by heat requires exposure to temperatures above 250°F for a minimum of 30 minutes. Some liquid disinfectants may be ineffective. Those disinfectants for which the spores are susceptible include 2% glutaraldehyde and formaldehyde solution and 5% formalin (37–50% solution of formaldehyde with 15% methyl alcohol). Chlorine and iodine are also effective sporicidal (spore killing) agents for decontamination of equipment. Iodine, to be effective, must be used at disinfectant strength; antiseptic strengths are not generally sporicidal. Chlorine's effectiveness may be reduced by the presence of organic materials. Overnight soaking of contaminated materials in the disinfectants is preferred. Keep in mind that these chemical disinfectants can have hazards of their own!

There is a cutaneous anthrax vaccine for humans that is licensed for use in the U.S. It is a cell-free (contains no dead or live bacteria in the preparation) filtrate that contains protective antigen and alum. The vaccine is reported to be 93% effective in protecting against cutaneous anthrax. Tests using animals indicate the vaccine may also protect against inhalation anthrax. The U.S. military has begun a program to vaccinate troops against anthrax, a process that will be very expensive and take several years to complete. It was halted for a period of time because many personnel refused the injections and there was some concern about the vaccine's safety. Injections of anthrax vaccine occur in six steps, administered at 0, 2, and 4 weeks, followed by 6, 12, and 18 months, followed by an annual booster. It is believed that after the first 3 doses, protection against cutaneous anthrax is achieved. Little data is available on the length of protection against inhalation exposure, although tests in primates suggest good protection can be attained after 2 doses with protection up to 2 years. It is possible that the vaccine could be overwhelmed by an extremely high dose of spores.

A new drug is under development for treatment of people exposed to anthrax. It is called ABthrax™, a human monoclonal antibody for the treatment and prevention of anthrax infections. Most anthrax fatalities are caused by the irreversible effects of the anthrax toxins. Research has shown that protective antigen is a central component of the anthrax toxins that contribute to the progression of anthrax infection at the cellular level. ABthrax specifically recognizes and neutralizes protective antigen. ABthrax has been shown in clinical trials and preclinical studies to provide significant survival benefit with minimal side effects in the event of an anthrax attack. ABthrax has received a Fast Track Product designation from the U.S. Food and Drug Administration for its potential use in the prevention and treatment of anthrax infection.

CDC recommendations for post exposure prophylaxis for prevention of inhalation anthrax after intentional exposure to Bacillus anthracis is as follows:

Adults
- Ciprofloxacin 500 mg po BID   60 Days
- Or Doxycycline 100 mg po BID

Children
- Ciprofloxacin 10–15 mg/kg po Q 12 hrs*   60 Days
- Doxycycline:
    - >8 yrs and >45 kg: 100 mg po BID
    - >8 yrs and <45 kg: 2.2 mg/kg po BID
    - <8yrs: 2.2 mg/kg po BID

---

* Ciprofloxacin dose should not exceed 1 gram per day in children.

Plague (Yersinia pestis) is a zoonotic bacterium that is normally spread among rodents by infected fleas. Zoonotic bacteria are capable of being transmitted from lower animals to humans under natural conditions. Transmission occurs through the bite of a flea or through inhalation. Three forms of the disease can affect humans:

- Bubonic
- Pneumonic
- Primary septicemic

Another type of plague called pharyngeal resembles acute tonsillitis. It often appears among Asian women who pick fleas out of each other's hair and bite the fleas to kill them. Plague was a part of the U.S. offensive biowarfare program in the 1950s and 1960s but was abandoned with the rest of the offensive program during the 1970s. It has been reported that the Japanese worked with the plague during World War II and had a plan to release plague-infected fleas on enemy troops. Periodic outbreaks of the plague occur naturally in rodent populations, which may result in a high death rate. Fleas that have lost their usual hosts pursue alternative sources of blood. When this happens, the risk to humans and other animals is increased. Epidemics of plague in humans commonly involve house rats and their fleas. Outbreaks of plague caused by rats continue to occur in underdeveloped countries, especially in rural areas. The disease is passed on to humans and other animals when they are bitten by a flea that has bitten an infected rat or other living thing. Animals prone to be carriers in the U.S. include rock squirrels, prairie dogs, and other burrowing rodents. During 1924 and 1925, the last epidemic in the U.S. occurred. Since that time there have been only isolated cases from wild rodents, reported usually in rural areas. Plague cases in the U.S. during the 1980s averaged around 18 per year, mostly in the southwestern states of New Mexico, Arizona, Colorado, and California. Highest rates of infection occur among Native Americans, particularly the Navajos. Others at risk include hunters, veterinarians, pet owners, campers, and hikers. Of those, most cases involved persons who were under the age of 20, with a fatality rate of 1 in 7. Death rates from bubonic plague can reach as high as 50–60% if not treated. When treated, the death rate is reduced to about 15%. If treatment is not begun within 24 hours after symptoms develop, pneumonic plague has a near 100% death rate. Throughout the rest of the world around 1,000–2,000 cases occur each year. From 1971–1995, 2,065 cases were reported to the World Health Organization (WHO) by 10 countries. Most of those cases occurred in underdeveloped regions such as Africa, Asia, and South America. Plague can also be transmitted when the organism enters the body through a break in the skin. This type of exposure occurs from direct contact with tissue or body fluids of a plague-infected animal, such as skinning a rabbit or other animal. This is, however, a rare occurrence. Plague can also be transmitted through inhalation by contacting infected droplets from a person or domestic animal coughing. Plague that develops from this type of exposure is called pneumonic. This infection involves the lungs as a result of inhalation of organisms, which results in primary pneumonic plague. Secondary pneumonic plague results from septicemia (blood infection) when the organisms spread to the lungs.

Symptoms from bubonic or septicemic plague exposure usually develop within 2–6 days following the exposure. Pneumonic plague occurs a little faster, from 2–3 days, which is also dependent on the amount of organisms inhaled. Symptoms of bubonic plague include:

- Rundown feeling
- Enlarged tender lymph nodes
- High fever, chills
- Prostration
- Staggering gait
- Delirium
- Mental confusion
- Shock
- Coma

Pneumonic plague symptoms are similar to bubonic and include:

- High fever
- Chills
- Headache
- Chest pain
- Nausea
- Vomiting
- Abnormal lung sounds
- Coughing
- Difficulty breathing
- Production of a bloody sputum
- Toxemia

Advanced symptoms include:

- Purpuric skin lesions
- Copious watery or purulent sputum
- Respiratory failure in 1–6 days

- Circulatory collapse
- Bleeding
- Diathesis
- Death

Symptoms may be followed by rapid shock and death if treatment is not begun early. Death results from respiratory failure, circulatory collapse, and a predisposition toward bleeding. Bubonic plague can progress spontaneously to septicemic plague accompanied by:

- Fever
- Chills
- Prostration
- Abdominal pain
- Shock
- Bleeding into the skin and other organs

Plague can also affect the central nervous system, lungs, and other parts of the body. As many as 80% of bubonic plague victims have positive blood cultures for septicemia. Approximately 25% of the patients will also have various types of skin lesions. Pustules, vesicles, eschars (dead tissue separating from living tissue), or papules (small elevations of the skin) containing leukocytes and bacteria may also be present near the site of the flea bite.

As soon as a case of plague is identified, the patient should be isolated for both respiratory and secretion precautions. Isolation should continue until the patient has been on antibiotics for at least 48 hours and symptoms have improved. The public health service should be notified as soon as plague is identified. Laboratory tests should be ordered for blood, sputum, or lesion fluid cultures and lymph node biopsy. Antibiotic treatment should begin as soon as possible. Streptomycin is the drug of choice, but others, such as tetracyclines, chloramphenicol, gentamicin, or one of the sulfonamides, might also be effective. Anyone suspected to have been in contact with the victim(s) should be located and evaluated. Contacts might need to be given antibiotic therapy to ward off the effects of the disease, particularly with pneumonic plague. All cases of the plague must be reported to the Centers for Disease Control (CDC) in Atlanta and, in addition, to the local health officials. A vaccine for the plague is available; however, it is only effective as a preventative measure. Once someone is exposed, the vaccine will not help. The initial dose of vaccine is followed by a second dose 1–3 months later and a third 3–6 months later. Booster shots are administered at 6, 12, and 18 months and then every 1–2 years. As with all vaccines, the level of protection is related to the size of the dose; vaccination defense could be overwhelmed by extremely high doses of the bacteria.

Plague would make an effective terrorist weapon, because, once infected through aerosol dissemination, people and animals could pass the disease to each other. Aerosol delivery would be the most effective, which would result in pneumonic plague developing in those exposed. Infected fleas could also be disseminated into a geographic area, and the bubonic plague would follow in those bitten by the fleas. The bacteria is fairly persistent and can survive in blood for 100 days and in human bodies for up to 270 days. It could remain viable in water and moist meals and grains for several weeks. The bacteria is sensitive to heat above 160°F for 15 minutes, sunlight for several hours, and disinfectants. Disinfection can be accomplished by using 1% sodium hypochlorite, 70% ethanol, 2% glutaraldehyde, iodines, phenolics, and formaldehyde.

Tularemia (Francisella tularensis), also known as rabbit fever, deerfly fever, and Ohara's disease, like the plague, is a bacterial infection that can occur naturally from the bite of insects, usually ticks and deerflies. The disease can also be acquired from contact with infected rabbits, muskrats, and squirrels; ingestion of contaminated food; or inhalation of contaminated dust. Once contracted, it is not directly spread from human to human. Tularemia remains infectious in the blood for about 2 weeks and in lesions for a month. It remains infective in deerflies for 14 days and ticks throughout their lifetime (about 2 years). The disease can occur at anytime of the year but is most common in the early winter during rabbit hunting season and in the summer when tick and deerfly activity is at its peak. Tularemia contracted naturally has a death rate of approximately 5%. The pneumonic form, which might be precipitated by a terrorist attack, would have a much higher death rate of 30% or greater. Tularemia was an agent in the U.S. biological weapons arsenal. Tularemia can appear in several different forms in humans depending on the route of exposure. The usual presentation is ulceroglandular, typhoidal, or septicemic. In humans, as few as 10–50 organisms can cause disease if inhaled or injected, but over 108 would be required for the disease if ingested. Ulceroglandular tularemia is acquired naturally from dermal or mucous membrane exposures of blood or tissue fluids of infected animals. The typhoidal form makes up 5–15% of naturally occurring cases, which result from inhalation of infectious aerosols. Pneumonia can result from any of the forms of tularemia but is most prominent in typhoidal. Incubation periods range from 2–10 days depending on the dose and route of exposure. The average incubation period occurs within 3 days. Symptoms of ulceroglandular disease include:

- Skin lesion
- Lymphadenopathy

- Fever
- Chills
- Headache
- Malaise

About 90–95% of patients may present cutaneous ulcers. When ulcers are absent, it is referred to as glandular tularemia. When symptoms are confined to the throat it is called primary ulceroglandular disease. Oculoglandular tularemia results from contact to the eyes from an infected fluid or blood. Typhoidal or septicemic tularemia produces fever, prostration, and weight loss, without adenopathy (any disease of the gland, especially a lymphatic gland). Diagnosis of primary typhoidal tularemia is difficult because the symptoms are very nonspecific. Serological (blood) testing may be the best diagnostic tool. After exposure, the usual treatment is 2 weeks of tetracycline. Streptomycin is given for more severe exposures. Aminoglycosides, genatamycin, kanamycin, and chloramphenicol are also effective antibiotics.

Once a person recovers, he or she has permanent immunity from the disease. Tularemia survives outside the host in carcasses and organs up to 133 days, in grain dust and bedbugs for 136 days, in rabbit meat for 31 days, in straw for 192 days, and in water for up to 90 days. The disease is susceptible to moist heat of 250°F for 15 minutes and dry heat of 350°F for at least 1 hour. Decontamination solutions that are effective include 1% sodium hypochlorite, 70% ethanol, glutaraldehyde, and formaldehyde. A vaccine is under development and has been successful during tests on more than 5,000 persons, without significant adverse reactions.

Cholera (vibrio cholera) is an incapacitating infection caused by the bacterium Vibrio cholerae that is contracted by ingestion of contaminated water or food or through inhalation. This bacteria has been considered in the past as a biological weapon. However, it does not spread easily from person to person and is not considered to be contagious. To be a serious biological terrorism threat, drinking water supplies would have to be contaminated with large amounts of the bacteria. Cholera occurs naturally in many underdeveloped countries and has caused widespread outbreaks in South America, with over 250,000 cases reported just in Peru. It can be spread through ingestion of food or water contaminated with feces or vomitus of patients, by dirty water, hands contaminated with feces, or flies. Cholera is an acute infectious disease, represented by a very sudden onset of symptoms. Victims may experience:

- Nausea
- Vomiting
- Profuse watery diarrhea with "rice water" appearance

- Rapid loss of body fluids
- Toxemia
- Frequent collapse

Not everyone exposed will show symptoms. In some cases, there may be as many as 400 people without symptoms for every patient showing symptoms. Where cases go untreated, the death rate can be as high as 50%. With treatment, the death rate drops to below 1%. While cholera itself is not lethal, the breakdown of medical treatment systems in large outbreaks can result in many deaths from dehydration, hypovolemia (loss of body fluid), and shock. Fluid loss can be as much as 5 to 10 liters per day, and IV fluids used to replenish fluids can be in short supply. The incubation period varies from 1–5 days depending on the dose of ingested organisms. An infectious dose is greater than 108 organisms to a healthy individual through ingestion. Treatment involves antibiotic and IV fluid therapy using tetracycline (500 mg every 6 hours for 3 days). Doxycycline (300 mg once or 100 mg every 12 hours for 3 days), IV solutions of 3.5 g NaCl, 2.5 g $NaHCO_3$, 1.5 g KCl, and 20 g glucose per liter are also appropriate treatments. Cholera shows a significant resistance to tetracycline and polymyxin antibiotics. Ciprofloxacin (500 mg every 12 hours for 3 days) or erythromycin (500 mg every 6 hours for 3 days) can be used as substitutes. Cholera is very sensitive to cold temperatures. Bacteria can remain active in dust for 3–16 days; feces up to 50 days; in glass up to 30 days; on metal coins for 7 days; on finger tips for 1–2 hours; and in soil for 16 days. It also survives well in water depending on the temperature. A vaccine is available for prevention, but it has not proven very effective. It offers only 50% protection for a period of up to 6 months.

Brucella (brucellosis), undulant fever, or Bang's disease, is a bacterial disease caused by any one of four species of coccobacilli. They are naturally occurring diseases, one normally a pathogen in cattle and the others in goats, pigs, swine, sheep, reindeer, caribou, coyotes, and dogs. The organisms can be contracted by humans through ingestion of unpasteurized milk and cheese, or from inhalation of aerosols generated on farms and in slaughterhouses. Skin lesions on persons who have come in contact with infected animals can also spread infection. This bacteria was also in the U.S. biological offensive weapons arsenal before the program was ended. If this bacteria was used by terrorists, it would have to be aerosolized for inhalation by victims or be used to contaminate food supplies. Brucella is present worldwide among the animal populations, but is especially prevalent in the Mediterranean countries of Europe and in Africa, India, Mexico, and South America. The disease is also common in populations that eat raw caribou. When the animal population has a high rate of infection, the rate of disease occurrence is also higher in humans. It is unknown what the infectious dose of brucella is. Symptoms are nonspecific and insidious upon onset (the disease is well established when the symptoms appear). Symptoms include:

- Intermittent fever
- Headache
- Weakness
- Profuse sweating
- Chills
- Arthralgia
- Localized suppurative (pus forming) infections

Incubation periods vary from 5–30 days, and in some cases, many months. Evidence of human-to-human transmission of the disease has not been documented. Side effects include depression and mental status changes. Osteoarthritic complications involving the axial skeleton are also common. Death is uncommon even in the absence of treatment. Treatment of brucellosis involves the administration of antibiotics tetracycline and streptomycin or TMP-SMX. The disease is resistant to penicillin and cephalosporin. Brucellosis bacteria remains active outside a host in carcasses and organs for up to 135 days, in paper 32 days, in soil for 125 days, and in blood for 180 days at 40°F. It is susceptible to moist heat of 250°F for at least 15 minutes, and dry heat of 320–340°F for a minimum of 1 hour. Effective disinfectants include 1% sodium hypochlorite, 70% ethanol, iodine/alcohol solutions, glutaraldehyde, and formaldehyde. There is no vaccine available for use in humans.

Q fever (Coxiella burnetii), query fever, rickettsia, is a bacterial disease that occurs naturally in sheep, cattle, and goats. It is present in very high concentrations in the placental tissues of these animals. Coxiella burnetii is the bacterial agent that causes Q fever and was also in the arsenal of the U.S. offensive biological weapons until the program ended. Incidence of the disease is worldwide, and it is likely that more cases occur than those reported. Many epidemics occur in stockyards, meat-packing plants, and medical labs using sheep for research. Transmission occurs from inhalation of airborne dissemination of rickettsiae in dust from contaminated premises. It can also be contracted by ingestion. Organisms can be carried in the air over a half-mile downwind. Infections are also contracted from contact with infected animals, their birth products (especially of sheep), wool from sheep, straw, fertilizer, and laundry of exposed persons. The disease has also been traced to unpasteurized milk from cows. Transmission from human to human is very rare. Several varieties of ticks may also carry the disease and transmit it from animal to animal. Mortality rates from this disease are very low, from 1–3%. It would, however, be an effective incapacitating agent because it is highly infectious when delivered through inhalation. As little as one organism can cause clinical symptoms. The usual infectious dose is considered to be 10 organisms through inhalation. To be used effectively as a terrorist weapon, it would have to be aerosolized. Symptoms are not specific to the disease, and it may be mistaken for a viral illness or atypical pneumonia. The incubation period is from 10–20 days. Patients may experience fever, cough, and chest pain as soon as 10 days after exposure. Although somewhat rare, other symptoms that may appear include:

- Chills
- Headache
- Weakness
- Malaise
- Severe sweats
- Hepatitis
- Endocarditis
- Pericarditis
- Pneumonitis
- Generalized infections

Patients are not critically ill, and in most cases the illness lasts from 2 days to 2 weeks. Diagnosis is confirmed through serology (blood work). Q fever is generally a self-limiting illness and will clear up without treatment. Antibiotics given during the illness can shorten the period of incapacitation. Tetracycline is the antibiotic of choice, and when given during the incubation period, may delay the onset of symptoms. Usual dosage is 500 mg every 6 hours or 100 mg doxycycline every 12 hours. Use of antibiotics will shorten the duration of the illness. Antibiotic treatment should be continued for 5–7 days. The disease is remarkably resistant to heat and drying and is stable under diverse environmental conditions. It can survive for months and even years in the environment. It also survives in dried sputum for 30 days, dust up to 120 days, dried urine for 49 days, feces of ticks 586 days, milk for 42 months at 45°F, and in wool for 12–16 months at 45°F. Disinfectants used for Q fever include sodium hypochlorite, formalin, and phenols (susceptibility varies), and it is also susceptible to ethanol, glutaraldehyde, and gaseous formaldehyde. It can be deactivated by using ether, chloroform, and gamma irradiation. Vaccines for humans are still in the development stages, although tests have shown promise. The International Society of Travel Medicine has reported that 10 cases of Q fever occurred between 1999 and 2003. Four patients had visited Bosnia; three, sub-Saharan Africa; and one each, French Guyana, Tunisia, and Reunion Island. Sources of exposure were farm animals, sheep and goats, and wild rodents. It is expected that the instances of Q fever in the world are likely under reported.

Salmonella spp. (Salmonellosis) is a naturally occurring bacteria that is present in a wide variety of animal hosts and environmental sources. There are over 2,000 strains of bacteria in the Salmonella family. Ten strains are responsible for most of the reported salmonella infections. We will limit our discussions here to the four most common strains: Salmonella spp, Salmonella typhi, Salmonella paratyphi, and Salmonella choleraesuis. Some strains may make humans and not animals sick, while others make animals sick and not humans. Bacteria that cause salmonella infections are single-celled organisms that cannot be seen with the naked eye, touched, or tasted. Salmonella bacteria occur naturally in the intestines and waste of poultry, dogs, cats, rats, and other warm-blooded animals. When live salmonella bacteria enter the body, which is usually the result of contaminated food, a salmonella infection occurs. Salmonellosis is the most common bacterial foodborne illness. Salmonella infections can be prevented by cooking food at the proper temperature and cleaning food utensils and preparation areas effectively. There are approximately 40,000 salmonella infections reported to public health officials each year in the U.S. Experts believe that between 500,000 and 4,000,000 cases go unreported. It is estimated that 2 of every 1,000 cases result in the death of the patient, over 500 annually. Salmonella affects those that are very young, those that are older, and most often those who have already been weakened by some other illness. Many of those who contract the illness believe they have the flu and never go to see a doctor. Major outbreaks have occurred in the U.S. over the years. One of the most recent involved ground beef used in many fast food restaurants across the country. Several people, including some children, died from the outbreak. The source of the contamination is thought to have been a midwestern meat distributor. CDC has reported over 120 major outbreaks of salmonella poisoning to date, many occurring in restaurants, and others in nursing homes, prisons, and hospitals. During one incident in 1984, 186 cases of salmonella were reported on 29 airline flights to the U.S. on a single foreign airline. Estimations indicate that 2,747 passengers were affected altogether. No specific food item was involved; however, food requested from first-class menus was heavily associated with the eruption of the illness. Salmonella was isolated from employees and patrons of three restaurants of a chain in Maryland during August and September 1985. Contaminated scrambled eggs from a breakfast bar resulted in 71 people becoming ill and 17 requiring hospitalization. Also during 1985, 16,000 people in six states became ill from ingesting low fat and whole milk from one dairy in Chicago. This was the largest outbreak of salmonella in U.S. history. During the 1990s salmonella outbreaks resulted from a Thanksgiving Day dinner in Nevada, consumption of raw eggs, raw ground beef, beef jerky in New Mexico, commercially and homemade ice cream, powdered milk products, and infant formula.

To be a terrorist agent, salmonella would have to be used to contaminate a food supply or private water supply (public supplies would kill the bacteria with chemical additives or filter them out). The only known route of exposure is ingestion. During September 1984 in a small town in northwest Oregon, terrorists from a local religious cult, the Rashneeshee, used salmonella to poison people in the community to keep them from voting on a political issue affecting the cult. They had cultured salmonella in their labs located in a facility at the edge of town. It was believed the salmonella would make the people too sick to vote. In the beginning, 4 or 5 cases were reported; during the first week 30 cases had been reported; within 2 weeks the total rose to over 200; ultimately, 751 persons including children and babies became ill. Over 1/10th of the population of the community was affected. Cult members took vials of the bacteria into several restaurants and poured it into salad dressing, on other items at the salad bar, and in the coffee creamer. It is believed the salmonella incident was just a warm-up for botulinum toxin, which was to be used the next time. Many people got sick from the bacteria. An informant told police of the plot, and members of the cult were arrested for the incident.

While there are many varied strains of salmonella, with a few exceptions, they produce similar symptoms. Incubation periods range from 6 hours to several weeks depending on the strain and the amount of bacteria ingested. The infectious dose varies widely, and there is no rhyme or reason for why certain people are affected by the bacteria. Some become ill with ingestion of as little as 10 organisms, while others have ingested food contaminated with millions of bacteria and experienced no adverse effects. There is not any particular type of food that contains salmonella. Infection can occur from any undercooked food, eating raw foods, or eating food contaminated by people preparing the food. Salmonella spp. (excluding s.typhi, s. choleraesuis, and s. paratyphi) causes acute gastroenteritis (inflammation of the gas-trointestinal tract). After exposure and the appropriate incubation period, the onset of symptoms are sudden, including:

- Abdominal pain
- Diarrhea
- Nausea
- Vomiting
- Dehydration, which can be severe in infants

The disease can occur anywhere in the world, but, most cases are reported in North America and Europe. Hosts range from humans to domestic and wild animals. The infectious dose is 100–1,000 organisms by ingestion. Symptoms can appear in 6–72 hours, and normally within 12–36 hours. Transmission occurs from eating food made from infected animals or food contaminated from feces of an infected animal or person. Infected animal feed and fertilizer prepared from contaminated meat scraps and fecal-oral transmission from person to person also occurs. The bacteria can survive for long periods of time in the environment. It is sensitive to moist heat, a minimum of 250°F for 15 minutes, and dry heat of 320–340°F for at least 1 hour. Salmonella bacteria is sensitive to antibiotic therapy using ampicillin, amoxicillin, TMP-SMX, and chloramphenicol. Effective disinfectants include 1% sodium hypochlorite, 70% ethanol, 2% glutaraldehyde, iodines, phenolics, and formaldehyde.

Salmonella chloeraesuis produces the following symptoms:

- Acute gastroenteritis (infection of the gastrointestinal tract)
- Sudden headache
- Abdominal pain
- Diarrhea
- Nausea
- Sometimes vomiting

This bacterial illness may develop into enteric fever with septicemia or focal infection in any tissue of the body. Outbreaks and locations are similar to those of the other salmonella bacteria. The infectious dose is 1,000 organisms by ingestion. Modes of transmission and incubation periods are similar to salmonella spp. Carriers are contagious throughout the infection, which can last for several days to several weeks. Antibiotic treatment can prolong the period in which the disease is contagious. Survival outside the host can occur for up to 450 days in pig meat and 38 days in sludge. Organisms can be excreted for over 1 year by 1% of the infected adults and 5% of the children. Sensitivities and disinfectants are the same as for salmonella spp.

Salmonella typhi is a generalized systemic infection which produces the following symptoms:

- Fever
- Headache
- Malaise
- Anorexia
- Enlarged spleen
- Rose spots on the trunk of the body
- Constipation

These symptoms are followed by more serious ones including ulceration of Peyer's patches in the ileum, which can produce hemorrhage or perforation. Mild and atypical infections can also occur with a death rate of 10% if not treated with antibiotics. Outbreaks and locations are similar to those of the other salmonella bacteria. Drug-resistant strains are appearing in several parts of the world. The infectious dose is 100,000 organisms by ingestion. Transmission occurs by ingesting food or water that have been contaminated with the feces or urine of a patient or carrier. Infection can also occur from food handlers who do not practice proper hygiene or flies contaminating foods. Incubation periods depend on the strength of the dose, but are usually 1–3 weeks. Antibiotic treatment with chloramphenicol, ampicillin, or amoxicillin is usually effective. Survival of the bacteria outside the host can occur for up to 130 days in ash, 17 days in rabbit carcass, 30 days in dust, 62 days in feces, up to 10 hours in linoleum flooring, 240 days in ice, and 10–20 minutes on the skin. Organisms can be excreted for over 1 week by 10% of the infected adults for up to 3 months, and 2 to 5% will become permanent carriers. Sensitivities and disinfectants are much the same as for salmonella spp.

Salmonella paratyphi is a bacterial enteric (intestinal) infection with an abrupt outbreak, which produces the following symptoms:

- Continued fever
- Headache
- Malaise
- Enlarged spleen
- Rose spots on the trunk of the body
- Diarrhea

These symptoms are very similar to those of typhoid fever, but the death rate is much lower. Mild and asymptomatic infections may also occur. Outbreaks and locations are similar to those of the other salmonella bacteria. The infectious dose is 1000 organisms by ingestion. Transmission occurs by direct or indirect contact with feces or, in rare cases, urine of patients or carriers. It is spread by food, especially milk and dairy products, shellfish, and in some isolated cases, water supplies. Incubation depends on the strength of the dose, but usually 1–3 weeks for enteric fever and 1–10 days for gastroenteritis. Antibiotic treatment with chloramphenicol, ampicillin, or TMP-SMX is usually effective. Survival outside the host can occur for up to 55 days in butter, 11 days in raw milk, 21 days in bed bugs, 48 hours in melon juice, and 10 days for flies. Organisms can be excreted for several weeks, commonly 1–2 weeks after recovery, and some victims become permanent carriers. Sensitivities and disinfectants are much the same as for salmonella spp.

Rickettsia are pleomorphic (come in many varying sizes) parasitic micro-organisms. A number of strains of this bacteria exist naturally. Rickettsia Canada, also known as louse-borne typhus fever and classical typhus fever, occur in areas of poor hygiene that are also louse infected. Outbreaks generally occur in Central America, South America, Asia, and Africa. The last epidemic in the U.S. occurred in 1921. It is primarily a disease of humans and squirrels. The body louse, pediculus humanus, is the primary carrier of the disease. It feeds on the blood of an infected patient with acute typhus fever and becomes infected. Once this occurs, the lice excrete rickettsiae in their feces, which is defecated as they feed. Infection occurs from feces left on the skin by the lice, which is rubbed in at the site of the bite or other breaks already existing in the skin, or through inhalation of infected dust. Squirrels become infected from the bite of the squirrel flea. The incubation period ranges from 1–2 weeks with an average of 12 days.

Rickettsia Canada cannot be directly transmitted from human to human, but it is a bloodborne pathogen, and universal precautions should be practiced. Victims are infective for the time in which the febrile (fever) illness is present and for 2–3 days after the body temperature returns to normal. Infection remains in the louse for 2–6 days after biting the source, although it may occur more quickly if the louse is crushed. Symptoms include:

- Headache
- Chills
- Fever
- Prostration
- Generalized pain

On the fifth or sixth day, a macular eruption (unraised spots on the skin) occurs on the upper trunk and spreads to the entire body (except for the face, palms of the hands, and soles of feet). The illness lasts for approximately 2 weeks. Without treatment, the fatality rate is about 10–40%. Treatment involves antibiotic therapy with tetracyclines and chloramphenicol. Decontamination solutions are 1% sodium hypochlorite, 70% ethanol, glutaraldehyde, and formaldehyde. The disease is susceptible to moist heat of 250°F for at least 15 minutes, and dry heat of 320–340°F for at least 1 hour. Rickettsia can continue to be viable in louse fecal substance and the dead louse for many weeks.

Glanders, Burkholderia (formerly Pseudomonas) mallei, is a gram-negative bacillus found naturally in horses, mules, and donkeys. Humans are rarely infected even during frequent and close contact with infected animals. No naturally occurring cases in humans have been reported in the U.S. for over 60 years, though sporadic cases continue to occur in Asia, Africa, the Middle East, and South America. It is believed to have been used during

World War I by the Germans to infect large numbers of Russian horses and mules on the eastern front. This affected troop supply and artillery movement, which were dependent on horses. Human cases increased in Russia during and after World War I. Japan also deliberately infected horses, civilians, and prisoners of war with the bacteria during World War II. The disease exists in four basic forms in humans and horses. Acute forms occur primarily in mules and donkeys and result in death in 3–4 weeks. Chronic forms occur in horses and result in lymphadenopathy (enlargement of the lymph nodes), skin nodules that ulcerate and drain, and induration (increase in fibrous tissue). Transmission to humans occurs through the nasal, oral, and conjunctival mucous membrane; by inhalation into the lungs; and breaks in the skin. Aerosols have been reported to be highly infectious in laboratory exposures and resulted in over 46% of the cases becoming severe. Because glanders is such an effective agent by aerosol exposure, it is viewed as a potential biological terrorist agent. There is no vaccine or effective treatment available. Incubation periods are from 10–14 days. Symptoms include:

- Fever
- Rigors
- Sweats
- Myalgia
- Headache
- Pleuritic chest pain
- Cervical adenopathy
- Splenomegaly
- Generalized papular/pustular eruptions

The disease is almost always fatal without treatment. Sulfadiazine may be an effective treatment in some cases. Ciprofloxacin, doxycycline, and rifampin have also been shown to be effective. Most antibiotic sensitivities are based upon animal studies, because of the low incidence of human exposure.

Glanders is the last of the bacterial agents that will be presented in this book. There are many other bacterial organisms occurring naturally throughout the world. Many of them are harmless, while others present a hazard to humans, plants, and animals. In a terrorist release of a bacterial agent, laboratory analysis will have to be conducted to positively identify the type of bacteria, which may take an extended period of time.

Viruses

Viruses are the simplest type of microorganisms and the smallest of all living things. They are much smaller than bacteria and range in size from 0.02–1 m (m = 1,000 mm). One drop of blood can contain over 6 billion viruses! Viruses were first discovered in 1898 and observed for the first time in 1939. Virus is a Latin word meaning "poisonous slime." Every living entity is composed of cells except for viruses. They are in fact totally inert until they come in contact with a living host cell. Hosts can include humans, animals, plants, or bacteria. The infection point created from the virus occurs at the cellular level. There must be an exact fit between the virus and the cell, or the invasion of the cell cannot occur. Viruses are unable to exist by themselves; they must find a suitable host cell in order to attach and thrive. After a virus attaches to a cell, the virus begins to reproduce itself, resulting in an acute viral infection. Viruses can also be cultivated on chorioallantoic membranes (fetal membrane) from fertilized eggs. Cultivating viruses in this manner is very expensive and time-consuming. Once a virus takes hold of the cell, it can cause the host cell to die. Common examples of viral agents include measles, mumps, meningitis, influenza, and the common cold.

Viruses that most people are familiar with today are HIV (the virus that causes acquired immune deficiency syndrome, AIDS), HBV (the virus that causes hepatitis B), and HCV (the virus that causes hepatitis C). These viruses would not be very effective terrorist agents because of the long incubation period and contraction methods required of AIDS, and the low lethality of the HBV virus. These viruses are not airborne and are usually very difficult to transmit. Very specific actions have to take place to transmit the viruses. HIV, HBV, and HCV are transmitted by contact with blood and body fluids. They are more commonly referred to as bloodborne pathogens. More likely virus candidates for terrorist agents would include Venezuelan equine encephalitis (VEE), smallpox, and those that cause hemorrhagic fevers. Viral hemorrhagic fevers are a group of viruses that include ebola, marburg, arenaviridae, Lassa fever, Argentine and Bolivian, Congo-Crimean, Rift Valley, hantavirus, yellow fever, and dengue.

Smallpox is a lethal infection caused by the variola virus, which has at least two natural strains, variola major and variola minor. Variola major has historically resulted in 30% or greater fatality rates among unvaccinated patients. It is highly contagious and spreads person-to-person by inhalation of submicron of water droplets (to which viral particles attach) exhaled by infected individuals. It can also enter the body through absorption. Spread of the virus can also occur through touching a contaminated object and then touching your own nose or mouth. Smallpox is the oldest-known human pathogen. Cases are first believed to have appeared around 10,000 BC in agricultural settlements in northeastern Africa. It was likely spread to India by Egyptian merchants. It is believed that smallpox is at least 3,000 years old. Smallpox was documented in China as early as 1122 BC. Scars from smallpox were found on the mummy of Pharaoh Ramses V, who died in 1157 BC. It

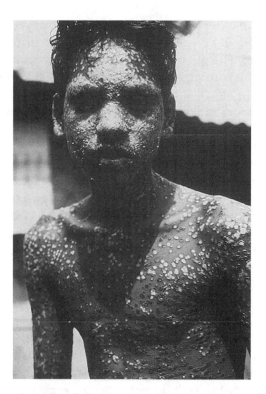

Figure 4.6 **(See color insert following page 236.)** Smallpox on the face and trunk of a small boy. (Courtesy Centers for Disease Control [CDC].)

was also found on other mummies from the 18th and 20th Egyptian Dynasties. During 1350 BC, the first known smallpox epidemic was recorded. During the Egyptian-Hittite war, Egyptian prisoners unwittingly spread smallpox to the Gittites. Smallpox devastated their civilization and led to the Egyptian victory. It is estimated that at least 400,000 people died from smallpox each year of the 18th century. Conquistadors brought the disease from Spain during the 1700s and it was transmitted to the American Indians, which wiped out over 90% of the population over the next 100 years. Naturally occurring smallpox was declared eradicated from the Earth in 1980 by the World Health Organization (WHO), a branch of the U.N. The last reported case in the world occurred in Somalia in 1977. Smallpox was the first and only disease ever intentionally eradicated from the face of the Earth: a scourge defeated in a remarkable, never-before-attempted campaign of generosity and cooperation by the nations of the world. It is quite possible that the "same hand of man that once rid the scourge of smallpox from the world, will be used to unleash this terror again on its unprotected citizens."

Two laboratories in the world still hold the last-known stocks of variola virus: the CDC in Atlanta and VECTOR in Novizbersk, Russia. Clandestine stocks could exist in other parts of the world but are as yet unknown. If they do exist, smallpox could come into the hands of terrorists and be used as a biological weapon. The WHO's governing body recommended the total destruction of the remaining stockpiles by the year 1999. Unfortunately, that did not happen. An effective vaccination is available for smallpox and has been used for years for the general population. Since it is primarily a children's disease, vaccinations were given during early childhood and were effective for about 10 years. Vaccination of civilians in the U.S. was discontinued in the early 1980s, although some military forces vaccinated until 1989 may still retain some immunity. Children, who are no longer vaccinated, would be at great risk from exposure to smallpox. The Japanese government considered using smallpox as a biological weapon during World War II, and the virus has been considered a threat to U.S. military forces for many years. Monkeypox and cowpox are closely related to variola and might be genetically manipulated to produce a smallpox-like virus.

Once exposure to the smallpox virus occurs, the incubation period is approximately 12–14 days on average. Those who might have contacted exposed persons are quarantined for a minimum of 16–17 days following the exposure. People are most infectious during the first 7–10 days of the rash. It is estimated that if a biological attack occurs using smallpox virus, each victim exposed will spread the virus to at least 10 others. During a recent exercise called "Dark Winter," three U.S. cities experienced smallpox outbreaks. Estimated results indicate that after three months the virus would have spread to 25 states and 15 countries, killing one million people. Critics say this is an extreme example of what may happen in a worst case scenario. Experts say it might not be that far-fetched. The level of U.S. preparedness has increased remarkably over the last several years. The CDC has launched a network of 50 specialized labs across the country for state-of-the-art analysis of samples from infected patients. Results would be available in 24 hours.

Symptoms of smallpox include:

- Malaise
- Fever
- Rigors
- Vomiting
- Headache
- Backache
- Delirium (hallucinations) (in about 15% of the patients)

In approximately 2–3 days, an enanthem develops concomitantly with a particular rash on the face, hands, and forearms. This is followed by eruptions on the lower extremities and the trunk of the body, which occur over a week's time. Lesions progress from discolored spots flush with the surface of the skin to raised spots on the skin, and finally to an inflamed swelling containing pus on the skin (skin blisters) (Figure 4.6). Lesions are more abundant on the extremities and face, which is important in the diagnosis of the disease. Within 8–14 days, scabs form on the skin blisters. Once the scabs fall off, a discolored depression is left behind. Smallpox is considered most infectious during the first week. However, as long as the scabs are in place the patient is considered contagious and should be isolated. An outbreak of smallpox would be a true international emergency and should be reported to the public health service. Few if any people in the general population have effective vaccinations against the disease. Transmission occurs from close person-to-person contact, and it is unknown if an airborne dispersion would be effective. About 30% of the people who get smallpox will die. Some people go blind, and the rash causes scarring for life. Most anitviral drugs for smallpox are experimental at the present time and would not be available for large numbers of victims. Vacinia-immune globulin (VIG) has shown to be effective prevention following an exposure to smallpox. It is recommended that 0.6 ml/kg of body weight be given to the victim intramuscularly within 24 hours of exposure. The U.S. military has a limited supply of VIG. There is no treatment available for smallpox. Research to evaluate new antiviral agents is ongoing. Patients with smallpox can benefit from supportive therapy (intravenous fluids, medicine to control fever or pain, etc.) and antibiotics for any secondary bacterial infections that might occur.

VEE is a virus that is transmitted from horse to horse in nature by mosquitoes. Humans can also get the virus from infected mosquitoes. Each year thousands of persons acquire the disease naturally from mosquito bites. Human outbreaks usually follow an epidemic among the horse population. Humans infected can infect mosquitoes for up to 72 hours. Once a mosquito becomes infected it remains so for life. VEE is considered to be a bloodborne pathogen. Universal precautions for bloodborne pathogens should be taken by emergency workers when around the VEE patient. Human-to-human transmission through inhalation of respiratory droplets can theoretically cause infection but has not been proven. For VEE to be an effective biological weapon, it would have to be aerosolized. The U.S. weaponized VEE during their offensive biological weapons programs. VEE is rarely fatal (less than 1%) and acts as an incapacitating agent. Nearly 100% of those exposed acquire the disease; however, only a small number actually develop encephalitis. Usually, young children are the most vulnerable for developing encephalitis. VEE is characterized by convulsions, coma, and paralysis. Encephalitis is characterized by inflammation of the meninges (surrounding membranes) of the brain and the brain itself, which produces central nervous system symptoms. Onset of symptoms is sudden, following an incubation period of 1–5 days. Symptoms are flu-like and may include:

- Malaise
- Spiking fevers
- Rigors (chills and severe shivering)
- Severe headache
- Photophobia (sensitivity to light)
- Myalgias (muscle pain)
- Nausea
- Vomiting
- Cough
- Sore throat
- Diarrhea

Complete recovery requires 1–2 weeks.

Diagnosis of the disease is difficult, as physical symptoms are nonspecific. White blood cell counts may show a striking leukopenia (abnormally low leukocytes in the blood) and lymphopenia (reduction in number of lymphocytes circulating in the blood). The virus can be isolated from the serum (fluid that forms blood clots). Because there are no drugs or specific treatments for the disease, treatment is supportive. Analgesics may be given to relieve headache and myalgia. Victims that develop encephalitis can be treated with anticonvulsants and fluid therapy for electrolyte balance. Two vaccines are available, but are still in the investigation phase of development. TC-83, a live vaccine, is given in a single dose 0.5 ml subcutaneously. A second vaccine, C-84, is used to boost those who do not respond to the TC-83. It is given 0.5 ml subcutaneously in 3 doses at 2–4-week intervals. Research is also underway using antiviral drugs that have shown some promise with laboratory animals. However, no human clinical data is available. VEE virus remains active outside the host in pharyngeal secretions, dried blood and exudates (fluids from wounds or pores of the skin). It can be inactivated with moist and dry heat. Disinfectant solutions include 1% sodium hypochlorite, 70% ethanol, 2% glutaraldehyde, and formaldehyde.

Viral hemorrhagic fevers (VHFs) are an assorted group of human diseases originated by viruses from several different families. Included are the Filoviridae family, which includes marburg and ebola, the Arenaviridae family, which encompasses lassa fever, as well as Argentine and Bolivian hemorrhagic fevers. Additionally, the Bunyaviridae family, which involves various members of the hantavirus genus, the Congo-Crimean hemorrhagic fever family from the Nairovirus genus, and the Rift Valley fever from the Phlebovirus genus are family members. The last family is the Flaviviridae, which includes yellow fever and the dengue hemorrhagic fever virus. Ebola virus first appeared in 1976 in the African states of Sudan and nearby Zaire. Another outbreak occurred in Zaire in 1979. In 1995, there were 316 cases of ebola reported in

Kikwit, Zaire, and are believed to have resulted from one person. The virus spreads through close personal contact with a person who is infected with the disease and can also be spread through sexual contact. Universal blood-borne pathogen precautions should be practiced when treating victims. It is not known what the natural host is for the virus or how a person initially contracts the disease. The incubation period is 2–21 days. It survives outside the host for up to 2 weeks in blood specimens, but does not survive long when dried out. Mortality rates in Africa from ebola range from 50–90% of those infected. Another strain of ebola, the reston, was reported among monkeys in the Philippines in 1989. This strain is not yet known to transmit to humans. African strains, on the other hand, have caused severe disease and death. Why the disease has only shown sporadic outbreaks is unknown.

Marburg virus has been reported to have caused infection in humans on four previous occasions. Three occurrences were in Africa and one in Germany, where the virus was named. Outbreaks first occurred in Germany and Yugoslavia, involving 31 reported cases, which occurred from exposure to African green monkeys. Seven people died. The incubation period for marburg is from 3–7 days. It can survive in blood specimens for 2 weeks at room temperature but does not survive long when dried out. Methods of transmission of these diseases are not well known. It is a bloodborne pathogen, and universal precautions should be used when treating victims. The disease is spread by direct contact with infected blood, secretions, organs, or semen.

Argentine hemorrhagic fever (AHF) is caused by the Junin virus, which first appeared in 1955 among corn harvesters in Argentina. The virus is spread naturally from contact with the infected excreta of rodents. Somewhere between 300 and 600 cases of AHF occur each year in the Pampas region of Argentina. A similar disease, Bolivian hemorrhagic fever, which is caused by the Machupo virus, appeared in northeastern Bolivia following the appearance of AHF. Another closely related virus is Lassa, which occurs over much of western Africa. Congo-Crimean hemorrhagic fever (CCHF) is a disease carried by ticks and transmitted by bites to humans. Infections occur primarily in the Crimea and other parts of Africa, and in Europe and Asia. The incubation period is 3–12 days. It is stable in blood up to 10 days at 105°F. Rift Valley fever also occurs only in Africa and results in sporadic widespread epidemics of the disease.

Hantavirus was first identified prior to World War II in Manchuria along the Amur River. U.N. troops reported the occurrence of the disease during the Korean conflict in the early 1950s. The disease has also been reported in Japan, Korea, and China since the war. Incubation periods vary from 5–42 days with 12–16 days being the average. The virus can survive outside the host in storage for 2–8 years if isolated from cells that have an immunologic function, but it is sensitive to drying.

Yellow fever and dengue fever are two diseases that are transmitted by infected mosquitoes. Yellow fever has an incubation period of 3–6 days. It does not survive outside the host for any period of time. Yellow fever is the only one of the VHFs that does have a vaccine available. Dengue fever virus has an incubation period from 3–14 days, with 7–10 being the average. The virus is stable in dried blood and exudates up to 2 days at room temperature. All VHFs except for dengue fever are capable of being spread by aerosolization and skin-crawling insects. Patients infected with VHFs other than hantavirus will have the virus in the blood, and it can be transmitted through contact with blood or body fluids containing blood. Bloodborne pathogen precautions should be undertaken when exposure to blood is a possibility. Routes of infection for the filoviruses in humans are not well understood at this time.

VHFs are feverish illnesses that are complicated by easy bleeding, petechiae (bleeding under the skin), hypotension (abnormally low blood pressure), shock, flushing of the face and chest, and edema (excess fluid in tissues). Diagnosis will involve the patient's history of travel, as well as a high level of suspicion. VHFs should be suspected in any patient having a severe fever-type illness and signs of vascular association. This is important if the victim has traveled to an area where the virus is known to occur, or where intelligence information indicates a biological warfare threat. Not all infected humans actually develop VHFs. The reason for this is not well understood. Congenital symptoms include:

- Malaise
- Myalgias
- Headache
- Vomiting
- Diarrhea

Symptoms may appear in association with any of the hemorrhagic fevers. Diagnosis relies on particular virologic (study of viruses and virus diseases) techniques for each virus. Treatment is supportive of the symptoms that are presented. Ribavirin may be effective antiviral therapy for Lassa fever, Rift Valley fever, and Congo-Crimean hemorrhagic fever viruses. During recovery, plasma may be effective in Argentine hemorrhagic fever. The only licensed VHF vaccine is yellow fever vaccine. Various viruses are susceptible to one or more of the normal disinfectants including 1% sodium hypochlorite, 70% ethanol, 2% glutaraldehyde, and formaldehyde. Once the specific virus is identified, the proper disinfectant can be selected.

Hoof-and-mouth disease, also known as foot-and-mouth disease in the U.K., is a highly contagious livestock disease. It is a viral infection that affects animals with cloven hooves such as cattle, pigs, and sheep. Symptoms include:

- Fever
- Blisters inside the mouth and on the feet

It is transmitted through fluids such as blood, saliva, and milk. Fluid from broken blisters has a particularly high concentration of the virus. The disease leaves the animals underweight and, in some cases, disabled. Hoof-and-mouth is not considered a fatal disease and clears up in the affected animals in a few weeks. Humans are not known to be susceptible to hoof-and-mouth, but humans can carry and transmit the disease without knowing it. This makes the disease even more difficult to contain.

Mad cow disease (Bovine Spongiform Encephalopathy/BSE)is a slowly progressive, degenerative, fatal disease affecting the central nervous system of adult cattle. There is a disease similar to BSE found in humans called Creutzfeldt-Jacob disease (CJD). A variant form of CJD (vCJD) is believed to be caused by eating contaminated beef products from BSE-affected cattle. To date, there have been 155 confirmed and probable cases of vCJD world-wide among the hundreds of thousands of people that may have consumed BSE-contaminated beef products. The one reported case of vCJD in the U.S. was in a young woman who contracted the disease while residing in the U.K. and developed symptoms after moving to the U.S. BSE is not transmitted in cow's milk, even if the milk comes from a cow with BSE. BSE in cattle was first reported in 1986 in the U.K. The exact origins of BSE remain uncertain, but it is thought that cattle initially may have become infected when fed feed contaminated with scrapie-infected sheep meat-and-bone meal (MBM). Scrapie is a prion disease in sheep similar to BSE in cattle. The scientific evidence suggests that the U.K. BSE outbreak in cattle then was expanded by feeding BSE-contaminated cattle protein (MBM) to calves. The definitive nature of the BSE agent is not completely known. The agent is thought to be a modified form of a protein, called a prion, which becomes infectious and accumulates in neural tissues causing a fatal, degenerative, neurological disease. These abnormal prions are resistant to common food disinfection treatments, such as heat, to reduce or eliminate their infectivity or presence. Research is ongoing to better understand TSE diseases and the nature of prion transmission. BSE is a Transmissible Spongiform Encephalopathy (TSE), a family of similar diseases that may infect certain species of animals and people, such as scrapie in sheep and goats, BSE in cattle, chronic wasting disease (CWD) in deer and elk, and variant Creutzfeldt-Jakob disease (vCJD) in people. To date, there is no scientific evidence that BSE in cattle is related to CWD in deer and elk. FDA is working closely with other government agencies and the public health community to address CWD in wild and domesticated deer and elk herds. Wildlife and public health officials advise people not to harvest, handle, or consume any wild deer or elk that appear to be sick, regardless of the cause, especially in those states where CWD has been detected. Both of those diseases are mentioned here because a terrorist could wreak havoc on the economy of countries and seriously affect the food supply by spreading these diseases among animals. In the case of mad cow disease, people could be affected as well.

Biological Toxins

Biological toxins are defined as any toxic substance occurring in nature produced by an animal, plant, or microbe (pathogenic bacteria), such as bacteria, fungi, flowering plants, insects, fish, reptiles, or mammals. Under the DOT/U.N. classification system, these materials would be classified as Class 6.1 poisons. Unlike chemical agents such as sarin, cyanide, or mustard, toxins are not man-made (Table 4.3). They occur naturally, which makes them readily available for potential terrorist activities. Toxins can be easily and cheaply produced without sophisticated laboratory equipment or training. Materials used to produce toxins are so common that their purchase would likely go unnoticed. Generally, toxins are not volatile and not considered a dermal exposure hazard (except for mycotoxins). Toxins as a family are much more toxic than any of the chemical agents, including VX and sarin (Table 4.4). Ricin, a biological toxin produced from the castor bean plant, can kill an individual with as little as a milligram (1/1,000 of a gram). Botulinum toxin is the most toxic material known to humans. One ounce of

Table 4.3 Comparison of Chemical Agents and Toxins

Toxins	Chemical Agents
Natural origin	Man-made
Difficult, small-scale production	Large-scale industrial production
None volatile	Many volatile
Many are more toxic	Less toxic than many toxins
Not dermally active*	Dermally active
Legitimate medical use	No use other than many toxins
Odorless and tasteless	Noticeable odor or taste
Diverse toxic effects	Fewer types of effects
Many are effective immunogens**	Poor immunogens
Aerosol delivery	Mist/droplet/aerosol delivery

* Exceptions are trichothecene mycotoxins, lyngbyatoxin, and some of the blue-green algae toxins. The latter two cause dermal injury to swimmers in contaminated waters, but are generally unavailable in large quantities and have low toxicity, respectively.

** The human body recognizes them as foreign material and makes protective antibodies against them.

Table 4.4   Toxicity of Chemical and Biological Agents Estimated Lethal Dose in mg/person*

Chemical Agents		1000 mg 100 mg 10 mg 1 mg	
		.1 mg .01 mg .001 mg .0001 mg	Toxin Agents
Biological		.00001 mg .000001 mg .0000001 mg .00000001 mg	

* One paper clip weighs approximately 500 mg.

botulinum toxin (.12 micrograms or 1,200 millionths of a gram) is enough to kill 60 million people. Mycotoxins are the least toxic of the toxins (thousands of times less than botulism). Routes of exposure also have a bearing on the level of toxicity. Some toxins are much more lethal when aerosolized and inhaled than when taken orally. Ricin, saxitoxin, and T2 mycotoxins are examples of these types of materials. Botulism, for example, has a lower toxicity through aerosolization and inhalation than through ingestion. When ingested, however, it is so toxic overall that it is a dangerous biological warfare and terrorist agent. Some toxins are limited in their usefulness as biological agents because it takes too much of the material to produce a toxic reaction. Saxitoxin, for instance, cannot be produced in large enough quantities to be useful. When looking at the potential toxicity of toxins, the lower the LD_{50}

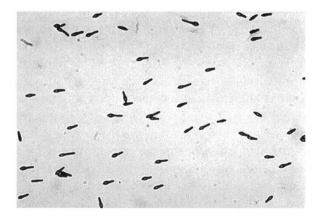

Figure 4.7   Botulinum bacteria under the microscope. (Courtesy Centers for Disease Control [CDC].)

Figure 4.8   Botulinum toxin being grown in fruit jars. (Courtesy Centers for Disease Control [CDC].)

in micrograms per kilogram of body weight, the less agent required to cover a large area. Conversely, some agents, such as ricin, would require great quantities (tons) for an aerosol attack out in the open. Toxins can be used either for their lethality or as an incapacitating agent. Some toxins are incapacitating at lower doses and would cause serious illness. Because of their lack of volatility, toxins would neither be a persistent threat nor likely produce secondary or person-to-person exposures.

Toxins can be divided into groups based upon the mechanism by which they function. Protein toxins are created by bacteria and are ordinarily harder to manufacture on a massive scale than are plant toxins. Because of its high level of toxicity, botulinum would be an exception. Protein toxins include botulinum (seven related toxins), diphtheria, tetanus, and staphylococcal enterotoxins (seven different toxins). Botulinum toxins are so lethal that it is technically possible to produce a toxic aerosol in quantities needed relatively easily. They function by paralyzing the respiratory muscles. Staphylococcal enterotoxins can incapacitate at levels at least 100 times lower than the lethal level. They too could be delivered as a breathable aerosol.

Bacterial toxins can be classified as membrane-damaging. This group includes Escherichia coli (hemolysins), aeromonas, pseudomonas, and staphylococcus alpha (cytolysins and phospholipases). Toxins from those bacterium are reasonably easy to produce but possess a varying degree of stability. Many of those toxins function by interfering with bodily functions and kill by creating pores in cell membranes. Their toxicity levels are much lower than the protein toxins and are less likely as terrorist threats. Marine toxins may be developed from marine organisms. Examples include saxitoxin, tetrodotoxin, palytoxin, brevetoxins, and microcystin. Saxitoxin is a sodium-channel blocker and is most toxic by inhalation compared to the other routes of exposure. Saxitoxin and tetrodotoxin are very similar in mechanical action, toxicity, and physical attributes. They can be lethal within a few minutes when inhaled. Saxitoxin could be used as a terrorist agent in localized scenarios. It has not yet been chemically synthesized efficiently, or easily created in large quantities from natural sources; therefore, it is not likely to be aerosolized and used over a large area. Palytoxin is produced from soft coral and is very toxic. It is, however, difficult to produce or harvest from nature and is an unlikely agent for large-scale terrorist use. The brevetoxins, hepatotoxins, and microcystin have limited toxicity and are unlikely agents for terrorist activities.

Trichothecene mycotoxins are created by numerous species of fungi. Over 40 toxins are known to be produced by fungi. T-2 is a stable toxin even when heated to high temperatures. Decontamination or disinfection requires very high concentrations of sodium hydroxide and sodium hypochlorite to detoxify the material. Aerosolization would not be a likely method of dissemination because of the potential low toxicity. However, unlike other toxins, the mycotoxins are dermally active. An aerosol dissemination can cause damage by contacting skin and mucous membranes. Once absorbed into the body, it would become a systemic toxin.

Plant toxins are derived from plants or plant seeds. Toxins developed from plants are easy to produce cheaply in large quantities without requiring a high level of technology. One of the premier plant toxins is ricin. It is a protein taken from the castor bean. Approximately 1 million tons of castor beans are grown annually worldwide for the production of castor oil. Castor beans necessary to grow the plants can be purchased through seed catalogs, from lawn and garden centers, and from agricultural co-ops. Waste mash resulting from the production of castor oil contains 3–5% ricin by weight. There are detailed videos and books available giving step-by-step instructions for producing ricin.

Animal venoms can contain protein toxins as well as nontoxic proteins. Many venom toxins can be cloned, created by molecular biological procedures, and manufactured by simple chemical synthesis. Venoms can be divided into groups — ion channel toxins, such as those found in rattlesnakes, scorpions, and cone snails; presynaptic phospholipase A2 neurotoxins, found in the banded krait, Mojave rattler, and Australian tiapan snake; postsynaptic neurotoxins, found in the coral, mamba, cobra, sea snakes, and cone snail; membrane-damaging toxins of the Formosan cobra and rattlesnake; and the coagulation/anticoagulation toxins, found in the Malayan pit viper and carpet viper. Many of these toxins cannot be produced in large enough quantities to create a battlefield threat; they could, however, be used by terrorists against small groups of civilian populations. Toxins are unlike chemical agents in that they vary widely in their mechanism of action (Table 4.5). Length of time from exposure to the onset of symptoms also varies a

Table 4.5   Comparisons of Chemical Nerve Agent, Botulinum Toxin, and Staphylococcal Enterotoxin B Intoxication Following Inhalation Exposure

	Chemical Nerve Agent	Botulinum Toxin	Staphylococcal Enterotoxin B
Time to Symptoms	Minutes	Hours (12–48)	Hours (1–6)
Nervous	Convulsions, Muscle twitching	Progressive paralysis	Headache Muscle aches
Cardiovascular	Slow heart rate	Normal rate	Normal or rapid heart rate
Respiratory	Difficult breathing, airway constriction	Normal, then progressive paralysis	Non-productive cough; Severe cases: chest pain, difficult breathing
Gastrointestinal	Increased motility, pain, diarrhea	Decreased motility	Nausea, vomiting and/or diarrhea
Ocular	Small pupils	Droopy eyelids	"Red eyes" conjunctival injection
Salivary	Profuse, watery Saliva	Normal, but swallowing difficult	May be slightly increased quantities of saliva
Death	Minutes	2–3 days	Unlikely
Response to Atropine/2PAM-CL	Yes	No	Atropine may reduce gastrointestinal symptoms

great deal. In battlefield scenarios, preparations can be made for treatments and preventive measures. However, with the terrorist threat, preparation is not as easy, because it is unknown when or where the terrorist will strike, or which agent would be used.

Saxitoxin acts very quickly and can kill an individual within a few minutes of inhalation of a lethal dose. It acts by blocking nerve conduction directly and causes death by paralyzing muscles of respiration. At slightly less than the lethal dose, the victim may not experience any effects at all. Botulinum toxin needs to invade nerve terminals in order to block the release of neurotransmitters, which under normal conditions control muscle contraction. The symptoms from botulinum toxin are slow to develop (from hours to days) but are just as lethal, causing respiratory failure. This toxin blocks biochemical action in the nerves, which activate the muscles necessary for respiration, which leads to suffocation. Unlike saxitoxin, toxicity for botulinum is greater through ingestion than inhalation. Neurotoxins are effective in stopping nerve and muscle function without producing microscopic injury to the tissues, where other toxins directly destroy or damage tissue. Microcystin is a toxin produced by blue-green algae. When it enters the body, it binds to an important enzyme inside the liver cells. No other cells in the body are affected by this toxin. If microcystin is not blocked from reaching the liver within 15–60 minutes of receiving a lethal dose, irreversible damage to the liver will occur. Damage to the liver from this toxin is the same, regardless of the route of exposure. With other toxins, the damage that occurs after contact may vary greatly depending on the route of exposure, even within the same toxin family. Death occurs from ricin because it blocks protein synthesis in many different cells within the body. However, no damage occurs to the lungs unless the route of exposure is inhalation.

There are bacterial toxins whose toxicity is too low to make them effective lethal terrorist agents. They still can produce illness and incapacitation at fairly low doses. Lethality is not the only threat to be considered when evaluating a toxin for potential terrorist use. Terrorists may just want to scare a group of people or incapacitate them for a period of time to show their vulnerability. For example, the staphylococcal enterotoxins can cause illness at very low concentrations, but require very large doses to be lethal. Trichothecene mycotoxins are the only biological toxins that are dermally active. Exposure results in skin lesions and systemic illness without being inhaled and absorbed through the respiratory system. Primary routes of exposure are through skin contact and ingestion. Because of the very low aerosol toxicity, large quantity production and aerosolization for inhalation exposure is very unlikely. Nanogram (one billionth of a gram) quantities per square centimeter of skin can cause irritation. One millionth of a gram quantities per square centimeter of skin can cause destruction of cells. Microgram doses to the eyes can cause irreversible damage to the cornea. Because most biological agents are not skin-absorbent hazards, simple washing of contaminated skin surfaces with soap and water within 1–3 hours of an exposure can greatly reduce the risk of illness or injury. In this book we will discuss in detail the four toxins that have been determined by the U.S. military as likely to be weaponized or used as terrorist agents. They are botulinum, staphylococcal enterotoxin B (SEB), ricin, and T-2 mycotoxins.

Table 4.6 Comparison of Biological Agent Characteristics

Disease	Dissemination Method	Infective Dose	Incubation Period	Lethality
Cholera	Food and water	106 organisms	1 week	Low when treated; high without
Brucella	Aerosol Food and water	Unknown	5–30 days	Very low
Plague	Aerosol	<100 organisms	1–6 days	High when not treated in 12–24 hours
Tularemia	Aerosol	1–50 organisms	1–10 days	Moderate
Q-Fever	Aerosol Food and water	10 organisms	14–26 days	Very low

Botulism is a deadly illness caused by any one of seven different but related neurotoxins (A through G). All seven types have similar mechanisms of action. They all produce similar symptoms and effects when inhaled or ingested but the length of time to development of symptoms may vary depending on the route of exposure and dose received. Toxins are actually chemical poisons, not biological organisms. Therefore, botulism is not spread from person to person. Botulinum toxins as a group are among the most toxic compounds known to humans. Lethal doses in research animals are 0.001 micrograms per kilogram of body weight, which will kill 50% of the animals. Botulinum toxins are 15,000 times more toxic than the lethal nerve agent VX and 100,000 times more toxic than sarin. Botulism occurs naturally in improperly canned foods and infrequently in contaminated fish, ingestion of which causes the illness. The CDC conducted studies on 706 cases of foodborne botulism that occurred in the Georgian Republic of Russia, along with the Republic of Georgia's National Center for Disease Control. Those patients that were at the highest risk of dying reported to the hospital with shortness of breath and impaired gag reflex; they did not report diarrhea. If these findings are validated in the U.S. and other countries as predictors of death, it would give doctors tools to help identify patients at highest risk of dying in a botulism outbreak. Although ingestion is the primary natural route of exposure, terrorists would likely aerosolize the manufactured toxin to produce the disease through inhalation. Low-dose inhalation might not produce symptoms for several days. Inhalation or ingestion of high doses would produce symptoms much more quickly. Contamination of food supplies is also a real possibility, because ingestion is a significant route of exposure. Botulism bacterium is commonly found in the soil. It is quite simple and inexpensive to produce.

Step-by-step instructions for producing botulinum toxin can be found on the Internet. Use of this recipe, even for experimental purposes, is not recommended. It is presented here for informational purposes only; making or possessing this material is illegal and very dangerous. Supplies needed to produce the toxin include cheap hamburger or low-quality cuts of meat that have a lot of fat; a handful of dirt taken from 6–12 inches underground; mason jars with sealable lids; a large pot or pressure cooker; coffee filters; and personal protective equipment. Preparation requires that the jars and lids be boiled for 45 minutes. Then place a fist-sized chunk of hamburger and a spoonful of the dirt into a mason jar. Fill the jar with water to the neck. Place the lid on the jar and repeat with the remaining jars. Place all of the filled jars into the large pot and boil for 45 minutes. When finished, let the jars cool and wrap them in aluminum foil or place them in a warm, dark place. They should be stored between 80 and 90°F during the incubation period. Leave the jars for about a week. When the meat in the jars starts turning black and a foul smell is coming from the jars, you know you have been successful. Filter the material in the jars through the coffee filters. The resulting product is botulinum toxin. This process produces a low-grade toxin that is still very lethal.

Three types of illness are associated with the botulinum toxin: foodborne, infant, and wound botulism. With foodborne the victim becomes ill by eating spoiled food that contains the toxin. Illness will occur within a few hours to several days. Foodborne botulism occurs in all age groups. There are a small number of susceptible infants each year who harbor C. botulinum in their intestinal tract. One source of these spores comes from the ingestion of honey. Spores are not normally toxic to adults. Wound botulism occurs when wounds are infected with C botulinum, which secretes the toxin. Iraq has admitted to U.N. inspectors that it had conducted research on the offensive use of botulinum toxins prior to the Persian Gulf War. Additional information has revealed that Iraq had actually filled and deployed over 100 munitions with botulinum toxin.

Botulinum toxins work by binding to the presynaptic nerve terminal at the neuromuscular junction and at cholinergic autonomic sites. They then act to stop the release of acetylcholine presynaptically, thus blocking neurotransmission. This function is quite unlike the action of the nerve agents, where there is too much acetylcholine due to the inhibition of acetylcholinesterase. What occurs with botulism is a lack of the neurotransmitter in the synapse. Therefore, using atropine as an antidote would not be helpful and could even provoke symptoms. When contaminated food is ingested by adults, the toxin is absorbed from the intestines and attaches to the nerves, causing the signs and symptoms of botulism poisoning. Symptoms include:

- Blurred vision
- Dry mouth and/or sore throat
- Difficulty swallowing or speaking
- Impairment of the gag reflex
- General muscular weakness
- Dilated pupils, double vision, photophobia (light sensitivity)
- Shortness of breath

Paralysis of the skeletal muscles follows with a proportional, downward, and growing weakness, which may result in sudden respiratory failure. Patients in respiratory failure will require ventilators. If there are multiple victims, multiple ventilators will be required. The planning process should identify the locations of these valuable resources. Incubation periods for botulinum range from 2–8 days. The time from the beginning of symptoms to respiratory failure can occur in as little as 24 hours after the toxin is

Table 4.7   Physical Properties of Nerve Agents

Property	Tabun	Sarin	Soman	GF	VX
Molecular weight	162.1	140.1	182.2	180.2	267.4
Density g/cm³*	1.073	1.089	1.022	1.12 0	1.008
Boiling-point °C	247	147	167	92**	300
Melting-point °C	−50	−56	−42	<−30	−39
Vapor pres. mm Hg*	0.07	2.9	0.3	0.06	0.0007
Volatility mg/m³*	600	17,000	3,900	600	10
Solubility in water %*	10	oo	2	~2	3 (oo<9.5°C)

* = at 25 °C.
** = at 10 mm Hg.

ingested. One-third of patients die within 3–5 days, although symptoms may not appear for 6–7 days, depending on the dose. Treatment for adults means hospitalization, usually in an intensive care unit. Individual cases could be mistaken for other neuromuscular diseases such as Guillain-Barre syndrome (muscle weakness and paralysis), myasthenia gravis, or tick paralysis. Mental status changes that occur with viral encephalitis should not be present with botulinum poisoning. Botulinum intoxication could also be confused with nerve agent or atropine poisoning. Nerve agent exposures produce copious amounts of respiratory secretions and miotic pupils, where there is a marked decrease in these fluids with exposure to botulinum. Atropine overdose produces hallucinations and delirium, which are absent from botulinum intoxication, even though the mucous membranes are dry in both cases. An antitoxin for botulism can be effective if administered quickly before the onset of symptoms. After the onset of symptoms, the antitoxin is not as effective. The bacteria that produce botulism survive well in soil and agricultural products. Botulism toxin can be destroyed by boiling for 10 minutes. Moist heat at around 250°F for 15 minutes will destroy the spores. Effective disinfectants include 1% sodium hypochlorite, 70% ethanol, and a solution of 0.1N sodium hydroxide. Experimental vaccines are also under development for prevention of botulinum intoxication.

Staphylococcal enterotoxin B (SEB) is a common cause of food poisoning. Cases have usually been isolated to a group of people exposed to contaminated food at some public event or through airline travel. While it can cause death, it is thought of as an incapacitating agent rather than a lethal agent. It could, however, make a large number of people ill for an extended period of time. The primary route of exposure is ingestion, although it can be aerosolized for inhalation exposure. Symptoms from inhalation exposure and ingestion are completely different. Either route of exposure may produce fatalities. Symptoms appear within 3–12 hours after aerosol exposure. They include:

- Sudden onset of fever
- Chills
- Headache
- Myalgia
- Cough

Some patients might also exhibit shortness of breath and retrosternal (behind the breast bone) type of chest pain. Fevers between 103 and 106°F generally last for 2–5 days, and cough may persist for several weeks. Ingestion produces nausea, vomiting, and diarrhea. Very large doses may result in pulmonary edema, septic shock, and possibly death. No antitoxin has been developed for this illness, so treatment remains supportive. No preventative vaccines are available. Diagnosis might be difficult because the symptoms are similar to a number of respiratory pathogens such as influenza, adenovirus (group of DNA-containing viruses, 47 distinct types), and mycoplasma. Generally, other respiratory illnesses occur over a longer period, and a small number of people are involved. In cases of SEB exposure, there could be a large number of victims over a 24-hour period. Naturally occurring food poisoning cases would not present with respiratory symptoms. SEB infection would have a tendency to develop quickly to a somewhat unchanging clinical condition, whereas pulmonary anthrax, tularemia pneumonia, or pneumonic plague would all advance if left untreated. Tularemia, plague, and Q fever would present with infiltrates on chest x-rays. Nerve agent exposure would bring about fasciculations (small bundle of nerves) and extensive secretions of mucus from the nose and mouth. Mustard would cause skin lesions in addition to pulmonary findings. SEB intoxication would not present any of these symptoms. Clear signs of muscular paralysis, bulbar palsies, absence of fever, and dry pulmonary tree due to cholinergic blockade would result from botulinum infection. Respiratory difficulties occur much later with SEB inhalation. Laboratory testing will provide limited data for diagnosing the disease. SEB toxin is very difficult to detect in serum when symptoms develop; however, a baseline specimen for antibody detection should be drawn anyway as early as possible after exposure. Additional specimens should be drawn during recovery. SEB can be detected in the urine, and a sample should be taken and tested. Test results might be helpful retrospectively in developing a diagnosis. High concentrations inhibit kidney function. Disinfectant solutions include 0.5% sodium hypochlorite for 10–15 minutes and/or soap and water.

Ricin (ricinus communis) is a protein toxin that is produced from the castor bean and functions as a cellular poison. One million tons of castor beans are processed globally each year to make castor oil. Ricin is a byproduct of castor oil production. Ricin is relatively easy to make from easily

Figure 4.9 **(See color insert following page 236.)** Castor bean plants growing wild on the Island of Oahu in Hawaii. Castor beans are used to produce the plant toxin ricin.

available castor beans and plants and can be deadly in very small doses. Castor bean plants grow wild in Hawaii and many other places (Figure 4.9). Routes of entry include inhalation, injection, and ingestion. Initial symptoms appear within 24–72 hours after exposure. Death can come between 36 and 72 hours, although some victims can linger for 10–12 days before death or recovery, depending on the dose. There is no known antidote or treatment. Ricin is widely available in any part of the world. It is very toxic and can enter the body by ingestion, inhalation, and injection. Inhalation from an aerosol dispersion would produce symptoms based upon the dose that was inhaled. During the 1940s, humans were accidentally exposed to sublethal doses which produced the following symptoms:

- Fever
- Chest tightness
- Cough
- Dyspnea
- Nausea
- Arthralgias within 4–8 hours

After several hours, profuse sweating occurred, which signaled the end of the symptomatic phase. Little data is available on human inhalation exposure, but victims would be expected to develop severe lung inflammation with a progressive cough, dyspnea, cyanosis, and pulmonary edema. When ricin enters the body through routes other than inhalation, it is not a direct lung irritant. Ingestion causes gastrointestinal hemorrhage with hepatic, splenic, and renal necrosis. Intramuscular injection would cause severe localized necrosis of muscle and regional lymph nodes with moderate visceral organ involvement. The toxicity of ricin compared to botulinum and SEB, based upon LD_{50} values, is much less. Natural intoxication from ricin can occur by the ingestion of the castor bean. This produces severe gastrointestinal symptoms, vascular collapse, and death. Terrorist uses may involve contamination of food or water supplies, use of ricin-laced projectiles, or aerosolization as a liquid or freeze-dried powder. When exposure to ricin occurs through inhalation of small particles, pathogenic changes can occur in as little as 8 hours. This is followed by severe respiratory symptoms and acute hypoxic respiratory failure. Intravenous injection may result in disseminated intravascular coagulation, microcirculatory failure, and multiple organ failure. Ricin is toxic to the cells in the body and acts by inhibiting protein synthesis. During tests conducted on rodents, ricin was more toxic through inhalation than ingestion. Little data is available to indicate the effects on humans.

During July 2004, two jars of baby food were found to be contaminated with ground up castor beans containing tiny amounts of ricin. The ricin detected was not in the purified form that can be deadly. It was instead a less toxic natural component of the castor beans, which can be obtained from ornamental plants (Figure 4.9). Small amounts of the food were eaten by babies but no symptoms were reported. Notes accompanying the jars of Gerber Banana Yogurt referred to an Irvine police officer. The officer is not a suspect. No motive has been determined at this time. Another incident involving ricin occurred during October 2003. A letter with a small amount of ricin inside a metal container was discovered by a clerk at a postal facility in Greenville, South Carolina. Inside the letter was a typewritten message addressed to the Department of Transportation demanding changes in truckers' sleep and work schedules not be implemented. The letter's author indicated they had easy access to castor pulp (waste of the castor bean processing, which can be used to make ricin). The FBI has offered a $100,000 reward for information leading to the capture of the person or persons responsible. None of the ricin escaped the container and no one was exposed. British police early in 2003 arrested seven members of an Algerian extremist group on charges of plotting to use ricin to kill a small number of people and terrify the London population. Instructions were also found in an al Qaeda safe house in Kabul, Afghanistan, according to the FBI. During the summer of 2002, a Washington state man was convicted of making and possessing about 3 grams of ricin, enough to kill 900 people.

Large numbers of victims seeking medical attention for lung injury should be an indication to medical personnel that a pulmonary irritant such as ricin might have been used as a terrorist agent. Keep in mind that other chemical and biological agents can also cause similar symptoms. These include SEB, Q fever, tularemia, plague, and some of the chemical agents. Treatment for victims of ricin poisoning remains supportive. For gastrointestinal exposure, the stomach should be irrigated along with oral administration of superactivated charcoal, followed by use of cathartics (purging or evacuation of the bowels) such as magnesium citrate. Fluids should be administered to replace GI fluids lost. A vaccine for ricin is under development but not currently available. RTA 1-33/44-198 has been tested on monkeys and is scheduled to go for clinical trials next. A vaccine would provide the best protection against ricin poisoning.

Trichothecene mycotoxins are toxins produced by several types of fungi (mold). They are the only group of biological agents that enter the body through skin absorption. Other routes of exposure include inhalation and ingestion. Most mycotoxins act by inhibiting protein synthesis and respiration. Fungi toxins most likely to be used by terrorists include diacetoxyscirpenol (DAS), Nivalenol, 4-Deoxynivalenol (DON), and T2. Of those listed above, T2 is the most likely candidate for terrorist use because of its stability. T2 could be aerosolized or used to contaminate food supplies. It is thought that mycotoxins were aerosolized-forming ("yellow rain"), producing casualties in Laos (1975–1981), Kampuchea (1979–1981), and Afghanistan (1979–1981). Victims included unarmed civilians and guerrilla forces located in remote jungle areas.

Mycotoxins are fast-acting and may produce symptoms within minutes of exposure. Initial symptoms include burning skin pain, redness, tenderness, blistering, and progression to skin necrosis (tissue death) with leathery blackening and sloughing of large areas of skin in lethal cases. When inhaled, the symptoms include:

- Itching and pain
- Sneezing, epistaxis (bleeding from the nose)
- Rhinorrhea
- Pulmonary/tracheobronchial toxicity by dyspnea
- Wheezing
- Cough

Mouth and throat exposures are characterized by pain and blood-tinged saliva and sputum. When the toxin reaches the gastrointestinal tract, symptoms include:

- Anorexia
- Nausea
- Vomiting
- Watery
- Bloody diarrhea
- Possible abdominal cramp pain

SEB and ricin can cause similar systemic symptoms; however, neither of them produce eye or skin symptoms. If the eyes are exposed, eye pain, tearing, redness, foreign body sensation, and blurred vision may result. Irrespective of the route of exposure, when the toxin reaches the rest of the body's systems it may cause weakness, prostration, dizziness, ataxia, and loss of coordination. When victims have been exposed to lethal doses, tachycardia, hypothermia, and hypotension follow. Death may occur in minutes, hours, or days.

Decontamination of victims is very important to remove the mycotoxins from the skin and eyes. Clothing should be removed and disposed of prior to decontamination. Skin should be completely washed with soap and uncontaminated water. Superactive charcoal can be administered orally to absorb ingested T2, and should be administered to victims of an aerosol attack as well. Eyes should be irrigated with normal saline for at least 15 minutes. No antidotes are known for mycotoxins. Treatment is supportive and symptomatic.

Biological agents and toxins are the most likely terrorist weapons for the future. They are inexpensive, do not require a great deal of technical expertise or equipment to manufacture, and can be produced without creating a lot of attention. Biological agents have the best potential as weapons of mass destruction and have the ability to inflict extremely high levels of casualties on a target population. It has been estimated by the WHO that "50 kilograms of aerosolized anthrax spores dispensed 2 kilometers upwind of a population center of 500,000 unprotected people in ideal meteorological condition, would travel greater than 20 kilometers downwind, and kill/incapacitate up to 125,000 people in the path of the biological cloud." It is estimated by the Defense Department that the amount of anthrax equal to a 5-pound bag of sugar in size would be enough to kill half of the population of Washington, D.C. To be effective against large numbers of people, biological agents must be properly disseminated. Conventional explosives could be used for this purpose, along with common agricultural and home garden spraying equipment modified to generate the smaller particle size of biological materials. Motorized vehicles, boats, and airplanes could also provide effective dissemination. Spray devices would require nozzles in the 1–10 micron range for optimum dissemination. Weather conditions are critical for the effective deployment of biological agents as aerosols. The ideal weather would occur during the early morning or evening hours.

The federal government has clamped down on the sale and use of biological agents in research facilities. A program has been developed to control the "Transfer or Receipt of Select Agents." The Anti-Terrorism and Effective Death Penalty Act of 1996 requires regulation of shipment and receipt of certain microorganisms and toxins, effective April 15, 1997 (a copy of the regulations covering the Select Agents can be found in Appendix E).

Explosive Terrorism

5

When terrorist bombings are discussed within the U.S., it immediately brings to mind the Unabomber; bombings at the World Trade Center in New York; the Alfred Murrah Federal Building in Oklahoma City; Olympic Park, the family planning clinic and the night club in Atlanta, Georgia; and the family planning clinic in Birmingham, Alabama. Secondary explosive devices were set up to injure or kill response personnel in two of the Atlanta incidents. During the bombing of the abortion clinic in Atlanta, the secondary device went off. A secondary device was found at the Otherside Lounge nightclub in Atlanta and was disposed of before it went off. Responders were aware of the possibility of secondary devices and took proper precautions. Secondary devices are quite common in other countries. British and Irish response personnel have been experiencing these types of devices for many years. But now it appears that American emergency response personnel have also become the target of terrorists and need to be alert to the possibility of secondary devices following a bombing incident.

Explosive devices used in the previously mentioned incidents included ammonium nitrate vehicle bombs at the World Trade Center and Murrah Building. A backpack with three pipe bombs inside and shrapnel was used in the Olympic Park bombing. Homemade pipe bombs and as many as 10–20 sticks of dynamite were used in the bombing of the family planning clinic and Otherside Lounge nightclub in Atlanta bombings and the family planning clinic in Birmingham. Responders should not only be aware of potential secondary devices but should also have a basic understanding of the characteristics and effects of explosives and explosive devices. Departments should have specific standard operating procedures (SOPs) that govern explosives incident scenes and actions responders should and should not take.

During the Olympics in Atlanta, a bomb was detonated in Olympic Park (Figure 5.3). Police and security officers already on duty in the park for the Olympics discovered the suspicious object just moments before the explosion and started to move back the crowd approximately 50 feet, which very likely saved lives. According to agents from the Baltimore office of the Bureau of

181

Figure 5.1 New York City police and firefighters inspect the bomb crater inside the World Trade Center after the explosion that killed six and injured more than a thousand. (Source: The New York City Fire Department, Firefighter John Strandberg, FDNY Photo Unit. Used with permission.)

Figure 5.2 Debris flies through the air seconds after a secondary device goes off just outside of the Atlanta Northside Family Planning Services clinic. Several emergency responders were injured by the blast. (Source: AP/Wide World Photos. Used with permission.)

Figure 5.3   Olympic Centennial Park bomb components. (Source: FBI.)

Alcohol, Tobacco and Firearms (ATF), an ATF agent actually had the opportunity to look into the satchel where the pipe bombs were placed, just before the explosion occurred. This is something that should never be attempted by emergency response personnel.

Initially, a security guard who found the explosive device was considered a hero, but was later suspected of being the bomber. He was eventually cleared of all connections with the bombing. As could be expected, the security for the Olympics in Atlanta was well planned with plenty of resources prepositioned for the event. Even with this large security presence, a bomb was still planted and detonated. The Olympic Park bombing shows just how vulnerable all locations throughout the U.S. are to acts of terrorism. If someone decides to plant a bomb or carry out some other act of terrorism, there might be little anyone can do to prevent it. For that reason, it is critically important for emergency responders to be aware of the potential locations where acts of terrorism might occur, be on the lookout for suspicious people, vehicles, or objects, and be aware of the danger of secondary devices.

For the first time in nearly 30 years, emergency responders were subjected to a secondary explosive device in Atlanta. It was 10:35 AM and the Fulton County, Georgia, Fire Department received a call for a transformer explosion at 275 Carpenter Drive in Sandy Springs. One engine company was dispatched, and as firefighters arrived they found extensive damage. It was clear that the type of damage found could not have been caused by an electrical transformer explosion. There was little doubt that a bomb had exploded at the Sandy Springs Professional Building. Targeted was the Atlanta Northside Family Planning Services center (Figure 5.4). This same family planning clinic had been bombed once before, 13 years prior. Firefighters and law enforcement personnel had been on the scene for about an hour when a second blast occurred, destroying the fire chief's car. Six people were injured — two

Figure 5.4   Sandy Springs Abortion Clinic bomb components. (Source: FBI.)

bystanders, one firefighter, one FBI agent, and one ATF agent. Dynamite had been placed in an old ammunition box near the west entrance of the building's parking lot (Figure 5.4). Two parked cars in the building's parking lot provided shielding from the brunt of the blast force for other response personnel, or there might have been many more injuries or deaths.

Following the family clinic bombing in Sandy Springs, two more bombings occurred — one in Atlanta and the other in Birmingham, Alabama. The second Atlanta incident also involved the placing of a secondary device. At approximately 10:00 PM, on February 22, 1997, an explosion occurred at the Otherside Lounge, a gay bar in Atlanta. Five patrons were injured when the bomb scattered large nails into a crowd of approximately 150 patrons. A secondary device was found in a backpack outside the building (Figure 5.5).

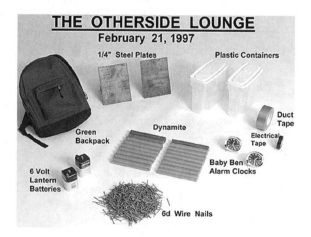

Figure 5.5   The Otherside Lounge bomb components. (Source: FBI.)

Police were able to destroy the device using a robot before it went off. The New Woman All Women Health Center in Birmingham was the target of a January 29, 1998, blast. That explosion resulted in the death of an off-duty police officer working as a security guard and the serious injury of a nurse. It was the sixth death involved in abortion clinic terrorism but the first involving a law enforcement officer. Bombing of the clinic occurred just one week after the 25th anniversary of the Supreme Court's decision in *Roe v. Wade*, legalizing abortion. The force of the blast blew a large crater in the ground and shook buildings a block away, including another abortion clinic, the Summit Women's Clinic, where things fell off the wall. ATF experts said the bomb was a small device that was designed to kill and injure. Once again, response personnel were cautious and searched for a secondary device. Bomb-sniffing dogs were hampered in the search because of explosive debris that had been scattered by the blast. A secondary device was located and rendered safe before an explosion could occur. Eric Rudolph was the prime suspect in the Birmingham bombing. A remote control device was used at the clinic. Rudolph planted a device at the clinic and then parked his car at a McDonald's. He returned to plant the second device then went up on a hill to wait. When the security guard and nurse arrived at the clinic and walked near the device in a flower pot, he detonated the device. A student walking by when the explosion occurred followed Rudolph back to the parking lot at McDonald's and got the license number of his vehicle. That is how Rudolph was identified.

Following the bombing in Birmingham, investigators were beginning to see similarities between the Birmingham bombing and the Atlanta area bombings. Evidence developed by the FBI and ATF eventually tied the bombings together. Components and tool markings collected from bomb fragments at both the Atlanta area and Birmingham bombings were matched. Indications are that the bombs were very similar in design. It was discovered that nails used as shrapnel from the casings on each of the bombs came from the same foundry. A group calling themselves the "Army of God" claimed responsibility for the bombings in the Atlanta area and in Birmingham, Alabama. Claims were sent through letters (Figure 5.6) sent to the *Atlanta Journal-Constitution* newspaper and Reuters news agency. Information in the letters indicated that the Sandy Springs, Georgia, explosion was carried out in retaliation for the "murder" of "3.5 million children" each year during abortions. It also indicated that the secondary bomb that exploded 67 minutes after the first "was aimed at agents of the so-called federal government," against which it had declared "total war." Further, the letter stated the gay nightclub bombing "was aimed at the Sodomite bar." The letters were turned over to federal authorities. The "Sons of Confederate Klan" (SOCK), a neo-Nazi Ku Klux Klan (KKK) organization based in Los

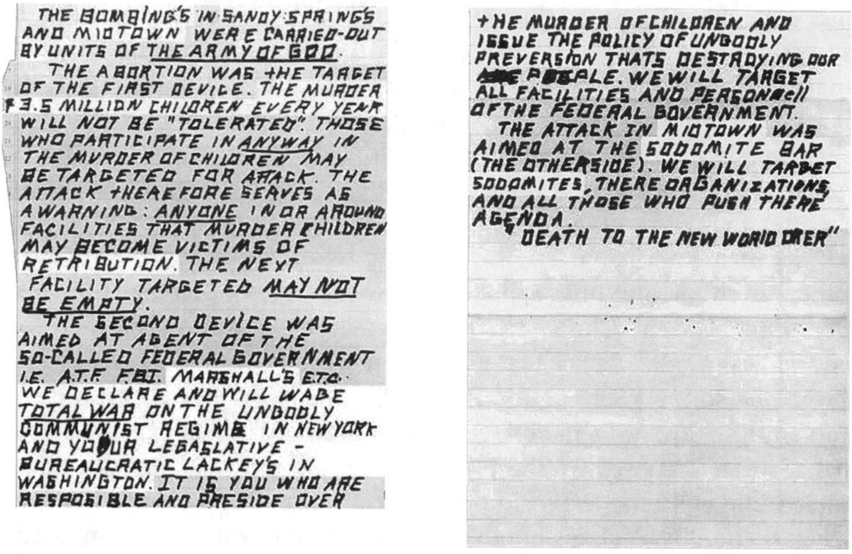

THE BOMBING'S IN SANDY SPRINGS AND MIDTOWN WERE CARRIED-OUT BY UNITS OF THE ARMY OF GOD. THE ABORTION WAS THE TARGET OF THE FIRST DEVICE. THE MURDER OF 3.5 MILLION CHILDREN EVERY YEAR WILL NOT BE "TOLERATED". THOSE WHO PARTICIPATE IN ANYWAY IN THE MURDER OF CHILDREN MAY BE TARGETED FOR ATTACK. THE ATTACK THEREFORE SERVES AS A WARNING: ANYONE IN OR AROUND FACILITIES THAT MURDER CHILDREN MAY BECOME VICTIMS OF RETRIBUTION. THE NEXT FACILITY TARGETED MAY NOT BE EMPTY. THE SECOND DEVICE WAS AIMED AT AGENT OF THE SO-CALLED FEDERAL GOVERNMENT I.E. A.T.F FBI. MARSHALL'S ETC. WE DECLARE AND WILL WAGE TOTAL WAR ON THE UNGODLY COMMUNIST REGIME IN NEW YORK AND YOUR LEGASLATIVE - BUREAUCRATIC LACKEY'S IN WASHINGTON. IT IS YOU WHO ARE RESPOSIBLE AND PRESIDE OVER

THE MURDER OF CHILDREN AND ISSUE THE POLICY OF UNGODLY PREVERSION THATS DESTROYING OUR PEOPLE. WE WILL TARGET ALL FACILITIES AND PERSONNEL OF THE FEDERAL GOVERNMENT. THE ATTACK IN MIDTOWN WAS AIMED AT THE SODOMITE BAR (THE OTHERSIDE). WE WILL TARGET SODOMITES, THERE ORGANIZATIONS, AND ALL THOSE WHO PUSH THERE AGENDA. "DEATH TO THE NEW WORLD ORDER"

Figure 5.6 Army of God letter, claiming responsibility for bombings in Atlanta. (Source: FBI.)

Angeles, also claimed credit for the gay nightclub bombing in Atlanta. However, following an extensive investigation, the FBI issued an arrest warrant for Eric Robert Rudolph, a suspected member of a Georgia militia group, charging him with the Birmingham bombing. A gray 1989 Nissan pickup registered in Asheville, North Carolina, was seen near the clinic just before the explosion. The truck was later found abandoned in the mountains of western North Carolina. Bomb-sniffing dogs detected a scent of explosive residue inside the truck. Rudolph was known to live in a trailer in Murphy, North Carolina, about four hours away from Birmingham. This region of Cherokee County has become known as a haven for political and religious extremists, tax protesters, survivalists, white supremacists, Freemen, and others. Rudolph's former school teachers said he had a strong distrust of governmental authority. A $1million reward was offered for information leading to the arrest of Rudolph. He was placed on the FBI's Ten Most Wanted Fugitive list and was the subject of an intensive manhunt in the backcountry of North Carolina during the summer of 1998.

On May 31, 2003, Rudolph was captured near Murphy, North Carolina. He was found while looking through a grocery store trash container for food by a local rookie law enforcement officer. Rudolph was charged with the bombings in the Atlanta area and the one in Birmingham, Alabama, which resulted in the death of an off-duty police officer and the serious injury of a nurse who worked at the clinic. Rudolph was not finished with his desire to spread terror through bombings. He had four separate stashes of explosives hidden in the North Carolina mountains where he was hiding out. One was located right above a National Guard armory where the Southeast Bomb Task Force had set up their command post. The constant pressure created by law enforcement's pursuit of Rudolph is credited with keeping him from bombing other targets.

Abortion clinic attacks are not new to Alabama or other parts of the country. In the summer of 1997, a clinic in Tuscaloosa, Alabama, was set on fire in a domestic terrorist attack. Two bombs were found at abortion clinics in Fayetteville, North Carolina, on October 4, 1998. Both clinics had been damaged in arson fires just a month before. Each bomb contained six sticks of dynamite wrapped with electrical tape, with a kitchen timer attached. The bombs were defused without incident by a military crew from Fort Bragg, North Carolina.

The Tippecanoe County Courthouse in Lafayette, Indiana, was the site of an attempted bombing on August 2, 1998. ATF agents recovered evidence from the scene and sent it to the ATF National Laboratory in Rockville, Maryland, for examination. A white male in his mid-40s was sighted near the scene around the time of the incident and was sought for questioning.

On October 28, 1998, two bombs were discovered in Concord, New Hampshire, libraries. The buildings were located about one block apart. Firefighters responding to a fire on a shelf of the Concord City Library discovered the first bomb. A second bomb was found about four hours later in the New Hampshire State Library. Police had received written threats, which were very generic and did not specify a location. Neither of the devices went off, and there were no injuries.

Bombing incidents are preceded by threats approximately 33% of the time. While the incidence of bombings decreased from 1994–1995, the lethality of the explosions increased. In 1994, 31 people died in bombings, and in 1995 this increased to 193. Over twice as many people were injured by bombings in 1995 compared to the previous year. Much of the increase in deaths and injuries between 1994 and 1995 can be attributed to the bombing at the Murrah Federal Building in Oklahoma City. In that incident alone, 168 people died, including many children, and 518 were injured. Besides causing death, injury, and destruction, explosive devices might also be used to deliver or disseminate chemical, biological, nuclear, and incendiary materials. Explosive devices and materials have been used over 70% of the time in cases of terrorism. FBI and ATF statistics show that in the U.S. alone, from 2000–2003, there were over 2,667 actual criminal bombing incidents, including those using incendiary devices. Total casualties from both actual and attempted bombings include 314 injuries and 51 deaths. Many of these could be categorized as terrorist attacks. Overall, however, bombing incidents increased 52% between 2000 and 2003, which is the most recent reporting

Figure 5.7 Demolition of the Murrah Federal Building in Oklahoma City, Oklahoma. (Courtesy FEMA.)

period. Deaths from bombings decreased 63%, and injuries decreased by 44%. Overall damage caused by the bombings remained constant over the four-year period. Abortion clinic bombing and arson seems to have peaked in the 1990s. From 2000–2004, there were only 16 attempts at bombing or arson at abortion clinics in the U.S.

Homemade bombs can take on any form and are limited only by the imagination of the person(s) making the bomb. Step-by-step instructions and diagrams are available from the Internet, books, and through videotapes for making many different types of bombs. These include exploding light bulbs, computer diskette bombs, tennis ball bombs, fertilizer bombs, napalm, mailbox bombs, car bombs, paint bombs, contact bombs, plastic explosives from bleach, and smoke bombs, to name a few. Instructions are also available to make your own potassium nitrate, a common ingredient of black powder. Emergency response personnel should be on the lookout for anything that appears unusual or out of place. Trained bomb technicians should make the determination as to whether a suspicious object might be a bomb. Do not take anything for granted. The era of the stereotyped bomb has passed, and bombs can look like anything, even being incorporated into a bicycle frame! Many bombing incidents are regional in nature and may only produce a short blurb on the national news or may not be mentioned at all. For every high-profile bombing, such as those mentioned at the beginning of this chapter, there are dozens of other bombing incidents that occur around the country every year. No area of the U.S. is immune to potential acts of terrorism. Many of these bombings are acts of domestic terrorism. Because of their size and limited impact on a community, they do not cause fear in the masses, but do affect individual groups of people. Abortion clinics around the country have been the target of bombings, arson, armed attacks, and attacks with chemicals and biological toxins. However, other facilities have also been targeted.

On November 13, 1995, in Reno, Nevada, two construction workers attempted to bomb the office of the Internal Revenue Service (IRS). A bomb fashioned from 100 pounds of fertilizer and kerosene was used. Fortunately, the bomb failed to ignite. Had the bomb gone off, authorities believe that many deaths and injuries would have occurred.

On January 6, 1996, in Espanola, New Mexico, a bomb did explode outside the U.S. Forest Service headquarters. Monetary loss from the bomb was $25,000, but there were no deaths or injuries. Another Forest Service employee had been the target of attempted bombings in Nevada. His office and a van outside his home were bombed, but both were unoccupied at the time, and no one was hurt in either incident.

A bomb went off outside an FBI field office in Laredo, Texas, on May 20, 1996. Twelve FBI agents were in offices of the FBI in Laredo at the time of the attempted bombing. However, no one was injured. A group calling themselves "Organization 544" claimed responsibility for the blast. During 1996 in Austin, Texas, a single suspect was convicted for plotting to blow up the IRS office.

Thanks to an off-duty NYPD officer equipped with a cell phone, police on Long Island caught a teenager they said had a carload of pipe bombs on July 15, 2001. Police said the NYPD officer spotted the driver spinning his car in circles and smoking his tires in an East Meadow, New York, parking lot at 2:25 PM. The officer followed the Honda to a dead-end street and called 911. Nassau County Police Officer Christian Migliore, responding to the call, said he saw a green military ammunition box in the car's backseat, with a "gray tubular metallic object" sticking out of it. After the driver was ordered out, Migliore searched the car and found that the ammunition box contained three pipe bombs. Police said they later found four more pipe bombs in the car, as well as fuses and bomb-making materials. The county bomb squad removed the devices, and police impounded the car. The 17-year-old driver was charged with seven felony counts of criminal possession of a dangerous weapon and one count of reckless endangerment. Nassau County police said they were not aware of any pipe bombs that had been detonated recently.

According to police in Philadelphia, about one-third of a pound of powerful military explosives was found in a suitcase at a bus station on October 20, 2001. The C-4 explosive, about the size of a bar of soap, was found in a suitcase along with about 1,000 feet of detonation cord. Police said there was no threat of explosion because no detonation cap was attached to the plastic explosive. Luggage claim workers opened the suitcase after the time limit for checked luggage in lockers had expired and found the explosive and detonation cord inside. They called police and evacuated the terminal. The bomb squad then removed the suitcase with the explosive. Police worked with the FBI and other federal agencies on the case.

Bombing of mailboxes in several Midwestern states was perpetrated by a college student from Minnesota. Luke Helder's cross-country bombing spree ended May 7, 2002, with a 40-mile high-speed chase across a Nevada desert highway. Behind him were 18 pipe bombs in five states, six of which exploded, wounding four postal workers and two Iowa residents. In the trunk of his father's car, which Helder was driving when he was caught, were six more bombs. According to affidavits filed in court, the University of Wisconsin-Stout junior admitted planting the bombs. A two-count criminal complaint was filed in federal court in Iowa, charging the student with using bombs to maliciously destroy property and to "commit a crime of violence" that injured a woman in rural Tipton. On April 1, 2004, a federal judge in Cedar Rapids, Iowa declared Helder incompetent to stand trial. Similar federal charges were filed against him in Illinois. In Nebraska, he faces another federal charge of interstate transportation of explosives. In Nevada, he faces a federal charge of possession of a firearm in the commission of a crime. The list goes on and on. The point is, acts of terrorism do not have to be the magnitude of Oklahoma City, and they can occur anytime and anywhere.

Law enforcement agencies have had some success in infiltrating militant organizations and through intelligence have foiled several potential bombing incidents. In Arizona during July 1996, 13 people were arrested for plotting to bomb state and federal government buildings in Arizona. They were charged with conspiracy to commit civil disorder and with firearms violations. All were reported to be members of the "Viper Militia." Police seized over 400 pounds of ammonium nitrate and other bomb-making components. Picric acid was found at one of the locations. It was used during World War II for making grenades. Picric acid is a high explosive, closely related to TNT in its potential power. The group was not suspected of any connection with the Oklahoma City bombing or the derailment of the Amtrak Sunset Limited in the Arizona desert. Several bombing plots against the U.S. have been discovered and stopped before they occurred. Ahmed Ressam, an Algerian living in Canada, planned to bomb Los Angeles International Airport (LAX). He was arrested at the U.S.-Canada border in Port Angeles, Washington, after crossing by ferry on December 14, 1999. Customs officials then found nitroglycerin and four timing devices concealed in a spare tire well of his automobile. He and three other Algerians stood trial for the crime. Ressam began cooperating with investigators in 2001. On July 27, 2005, he was sentenced to 22 years in prison. In Yemen, members of the group planned to bomb USS The Sullivans with a boat laden with explosives. Militants deployed a bomb-laden boat on January 3, 2000, but the overloaded bomb boat sank before detonating. After the attack on The Sullivans failed, al Qaeda tried the same type of attack a second time. They successfully bombed the USS Cole on October 12, 2000. While in prison, Ressam revealed that al

Qaeda sleeper cells existed within the U.S. Richard Colvin Reid, also known as the shoe bomber, was a Muslim allegedly working for al Qaeda. He was arrested on December 22, 2001 for attempting to destroy a passenger airliner by igniting explosives hidden in his shoes. According to the FBI he has used the aliases Tariq Raja and Abdel Rahim. The flight was American Airlines Flight 63 going from Charles De Gaulle International Airport near Paris, France, to Miami, Florida's Miami International Airport. He was caught when a flight attendant saw him attempting to light a match on the tongue of his sneaker. She tried grabbing his shoes, but he pushed her to the floor, and she screamed for help. When another flight attendant tried to stop him, he fought her and bit her thumb. The 6-foot 4-inch Reid was eventually subdued by other passengers on the airliner, two of whom were doctors who injected him with sedative drugs. Authorities later found plastic explosives with a triacetone triperoxide (TATP) detonator hidden in the lining of his shoes. On January 30, 2003, he was found guilty on terrorism charges at a federal court in Boston, Massachusetts, and sentenced to life in prison. During the sentencing hearing he openly stated that he was an Islamic fundamentalist and declared himself an enemy of the U.S. and in league with al Qaeda and Osama bin Laden.

Bombings have been the primary terrorist activity involving American facilities in foreign countries. During 1996, in Saudi Arabia, U.S. troops housed in the Khobar Towers were preparing to return home. A truck bomb exploded outside, sending a shock wave from over 20,000 pounds of TNT against the concrete building. Nineteen American Air Force personnel were killed in the blast. Two massive bombs exploded minutes apart outside the U.S. embassies in Kenya and Tanzania on August 8, 1998, killing at least 80 people, eight of them American. According to unnamed U.S. officials, they were coordinated terrorist attacks. In Nairobi, an enormous explosion ripped through downtown at about 10:35 AM, turning busy Haile Selassie Avenue into a scene of death and destruction that left more than 1,600 people injured and dozens unaccounted for long into the night. The blast, which leveled a three-story building containing a secretarial school and gutted the rear half of the U.S. embassy next door, dismembered more than a dozen people passing on foot and incinerated dozens of others in their seats in three nearby buses. Just minutes earlier, a bomb reportedly planted in a gasoline tanker detonated near the front entrance of the U.S. embassy in the Tanzanian capital of Dar es Salaam. The explosion destroyed the front of the building and demolished a side wall, throwing charred debris down the street, setting cars ablaze and knocking down trees. At least seven people were killed and 72 injured, none of them American. U.S. officials said they believed the bombings were a terrorist attack. Although they did not identify any suspects, the newspaper Al-Hayat, based in Cairo, Egypt, reported that it had received a call claiming responsibility for the bombings from a previously unknown group called the Liberation Army of the Islamic Sanctuaries.

Another bombing occurred at the First Battalion, 8th Marine Headquarters building in Beirut, Lebanon, on October 23, 1983, killing 241 U.S. marines, sailors, and soldiers outright, and another 29 died later from injuries suffered in the explosion. A terrorist drove a truck laden with "compressed gas-enhanced explosives" near the military compound at the airport and detonated the explosives. Because this type of truck is often seen at the airport, it attracted no unusual attention. Suicide bombings carried out by Islamic fundamentalists occurred twice at the American Embassy in Beirut, Lebanon, in the early 1980s, killing 74 people. In the mid-1980s a German nightclub was bombed, killing two U.S. servicemen and injuring 200 others. That bombing was blamed on Libya.

Terrorist attacks are not limited to military and government targets. On August 25, 1998, the American restaurant chain Planet Hollywood was targeted by terrorists in Cape Town, South Africa. One woman was killed and 25 people were injured in the blast, including several children. There were more than 150 people in the restaurant at the time of the explosion. A local radio station received two calls claiming responsibility, one from the group Muslims Against Global Oppression and another from a man calling himself "Jihad," which means "holy war" in Arabic. The second caller said the blast was in retaliation for the U.S. attacks in Afghanistan and Sudan. This explosion had a ripple effect in Hollywood, where Daily Variety contained the headline "H'Wood on Alert." Since the U.S. missile strikes in Sudan and Afghanistan, the American entertainment industry has been concerned about being targeted by terrorists. Planet Hollywood might only be the beginning. Disney cancelled appearances by Mickey and Minnie Mouse at a shopping mall in the United Arab Emirates. Security was increased at all Disney theme parks in light of the threats against American interests worldwide. Other American companies with many interests throughout the world include McDonald's and Coca-Cola. The August 1998 embassy bombings in East Africa have shown just how unprepared we are to deal with acts of terrorism. These embassies were not considered high risks, which is just the type of target a terrorist might look for. No place in the U.S., or the world for that matter, is completely safe from potential acts of terrorism. Terrorists may choose to strike in some out-of-the-way community because no one expects it. This tactic would add to the impact of the event because of the element of surprise, leaving the community feeling violated.

Threats of bombings should be taken very seriously, no matter how often they occur or what the targets might be. When a bomb threat is received, there are three alternatives for building owners and response personnel: ignore the threat, evacuate immediately, or search and evacuate if warranted.

If it is determined that a search will be conducted, occupants of the area in question should assist in the search. They know the surroundings, what is usually there, and what would be suspicious. Warnings of bombs generally come from phone calls to the target; however, they can also be made in writing or by recorded message. Bomb threats are made for two general reasons. First, the person making the call knows or believes that an explosive device has been or will be placed in a specific location. Their reason for making the call is to reduce the chances of injury or property damage from the bomb. Calls may come from those responsible or someone who has obtained information concerning a bomb placement. Secondly, the person making the call wants to create fear and terror, which will result in disruption of activities at the facility where the threat is made. This will result in emergency response, evacuation of the facility, traffic tie-ups, and disruption of business activities. Over the past two years in Anne Arundel County, Maryland, the school system has been inundated by bomb threats. They were made by many different students who wanted to disrupt the school day. On several occasions, multiple threats occurred on the same day. Even though responders may have suspected each call was just another hoax, they still had to treat each occurrence as if it were real. Because of the potential for terrorism, sooner or later there might be a real bomb.

Dispatch personnel should be trained in proper procedures for handling bomb-threat calls. More than one person should listen to an incoming call. Keep the person on the line as long as possible. If the location of the bomb is not given, ask the caller where the bomb is located. Inform the caller that the building is occupied, and detonation of the device could result in death and injury to occupants. Listen for background noises, such as music, equipment, public address announcements, traffic, aircraft, and anything else that might help identify the caller's location. Pay attention to the caller's voice — is it male or female, with accents or speech impediments? Below is a checklist developed by ATF for dispatch personnel to follow to obtain the best information from a bomb-threat caller.

ATF Bomb Threat Checklist

Exact time of call: _____

Exact words of caller: _____

Questions to ask:

   1. When is the bomb going to explode? _____

   2. Where is the bomb? _____

   3. What does it look like? _____

4. What kind of bomb is it? _____

5. What will cause the bomb to explode? _____

6. Did you place the bomb? _____

7. Why? _____

8. Where are you calling from? _____

9. What is your address? _____

10. What is your name? _____

Caller's voice (circle):

Calm	Slow	Crying	Slurred
Stutter	Deep	Loud	Broken
Giggling	Accent	Angry	Rapid
Stressed	Nasal	Lisp	Excited
Distinguished	Sincere	Squeaky	Normal

If voice is familiar, whom did it sound like? _____

Were there any background noises? _____

Remarks:

Person receiving call: _____

Telephone number call received at: _____

Date: _____

During the bombing at the Olympics in Atlanta, a call was received by 911 operators for a bomb in Olympic Park. The threat claimed that an explosion would take place in 30 minutes. In reality, there was only a 20-minute period between the warning and the blast. Perhaps the caller misled dispatchers about the 30-minute period to catch response personnel at the scene when the bomb went off. It took dispatchers 10 minutes to determine the location of the pay phone where the call originated. The 911 system requires an address be entered before the call can be transferred to dispatchers. An officer arrived at the pay phone where the call came from at 1:12:52 AM. Once the phone was located, officers were dispatched from other locations in the city to the park, instead of contacting police already in the park.

A police officer in Canada lost his life when he opened a suspicious bag that contained an explosive device. When he opened the bag, the device detonated, killing him. Suspicious packages or other potential explosive devices should only be handled by experienced bomb technicians. When a package needs to be opened, it should first be x-rayed in place and then opened remotely using a robot or water cannon if the package is still suspicious following x-ray.

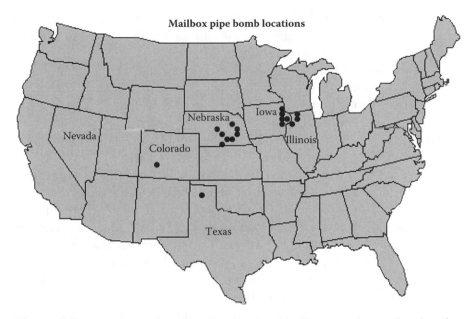

Figure 5.8 Locations of mailbox bombs placed in five states by mailbox bomber Lucus Helder during the summer of 2002. He was captured in Nevada.

During the summer of 2002, a 21-year-old college student from Minnesota accused of putting pipe bombs in mailboxes in five states told authorities he was trying to make a "smiley face" pattern on the map, according to a sheriff involved in the investigation. The first 16 bombs were arranged in two circles, one in Illinois and Iowa and the other in Nebraska. On a map, the circles could resemble the eyes of the popular 1970s happiness symbol. The final two bombs, found in Colorado and Texas, form an arc that could be the beginning of a smile. The FBI said Helder placed 18 pipe bombs in mailboxes in Iowa, Illinois, Nebraska, Colorado, and Texas, along with antigovernment notes. Six of the bombs exploded on one day, injuring four letter carriers and two residents. The eight bombs in Iowa and Illinois were found in rural locations that form an uneven ring about 70 miles in diameter. The Nebraska bomb sites — about 350 miles away — form a ring about 90 miles across. The other bombs were found hundreds of miles away — one in Salida, Colorado, the other in Amarillo, Texas. The FBI issued an alert for Helder after his father called police about letters from his son that included references to death, antigovernment comments, and the phrase "mailboxes are exploding." The bombs were reported to have been accompanied by a typewritten note that read: "Mailboxes are exploding! Why, you ask? If the government controls what you want to do they control what you can do. I'm obtaining your attention in the only way I can.. More 'attention getters' are on the way. If I could, I would change only one person, unfortunately the resources are not accessible. It seems killing a single famous person would get the same media attention as killing numerous un-famous humans." The same phrase was in the notes found with the bombs.

Authorities said Luke Helder confessed to making 24 pipe bombs out of smokeless gunpowder, BBs or nails, paper clips and Christmas tree bulbs. The final 10 bombs found in mailboxes, and the six found in his car, had different detonation mechanisms and were not rigged to explode but were still dangerous, authorities said. "Same pipe bombs, but he did not hook the battery to them," said Terry Hulse, the FBI agent in charge in Las Vegas. "The difference is when people opened the mailbox, they found them laying there." In a competency hearing, U.S. District Judge Mark Bennett ruled Helder was mentally unfit to stand trial. Bennett also ordered that Helder undergo another round of psychological testing at the Federal Medical Center in Rochester, Minnesota, where he has been held for more than a year. Doctors will determine whether Helder poses a substantial risk to society.

The mailbox bombings also produced some copycat attacks by kids in several states. Authorities in Sioux City, Iowa, blew up a pipe with no explosives, found by three young boys, and three small bombs made with drain cleaner exploded in mailboxes north of Spokane, Washington. There were no injuries in either case. Indiana State Police also said that at least two juveniles were suspected of planting two pipe bombs in roadside mailboxes. One of the bombs exploded, but there were no injuries.

In recent years the U.S. has been prone to bomb attacks carried out by its own citizens. In 1998, Theodore Kaczynski, known as the Unabomber, was sentenced to four terms of life in prison without parole for a 17-year bombing spree that left three people dead and many injured. Gulf War veteran Timothy McVeigh was executed for the 1995 bombing of a federal building in Oklahoma that killed 168 people and injured hundreds of others. Following the September 11 attacks on the U.S., the country was hit by a series of anthrax attacks. The FBI has said it believes those attacks were probably the work of a U.S. national.

Characteristics of Explosions

Definitions

An explosive material is identified by the U.S. Department of Transportation in 49 CFR 173.50 as "any substance or article, including a device, which is designed to function by explosion or which, by chemical reaction within itself, is able to function in a similar manner even if not designed to function by explosion." This definition of explosive, according to the DOT, applies only to chemical explosives that were designed to create explosions and are

Table 5.1   Examples of Overpressure Damage to Property

0.5–1 psi	Window glass breakage
1–2 psi	Buckling of corrugated steel and aluminum
	Wood siding and framing blown in
2–3 psi	Shattering of concrete or cinder block walls
3–4 psi	Steel panel building collapse
	Oil storage tank rupture
5 psi	Wooden utility poles snapping failure
7 psi	Overturned loaded rail cars
7–8 psi	Brick walls shearing and flexure failures
	Injuries and Deaths to Personnel
1 psi	Knockdown of personnel
5 psi	Eardrum rupture
15 psi	Lung damage
35 psi	Threshold for fatalities
50 psi	50% fatalities
65 psi	99% fatalities

transported in commerce. However, it could easily be applied to explosive materials and devices used in acts of terrorism. Another definition taken from the National Fire Academy Tactical Considerations Student Manual is "a substance or a mixture of substances which, when subjected to heat, impact, friction, or other suitable initial impulse, undergoes a very rapid chemical transformation, forming other more stable products entirely or largely gaseous whose combined volume is much greater than the original substance." An explosion is defined in the NFPA Fire Protection Handbook as "a rapid release of high-pressure gas into the environment." This release of high-pressure gas occurs regardless of the type of explosion. The high-pressure energy is dissipated by a shock wave that radiates from the blast center. Shock waves create an overpressure in the surrounding area, which can affect personnel, equipment, and structures (Table 5.1). Overpressure of just 0.5–1.00 psi can cause windows to break and knock down personnel. Overpressures of just 5 psi can rupture eardrums and snap wooden utility poles in two. Ninety-nine percent of people exposed to overpressures of 65 psi or greater die.

Categories of Explosions

According to the NFPA Fire Protection Handbook, there are two general categories of explosions, physical and chemical. In a physical explosion, the high-pressure gas released is produced by mechanical means. That is to say, even if chemicals are present in the container, they are not affected chemically by the explosion. In a chemical explosion, the high-pressure gas is generated by the chemical reaction that takes place within the fuel or explosive material.

Categories of Explosives

An explosive material is able to undergo a powerful decomposition, which might result in the production of thermal energy and shock waves, which can be followed by a deafening noise. Additionally, a ground shock or seismic shock can be recorded by seismic detection equipment many miles from the site of the explosion. During the Oklahoma City explosion, the size of the blast was so great that it registered 3.5 on the Richter scale in Denver, Colorado, which is more than 500 miles away. Local effects of ground shock and shock wave were evident in the damage that occurred to over 800 buildings in Oklahoma City. Decomposition of an explosive material is really an extremely rapidly burning fire. Chemical oxidizers that must be present in explosive materials allow for the rapid acceleration of combustion required for the explosive decomposition to occur. This is sometimes referred to as a "sudden and violent release of gas," which takes place during the decomposition reaction. A chemical explosion, like fire, requires similar components to be present before decomposition can take place. In a fire, there must be oxygen (usually atmospheric), fuel, and heat (an ignition source) to allow combustion to take place. Once ignition occurs, a chemical chain reaction will begin. For a chemical explosion to occur, there must be oxygen present in the compound (in this case a chemical oxidizer, because atmospheric oxygen will not provide enough oxygen), fuel or combustible filler, an ignition source, and, most importantly, confinement of the oxidizer and fuel. Without confinement, the materials will not explode; they will merely burn with great intensity. Bombings at the World Trade Center and Murrah Federal Building involved a chemical blasting agent. The bombs were made up of ammonium nitrate or urea nitrate (the oxidizer) and fuel oil, which provides the fuel. It is estimated that the World Trade Center bomb contained 1,200 pounds of urea nitrate, and the Oklahoma City bomb over 4,800 pounds of ammonium nitrate. The bomb that destroyed the 8th Marine Headquarters in Beirut, Lebanon, contained approximately 12,000 pounds of yet unidentified explosives.

Between February 13 and February 16, 1998, the ATF reported the largest theft of explosives in many years had occurred from the C and K Coal Company in West Sligo, Pennsylvania. Items taken included 2,000 pounds of explosive materials, ANFO (commercial grade ammonium nitrate blasting agent), 560 electric blasting caps, 1,500 feet of noiseless fuse line, and 13,000 feet of detonating cord. It is unknown what the motive was for the theft, but terrorism could certainly be a possibility.

Table 5.2   Characteristics of High and Low Explosives

	High	Low
Initiation Method	Primary by ignition Secondary by detonation	By ignition
Conversion to gas	Microseconds	Milliseconds
Consumption velocity	1–6 miles/second	Few inches to feet per second
Velocity of flame front	1–6 miles/second	1/3–1 mile per second
Pressure of explosion	50,000 to 4,000,000 psi	Up to 50,000 psi

Types of Explosives

Explosives can be divided into two primary groups based upon the speed in which the chemical decomposition takes place, usually expressed in feet per second. These groups are known as high explosives and low explosives (sometimes referred to as high order and low order fillers) (Table 5.2). Low explosives change physical state from a solid to a gas rather slowly. The low explosive burns gradually over a somewhat sustained period of time. This action is typically used as a pushing and shoving action on the object against which it is placed. Primary uses of low explosives are as a propelling charge and for powder trains such as time fuses. Reactions of this type generally are referred to as deflagrations and may occur without complete decomposition of the fuel. Unexploded fuel can prove a danger to responders as the material may still explode. Examples of low explosives include black powder and smokeless powder. There are three types of high explosives — primary, booster, and secondary. Primary explosives are extremely sensitive to shock, vibration, heat, and electricity. Primary explosives are usually contained in a small metal tube and are electrically ignited. They are used to initiate another, less sensitive high explosive, called the secondary explosive. Sometimes the secondary explosive is so insensitive it needs a booster explosive to set it off. In other words, the primary sets off the booster, which sets off the secondary. This process is known as the explosive train. Booster explosives are themselves secondary explosives. High explosives change from a solid to a gas almost immediately, and the process is generally a complete decomposition of all the fuel or filler. This action is often referred to as a detonation. A high explosive is detonated by heat or shock, which sets up a detonating wave. The wave passes through the entire mass of explosive material instantly. Sudden creation of gases and their extremely rapid extension produces a shattering effect, which can overcome great obstructions in their path. Examples of primary high explosives include mercury fulminate, lead azide, almost any azide, lead picrate, lead styphnate, DDNP, HMTD (hexamethylenetriperoxidediamine), TACC (tetraminecopper [II] chlorate), and double salts. Examples of booster and secondary explosives include nitroglycerine, TNT

Table 5.3   Improvised Explosive Device (IED) Safe Standoff Distance Cheat Sheet

	Threat Description	Explosives Mass[1] (TNT equivalent)	Building Evacuation Distance[2]	Outdoor Evacuation Distance[3]
High Explosives	Pipe bomb	5 lbs (2.3kg)	70 ft (21 m)	850 ft (259 m)
	Suicide belt	10 lbs (4.5 kg)	90 ft (27 m)	1080 ft (330 m)
	Suicide vest	20 lbs (9 kg)	110 ft (34 m)	1360 ft (415 m)
	Briefcase/suitcase bomb	50 lbs (23 kg)	150 ft (46 m)	1850 ft (564 m)
	Compact sedan	500 lbs (227 kg)	320 ft (98 m)	1500 ft (457 m)
	Sedan	1000 lbs (454 kg)	400 ft (122 m)	1750 ft (534 m)
	Passenger/cargo van	4000 lbs (1814 kg)	640 ft (195 m)	2750 ft (838 m)
	Small moving van/delivery truck	10,000 lbs (4536 kg)	860 ft (263 m)	3750 ft (1143 m)
	Moving van/ water truck	30,000 lbs (13,608 kg)	1,240 ft (375 m)	6500 ft (1982 m)
	Semi trailer	60,000 lbs (27,216 kg)	1,570 ft (475 m)	7000 ft (2134 m)

	Threat Description	LPG Mass/Volume[1]	Fireball Diameter[4]	Safe Distance[5]
*LPG	Small LPG tank	8	40 ft (12m)	160 ft (48 m)
	Large LPG tank	100 lbs/25 gal 45 kg/95 l	69 ft (21 m)	276 ft (84 m)
	Commercial/ residential LPG tank	2000 lbs/500 gal (907 kg/1893 l)	184 ft (56 m)	736 ft (224 m)
	Small LPG truck	8000 lbs/2000 gal (3630 kg/7570 l)	292 ft (89 m)	1168 ft (356 m)
	Semi tanker (MC 336)	40,000 lbs/10,000 gal (18,144 kg/37,850 l)	499 ft (152 m)	1996 ft (608 m)

*   Liquefied petroleum gas (LPG) (mixture of petroleum gases) or propane or butane.

** Trinitrotoluene (TNT) equivalent.

[1] Based on the maximum amount of material that could reasonably fit into a container or vehicle; variations possible.

[2] Governed by the ability of an unreinforced building to withstand severe damage or collapse.

[3] Governed by the greater of fragment throw distance or glass breakage/falling glass hazard distance. These distances can be reduced for personnel wearing ballistic protection. Note that the pipe bomb, suicide belt/vest, and briefcase/suitcase bomb are assumed to have a fragmentation characteristic that requires greater standoff distances than an equal amount of explosives in a vehicle.

[4] Assuming efficient mixing of the flammable gas with ambient air.

[5] Determined by U.S. firefighting practices wherein safe distances are approximately 4 times the flame height. Note that an LPG tank filled with high explosives would require a significantly greater standoff distance than if it were filled with LPG.

Source: U.S. Army National Ground Intelligence Center (NGIC).

(trinitrotoluene), RDX/cyclonite/cyclotrimethylenetrinitramine, PBX, PETN (pentarytritholtertranitrate), nitrostarch, cellulose nitrate (guncotton), ammonium nitrate, potassium chlorate, amatol, urea nitrate, and others. Nitroglycerine is the most powerful of all explosives known. Nitro is the standard against which all other explosives are measured.

Types of Chemical Explosions

Detonation is an instantaneous decomposition of the explosive material. All of the solid material changes to a gas instantaneously, with the release of high heat and pressure shock waves. Detonation is the only type of chemical explosion that will produce a true shock wave. A material that detonates is considered a high-yield explosive. Blast pressures can be as much as 700 tons per square inch. Pressure and heat waves and shrapnel or fragments, travel away from the center of the blast equally in all directions. The reaction occurs at supersonic speed or, in other words, faster than the speed of sound, which is 1,250 feet per second. Many of the reactions occur above 3,300 feet per second, up to 29,900 feet per second, or over 20,300 miles per hour. At that speed you could travel from Los Angeles to New York in 7 $^1/_2$ minutes. Often the terms explosion and detonation are used interchangeably, which is not accurate. An explosion may very well be a detonation; however, an explosion that is not a detonation can occur. In either case, the explosions occur very rapidly, and the difference cannot be distinguished very well by the human senses. The only way you can tell the difference between a detonation and a deflagration is by hearing the sound of the explosion. During a detonation the explosion will be seen and the shock wave sent off before the explosion is actually heard. During a deflagration, the explosion will be heard almost immediately. Detonation and deflagration are terms that only apply to the speed of the explosion and some of the characteristics; they do not infer that one is any less dangerous than the other.

Deflagration is a rapid auto combustion, which occurs at a subsonic speed (less than the speed of sound), or less than 1,250 feet per second. The solid material changes to a gas relatively slowly. A material that deflagrates is considered a low-yield explosive. Explosive material that is designed to deflagrate may, however, under the right conditions produce a detonation. Explosions that occurred at the World Trade Center and the Murrah Federal Building were caused by what are considered to be low-yield fillers that deflagrate. However, the material that was used in those bombings detonated, producing a great deal of physical damage to the structures, more so in Oklahoma City than at the World Trade Center. The bomb used in the Oklahoma City bombing was four times larger than the World Trade Center bomb.

Two Phases of Explosions

An explosion creates two phases of blast pressure, the positive and the negative. The positive phase occurs first as the blast wave travels outward, releasing its energy to objects that it comes in contact with. This is also known as the blast pressure. Blast pressure is generally the most destructive element of an explosion. If an explosion is a detonation, blast waves will travel outward equally in all directions away from the center of the explosion. The negative phase begins as the outward movement reaches its maximum range. A partial vacuum is created near the center of the explosion by all of the outward movement of air from the blast pressure. During the negative phase debris from the explosion, smoke, and gases produced by the positive phase of the blast are drawn back toward the center of the explosion's origin by the subsequent vacuum. All of the smoke, gases, and debris then rise in a thermal column vertically into the air and are eventually carried downwind by air currents. The negative phase may last up to three times longer than the positive phase. If the explosion is a result of an exothermic (heat producing) chemical reaction, which usually occurs as the result of a detonation, the shock wave may be preceded by a high temperature thermal wave, which can ignite combustible materials. The amount of heat produced depends on the ingredients used to make the explosive material. Heat generated by high explosives is generally greater than that of low explosives; however, the thermal effects from low explosives tend to last longer. Explosive devices may be designed to spread shrapnel when the explosion occurs. Examples are anti-personnel munitions, hand grenades, and pipe bombs filled with nails, screws, glass, and other sharp materials. Explosive materials may be placed in metal, plastic, wooden, glass, or cardboard containers to provide the necessary confinement for an explosion to occur. Fragments of these containers may become projectiles when an explosion occurs. Projectiles from an explosion travel out equally in all directions from the blast center as do the blast and thermal waves. Homemade explosive devices that may be designed by terrorists to produce fragmentation include vehicle bombs, pipe bombs, satchel devices, and others of types limited only by the imagination of the terrorist. Blasts that occur in structures can also produce flying debris from the construction components of the building, which are torn apart by the force of the explosion and can cause injury and death.

In order for responders to have maximum protection in terms of distance from the effects of an explosion, the isolation areas must be a 360° circumference around the center of the blast or explosive object. In order for the waves or projectiles coming off an explosion to travel equally in all directions, the velocity (speed) of the release of high-pressure gases must be supersonic, or faster than the speed of sound. This occurs only in a detonation, not in a

Figure 5.9 Briefcase bomb with steel nuts for fragmentation and triggered by a cell phone.

deflagration. However, responders may not know the type of explosive material that has been used, so they should always use the 360° isolation area. Distances can be found in the Emergency Response Guide Book, but in no case should be less than 1,000 yards.

In April 1996, a pipe bomb exploded outside the city hall in Spokane, Washington. The blast caused minor damage, blowing out the windows in the front door, but no one was hurt. This was largely because the bomb went off between 3:30 and 5:45 AM, before any employees reported for work. Shrapnel, which included construction nails, was found 100 yards away from the scene of the blast. No one called to warn of the bomb or to claim responsibility after it went off. The incident might have been related to two other bombings in Spokane Valley earlier in the month. In those incidents, a bank and newspaper office were targeted. No injuries were reported in any of the bombings. Later in the day about 40 guests of the West Coast Ridpath Hotel were evacuated when a suspicious briefcase was discovered in the lobby. It turned out that it was not dangerous.

Yield vs. Order

The yield of an explosive material is associated with the rate or speed in which the explosion involving the material occurs. This is an indication as to whether an explosive will detonate or deflagrate. A high-yield explosive material detonates, and the blast pressure shatters materials that it contacts. Examples of high-yield explosives are dynamite, trinitrotoluene (TNT), nitroglycerin, detchord, C-3, C-4, Semtex, RDX (cyclonite), PETN (Pentaerythrite tetranitrate), and military bombs. According to the American

Broadcasting Company (ABC) News, Semtex is one of the most powerful plastic explosives in the world. It is suspected of being the material used in the bombings of the Pan American flight over Lockerbie, Scotland; the explosions in Riyadh, Saudi Arabia; and the summer 1998 bombings of U.S. embassies in Kenya and Tanzania. The two primary components of Semtex are RDX and PETN, which are powerful explosives in their own right. Explosive devices and materials can be manufactured inexpensively by someone with the appropriate chemical background using a simple laboratory. Semtex is a favorite choice of terrorists because x-ray machines and chemical "sniffing" instruments might not detect it. It appears that only specially trained dogs can detect its weak odor. Semtex is similar to the American-made C-4 plastic explosive, which is safe to handle and can be burned without exploding. In fact, American servicemen commonly burned C-4 as a fuel for heating C-rations during Vietnam and other wars. It is estimated that only 45 pounds of Semtex was used to bomb the Saudi military building in Riyadh. Seven people, including five U.S. military advisors, were killed in the explosion. The entire front side of the three-story building was blown away by the relatively small amount of Semtex. A much smaller amount was used to down Pan American Flight 103 over Lockerbie, Scotland in 1988, where 270 people lost their lives. It is suspected by the Jane's Information Group that some three metric tons of Semtex is in the hands of the Irish Republican Army (IRA).

A low-yield explosive material deflagrates and is used to push and shove materials. Examples of low-yield explosives are black powder and commercial grade ammonium nitrate (ANFO). Ammonium nitrate is an explosive material that can also be made by terrorists using ammonium nitrate fertilizer and fuel oil or other hydrocarbon fuel. Deflagrating materials are often used to move rocks in road construction, quarries, and mining operations.

The term order refers to the extent and rate of a detonation. A high-order detonation is one in which all of the explosive material was consumed in the explosion, and the explosion occurred at the proper rate. Proper rate in this case would be at supersonic speed. So, a low-order explosion would occur as an incomplete detonation or at less than the desired rate. Yield involves the specific explosive material that is used, and order indicates the way in which the explosive detonated. The hazards to emergency responders are obvious. If an explosion is low order, not all of the explosive material has been consumed; therefore, the remaining material presents a hazard. High- or low-yield, high- or low-order explosives should all be treated as high-yield, high-order explosives by emergency responders, because there may be no means of telling the difference. The explosives used in the World Trade Center and Oklahoma City bombings were considered low order.

Improvised Explosive Devices

Bombs used in the New York City and Oklahoma City explosions were vehicle bombs. These types are characteristically large and powerful. Vehicles are fitted with quantities of explosive materials, coupled with timed or remote triggering devices. In both of the above cases, the vehicle used was a rented moving-type truck. More commonly, however, the explosive device chosen by terrorist bombers is the pipe bomb. Pipe bombs are very easy to make; the components for confining the black powder can be obtained at almost any hardware store. A recent report from the U.S. Air Force Office of Special Investigations shows an increase in the use of flashlights as housings for explosive devices (Figure 5.10). Typically, the flashlights will be left at the crime scene of an arson or explosion to kill or injure unsuspecting response personnel. One law enforcement officer has been killed, several injured, and a number of civilians injured from these devices. The flashlights are metal, similar to the Mag lights used by many response organizations. Batteries are removed, and a small pipe bomb is inserted. The device is then set to go off when the switch is turned on or when the flashlight is moved. When flashlights are found at the scene of an arson or bombing, do not touch them. Contact appropriate bomb technicians for examination and disposal if needed. ATF has reported about 20 such devices found between 1997 and 1998. The typical person making a pipe bomb is a young, white male. Many people get hurt experimenting with construction of pipe bombs. Pipe bombs have been used to intimidate people, particularly in the illegal drug trade. They have become a popular weapon of the terrorist, both domestic and international. However, they are usually more unstable and dangerous than some military explosives.

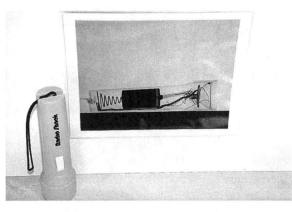

Figure 5.10   X-ray of flashlight bomb.

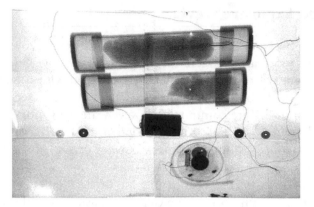

Figure 5.11 X-ray of briefcase bomb.

Between 1990 and 2004, 49 people were killed and another 434 injured during 1,863 pipe bombings reported to the ATF. Another 844 reports of attempted bombings were recorded. Pipe bombs are commonly small in nature and explosive power but can still be deadly to anyone in the vicinity when the device explodes. They can be filled with low-order gunpowder or higher-order plastic explosives. Timing devices can be attached and rigged to go off at any time. Often the pipe bombs are laced with nails, screws, glass, or other sharp objects designed to cause injury to people. The device used in the Olympic Park bombing was actually three pipe bombs placed in a satchel or canvas backpack. Backpacks are presently very popular with almost all age groups and would not be considered uncommon or out of place in almost any setting, which makes satchel and backpack explosive devices all the more dangerous. Almost any type of container that would provide confinement for an explosive material could also be used to fashion a homemade explosive device. These include glass jars, pieces of metal and plastic pipe, cardboard tubes, and various tools and appliances.

Letter and Package Bombs

While it is important to watch for suspicious items in the mail, it is very rare for the mail to be used to send explosive devices. Postal inspectors investigate, on average, 16 mail bomb incidents each year. This is in contrast to over 170 billion pieces of mail processed. Therefore, the chance of receiving a piece of mail that actually contains a bomb is less than one in 10 billion. However, it is still important to be on the lookout for suspicious articles of mail (Figure 5.12). During 1991, in Dumfries, Virginia, a postal worker noticed a suspicious package in a mail collection box. It contained a bomb intended for the sender's former husband. Quick action by the letter carrier may have saved

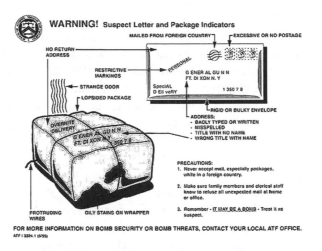

Figure 5.12   Letter bomb warning signs. (Source: ATF.)

the man's life. Package or letter bombs can be built to resemble almost anything that the terrorist wants them to be. They can be delivered in many different ways. In fact, when watching for a mail device, it may be very difficult to find one that looks like a stereotypical bomb. There might only be one common thread among all mail bombs, and that is they are designed to explode. The vast majority of mail bombs used during terrorists attacks or during criminal activity are homemade. The design of the explosive device is limited only by the imagination of the bomber and what he or she wants to accomplish. When an unexploded mail bomb is suspected, look for anything that is unusual about the article. Once a suspicious letter or package is located, the bomb squad determines if the object is a bomb or not. Most mail bombs are not actually delivered by the Postal Service; the bombers prefer to set up and deliver the devices themselves. Shown below is a list that ATF and the Postal Service have developed for characteristics of mail bombs, which have appeared time and time again.

- If delivered by carrier, inspect for lumps, bulges, or protrusions, without applying pressure.
- The postmark might show a different location than the return address.
- Mail bombs might display distorted handwriting, or the name and address might be prepared with homemade labels or cut-and-paste lettering.
- Parcel bombs might be unprofessionally wrapped with several combinations of tape used to secure the package, and might be endorsed "Fragile — Handle With Care" or "Rush — Do Not Delay."
- Letter bombs might feel rigid, or appear uneven or lopsided.

- If delivered by carrier, and is lopsided or heavy sided
- Handwritten addresses or labels from companies are improper. Check to see if the company exists and if they sent a package or letter.
- Packages wrapped in string are automatically suspicious, as modern packaging materials have eliminated the need for twine or string.
- Excess postage on small packages or letters indicates that the object was not weighed by the Postal Service.
- No postage or non-canceled postage.
- Any foreign writing, addresses, or postage.
- Handwritten notes, such as: "To Be Opened in the Privacy of ...," "CONFIDENTIAL," "Your Lucky Day is Here," "Prize Enclosed," etc.
- Improper spelling of common names, places, or titles.
- Generic or incorrect titles.
- Leaks, stains, or protruding wires, string, tape, etc.
- Hand delivered or dropped off for a friend.
- No return address or nonsensical return address.
- Any letters or packages arriving before or after a phone call from an unknown person asking if the item was received.

Because of the sheer volume of mail, the Postal Service cannot screen each piece. However, if a suspicious piece of mail is detected, postal inspectors can respond quickly. Each inspection service field division has trained and equipped bomb specialists to provide assistance. If for any reason a suspicious letter or package is found, the following safety precautions should be taken.

- Do not open the article.
- Isolate the suspect parcel or letter and evacuate the immediate area.
- Do not put, move, or attempt to place it in water or a confined space, such as a desk drawer or cabinet.
- If possible, open windows in the immediate area to assist in venting potentially explosive gases.
- Do not worry about possible embarrassment if the item turns out to be innocent. It is better to be safe than sorry.

If you have a suspicious letter or package, call 911 — ISOLATE — EVACUATE!

During January 1997, two greeting-type cards were found at the Washington, D.C. headquarters of the *Al-Hayat* newspaper at the National Press Building. Two others were discovered later in the afternoon at the same address. One additional card was located at the Brentwood Postal Facility in northeast Washington. At the Federal Penitentiary at Leavenworth, Kansas, two more cards were found addressed to the parole officer. One of the cards had been partially opened at the newspaper office, and an employee noticed wires inside the envelope. The card was turned over to the FBI and determined to have contained a bomb. All of the other cards were seized before they were opened. None of the devices exploded. Plain white envelopes contained the cards and disguised bombs. They measured 5 $^1/_2$ × 6 $^1/_2$ inches and had computer-generated addresses on the front. There was no return address, and the cards were postmarked Alexandria, Egypt, December 21, 1996.

Explosives under ATF Jurisdiction

The ATF publishes, at least annually, a listing of explosives determined to be within their jurisdiction under 18 U.S. Code (U.S.C.) Chapter 40 (a listing of ATF-regulated explosives can be found in Appendix D). This Federal Code covers the importation, manufacture, distribution, and storage of explosive materials. It covers not only explosives but also blasting agents and detonators. Explosive materials can be identified by their reaction, composition, or military use. New regulations introduced late in 1998 have a direct impact on fire departments across the country. Effective December 22, 1998, anyone who stores explosives must notify the local fire department of the location(s) of explosives' storage or manufacturing. Information can be obtained from the ATF Web site at www.atf.trea.gov or by calling the ATF Public Affairs Office at 202-927-8500.

Ammonium nitrate is generally considered to be a fertilizer in its simplest form. It is available from almost any agricultural supply store, home garden center, and local discount store. Ammonium nitrate is also considered a strong chemical oxidizer (one of the necessary ingredients for a chemical explosive). When contaminated, or purposely mixed with fuel oil or other hydrocarbon, an explosive mixture is formed. A commercial-grade explosive made from ammonium nitrate and fuel oil is also available but requires a license to purchase and use. Whether homemade or commercial grade, ammonium nitrate is a powerful low-order blasting agent. Ammonium nitrate is a colorless-to-white crystal solid that is soluble in water (Figure 5.13). It may explode when confined or exposed to high temperatures, but it does not easily detonate. When contaminated or prilled (coated with wax), it explodes much more readily. Ammonium nitrate and fuel oil mixtures were used in both the Oklahoma City and World Trade Center bombings. There are not any restrictions on the purchase of fertilizer-grade ammonium nitrate, so it can be easily obtained and mixed with fuel oil to make an explosive mixture.

Black powder is a low-order explosive filler made up of a mixture of potassium nitrate ("salt peter") or sodium nitrate, charcoal, and sulfur in 75,

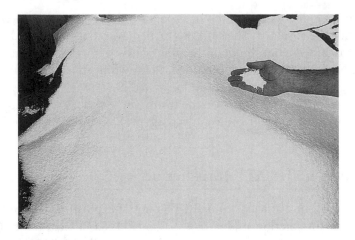

Figure 5.13   Pure ammonium nitrate before mixing with fuel oil.

15, and 10% proportions. Its consistency varies from a fine powder to dense
pellets, which can be black or grayish black. Sometimes powdered aluminum
or other metals may be added to improve the explosive punch. Danger from
fire and explosion is very high, it is sensitive to heat, and it will deflagrate
rapidly. Black powder is one of the most common explosive materials used
in the building of a pipe bomb. It can be made easily without the use of any
sophisticated equipment, with chemicals commonly found in any chemical
supply catalog. Some ingredients, such as the potassium nitrate or sodium
nitrate, may be purchased at some local drug stores.

Nitrogen triiodide, black unstable crystals, explode at the slightest touch
when dry. When handled, it is kept wet with ether. It is too sensitive to be
used as an explosive because it cannot be stored, handled, or transported.
Azides, such as lead azide and hydrazoic azide, are very unstable. Lead azide
is a severe explosion risk, should be handled under water, and is also a
primary detonating compound. Hydrazoic acid or hydrogen azide is a dangerous explosion risk when shocked or heated. Metal fulminates, such as
mercury fulminate, explode readily when dry. It is used in the manufacture
of caps and detonators for producing explosions. Ammonium chlorate,
which is shock-sensitive, can detonate when exposed to heat or vibration. It
is used in the production of explosives. Ammonium perchlorate is also shock-
sensitive and may explode when exposed to heat or by spontaneous chemical
reaction. This is the material that was involved in the explosion at the Pepcon
plant in Henderson, Nevada. It is used in the production of explosives,
pyrotechnics, etching, engraving, and jet and rocket propellants. Diethylene
glycol dinitrate is a severe explosion hazard when shocked or heated. It is
used as a plasticizer in solid rocket propellants.

Dynamite is moderately sensitive to shock and heat and may also ignite when in contact with powerful oxidizing agents. It is primarily made of nitroglycerin (straight dynamite) combined with a porous filler such as sawdust, as a desensitizer, or with special formulations made up of sensitized ammonium nitrate (ammonium gelatin dynamite) dispersed in carbonaceous materials. Dynamite is packaged in cylindrical cartridges, approximately 1 inch in diameter and 8 inches in length, and enclosed in a heavy water-repellent paper. An indication that dynamite is old is the appearance of an oily substance on the casing of the cartridges, or stains on the wooden packing case. This can be attributed to the separation of the nitroglycerin from the porous base. Dynamite in this state is extremely sensitive. Unstable dynamite should be destroyed immediately by explosives-handling experts.

Nitroglycerin is a pale yellow, viscous liquid. It is slightly soluble in water with a specific gravity of 1.6, which is heavier than water. It is a severe explosion risk, and will explode spontaneously at 424°F. It is much less sensitive to shock when it is frozen. Nitroglycerin freezes at about 55°F. It is highly sensitive to shock and heat. It is toxic by ingestion, inhalation, and skin absorption. The TLV is 0.05 ppm in air. The primary uses are in explosives and dynamite manufacturing.

Trinitrotoluene (TNT) is flammable, a dangerous fire risk, and a moderate explosion risk. It is a light cream-to-rust color and is usually found in $1/2$- or 1-pound blocks. It is fairly stable in storage. TNT will detonate only if vigorously shocked or heated to 450°F. TNT is toxic by inhalation, ingestion, and skin absorption. The TLV is 0.5 mg/m^3 of air. TNT is one of the common ingredients used in military explosives, and is used as a measurement to calculate the blast effects of other explosives.

Trinitrophenol (picric acid) is composed of yellow crystals that are soluble in water. It is a high explosive that is shock and heat sensitive and will explode spontaneously at 572°F. Trinitrophenol is reactive with metals or metallic salts and is toxic by skin absorption. The TLV is 0.1 mg/m^3 of air. When shipped in 10–30% water, it is stable unless the water content drops below 10%, or it dries out completely. The primary uses are in explosives, matches, electric batteries, and etching copper. Picric acid is often found in chemical labs in high schools and colleges and can be a severe explosion hazard if the moisture content of the container is gone. Picric acid was used by the Japanese during World War II as a main charge explosive filler. When in contact with metal, picric acid will form other picrates that are extremely sensitive to heat, shock, and friction. Great care should be used when handling World War II souvenirs because of the possible presence of these picrates. When the structure of picric acid is compared with the structure of TNT, the only difference is the fuel that the nitro functional groups are

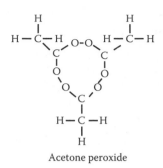

Acetone peroxide

Figure 5.14   Acetone peroxide structure.

attached to. The number of nitro groups are exactly the same. The explosive power of picric acid is very similar to that of TNT.

Acetone peroxide, also known as "Mother of Satan," 3,3,6,6,9,9-hexam-ethyl 1,2,4,5,7,8- hexaoxyacyclononane (tri-acetone tri-peroxide) (peroxy-acetone) (TATP) ($C_9H_{18}O_6$), is an organic peroxide. Acetone peroxide is one of the few explosives that can be quite easily made from materials that can be readily bought with no questions asked. It is a primary explosive that can be made from hair bleach (hydrogen peroxide, 27–30% works the best, although most "recipes" call for 3% because it is most common) easily obtained from drug stores and hair supply stores. Acetone (CH_3COCH_3) is a colorless, volatile, extremely flammable liquid ketone. It is often used as a solvent, which is why it is available in paint thinners that can be obtained from hardware stores and drug stores. Acetone is also a primary ingredient in nail polish remover, but 100% acetone is needed for the mixture. Sulfuric acid (H_2SO_4) is available from hardware stores and can be derived from clear battery acid boiled until white fumes appear (although battery acid is only a 40% concentration). Eighty-five percent concentration or higher is necessary for best results. This strength may be the most difficult of the three ingredients to locate. Ninety percent or higher sulfuric can be found in some drain cleaners. The structure for acetone peroxide is shown in Figure 5.14.

This explosive is primarily used in the fabrication of detonators. It is considered to be a primary explosive as well. Primary explosives can be used on their own, or in percussion caps, primers, and blasting caps to initiate secondary explosives. There are numerous sources on the Internet that give instructions for formulation of this explosive material. Acetone peroxide has been used by the Palestinians for many years in construction of bombs used against Israel. It is also the explosive material used by the bombers who attacked the London subway system and buses during the summer of 2005.

In the occupied Palestinian territories, you can tell who the "engineers" are; they are the ones covered in burn marks who might be missing fingers or even a whole hand. The engineers are the bomb makers for the young suicide bombers sent to kill Israelis by the Islamic militant organizations such as Hamas. Their explosive of choice is triacetone triperoxide (TATP). TATP generally burns when ignited unconfined in quantities less than about 2 grams. Above this it will usually detonate, although even slight confinement will promote detonation in smaller quantities. Completely dry TATP is much more prone to detonation as opposed to fresh product still wetted with water or acetone. The explosive decomposition of TATP, in contrast, results in "formation of acetone and ozone as the main decomposition products and not the intuitively expected oxidation products." It is the rapid creation of gas from a solid that creates the explosion. Very little heat is created by the explosive decomposition of TATP. Recent research describes TATP decomposition as an entropic explosion. The extreme shock, heat, and friction sensitivity are due to the instability of the molecule. Big crystals, found in older mixtures, are more dangerous, as they are easier to shatter and initiate than small ones. Many people have been killed or permanently injured by accidents with acetone peroxide. There is a common myth that the only "safe" acetone peroxide is the trimer, made at low temperatures. If one is making tricycloacetone peroxide, the temperature must be less than 10°C at all times, otherwise the product formed will be dicycloacetone peroxide, which is so unstable and sensitive that it has no uses in the field of explosives: dicyclo-acetone peroxide has been known to explode spontaneously. The trimer is the more stable form, but not much more so than the dimer. All forms of acetone peroxide are very sensitive to initiation and degrade in long-term storage, so they are used as explosives only by unconventional forces (e.g., guerrillas, freedom fighters, and terrorists) and curious amateurs. At the same time, no form of acetone peroxide will truly explode spontaneously. Acetone peroxide can also occur accidentally, when suitable chemicals are mixed together: for example, when methyl ethyl ketone is mixed with acetone when making fiberglass, and left to stand for some time, or when a mixture of peroxide and hydrochloric acid from printed circuit board etching (the $FeCl_3$ method is less smelly, more accurate, but slower) is mixed with waste acetone from cleaning the finished board and allowed to stand. While amounts obtained this way are typically much smaller than from intentional production, they are also less pure and prepared without cooling and, hence, very unstable. It is also a hazardous by-product of isosafrole oxidation in acetone, a step in illicit synthesis of MDMA, the street drug ecstasy. Acetone peroxide is not easily detected by currently trained explosives or bomb trained dogs. An Israeli scientist has developed a "pen" that is very effective in detection of acetone peroxide. This device is discussed in detail in Chapter 8.

Emergency responders encountering the above-mentioned ingredients or individuals presenting with the wounds described under suspicious circumstances should be extremely cautious and ensure to request police assistance.

Military explosives can be divided into two groups, high and low, based upon their rates of decomposition. They are noted for their high shattering power accompanied by rapid detonation velocities. Because they are often kept in storage for long periods of time, they must be very stable and safe for the personnel using them. Due to their intended use, they must detonate dependably after being stored and do so under a variety of conditions. Military explosives may release large quantities of toxic gases when they explode. Military explosives used most commonly are TNT (trinitrotoluene), C-3, C-4, and RDX cyclonite.

Nuclear Terrorism

6

Terrorists have shown a great degree of willingness to use violence and accept the idea of victims among innocent bystanders and emergency responders. Approximately 70% of all terrorist incidents have involved conventional explosives. Some have involved biological materials, nerve agents, and incendiary devices. However, terrorists have not yet been successful in the use of nuclear terrorism. This may not be because they do not want to; perhaps they have just not developed the technology or acquired the nuclear fuel yet in order to carry out such attacks. Terrorists have three general options when it comes to nuclear terrorism. These options include a nuclear device, a radioactive dirty bomb, or an attack on a nuclear power plant, resulting in the release of nuclear material into the atmosphere.

It is unknown if any terrorist organization has obtained the materials to construct a nuclear device. To build a nuclear device would require some technical expertise and the ability to acquire a suitable quantity of weapons-grade nuclear materials. There has been much discussion as to just how much nuclear material is necessary to develop an effective nuclear bomb. Some scientists have suggested one could be constructed with as little as 1 pound of weapons-grade material. Several seizures of nuclear materials have occurred in the world since 1992. Smugglers were arrested on December 14, 1994, in the Czech Republic possessing 2.72 kilograms (approximately 6.6 pounds) of highly enriched uranium (HEU). While the material was nearly 90% enriched with uranium-235 isotopes, by some accounts it would not be nearly enough material to build an atomic bomb. It has been reported by some research sources that 44 pounds (20 kilograms) of HEU would be needed to make a nuclear bomb. The source of the confiscated nuclear materials was thought to be the former Soviet Union. Research teams at the University of California report that, theoretically, as little as 3 kilograms could be used to produce a nuclear bomb. Computer modeling showed a nuclear yield equivalent to more than 100 tons of high explosives could be achieved with only 1 kilogram of HEU. Researchers believe that a nuclear bomb can be produced with much less HEU than previously thought. If, however, the materials could be obtained, that would be the most difficult portion of the equation. Without HEU or plutonium, building a nuclear bomb would be impossible. Even a crude nuclear device, built by terrorists that had no previous experience designing or building nuclear bombs, theoretically could still provide a yield of about 10 kilotons of TNT. Even if the bomb failed to produce its maximum explosive potential, a blast in the 100-ton range might still be expected from a crude device.

It is unknown if terrorists have actually obtained nuclear devices from the former Soviet Union or the black market. However, such devices would require codes to activate them, which further makes it unlikely terrorists could even use the devices if they had them. However, it is likely that if terrorists had possession of a device, they would certainly use it. Dirty bombs provide a much more likely scenario. Dirty bombs are composed of conventional explosives used to disseminate radioactive materials. Radioactive materials could potentially render an area uninhabitable for many years. The National Academy of Science reports that few, if any, people would actually die from radiation in a dirty bomb attack. Contamination is the real issue, and decontamination would be the difficult task. Environmental Protection Agency (EPA) guidelines indicate that decontamination would be necessary for contamination levels above 15 millirem of material. Therefore it is not necessary for everyone to go out and purchase potassium iodide, which is one type of antidote for radiation exposure (this will be discussed in detail later in the chapter). If an attack were to occur, it would be best to stay inside a building and wait for official instructions. Materials for dirty bombs could be obtained from a number of sources, the black market, medical isotopes, and industrial sources. Some medical isotopes might be useful, but most are too small to be used in dirty bombs. It would take approximately 1 curie of radioactive material to produce an effective dirty bomb.

Countries such as Iraq have spent large sums of money and have tried for years to develop a nuclear capability. As yet they have not been successful. How is it, then, that we could expect terrorist groups to have this capability? Intelligence sources have revealed that terrorist organizations, particularly al Qaeda, have shown an interest in nuclear power plants. Nuclear power plants would be particularly vulnerable to a September 11-type of aircraft assault. Mounting a ground assault would be much more difficult, but possible.

As convincing as the argument is that terrorists may resort to forms of nuclear terrorism to make clear their demands, to date no incidents have occurred in the U.S. involving the release of any form of nuclear materials. In fact, up to this time, there is no evidence or single case where a nongovernmental organization, a terrorist group, or an individual offender has come anywhere close to attaining "nuclear capability" through theft or through a "homemade" device. Nor has there been any attempt to contaminate public water or food supplies using nuclear materials. In other parts of the world terrorists have been a little more active with efforts to use nuclear terrorism. During the summer of 1994, three seizures of plutonium and one of HEU occurred in Germany. The amounts involved in these cases were small, less than a gram in quantity, and the source once again was suspected to be the former Soviet Union. Additional seizures occurred in St. Petersburg during March 1994 where 6 pounds of HEU were recovered. Three pounds of HEU were recovered near Moscow in December 1992, and 4 1/2 pounds recovered in Lithuania, also during 1992. Weapons-grade uranium in quantities necessary to construct a bomb would be very difficult to transport. Uranium-235 weighs approximately 18.7 times more than water, which is approximately 8.35 pounds per gallon. One gallon of uranium would weigh 156 pounds and a 55-gallon drum of uranium weighs 8,580 pounds.

Terrorist sources for nuclear materials could include hijacking spent nuclear fuel, acquiring it on the black market, or stealing the material from secure facilities. It is highly unlikely that spent nuclear fuel shipments or black market nuclear materials would be weapons grade, so further refining would be needed. This would require special technical information, specialized equipment, and financial backing. Even if terrorists were able to acquire the necessary amount of nuclear fuel to make a bomb, the weapon would function correctly only if the material is machined into exact geometric forms with correct quantities of explosives placed around the fuel. Placement is critical to ensure the proper creation of critical mass during the brief time necessary for the reaction to occur. Without following the proper procedures, the nuclear bomb will simply act as a dispersion device and scatter radioactive material around rather than creating a nuclear detonation. Obtaining an operational atomic bomb would be even more difficult to accomplish than making your own! Security surrounding atomic bombs in this country and other nations is so tight that it is not likely that a complete bomb could be obtained. If someone were able to acquire an atomic bomb, it is highly unlikely they would be able to get the access codes necessary to activate the device. Allied and Russian nuclear devices use the permissible action links (PAL) security system, which requires specific codes before the devices can be put to use.

The second type of potential nuclear terrorism involves using a conventional explosive device to disperse nuclear materials. This is a much more realistic scenario than the nuclear bomb detonation. Terrorists would pack radioactive materials around conventional explosives. When the device detonates, the nuclear materials would be dispersed over a specific area, based on the strength of the explosive and the amount of radioactive material present. Terrorists would not have to build a device that would produce a nuclear yield; they could just use a device to disperse lethal amounts of radioactivity over several hundred yards. According to the Department of Defense, a radiological dispersal device (RDD) is defined as "any device, including weapons or equipment other than a nuclear explosive device, that is specially constructed to scatter radioactive material to cause destruction, damage, or injury by means of radioactive decay." Almost any type of radioactive material could be used as the source of radiation fission products, including spent nuclear fuel from reactors, low-level medical, research, and industrial waste. Scattering of the radioactive material through the use of a dispersion device would cause widespread contamination over a large area. Radiation sickness could also be caused to those exposed. Different types of radioactive materials would produce different degrees of lethality. If two RDDs were exploded at the Washington Monument in Washington, D.C., using 100 pounds of high explosives and two different radioactive sources, the lethality caused by each explosive would be vastly different. For example, cobalt-12 would produce a maximum dosage at the point of detonation of 12 rem, which would result in no deaths. However, a RDD using spent nuclear fuel rods would produce a dosage at the point of detonation of 3,064 rem — six times the lethal dose! This lethal dose would extend a distance of potential death approximately 1 kilometer into the surrounding area of the capital.

Radiological effects that might occur among the population exposed to radiation can be short and long term. In the short term, people can experience radiation burns and acute poisoning. Long-term effects include the development of cancer. Another danger to the public would be the contamination of water and food supplies by radioactive particles. When the Chernobyl nuclear power plant disaster occurred, a large amount of nuclear material was released, and the environment remains damaged to this day. When a nuclear power plant reactor explodes or is damaged such as in Chernobyl, iodine 131 and cobalt are released. Following Chernobyl, 25 m curries of iodine 131 were detected in Sweden and Denmark. Forty million curries were released. Responders were exposed to 12,000 rads. There are still spots of 10,000 rads at the site to this day. Helicopter pilots received 1,800 rads per hour at the site. This type of material certainly could come into the hands of terrorists. In November 1995, a conventional bomb containing radioactive cesium (a source of gamma radiation) was found in Ismailovsky Park in Moscow. Fortunately, it was discovered before it exploded.

Terrorists might choose a third form of unleashing nuclear terrorism by targeting facilities that have nuclear materials (Figure 6.1). These include military installations, nuclear-powered ships, power plants, waste facilities, fuel processing plants, university research centers, and weapons construction and maintenance facilities. Recently, the U.S. Nuclear Regulatory Commission (NRC) took action to protect nuclear power plants from truck or vehicle bombs. Two unrelated incidents in 1993 caused Congress to take an interest

Figure 6.1 Truck transporting spent nuclear fuel rods, which could become the target of a terrorist highjacking.

in the security of nuclear power plants. On February 7, 1993, an unarmed intruder crashed through a gate at the Three Mile Island nuclear power facility near Harrisburg, Pennsylvania, and crashed his car into the turbine building. Experts have long contended there are two potential threats to nuclear power plants. First would be a vehicle crashing through fences and other barriers to gain access to a facility. Second is the concern that a bomb could be placed in a vehicle outside the security area of the facility. Many of the safeguards required by the NRC are not public information for obvious reasons. Security measures have been developed to protect nuclear power plants. Phase I security actions include preventing vehicle intrusion and vehicle bombs. Phase II actions will require protection against large groups of intruders using sophisticated weapons. Negotiations between the nuclear power industry and the NRC resulted in a compromise. The industry was favored in the decisions, which involved a reduction of the size of the bomb they were required to protect against. Construction features of nuclear power plants that provide safety to the public during normal operations also make them unattractive targets for terrorists. Reinforced concrete containment structures, along with redundant safety and shutdown systems, have been designed to permit a facility to withstand the impact of earthquakes, hurricanes, tornadoes, floods, and plane crashes. Commercial nuclear power plants have highly trained and well-armed security forces that protect reactor sections of the facilities. Perimeter fences are patrolled and monitored by closed-circuit television and alarm devices. Access to sensitive areas of the plants are controlled by security forces that search all people and vehicles entering or leaving the facility. An attempted intrusion at the Three Mile

Figure 6.2   Nuclear power plants may become the target of terrorism.

Island Nuclear Power Plant in 1993 was foiled by security forces. The NRC investigation indicated that the security forces and systems functioned as they were supposed to, and the incident was termed "insignificant" in terms of public health and safety.

In the U.S., approximately 20% of our power is produced by 103 nuclear power plants. Presently, there are nuclear power plants in 31 states, while the remaining 19 states have no nuclear power capability. The first plant opened in the U.S. in 1954 in Shippingport, Pennsylvania. By the late 1960s, there were 13 plants; in the 1970s, this figure grew to 70. Because of the heavy security involving the sensitive areas of the plants, it is unlikely that a terrorist could cause the release of any nuclear radiation by any covert actions at a nuclear power plant. They could still disrupt the operation of the plant, resulting in the loss of power for many thousands of customers (Figure 6.2). If an attack force was large enough, they could possibly overpower the security at a nuclear power plant.

An incident was reported at Brown's Ferry Nuclear Power Station, Unit 2, on April 6, 1981. Investigation by the FBI revealed two switches controlling the circulating water system failed, resulting in the tripping of two circulating water pumps at the intake structure. A third pump remained in service. Tampering with the switches did not pose a safety threat to the facility at any time. No evidence was found by the FBI that would indicate who might have been responsible. On April 19, 1983, another report of intentional damage was reported from Diablo Canyon, Unit 1. Workers found damage to a piping surface in the form of an inch deep by 2-inch long gouge alongside a smaller gouge. Investigation determined that the gouges could have not been accidental. A fire occurred at the Brown's Ferry, Unit 2, on November 2, 1987. The 30-minute fire resulted in damage to hundreds of safety and nonsafety cables. Intensity of the fire caused suspicion that an accelerant might have been used, and tests revealed the presence of gasoline in samples of the affected cables. It is not known if any of these incidents were acts of terrorism. Even so, a nuclear power plant could become a terrorist target. The motive might not be to spread nuclear radiation, but could be to disrupt power to a large number of customers. One of the best-known nuclear power plant accidents in the U.S. occurred at Three Mile Island in 1979. Doses of 1.5 millirem occurred to people living within 50 miles of the power plant. Subsequent studies have shown that there are no unusual increases in cancer rates to those exposed as a result of the accident.

Definition of Radioactive Material

According to the U.S. Department of Transportation (DOT), a radioactive material is "any material having a specific activity greater than 0.002 microcuries per gram." Specific activity of a radionuclide means "the activity of the radionuclide per unit mass of that nuclide." Simply stated, a microcurie is a measurement of radioactivity. When a radioactive material emits more than 0.002 microcuries per gram of material, which is a term of weight, the material is then regulated in transportation by the DOT. The NRC regulates radioactive materials and wastes used and stored in fixed facilities. Radioactive materials in the U.S. are used at medical facilities, nuclear power plants, research facilities, agriculture, industry, and found in consumer products. Medical uses will be discussed later in this chapter. Nearly 100 Navy submarines and five surface ships powered by nuclear fuel are in use by the U.S. and its allies. Industrial uses of radiation include high-precision measurements and imaging. Radiation is used to detect structural cracks and stresses in airplanes, pipelines, and other critical equipment. Smoke detectors rely on a tiny radioactive source of americium-241 to sound the alarm when smoke is sensed. Radiation is used to sterilize baby powder, bandages, contact lens solutions, and many cosmetics, including false eyelashes, mascara, and hair products. Small amounts of radiation are used in photocopiers to reduce static and keep paper sheets from sticking together, which could otherwise jam the machine. Radiation is used to toughen rubber and make tires on our vehicles safer. Reflective traffic signs and glow-in-the-dark exit signs are made up of radioactive materials to improve visibility at nighttime. With so many uses and sources of radioactive materials, it would not be difficult for a terrorist to obtain small amounts.

History of Radiation

Radiation is a phenomenon characterized more by its ability to cause biological effects than where it originates. Radiation was first discovered by

German scientist Antoine Henri Becquerel, who received the Nobel Prize of Physics in 1903 for his work. Many of the terms associated with radioactivity come from those early pioneers in radiation physics, including Wilhelm Conrad Roentgen (1845–1923) as well as Pierre (1859–1906) and Marie Curie (1867–1934), who also received the Nobel Prize in Physics in 1903 for their work on radiation. Ernest Rutherford (1871–1937) is considered the father of nuclear physics. He developed the language that describes the theoretical concepts of the atom and the phenomenon of radioactivity. Particles named and characterized by him include the alpha particle, beta particle, and proton. Rutherford won the Nobel Prize for Chemistry in 1909 for his work. The effects of radiation have been studied for over 100 years. Scientists know a great deal about how to detect, monitor, and control even the smallest amounts of radiation. More is known about the health effects of radiation than any chemical or biological agent. Radiation is naturally occurring and is a part of everyday life. It is present in the earth's crust, travels from outer space, and is in the air and rocks. Radiation can also be human made. Our way of life is characterized by the many uses of human-made radiation. Radioisotopes are used in medicine, scientific research, energy production, manufacturing, mineral exploration, agriculture, and consumer products. Radioisotopes can come from three sources. They are naturally occurring, such as radon in the air or radium in the soil. Linear accelerators and cyclotrons can produce radioisotopes as well as a nuclear reactor. Forty-seven nuclear reactors, primarily located in colleges and universities, are licensed in research facilities around the U.S. by the NRC.

While highly unlikely, if a terrorist or foreign country did obtain a nuclear device, the damage could be significant. A nuclear detonation involves energy being released from a nuclear reaction — either fission or fusion — rather than a chemical reaction. Changes that occur during the nuclear reaction are the result of changes in the nuclei of the reacting material rather than changes in the electron shells, which is what happens during a chemical reaction. Energy produced from a nuclear reaction is many times greater than what would be produced from a chemical reaction. To understand the concept of nuclear reaction, it is necessary to study the elements (particularly those that are radioactive) and atomic structure. Elements are the building blocks of all matter on the earth. There are 109 identified elements listed on the periodic table of elements. Of the 109 elements, 92 occur in nature.

Atomic Structure

The smallest part that any element can be reduced to is an atom of that element. An atom can also be broken down into its component parts, sometimes referred to as subatomic particles. Atoms contain a nucleus and varying orbitals of electrons around the outside of the nucleus. Generally, chemical reactions involve the electrons in the outer shell of any given element. Radioactivity, on the other hand, involves the nucleus of the atom. Within the nucleus there are two subatomic particles, protons and neutrons. Protons have a positive charge, while neutrons do not have a charge and are considered neutral. Electrons orbiting around the outside of the nucleus are negatively charged. An atom must be electrically balanced and therefore must have an equal number of negative charges in the electrons orbiting the nucleus as there are positive-charged protons in the nucleus. Numbers of protons within the nucleus of atoms vary from element to element. It is, in fact, the number of protons within an element's nucleus that identifies that element. The atomic number of an element is the number of protons present in the nucleus of an atom. The number is located on the periodic table of elements and is the whole number by the element without any decimal points. Atoms of the same element may contain varying numbers of neutrons in the nucleus. When the number of neutrons differs from the normal, but the number of protons is the same, it is said to be an isotope of that element. Atomic weight or mass of an element is determined by the combined weights of the protons and neutrons in the nucleus. Neutrons and protons of an element are represented on the periodic table by the atomic weight. This is the number by the element symbol with a decimal point.

Most chemical elements, in fact, exist as mixtures of isotopes. Less than 25% of the elements exist as a single isotopic form. Most isotopes are not radioactive and therefore do not emit any radiation. Isotopes that do not emit radiation are considered to be stable isotopes. Those isotopes that do not have a stable nucleus are considered to have a degree of nuclear instability, which manifests itself as radioactivity. Everything in nature must be stable, so the isotope with the excess neutrons tends to throw out the material from the nucleus. Isotopes that emit ionizing radiation spontaneously from the nucleus are considered radioisotopes. Material thrown out from the nucleus of an atom is known as radioactivity and is emitted in the form of ionizing radiation. Ionizing radiation is radiation capable of removing an electron from a target atom or molecule, forming an ion pair. This process of emitting ionizing radiation may also be referred to as radioactive decay. The process of radioactive decay varies in terms of time it takes to emit all of the excess material in the nucleus.

Radioactive half-life is a term used to express the time it takes for half of the atoms of a given sample of an isotope to decay. Half-life can range from fractions of a millionth of a second to billions of years. No matter what the half-life, some small amounts of nuclei would still remain. It remains theoretically possible that given enough time, all of the atoms would eventually decay. Potassium-40, a radioisotope, has a half-life of 12,500 years. During the first 12,500 years, half of the potassium-40 decays, which means that 50% of the potassium-40 still exists. During the next 12,500 years, that will be reduced by half. The remaining potassium-40 after 25,000 years will be 25%. Each additional 12,500 years will reduce the remaining amount by half. Other radioisotope half-lives include uranium-235 (235U) (704 million years), uranium-238 (238U) (4,470 million years), thorium-232 (232Th) (14,010 million years), and rubidium-87 (87Rb) (48,800 million years). Potassium is an element that has three naturally occurring isotopes: potassium-39 (39K), potassium-40 (40K), and potassium-41 (41K). Potassium-39 and -41 are stable isotopes and comprise 99.99% of all isotopes of potassium. Potassium-40 exists in only 0.01% of all isotopes of potassium but emits radiation and is considered a radioisotope of potassium. These percentages of potassium isotopes are constant in all encounters with potassium. So, since the human body has approximately 150–200 grams of potassium, 15–20 milligrams exist as the radioisotope potassium-40. There is also radioactivity in the air we breathe. Radiation from the sun causes atmospheric nitrogen to produce the carbon radioisotope, carbon-14 (14C) and radioactive hydrogen (tritium, 3H) through a nuclear reaction. Carbon-14 enters the Earth's carbon pool and is fixed by photosynthesis in green plants, which are then consumed by humans and animals. Human exposure also occurs by eating the animals that have eaten the carbon-14 present in the plants. Throughout our lifetimes we absorb and excrete carbon-14 to the point that it reaches an equilibrium level. The half-life of carbon-14 is 5,730 years, so we do not notice any decay during our life. Once we die and do not absorb any more carbon-14, the amount of its decay in the body can be measured and the age determined, based upon the amount of decay that has taken place. The age of objects and people can be determined by a method that is often referred to as carbon-14 dating. Most background radiation comes from naturally occurring radon-222 (222Rn) and radon-220 (220Rn). These radioactive gases seep from rocks that contain uranium and thorium and account for 50–80% of the background radiation exposure. The average individual exposure from background radiation is 360 millirems per year.

Radioactive materials have been the backbone of almost all medical advances that have occurred in the past 50 years. Nuclear technology plays a key role and often saves lives in medical clinics, hospitals, operating rooms, and pharmaceutical development. In addition to using radiation to diagnose medical problems, it is also used as a treatment for many diseases. Almost half of all Americans diagnosed each year with cancer undergo radiation therapy. Every hospital in this country has some type of radiation unit. Radioisotopes are administered to humans during medical procedures to either aid in the diagnosis of a disease or provide a treatment for a disease.

This process is referred to as nuclear medicine. As a rule, radioisotopes used in medicine have very short half-lives (most times in terms of hours). They do not emit either alpha or beta radiation because these particulate radioactive materials would be deposited in the tissue of the body and cause serious damage. These isotopes are gamma emitters, which allow the medical procedure to obtain the best results. Radioisotopes used in medical procedures are usually not toxic and do not cause any pharmacological response in the patient. On the other hand, radioactive materials used for therapeutic purposes do emit alpha and beta particles as well as gamma rays. Primarily, the radioisotope technetium-99 (99Tc) is used in almost 80% of all daily diagnostic studies worldwide. Other radioisotopes used include thallium-201 (201Tl), gallium-67 (67Ga), indium-111 (111In), and iodine-123 (123I). Therapeutic procedures involve the use of the radioisotopes iodine-131 (131I), phosphorus-32 (32P), and yttrium-90 (90Y). Controls on the use, storage, and disposal of medical radioactive materials are tight. Terrorists could attempt to steal these materials for use in a nuclear dispersion device.

Nuclear Fission

Fission is a nuclear reaction that occurs when a heavier unstable nucleus divides or splits into two or more lighter nuclei. Splitting of the nucleus occurs when a free neutron enters the nucleus of a fissionable atom. This makes the nucleus of the atom unstable because of the extra neutron. Because of this imbalance, the nucleus then splits into two or more lighter nuclei. When this occurs, very large amounts of energy can be released along with more free neutrons. Newly released electrons then enter the nucleus of other atoms, causing more splitting, more released energy, and more free neutrons. Fission is the process that produces the nuclear chain reaction that results in a nuclear explosion. A chain reaction initiates its own repetition. Elements used to produce a nuclear explosion by fission are the isotopes of uranium-235 or plutonium-239, which experience fission much more easily than other isotopes of the same elements. Nuclear explosions are a chain reaction of numerous fissions taking place among the isotopes of uranium-235 or plutonium-239. Collectively, these fissions can produce enormous amounts of energy. Each time a nucleus is split, energy is released, resulting in many more fissions taking place feeding upon each other to produce the awesome power of a nuclear explosion. In order for fission reactions to take place, there must be an appropriate amount of fissionable material (i.e., uranium-235 or plutonium-239) in the appropriate configuration so that free neutrons will be produced, which can cause equal or increased numbers of fissions. The amount of material needed to sustain the chemical reaction is termed as the critical mass. Nuclear fission can produce two million times more energy than a chemical reaction. However, there still must be an enormous number of fissions to produce a significant amount of energy release. The process of fusion in general may be thought of as the opposite of fission. Instead of splitting the nucleus, two light nuclei come together to form a heavier nucleus. In order for fusion to take place, there must be enough energy to force the nuclei together and overcome the electrostatic forces of repulsion. Two forces are necessary in order for fusion to take place. First of all, there must be high temperatures to accelerate the nuclei, and, second, there must be high-pressure density to increase the probability of interaction between the nuclei. Interestingly, the only way for the types of temperature and pressure to be generated for a fusion reaction is to create a fission reaction first. Therefore, weapons containing a fusion element must also contain a fission element. The energy from the fusion-fission reaction is generated in approximately equal amounts from each process.

Types of Radiation

Most, if not all, of the fission products yielded by a nuclear reaction are radioactive. So the question is what is radiation or radioactivity? Radiation is ionizing energy spontaneously emitted by a material or combination of materials. A radioactive material, then, is a product that spontaneously emits ionizing radiation. There are two types of radiation, ionizing and nonionizing. Ionizing radiation involves particles and "waves of energy" traveling in a wavelike motion. Examples are alpha, beta, gamma, x-ray, neutron, ultraviolet, and microwave. Nonionizing radiation is also made up of "waves of energy." Examples include ultraviolet, radar, radio, visible light, and infrared light. While all radioactive waves travel in a wavelike motion, radioactivity travels in a straight line.

There are three primary types of radioactive emissions from the nucleus of radioactive atoms. The first is the alpha particle, which resembles an atom of helium stripped of its electrons, with two protons and two neutrons remaining (Figure 6.3). They are held together tightly by nuclear forces. Alpha particles are positively charged and emitted from the nucleus of some radioactive elements. As the alpha particle is ejected from the nucleus, it is accompanied by one or more types of energy in the form of radiation. Heavy elements such as radium and uranium usually emit alpha particles when they decay. Others may decay by spontaneous fusion, which results in the emission of neutrons. Alpha particles are large in size and therefore will not penetrate as much or travel as far as beta or gamma radiation. Alpha particles travel 3 to 4 inches and will not penetrate the skin. Complete turnouts, including

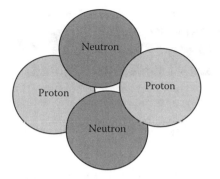

Figure 6.3 An alpha particle resembles a helium atom stripped of its electrons.

SCBA, hood, and gloves, will protect responders from external exposure. However, if alpha particles are ingested or enter the body through a broken skin surface, they can cause a great deal of damage to internal organs.

Beta particles are negatively charged and smaller, travel faster, and penetrate farther than the alpha particle. A beta particle is 1/1800th the size of a proton or roughly equal to an electron in mass. In fact, the beta particle is formed when a neutron is changed into a proton and electron within the nucleus of the atom. The proton remains in the nucleus while the beta particle (electron) is ejected from the nucleus. A beta particle is less ionizing than an alpha particle but can penetrate farther. Lighter elements tend to emit beta particles. Beta particles will penetrate the skin and travel from 3–100 feet. Full turnouts and self-contained breathing apparatuses will protect against penetration of alpha but will not provide full protection from beta particles.

Particulate radiation results in contamination of personnel and equipment where the particles come to rest. Response personnel and citizens exposed to particulate radiation by the detonation of a radioactive dispersion device will require decontamination. Efficiency of decontamination can be monitored using radiation meters. Energy waves of radiation do not cause contamination and do not make anyone or anything radioactive. It is likely that elements that emit alpha and beta particles will also emit some gamma

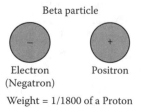

Figure 6.4 A beta particle is negatively charged and is smaller, travels faster, and penetrates further than the alpha particle.

Electromagnetic-energy waves

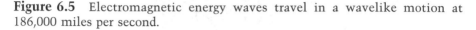

- Speed = 186,000 miles per second
- The energy of gamma is greater than visible light

Figure 6.5 Electromagnetic energy waves travel in a wavelike motion at 186,000 miles per second.

or x-ray photons. Gamma and x radiation are the primary casualty-causing forms of ionizing radiation produced by a nuclear explosion. Gamma and x radiation are basically identical in form and differ only in their source of origin. Gamma photons are produced from the decaying nuclei of atoms, and x-rays are produced from the electron shells surrounding the nuclei.

The third type of radioactive particle does not occur naturally. The neutron particle is the result of an atom being split in a nuclear reactor or accelerator, or may also be produced by a thermal nuclear explosion. During the fission process, neutrons are released and are the primary portion of the total amount of radiation released from the reaction. When an atom is split by fission, neutron particles are thrown out. Someone would have to get inside a nuclear reactor or experience a thermal nuclear explosion to be exposed to neutron particles. Even if someone were to be exposed to neutron particles from a thermal nuclear blast, they would not need to worry, because they would be either vaporized by the heat or torn apart by the blast pressure!

Gamma radiation is a naturally occurring, high-energy electromagnetic wave that is emitted from the nucleus of an atom (Figure 6.5). It is not particulate in nature and has high penetrating power. Gamma rays have the highest energy level known and are the most dangerous of the common forms of radiation. Examples of other electromagnetic energy waves include ultra-violet, infrared, microwave, visible light, radio, and x-ray. Gamma rays travel at the speed of light, or more than 186,000 miles per second, and will penetrate the skin and injure internal organs. No protective clothing can be worn by emergency responders to protect against gamma radiation. Shielding from gamma radiation requires several inches of lead, other dense metal, several feet of concrete, or several feet of earth (Table 6.1). Gamma radiation does not result in contamination because there are no radioactive particles, only energy waves. Little difference exists between gamma rays and x-rays; x-rays are produced by a cathode ray tube. To be exposed to x-rays there has to be electrical power to the x-ray machine, and the machine has to be turned on. If there is no electrical power, there is no radiation, because there is no radioactive source.

Table 6.1 Radiation Shielding Protection Values of Common Materials

Material	Half-Value Thickness*
Steel	.79 in.
Concrete	2.36 in.
Earth	3.15 in.
Water	4.72 in.
Wood	8.66 in.

* Thickness of material necessary to reduce the dose rate by one-half.

Measurements of Radioactivity

Internationally, there is a system of measurement based upon the meter and kilogram; additional units of length, mass, and time are known as Systems International (SI) measurements (Table 6.3). In the past, several terms have been used to express the intensity of radiation (Table 6.2). Radiation level is a term often substituted for dose rate or exposure rate. It is generally referred to as the effect of radiation on matter (i.e., the amount of radiation imparted from the source and absorbed by matter due to emitted radiation per unit of time). A dose occurring as a result of a nuclear detonation can be divided into two parts, neutrons and gamma rays. A curie is 37 billion disintegrations

Table 6.2 Conversion Table for Radiation Terms

1 curie = 3.7×10^{10} disintegrations per second	1 becquerel = 1 disintegration per second

1 millicurie (mCi) = 37 megabecquerels (MBq)

1 rad = 0.01 gray (Gy)

1 rem = 0.01 sievert (Sv)

1 roentgen (R) = 0.000258 coulomb/kilogram (C/kg)

1 megabecquerel (MBq) = 0.027 millicuries (mCi)

1 gray (Gy) = 100 rad

1 sievert (Sv) = 100 rem

1 coulomb/kilogram (C/kg) = 3880 roentgens

Table 6.3   Biological Effects of Acute, Total Body
Irradiation

Amount of Exposure	Effect
25 REM (0.25 Sv)	No detectable injury or symptoms (maximum single lifetime exposure)
50 REM (0.50 Sv)	Elevated temperature, fatigue, WBC reduction
100 REM (1 Sv)	Nausea and vomiting initially, deficiency of white blood cells and platelets
200–250 REM (2–2.50 Sv)	Fatal to some in 30 days, hair loss, severe WBC reduction, all sick
500 REM (5 Sv)	50% dead in 30 days
600 REM (6 Sv)	All will die
1000–2000 REM (10–20 Sv)	All will die 4–14 days
2000 or more	Immediate death

per second. The curie is a physical amount of material required to produce a specific amount of ionizing radiation; 1 millicurie = 0.001 curie, and 1 microcurie = 0.000001 curie. Several hundred pounds of one radioactive material might be required to produce the same amount of curies as 1 pound of another radioactive material. New terminology from SI for the amount of radioactivity in a given sample of radioisotope is expressed in terms of the becquerel (Bq). One becquerel of a radioisotope is the exact quantity that produces 1 disintegration per second; 37 billion (3.7×1010) becquerels = 1 curie (Ci). Additional prefixes may be used to identify other amounts of disintegrations per second. They are micro (u), milli (m), kilo (k), mega (M), and giga (G). When a nuclear detonation occurs, large amounts of radioactive materials are produced. Terminology used to identify large amounts of radio-activity includes petabecquerel (PBq) and exabecquerel (EBq). Previously, the term megacurie (MCi) was used for large amounts. While a curie is a measure of the physical amount, the roentgen is a measure of the amount of ionization produced by a specific material. It is the amount of x-ray or gamma radiation that produces 2 billion ionizations in 1 cm^3 of dry air. A RAD is the radiation-absorbed dose (roughly equal to a roentgen) (i.e., how much radiation someone has been exposed to or, in other words, the radiation dose). The radiation equivalent man (REM), also roughly equal to a roentgen, is a term for how much radiation has been absorbed or the biological effect as a result of the dose. When radioactive materials are released, the human senses *cannot* detect radioactivity. The only way responders will know if radioactive materials are present is with the use of instruments specially designed to detect radioactivity.

Table 6.4 Biological Effects of Acute, Total Body Irradiation

Amount of Exposure	Effect
50 mGy (5 rads)	No detectable injury or symptoms
1 Gy (100 rads)	May cause nausea and vomiting for 1–2 days and temporary drop in production of new blood cells
3.5 Gy (350 rads)	Nausea and vomiting initially, followed by a period of apparent wellness; at 3–4 weeks there is a potential for deficiency of white blood cells and platelets; medical care is required
Higher levels of exposure can be fatal; medical care is required	

Biological Effects of Nuclear Explosions

Blast waves created by nuclear explosions can produce serious injury and death to those close to the point of detonation. Even those who might be protected from the initial blast wave by fortified buildings or heavy vehicles can be affected by the atmospheric overpressure created by the blast. The blast wave can enter buildings and vehicles and be reflected and reinforced within. Injuries to humans from blast waves vary based upon changeable susceptibility from person to person, accounting for age, physical condition, and the existence of disease or other injury in the victim. When the blast wave comes into contact with the human body, there is first a rapid compression followed by decompression, resulting in the transmission of pressure waves through body tissues. Sites where damage occurs includes junctions of different tissues such as bone and muscle, or where tissue and air spaces intersect. Lungs and gastrointestinal components are very susceptible because of the amount of air present within. Hemorrhage or air embolism can occur, which can be fatal. While not serious, eardrum perforation can occur from blast overpressurization of the surrounding atmosphere. Pressures of 193 kPa (1.9 atm) can be fatal. There have been people, however, who have survived overpressures of 262 kPa (2.5 atm). As it turns out, the body is quite resilient to blast pressures when compared to something like a concrete block wall. Blast overpressures of 10.1–20.2 kPa (0.1–0.2 atm) can shatter a concrete block wall. Overpressures much less than those that are lethal can cause serious injury to those exposed. Lung damage can occur at 68.9 kPa, while eardrum rupture occurs at 22 kPa (0.2 atm), with a 50% chance of eardrum rupture from 90–130 kPa (0.9 to 1.2 atm). It is therefore likely that overpressures above 70 kPa will produce injuries. Radiation and thermal injuries will make up the largest portion of injuries produced by a nuclear explosion.

Additional injuries can also be expected from flying debris and crushing caused by collapsing structures and vehicles.

Health effects of exposure to radiation can vary. Nonionizing radiation comes from ultraviolet and infrared energy waves. This type of radiation causes a sunburn type of injury. Because of this, PPE should not be a major concern for hazardous materials responders. Ionizing radiation comes from alpha, beta, and gamma sources. When ionizing radiation is released, it interacts with surrounding matter. Ionizing radiation is either dispersed by the contact or absorbed into the matter. When ionizing radiation contacts the body, it is absorbed and results in physiological damage. Ionization damage occurs at the cellular level. There can be four types of short-term effects that occur to the cells. The first leaves no damage at all; the ionization passes through the cell. Second, there can be repairable damage. Third, certain irreparable damage to the cells does not cause death, but results in permanent damage. Fourth is the destruction of the cells. There are also long-term effects from ionizing radiation. Exposures can cause cancer and birth defects of a teratogenic or mutagenic nature. Teratogenic birth defects result from the fetus being exposed to, and damaged by, radiation. The child is then born with some form of birth defect as a result of the exposure. Provided no further exposures occur, future children may be born normal. Mutagenic damage occurs when the DNA or other part of the reproductive system is damaged by exposure to radiation. The ability to produce normal children is lost; the damage is permanent.

Radiation Exposure

Routes of entry into the body for radioactive materials are much the same as they are for poisons. However, the radioactive source or material does not have to be directly contacted for radiation exposure to occur. Exposure occurs from the radiation being emitted from the radioactive source. Once a particulate radioactive material enters the body, it is very dangerous because the source now becomes an internal source rather than an external one. You cannot protect yourself by time, distance, or shielding from a source that is inside your body. Contact with a radioactive source or ingestion of a radioactive material does not make you radioactive. People may become contaminated with radioactive particles, but those can be successfully removed with proper decontamination. After particles are removed, they cannot cause any further damage to your body. Because radiation exposure can be cumulative, there are no truly safe levels of exposure to radioactive materials.

Radiation does not cause any specific diseases that can be attributed to contact. Symptoms of radiation exposure can be the same as those from

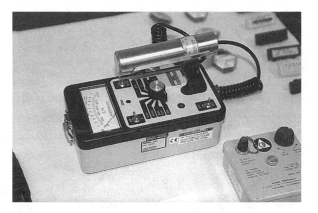

Figure 6.6 All response organizations should have a radiological monitoring instrument in order to scan for radioactive materials at an incident scene.

exposure to cancer-causing materials. Tolerable limits for exposure to radiation that have been proposed by some scientists are very arbitrary. Scientists concur that some radiation damage can be repaired by the human body. Therefore, tolerable limits are considered acceptable risks when the activity's benefits outweigh the potential risks. The maximum annual radiation exposure for an individual person in the U.S. is 0.1 REM. Maximum exposures for workers in the nuclear industry is 5 REMs per year. A one-time emergency exposure of 25 REMs has been established by The National Institute of Standards and Technology for response personnel. This type of exposure should be attempted under only the most dire circumstances, such as a life-or-death rescue, and should occur only once in a lifetime.

Effects of exposure to radiation on the human body depend on the amount of material the body was exposed to, the length of exposure, the type of radiation, the depth of penetration, and the frequency of exposure. Cells that are the most susceptible are the rapidly dividing type, such as the bone marrow. Children are more at risk than an adult, and the fetus is the most sensitive of all. Symptoms of radiation injuries frequently do not present themselves for quite a long time after exposure. Varying levels of illness will occur from radiation exposure depending on the dose:

- No detectable symptoms are the result of up to 25 REM exposure.
- Elevated temperature and changes in blood count occur from 50 REM.
- Nausea and fatigue result from 100 REM.
- Two hundred to 250 REM results in sickness to all exposed and death to some within 30 days.
- Exposure to over 600 REM results in death of all exposed.

It can be years or even decades before symptoms appear. Cancer is one of the main long-term effects of exposure to radiation. Leukemia may take from 5–15 years to develop. Lung, skin, and breast cancer may take up to 40 years to develop.

Radiation burns are much like thermal burns, although they can be much more severe. Effects of radiation thermal burns on the body depend on several factors. First, the area of the body affected by the burns is expressed in a percentage of body surface involved. Second, involvement of critical organs, such as the head, neck, respiratory tract, genitalia, hands, and feet, is considered. Third, the depth of the burn is determined: superficial (first- or second-degree), deep (second-degree) or full thickness (third-degree). First-degree radiation burns result from an exposure of 50–200 RADs. Second-degree burns result from 500 RADs, and third-degree burns result from 1,000 RADs. Burns that affect over 20% of the body can be fatal if not treated. Even with treatment, deaths from extensive burns will be high, especially among the very young and the elderly. Treatment of burns is much the same as the treatment for thermal burns and may require extended hospitalization, debreeding, and skin grafts. Thermal radiation can affect the human body in two ways: direct absorption of the thermal energy through flash burns to exposed surfaces (skin and tissue), and indirect action from fires caused in the exposed environment (flame burns). If a nuclear detonation occurs in an area of highly flammable materials, the flame burns could outnumber the flash burns. Thermal radiation travels in a straight line away from the fireball and rapidly decreases in intensity with distance. Objects close to the fireball will be incinerated by the enormous thermal output. Lethality would be 100% within this range and would continue for a distance beyond the fireball. Actual ranges will vary based upon the yield of the device, position of the burst, weather conditions, and environmental factors. Two things determine the degree of burn injury from a given nuclear burst: the amount of thermal energy per square centimeter and the duration of the thermal pulse. Radiation doses required to produce a flash second-degree burn vary from less than 16.7 joules (change in temperature per atmosphere change of pressure)/cm^2 to more than 29.3 joules/cm^2 depending on the yield of the device. Clothing may provide some protection at temperatures less than those required to ignite the clothing. Some flash burns may occur even to skin covered by clothing, depending on the thermal energy conducted across the clothing and the amount absorbed by the clothing. Indirect or flame burns result from fire caused by thermal effects in the environment, particularly from ignition of clothing. Large-yield devices could cause conflagrations and firestorms over large areas.

Two types of thermal/visual radiation can affect the eyes — flash blindness and permanent retinal scarring. Flash blindness is caused by the initial brilliant flash of light produced by a nuclear detonation. More light energy is transmitted to the retina than can be tolerated but less than what would be required for permanent damage. The retina is sensitive to visible and short wavelength infrared light. Exposure causes bleaching of the visual pigments and temporary blindness. Usually during daylight hours, the effect does not last more than 2 minutes and usually corrects itself within seconds. Because the pupils are dilated to adjust to darkness, flash blindness can last from 3–10 minutes with longer lingering effects after dark. In some cases, it might take 15–35 minutes for full night vision to return to normal. Retinal burns that cause permanent damage from scarring are fairly uncommon occurrences. Persons exposed would need to be in view of the fireball, but damage can occur from an exposure a considerable distance from the detonation. The size of the fireball, which results from the yield and detonation, will determine the degree and extent of retinal scarring. Location of the scarring will determine the degree of interference with vision.

Effects on the human body from exposure to radiation range from rapid death as a result of high doses being absorbed into the body to normal life for a variable period of time until delayed effects develop. Significant variations of effects occur depending on the age of victim, biological makeup, dose, time of exposure, and the source and type of radiation. Gamma radiation, produced during a nuclear detonation or from its fallout, is highly energetic and very penetrating. Much of it passes through the body without interacting with tissues or cells. Either internal or external sources of gamma radiation can result in whole-body exposure. Neutrons may also result in whole-body radiation. Alpha and beta radiation, on the other hand, do not result in whole-body radiation because they are particles rather than energy waves. Tissue damage will occur around the location of the radioactive particle(s). Alpha radiation is not an external hazard, as the particles are too large to penetrate intact skin tissue. If alpha radiation enters the body through ingestion or broken skin, damage can occur to tissues immediately surrounding the alpha source. Cell death can occur around the alpha radiation, but does not seriously affect the organism unless the cells are part of a highly critical system. Alpha-emitting materials can, however, emit gamma radiation in addition to the alpha. Because the gamma radiation has much greater penetrating power compared to the alpha radiation, the total volume of tissue damage may be much greater. Beta particles lose much of their energy after penetrating only a few inches into the tissue. Beta radiation on the surface of the skin will cause a first- or second-degree thermal burn type injury. If the beta particle gets inside the body, much more significant injury can occur. Damage will occur in the tissue surrounding the radioactive source, and target organ damage will depend on the chemical nature of the radioactive material.

Cellular effects of ionizing radiation range from cell death to changes in cell function. Some of the damaging effects to cells that result in cell death include pyknosis, karyolysis, protoplasmic coagulation, karyorrhexis, and cytolysis. Pyknosis occurs when the nucleus becomes contracted, spheroidal, and filled with condensed chromatin. Karyolysis involves the swelling of the nucleus, which results in the lose of its chromatin. Protoplasmic coagulation is an irreversible gelatin formation that occurs in the cytoplasm and nucleus. Karyorrhexis occurs when the nucleus becomes fragmented and spread throughout the cell. Cytolysis occurs when the cells swell until they burst and slowly disappear. Changes in cell function can occur from nonlethal lower doses of radiation. These include delays in certain phases of the mitotic cycle, disrupted cell growth, permeability changes, and changes in motility. Additionally, exposure to various levels of radiation can result in damage to the chromosomes and DNA, resulting in mutated cells and, in some cases, damage to the reproductive system of those exposed. During a normal cell life cycle, different systems of the body produce cells in the following cycle: formation, proliferation, maturation, and cell death. Central nervous system cells, like some other systems in the body, stabilize at the end of maturation. Any cells lost or destroyed are not replaced. Liver cells, which are not normally produced at a very rapid rate, can reproduce large numbers of cells when existing cells are damaged. Body systems such as the bone marrow, skin, reproductive system, gastrointestinal tract, and the hematopoietic system all have a high cell turnover rate. Whole-body radiation effects cause primary damage to the bone marrow and gastrointestinal systems. Bone marrow contains three cell-renewal systems: the erythropoietic (red cell), the myelopoietic (white cell), and the thrombopoietic (platelet). Mature red cells are produced over 4–7 days and have a lifespan of approximately 120 days. Damage to the bone marrow can result in death of the victim. In some cases, bone marrow transplants can induce new cell production and the victim can be saved. Following the Chernobyl incident in Russia, several American doctors went to Russia to perform lifesaving bone marrow transplants. The small intestine is particularly vulnerable to exposure to radiation. Within 1–2 weeks after irradiation, hemorrhage can occur, along with loss of fluid and electrolyte loss, which contributes to shock.

Whole-body radiation exposure is the most important aspect, because it is the most damaging. Partial body and specific organ irradiation can also occur, causing serious damage, particularly from internal deposits of radioactive particles or fission products. Radiation sickness might also occur from partial body exposures from lesser amounts of radiation exposure. Radiation sickness has three phases associated with exposures: prodromal, latent, and manifest. Prodromal, known as the initial phase, happens during the first few hours after exposure and can result in nausea, vomiting, and malaise, depending on the dose and length of time of exposure. These symptoms can develop within 2–12 hours from exposures of 100–200 cGy (centigray) and

Figure 1.1 Smoke billows from one of the towers of the World Trade Center, and flames and debris explode from the second tower. (Source: AP/Worldwide Photos. Used with permission.)

Figure 2.6 To the side of the reflecting pond are 168 bronze colored chairs each engraved with the name of one of the 168 victims of the terrorist attack.

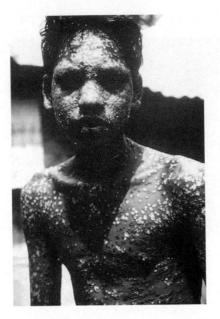

Figure 4.6 Smallpox on the face and trunk of a small boy. (Courtesy Centers for Disease Control (CDC).)

Figure 4.9 Castor bean plants growing wild on the Island of Oahu in Hawaii. Castor beans are used to produce the plant toxin ricin.

Figure 10.7 Sacramento County Fire Department's new hazmat unit with closed circuit television, complete analytical laboratory, light towers and other typical hazmat equipment.

Figure 11.9 A jet airliner on one of the World Trade Center towers in New York, September 11, 2001. In the most devastating terrorist onslaughts ever waged against the U.S., knife-wielding hijackers crashed two airliners into the World Trade Center, toppling its twin 110-story towers. (Source: AP/Wide World Photos. Used with permission.)

usually subside after one day. Vomiting, which occurs within the first 2 hours, should be associated with a high dose of radiation. Doses of radiation over 200 cGy can result in hyperthermia. High doses may also produce fever and chills within the first day of exposure. Whole-body exposures of 1,000 to 2,000 cGy can produce erythema (sunburn type injury) within the first day. Hypotension (lowered blood pressure) develops from supralethal whole-body radiation doses. Severe hypotension resulting from radiation exposure is usually associated with a poor prognosis. Victims who show symptoms of central nervous system damage within the first hour have likely received a superlethal dose. The prodomal phase lasts only a few hours. While the preliminary symptoms of nausea, vomiting, and malaise are nonspecific, when nuclear exposure is suspected and in the absence of other causes, radiation exposure should be considered. A triage of suspected radiation victims can be placed in three categories: Radiation Injury Unlikely, Radiation Injury Probable, and Radiation Injury Severe. The latent phase may last for 2–6 weeks, where the victim will not show any symptoms. Following the latent phase, the manifest phase develops in which the bone marrow, intestines, and neurovascular systems become affected by the radiation exposure. Diagnosis of radiation sickness will be based on the symptoms exhibited by the patient. Exposure history will also be helpful if available. Certainly patients exposed to a conventional explosion who develop radiation sickness symptoms should be evaluated for radiation exposure. The explosive device may have been used to disseminate nuclear materials. When comparing effects of radiation exposure, often the term LD_{50} is used to express the lethal dose to a given population. This term expresses the dose of a radioactive material that would cause death to 50% of the population that is exposed. An additional expression of time is also identified with the 50%, indicating the time period it takes for the deaths to occur. This can range from 5–60 days in length. The value $LD_{50/30}$ would mean that 50% of the exposed population would die within 30 days of the exposure. These values assume that the victim does not receive any other injuries or treatments.

Other terms of significance in radiation exposures are LD_5 and LD_{95}. Doses of 200–300 cGy (free in air) is the amount which would cause no deaths, or the LD_5. Doses of 600–700 cGy (free in air) is the amount that would result in the deaths of nearly everyone exposed, which is known as the LD_{95}. Exposures to radiation can result in delayed effects that present months or years after the exposure. Types of effects are based upon the dose of the exposure and the length of time of the exposure. Effects can include shorter life span, development of cancer, formation of cataracts in the eyes, radiation-induced chronic dermatitis, decreased fertility, and genetic mutations. There is a period of time between irradiation and the development of cancer, as well as a variance based upon dose and cancer site. Skin cancer latency can range from 12–56 years. Bone tumors might take 15 years to develop. Leukemia resulting from radiation exposure can develop within 5–6 years depending on the dose and length of exposure. Cataract formation as a result of radiation exposure takes from 6 months to several years following exposure. Dermatitis as a result of radiation occurs when the bare skin is exposed to heavy contamination from a beta emitter material from fallout or other beta source. Decontamination would greatly reduce the chances of damage.

When radioactive materials enter the body and remain for extended periods of time, significant injury can occur to specific tissues that are exposed to the radiation. Many medical isotopes have short half-lives and do not cause any permanent damage to cells or tissues. Radioactive materials enter the body through inhalation, ingestion, or skin absorption. Once inside the body, the material may enter the bloodstream, depending on the solubility of the material. Materials that are insoluble are not absorbed and may be eliminated from the body through the respiratory or gastrointestinal tracts. Insoluble materials in some circumstances can remain in the body at or near the site of deposition (i.e., the lungs or wounds) or transferred to the lymph nodes, where they can cause additional radiation damage to tissue. In order to eliminate the radioactive hazard within the body, the material must be removed. There are no antidotes for radioactive materials. Some chemicals can be removed from the body through detoxification; however, radioactivity is not affected by chemical changes. Some soluble radioactive materials can be excreted from the body through the kidneys. Materials in the intestines or liver can be eliminated through feces. Volatile materials and gases can be exhaled through the lungs. Chelating agents (e.g., calcium or zinc DTPA [diethylenetriamine pentaacetic acid]), if administered soon after exposure, can be effective in elimination of certain radioactive isotopes. This process will not be very effective against materials deposited in organs, tissues, and the bones. Victims from a nuclear explosion will also find little help from chelating agents. During 2001, the Food and Drug Administration (FDA) issued new instructions for the use of a drug that can protect against thyroid cancer in case of a nuclear accident or terrorist attack. These new instructions deal with the release of radioactive iodine. If this radioactive compound is inhaled or ingested through contaminated food or milk, it can cause people to develop thyroid cancer. Children are the most at risk and can be affected by doses much lower than those that might affect adults. Potassium iodide (KI) has been recognized to reduce the risk of cancer for quite some time. It has been used as a radiation antidote following nuclear accidents. The changes primarily deal with the dose given following exposure. Instead of one dose for babies and another for all other children of all ages, the FDA now recommends far different doses for children of different ages. Adults over 40 would not need the antidote unless they were exposed to massive amounts of radiation. In addition to other protective measures, such as evacuating people out of danger zones and providing safe food, newborns would need a daily dose of 16 milligrams of KI until exposure was deemed over. Children ages one month to three years would get twice that dose at 32 mg; children ages 3–18 would get 65 milligrams; and 130 milligrams would be administered to adults. Radioactive iodine is produced as a by-product of nuclear fission and would only be released from the meltdown of a nuclear reactor or the detonation of a thermal nuclear weapon. Since there is no fission in a dirty bomb, no radioactive iodine would be produced. Additionally, radioactive iodine decays quickly (8 day half-life) so it would be difficult for a terrorist to use.

Rates at which radioactive isotopes are eliminated from the body are expressed as the biological half-life. That is the time it takes one-half of the material to be excreted or expelled from the body. During each additional half-life, an additional one-half of the material is eliminated. Not all isotopes are removed in an exponential fashion, but the biological half-life theory is accurate enough to be used with most soluble isotopes. Insoluble heavy metals such as plutonium will not be removed in this manner and will remain in the lungs and bone for a long period of time. Biological half-life depends on the body's ability to process water and remove it through the kidneys. This can take as long as 18 days or can occur in as little as 4 days. Removal rates of water from the body depends on the volume taken in, the state of hydration, and kidney function. Intakes of large amounts of water can accelerate the process. Another factor considered in the elimination of radioactive isotopes from the body is the radiological half-life of the isotope. The two terms factored together are expressed as the "effective half-life." This relationship is expressed in the following equation:

$$\text{Effective half-life} = \frac{\text{Biological half-life} \times \text{Radiological half-life}}{\text{Biological half-life} + \text{Radiological half-life}}$$

Radioisotopes can be effectively blocked from entering the body in some cases. For example, the administration of potassium iodide or iodate before or soon after the intake of radioiodine will reduce the uptake of the radioiodine by the thyroid gland. Prussian blue will likewise reduce the absorption of cesium from the intestines, and alginate will reduce strontium absorption.

Effects of Nuclear Explosions

Damage from conventional explosives almost entirely occurs from the transmission of energy in the form of a blast pressure or blast wave, which results in mechanical damage to structures. Some types of conventional explosives can also produce thermal waves. Nuclear explosions produce blast waves and thermal radiation (heat), like some conventional explosions, and also ionizing radiation, which is totally unique. It is the ionizing radiation that can produce additional injuries beyond those produced by blast and thermal waves. Energy from a nuclear detonation is distributed into the environment by three distinct methods: blast, thermal radiation, and nuclear radiation. The allocation from the blast to these three forms is a direct result of the yield of the nuclear device, the location of the explosion (air burst or ground burst), or the characteristics of the environment. For example, a low altitude detonation of a moderate-size device (kiloton range) would produce a distribution of approximately 50% blast, 35% thermal radiation, and 15% nuclear radiation. Of the 15%, 5% is initial ionizing radiation consisting of neutrons and gamma rays being emitted during the first minute after the detonation, and 10% is residual nuclear radiation, which is the hazard with nuclear fallout. Thermal radiation is composed of infrared, visible, and ultraviolet light, along with some soft x-ray that is emitted at the time of the explosion. Outcomes will vary with the size and location of the explosion. Some weapons are designed to produce more radiation than others. Enhanced radiation devices would produce a 30% blast, 20% thermal, 45% initial radiation, and 5% residual radiation. Because of the very high temperatures and pressures created by a nuclear blast, the hot gaseous residues move away from the center of the blast at very high velocities. Initially, the shock wave stays behind the fireball, but within a matter of milliseconds after the blast, the fireball slows down and the shock wave catches up. At this point the shock wave moves ahead of the fireball, even obscuring its view for a fraction of a second, which accounts for the characteristic double peak of light viewed from a nuclear detonation. Much of the destruction of a nuclear blast comes from the initial blast pressure. Blast winds can exceed several hundred km/hr. The range of the blast's effects increases proportionately with the size of the device. During surface or subsurface bursts, most of the yield of the blast is transmitted in the form of ground or water shock (Figure 6.7). A crater is formed with the size increasing in proportion to the size of the device. Most of the ground shock effects from the surface blast will be limited to approximately three crater diameters away from the center of the blast. The balance of the damage will occur from the shock wave. With the subsurface blast, the shock wave damage is limited to ground shock, which will be confined to the area close around the site of the detonation.

Large amounts of thermal energy or electromagnetic radiation in the form of visible, infrared, and ultraviolet light are emitted from the fireball within the first minute or less after the nuclear explosion. This radiation travels out from the center of the blast at the speed of light, 300,000 km/sec.

Figure 6.7   Nuclear test blast at the Nevada test site during the 1950s. (Source: U.S. Department of Energy.)

The primary hazard of the thermal radiation is burns to skin and eye injury to people exposed. Combustible materials can also be ignited from the effects of the thermal energy. Large fires can result from burning debris. As thermal radiation strikes an object, some will be transmitted, and the remaining amount will be absorbed by the object. The makeup and color of the object determines how much radiation will be absorbed. Thin materials transmit most of the radiation that strikes them. Light-colored materials reflect much of the radiation and escape most of the damage. Thermal damage occurs because large amounts of thermal energy are absorbed into objects within a very short period of time. Absorbed radiation raises the temperature of the absorbing material, which results in scorching, charring, and possible ignition of combustible materials such as wood, paper, and fabrics. These effects of thermal radiation increase as the size of the device increases. Low-altitude bursts generate the greatest thermal effects. Surface bursts create much less thermal effect, and subsurface blasts do not create much thermal effect at all. Much of the thermal effect of a high-altitude burst is absorbed into the surrounding atmosphere. Temperatures produced by a nuclear detonation can reach to millions of degrees centigrade in the immediate area around the blast center. In contrast, a conventional explosion produces temperatures only in the low thousands of degrees. After the initiation of a blast, the fireball is formed within milliseconds. A fireball from a 1 megaton (Mt) air burst can develop from 150 m to over 2,200 m within 10 seconds, while rising at a rate of 100 m/sec. This initial rapid expansion of the fireball compresses the surrounding air, which produces a powerful shock wave. Enormous amounts of radiation, similar to the light spectrum of sunlight, are emitted from the fireball in the form of thermal radiation. Visible light accounts for the blinding flash and bright fireball that occurs with the initial blast. The infrared light results in widespread burns and incendiary effects. As the fireball reaches its maximum expansion, temperatures start to cool, and the level of thermal radiation is reduced.

Upward movement and cooling of the fireball results in the formation of the characteristic mushroom cloud (Figure 6.7). The cloud continues to rise for approximately 10 minutes, depending on the thermal release of the device and weather conditions. Growth will continue, laterally forming the familiar mushroom shape, which can remain intact for an hour or longer depending on atmospheric conditions. Clouds resulting from a 1 Mt blast can reach an altitude of over 20 kilometers (km) and have an average horizontal diameter of 35 km. As the temperature of the cloud cools further, the materials that were vaporized by enormous heat from the blast condense, forming a cloud of solid materials, which then starts to move away from the blast center according to atmospheric conditions. In the case of an air burst, the solid materials are droplets of water. If the explosion was a ground burst, the cloud would also contain dirt and other debris vaporized by the heat when the fireball touched the surface and was sucked up into the cloud by the updraft. This material would then become contaminated by the radiation created during the blast. As the cloud condenses and moves away, the material would return to earth in the form of radioactive fallout. This fallout would then cause contamination of anything or anyone that it touched.

Four types of nuclear blasts can occur based upon the tactical objective of the deployed weapon. These blasts include air bursts, surface bursts, subsurface bursts, and high-altitude bursts. An air burst is a nuclear explosion that takes place below 30 km in altitude, but the fireball does not touch the ground. This type of blast can cause considerable damage over a very large area and injury from the blast pressure. Injuries from an air burst can include burns to exposed skin and eye injuries. Radiation will be produced from the blast; however, there is no fallout from an air burst. A tactical air burst would be used in warfare to incapacitate ground troops and knock out electronic equipment. Surface bursts occur when the nuclear device is detonated at ground level or slightly above. The resulting fireball will touch the ground and any water surface that might be present. Areas affected by the explosion will be less extensive than those from an air burst of an equal size. Damage will be concentrated to a smaller area than from an air burst. The surface burst would result in blast pressure damage, thermal radiation, and initial nuclear radiation. Unlike the air burst, the surface burst creates radioactive fallout, which can blanket a large area downwind from the blast. Subsurface bursts occur below the surface of the ground or water. A crater will be produced just as in the surface burst. If the force of the blast does not break the surface of the ground, the only hazard produced will be ground or water shock. Water shock can produce a tidal wave and ground shock can produce earthquake-type damage. If the burst does penetrate the surface, blast pressure, thermal wave, and initial nuclear radiation can be produced. The amounts will be less than those produced by a surface blast of similar size. Local fallout produced from the subsurface blast that breaks the surface of the ground will be very heavy. High altitude bursts occur above 30 km, which allows initial soft x-rays created by the blast to spread heat energy over a much larger area. Fireballs created by high-altitude bursts are much larger and travel much faster than those of the other air bursts. Ionizing radiation is distributed over hundreds of miles before being absorbed. Ionization of the upper atmosphere (ionosphere) can also occur. Most modern communications equipment is destroyed by the intense electromagnetic pulse (EMP) created by a high-altitude burst. This EMP does not have any biological effect on the body, but can destroy medical equipment, resulting in deaths of those depending on the equipment for life.

Because of the physical characteristics of radioactive materials, protection can be provided by taking a few simple steps. These steps are commonly referred to as time, distance, and shielding. These terms for protective measures can be applied to other forms of terrorism, including biological, chemical, incendiary, and explosives. **Time** refers to the length of exposure to a radioactive source. Time also refers to the half-life of a radioactive material. A half-life is the length of time necessary for an unstable element or nuclide to lose one-half of its radioactive intensity in the form of alpha, beta, and gamma radiation. Half-lives range from fractions of seconds to millions of years. In 10 half-lives, almost any radioactive source will no longer put out any more radiation than normal background. **Distance** is the second protective measure from radiation. As was previously mentioned, radiation travels in a straight line, but only for short distances. Therefore, the greater the distance from the radioactive material, the less the intensity of the exposure. There is a "law" in dealing with radioactivity known as the "inverse square law." This means that as the distance from the radioactive source is doubled, the radiation intensity drops off by one-quarter. If the distance is increased 10 times, the intensity drops off to 1/100 of the original intensity.

Shielding is the third protective measure against radiation. Shielding simply means placing enough mass between personnel and the radiation, which will provide protection from the radiation (Figure 6.8). In the case of alpha particles, your skin or a sheet of paper will produce enough shielding. Turnouts, if worn, will provide extra protection. Ingestion is the major hazard of radioactive particles, and wearing SCBA will prevent ingestion. Beta particles require more substantial protection from entering the body. A 1/24-inch-thick piece of aluminum will stop beta radiation. Turnouts will not

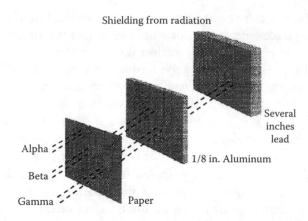

Figure 6.8 Alpha particles are stopped by a sheet of paper and the skin. Beta particles are stopped by 1/2-inch of aluminum. Gamma rays are stopped by several inches of lead.

provide adequate protection. Gamma radiation requires 3–9 inches of lead or several feet of concrete or earth.

From state to state, the agencies responsible for response and handling of radioactive emergencies, other than fire, police, and EMS, may vary. Emergency first-responders must stay aware of the dangers of radioactive materials and know how to protect themselves from radiation. Each state has radiological response teams that handle radioactive emergencies. They may be a part of the emergency management agency, the health department, the department of environment, etc. Federal interests are represented by the U.S. Nuclear Regulatory Commission (NRC), Office of Public Affairs (OPA), Washington, DC 20555, toll-free: 800-368-5642; local: 301-415-8200; TDD: 301-415-5575. Incidents involving weapons are handled by the Department of Defense Joint Nuclear Accident Center, 703-325-2102.

Incendiary Terrorism 7

Arson fires have plagued the fire service almost from the beginning (Figure 7.1). Each year in the U.S., there is an average of 276,000 arson fires resulting in 475 deaths, 2,000 injuries, and $2 billion in property damage. Arson fire deaths are the second leading cause of deaths in fires. Outside fires account for 50% of arson cases, inside fires 30%, and vehicle fires 20%. Half of all arson arrests are juveniles. Terrorists may also choose to use fire and incendiary devices to perpetuate acts of terrorism. If response personnel are not aware of the potential occupancies and locations where terrorist acts might occur, the arson might go undetected. Signs of arson and terrorism are often subtle and easily overlooked. Arsonists set fires for many different reasons. Concluding that arson has occurred involves determination of motive. Therefore, a fire set by a terrorist becomes a terrorist event rather than just an arson case, because of motive. During September, 2004 five governors were sent letters rigged with matches designed to ignite when opened. They were sent to governors in Montana, Idaho, Nebraska, Washington, and Utah. The letters appeared to have been mailed from a maximum security prison in Nevada. While this appears not to be a terrorist incident, it is certainly the type of thing a terrorist might choose to do to set a fire. Before discussing the terrorist side of incendiary fires, it is appropriate to review some background information concerning fire cause and arson investigation.

What Is Arson?

The common law definition of arson is generally accepted as "the willful and malicious burning of the house of another, including all outhouses or outbuildings adjacent thereto." In this definition, the emphasis is on "another's dwelling." This definition did not cover commercial properties, churches, schools, and other occupancies. Common law courts began to recognize the crime of arson as the burning of another's home or possessions. Today, the crime of arson is defined as "the willful and intentional burning of all types of structures, vehicles, forests, fields, etc." Most modern state arson laws

Figure 7.1   Arson fires account for almost one quarter of all fires in the U.S.

define arson as the willful and intentional damage or destruction of property. In the U.S., arson is the second leading cause of residential fires. Incendiary fires are the leading cause of monetary loss from fire, exceeding $2 billion annually. During 2004, 320 people died as a result of over 72,500 arson fires in the U.S., according to the U.S. Fire Administration (USFA). Approximately one in every four reported fires is caused by arson. There were 36,500 structure fires resulting in $714 million in damage and 36,000 vehicle fires resulting in $165 million in damage. Because arson is so common, any fire scene could potentially become an arson or crime scene. If a terrorist uses arson as a weapon, this would also be considered a crime scene. The real difference between arson and terrorism might not be known until the motive is determined. However, it is important that responders and fire investigators not develop a predetermined cause of the fire before a thorough examination of the evidence is complete. In reality, the fire investigator does not set out to determine the cause of a fire, but rather seeks to determine what was not the cause. By process of elimination, the fire cause will become apparent. Catching an arsonist, or terrorist for that matter, is difficult. Only 17% of arson cases result in arrests. Juveniles account for 50% of all arson arrests. Only 2% of the arrests result in convictions.

The Firefighter's Role

People who set fires do so for many different reasons — mental illness, sexual gratification, revenge, insurance company fraud, murder, etc. Terrorists might choose incendiary devices to carry out acts of terrorism or might create other types of terrorist events that might also produce the risk of fire. Terrorists might use a combination of explosive devices and flammable fuels to

Figure 7.2 New Orleans, LA, September 21, 2005 — New Orleans homes are burning in this aerial photograph. Arson was still a problem two weeks after Hurricane Katrina made landfall near the city. (Photo by Greg Henshall/FEMA.)

Figure 7.3 Fires can be accidental, intentionally set by arsonists, or set as an act of terrorism. (NOAA News Photo Courtesy FEMA Photos.)

create an incendiary incident. There might not be any obvious signs that separate an arson fire from a terrorist event. It will be difficult for responders and investigators to determine from physical evidence whether the fire is a "common" arson or an act of terrorism. Attention needs to be paid to locations and timing of such incendiary fires. The investigator will need to look carefully at the location, time of day, day of week, and type of business operations for possible clues. Intelligence gathered on local militia and other antigovernment or religious group activities, warning calls, or claims for responsibility may help in the determination of the motive.

Responders should be alert for signs of a set fire when responding to fires in churches, public buildings, historical buildings, landmarks, colleges and universities, abortion and related clinics, hospitals, doctors' offices, public utilities, and locations of important infrastructure, such as tunnels, bridges, and water treatment plants. According to FBI statistics, 20–25% of all bombing incidents in the U.S. involve incendiary devices. These devices ignite with a 75% rate of efficiency. Unlike other types of bombings, only about 5% of the incendiary incidents are preceded by a warning or threat. This lack of warning increases the chance that there will be casualties.

History of Incendiary Terrorist Incidents

Terrorists have used incendiary devices throughout history. Fire can cause damage to property, disrupt normal business operations, result in injury and loss of life, and create panic among the public. The Ku Klux Klan (KKK) has used fire for over 100 years to spread terror among the African American population across the country. The rash of recent incendiary fires in churches across the U.S. could be termed acts of incendiary terrorism. According to the National Fire Protection Agency (NFPA), arson is the leading cause of fires that occur in churches and related buildings, resulting in $38 million in property damage in 2002. There are over 300,000 churches in the U.S., and 1 fire occurs for every 150 churches each year. Overseas, the Irish Republican Army (IRA) uses incendiary devices around Europe to cause death, injuries, property destruction, and significant monetary loss. During the 1970s in Philadelphia, a group of antitechnology, back-to-nature activists were operating in the city. The group was referred to as MOVE. It is reported that members felt harassed and threatened by the City of Philadelphia and the police department. During 1978, a police officer was shot by MOVE members as police tried to make arrests for possession of illegal weapons. MOVE has been called everything from advocates to cultists to activists. In reality, they were a group of domestic terrorists whose final confrontation with police resulted in a conflagration from the use of incendiary devices. During the 1981 conspiracy trial of MOVE leader John Africa, Bureau of Alcohol, Tobacco and Firearms (ATF) agents testified that 12 pipe bombs, 24 readily assembled bombs, 17 hooking devices to wire bombs together, and components for 41 additional bombs, including 15 pounds of black powder, were found in the basement of a MOVE house and two automobiles driven by members. During 1985, MOVE members barricaded themselves in a house in west Philadelphia, holding their own children hostage. Windows were barricaded, gasoline cans were placed on the roof, and bunkers were constructed, threatening a gun battle as well as incendiary fire. Fires would eventually claim 11 lives and destroy an entire Philadelphia neighborhood as a result of nothing less than an act of terrorism using incendiary materials.

Abortion clinics and animal research facilities have been the target of terrorists using incendiary devices to further their cause. During July 1993, members of the Animal Liberation Front (ALF) set fire to an animal research facility at Michigan State University. Abortion clinic fires investigated by ATF during 1995 include incidents in several California communities, Albuquerque, New Mexico, and Norfolk, Virginia. During October 1998, bombs were found at two abortion clinics in Fayetteville, North Carolina. These same abortion clinics had been the scene of incendiary fires just one month before. Fire was set on the roof of one clinic and burned through, causing damage to interior walls. The second clinic sustained damage to two doors at the rear of the building. No one has claimed responsibility for either the fires or the attempted bombings.

On July 8, 2004, an early morning fire hit the recycling building on the campus of Brigham Young University in Provo, Utah. The letters "ALF," thought to represent the Animal Liberation Front, were found spray-painted in red at seven locations near the building, according to BYU police captain Michael Harroun. Fire damage was limited to a corner of the building where bundles of recycled cardboard were stored to be shipped, and in a nearby stall where two small tractors also were set on fire. No animals were kept in the building. The fire was suspicious in nature. The letters "ALF" were found on a bed of a truck, outside a nearby horse barn, on a concrete ramp, on a trailer, on the sides of two sheds, and on a roll-up door. This was the third incident attributed to the sister organization of the environmental radical group Earth Liberation Front. The ELF took responsibility for a $1.5 million lumber yard fire that occurred during June 2004 in West Jordan, Utah. According to BYU police, over a six-week period at BYU, someone broke into a horse barn and released animals, and later, equipment that researchers were using to test the breeding habits of fish were removed from an aquarium.

Types of Incendiary Devices

Just like homemade bombs and explosives, incendiary devices can take on many shapes and forms, limited only by the imagination of the terrorist. Generally, an incendiary device requires an ignition source, combustible fuel, and some type of housing or container. Materials to make incendiary devices are generally common, cheap, and easy to obtain without causing suspicion. Fuels can be flammable or combustible liquids (Figure 7.4), combustible solids and metals, combustible gases, and combustible dusts. Components used to assemble devices can include any of the following:

Figure 7.4 Flammable liquids ignited by explosives can produce overpressure damage, as well as set fires from the fireball.

- Flares used by police at accidents
- Motor fuels, such as gasoline and diesel
- Electric light bulbs and matches
- Electrical appliances and components
- Fireworks
- Reactive chemicals
- Propane and butane cylinders
- Plastic pipes, bottles, and cans

These are just a few of the many common materials that could be used to construct an effective incendiary device. Ignition of an incendiary fire can occur from chemical reactions, electronics, and mechanical devices. They can be delivered as stationary, hand-thrown (Molotov cocktail), or self-propelled (rocket, etc.) weapons. Emergency responders will need to recognize situations that might indicate an incendiary fire has occurred. Outward warning signs of a terrorist incendiary fire are much the same as those for arson fires. These include multiple fire origin locations, signs of accelerants, flammable liquid containers, splatter or burn patterns on floors, fusing residue, trailers, forced entry into a structure, and electrical appliances or devices that are out of place.

Chemistry of Fire and Fire Behavior

In order to better understand some of the clues to look for in determining when a fire is of incendiary origin, it is necessary to review some of the basic concepts of the "chemistry of fire and fire behavior." Without this background, the first responder or the fire investigator's success in determining incendiary fires or acts of terrorism will at best be accidental. Since this is not a text for teaching fire investigation, the purpose here is to review some of the basic subjects of fire behavior and fire investigation. Four conditions have to be met in order for a fire to occur in the first place. There must be fuel, heat (ignition source), oxygen (from the air or from a chemical compound), and a chemical chain reaction present. The chemical chain reaction results from the combination of the oxygen, fuel, and ignition source. Knowing the physical state of the fuel in an incendiary fire is quite important in determining the ease of ignition. Fire fuels can be solids, liquids, or gases. Liquids and gases are easier to ignite than a solid material. Gases are easier to ignite than a liquid material. The fire investigator, as well as firefighters, should have knowledge of fire fuels and their physical and chemical characteristics. Just because a fuel is available does not mean fire will automatically occur. Fuel must be in an appropriate physical state in order to burn. Solid and liquid materials do not burn, so the fuel must be vaporized in order for combustion to occur.

Heat Transfer

Fire travels through a structure by three methods: conduction, convection, and radiation. Conduction is a process by which heat travels through a solid medium or solids in contact with each other. Not all materials conduct heat in the same way. How well a material conducts heat is determined by the temperature difference and density of the solid and whether the material is a good conductor of heat. Solids conduct heat much better than gases. Through convection, heat is transferred through a medium such as a gas or liquid. Air in the atmosphere is composed of gases; when heated, the gases expand and rise. Generally within a structure, heated air, fire gases, and smoke rise to the upper parts. When conduction of heat between combustion products and other solid materials occurs, the fire is spread. Most people at one time or another have witnessed heat, smoke, and thermal columns rising from campfires, rubbish fires, or a smoke stack. These examples provide a good illustration of how a convection current or a thermal column develops and travels from a fire. The convection process also moves products of combustion, in the form of smoke and gases, to other parts of the structure. Smoke and gases continue to rise until they encounter a solid object, such as the ceiling. At that point, the gases spread horizontally and then bank down again until the whole room may be filled with smoke and hot fire gases. Once the ignition temperature of these gases is reached, flashover occurs. Generally, ordinary combustible materials tend to burn above the floor level, even when flashover occurs. These materials rarely burn up completely without the help of an accelerant. Ash and burned materials from the upper parts of the room tend to protect the floor from burning. Temperatures encountered in an "ordinary" dwelling fire can reach between 1,000–1,600°F in the upper parts of rooms. Floor temperatures, however, will be much lower, between 100–250°F.

Radiant heat generally does not penetrate smoke and steam. In a room with minimum smoke presence, radiant heat can cause char and burn patterns on the floor, and mislead an inexperienced fire investigator. Radiation, in terms of fire behavior, is a process by which heat is transferred from a hot object to a cold object. Radiation is a type of visible light. Radiant heat can cause fire to communicate between buildings as far as 100 feet apart. Heat radiated to another object causes pyrolysis (chemical decomposition of the material), which is really the vaporization of the cold object allowing it to burn. Most solid materials do not burn; they must be heated to the point at which they produce vapors. Once produced, it is the vapors that burn. It is the pyrolysis process, which is relatively slow, that produces the vapors. Once the ignition temperature of the vapors is reached, they will burst into flames. However, it is the vapor — not the object — that is burning. Fuel above the flames of a fire are pyrolized, where the fuel below generally is not. Radiated and conducted heat, unlike convected heat that rises, can travel in any direction.

Stages of Fire Development

There are three stages of fire development: beginning or incipient stage, free-burning stage, and smoldering stage. During the incipient stage, fire is localized to the point of origin. At this point, there is plenty of oxygen present for the fire to burn and little smoke being produced. Hot gases are rising in a thermal column away from the fire. Convection moves these gases to the upper parts of the room or within the structure. If a solid fuel exists above the flames, convection and direct flame contact spread the flames up and out from the source in a typical "V" pattern of char. This "V" pattern can be a virtual "neon" sign pointing back to the fire origin. Care should be taken in examination of "V" patterns because they can also be misleading if taken out of context with the other clues present. During the free-burning stage, the fire grows in intensity and spreads through the fuel in the room. Other fuels in the room are heated until they reach their ignition temperatures (Table 7.1). Smoke and fire gases continue to rise in the room, until they reach the ceiling and begin to bank down. When these gases reach their ignition temperatures, flashover occurs in the room. After flashover, the fuels in the room will continue to burn as long as oxygen and fuel are present.

**Table 7.1   Ignition Temperatures of
Common Combustibles**

Wood	392°F
#1 fuel oil	444°F
Paper	446°F
60 octane gas	536°F
Acetylene gas	571°F
Wheat flour	748°F
Corn	752°F
Propane gas	871°F

After a period of time, the fuel will be consumed and the open flame burning will subside: this is known as the smoldering stage. Once the oxygen level of the room goes below 16%, open flame combustion will stop. Combustion taking place at this point is referred to as glowing combustion. Temperatures in the room remain very high. If not ventilated, hot fire gases and products of combustion can deflagrate into a secondary fire in the presence of an ignition source, which will likely result in what is known as a backdraft or smoke explosion.

Several environmental factors affect the way a fire will burn, such as temperature, humidity, and wetness of fuel. Fires may become more severe on hot days rather than cold days. Heat causes dehydration of fuels and a heated environment is much dryer than a damp environment. Dry materials are more likely to combust than wet materials. When investigating a fire where wetted materials have burned, there should be some question as to the possible use of an accelerant. Wetted materials generally do not burn well by themselves. Heat can cause materials to be dried in the path of the fire if the wet conditions are not maintained. Humidity is a factor that will affect fire potential. When the humidity is low, fires are more likely to occur than when the humidity is high. This fact has more bearing on external fires than structural fires. Humidity is a measure of the amount of water vapor present in the air. As the temperature of the air increases, so does the ability of the air to hold more water, without developing a fog or mist condition. This is why fog generally forms at night and early morning, when the humidity is high and the temperature is low. When exposed to low humidity for long periods of time, fuels dry out and are much more susceptible to combustion than when they are wet. Wetness of fuel should not be confused with humidity, which causes the surface of a material to become wet. When a fuel is wet, it has absorbed moisture to its interior and is much more difficult to ignite than a material that just has a wet surface. Material that is wet throughout will require much more heat, over a longer period of time, to boil off the moisture and ignite the material. The presence of an accelerant may provide the heat necessary to dry out the material or cause charring on the surface.

Table 7.2   Physical Characteristics of Some Common Fuels

	Gasoline	Kerosene	Fuel Oil #4	Jet Fuel
Boiling point	100–400°F	338–572°F		250°F
Flashpoint	–45°F	100–150°F	130°F	100°F
Ignition temp	536–853°F	444°F	505°F	435°F
Vapor density	3.0–4.0	4.5		1.0
Specific gravity	0.8	0.81	<1	0.8
LEL	1.4%	0.7%		0.6%
UEL	7.6%	5%		3.7%

Hydrocarbon fuels that might be used as accelerants have distinct heat outputs, sometimes referred to as the heat of combustion. NFPA's Fire Protection Handbook defines heat of combustion as "the amount of heat released during a substance's complete oxidation" (combustion, i.e., conversion to carbon dioxide and water). The importance of heat of combustion to the fire investigator or fire officer is in the comparison of the intensity of the burn to the potential fuels that were normally present. In other words, if the damage from a fire is more significant than would be expected from ordinary combustible materials, an accelerant may have been used. Volatile materials, such as gasoline, are easy to ignite because of low boiling points and flashpoints, but they do not produce as much heat as do kerosene-like fuels (Table 7.2). One of the characteristics of gasoline is that it will explode, something that many arsonists do not realize. Gasoline can also be used as an explosive fuel with some type of explosive device as an ignition source. This type of device will create an explosion and fire. Gasoline mixed with soap flakes, forming a paste, can be used as an antipersonnel device which inflicts deep skin burns. Kerosene-type fuels include diesel fuel, paint thinners, mineral spirits, charcoal lighters, and fuel oils. These fuels should be mixed with a small amount of gasoline to help ignite the fire. Because of their low volatility, when these fuels are used as accelerants the person setting the fire is not in as great a danger to injury as with gasoline or other highly volatile fuels. Low volatility liquids are persistent because they are not readily vaporizing, and there is no hurry to ignite them. Danger of explosion from the vapors is also much less than for gasoline. Kerosene-type liquids have heavy molecular weights with lots of carbon and hydrogen. Liquids with large amounts of carbon and hydrogen tend to burn hot and produce many more BTUs per equivalent quantity than gasoline. Heavy fuels are used most often in the setting of incendiary fires and are likely to be the choice of terrorists who choose fire as their weapon for destruction. Skills of the arsonist or terrorist can be learned from the type of fuel used to set the fire. Professionals would use harder-to-obtain fuels. The amateur fire setter would use fuels that are present at the scene or are easy to obtain, such as gasoline and diesel.

Clues to Arson and Terrorism

Firefighters should be observant when approaching all fire scenes. Many clues indicating a fire has been set may be present but easily overlooked if firefighters are not observant. Flame color can be a key indicator of the presence of an accelerant. Normally, the color of flames from an "ordinary" fire contain variations of yellow and orange. Generally, hydrocarbon accelerants produce a yellow-to-deep red flame. Deep red flames in combination with dense black smoke might indicate the presence of petroleum products, tar, rubber, or plastics. While the color of the smoke from a fire is determined by the type and nature of fuel, often materials high in carbon content burn with a heavy black color. This does not automatically mean an accelerant was used, but should be noted. Alcohols, which may be used as accelerants, burn with a blue or purple flame. Heavy brown smoke accompanied by deep red flames indicates nitrogen products are present. White smoke with bright white flames, which produces a water reaction, is usually magnesium. Black smoke with red and blue-green flames indicates asphalt shingles. Normal fire smoke colors that change to yellow or grayish-yellow usually indicate that "backdraft" conditions might be present. Other materials present in a fire may produce colors other than the normal yellow and orange. Sodium metal present in a fire produces a yellow flame, which is difficult to distinguish from the yellow produced by carbon. Strontium salts produce a bright red color, which is the source of the red color in roadway flares and pyrotechnic devices. Copper halides produce a green color, while potassium gives off a violet or purple color, and barium salts produce a yellow-green color. The presence of any particular color of flame by itself is not significant, but it should be noted as unusual and can assist in determining the cause of the fire. Smoke colors from a fire are generally white, gray, or black. As mentioned earlier, black generally is an indication of hydrocarbon materials present. Many materials found within a structure or vehicle are carbon based and can produce dense black smoke. However, if heavy black smoke is encountered in an area where it might not be expected, then further investigation is warranted. Smoke that contains colors other than white, gray, or black should also be noted.

Fire investigators are not routinely dispatched to structural fires. They are called by firefighters at the scene who have determined that the circumstances surrounding the fire are suspicious. When the investigator arrives, the fire is usually over. He or she does not know anything about how the fire developed or progressed, what difficulties firefighters might have had extinguishing the fire, or any other details about the event. First responding fire personnel therefore play a significant role in determining the potential for incendiary fires by noting unusual colors of smoke and flame, coupled with other signs and clues. Information developed for the fire investigator begins before arrival of the fire department at the incident scene. Dispatch information can be very important to the fire investigator. Who made the call reporting the fire? What is the date, time, day of the week, and location of the incident? What events occurred upon approach to the incident scene? Weather conditions can play an important part in the fire investigation. Factors such as rain, snow, ice, wind, humidity, and atmospheric inversion can affect the fire conditions.

When approaching the scene, responders should be alert for anyone leaving the scene in a hurry. Make note of vehicles or other obstructions placed in such a manner that access to hydrants, sprinkler connections, streets, driveways or the building itself is impaired. Find out who reported the fire. Were they still on the scene when the firefighters arrived? Is the person who discovered the fire the one who reported the fire? If not, who told the person to call the fire department? Often, the person who started the fire stays around to watch the fire department. Sometimes he may even try to assist the fire department in extinguishing the fire. This is unlikely to happen if the fire is a terrorist incident. Listen for comments made by people on the incident scene — sometimes they can be important. Was the owner of the building or structure at the fire scene? How did he learn about the fire? If the fire occurred at night, were the occupants dressed in night clothes? Were they acting normally based upon the severity of the event? Were they calm or were they excited or hysterical? One would expect that those watching their home or business burning would be very upset. Have there been any threats against the person or business? Does the person who owns the property have financial difficulties?

Witnesses might also be able to identify colors of flame or smoke that might have been present in the initial phases of the fire. Information that can be valuable to the investigator also becomes available on the scene while fighting the fire. Fires started in several unconnected locations are usually an indication of an incendiary fire. Was it necessary to use forced entry to get into the structure or was the door unlocked? Were there signs of forced entry to the building before fire department arrival, such as marks on doors or windows, broken or damaged doors, or broken windows, not caused by the fire? Are there signs inside the structure of a burglary, such as an open safe or cash register? Business records placed on a desk or scattered throughout an office can also be a sign of an incendiary fire. Did the fire spread more rapidly than might be expected in this type of occupancy? Was the fire burning hotter than might have been expected from the fuel present? Were there any unusual odors at the fire scene? Arsonists sometimes try to hide the smell of accelerants by using perfume, ammonia, or similar materials with strong odors. Was there any unusual configuration of contents of the structure? Are any appliances or items of furniture out of place? Were sprinkler valves found in the closed position, or was there any damage to the fire suppression systems in the structure? Were fire doors in the building open or closed? Were open doors blocked open, or had the closing devices been damaged to prevent closing? When first attempts were made to extinguish the fire, how did it behave? Was it difficult to extinguish, did it spread, or were explosions encountered when the fire was hit by hose streams? Finally, what information was discovered during overhaul and after?

Firefighters should perform only the overhaul necessary to extinguish the fire before the fire investigator arrives. Care should be taken not to move anything that was in place before the arrival of the fire department. Doing too much overhaul or cleanup at a scene might please the building owner, but it might also satisfy the arsonist because the evidence might be destroyed. The fire scene where a fire is suspicious could also be a terrorist incident, but in either case it is still a crime scene. All response personnel should be aware of this potential and secure the area. Keep unnecessary personnel, the owners, and anyone else who has no business there out until the investigation of the scene is over. Many signs and bits of evidence are present on the scene that might be helpful to investigators. They include multiple fires, distinct odors, undue wood charring, uneven burning, inoperative sprinklers, tracks, footprints, evidence of a burglary, and many others. Physical evidence should be left where it is found and not touched or handled by firefighters. All of the information collected by firefighters on the scene needs to be preserved and accurately documented by responders and passed on to the investigator. Unless someone claims responsibility for the fire, even if determined to be incendiary, it might not be known for some time, if ever, that it might have been an act of terrorism. Only when those responsible are caught will their motives be discovered.

Fire Causes

Fires in general can be divided into three causes: an act of God, an accidental origin, or an incendiary origin. Fire investigators must therefore eliminate all natural and accidental causes before they can look at potential incendiary causes. The entire fire scene and surrounding area must be thoroughly searched to identify clues to its origin. Fire scene investigation begins with the area outside the structure or vehicle and works toward the area of the burn. Many clues can be found in unburned areas, such as abandoned containers, cigarettes, footprints, tire tracks, and others. With the potential for terrorism, the location of the incident scene should be considered, as well as dates, times, and days of the week. Is there anything about the scene, event, or dates and times that would point to possible terrorist activity? For example, a fire in a laboratory that does research on animals might be the work of an animal rights group. Fires in abortion clinics should also be suspected as being terrorist events. When a fire occurs in a church, it should be considered suspicious. These types of acts might be the work of domestic terrorists trying to create fear among a group of people or to further their moral and political viewpoints. Keep the goals of the terrorist and the types of terrorist targets in mind when investigating fires.

Ultimately, the investigator wants to determine where the fire originated or where it started. Once the area of origin is identified the investigator wants to know what the source of ignition was. This can be determined by eliminating all other sources of ignition — the last possible source becomes the probable source. No matter what the fuel might have been, there must be something that ignited the fire. Generally, the source will be either some type of flame, a spark, heat, or a hot object. Heat is the primary source of ignition in almost every fire. The source of the heat can be open flames, hot surfaces, electricity, mechanical sparks, lightning, static electricity, friction, spontaneous heating, chemical reactions, polymerization, oxidizing agents, compression of gases, or water reactivity.

Fuels, whether wood, paper, plastics, liquids, or gases, all have ignition temperatures. The ignition source (heat source) of a fire must be at or above the ignition temperature of the fuel in order for combustion to occur. Most set fires are started by the heat from a small flame coming from a match or lighter. When matches are used, the match might not be fully consumed by the fire. In their search of the point of origin, investigators should be very meticulous in seeking small pieces of matches or cigarettes that might have been the source of ignition. Lighters are generally not left behind in the building or vehicle, but might have been discarded outside the area. Remaining significant sources of heat ignition include electrical, arcs, and lightning (Table 7.3).

Electrical distribution systems have many safeguards built into them to help prevent fire. Someone who wants a fire to occur could compromise some of these safeguards. Tampering with circuit breakers or fuses can cause a fire to start. Undersized electrical cords, extension cords, oversized light bulbs, or placement of a combustible material against a hot light bulb can

Table 7.3 Temperatures of Common Ignition Sources

Lighted cigarette, no drafts	550°F
Lighted cigarette, with drafts	1350°F
Struck match	2000°F+
Electric arc	2000°F+

all be efforts to start an incendiary fire. The investigator needs to look carefully at the electrical system for signs of tampering or electrical shorts that might not be explainable by natural causes. Spark is a term that has several definitions and must be further explained. A spark can refer to an electrical spark, which is the discharge of electrical current through the air or another insulator. Another type of spark is a small particle of a burning or glowing solid material moving through the air. Both of these types of sparks are likely to be hot enough to ignite vapors and some solid fuels. Particulate sparks can be produced from two dissimilar materials, such as flint and steel, or by significant frictional contact between two materials.

Many chemical reactions are exothermic (heat producing) and can be an ignition source for natural fire causes and incendiary fires. Animal and vegetable oils are subject to spontaneous ignition (spontaneous heating) and have been the source of many fires in restaurants, laundries, and other locations. The fire that occurred in the 1 Meridian Plaza Building in Philadelphia and killed three firefighters was caused by the spontaneous ignition of linseed oil-soaked rags that had not been properly disposed of after use. This chemical reaction is slow oxidation involving the oxygen in the air reacting with the bonding of the animal or vegetable oils, resulting in the combustible material, such as a rag being heated slowly to its ignition temperature, leading to spontaneous fire. Carbon-based materials, such as charcoal used for cooking on a grill, can undergo slow oxidation in the presence of moisture and spontaneously combust, igniting other combustible materials in the vicinity. Care should be taken to eliminate these types of materials as possible sources of ignition.

Polymerization is a chemical reaction in which a chemical reacts with itself, creating an enormous expansion of the material and the production of heat. Chemical oxidizers may also be incorporated into the arson fire to act as the ignition source and accelerate the rate of combustion. Some oxidizers are water reactive and, when in contact with water, produce heat. This heat can be significant enough to ignite ordinary combustibles. Contact with water also causes some oxidizers to release oxygen. Many common oxidizers include bromates, chlorates, chlorites, hypochlorites, nitrates, nitrites, perborates, perchlorates, peroxides (both organic and inorganic), permanganates, and persulfates.

Calcium hypochlorite is a common swimming pool chlorinator. It is also a strong oxidizer and, in contact with hydrocarbon materials, can ignite spontaneously. Two tablespoons of brake fluid poured into 2 cups of calcium hypochlorite causes a violent orange-red flame that can extend 4–6 feet above the container, producing an enormous amount of heat. Depending on the environmental conditions, the reaction takes from 45 seconds to 5 minutes to start. Reactions between other oxidizers and hydrocarbons would produce similar results. Using gaseous oxidizers such as oxygen, or liquid oxygen, chlorine, fluorine, and bromine can significantly increase the rate of combustion and increase the heat output of the fire. Oxidizers in contact with hydrocarbon fuels such as gasoline, diesel, kerosene, and others can create a chemical reaction that will result in a fire. Some, if not all, of these chemical reactions could be used by an arsonist or a terrorist to start an incendiary fire. If the fire cannot be attributed to any natural causes, then it is quite possible that an incendiary fire or a terrorist event has occurred. The investigator must then ask what is unusual about the fire and what is not normal? Perhaps the fire occurred in an area where no natural ignition source was present, such as in an abandoned building where all electrical power and heating fuel was shut off. Fires that occur within structures where no electrical or heat source is present at the point of origin are suspicious. Certain areas within structures are unusual for fires to occur. These include unfinished basements and crawl spaces, common areas of a building, closets, bathrooms, water heaters, stairwells or hallways, and behind or underneath stairs.

Thermal damage to a building and contents can also give clues to the cause of the fire. No single clue is conclusive in determining the cause of a fire; however, all of the clues evaluated together may yield the probable cause. Firefighters should be interviewed to determine what tactics were used in fighting the fire and where they concentrated their efforts. Surfaces of building contents will generally be burned more on the end facing the oncoming fire. Heat and smoke travel up within a structure. In a building not completely destroyed, heat damage will generally occur high in the room or structure. If there is low burning, the area should be thoroughly examined because this might lead to the point of origin. Floors should have much less burn damage than walls and ceilings. Burning on the floor, or walls burned down to the floor, should be considered suspicious. Low burns are very unusual in a structure and should be given careful consideration, especially when there are burn marks on the bottom of a door, which is highly unusual. Burning on the floor can be caused by the pooling of a flammable liquid. When a floor is burned through, it is important to observe if the underside of the floor is burned, to determine if the fire came from above or below the floor.

Char depth can be useful in determining the point of origin of a fire. As wood is exposed to fire, it burns at the rate of approximately 1 inch deep in 45 minutes. The area that has the deepest charring may likely be where the fire burned the longest. This usually occurs near the point of origin. When concrete or other masonry surface is exposed to fire or heat, it goes through a process of chipping or crumbling. Spalling can be an indicator of localized heating, which might be the result of a chemical incendiary material or volatile petroleum liquid. When a flammable liquid burns on a surface it protects the area underneath. The burning takes place at the surface of the

Table 7.4   Incendiary Incidents Investigated by ATF 2000–2003

	2000	2001	2002	2003
Incidents	1604	1555	1823	1884
Injured	338	4624*	311	642
Killed	161	3396*	191	299
Property Damage	633 M	23 B	7 B	749 M

* Injuries and deaths included from World Trade Center attack September 11, 2001.

liquid where the vapor is being produced and mixes with the air. This process may produce irregular unburned areas on the floor that were protected by the flammable liquid. When this occurs, it is a good indication that an accelerant might have been used. Springs in furniture might also hold some clues as to the temperature of the fire. When steel springs are heated, they will reach a temperature well below their melting point, in which they will lose their "spring." This temperature is referred to as the "annealing" temperature. Between 1100 and 1200°F, the spring will collapse from any applied weight. The collapse of the springs can be an indicator of whether the fire started within the furniture or from the outside. When a smoldering fire occurs within the furniture, intense heat will produce a localized area of spring collapse surrounded by springs that have not collapsed as much. Heating from an external source will tend to be less intense and, in general, the collapse of the springs is minimal. Even if the external fire does develop high heat, the spring collapse will be uniform throughout. If something falls on the furniture, this can change the whole picture.

Glass is found in almost any type of vehicle or structure. While it looks like a solid, it is really a super-cooled liquid. When glass is exposed to external stress, it has a degree of flexibility before it will break. As glass breaks, certain lines are formed, which can indicate from which side the blow came that caused the glass to shatter. This can help the investigator determine if there might have been a break-in. Glass can be recovered from the scene and sent to the lab for reconstruction, which will reveal the side where breaking started. Thermal stress can also cause glass to break. Breaking lines are almost always curved randomly throughout the pane from heat exposure; when the stress is mechanical, the breaking lines are usually straight. Glass broken from the heat of a fire will almost always be covered with soot, charring, or ash residue. If broken glass is found under other burn debris and has not been stained, it is very likely that it was broken before the fire. Glass on top of burn debris very likely was broken during suppression operations. If the fractures in the glass resemble a complex road map, this might indicate a rapidly developing fire with a lot of heat. When craters or spalling occur in the glass, it is likely due to water hitting the hot glass during suppression efforts. Slivers of glass that are narrow and in long pieces suggest that some type of explosion might have occurred. If they are covered with soot or varnish, it means the explosion occurred late in the fire. Absence of soot or light soot would indicate the explosion happened early in the fire, which might have been the result of an explosive device or gasoline vapor explosion. The meticulous investigator will take the time to evaluate the clues indicated by the presence and condition of glass at the fire scene. Melting glass can also present some helpful clues as to the progress and origin of the fire. Whether from a window, lamp, furnishing, or a light bulb, glass will generally melt in the direction of the heat source. This can point to where the heat came from and possibly the origin of the fire. When glass reaches its melting temperature of approximately 1400°F, it will melt on the side facing the source of the heat. Melting points of other common materials that might be found in fire debris include aluminum, 1220°F; copper, 1625–1780°F; and cast iron, 2200–2700°F. Fires involving wood and charcoal that have plenty of oxygen can produce temperatures in excess of 2400°F. Therefore, melting of metals may occur from the heat developed in an ordinary fire. Melting of metals and glass can be an indicator of temperatures reached at specific locations in the vehicle or structure. Inventories of structures should be evaluated to determine if things had been removed from the structure before the fire or if a theft might have occurred.

The fire scene should be carefully searched for clues to the origin and cause of the fire. Whether the act is arson or terrorism, it should be considered a crime scene, and only those who need to be on the scene should be allowed there. Acts of terrorism are under the jurisdiction of the FBI, and they should be called when terrorism is suspected. Evidence should be preserved and carefully removed for analysis at the crime lab if needed. Convictions on charges of arson or incendiary terrorism will likely be based heavily on circumstantial evidence. The better the job firefighters and investigators do to preserve the crime scene and evidence, the better the chances for a conviction. Firefighters should be familiar with the signs of arson or incendiary fires. They should also be familiar with potential terrorist targets in the community.

The ATF has established a new fire research laboratory (FRL) that is the first scientific research laboratory in the U.S. dedicated to supporting the unique needs of the fire investigation community. The new laboratory has established the following goals:

- Serving as a national and international model for forensic fire researching
- Conducting scientific research directed at the determination of fire causes, fire development, and other fire phenomena that validates fire scene indicators and improves fire evidence analysis

- Establishing a central repository of fire investigation test and research data
- Developing an internationally recognized research and education center for the advancement of knowledge and technology transfer related to fire cause investigation and fire scene reconstruction
- Operating as a full-scale testing laboratory conducting reconstruction analysis to determine where additional research on fire science and fire investigation is needed

The FRL will work in cooperation with the International Association of Arson Investigators (IAAI), U.S. Fire Administration (USFA), National Fire Academy (NFA), and the National Fire Protection Association (NFPA) to develop enhanced investigative, prosecutorial and training methodologies. The FRL will join two existing laboratories that will occupy ATF's National Laboratory Center (NLC) complex on a 35-acre site in Ammendale, Maryland. The NLC will house the ATF Alcohol and Tobacco Laboratory (ATL), the Forensic Science Laboratory (FSL)–Washington, and the new Fire Research Laboratory. The FRL will occupy approximately 50,000 gross square feet of the facility and will encompass three fire test (burn) cells and administrative office space. A number of scientists with disciplines in fire protection engineering, mechanical engineering, chemical engineering, electrical engineering, materials engineering, physics, and metallurgy will staff the facility. The FRL will provide fire scientists, engineers, researchers, and investigators with the capability to perform a wide range of standard and unique tests. These potential tests range from small-scale fire tests to full-scale testing of entire residential structures. The FRL will have several large test cells (rooms) where full-scale test fires will be conducted. This unique capability will provide ATF the versatility necessary to reconstruct and test key aspects of most of the fire scenarios encountered by fire investigators in the field. Using these test cells, the FRL will have the ability to evaluate a wide variety of fire scenarios, ranging from a simple burning trash can to a complete furnished room to a full-scale structural mock-up. The lab will be equipped with state-of-the-art hood/exhaust systems, data acquisition systems and instrumentation to facilitate the measurement of heat release rate (HRR), burning rate, heat flux, and temperatures of burning materials. In addition to the large test cells, the laboratory will have reconfigurable small-scale test areas and bench-scale test equipment necessary to predict large-scale fire behavior and perform computer fire modeling for use in fire scene reconstruction and test validation. The FRL will also utilize a 1–10 scale model of its medium and large burn rooms (including hood systems) to effectively predict fire behavior and smoke movement within the laboratory itself. Additional support space in the FRL will include:

- An electrical testing laboratory to facilitate testing and failure analysis of residential and commercial electrical products, components, equipment, and wiring
- A state-of-the-art fire control room, fire safety suppression system, and on-site air and water pollution treatment facilities
- Classroom/training space for delivery of fire investigation training and educational programs
- Support spaces that include shop areas, locker rooms and showers, instrumentation rooms, conditioning rooms, construction and test materials storage, and evidence storage areas

The Fire Research Laboratory will provide a controlled environment where fire investigation theories can be evaluated and fire cause determination scenarios can be reconstructed and tested on a large scale by fire scientists, engineers, and investigators. The FRL staff will also provide training that will produce a cadre of accredited and certified fire investigators. The FRL will serve as a central repository of scientific information related to fire incident investigation, analysis, and reconstruction research. The FRL will disseminate the knowledge derived from this research through scholarly publication in scientific and investigation literature and through the delivery of training and education programs. The FRL will continue to work in close cooperation with NIST to support joint research projects and other initiatives designed to improve fire scene investigation, reconstruction, and analysis. The FRL will be an active participant in the worldwide community of fire research laboratories and will serve as an international model in the training of personnel, in the development of research and testing protocols, and in fostering technical partnerships.

Monitoring and Detection Equipment for Terrorist Agents

8

One of the most important functions at any hazardous materials incident is air monitoring and liquid sampling for known and unknown hazardous materials. Air monitoring and liquid sampling are just as important for radiological, chemical, and biological terrorist events as they are for unknown hazardous materials. Providing a safe and efficient monitoring effort requires a systematic approach. Some things must be done either before or simultaneously with others. Monitoring device priorities, assigned in the interest of safeguarding instruments for unknown materials, are as follows:

- Corrosive vapor
- Radioactivity
- Combustibility (flammability)
- Oxygen levels, both deficient and rich
- Corrosive liquids
- Other chemical products

Testing for corrosive vapors first is important to protect the monitoring instruments. If an atmosphere is corrosive, it can damage other instruments, and information gathered might not be accurate. Obviously if you have a pretty good idea of what has occurred, you can use a specific monitoring instrument to look for the suspected material. If an explosion has occurred, the site should be monitored for radiation at the same time the site is being cleared by the bomb squad. Releases of some type without illness should be monitored for radiation and biological materials. If you see liquids or solids, monitoring can be more specific, depending on what type of material is suspected. Without the appropriate monitoring equipment or personnel skilled in its use, it must be assumed that terrorist agents are present and proper precautions should be taken. Terrorism and use of monitoring instruments for chemical and biological agents are rather new to emergency responders. Personnel should be aware that new developments in agent monitoring are occurring almost daily. Technology is evolving, and it is important to keep up with the information as it comes out. Each type of monitoring device requires calibration, testing, setup, and training for proper use. Responders must be aware of the types of monitors available, their capabilities, and limitations.

Generally, monitors are designed to sample the air for one specific gas or a small number of gases. If limitations and operations of monitoring equipment are not understood, it could become more dangerous than not monitoring at all. For example, if you were monitoring for a flammable gas, and did not understand the concept of flammable range and how it relates to the meter readings, you might find yourself in the middle of the flammable range! Remember that all monitoring instruments have their differences and should be calibrated, tested, cleaned, and maintained on a frequency recommended by the manufacturer. Personnel who test and maintain monitoring instruments should be trained. Untrained people calibrating, maintaining, and repairing instruments might void the warranty, and more importantly, might render the instrument useless to emergency personnel, placing their lives in danger.

pH

One of the most basic liquid tests to verify or eliminate a class of chemicals is the pH reading. pH ranges can be determined by simple and inexpensive papers or a variety of meters. All that is really important to know about pH in the field is that it tells us the relative acidity and alkalinity of a given liquid material. pH is based on a reverse logarithm scale of 0–14. Readings on the scale from 0–6.9 indicate that the material present has a degree of acidity. The lower the number value, the higher the level of acidity, or the more corrosive the material is in terms of damage to body tissues and metals. A reading of 7 on the pH scale indicates that the material is neutral — neither acidic nor alkaline. Pure water would have a pH of 7.0. As the numbers increase above 7.1 the liquid material identified is alkaline. The higher the number, the higher the level of alkalinity and the more corrosive the material will be. It is important that response personnel understand the pH scale and what resources they have in their departments to test for pH (Figure 8.1).

Monitoring for Oxygen Levels

Everyone knows that there must be enough oxygen in the air to sustain life. At times, it is important for response personnel to monitor the air or a

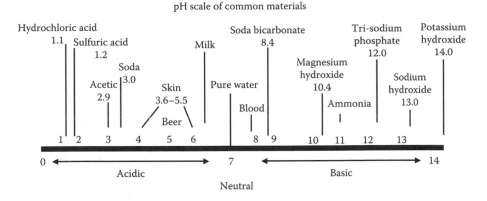

Figure 8.1 pH scale of common materials.

confined-space atmosphere to determine the oxygen level. Too much oxygen, just as not enough oxygen, can present dangers. Normal air contains approximately 20.5% oxygen. Levels below 19.5% are considered oxygen deficient and dangerous to health. Levels of oxygen above 23.5% are considered oxygen enriched and present an extreme fire hazard. While they are not flammable themselves, oxygen and other oxidizers drastically increase the rate of combustion. In fact, some materials that are normally considered noncombustible will burn very well in oxygen-enriched atmospheres. If personnel are involved in monitoring for oxygen levels, they should do the monitoring while wearing a self-contained breathing apparatus (SCBA), in case an oxygen-deficient atmosphere is encountered. This is especially true in atmospheres less than 19.5%. When monitoring excess oxygen levels between 19.5 and 25.0%, it is not necessary to wear SCBA, but it should be worn as a precaution.

Monitoring for Flammable Atmospheres

The instrument usually chosen for monitoring flammable atmospheres is referred to as the combustible gas indicator (CGI). This comes in many sizes and shapes with diverse operating features, but all perform pretty much the same function: they check for a percentage of the lower explosive limit (LEL). CGIs are intended for use only in normal oxygen atmospheres. Oxygen-deficient atmospheres will produce readings that are lower than correct. When a flammable atmosphere is suspected, it is necessary to use a CGI to determine what percentage of the LEL may be present. Every flammable vapor has a flammable range. Some materials have a narrow range, and some a wide range. The wider the range, the easier it is for combustion to occur. Materials with wide ranges generally burn rich and may burn within containers. Flammable materials have an LEL and an upper explosive limit

(UEL).Below the lower limit, there is enough oxygen but not enough fuel to burn. The vapor is considered too lean to burn. Above the UEL, there is enough fuel but not enough oxygen to burn; the vapor is considered too rich to burn. However, somewhere between the upper and lower explosive limits there is just the right mixture of fuel vapor and oxygen for combustion to take place. Combustible gas indicators measure a percentage of the LEL. The U.S. Environmental Protection Agency (EPA) has issued guidelines for response personnel to keep them from getting into a dangerous flammable atmosphere. When the reading on the combustible gas indicator reaches 10% of the LEL, monitoring should continue cautiously. Between 10 and 25% of the LEL, monitoring should be continued with extreme caution, particularly as levels get higher. When the monitor reads 25% of the LEL, there is a potential vapor explosion hazard and personnel should withdraw at once. There are several monitoring instruments that use the CGI principle; they include photoionization detector (PID), flame ionization detector (FID), organic vapor analyzer (OVA), and catalytic combustion detectors (CCD). Photoionization detectors measure the amount of energy used to remove the outermost electron from a molecule. The energy required to accomplish this is referred to as the "ionization potential," measured in electron volts (eV). PIDs use a fan or pump to draw air into the detector where the contaminants are exposed to ultraviolet light. The resulting negatively charged particles (ions) are collected and measured. As the sample is drawn into the instrument it passes over the lamp to be ionized, dust in the atmosphere can collect on the lamp and block the transmission of ultraviolet light. This causes a reduction in instrument reading. Fortunately, the problem can be detected during calibration, and the lamp should be cleaned on a regular basis. Humidity can also affect the efficiency of the device. The presence of moisture on the lamp will confuse the device into believing that there is product present. Moist air also causes a reduction in the ionization of chemicals, which in turn produces inaccurate readings.

Flame ionization detectors (FID) use combustion to ionize airborne contaminants. Once ionized, they are detected, and their numbers are measured electronically. Inside the detector chamber, the sample is exposed to a hydrogen flame, which ionizes the organic vapors. As they burn, positively charged carbon-containing ions are produced. These are collected on a negatively charged electrode, and a current is generated. This measurable change in current then causes the meter gauge readout to change. Flame ionization detectors are best suited for use with simple saturated and unsaturated hydrocarbons. Much of the device's sensitivity is lost, however, when dealing with functional derivative compounds.

Organic vapor analyzer (OVA) is factory-calibrated to methane. Consequently, all responses that it provides are relative to methane and are given in percentage, with methane at 100%. The OVA operates in two different modes. In the survey mode, it can determine approximately total concentration of all detectable gases in air. With the gas chromatograph option, individual components can be detected and measured independently, with some detection limits as low as a few parts per million (ppm).

Monitoring Toxic Atmospheres

Toxic sensors are available for many different toxic vapors. They include carbon monoxide, hydrogen sulfide, chlorine, sulfur dioxide, hydrogen chloride, hydrogen cyanide, nitrogen dioxide, and others. No matter which type of toxic sensor is being used, they all display in parts per million (ppm). Those who have taken a course on the chemistry of hazardous materials should remember the family effect of pure elements on the periodic table of elements. For example, chlorine is in family 7 on the periodic table. Also in family 7 are fluorine, bromine, and iodine. Astatine is also in family 7 and has the same family effects, but it is so rare that it will not likely be encountered by emergency responders. All elements in the same family on the periodic table would have similar characteristics. There are monitoring instruments available that detect chlorine. Those same instruments would also detect fluorine, bromine, and iodine, because of the family effect. PIDs use an ultraviolet (UV) lamp to ionize contaminants present in the environment. When the contaminant particles are ionized, they develop an electrical charge that can be read by the instrument. PIDs register toxic materials, but they also pick up hydrocarbons such as gasoline and motor oil. Pesticides that are mixed with xylene, trimethyl benzene, and emulsifiers in a 1–50% concentration can be detected by the PID. This instrument is useful because it detects a wide variety of vapors in relatively small amounts. The PID does not detect specific materials, but it does indicate when there is a contaminant in the environment and expresses a value in parts per million. Readings can be detected from 0.1–10,000 ppm, depending on the manufacturer. Permissible exposure limits (PEL) and threshold limit values (TLV) that are listed at 500 ppm or below are considered toxic. There needs to be a minimum of 10% oxygen in the air for the PID to function.

Gas Chromatography/Mass Spectrometry

One instrument that is valuable in terms of chemical and biological agents is gas chromatography/mass spectrometry (GC/MS). In the past, it has been primarily used in analytical laboratories and was difficult to transport to an incident scene because of its size and sensitivity. Products continue to be developed to make such technology more readily available for field applications. The GC/MS uses a column where the sample gas is passed. Gas samples will have varying degrees of attraction to the material making up the column. Travel time through the column will be unique to each type of gas. As the gas leaves the column, the time of travel is compared to known travel times of specific gases programmed into the instrument to try and find a match. When multiple gases may be present, each will "boil off" at different times and temperatures, resulting in an individual mark on the readout paper. Running time for samples can range from 10–20 minutes. This type of testing is used after all other methods of identifying an unknown have been exhausted. If a sample of the gas being tested is not available for comparison in the instrument, the test will not produce any results. GC/MS is available for limited field use; however, it is very technical in nature and requires experienced operators to produce reliable results.

Colorimetric Sampling Tubes

Colorimetric tubes have been used in hazardous materials response for many years. They are glass tubes with a type of reagent, powder, or crystal that

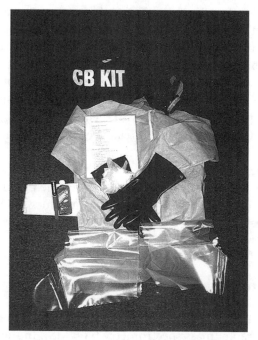

Figure 8.2   Chemical/biological (CB) personal protective equipment kits can be prepackaged for quick use by emergency responders when conducting on-scene testing of samples.

Table 8.1

Agents	Draeger Tube	Part Number
Lewisite (L)	Organic arsenic compound	CH26303
Sulfur mustard (HD)	Thioether	CH25803
Nitrogen mustard (HN)	Organic basic nitrogen compounds	CH25903
Sarin (GB), soman(GD), Tabun (GA)	Phosphoric acid estes	6728461
Cyanogen chloride(CK)	Cyanogen chloride 0.25%/a	CH19801
Phosgene (CG)	Phosgene 0.25/b	CH28301
Hydrogen cyanide (AC)	Hydrocyanic Acid 2/a	CH25701

Source: National Draeger, Inc.

detects certain vapors in the air. A vacuum pump is used to draw an air sample across the reagent, and the color indicated by the reagent reaction with the sampling of air indicates the level of material in the sample. Colorimetric tubes are made for a wide variety of chemicals, including many chemical agents. The tube used to take a sample is identified for the material that is suspected to be in the air. Colormetric tubes not only can be used to determine what chemical is present, but by not reacting to an air sample, they can eliminate a particular type of chemical from consideration. Several companies manufacture colorimetric tubes, including MSA and National Draeger. For departments that cannot afford to buy expensive detection instruments for chemical agents or support a program to maintain them, the less expensive alternative could be a combination of M-8 test strips and colorimetric tubes. Most tubes have a shelf life of 2–5 years, so someone would have to be assigned to oversee replacement of sample tubes as they expire. Many colorimetric tube systems are already in use by hazardous materials teams, so they may be readily available. Response times for detection of vapors from individual agents can vary, and it is important to read manufacturer's instructions for using colorimetric tube equipment. Listed in Table 8.1 are examples of colorimetric tubes for chemical agents by National Draeger.

Chemical Agent Detectors

Five types of detection methods are used by the military for chemical agent monitoring:

- Test strips
- Colorimetric sampling
- Direct-read instruments

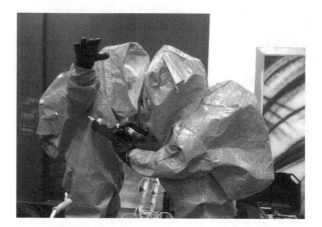

Figure 8.3 Hazmat technicians use an APD 2000 chemical agent monitor to detect chemical agents on Level A suit.

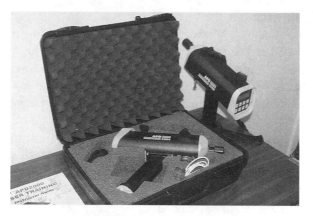

Figure 8.4 APD 2000 Chemical Agent Monitors.

Figure 8.5 MultiRae Chemical Agent Monitor.

Table 8.2

Device	Agent	Approximate Cost
Chemical Agent Monitor (CAM)	Nerve and Blister Agents	$7000
Improved Chemical Agent Monitor (ICAM)	Nerve and Blister	$9000
Individual Chemical Agent Detector (ICAD)	Nerve, Blister, Choking, and Blood	
SAW Mini-Chemical Agent Monitor (CAM)	Nerve, Blister, and Choking	$6300
M8A1	Nerve and Aerosols	
M21 RSCAAL	Nerve and Blister	$170,000
APD2000 Mace and Pepper Spray Detector	Nerve, Blister, Mace, Pepper, and Gamma	$6000

- Test kits
- Field/lab analysis

Direct-Read Instruments

Much of the chemical agent detection equipment that is available to civilian emergency response organizations comes from military technology. Direct-read instruments can be divided into two groups: those used in emergency response and those that are prepositioned for particular purposes. For example, at the nation's chemical stockpile locations, detection equipment with alarms are in place to sense any leaks that might occur from weapons or storage containers of nerve and mustard agents. High-profile events such as the Olympics or presidential inaugurations might benefit from the placement of agent monitors in case a terrorist attack were to occur. At some point in the future, vulnerable exposures, such as subway systems, might routinely install fixed chemical agent monitors for early warning of dangerous conditions. These might become as commonplace as smoke, heat, and carbon monoxide detectors. Many direct-reading devices do not provide a readout of how much agent is present but rather act as a warning that a suspected agent is present in some quantity. Examples of direct-read monitors and their approximate costs are listed below.

The Chemical Agent Monitor (CAM) (Figure 8.6) is a handheld, gross-level, NRT chemical agent detector. It is used to automatically monitor and recognize concentrations of nerve or blister agents (i.e., sarin [GB], VX, or mustard [HD]). The CAM verifies the presence of chemical agent by a bar display on the face of the meter. There is no relationship between the bar readout and ppm that might be present in the air. However, the military

Figure 8.6   Chemical Agent Monitor (CAM).

reports that a skilled and experienced operator can use the bar readout as a determination of when personnel protective clothing should be donned. Detection of an agent by the CAM takes approximately 1 minute. The CAM is known to give false positive readings for many common chemicals including aromatic hydrocarbons (benzene, toluene, xylene, styrene), solvents, and cleaning solutions. This monitor will detect only one agent at a time, so if multiple agents are deployed, they might not be individually detected. An improved version of the CAM is the APD2000 Mace and Pepper Spray Detector. This device will detect riot control agents, nerve and blister agents, and gamma radiation. It has the same response time as the CAM and responds to the same false positive chemicals. A larger version of the CAM is the Improved Chemical Agent Monitor. This unit boasts an improved sampling mechanism with an agent response time of less than 1 minute. It is also designed to reduce the number of false positive responses. Another type of meter available is the Individual Chemical Agent Detector (ICAD). This device detects nerve, blister, choking, and blood agents. Response time to the presence of an agent is 15–120 seconds. False positives given are the same as for the CAM.

A recent addition to the arsenal of chemical agent monitors is the Surface Acoustic Wave (SAW MINICAM) (Figure 8.7). It is much more dependable than its counterparts mentioned above because it is less prone to giving false positives. This instrument can detect nerve and blister agents at the same time. The SAW MINICAM is not in use by the military and has not been tested by them for use against chemical agents. Response time is less than 1 minute and false positives are given for aromatic hydrocarbons.

Handheld Raman Spectroscopy System. Recently, at the University of Maryland, I had the opportunity to participate in a demonstration of a newly developed weapons of mass destruction (WMD) monitoring device. I was impressed with the unit's ease of operation, rugged construction, and that it has applications in both WMD and hazardous materials incidents. The fact

Figure 8.7 SAW MINICAM Chemical Agent Monitor.

that you can program additional chemicals into the unit is also a plus. The "First Defender" model Raman spectroscopy system (Figure 8.7) is designed for the identification of solids, liquids, and mixtures on the incident scene. Spectroscopy is an analytical technique arising from the interaction of a substance with electromagnetic radiation. The electromagnetic radiation absorbed, emitted, or scattered by the molecule is analyzed by the device. Typically, a beam of radiation from a source, such as a laser, is passed through a sample, and the radiation exiting the sample is measured. First Defender has the capability of identifying substances in air, and through bags, bottles, and other containments, without the user or the spectrometer being exposed to the substance. Sampling is nondestructive, does not require contact of the substance, and requires no sample preparation. However, responders still need to wear proper protective clothing for the hazard present when using the First Defender and all monitoring instruments. Start-up time for the monitor is less than 1 minute. The First Defender, made by Ahura Corporation,* was developed with the input and assistance of first responders and is designed for use by fire, EMS, hazardous materials teams, law enforcement, and homeland security personnel in the field. First Defender has an extensive library of substances, including WMD, chemical weapons, explosives, toxic chemicals, white-powders, and other common hazardous materials. Users can add to the library by using the monitor on known substances and programming them into the database. The manufacturer reports that the device is highly accurate and not subject to false positives or false negatives. Frost & Sullivan has awarded the 2005 Product Innovation Award for Homeland Security Technologies in recognition of the company's development of the innovative First Defender handheld Raman instrument.

---

* Ahura Corporation, 978-657-5555 ext. 120, eschmidt@ahuracorp.com.

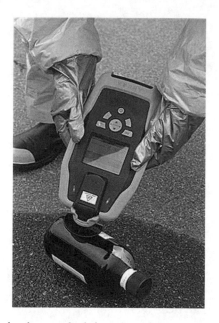

Figure 8.8 First Defender is ideal for identification of potentially hazardous materials directly through the container. (Courtesy AHURA Corporation, used with permission.)

The M8A1 Automatic Chemical Agent Alarm is primarily used as a fixed-site perimeter monitoring device. It is used by the military and may be the primary instrument available when the military is called to assist at a civilian terrorist incident or prepositioned for a high-exposure public event. It will detect nerve agents and aerosols with a 2-minute response time. The unit will give false positives for smoke, internal combustion engine exhaust, and a nuclear blast. The last direct-reading monitor is the M21 Remote Sensing Chemical Agent Alarm (RSCAAL). This unit is also primarily a fixed-site prepositioned device. It will detect nerve or blister agents with a response time of less than 1 minute. False positives occur from halon and organophosphate pesticides such as malathion and parathion.

Test Kits

Another fairly new monitor for chemical agent detection is the Travel IR HCL™, which provides portable laboratory-type identification in the field. It is capable of identifying solids, liquids, pastes, and powders in a matter of seconds. Toxic industrial chemicals, explosives, drugs, and chemical warfare agents are identified easily by response personnel. Travel IR only requires a very small sample for analysis, requiring less decontamination and cleanup.

The device hooks up to a laptop computer and uses simple software to identify materials by "molecular fingerprinting." Sampling procedures are simple, requiring three steps and taking only about 30 seconds. No sample preparation is required. Responders place a sample of the unknown material directly on the analysis area. The Travel IR* records a graph, known as a spectrum, which is the fingerprint of that material. It is then compared to spectrums in the libraries of known materials, and the best match is given as the likely identity of the substance. Additional materials can also be placed in the library. Travel IR is compact, weighing only 26 pounds, and can be used at the sampling location or on the hazmat unit. While this device does not identify biological materials, it can identify white powders after other tests rule out biological materials.

The primary test kit used by the military is the M256A1. The kit contains 12 disposable plastic sampler-detectors, 1 booklet of M8 paper, and a set of instruction cards attached by lanyard to a plastic carrying case. Each sampler-detector contains a square test spot to detect blister agents, a circular test spot to detect blood agents, a star test spot to detect nerve agents, and a tablet with a rubbing tab to detect lewisite. The M256A1 is used to detect and identify gross-level concentrations of GB, VX, H, L vapors, and blood agents. Contents of this kit include M8-detector paper for liquids and enzyme tickets for vapor detection. Wet chemistry is used with this kit to detect the presence of nerve, blister, and blood agents in the air. Enzyme tickets are used to detect GB, VX, H, and L, and blood-agent vapors. Tickets are divided into three sections for detection — blister, blood, and nerve. To test for a specific agent, ampoules are crushed and allowed to react with the air. Reagents placed on the test spot will change color if the agent is present in the air. Testing for an agent requires approximately 15 minutes to go through the entire process, except for hydrogen cyanide, which takes 25 minutes. A timer is needed to monitor the steps. Determination of agent presence is made by watching for color changes or a lack of color change, depending on the agent being tested. False positives can occur from smoke, high temperatures, petroleum products, and organophosphate pesticides. Cold temperatures can also affect the chemicals in the M256/M256A1 chemical agent detection kits, making them unreliable. The cost of the kit is approximately $14 per test card. Sensitivities for selected chemical agents are shown in Table 8.3.

---

* Sold by Smiths Detection, 203-207-9726, missy.robinson@smithdetection.com.

Table 8.3

Agent Class	Agent Detection	Sensitivity
Blister	CXHD L	1.0PPM 0.5 PPM 2.0 PPM
Blood	ACCK	10.0PPM 4.0 PPM
Nerve	GBVX	0.0008PPM 0.0018 PPM

Table 8.4   Thirteen Most Common Suspicious Powders

1. Carnation powdered milk
2. Cremora powdered coffee creamer
3. Johnson & Johnson baby talcum powder
4. Gold Medal All-Purpose Flour
5. Arm & Hammer Baking Soda
6. Dominos Powdered Sugar
7. Fleischman's Brewer's Yeast
8. Dry wall dust
9. Morton's Iodized Salt
10. Chalk dust
11. Gold Bond Medicated Foot Powder
12. Ajax cleaning powder
13. Aerosil Silica Powder

Test Strips

Two types of test papers are used to determine the presence of nerve and blister agents, M-8 and M-9. They function much the same as pH paper. When the M-8 test strip is dipped into a liquid agent, there will be a color change if a nerve or blister agent is present. Color change will identify which agent is detected. Test strips come prepackaged in a booklet of 25, with a color comparison chart inside the front cover (Figure 8.10). It is recommended by the Biological Defense Information Analysis Center (BDIAC) that test strips not be used as the sole method of detecting chemical agent presence because of potential false positive readings. Response time for a color change is approximately 30 seconds or less. False positives can occur from aromatic hydrocarbons, solvents, cleaning solutions, and pesticides. Each pack costs $1. M-9 test strips function in much the same way as the M-8. They are packaged in a roll with adhesive backing and can be wrapped around wrists, cuffs, and boots. The M-9 paper is a little more sensitive and reacts somewhat faster than the M-8. It does not, however, identify which agent is detected. There is also a commercial version available.

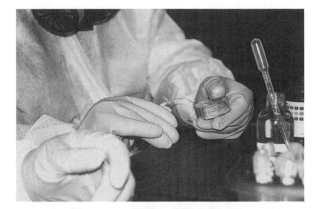

Figure 8.9 A CDP student using a test strip to check for protein content compares his findings to a container comparison chart. Determining protein content helps emergency responders evaluate suspect powders.

Figure 8.10   Responder in proper protective clothing using M-8 paper and comparing results to chart inside front cover.

CDP Five-Step Process for Biological Materials

Following the anthrax mail attack on the eastern U.S. in September 2001, emergency response organizations across the country were inundated with "white-powder" incidents. All but a few of the calls, related to the actual anthrax attack on the East Coast, were hoaxes. Responding to the extremely high number of white-powder incidents taxed the resources of many response organizations. There were so many requests for assistance that the FBI could not respond to all of them; the bureau wanted to be notified only of "credible" incidents. Analytical laboratories that were asked to identify samples from

**Table 8.5   Equipment Inventory Five-Step
Test for Suspicious Powders Kit**

Magnifying glass — 1 each
Sample tubes — 2 each
Tube stand — 1 each
Spatula — 1 each
Scopula — 1 each
Pipette — 1 each
Bottle of distilled water — 1 each
DiaScreen Reagent Strips — 2 bottles (2GP and 3)
pH paper — 1 roll
Flashlight — 1 each
Pen — 1 each

incidents were overwhelmed by the number of requests. Field tests available at the time to test for anthrax spores were unreliable and resulted in many false positives. Lab test equipment that could be used in the field to test for anthrax is very expensive and not available in most areas outside the military.

Personnel at the Center for Domestic Preparedness (CDP) in Anniston, Alabama, saw the need for a better way to deal with white-powder incidents. CDP, a component of the Office for Domestic Preparedness, is the U.S. Department of Homeland Security training center for WMD. It is the only emergency responder training center in the world that provides live-agent training using sarin and VX nerve agents. The center opened in 1998 and has trained 186,000 emergency responders through on- and off-campus training opportunities. The facilities are situated on 62 acres at the site of a former army base, Fort McClellan. Plans are in the works to acquire an additional $23^{1}/_{2}$ acres at the fort, with buildings that will be used for hands-on training. In addition, CDP conducts WMD equipment evaluation using first responders to determine the usefulness of various items on the market. Equipment is obtained from manufacturers, and emergency responders assess them under realistic conditions. Responders wear full personal protective equipment (PPE) when appropriate. While I was there, responders were evaluating equipment for carrying nonambulatory patients out of incident hot zones, through decontamination, and on to triage and treatment.

To deal with problems associated with white-powder incidents, CDP assembled a working group in December 2002 to develop a protocol for use by emergency responders at incident scenes. The goal was to pursue a low-cost way to detect anthrax spores in the field. Members of the working group included scientists, representatives from the fire service, law enforcement, EMS and hazardous materials response organizations, and emergency response educators. An analysis of responses to white-powder/biological-agent incidents yielded weaknesses in preparedness at the local level, including:

- Lack of standardized protocols for response to biological incidents.
- Large numbers of responses exceeded local capabilities.
- Mid-sized and small communities lacked means of analysis to rapidly screen materials in the field to differentiate between potential hoax materials and real biological materials.
- Lack of safety guidelines for response to white-powder incidents, resulting in both overreaction and underreaction.
- Confusing and conflicting information from emergency responders resulted in skepticism among members of the public.
- Some detection equipment sold on the market is unregulated and invalidated.

Beginning the problem-solving process, the working group established two objectives:

1. Determine how a "typical American community's" responders might quickly distinguish a hoax biological event from the real thing, given their current resources.
2. Develop a consensus field analysis protocol for responding to a potential anthrax letter.

By the summer of 2003, as a result of the working group's efforts, a five-step biological field test system was proposed. First of all, it is important to note that the field test does not specifically identify anthrax spores or any other biological agent. What the field test system does is "rule out" the presence of biological materials in a sample from a suspected white-powder or biological agent. Several factors regarding biological agents were addressed in the development of the testing system. First, biological agents are living organisms that typically survive and multiply within a pH range of 6.5–8.0. They contain protein and other components, such as carbohydrates, fats, and nucleic acids (DNA and RNA). Most biological materials, including anthrax spores, create a turbid (opaque or muddy) suspension when placed in water. Based on the natural characteristics known about potential biological materials, the working group established test procedures designed to "rule out" the presence of biological agents. These procedures focus on particle size, water solubility, pH, and protein content to assist emergency responders in evaluating unknown suspect powders. The Five-Step Testing Process is presented in Table 8.6. The Five-Step Process is designed to be simple to conduct with minimal equipment. Supplies for the test kit include 3-milliliter glass or borosilicate vials; pH paper test strips with a container comparison chart; protein test strips with a container comparison chart; a small disposable spatula or scoop; distilled water; a magnifying glass (10 or 20×); and a

Table 8.6   Five–Step Process Biological Field Test

Test to be Conducted	Possibly a Biological (or of Respirable Size)*	Not Likely to be a Biological (or not of Respirable Size)*
Step 1) Collect two samples: sample 1 for reference laboratory analysis**; a volume equal to 1 restaurant sugar packet (ca. 1 gm) or more if available; sample 2 for field analysis; a volume similar to the size of a small pea or kernel of corn		
*Step 2) Place material to be analyzed in a dry ca. 3 ml clean glass vial and secure lid; shake vigorously for a few seconds and observe	Fine cloud or haze hangs above the sample for several seconds after shaking has stopped	All material falls to the bottom of the vial, like salt in a salt shaker, after shaking; air above material is clear
Step 3) Remove lid, fill vial (ca.2 ml) with distilled water and resecure lid; shake vigorously for 15 seconds and observe	Sample appears to mix with water but does not dissolve; liquid contents remain turbid or cloudy	Sample dissolves in water and becomes clear with or without larger particles settling to the bottom
Step 4) Remove lid of vial and dip pH test strip into water; remove strip, wait 30 seconds, and read result on pH strip container	pH between 5 and 9	pH less than 5 or greater than 9
Step 5) Remove lid and dip 1 protein test strip; remove strip, wait 30 seconds, and read result on protein strip container	Protein is present	Protein is not present

*   The shaking of powder in vial as described in Step 2 provides only an indication of particle size. This part of the test protocol does not provide an indication regarding the potential for the material being of biological origin.

** Standing procedures that address packaging, chain of custody and decontamination for suspect samples should be established with the local FBI in advance of an event.

flashlight. A minimum of Level C personal protective clothing and respiratory protection with appropriate filters needs to be worn during sampling and testing procedures. Tests should be performed at the site where the powder or container of powder is located (within the "hot zone") so that contamination is not spread. This testing process does not eliminate the need to take a sample or for samples to be sent out for laboratory analysis, so in addition to the test sample, response personnel should have the necessary supplies for collecting a sample to go to the lab. Labs should have been contacted in advance of an incident to determine if they can test for biological materials and what they require in the way of sample collection, preservation, and sample size. Standing procedures that address packaging, chain of custody and decontamination for suspect samples should be established with the local FBI or other law enforcement agencies in advance of an event.

Biological experts have validated the effectiveness of the field-test procedures in the laboratory, with a confidence level of 99%. That is to say if all of the steps in the Five-Step Process produce negative results, there is a 99% chance that there is no anthrax or other biological agent present. Live anthrax spores were used to test the effectiveness of the test kit in the laboratory setting. CDP has developed a chart titled *Simple Biological Field Test System Confidence Factors* to help response personnel interpret unclear test results and make decisions regarding white-powder incidents (Table 8.7). The shake test is used to determine particle size. Solubility, pH, and protein test results, no matter in what order conducted, can be evaluated by comparing results to Table 8.7. This will ascertain the approximate likelihood that the sample does not contain anthrax spores. Test scores that are in the red zone are considered to be dangerous and should be treated as such. Those in the amber and yellow zones should also be considered potentially dangerous. Green zone scores are considered very unlikely to be a biological threat, and may be treated as such. Once the working group reported its findings and the procedures were validated by biological experts, the next step was to determine how effectively emergency response personnel could utilize the procedure in the field. I was invited by the CDP to witness the testing process and prepare an article for Firehouse® Magazine to get the word out regarding this revolutionary new testing procedure.

A group of hazardous materials technicians attending CDP the week of June 21–25, 2004, were asked to stay an extra two days following their terrorism training class to perform operational tests using the Five-Step Process. Responders were provided with an overview of the test-development process, instructions for conducting the tests, test kits, and personal protective equipment. Responders were divided into pairs, and unmarked test samples were provided from the 15 most common substances used in white-powder incidents. Harmless biological materials were also present among the test samples to show positive results from the testing process. For security purposes those materials will not be identified here. The testing apparatus and procedures did not appear to cause any significant difficulty for response personnel (Figure 8.12). Each group of responders conducted tests on some of the 15 samples without protective equipment to become familiar with the procedures. Each responder was then given Level C protective clothing, a cartridge respirator, protective booties, and two layers of gloves. An additional layer of latex gloves was placed on the outside of the butyl rubber gloves to make it easier to handle the test equipment and materials with gloved hands.

Table 8.7 Simple Biological Field Test Confidence Factors

	VERY HIGH THREAT — Credible threat means other confirmed attacks	HIGH THREAT — Credible threat but no similarities to other confirmed attacks	MODERATE THREAT — Threatening but assessed as possible copy cat	LOW THREAT — Same as other confirmed suspicious materials	VERY LOW THREAT — Other indications that there is no threat
HIGH-RISK LOCATION					
Federal or state government's offices of courts, major business locations similar to other confirmed attacks; other hot spots such as transportation hubs, women's health clinics, or genetic organs research centers	+ Turbidity + Protein + pH	+ Turbidity + Protein + pH	+ Turbidity − Protein + pH or − Turbidity + Protein + pH	+ Turbidity − Protein + pH or − Turbidity + Protein + pH	− Turbidity − Protein − pH or + Turbidity − Protein − pH or − Turbidity + Protein − pH

MODERATE-RISK LOCATION

Local government offices and courts, controversial local businesses, or institutions, schools	+ Turbidity + Protein + pH	+ Turbidity − Protein + pH or − Turbidity + Protein + pH	+ Turbidity − Protein + pH or − Turbidity + Protein + pH	− Turbidity − Protein − pH or + Turbidity − Protein − pH or − Turbidity + Protein − pH

LOW-RISK LOCATIONS

Private homes, small businesses	+ Turbidity + Protein + pH	+ Turbidity − Protein + pH or − Turbidity + Protein + pH	+ Turbidity − Protein + pH or − Turbidity + Protein + pH	− Turbidity − Protein − pH or + Turbidity − Protein − pH or − Turbidity + Protein − pH

Source: Homeland First Response July/August 2003.

Figure 8.11   Draeger Civil Defense colorimetric tube kit for chemical agents.

Figure 8.12   During training at the Center for Domestic Preparedness (CDP) in Anniston, AL, an emergency responder in Level C protective clothing uses a flashlight to better view turbidity in a test sample.

Five-Step Testing Process

Step 1) Collect two samples: sample 1 for reference laboratory analysis*;
a volume equal to 1 restaurant sugar packet (ca. 1 gm) or more if
available. Sample 2 for field analysis; a volume similar to the size of
a small pea or kernel of corn.

Step 2) Place material to be analyzed in a dry ca. 3 ml clean glass vial
and secure lid; shake vigorously for a few seconds and observe.†

Step 3) Remove lid, fill vial (ca. 2 ml) with distilled water and resecure
lid; shake vigorously for 15 seconds and observe.

Step 4) Remove lid of vial and dip pH test strip into water; remove strip,
wait 30 seconds and read result on pH strip container.

Step 5) Remove lid and dip 1 protein test strip; remove strip, wait 30
seconds and read result on protein strip container.

Once again there did not appear to be any major problems with response
personnel conducting the tests using full Level C personal protective equipment. The complete test was conducted in a much shorter time than predicted
by Centers for Disease Control and Prevention (CDC) staff. Results of the
operational testing conducted by the emergency responders will be evaluated
by scientists at the Aberdeen Proving Ground in Maryland. Initial findings
from the laboratory and operational testing indicate the process is effective
at ruling out anthrax, specifically, and other biological agents, generally. Further tests are ongoing to ensure that the best methods of employing the entire
process are developed and documented prior to release of the final reports.

Agent Characteristics for Monitoring

Detection of chemical agents in the atmosphere is directly related to the
ambient temperature, freezing point, and volatility of the agent. Agent volatility is based upon its vapor pressure. The lower the vapor pressure of a
given agent, the more likely it will not produce significant vapor above and
beyond the surface of the liquid. When monitoring for a low-vapor-pressure
agent such as VX, the inlet for the detection device must be very close to the
surface of the liquid in order to detect any vapor. HD mustard has a much
higher vapor pressure than VX, but its freezing point is also much higher. At

---

* Standing procedures that address packaging, chain of custody and decontamination for
suspect samples should be established with the local FBI in advance of an event.
† The shaking of powder in the vial as described in Step 2 provides only an indication of
particle size. This part of the test protocol does not provide an indication regarding the
potential for the material being of biological origin.

ambient temperatures below 58°F, HD mustard agent is a solid. Agent GB, or sarin as it is commonly known, has the highest vapor pressure of the mustard and nerve agents and is easily spotted by most chemical agent detectors. When an agent liquid is released or splashed on personnel or civilians, monitors might not detect the agent if the ambient temperature is too low.

Chemical agent monitoring methods rely primarily on colorimetric reactions in detector paper, colorimetric tubes, and detection of specific atoms of elements via gas chromatography. For example, the phosphorus atom contained in GB or VX molecules or the sulfur atom present in HD molecules might be detected. Remember, though, that nerve agents are closely related to pesticides in chemical makeup, and pesticides can cause false readings on nerve agent monitors. Monitor operators should become familiar with chemical compounds that can cause a false reading. All types of detection systems can experience false positive readings from certain materials. Chemical agent detection systems are helpful in determining hazardous concentrations of agents; still, they do have limitations.

There are two levels of agent detection systems — gross-level and low-level systems. Gross-level systems are qualitative or, in other words, detect the vapor by its quality. These systems are able to detect high concentrations of vapor, which would be in the range immediately dangerous to life and health (IDLH). Gross-level detectors supply rapid notification when agents are present at these levels. This response can range from 3–15 minutes, depending on which system is used. Gross-level monitoring systems include the M8A1 alarm (M43A1 detector), Chemical Agent Monitor (CAM), M256A1 Chemical Agent Detector Kit, the M18A2 Chemical Agent Detector Kit, and M-8 detection paper. Because of their relatively high-level detection capability, use of these monitors to check for proper decontamination is not dependable. Low-level detection systems are both qualitative (quality of vapor) and quantitative (amount of vapor). These detectors have the capability to detect low concentrations of agent vapor. When agent vapors are present at the airborne exposure limit (AEL) level or below, it can take 3 minutes to 1 hour before a response is indicated, depending on the type of system used. There are some low-level detectors that require sample collection and analysis at an off-site laboratory. The Miniature Continuous Air Monitoring System (MINICAMS) is an example of a low-level monitoring system.

Some agent detection systems are designed only for certain agents. The M8A1, for example, detects only GB and VX; it does not detect HD. Other detectors detect only G-series, H-series, or V-series agents. Liquid chemical agents can be detected with M8 Chemical Agent Detection Paper and the ABC-M18A2 Chemical Agent Detector Kit. Both are classified as gross-level agent detection equipment. For the M-8 paper to work, it must be in contact with the liquid. It is capable of detecting and identifying 0.02 ml of liquid chemical agents within 30 seconds. The resulting colorimetric change is then compared to a color chart on the inside cover of the paper booklet. M-8 papers turn yellow in the presence of G-agents, red for liquid H blister agents, and green for liquid V-agents. False positives may result from cleaning solvents, insect repellent, DS2, and petroleum products. M-8 papers will not detect chemical agents in water or aerosol agents in the air. M-9 detection paper contains an indicator dye that is suspended in the paper matrix. The paper responds to a liquid sample with a contrasting color change. Red or pink spots will appear on the green paper when nerve agents are present in as little as 100 microns. These papers will not respond when wet and can give false positives for a number of materials. Brake fluid, cleaning compounds, DS-2, gasoline, grease, hydraulic fluid, insect repellent, insect spray, lubricating oil, FS smoke, defoliant, ethylene glycol, and camouflage stick can all cause a false positive reading.

ABC-M18A2 Chemical Agent Detector Kit is used to monitor and recognize gross-level concentrations of GB, VX, and HD. It is designed to detect dangerous concentrations of vapors, aerosols, and liquid droplets of chemical agents. The kit is comprised of M-8 detector paper for liquids, detector tickets, assorted color coded tubes, reagent powders, bottles, and tablets. This kit also has an apparatus for testing the presence of blood agents. Detector tickets are designed to detect gross-levels of GB and VX vapors within 3–5 minutes. They are prepared with a liquid reagent prior to use. An aspirator bulb is provided to draw an air sample over the chemically treated ticket. If nerve agents are present, the ticket will change colors. Detector tubes are color coded and are used to detect GB vapors within 3 minutes by drawing an air sample into the tube. White-banded tubes are used to test for the presence of GB. Sampling consists of 60 compressions of the aspirator bulb. A drop or two of reagent is then added to the sample, and a color change indicates the presence of GB in the air sample. No tubes are available to detect for VX, so the detector tickets are the only choice. Blue-banded tubes are used to test for HD. Mustard (HD) is detected at a slightly lower concentration with the tube than sarin (GB). False positives maybe given for smoke and decontaminants. Sensitivity of the M18A2 Kit for detecting chemical agents is shown in Table 8.8.

M8A1 Automatic Chemical Agent Alarm is comprised of the M43A1 detector unit and the M42 alarm unit. It will automatically detect gross-level vapor concentrations of GB and VX and sound an audible alarm. These units are generally used for fixed location detection of agents. Chemical stockpile sites around the country use M8A1 detectors to monitor for leaks in containers and munitions. The M8A1 can also detect blister agents if the vesicant agent detector is attached. A radioactive source, Americium 241 (Am 241),

Table 8.8

Agent	Detection Sensitivity* (PPM)	Response Time (Minutes)
GB (Tube)	0.17	2
GB/V (Ticket)	N/A	4
CG	3.0	1
HD	0.08	3
L	1.0	1
AC	7.0	1

* Based on one minute exposure time.

is used for detection of nerve agents in the M43A1 detector. Air is automatically drawn into the detector from the surrounding atmosphere through an inlet at the top. Air samples are ionized by the radioactive source and electronically analyzed for the presence of nerve agents. When agents are detected, the system activates an audible alarm.

Many of the monitoring instruments for chemical agents require regular testing and maintenance. For example, the CAM needs to be operated a minimum of 10 hours a week to be ready for use when needed. Some fire departments in larger cities might be able to provide this type of maintenance; however, the vast majority of fire departments in this country are volunteer and would have a difficult time maintaining the equipment, as would smaller career departments. If a terrorist event occurs, it is likely to be a one-time situation for any given community. When preparing plans for terrorism response, thought has to be given to the practicalities of owning monitoring equipment before large amounts of money are committed. If the monitoring equipment is just going to sit in a compartment on the apparatus until the event occurs, it will be of no use.

Biological Agent Detectors

Technology for field detection of biological agents and biological toxins is still developing, with new information becoming available almost daily. Detecting biological agents is difficult because the monitor has to differentiate between the artificially generated biological agent cloud and normal background organic matter present in the atmosphere. Because of this, detection methods must be used in conjunction with medical protection (vaccines and other chemoprophylactic measures), intelligence, and physical protection to provide a layered defense against a biological release. Detection systems need to exhibit a high degree of selectivity and be able to discriminate between biological agents and other harmless biological and non biological material

Table 8.9   Agent Effect Values for Monitoring

Agent	PEL (PPM)	IDLH (PPM)	LCt50 (PPM)	ICt50 (PPM)
Phosgene	0.1	2	791	395
Chlorine	0.5	10	6551	620
Sarin	0.000017	0.03	12	8
Tabun	0.000015	0.03	20–60	45
Soman	0.000004	0.008	9	4
VX	0.0000009	0.0018	3	2
Mustard	0.0005	0.0005	231	30
Lewisite	0.00035	0.00035	141–177	<35
Hydrogen cyanide	10	45	3600	
Cyanogen chloride	0.2	Unknown	4375	2784

Source: National Fire Academy Emergency Response to Terrorism: Tactical Considerations: Hazardous Materials Student Manual.

present in the environment. Biological agents are effective in very low doses. Therefore, biological agent detection systems need to exhibit high sensitivity; that is to say, they need to be able to detect very small amounts of biological agents. Biological detection also needs to be able to analyze and report on findings in a timely manner.

Currently under development is the Long-Range Standoff Detection System (LRSDS), which will provide the first standoff early warning of the presence of biological materials. It uses an infrared laser to detect aerosol clouds at a distance of up to 30 kilometers. An improved version is also under development that would increase the standoff distance to 100 kilometers. When fielded, the system will be available for fixed site installations or mounted on vehicles and fixed wing and rotary aircraft.

Another biological monitor in development is the Short-Range Biological Standoff Detection System (SRBSDS). This technology utilizes an ultraviolet and laser-induced fluorescence to detect biological aerosol clouds at distances up to 5 kilometers for early warning. The military has also developed a response vehicle that contains detection devices for biological agents. The biological agent detection capability alone costs in excess of $100,000 per vehicle. This does not include any other equipment that might be needed or the cost of the vehicle. Portable testing devices are also available, but have not been proven under response conditions.

Most emergency responders at the present time will still have to rely on laboratory analysis of samples of biological agents, which may take days or even weeks to complete. It is important to identify where the nearest testing laboratory is located that can conduct these types of tests. Twenty-four-hour contact information for emergencies involving biological or toxin materials should be identified. Currently, there are four inexpensive biological field tests available that could be used by emergency response personnel to detect certain biological agents. "SMART™ tickets" are used for initial field testing for anthrax, staphylococcal enterotoxin B (SEB), botulinum toxin, and Y-Pestis (plague). These "tickets" take from 5–15 minutes for a response to a sample, which results in a color change. Other biological agents and toxins can cause a false positive. They have a 1-year shelf life and cost about $300 per pack of five. On October 18, 2001, the Centers for Disease Control and Prevention (CDC) issued a health advisory concerning "smart tickets." This advisory stated that these assays are intended only for the screening of environmental samples. First responder and law enforcement agencies using these devices should forward any positive samples to authorities for more sensitive and specialized confirmatory testing. (Samples should always be sent to a testing laboratory even if tested negative in the field for verification). Also, some incidents have occurred where the smart ticket showed a positive indication, when in fact it was harmless non-anthrax Bacillus bacteria found in the environment. The analytical sensitivity of smart tickets is such that a minimum of 10,000 spores is necessary to generate a positive signal. Since the actual number of spores required to make any one person sick is really unknown, it is important to know well below 10,000 how many spores are present.

The results of field assays should not be used to make decisions about patient management or prophylaxis. Patient treatment should only be undertaken based upon positive laboratory testing results. CDC is conducting an evaluation of handheld assay devices, although results are not expected in the near future. On July 19, 2002, the International Association of Fire Chiefs issued a statement reporting that handheld anthrax detectors are not reliable. The Federal Bureau of Investigation (FBI), in collaboration with the Department of Health and Human Services (HHS) and the CDC, conducted experiments to validate the performance of commercially available handheld assays for the detection of Bacillus anthraci, or "anthrax," available prior to July 2002. This study resulted from the anthrax attacks of September and October 2001 and was meant to apply to situations where anthrax was present in quantities that are not detectable by current technology. These studies found that all of the commercially available assays had low sensitivities, most had the potential to produce false-positives, and some produced false negative results on samples that were truly positive. Other tests are under development for ricin, Venezuelan equine encephalitis (VEE), brucella, and others. Keep in mind this is an emerging technology, and someone within your organization needs to keep on top of new developments.

The BioWarefare Agent Detection Device (BADD™) Anthrax Test was developed at Dugway Proving Ground in Utah from 1994–1997. The purpose of the test is intended for visible quantities of suspicious substances. Accord-

Figure 8.13 Tetracore Guardian biological test kits with reader for ricin, plague, tulaemeria, anthrax, and brucella.

ing to the manufacturer, Osborn Scientific Group, the test will detect .25 micrograms (about one quarter the size of a spec of dust) of anthrax spores on a smooth surface or 1.0 micrograms per milliliter in solution. The spore count is considered to be as follows:

- 1 speck of dust: = 1 microgram =1000 nanograms
- 1 infectious dose (ID) =10,000 spores = 10 nanograms
- 1000 nanograms= 1 million spores = 100 ID

The BADD test, according to tests conducted at Dugway Proving Ground, will detect levels of anthrax at 0.1 ID (1 nanogram). That is 1/10th of an ID or 1/1000th of a speck of dust. Technology of the BADD test is much like an over-the-counter pregnancy test, leveraging special antibodies developed by Osborn Scientific Group that detect biowarfare agents. Test results are available on scene within 1–30 minutes (usually 15 minutes or less). No reader or other equipment is required. Tests are also available for ricin toxin and botulinum toxin. Remember that these tests are designed only for visible quantities of suspicious substances.

Table 8.10　Procedures for Personnel Monitoring Using Radiation Detection Devices

- Have person stand on clean surface.
- Instruct the person to stand straight, feet spread slightly, arms extended with palms up and fingers straight out.
- Monitor both hands and arms; then repeat with hands and arms turned over.
- Starting at the top of the head, cover the entire body, monitoring carefully the forehead, nose, mouth, neckline, torso, knees, and ankles.
- Have the subject turn around, and repeat the survey on the back of the body.
- Monitor the soles of the feet.

Radiation Detection Equipment

If radioactive materials are released during a terrorist incident, the human senses would not be able to detect them. It would be almost impossible to determine what radioactive material was present. Nevertheless, response personnel can monitor to determine if any radiation is being produced. Radiation released in the air produces charged particles. Monitoring instruments can detect and measure these particles produced within a volume of gas within the instrument. Two types of information are needed for evaluation and control of a radiological hazard. First, the intensity of the radioactive field needs to be measured; this is commonly known as the exposure rate. Second is the total amount of exposure that has occurred to any individual. Two separate instruments are required for these measurements because no single monitor has been developed. Survey meters are used to measure the level of radioactive intensity. The dosimeter is used to measure the radiation dose from the exposure. The most common types of survey meters are the Geiger-Mueller meter (GM), or Geiger counter, and the ionization chamber. Each detects radiation by collecting charged particles. The Geiger-Mueller meter detects low-level radioactive materials. Ionization chambers are used for medium- and high-level radiation detection. Instruments report in roentgens, rads, rems, milliroentgens, or millirads per hour, or counts per minute. Dosimeters monitor the total exposure of an individual to radiation during the monitoring operation. These devices should be worn whenever monitoring is being conducted. Dosimeters measure the radiation exposure, much like the odometer on a car, which tabulates the total miles traveled. Dosimeters are available for both low-level and high-level exposures.

The only way to determine if radioactive materials are present is with the use of instruments specially designed to detect radioactivity. There are two types of civil defense meters widely available to emergency responders in most communities, but it must be noted that the Federal Emergency Management Agency (FEMA) is phasing out its program of maintenance and calibration of those instruments. Responders will need to locate other source(s) for calibration and may have to pay for this maintenance in the future. Civil defense meters include the CD V-700 and the CD V-715. Neither of these instruments can detect alpha radiation. The CD V-700 survey meter has a range of 0–50mR/hour. An experienced operator can detect beta radiation with the CD V-700 through a process of elimination. If you check for radiation with the Geiger-Mueller (GM) tube on the CD V-700 with the window closed and no radiation exists beyond normal background, then no gamma radiation is present. If the window is opened, another reading taken, and radiation detected, then it is beta radiation. The CD V-715 survey meter has a range of 0.05–500R/hour or 50 to 500,000 mR/hour. Radiation is detected through an ionization chamber much like the ionization chamber of a smoke detector. This unit is designed to detect gamma radiation from fallout in a nuclear attack. Dosimeters are used in conjunction with survey meters to monitor levels of exposure to personnel. Two types of civil defense dosimeters are available with different monitoring scales. The CD V-138 is used for monitoring relatively low levels of exposure and has a minimum scale reading of 200 mR. The CD V-742 has a range up to 200 R (200,000 mR) and is used for high levels of personnel exposure. Both meters should be worn by responders to ensure proper protection. There are similar commercial monitoring instruments available, including those sensitive enough to detect alpha radiation. Survey meters measure the exposure rate or radiation intensity at a given location at a specific time. Survey meters work much like the speedometer of an automobile, which measures miles per hour. The survey meter measures radiation exposure in terms of roentgens per hour. Calibration of survey meters is either in roentgens per hour (R/hr) or milliroentgens per hour (mR/hr). Whether the meters used are the civil defense meters or those commercially available, they should be able to be read at a range of a minimum of 0–50 millirems per hour. All personnel should be familiar with the models available and trained in their use.

Air Monitoring during Terrorist Incidents

If a terrorist act occurs in your community, it is quite likely the agent will be unknown when responders arrive. It is even more likely that a hoax event could happen before a real chemical agent or biological agent attack would occur. The hoax incident can have just as great an impact on the community resources as a real incident might. Both a hoax and real chemical or biological incident require identification or confirmation that an agent has actually been released. When monitoring, a determination is made that either no agent is present, or it is present in a form that does not present a credible risk. At that point, the incident response can be greatly scaled back and the community returned to normal in a short time. There have been no large-scale releases of chemical or biological agents reported in the U.S. Several small incidents involving ricin have occurred, along with several hoaxes involving the threatened release of sarin and anthrax. The vast majority of incidents up to this time have been bombings. Without some kind of monitoring equipment, response personnel will have to rely on awareness of potential terrorist targets and victims' symptoms to get some idea of what type of incident might have occurred. When sampling equipment is available, it is important that personnel follow the following basic rules when monitoring for an unknown agent:

- Respiratory protective equipment should always be worn.
- As with all hazardous materials, avoid contact with visible product.
- Emergency decontamination should be available.
- Any field tests for terrorist agents should be followed up with a laboratory verification.
- Monitoring usually does not occur until the hazmat team arrives. Always make sure the scene is monitored first for oxygen, radiation, LEL, pH of any liquids, and some toxic substances, at a minimum. Availability of these types on monitoring instruments should be identified during the planning process.
- Inexpensive monitoring can be done with the M-8 or M-9 test strips, the M256A1 kit, or colorimetric tubes to help isolate an unknown material (Table 8.1).

Do not make statements about the identity of the suspected substance until all of the test data is available. Most departments can afford to have M-8 and M-9 test strips, the M256A1 kit, and colorimetric tubes to check for chemical agents. Protection of personnel and prompt patient treatment may depend on it. The reality is that while the expensive instruments are most effective, they will be few and far between in many parts of the country. Prompt emergency decontamination procedures and appropriate respiratory protection and chemical protective equipment will help safeguard responders and allow treatment of victims.

Explosives Monitoring

Acetone peroxide (TATP) is a powerful explosive that is easily made from common materials that can be purchased without suspicion. It is very difficult for bomb dogs and existing monitors to detect TATP. Ehud Keinan, a chemistry professor from Israel, has developed a device that detects peroxide explosives, called the Peroxide Explosive Tester (PET). The device looks like an oversized pen with three levers at one end and a removable rubber cap at the other. The cap has a stick surface designed to collect material; the levers release three solutions that wash over the cap when it is reattached to the PET. The first solution is an acid that breaks down TATP into acetone and hydrogen peroxide. The second solution contains a pigment that turns green when oxidized, and the third solution contains an enzyme that, when exposed to hydrogen peroxide, catalyzes oxidation in the pigment. PET is meant to be a cheap disposable device that will cost $10–15 once on the market.

Biochip technology developed at Argonne National Laboratories is designed to provide rapid identification of biological and chemical agents using reusable biochips and a portable reader. The portable biochip reader is smaller than a shoebox and is able to analyze a single sample droplet for thousands of biological agents simultaneously. Results are available in less than 2 hours. Each biochip contains hundreds to thousands of gel pads. Each gel pad has inserted into it a segment of DNA strand, protein, peptide, or antibody, which tailors the pad to recognize a specific biological or chemical agent signature. Pads are in a known position on the chip so that when a sample reacts, the reaction position can detected, identifying the sample. The estimated cost of the system field portable system is $12,000 and $2–3 per test.

Anthrax Field Test Update

Much confusion exists concerning the field-testing for the presence of anthrax spores, particularly with handheld devices. According to the *Washington Post*, the White House has issued a memo to federal agencies, firefighters, police, and local officials warning that commercially available anthrax field tests might produce unreliable results in certain circumstances. A previous health advisory from the CDC indicated that they do not have enough scientific data to recommend the use of these field assays. The CDC has been asked to evaluate the sensitivity and the specificity of the commercially available, rapid, handheld assays for anthrax. However, conclusions from this study are not expected in the near future. No other federal agency has claimed oversight of the test devices; however, the Food and Drug Administration (FDA) is evaluating whether the devices should be declared medical tests, and therefore come under their jurisdiction for approval and regulation.

Manufacturers' data indicate most of the handheld field tests require the presence of at least 10,000 spores to generate a positive signal. That would indicate a heavy contamination of the area or sample. A negative signal from the field tests, on the other hand, does not rule out the presence of anthrax spores. There could be levels of anthrax spores present in quantities less than what can be identified by the tests. In the past it has been believed that 8,000–10,000 spores is the lethal dose for exposure to anthrax. There is limited data available on human exposure to inhalation anthrax, because it rarely occurs naturally, and the case history is limited. There is no way to determine what the dose was for those who developed inhalation anthrax in the fall of 2002. It is now believed by some epidemiologists that the dose, which causes infections, could be as low as 200 spores. According to manufacturers' data, there are currently no handheld field tests that can detect anthrax spores at that level of concentration. One company claims their device can detect a level of 250 spores. Testing by the army indicated it might even be lower. Regardless of the results of field tests for anthrax spores, no decisions involving patient management or prophylaxis should be made based upon field tests. In all cases of suspected anthrax contamination, samples should be sent to a qualified laboratory for confirmation.

Personal Protective Equipment (PPE) and Decontamination for Terrorist Agents

9

Personal Protective Equipment (PPE)

Personal protective equipment (PPE) is any type of clothing or device worn by emergency personnel to protect them from the hazards that might be present on the scene of an emergency. All response personnel on the scene of a terrorist incident will require some form of respiratory and dermal protective equipment. They will also need to have established policies and procedures to ensure that personnel do not become victims, further taxing already short resources. Wearing chemical personal protective equipment (PPE) can create some significant psychological and physiological hazards. This is especially true for those who are not used to wearing PPE, such as law enforcement officers and EMS personnel. Wearing PPE can cause claustrophobic reactions, hyperventilation, heat stress, contact dermatitis, and reduced physical performance. Heat stress is one of the most hazardous complications from wearing chemical protective clothing, particularly Level A. When using chemical clothing with air-purifying respirators (APRs) and positive pressure air-purifying respirators (PAPRs) (Figure 9.1), work times should be limited, based upon ambient temperature, to reduce the effects of heat stress. The following chart may be used to determine work times based upon ambient temperature.

Positive air-purifying respirator (PAPR) for respiratory protection against chemical and biological agents. The amount of heat built up and retained in the body is affected by the following factors:

- The measure of physical activity being performed

299

Table 9.1

Temperature Range	Work Time	Rest Time
50–70°F/10–21°C	30–45 minutes	10–15 minutes
70–85°F/21–29°C	20–30 minutes	40–60 minutes
85–100°F/29–38°C	15–20 minutes	Indefinite

Figure 9.1 Positive Air Purifying Respirator (PAPR) for respiratory protection against chemical and biological agents.

- Time spent in the suit
- Amount of hydration or lack of hydration in the body prior to PPE use
- Type of PPE worn
- Physical amount of material being carried
- Degree of heat acclimation, physical fitness, and fatigue by the wearer
- Terrain and weather conditions

Terrorist attacks involving chemical, radiological, and biological agents will require that personnel wear appropriate body and respiratory protection. Those personnel who need protection include law enforcement, EMS, firefighters, hospital emergency room staff, doctors, and anyone else who might be exposed to the agents. All persons required to wear PPE, including respiratory protection, will need to be trained in its use. Occupational Safety and Health Administration (OSHA) Standard 29 CFR 1910.134 (b) requires that all persons who use respirators must have a medical exam that certifies that they are physically fit to do so. Local medical personnel will determine what tests are necessary for the certification. Persons wearing respirators will also have to be fit-tested for their masks to ensure a tight seal around the face. Details are also found in OSHA respiratory regulations. When dealing with potential chemical, biological, or radioactive materials, the respiratory system is the most important part of the body to protect. All of the chemical, biological, and nuclear materials are serious inhalation hazards. Firefighters generally have respiratory protection available through use of their self-contained breathing apparatus (SCBA). Law enforcement and EMS personnel might not have respiratory protection readily available unless jurisdictions take action to provide such protection. Protective equipment is selected based upon the anticipated hazard on the incident scene. The National Fire Academy, as part of its Initial Response to Hazardous Materials: Basic Concepts course (IRHMI:BC), uses the acronym TRACEM to identify potential hazards that could occur in the hot zone of a hazardous materials incident.

T — Toxic
R — Radiation
A — Asphyxiation
C — Chemical
E — Etiological
M — Mechanical

This same concept can be readily adapted for use during acts of terrorism, because many of the same hazards are also present at those incidents. Chemical agents and biological toxins are poisonous materials. Radiological materials and nuclear devices can produce radiation and radioactive contamination. Explosives are chemicals that produce mechanical damage when they go off. Etiological materials are living organisms that can be biological terrorist agents. Respiratory protection is by far the most important aspect of personal protective equipment for emergency response personnel called to a terrorist incident.

Respiratory Protection

Inhalation is one of the primary routes of exposure for chemical and biological agents. Inhalation hazards can be classified into three groups: airborne contaminants, inhalation of gases or vapors, and oxygen-deficient atmospheres. Airborne contaminants can be dusts, mists, fumes, fiber, irritating smoke, or an aerosol agent. Dusts are solid particles that have been suspended in the air. Mists are formed from the suspension of liquid particles in the air through atomization, condensation, or mechanical means. This is the most effective form for dissemination of chemical and biological agents. Fumes are suspended liquid droplets, formed when a liquid material is vaporized in the air and then condensed as the air cools. Fibers are particles, defined by having a length three times that of their width, that have been suspended in air. Irritating smoke is an aerosol that is created by the burning of an organic material.

Vapors and gases comprise the second type of inhalation hazard. By definition, a gas can be expanded indefinitely, readily mixes into other gases, conforms to the shape of a container, and will expand or contract depending on the temperature and pressure to which it is exposed. Vapors differ from gases, because they are usually liquids and solids at normal temperatures and pressures. Protection from gases or vapor exposure is based upon the type or form of gas or vapor present. Vapors may be filtered out by cartridge respirators, where gases may require a SCBA or supply line respirators.

The third type of inhalation hazard is the oxygen-deficient atmosphere. Normally, the oxygen content of the air is 20.5% at sea level. By OSHA definition, an oxygen-deficient atmosphere is one where the oxygen content falls below 19.5%. A lack of oxygen in the air usually results in the health hazard referred to as simple asphyxiation. The body does not have enough oxygen from the air to continue to breathe. Chemicals that enter the body can also inhibit body systems from making use of the oxygen that might be in the blood. Atmospheric oxygen is plentiful, but the chemical in the blood interferes with the uptake into the cells. The result remains much the same: the person could die from the lack of oxygen in the cells. This type of health effect is referred to as chemical asphyxiation.

Personal protective equipment for hazardous materials technicians operating at a terrorist event is much the same as that used for other types of hazardous materials. First responders, however, are limited in chemical protection by their turnouts unless specialized chemical protection for terrorism has been provided by the jurisdiction. Their breathing protection is the highest level available if they are using positive pressure SCBAs; even so, they are limited by the amount of air supply. Biological agents are generally not considered skin absorption hazards. Turnouts will provide adequate protection against biological agents except for mycotoxins.

Tests conducted at Fort Detrick, Maryland, by the U.S. Army showed that just two layers of army issue green t-shirts provided good protection against bio agents if used to cover nose and mouth. The Centers for Disease Control and Prevention (CDC) recommends that a half-mask or full-face piece air-purifying respirator with particulate filter efficiencies ranging from N95 (for hazards such as pulmonary tuberculosis) to P100 (for hazards such as hantavirus) be used as a minimum level of respiratory protection. At any suspected terrorist event, all personnel, including EMS, should wear respiratory protection appropriate for the suspected hazard. Respiratory protection should be worn for patient evaluation, treatment, and decontamination. SCBA is the best choice for maximum respiratory protection. The only drawbacks of SCBAs are the length of time in which they can be worn without changing the bottles (30–60 minutes) and their weight (approximately 30–40 pounds). Supplied air respirators are also an option, providing the protection of a SCBA, with an extended air supply from an air cascade system. However, those types of systems are not widely available for most departments. The most protection that can be supplied for the longest period of working time is the military gas mask. This mask is available as a canister air purifying respirator (APR), which is a negative pressure mask, or as a positive pressure air purifying respirator (PAPR); both will allow longer work periods in the contaminated area than a SCBA, without having to change a bottle or cartridge. APRs and PAPRs can be worn for up to 16 hours without being taken off for service. Their downside is that they do not provide protection in an oxygen-deficient atmosphere. Cartridges have to be appropriate for the concentration and chemical or biological agent that is present. Generally, APRs and PAPRs are not effective in IDLH (immediately dangerous to life and health) atmospheres. The chemical also has to be identified; respirators will not provide adequate protection for unknown materials. They can lead to heat stress and fatigue because of the long work periods they allow. APRs can be a full- or half-face piece, with a filter cartridge and exhalation valve. Cartridge filters screw into the face piece and can only be changed in an uncontaminated atmosphere. If the filter elements are immersed in water, they must be replaced. PAPRs have a full-face piece very similar to the SCBA mask. PAPRs have a pump, which blows fresh air through a filter cartridge system into the face piece. Blowing air into the face piece can also have a cooling effect on the wearer.

The PAPR consists of the following parts:

- Full face piece that can be fitted with a spectacle kit with corrective lenses
- Blower unit attached to a waist belt
- Battery pack with battery charger or lithium batteries
- Breathing tube assembly
- Air filtering devices
- All but the battery charger are assembled to make complete respirator

Benefits of using APRs and PAPRs include:

- Economical to purchase
- Not as heavy as SCBAs
- Longer working times

Restrictions for using APRs and PAPRs include:

- Cannot be used where oxygen is deficient (below 19.5%)
- Cannot be used in IDLH atmospheres

- Cannot be used in flammable or explosive atmospheres
- Can be come impregnated with particles and contaminants
- Must have appropriate canisters and filters

Those responders who are near the nine chemical stockpiles around the country mentioned in Chapter 1 have been provided with PAPRs for respiratory protection in case of an accidental release from one of those facilities. Periodic releases do occur, even though to date there have not been any serious exposures beyond the boundaries of the military facilities. Most recently, on September 9, 1998, 11 gallons of the nerve agent sarin leaked from a "popped cork" on the container onto the floor of a storage bunker at the Tooele Army Depot, approximately 15 miles south of Tooele, Utah (west of Salt Lake City). This was the largest spill to occur at Tooele since a 1-ton container of mustard agent spilled onto the floor of a bunker in September 1995, 5 years earlier to the day. Sarin was detected with mobile monitors 600 feet away from the storage bunker. Personnel at the depot evacuated the 1,000-acre storage area, home to 208 bunkers with 31,495 tons of chemical agents, approximately 40% of the nation's stockpile. Workers entered the bunker with protective equipment, plugged the container, and cleaned up the spill. This incident was a "Level 2" event out of 4 possible levels. None of the agent was detected off of the base.

Body Protection

Most chemical agents are skin absorbents. If exposure to liquid agents or aerosols is possible, chemical protective clothing will be required to protect emergency response personnel. Studies conducted at Aberdeen Proving Ground in Maryland with chemical nerve agents have shown that when exposed to vapor only, firefighter turnouts provide a high degree of protection against those agents. They developed what was referred to as the 3/30 Rule. Turnouts and SCBA might be the only protection available for first responders in many parts of the country.

IAFF Concerns about the 3/30 Rule

During 1998 and 1999, the U.S. Army Soldier and Biological Chemical Command (SBCCOM) studied the safety of firefighter turnout gear in an atmosphere of chemical warfare agents. Results of the testing were released in a document titled *Guidelines for Incident Commanders Use of Firefighters Ensemble (FFPE) With Self-Contained Breathing Apparatus (SCBA) for Rescue Incidents During a Terrorist Chemical Incident*, which became widely known as the 3/30 Rule. The context of the 3/30 Rule is outlined in the following paragraphs.

- Standard turnout gear with SCBA provides a first responder with sufficient protection from nerve agent vapor hazards inside interior or downwind areas of the hot zone to allow 30 minutes of rescue time for known live victims.
- Self-taped turnout gear with SCBA provides sufficient protection in an unknown nerve agent environment for a 3-minute reconnaissance to search for living victims (or a 2-minute reconnaissance if HD — distilled sulfur mustard agent — is suspected).

Following the release of the test results and the 3/30 Rule, the International Association of Fire Fighters (IAFF) expressed concern over the use of turnout gear in a chemical agent atmosphere. They said that it was their position that the "3/30 Rule and its modifications were inappropriate and unacceptable as the basis of a protective strategy for use by firefighters and other first responders." Following the concerns expressed by IAFF, SBCCOM withdrew the 3/30 Rule in the spring of 2003. During June 2003 SBCCOM released another document titled *The Risk Assessment of Using Firefighter Protective Ensemble with Self-Contained Breathing Apparatus for Rescue Operations During a Terrorist Chemical Agent Incident.* According to IAFF, the "new" report was still based upon the same limited testing data of the 3/30 Rule. IAFF objections to the SBCCOM test reports are summarized below.

- Chemical agent exposures used in the testing process were based upon military battlefield conditions, not the urban settings that would be encountered by first responders. Higher concentrations would be expected inside buildings and in the confinement of urban settings vs. the openness of the battlefield.
- Military percutaneous vapor toxicity estimates are not appropriate for assessment of firefighter protective ensembles for two reasons: 1) The severe effects evaluated are set for levels that allow injuries (unfit for duty) to the protected and exposed individual. 2) The evaluated threshold levels are based on a lethal dose representing only 50% of the population and therefore assume that some effects will occur for at least half of the population in the emergency response community using the selected firefighter protective ensemble.

The IAFF recommends that all fire departments regard the 3/30 Rule and its modifications with extreme caution. The complete IAFF position paper can be accessed on the Internet at http://www.iaff.org/safe/pdfs/3_30Rule.pdf.

Response personnel should avoid contact with liquid agents or contaminated victims. EMS personnel also need to have respiratory and body protection when treating victims of chemical or biological attacks. Treatment should not begin if contaminated victims have not undergone emergency decontamination and response personnel do not have access to the appropriate protective equipment. If monitoring devices are not available, then all victims must be assumed to be contaminated and must undergo emergency decon, and personnel must have body and respiratory protection. Once victims' clothing has been removed and victims have gone through emergency decon, universal precaution protective equipment used for bloodborne pathogens, supplemented with breathing protection as needed, should provide adequate protection for EMS personnel. Unless they have not had terrorism awareness training and become contaminated, law enforcement personnel are not likely to encounter chemical nerve and blister agents in the liquid form or above the IDLH level. They are more likely to be exposed to agent vapors while securing the area, providing security for perimeters, conducting evacuations, or directing traffic control operations. Supplying them with PAPRs or cartridge respirators would give them a high degree of respiratory protection against nerve and blister agents. Depending on the agent concentrations, they might also need to wear disposable chemical protective clothing.

According to the Environmental Protection Agency (EPA), there are four levels of chemical protective clothing. The National Fire Protection Association (NFPA) also has standards for chemical protective clothing. NFPA 1991 is the Standard on Vapor-Protective Suits for Hazardous Chemical Emergencies. The U.S. Department of Homeland Security (DHS) adopted five NFPA standards for personal protective equipment for first responders to assist state and local procurement officials in selecting the best available protective equipment. The standards, the first of their kind to be adopted by DHS, will protect first responders against chemical, biological, and other hazards at emergency incidents.

The five standards are:

- *NFPA 1951, Standard on Protective Ensemble for USAR Operations.*
- *NFPA 1981, Standard on Open-Circuit Self-Contained Breathing Apparatus for Fire and Emergency Services*
- *NFPA 1991, Standard on Vapor-Protective Ensembles for Hazardous Materials Emergencies*
- *NFPA 1994, Standard on Protective Ensembles for Chemical/Biological Terrorism Incidents*
- *NFPA 1999, Standard on Protective Clothing for Emergency Medical Operations*

NFPA 1951, Standard on Protective Ensemble for USAR Operations

Based on work begun in 1997, this standard answers the need for personal protective equipment for fire and emergency services personnel operating at technical rescue incidents involving building or structural collapse, vehicle accidents, confined spaces, trench cave-ins, scaffolding collapses, high-angle climbing accidents, and similar incidents. The first edition of this standard was issued in July 2001.

NFPA 1981, Standard on Open-Circuit Self-Contained Breathing Apparatus for Fire and Emergency Services

Based on work begun in 1975, this standard specifies the minimum requirements for the design, performance, testing, and certification of open-circuit SCBA and combination open-circuit self-contained breathing apparatus and supplied air respirators (SCBA/SAR) for the respiratory protection of fire and emergency responders where unknown, IDLH (immediately dangerous to life and health), or potentially IDLH atmospheres exist. The first edition was issued in July 1981, and the current edition, issued in July 2002, is the fifth edition.

NFPA 1991, Standard on Vapor-Protective Ensembles for Hazardous Materials Emergencies

Based on work begun in 1986, this standard specifies the minimum requirements for the design, performance, testing, and certification of vapor-protective ensembles and individual protective elements for chemical vapor protection for fire and emergency service personnel. Additional optional criteria are provided for ensembles and individual protective elements that provide protection for chemical flash fire escape, liquefied gas, chemical and biological warfare agents, and chemical and biological terrorism incidents. The first edition was issued in January 1990, and the current edition, issued in January 2000, is the third edition.

NFPA 1994, Standard on Protective Ensembles for Chemical/Biological Terrorism Incidents

Based on work begun in 1998, this standard specifies the minimum requirements for the design, performance, testing, and certification of protective ensembles for fire and emergency services personnel operating at domestic terrorism incidents involving dual-use industrial chemicals, chemical terrorism agents, or biological terrorism agents. The intent is that the ensembles would be available in quantity, easily donned and used, and designed for single exposure use. The first edition of this standard was issued in July 2001.

NFPA 1999, Standard on Protective Clothing for Emergency Medical Operations

Based on work begun in 1990, this standard specifies the minimum requirements for the design, performance, testing, and certification of new single-use and multiple-use emergency medical protective clothing, including garments, gloves, footwear, and face protection devices used by fire and emergency services personnel performing patient care during emergency medical operations for protection against exposure to blood and body fluid-borne pathogens. The first edition was issued in July 1992, and the current edition, issued in January 2003, is the third edition.

All of the above- mentioned standards are available on the NFPA Web site as read-only documents for all emergency responders to view. In addition, DHS adopted three other standards, from the National Institute of Occupational Safety and Health, (NIOSH), for respirators to protect against chemical/biological/radiological/nuclear environments. The standards adopted today will also provide manufacturers with requirements for the design, performance, testing, and certification of equipment.

Listed below are the four levels of EPA chemical protective clothing.

- Level A   Fully encapsulated vapor-proof suits worn with SCBA
- Level B   Splash-protective suits worn with SCBA
- Level C   Splash-protective suits with cartridge respirators
- Level D   Street clothing

Level A suits (Figure 9.2) are worn when the atmosphere contains toxic vapors or gases above the IDLH and for long-term work at levels greater than

Figure 9.2   Level A personnel protective chemical suits for vapor exposure to chemical agents.

Figure 9.3 Kappler Responder civilian chemical suit with military hood and PAPR for protection against mustard and nerve agents.

the short-term exposure limit (STEL). This level provides the highest level of full-body protection against chemical and biological exposures. However, Level A might not always be necessary for chemical agents, and might only be worn by hazardous materials technicians and military personnel for biological agents. Respiratory protection with Level B is the same as for Level A. However, body protection is reduced because the suits allow only for splash protection, not vapors or gases. Level B suits can be either fully encapsulating or unencapsulated. Either way, they still do not provide vapor or gas protection. Level B is really the minimum level of protection that should be considered for an entry into a chemical or biological agent scene. Level C can be used when the chemical or biological agent has been positively identified, and the concentrations are known to fall within the range allowed by respirator cartridges. With Level C protective clothing, great care should be taken to ensure that there is little danger of a liquid spill of chemical agent. Level C does not provide splash protection as well as Level B. The army has tested several different chemical protective suits, challenged the suits with chemical warfare agents, and approved them for civilian response personnel.

The U.S. military also has specially designed suits effective for both chemical and biological agents. Respiratory protection used by the military

Table 9.2   Chemical Agent Breakthrough Times
for Gloves; Minimum Breakthrough Times (min)

Glove Thickness (mil)	Mustard (HD)	Nerve (GB)
25	360	450
14	240	450
7	75	360

Source: Argonne National Laboratory (August,1994).

is strictly APR or PAPR — they generally do not use SCBAs. Chemical and biological body protection is provided by an ensemble of overgarments, mask, hood, overboots, protective gloves, individual decon kits, detection equipment, and antidotes (primarily for chemical agents). Butyl rubber provides good protection against nerve and blister agents. Gloves made of this material are recommended when the type of agent is known. Military gloves come in two thicknesses, 7 mil and 14 mil, and come in four sizes. Both gloves protect against agents; however, the breakthrough time for the 7 mil is 6 hours, and for the 14 mil is 24 hours. Boots used by the military are designated as green vinyl overshoe (GVO) made from butyl rubber and are available in only one size. The overshoes provide up to 12 hours of protection from contamination. If unexposed, the boots can be worn for 14 straight days without being changed. In addition to the boots and gloves, the military ensemble includes a hood that protects the head and neck from agent exposure. The hood is used in conjunction with the PAPR and has been approved for civilian use as well. Development and testing by NIOSH is underway for a hood that does not require a face piece and is used with the PAPR blower to provide filtered air into the hood. Many of the Chemical Stockpile Emergency Preparedness Program (CSEPP) emergency responders use the hood in conjunction with Level B civilian chemical protective suits (Table 9.3). The CSEPP ensemble, while tested for chemical agents, will also provide adequate protection against biological agents. Most CSEPP civilian response organizations use the Kappler Responder Suit in conjunction with the PAPR, GVO boots, butyl gloves, white cotton glove inserts, and hood.

Because all responders look alike in protective equipment, response organizations involved in the Utah CSEPP program initiated a program of providing stickers on the outside of chemical suits to identify response organizations. They are approximately 3–4 in. in diameter, color-coded, and show the words police, fire, or EMS. This allows for easy on-scene identification of personnel (Figure 9.4).

The primary component of the military ensemble is the battle dress overgarment (BDO) (Figure 9.5) and the chemical-protective overgarment (CPOG). The BDO is a camouflage-colored (woodland or desert), disposable, two-piece unit consisting of a coat and one pair of pants. This garment

Table 9.3 Breakthrough Times for GB and HD on Selected PPE

Suit Type	Incapacitation GB Minutes	Erythema HD Minutes
25-mil chemical gloves	>480	360
Kappler Suit Model 42483	350	330
TYCHEM 12645	>480	330
Trellchem HPS suit	>480	>480
Ready 1 Suit Model 91	>480	125
First Team XE Suit	>480	385
Commander Ultrapro Suit Style 79102	>480	280
Kappler Suit Model 50660	>480	435
TYCHEM No. 11645	>480	>480
Trellchem TLU Suit	>480	>480
Chemturion Suit Model 13	>480	110
Chempruf II BETEX Suit	225	125
Commander Brigade: F91	>480	>480

Source: U.S. Army SBCCOM.

Figure 9.4 Response personnel all look the same when wearing chemical protective clothing. These labels help identify different organizations.

is constructed of an outer layer of nylon/cotton and an inner layer of charcoal-impregnated polyurethane foam, and is available in eight sizes. It is usually worn over the soldier's uniform, but in hot weather can be worn over underwear. During cold weather, the BDO can be worn underneath winter coats. BDOs provide protection against chemical agent vapors, liquid droplets, biological agents, toxins, and radioactive alpha and beta particles. Once removed from its storage bag and donned, its protection will last for approximately 30 days. When exposed to a liquid chemical agent, the BDO should be changed after 24 hours. Just like other forms of chemical protective suits, if the BDO is ripped, torn, or otherwise damaged, it will not provide full protection and should be discarded. Characteristics of the CPOG are much

Figure 9.5 Military BDO chemical and biological protective clothing. (Source: U.S. Army.)

the same as for the BDO, but it is a plain green color. Just as with all types of hazardous materials, even when protective equipment of any type is worn, contamination should be avoided whenever possible.

Guidelines for Choosing Chemical and Biological Agent Protective Clothing

- Identify the agent and its chemical, physical, and toxicological characteristics
- Determine the agent vapor pressure

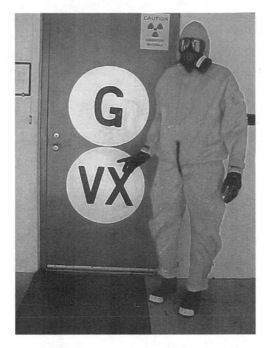

Figure 9.6   Civilian version of the military BDO with cartridge respirator. (Source: Center for Domestic Preparedness.)

- Is the agent a skin hazard?
- Choose the best protection available
- Determine what EPA level of protection is required

Indications Requiring Maximum Body Protection (Level A):

- Presence of vapors, gases, dust, or smoke.
- Positive instrument reading for airborne contaminants.
- Containers or other indication of a gas or pressurized liquid.
- Confined spaces where toxic vapors, gases, and contaminants accumulate.
- Skin, eye, or mucous membrane exposure is a high risk.
- Unknown types or concentrations of agents are suspected.
- Heat stress is not a major concern.

PPE Required for Protection from Specific Agents

Nerve agents (GA [tabun], GB [sarin], GD [soman], GF, and VX) require both respiratory and dermal protection. They are thick viscous liquids at normal temperatures and pressures. Liquid droplets can be absorbed through intact tissue. Vapors will enter the body through the lungs. Level A protective clothing or military BDO with SCBA, APR, or PAPR with hood will provide appropriate body and respiratory protection when entering the hot zone. The level of protection may be downgraded based upon agent identification, concentration, and with approval of the safety officer and the incident commander. Personnel in the CSEPP program operating outside the hot zone use Level B protection for firefighters, EMS, and law enforcement personnel. Butyl rubber gloves should be worn along with butyl rubber boots.

Blister agents (mustard) cause both internal and external damage to tissue and organs. Mustards are thick viscous liquids at normal temperatures and pressures. They present both a respiratory and dermal exposure threat. Level A protective clothing or military BDO with SCBA, APR, or PAPR and hood will provide appropriate body and respiratory protection. The level of protection may be downgraded based upon agent identification, concentration, and with approval of the safety officer and the incident commander. Personnel in the CSEPP program operating outside the hot zone use Level B protection for firefighters, EMS, and law enforcement personnel. Butyl rubber gloves should be worn along with butyl rubber boots.

Choking agents (phosgene, chlorine) are primarily inhalation or respiratory hazards. They are gases at normal temperatures and pressures. Some skin irritation or damage might occur; however, the major concern is the respiratory hazard. Level B protection and SCBA is required for choking agents.

Blood agents (hydrogen cyanide, cyanogen chloride) are primarily tissue-absorbent hazards. They are extremely volatile and will dissipate quickly in the air. Level B protective clothing should be worn along with SCBA, and APR or PAPR, only if they are proven effective against those agents.

Radiological agents, which emit alpha and beta particles, can enter the body through breaks in the skin, inhalation, or ingestion. Gamma radiation, which is an electromagnetic energy wave, enters the body by passing through the skin. HEPA filters, Level C protective clothing, and firefighter turnouts will provide protection from alpha particles. Nothing worn by response personnel will protect against gamma rays, and protection from beta particles is not guaranteed by Level C or turnouts.

Biological agents can enter the body through inhalation, breaks in the skin, or ingestion. They are not generally a dermal hazard when the skin is intact, except for the mycotoxins. HEPA filters and Level C body protective clothing will give adequate protection. SCBA and full turnouts worn by firefighters will also give a high level of protection for biological agents.

CDC Interim Recommendations for the Selection and Use of Protective Clothing and Respirators against Biological Agents

When using respiratory protection, the type of respirator is selected on the basis of the hazard and its airborne concentration. For a biological agent, the air concentration of infectious particles will depend upon the method used to release the agent. Current data suggest that the SCBA, which first responders currently use for entry into potentially hazardous atmospheres, will provide responders with respiratory protection against biological exposures associated with a suspected act of biological terrorism. Protective clothing, including gloves and booties, also may be required for the response to a suspected act of biological terrorism. Protective clothing may be needed to prevent skin exposure or contamination of other clothing. The type of protective clothing needed will depend upon the type of agent, concentration, and route of exposure. The interim recommendations for personal protective equipment, including respiratory protection and protective clothing, are based upon the anticipated level of exposure risk associated with different response situations, as follows:

- Responders should use a NIOSH-approved, pressure-demand SCBA in conjunction with a Level A protective suit in responding to a suspected biological incident where any of the following information is unknown or the event is uncontrolled:
  - The type(s) of airborne agent(s)
  - The dissemination method
  - If dissemination via an aerosol-generating device is still occurring, or it has stopped but there is no information on the duration of dissemination, or what the exposure concentration might be
- Responders may use a Level B protective suit with an exposed or enclosed NIOSH-approved pressure-demand SCBA if the situation can be defined in which:
  - The suspected biological aerosol is no longer being generated
  - Other conditions might present a splash hazard
- Responders may use a full-face piece respirator with a P100 filter or powered air-purifying respirator (PAPR) with high efficiency particulate air (HEPA) filters when it can be determined that:
  - Anaerosol-generating device was not used to create high airborne concentration
  - Dissemination was by a letter or package that can be easily bagged

These types of respirators reduce the user's exposure by a factor of 50 if the user has been properly fit-tested. Care should be taken when bagging

Figure 9.7 Firefighter turnouts do not provide adequate protection against chemical agents. They do however provide a high level of protection against biological agents.

letters and packages to minimize creating a puff of air that could spread pathogens. It is best to avoid large bags and to work very slowly and carefully when placing objects in bags. Disposable hooded coveralls, gloves, and foot coverings also should be used. NIOSH recommends against wearing standard firefighter turnout gear into potentially contaminated areas when responding to reports involving biological agents.

Heat and Cold Stress

There are four types of heat stress-related conditions: heat rash, heat cramps, heat exhaustion, and heat stroke. **Heat rash** is not a life-threatening type of illness and is really nothing more than a nuisance. It results in skin irritation, sometimes referred to as "prickly heat," and can be aggravated by chaffing. There is no increase of the body's internal temperature. Chaffing areas and broken skin can result in bacterial and fungal skin infections if not kept clean. **Heat cramps** are an indication that the body has lost fluid and electrolytes through sweating. This condition can signal the beginning of a hypovolemic reaction. As sodium chloride is lost through perspiration, cramping and pain develop. This occurs primarily in the abdomen and extremities. There is usually not an increase in body temperature with heat cramps. Fluid and electrolytes should be replaced, but salt pills or tablets should not be taken. **Heat exhaustion** (prostration) is a serious medical emergency. The outer body temperature is near normal, but there is an increase in body core temperature. A hypovolemic reaction may occur in some people. The victim's pulse is weak, rapid, and thready. Muscles are tense and may experience cramping. Blood pressure readings are low, and respirations are shallow. Pupils are usually equal and reactive. Skin is pale, cool, and clammy to the touch and may be associated with profuse sweating (diaphoresis). Victims of heat exhaustion should be removed from the heat as soon as possible, preferably to an air conditioned environment, and be rehydrated with electrolyte solutions. They should rest in a supine position with their feet and legs elevated to treat for shock. If treatment is not implemented in a timely fashion, heat exhaustion can be fatal. **Heatstroke** is an immediate life-threatening condition. The body's cooling system has completely failed. If victims are not treated at once, they will die. Heat stroke is also referred to as hyperthermia. Symptoms include red, hot, and dry skin, and even though the victim has come out of a very hot atmosphere inside a chemical suit, they are not sweating. The body core temperature can be as high as 106–110°F. Pulse is fast, bounding, and strong, and blood pressure is elevated. Muscles are tense and can be convulsive. Pupils are dilated. The patient may be unconscious, unresponsive, delirious, or convulsive. Irreparable brain damage can occur if the body temperature is not lowered immediately. This person should be cooled by any way possible: air conditioning, ice packs, fans, etc. Transport to the hospital should be in the head-up position. Rehydrate with normal saline IV and do not allow body temperature to go below 101°F. It cannot be over emphasized that this patient is critical — medical attention and body cooling has to occur at once, or this person will die. Emergency medical people who are assigned to take care of personnel wearing PPE should be keenly aware of heat stroke signs, symptoms, and treatment protocols for their area.

In addition to heat stress factors, cold stress should also be considered when the weather is freezing. The complications presented by cold stress are far less serious than heat stress but can be just as deadly. Extended exposure to cold temperatures can lower the body temperature, sometimes to a dangerous level. Wind, rain, snow, and ice can also accompany cold weather and cause difficulties for response personnel in chemical suits. Chemical suits can become rigid when temperatures are cold, and it becomes more difficult to function. Physical conditioning and health are the two most important factors in withstanding the extremes of heat and cold. Others will need to rely on shorter work periods, fluid replenishment, and proper rest. In addition to receiving medical physicals to determine fitness for using respirators, personnel donning PPE should also undergo medical surveillance before getting into the suits. Once the work period is over, personnel are decontaminated and the suit is removed, post-entry medical surveillance should also be performed by EMS personnel.

PPE of the Future

North Carolina State University, Globe Firefighter Suits, and DuPont have partnered to produce a turnout providing protection from fire with additional features for withstanding chemical and biological agents. Funding was provided by the DHS. The project goal was to create a rugged, lightweight, and user-friendly turnout that meets all of the requirements for structural firefighting ensembles, while providing escape and rescue capability from chemical and biological threats. The turnouts were unveiled at the International Association of Fire Chiefs (IAFC) Fire-Rescue International 2004 in New Orleans, Louisiana. Response to prototype turnouts has been very positive.

Decontamination

Decontamination includes many related activities on the incident scene. Emergency decon is performed by first responders without any elaborate decon stations or chemical protective equipment. The decontamination solution is usually water, which is delivered through hose lines. Technical decon involves setting up one or more decontamination corridors and cleaning personnel, victims, tools, suits, and other equipment. Local protocols should be developed to cover decontamination procedures. Sources of information for proper solutions and decontamination procedures for chemical and biological terrorism can be obtained from the U.S. Public Health Service, the CDC, or the U.S. military, and should be incorporated into local standard operating procedures. Information on responding to terrorist incidents is also available from the Federal Bureau of Investigation (FBI).

Whether you are a member of a hazardous materials response team or a first responder, decontamination is one of the most important actions taken by emergency personnel during a hazmat or weapons of mass destruction (WMD) incident. Decon reduces the effects of hazardous materials and terrorist agents when response personnel and the public become contaminated.

Decon also confines the hazardous materials or WMD agent to the "hot zone" and "warm zone" and prevents cross contamination. When emergency personnel arrive on the scene of a hazardous materials incident or terrorist attack involving chemical or biological agents, perimeters and zones are set up to help control the spread of contamination. One of the best ways to accomplish decontamination is to avoid contamination in the first place. This is most appropriate for emergency response personnel. According to the U.S. Occupational Safety and Health Administration (OSHA), "Decontamination means the removal of hazardous substances from employees and their equipment to the extent necessary to preclude the occurrence of foreseeable adverse health effects." The NFPA defines decontamination as the "physical or chemical process of reducing and preventing the spread of contaminates from persons and equipment used at a hazardous materials incident."

Contamination, or the event that makes decon necessary in the first place, occurs in the hot zone. Three distinct zones are established during a hazmat or WMD incident: hot, warm, and cold. Anything or anyone who has been contaminated, including responders and victims and the product and container, are located in the hot zone. Anything or anyone in the hot zone should be decontaminated to reduce the chances of creating additional contamination beyond the hot zone. Equipment and the environment are secondary concerns. Entry-team personnel, even with proper PPE, should not come in contact with hazardous materials in the hot zone unless they absolutely must as part of mitigation efforts. This will help keep contamination to a minimum and make decon easier.

The warm zone surrounds the hot zone and is where decon occurs. It is sometimes referred to as the contamination-reduction corridor. Outside of the hot and warm zones is everything else. No contamination should be present, and it should be a reasonably safe area. This area is referred to as the cold zone.

Two types of contamination can occur when dealing with chemical, biological, or radioactive agents. The first is direct contamination, which occurs when response personnel or civilians come in direct contact with the hazardous materials or terrorist agent. Cross-contamination occurs when proper decontamination has not been accomplished and contamination is spread beyond the incident scene. Therefore, the real mission of decontamination is to prevent cross-contamination from occurring in the first place. Decontamination (Figure 9.8) is a procedure for eliminating or neutralizing harmful chemical or biological materials that have accumulated on personnel, victims, or equipment during a response to a hazardous materials or terrorist incident. The primary reason for doing decontamination is to reduce injury to those exposed and to prevent cross-contamination. Wearing appropriate PPE and conducting decontamination will help to prevent further

Figure 9.8   Decontamination might be necessary for many chemical agents.

contamination. When terrorist events involve contamination of victims, decontamination must occur before treatment begins. This is unlike most other types of emergencies where patient treatment comes first. Once decontaminated, patients can be triaged, treated, and transported to medical facilities as necessary. Besides the two types of contamination, there are also two primary types of decontamination — technical and emergency.

Technical Decontamination

Technical decontamination occurs when the hazmat team arrives on scene. It may involve decontamination of response personnel only or of responders and victims. When victims require decontamination, two or more decon lines will need to be established, one for personnel and the others for victims. Victims may be ambulatory or may need to be removed by properly protected responders through the decon line. Either specially trained decon personnel or hazmat team members will set up technical decontamination while the entry team is dressing out and preparing for entry. Technical decontamination should be fully operational before the entry team begins operation in the hot zone. Some departments have developed trained decon units that respond when the hazmat team is dispatched on an alarm. They perform only decon functions. Decon personnel should not go on air supply until the entry team is preparing to exit the hot zone. This is done to ensure that decon team members have enough air supply to perform decontamination on entry personnel and themselves. Technical decontamination is performed with equipment carried on the hazmat or decon units for just that purpose. It has little other value in any other type of operation.

Equipment is not highly technical and does not have to be expensive. The process requires a device to catch contaminated water; buckets and hose; tarps to set collection devices on; and soap, scrub brushes, and trash containers. Water-catching devices or pools are available commercially that have steel frames and plastic liners. Children's swimming pools, both rigid and inflatable, also work well, are disposable, and are available at toy stores. Other supplies and equipment can be purchased from home improvement or hardware stores.

Decontamination relies heavily on water, so a supply must be established from a domestic source, fire hydrant, or fire apparatus. Volume should be kept to the minimum necessary to accomplish the job as the runoff might need to be contained. Following the incident, environmental or health officials should be consulted for disposition of decon runoff. Soap and water are the only decon solutions that should be used on victims or personnel in PPE. Bleach should not be used on victims, even if a chemical or biological agent is involved. Bleach can cause injury and even blindness if it gets into the eyes.

Emergency Decontamination

Emergency decontamination has become a major response objective of first responders to terrorist incidents. Initially, from a priority standpoint, emergency decontamination is more concerned with reducing the effects of hazardous materials or terrorist agents on victims. Preventing cross-contamination becomes a secondary issue. The idea is to get the hazardous materials off of the person or persons contaminated as quickly as possible so the damage to the affected area can be minimized. Emergency decontamination should be conducted upwind and uphill from victims. Responders should avoid contact with victims, runoff, or spray from the decon operation. One of the few clues that might be present as to what has happened on a potential WMD incident scene might be the symptoms of victims. If victims are exhibiting symptoms, then emergency decontamination should be performed. If no symptoms occur and there is no obvious contamination present, then victims can wait for technical decontamination. When a hazardous material or terrorist agent comes in contact with the skin, it can cause damage at the point of contact, be inhaled, or be absorbed into the body and move to a susceptible target organ. Emergency decontamination applied quickly upon arrival will help reduce the effects of agents on the body. Emergency decontamination also works well for hazmat incidents where someone has been splashed with a corrosive or other material that is absorbed through the skin. Damage to exposed skin can continue as long as the material in on the person. Copious amounts of water should be applied to counter the effects and remove the material. Emergency decontamination can be accomplished with equipment carried on apparatus for firefighting and rescue operations. Aerial master streams with adjustable nozzles can be put on wide-angle fog patterns and sprayed toward the ground, creating a decon shower. Nozzles can also be placed on the discharge ports of engines. Commercial devices also are available specifically for emergency decontamination. Such devices provide a wide spray pattern for mass decontamination. They can be attached to a ladder pipe on an aerial apparatus or a discharge port on an engine, or hooked directly into a hydrant to free apparatus for other functions (Figure 9.9).

Figure 9.9   Trident/One Mass decontamination device that hooks onto a fire hydrant so an engine company is not tied up. Also works well for fixed facilities such as hospitals and chemical plants.

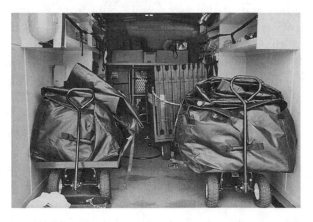

Figure 9.10   Portable mass decontamination tents on handdrawn carts for quick deployment.

Figure 9.11 Hydrant steamer caps with modifications to produce mass decontamination spray pattern.

Removing Clothing

The first step in technical or emergency decontamination of victims is to remove their outer clothing. Most of the contamination will likely be on the clothing of victims. Once removed, clothing and other personnel belongings should be bagged and marked for later disposal upon consultation with health and environmental officials. Removing outer clothing of victims, while reducing the hazard, raises the question of privacy. Victims might be children or adults. Provisions need to be made so that victims are segregated by age and gender. Children will be apprehensive of the decon process and the removal of outer clothing; the younger they are, the more apprehensive they might be. In some cases, children may be allowed to participate in some stages of decon, such as rinsing one another with a hose. Letting children participate in the decon process can greatly reduce the chaos and make the situation seem fun while accomplishing the task at hand. Privacy for victims can be accomplished in a number of ways. Most fire department companies carry tarps of various sizes. With a little preparation, procedures can be developed to use tarps in combination with ladders, fire apparatus, or natural features at the site to provide privacy screens. For example, the Seattle Fire Department has developed a procedure for setting up a privacy corridor using an aerial ladder extended straight out horizontally. Tarps are hooked to the ladder with prefabricated hooks. The base of the tarp is held in place with a charged 2 1/2-inch houseline. Commercially available tents (Figure 9.12) and decon trailers (Figure 9.9) can also be used to provide privacy. Once the decon process is complete, victims will need to be covered with some type of temporary clothing. Paper clothing is available, as are hospital gowns and scrubs. Plastic trash bags with holes cut for head and arms can also be useful.

Figure 9.12   Portable mass decontamination tent with nonambulatory patient decon setup.

Tarps and plastic sheeting can be used to help control runoff from emergency decontamination. However, the number one priority is the decontamination of victims; if personnel and equipment are not available for controlling runoff, then it should not be a concern at that point. Victims should always take priority over property or the environment.

Several mechanisms can be utilized to accomplish decontamination. These include emulsification, neutralization, chemical reaction, disinfection, dilution, absorption, and adsorption. Emulsification is a process of using soap and water to remove the contaminant from the surface of the person or object. This type of decontamination is used most often for contaminated victims and personnel. Neutralization, in terms of nerve and blister agents, involves the use of 0.5% bleach solutions on equipment after it has been exposed to the emulsification process. Chemical reaction is used to neutralize, degrade, or otherwise chemically alter the contaminant. Chemical reactions and bleach solutions should not be used for people, only equipment. Disinfection destroys the biological contamination because the disinfectant solution kills the microorganism or its toxin. Bleach is the most common disinfectant used. Dilution involves reducing the concentration of the contaminant and is usually accomplished with water. It works the best with polar compounds and other materials soluble in water. Flushing with water or IV solutions is most often used on human tissue and is continued for a minimum of 15 minutes. Since flushing or dilution does not neutralize the agent, the runoff water will have to be contained and neutralized. Absorption is the penetration of a liquid or gas into another substance (usually dry) with absorbent properties. This process is much like using a sponge to clean up a liquid material. Adsorption is the process of using an adsorbent substance that will stick to the surface of the chemical or biological agent, and then both are removed together, much like a magnet causes metal to stick to its surface.

It is most important to control the spread of contamination that may be present on the incident scene. When victims are involved, a thorough job of decontamination should be performed. Sufficient decontamination involves ensuring that the victim is as uncontaminated as possible. This infers that the contamination has been decreased to a point that is no longer a danger to the victim or the response personnel. On many occasions, contaminated victims have been successfully extricated from emergency scenes and transported to medical facilities, only to have emergency rooms and personnel, ambulances, firefighters, and EMS personnel contaminated along the way. Proper decontamination can prevent this type of nightmare from happening again. Unless it is known that a victim received only a vapor exposure, it must be assumed that there may be contamination on the victim's skin and clothing. Contamination can be transferred to emergency response personnel if proper precautions are not taken. During mass casualty incidents that require decontamination, multiple teams might be required to rotate in and out of PPE. Controlling additional contamination will reduce the potential for responders becoming casualties. Reducing the spread of contamination also aids in the restoration phase of cleanup. Contamination of victims results from contact with the chemical agent liquid or droplets resulting from aerosolization of biological agents or their toxins. Liquid contamination can be minimized by shielding the response personnel using respiratory protection and chemical protective clothing or swift decontamination of the victim.

Chemical agents of any kind splashed in the eyes is always treated by flushing with water for 10–15 minutes. Some of the skin contact decontamination procedures are listed below. Keep in mind decontamination solutions are meant for equipment, and they are all chemicals and have hazards associated with their use. Response personnel should wear the appropriate PPE and respiratory protection when performing decon. Care should also be exercised to make sure chemical damage does not occur to victims.

Nerve Agents: Decontamination of equipment and surfaces is accomplished with a 10% by weight aqueous solution of sodium hydroxide. If this is not available, the following are listed in order of preference: military Decontaminating Agent, DS (DS2), 10% sodium carbonate, and Supertropical Bleach Slurry (STB), or mixtures of HTH, or household bleach of 5% solution.

Blister Agents: For phosgene oxime, flushing contaminated skin with large amounts of water is required. Lewisite is removed by soap and water for 3–4 minutes. This is followed by removal of the clothing and continued flushing with the 0.5% hypochlorite solution. Contaminated skin areas should then be washed with soap and water.

Riot Control Agents: These chemical agents are actually solid materials suspended in an aerosol gas. When the agents are released, contamination of people and the surrounding area occurs. Decontamination of victims involves removal of clothing and flushing with a mild soap and water.

Skin Decontamination Solutions and Agents

Soap and detergents can be used on personnel, victims, or equipment. They are effective against all agents when scrubbed into the surface. When the agent gets into solution it is much more easily hydrolyzed. Hydrolysis is a chemical action in which water reacts with a substance to form two or more new substances. In the case of agents the new substances are less harmful than the agents. Soap and detergents remove contaminants; however, they do not usually neutralize them. Collection of the runoff will be necessary.

Sodium hypochlorite (household bleach) can be used for equipment decontamination. It is effective against all chemical and biological agents. As with HTH, bleach reacts quickly with blister, G, and V agents but requires 15 minutes of exposure for biological agents. Bleach can be applied undiluted with brooms, brushes, or swabs. For chemical agents, no special preparation is required. For biological decontamination, a solution of 2 parts bleach to 10 parts water should be used.

M258A1 Skin Decontamination Kit is designed to remove chemical agents from skin surfaces. It is a military kit that contains three number one liquid packets and three number two liquid packets. Packet number one (hydroxyethane, phenol, sodium hydroxide, and ammonia) will neutralize G agents by hydrolysis. Packet number two (chloramine B, hydroxyethane, and zinc chloride) will neutralize VX and mustard agents by oxidation. The kit contents are very corrosive and should not be used near wounds, eyes, or mouth.

M291 Skin Decontamination Kit is also a military kit with three decontamination packets. This is a dry decontamination system. The powder both absorbs and neutralizes chemical agents. Each packet contains a black resin, which is a carbon-based adsorbent, a polystyrene polymeric compound, and an ion exchange resin, which is both active and adsorbent. Decontamination is accomplished by opening the packet and scrubbing the skin surface with an applicator pad, creating a smooth coating of resin. The powder should be kept from wounds, eyes, and mouth.

Equipment Decontamination Solutions and Agents

Calcium hypochlorite (HTH) is one of the most versatile decontamination solutions that can be used for all chemical and biological agents. It reacts

quickly with blister agents but requires a 15-minute exposure time for biological agents. HTH is one of the military's primary decontamination solutions. Solutions for chemical agent contamination of equipment are 5%
HTH. Five pounds of HTH is mixed with 12 gallons of water, or 48 ounces
is mixed with 5 gallons of water. Biological agent-contaminated equipment
is decontaminated with a 2% solution of HTH. This is made by mixing 1
pound of HTH with 6 gallons of water. For personnel, the same solution is
used as for chemical agents. A paste can be made for treating horizontal
surfaces from 3 parts of HTH and 97 parts of water.

Acetone and ether can be used for equipment decontamination only.
They are solvents that can dissolve and flush chemical-based contaminants.
They do not neutralize the agents, and runoff should be controlled and
neutralized. Both acetone and ether are extremely flammable. Ethylene glycol,
also known as antifreeze, can be used for equipment decontamination only.
It is also a solvent that can dissolve and flush chemical agents. This chemical
does not neutralize, so runoff needs to be controlled and neutralized so as
not to cause environmental damage.

Formalin (formaldehyde) is used for equipment decontamination only.
It is sufficient for delicate equipment in neutralizing biological agents, including spores. Formalin vapors must remain in contact with the agent for a
minimum of 16 hours when temperatures are above 70°F. When temperatures are below 60°F, the minimum time is increased to 24 hours. Formalin
vapors are flammable and toxic.

Sodium and potassium hydroxide are used for equipment decontamination only. Sodium hydroxide (NaOH) is sometimes called caustic soda, and
potassium hydroxide (KOH) is called caustic potash. Both are effective
against G agents, V agents, lewisite, and all bacterial agents including spores.
G agents are neutralized upon contact with either hydroxide. When lewisite
is the agent, it must remain in contact for a minimum of 15 minutes. Ten
pounds of lye added to 12 gallons of water will produce a 10% solution.
Hydroxide solutions should be used in conjunction with a 10% alcohol
solution. Hydroxide solutions are very corrosive and can damage skin, eyes,
and the respiratory system.

Sodium carbonate is used for equipment decontamination only.
Sodium carbonate (Na_2CO_2) works only with the G agents. It must remain
in contact for a minimum of 5 minutes. Solutions of 10% can be made by
mixing 10 pounds of sodium carbonate to 12 gallons of water. It is also
used with a 10% alcohol solution. If applied to VX, it can produce extremely
toxic by-products.

Ammonia is used for equipment decontamination only. Ammonia solutions and ammonium hydroxide are variations of common household
ammonia cleaners. They are very effective against G agents and nonspore

producing biological agents. Ammonia is an inhalation hazard in confined areas. Ammonia and bleach mixed together produce toxic fumes.

Decontaminating Solution No. 2 (DS-2), a military decon solution for equipment decontamination only, can be used to decontaminate both chemical agents and biological agents, except spores. It must remain in contact with the surface for a minimum of 30 minutes to be effective. DS-2 can be used at temperatures above −250°F. The solution is usually applied with a spray device, broom, or scrub brush. Scrubbing action increases the effectiveness of the solution. DS-2 is an eye and skin irritant. When in contact with M-8 paper, it produces a green-to–black color change. In contact with super tropical bleach (STB) or calcium hypochlorite (HTH), both strong oxidizers, it will spontaneously combust. It is also very flammable.

Supertropical bleach (STB) is used for equipment decontamination only. STB is known as chlorinated lime. There is approximately 30% chlorine in the compound. It is effective against V agents, G agents, and biological agents. When mixed with water, it forms a paste that should remain in contact with a surface for a minimum of 30 minutes. Several solution concentrations can be mixed depending on the agent that is present. When in contact with G agents, toxic vapors are generated.

Physical methods can also be employed to eliminate contamination from biological agents. This is accomplished through the use of heat or radiation. Dry heat of 160°C for a period of 2 hours will render most biological agents harmless, except for spores. If steam is used at 121°C with an increase of 1 atmosphere of pressure, the time can be reduced from 2 hours to 20 minutes. This process is known as autoclaving. Ultraviolet radiation that reaches the earth from the sun can have a disinfectant effect when accompanied by drying. However, this is difficult to duplicate into a disinfectant procedure that can be quality controlled.

Incidents where a radiological dispersion device was used and contamination has resulted may require decontamination of victims. If the radiation involved is in the form of alpha or beta particles, there will be contamination. Radiation detection instruments can be used to determine contamination on victims and at what point a complete job of decontamination has occurred. Note that civil defense meters will not detect alpha radiation. Standard operating procedures should be developed for radiological monitoring of the incident area, victims, and personnel. In many jurisdictions this is not a fire department function. Radiological monitoring may be conducted by the state or local health department, emergency management agency, or department of the environment. Responders should be familiar with who does the radiological monitoring in their area and how to notify them of an emergency. Personnel working in a potentially contaminated area, or where a radioactive source may be emitting radiation, should enter with monitoring instruments and dosimeters. Personnel should limit time in radiation exposure areas and rotate crews to reduce the chance of over-exposure of any individual. Entry times and dosimeter readings should be documented. Exposure records should be kept on file to ensure that no personnel are exposed above the quarterly and annual limits. Nothing should leave the hot zone unless it has been monitored for contamination. This includes clothing, equipment, supplies, victims, and personnel. The following actions for radiological decontamination are recommended by the International Association of Firefighters in their training course, Training for Hazardous Materials Response: Radiation:

- Designate a decontamination area.
- Assign responsible, knowledgeable personnel to monitor and coordinate decontamination.
- Provide plastic bags, drums with lids, and other supplies to hold clothing and equipment suspected of being contaminated.
- Monitor each person who worked in the hot or warm zone with a GM counter and, if possible, an alpha meter — remember that the alpha meter is more difficult to use properly.
- Monitor everyone twice — once on exiting the hot zone while wearing protective clothing and equipment, and again after its removal. A third monitoring can be done after the personal hygiene shower.
- Monitor emergency apparatus, equipment, and tools, and decontaminate as necessary.

Just as with chemical agents, when patients are contaminated, clothing will have to be removed. Clothing and equipment that has become contaminated with radioactive particles will have to be bagged and properly disposed of. Hospitals should be notified as far in advance as possible that victims contaminated or exposed to radiation will be brought in. The hospital must prepare a radiation emergency area, which may take as much as 30 minutes or more to accomplish depending on their staffing and other patient traffic.

Decontamination Corridor Setup

Decontamination procedures for chemical, biological, and radiological agent contamination are not significantly different from other types of hazardous materials. Decontamination personnel must wear the appropriate PPE; decon solutions have to be chosen based upon whether it is equipment or human tissue that is being decontaminated; and care must be taken to control runoff from decon operations. The primary difference will likely be the large numbers of potential victims from a terrorist attack vs. the relatively few victims from most hazardous materials incidents. When an incident involves contaminated victims, two or more decontamination corridors will need to be established to accommodate rescue personnel who have entered the hot zone and victims. Victims can be divided into two groups: those who can move around on their own and those that cannot. If both types of victims are present, then two different decontamination corridors might have to be established to decontaminate victims. One type of corridor will accommodate the "walking wounded"; the other, litter patients.

Clothing can be contaminated with agents and must be removed from victims, at a minimum down to their underwear, and bagged for disposal. Significant contamination might require total clothing removal. Victim privacy is a major issue when establishing both technical and emergency decontamination. Victims should be washed down with soap and water at the incident scene. Contaminated patients should not be treated or transported to the hospital until they have been decontaminated. When emergency decontamination becomes necessary, firefighters can rig a privacy corridor with ropes tied between apparatus and salvage covers or tarps to provide victim privacy. Separate lanes can be established within the privacy area for men, women, and children, if necessary. It is important that the decision to do an emergency decontamination is made quickly and the setup assembled in a very short period of time. The importance of removing chemical agents from victims' bodies as quickly as possible cannot be overstated.

Equipment used for performing decontamination can range from hose lines off engine companies to ladder pipes in a fog pattern to elaborate decontamination trailer setups. Numerous fire departments around the country have placed decon trailers in service. Lincoln, Nebraska, has a decon trailer (Figure 9.13) equipped with mass decontamination showers on the outside; undressing areas; contaminated clothing chutes; heated showers; emergency generator; portable bladder to collect contaminated drainage from showers; dressing area; and disposable paper clothing for victims, once they shower. MODEC Corporation of Denver, Colorado, manufactures an automated mass decontamination system. Their decontamination shelters are either trailer-mounted or inflatable, with a compact portable solution spray system. Automatic bleach injectors can deliver up to 3,840 gallons per hour of heated decontamination solution at the appropriate mixture proportions coupled with fresh rinse water, without operator oversight or mixing. This unit has a capacity to decontaminate thousands of chemical or biological agent victims over extended scene operation times. Water heating capacity is 64 gpm from a 1.32 million BTU water heating system continuously, with no required heater recovery time. The system allows victims to self-decontaminate, reducing greatly the demand on response personnel resources.

Figure 9.13 Mass decontamination trailer used by the Lincoln Fire Department, Lincoln, Nebraska.

Setup time is minimal, and the unit can be operational within 5 minutes. Thirty-six people can be simultaneously decontaminated. With industrial and military design input, MODEC is the leading provider of consequence management tools designed for first responders and medical personnel involved in mass casualties resulting from the terrorist use of chemical, biological, or radiological materials. MODEC units are in use by the National Metropolitan Medical Strike Teams, the U.S. Secret Service, Fire Department New York (FDNY), CSEPP, and many others.

Binary Ionization Technology (BIT) is reported by the manufacturer to be "the most advanced sanitizing system available for on-scene decontamination of equipment and HAZMAT personnel." Utilizing a "spray gun," this portable system produces a water-based mist that contains "transient hydroxyl radicals," OH, a radical consisting of one hydrogen atom and one oxygen atom which does not normally exist in a stable form.

Hydroxyl radicals are among the most reactive chemical species known to science. As the spray mist contacts a microbe, cell walls are broken down, leading to the death of the organism. This process occurs within seconds of contact. Cleanup is not necessary because the remaining hydroxyl radicals bond with each other, forming oxygen and water. According to the manufacturer, the system "is not harmful to the building, its contents, or occupants." This product has not been approved by the EPA or FDA and has not been tested for effectiveness against all biological materials that might be found at an incident scene. A listing of biological materials tested for the use of this technology can be found on the manufacturer's Web site, http://www.alexeter.com.

Sandia National Labs has developed a decontamination foam for WMD incidents.

Researchers at the Department of Energy's Sandia National Laboratories have created a type of foam that begins neutralizing both chemical and biological agents in minutes. Because it is not harmful to people, it can be dispensed on the incident scene immediately, even before casualties are evacuated. The foam, comprised of a cocktail of ordinary substances found in common household products, neutralizes chemical agents in much the same way a detergent lifts away an oily spot from a stained shirt. Its surfactants (like those in hair conditioner) and mild oxidizing substances (like those found in toothpaste) begin to chemically digest the chemical agent, seeking out the phosphate or sulfide bonds holding the molecules together and chopping the molecules into nontoxic pieces. How the foam kills spores (bacteria in a rugged, dormant state) still is not well understood. The researchers suspect the surfactants poke holes in the spore's protein armor, allowing the oxidizing agents to attack the genetic material inside.

Clothing may have to be disposed of, so victims should remove valuables before removing clothing and going through decontamination. Police officers will have equipment, such as guns and handcuffs that need to be secured. Remember that when decontaminating victims, water is good, soap and water is better, and bleach solutions in combination with soap and water are best (Table 9.4).

Weather can provide challenges for responders for both emergency and technical decontamination. Cold weather climates are a particular problem. Ice can form from runoff, creating a dangerous fall hazard for responders and victims. Cold climates also present an exposure problem for victims, particularly during emergency decontamination. If heated water is available, it should be used during cold weather, but responders might have to be creative. Decon tents and trailers are usually outfitted with water-heating capability. Pools and makeshift emergency decontamination lines usually do not have heated water available. Water-heating decon devices are available commercially, independent of trailers or tents, but they can be expensive. If you are in a cold climate, you need to make some provision for heating decontamination water. The Anchorage Fire Department in Alaska has developed a dry-decontamination process for cold weather to use on personnel who have been exposed to vapors or gases (Figure 9.14). This process makes use of positive-pressure smoke evacuation fans that blow vapors and gases off of protective equipment. Personnel are then assisted with undressing, and protective clothing is bagged for evaluation or disposed of if the PPE is disposable.

Table 9.4 Decontamination Agents for Chemical Agent Contamination (in Order of Preference)

Agent	Decontaminant
Blister, H-HN-HD-HT-HL-L	1. HTH-HTB solution (calcium hypochlorite)
	2. DS-2 (decontamination solution)
	3. STB slurry (super tropical bleach)
	4. Commercial or household bleach solution (sodium hypochlorite)
Nerve, GA, GB	1. Caustic soda solution (sodium hydroxide)
	2. DC-2 (Decontamination Solution No. 2)
	3. Washing soda solution (sodium carbonate)
	4. STB (super tropical bleach) slurry
	5. Not soapy water
VX	1. HTH-HTB solution (calcium hypochlorite)
	2. DS-2 (Decontamination Solution No. 2)
	3. STB (super tropical bleach) slurry
	4. Commercial or household bleach solution (sodium hypochlorite)
Blood AC, CK	1. DS-2 (decontamination solution)
	2. Caustic soda solution (sodium hydroxide)
Choking CG	
Riot Control DM, DA	1. DS-2 (decontamination solution)
	2. Caustic soda solution (sodium hydroxide)
CS	1. DS-2 (Decontamination Solution No. 2)
	2. Alcoholic caustic (alcohol mixed w/sodium hydroxide solution)
	3. Hot soapy water
	4. 5% sodium bisulfite solution
CN	1. Caustic soda (sodium hydroxide) solution
	2. Washing soda (sodium carbonate) solution
	3. Hot soapy water
Incapacitating Agent, BZ	1. Alcoholic caustic (alcohol mixed w/sodium hydroxide solution)
	2. Sulphuric acid 1% solution
	3. Hot soapy water

Decontamination can present many challenges, but they can all be overcome with the proper planning, training and equipment. Every fire department, large and small, should be able to conduct an effective emergency decontamination with equipment already available.

Figure 9.14 Anchorage, Alaska, hazmat team members use positive pressure fan for decontamination during cold weather, which can reach well below zero.

Response Tactics for Terrorism: "The Rules Have Changed"

10

One simply has to read the newspapers or watch television to recognize that terrorism is for real. It occurs not just in the rest of the world, but right here in the U.S. Realistically, optimal preparation for a terrorist incident cannot be justified. The low likelihood of incidence and the great financial outlay it would take to prepare every community in the U.S. for every possible occurrence make preparation impractical. We can, however, lessen the impact of a terrorist incident by taking appropriate actions if one does occur. Exercising precautions based upon the hazards presented by terrorist weapons will protect emergency response personnel and minimize the danger. Acting Secretary of the Army Mike Walker once said, "I keep on my desk a jagged piece of glass which the FBI gave me from the childcare center in the Murrah Federal Building in Oklahoma City. I keep it there as a reminder of what can happen in America. One hundred and sixty-eight people died that day in Oklahoma City. But 5,000 would have died if that bomb had been a chemical weapon. So that is what we face with the potential of weapons of mass destruction."

Weapons that have been referred to as weapons of mass destruction (WMD) include chemical, biological, and nuclear materials. Terrorist incidents can also involve the use of explosives and incendiary devices. Safety of response personnel is the number one priority during a terrorist incident, just as it should be in all other types of emergency response. During the sarin attack in the Tokyo subway system, 10% of the emergency responders became victims. They had no idea when they arrived what had happened or that they were being exposed to a chemical nerve agent. It was, in fact, much later at the hospitals when doctors realized that nerve agent was responsible for the widespread illness. There were 1,364 emergency responders from the Tokyo Fire Department who responded to that incident. One hundred thirty-five of those first responders were injured and could no longer help each other or the public. That is more injuries than the entire Tokyo Fire Department experiences in a typical year. The importance of using proper protective equipment and standard operating procedures for response to WMD cannot be overestimated. We will not be able to wait for the military, National Guard, FBI, or any other state or federal resource. The local emergency response organizations must be prepared.

Firefighting by itself is a very dangerous vocation. Each year, on average, between 80 and 100 firefighters lose their lives in the U.S. responding to or fighting fires and returning to their stations. EMS scenes also present significant dangers in the form of mechanical hazards, hazardous materials, electrical hazards, combative victims, and bloodborne pathogens, to name a few. Hazardous materials personnel risk encounters with chemicals, etiological agents, and thermal and mechanical hazards at the incident scene. Law enforcement officers face potential gunfire, physical attack, or a vehicle accident each time they respond to a call. However, all of those dangers combined do not come close to the potential hazards and long-term impact that emergency responders could encounter on the scene of a terrorist attack. On September 11, 2001 in New York City, 343 firefighters, 21 police officers, and 37 port authority police officers died in the attacks on the World Trade Center, which resulted in the total collapse of both towers. Many others experienced psychological effects and long-term health effects from airborne contaminants. Potential lethality for responders and the public is much greater than during any other type of emergency. That is not to say that any more extraordinary care should be taken at a terrorist incident vs. other types of emergencies; just realize that there are some new and somewhat different circumstances surrounding a terrorist event. One major difference between a terrorist attack and other types of emergencies is that response personnel might be targeted by the terrorist. Being a target is nothing new for law enforcement personnel. Even firefighters and EMS personnel have been subjected to "potshots" from snipers during civil disturbances. Booby traps are a common concern during clandestine drug operations and have presented danger to police, fire, and EMS personnel for some time. However, the terrorist is literally painting a "bull's-eye" on the body of every emergency responder and considers them fair game as part of the attack. Bombing incidents that took place in Atlanta, Georgia, and Birmingham, Alabama, have brought this to a painful reality. Secondary bombing devices were placed and timed for the sole purpose of killing and injuring emergency response personnel. When a bomb exploded at an Atlanta nightclub, it sprayed large nails into the crowd. The secondary device that had been set for responders also contained the same large nails. It was found in a backpack outside the building but was disarmed before it could go off. As emergency personnel approach an emergency scene, they must be alert for signs of terrorism and secondary devices, which may be in many different types of containers and locations.

The goals of emergency responders for handling terrorist incidents should be self-protection, saving lives, and preserving the crime scene. Early on, responders must gain control of the terrorist incident scene and deny entry to anyone who does not belong there. Some of these same procedures are also practiced during a hazardous materials response. However, establishing security and denying entry in the case of terrorism may require armed law enforcement personnel, the National Guard, or even the military. Because a terrorist event is also a crime scene, care must be taken to preserve and protect evidence. Responders are not unfamiliar with crime scenes. Arson is a crime, and firefighters are trained to watch for the signs of arson and to preserve the scene and the evidence. Law enforcement personnel and other responders should be alert for suspicious activities that might be preparation for a terrorist act. Certainly large vehicles parked in front of "target" buildings or locations should be checked out. The Department of Defense (DOD) Security Institute reports the following situations should trigger reporting to the appropriate security or law enforcement agencies:

- Anonymous tips, phone calls, or notes of a threatening nature that might identify groups or carry extremist messages
- Surveillance by suspicious persons of federal offices or federal employees performing official duties
- Unidentified or unattended packages, cans, or other containers left in or near government offices
- Unattended and unoccupied vehicles parked in unauthorized or inappropriate locations, particularly those in close proximity to buildings or other structures
- Requests for plans, blueprints, or engineering specification for federal buildings or commercially owned buildings that house government offices by those who have no official reason to possess such information
- Unauthorized access even to unsecured areas by unknown or unidentified persons who have no apparent reason for being there
- Packages or heavy envelopes that arrive in the mail from unknown senders or that have a peculiar odor or appearance — often without a clear return address
- Confrontation with angry, aggressively belligerent, or threatening persons by federal employees in the performance of their official duties
- Extremely threatening or violent behavior by coworkers who indicate that they might resort to revenge against a group, company, or government agency

Response to a terrorist incident is much like the response to a hazardous materials incident in many ways. It is also potentially a mass-casualty EMS incident, confined-space incident, urban search and rescue incident, and law enforcement crime scene all rolled into one. It is unlikely that dispatch information will indicate that a terrorist incident has occurred. Once again, it will be the local emergency responders who will be first on the scene, and they will need to determine what has happened. Additional resources might be minutes, to hours, to days away in some cases. Local responders will have a great deal to do on the terrorist incident scene, particularly if there are victims, before the federal, state, and other resources arrive.

Approaching the Scene

Methods by which response personnel approach the scene of a potential act of terrorism and deal with the hazards might determine the success of the ultimate outcome. Like all other hazardous materials incidents, the scene should be approached from upwind and uphill directions if at all possible. The type of suspected incident will dictate the size of the isolation zone and downwind evacuation/protection distances. Incidents involving explosive materials or potential bombs will have greater isolation and evacuation distances than liquid spills of nerve or blister agents. Vapor releases from nerve or blister agents will require greater isolation and downwind distances than would a liquid spill. Distances are all relative to the hazard, just as with any other type of hazardous material. Detection devices, if available to the first responders, will help in determining presence of agents and assigning isolation and evacuation distances. However, there are not many first response units in this country that have access to monitoring instruments of any kind, let alone those necessary to detect chemical or biological agents.

The best method of detection for first response personnel is the use of their eyes and ears. Be aware of circumstances on the incident scene. Know signs and symptoms of agents. Use of the Emergency Response Guide Book (ERG) will give responders basic isolation and downwind protection distance information for initial response. They will need to know which hazard classes the agents fall into in order to determine distances. This might be the only information immediately available. Local standard operating procedures (SOPs) can be developed for dealing with different types of terrorist agents. In Atlanta, they have identified 1,000 feet horizontally and vertically in all directions for the isolation distance involving bombing incidents. When a bomb is suspected, priorities should be established upon arrival on the scene.

- Priority 1: Protect personnel, and establish the command post and all nonessential personnel 3,000 feet from the location of the explosion.
- Priority 2: Identify locations and numbers of victims. If it can be done safely, move them to a safe area before any treatment is begun. Use the "Load and Go Method."
- Priority 3: Provide a staging area for all incoming ambulances at least 3,000 feet from the explosion scene.
- Priority 4: Be aware of secondary explosive devices, and do not search or attempt to move anything unusual.
- Priority 5: Establish the hot zone and perimeter areas.
- Priority 6: Begin immediate evacuation of the surrounding area.
- Priority 7: Determine hazards in the area of the explosion, such as gas lines, electrical wires, unstable building components, and any hazardous materials that might be present.

Responders should be aware of the types of facilities that might be terrorist targets, such as government or other public buildings, places of assembly, symbolic or historic locations, national and other monuments, tourist destinations, and high-profile events such as the Olympics, fairs, carnivals, and festivals. Controversial businesses and locations, such as colleges and universities where animal research takes place might also be threatened. Embassies and consulates or state, local, and federal court buildings could become targets. Abortion clinics and fur stores might also be potential targets. Infrastructure locations, such as public safety buildings, transportation facilities and networks, and communication centers could be disrupted. Public utilities, nuclear and conventional power plants, and transmission lines might also be targeted. When emergency responders are dispatched to these types of locations for explosions, incendiary events, firearms incidents, and non-trauma mass-casualty incidents, they should suspect a terrorist act. Commemorating anniversary or historically significant dates may be the reason for an attack. Bombing of the Murrah Federal Building in Oklahoma City occurred on the anniversary date of the tragic conclusion of the Waco, Texas, incident, just 2 years earlier. Days of the week and time of day can also be significant; for example, fires in government buildings on weekends when no one is there may be suspicious.

Upon arrival on the scene, a thorough job of size-up should be undertaken. Our best detection equipment, when first on the scene, might be our eyes and ears. Look for unusual items or circumstances such as dead animals, birds, or fish. Lack of insects should also be a concern, especially in the summertime. After all, nerve agents are related to insecticides. Discoloration or defoliation of ground cover, trees, and bushes should be noted. So should unusual weather conditions, such as fogs, low-lying clouds, or mists on what was thought to be a clear day.

Most firefighters understand what is involved in size-up of a fire or other emergency scene. EMS personnel evaluate incident scene safety, patient conditions, and triage, which are forms of size-up. Response to hazardous materials incidents, which also include terrorist incidents, should also involve sizing up the situation upon arrival. Be aware of circumstances. Know the signs, symptoms, and dangers of chemical and biological agent exposure. Upon arrival, determine what has happened. Go through a mental checklist or ask yourself some questions. Are there any hazardous materials involved? Was there an explosion? Who and how many are injured? Are there victims as a result of trauma or are they experiencing nontrauma illness? What structures are involved? Is there any property damage? Did an explosion occur with little or no property damage? Are there unexplained patterns of sudden onset of illness or death involving large numbers of victims?

Watch and listen for clues to what might have happened. Take note of reports of unusual odors or tastes, unexplained signs and symptoms of skin, eye, or airway irritation, which can all be clues of a terrorist agent. Unexplained vapor clouds, mists, plumes, chemical containers, abandoned spray devices, or lab equipment in unusual locations are also clues. Items or containers that appear to be out of place at unusual incidents might be an indicator of a secondary device. Reports of an explosion with little physical damage. Reports of unscheduled spraying (time/location inconsistent with normal pesticide spraying). Discovery of abandoned spraying equipment or discarded protective suits, biohazard bags, or laboratory equipment are indicators that might identify the use or development of biological agents. The presence of unusual swarms of biting insects, as they may be used as a mechanism for dissemination. Observation of unusual numbers of sick or dying animals, often of different species. Most biological warfare agents are capable of infecting a wide range of hosts, and sometimes animals are more susceptible; therefore some animals might be affected before humans. Any unexplained outbreak of respiratory or flulike illness. Spot fires, or multiple fire locations, unusual fire behavior, or just a gut feeling that something is not right, should be investigated further. There might be multiple incident locations, as occurred during the sarin incident in Tokyo. Sarin placed in small glass containers, wrapped in newspapers, and covered with plastic bags, about the size of lunch boxes, were placed at 15 stations on three subway lines. Sarin placed in the subways was in a binary form, in which several glass containers contained different chemicals. The containers had to be broken, which would mix the chemicals together to produce sarin.

Significant periods of time might pass before response personnel realize there is more than one incident scene. Acts of terrorism first come to the

Table 10.1   Some Characteristics of Suspicious Packages and Letters

- Excessive postage
- Handwritten or poorly typed addresses
- Incorrect titles
- Title, but no name
- Misspellings of common words
- Oily stains, discolorations or odor
- No return address
- Excessive weight
- Lopsided or uneven envelope
- Protruding wires or aluminum foil
- Excessive security material, such as masking tape, string, etc.
- Visual distractions
- Ticking sound
- Marked with restrictive endorsements, such as "Personal" or "Confidential"
- Shows a city or state in the postmark that does not match the return address

attention of emergency response organizations through 911 or other dispatch centers. Dispatchers need to be alert for indications that a terrorist incident might have occurred. They should ask for as much information about the potential incident as possible. Dispatchers should be trained to recognize when reports of similar incidents are coming in from different locations; they could be related to terrorist activity. Training for dispatchers should involve the same awareness techniques taken by on-scene responders. A tie-in might exist between incidents, and the dispatcher might be the first person to recognize the connection.

When they arrive on the scene, responders must get a quick handle on the incident situation. An understanding of what needs to be done to protect themselves, treat the victims, stabilize any hazardous materials, or perform rescue from damaged structures is critical. Response personnel must take actions to protect themselves. While firefighter turnouts, including SCBA, are neither explosion-proof nor chemical-proof, they will certainly improve the chance for survival in some cases. Tactical decisions need to be based upon good, sound information gathered from the incident scene and from those involved. The terrorist might also use deception as a tool to confuse or distract response personnel from the task at hand. Incidents have occurred recently in which terrorists claimed to have a chemical or biological material or threatened use of a chemical or biological attack. Letters and small packages have been sent through the mail that were marked to indicate a chemical or biological material, when in fact they were not. Merely the threat of a terrorist attack can have a significant impact on a community, even if there is not any agent or device.

On February 8, 1998, FBI agents in Las Vegas arrested two suspects on suspicion of possessing anthrax. Larry Wayne Harris, who was on probation for attempting to purchase bubonic plague the previous year in Ohio, was one of the suspects. He had been bragging to a television reporter earlier in the day about how dangerous anthrax was. Both suspects claimed that the suspected anthrax was actually a vaccine for anthrax that was being tested. As it turns out, the material was not anthrax at all, but it took the FBI over 30 hours to make that determination. Emergency services from Clark County, Las Vegas, Nellis Air Force Base, an Army Technical Escort Unit, and FBI resources were tied up for several hours.

Another deceptive incident occurred on August 8, 1998, in Wichita, Kansas. A state office building had to be evacuated when an envelope containing a white powder and a note claiming the powder was anthrax was found in a stairway in the building. According to FBI reports, 20–25 people might have been exposed to the powder. The material had to be sent to Washington, D.C., for analysis. No symptoms were reported from the victims, but all were decontaminated and received medical attention. Approximately 200 people were evacuated from the building. Analysis of the white powdered material revealed it was not anthrax. The impact of this problem is that anyone could become a terrorist with just the will to do so, without any explosive, chemical, radiological, or biological material. Threats, no matter how likely or unlikely they might seem, must be investigated. That fact makes the aforementioned incidents acts of terrorism, even though the terrorist did not possess any actual chemical or biological agents.

Response personnel can minimize the impact of real or threatened acts of terrorism on the community by understanding the characteristics and symptoms of WMD agents. Responders need to be able to determine if a threat is credible or not. For example, if someone reported to have released sarin into a population, yet no one was experiencing symptoms, responders should recognize it as unusual. If significant concentrations of nerve agent have been released, victims would at least be experiencing some miosis and runny noses. Responders should investigate further for other clues to what might have occurred. On the other hand, if the threat is reported to be anthrax, and citizens or responders are reporting immediate symptoms, that would be unusual. Anthrax and most other biological agents do not produce immediate symptoms. They all have varying incubation periods that last for more than one day. Either case could be the release of one agent and the claim of another, or the whole thing could be a hoax.

On October 30, 1998, letters claiming to contain anthrax were sent to abortion clinics in three states. Clinics in New Albany, Indiana, Indianapolis, Indiana, Louisville, Kentucky, and Knoxville, Tennessee, all received the letters, which bore the postmark of Cincinnati. The substance in the envelopes was reported to be a white powder. At the Planned Parenthood Clinic in Indianapolis, after the letter was opened, employees and patients had to be stripped down and decontaminated as a precaution. Two police officers and a postal carrier were among 31 people treated in the Indianapolis incident. None of those exposed was experiencing symptoms, and if it was really anthrax, that would be expected. Anthrax has an incubation period of 2–5 days. All of those exposed were transported to hospitals and given antibiotic treatment as a precaution. One employee and a mail carrier from the Women's Health Services in Louisville were taken to University of Louisville Hospital, again as a precaution, and were given antibiotics and released. The clinic in New Albany, which is right across the Ohio River from Louisville, was not evacuated because the letter had not been opened, so no one was exposed. Unless aerosolized and inhaled by victims, anthrax is a minimal hazard within a container such as an envelope. Anyone who may touch anthrax could be infected if they had a break in the skin, although anthrax is generally not absorbed through intact skin. Anthrax in its deadly spore form is a light tan color and would have a consistency very much like cocoa powder, used for making hot chocolate, or the common spice cinnamon. However, if some other material was used as a medium, such as talcum powder, the mixture claimed to be anthrax could be white in color. As it turns out, the white powder was not anthrax in any of the incidents. During December 1998, Southern California experienced a series of similar anthrax threats. Telephone threats were called in to a dance club in Los Angeles County, requiring the quarantine of 800 people for several hours. No trace of anthrax was found. Two Van Nuys courthouses were also targeted, resulting in the quarantine of 1,500 people for several hours. Another threat occurred at a bankruptcy court in Woodland Hills resulting in antibiotic administration to approximately 90 people. An office building in the Westwood area of Los Angeles received a letter threatening exposure to anthrax. In Riverside County, a Perris School District secretary opened a letter that read: "You've been exposed to anthrax." Other hoaxes have also occurred in Colorado, Kentucky, and Tennessee.

Because of the rash of anthrax scares around the country in the late 1990s, the FBI WMD Operations Unit and the National Domestic Preparedness Office (NDPO), in coordination with the Centers for Disease Control and Prevention (CDC), the Department of Health and Human Services/Office of Emergency Preparedness, and the U.S. Army Medical Research Institute of Infectious Diseases (USAMRIID) issued guidelines for dealing with similar incidents. Following the anthrax attacks of 2001, the following same guidelines were reinforced as being correct.

1. If an envelope or package suspected of containing anthrax remains unopened, no action should be taken by first responders.
   - The FBI should be notified immediately.
   - NO evacuations, quarantines, decontamination, or chemoprophylaxis should be undertaken.

- Anthrax, if present, will appear as a powder or powder residue.
- Without any presence of powder, it is unlikely that anthrax is present.

2. If packages or letters are opened with evidence of powder, and a threat of anthrax is indicated, certain actions should be taken by emergency response personnel.
   - Anthrax spores are harmful only if inhaled, ingested, or injected through openings in the skin.
   - Anyone exposed to anthrax is not contagious, and quarantine is not appropriate. Response personnel should follow the same protocols for any type of biological hazardous materials incident.
   - A thorough hazard risk assessment should be conducted upon the receipt of a threat of anthrax.
   - Any contaminated evidence gathered at the scene should be triple-bagged.

No actions should be taken based solely on field test results. Some biological field tests are subject to false positives and false negatives. Field tests such as the CDC test in Chapter 9 can be conducted by companies responding to large numbers of white powder calls to screen out some materials. Also remember that some field tests have a limit to the size of the spore count they can detect. Because of the level of technology currently available for biological field tests, all samples of suspicious powders should undergo laboratory analysis, which usually takes from 24–48 hours. Those exposed should wait until results are available before treatment is administered. They do not need to be given antibiotics until it is confirmed that anthrax was present. Instructions should be given to victims as to what they should do if symptoms appear before laboratory test results are available. The health department should be notified, and the victim experiencing symptoms should go to a predesignated emergency department, where they should inform staff of their potential exposure. Response personnel can protect themselves by donning splash protection, gloves, and a full-face respirator with high efficiency particulate air filters (HEPA) or self-contained breathing apparatus (SCBA). Victims in the immediate area of the opened envelope or package are potentially contaminated and should be decontaminated with soap and water. Technical assistance can be obtained by contacting the National Response Center at 1-800-424-8802.

During September 2001, shortly after the attacks of September 11, seven letters, all mailed from Trenton, New Jersey, started arriving at locations up and down the East Coast from Florida to New Jersey to New York. News media outlets were targeted first in Florida and then in New York, then the U.S. Capitol and offices of senators. ABC News, CBS News, NBC News, and the

Figure 10.1   Anthrax letter sent to Senator Tom Daschle. (*Source:* FBI.)

New York Post were all sent letters. Of these, only the NBC and *New York Post* letters were recovered. One letter was addressed to NBC news anchor Tom Brokaw. He had actually handled the letter, so he was administered antibiotics and did not become ill. The letter sent to Tom Brokaw contained a brown, granular material, which later was positively identified as anthrax. One thing that caught the attention of officials was the misspelling of several words on the envelope containing the anthrax. Letters believed to be addressed to ABC News and CBS News offices caused two persons to develop anthrax infections. One was a seven-month-old boy brought in by his mother, a producer at ABC News; the other was an assistant to Dan Rather at CBS. Those letters were never found and were likely discarded. All of the letters contained powders that turned out to be weapons grade anthrax spores. It was the first confirmed biological attack by suspicious letters with powders that ever occurred in the U.S. The first victim was an employee of a supermarket tabloid at American Media Inc. in Boca Raton, Florida. It is suspected that he inhaled a large dose of the anthrax, and there was nothing anyone could do to save him. When it was all over, the number of confirmed cases of anthrax was at 22 (11 deadly inhalation and 11 cutaneous); 5 of the victims died. In spite of a $2.5 million reward offered by the federal government, no one has been charged with the anthrax attacks. Following the anthrax attacks of September 2001, emergency responders across the country were inundated with suspicious powder and package calls. The volume was so intense that the FBI would not respond until it was determined to be a credible incident. Many agencies treated the calls as nonemergency and sent one company or officer to investigate.

Establishing Scene Control

When responders first arrive at an incident, it is important that they take control of the scene. During the early stages of a terrorist incident, there is

Table 10.2

Radio Transmission Wattage	Stand-Off Distances
5–25	100 ft
50–100	220 ft
250–1000	450 ft

likely to be chaos. Officers should make sure personnel do not rush into the situation and become part of the problem. According to William M. Martin, in an article in *Fire Journal*, responders might be confronted with numerous operations at the scene of a terrorist incident. These include "fire suppression; search, rescue, and extrication; triage and medical treatment; hazardous materials control; crowd control; logistical support; and incident scene command and management." In addition, responders themselves might be the target of armed terrorists or secondary devices. Emergency personnel might be faced with multiple nontrauma casualties, which could require emergency decontamination in addition to other first-responder actions. Like any other hazardous materials incident, responders must recognize when a terrorist incident has occurred. Proper notifications must take place before response personnel begin dealing with the incident scene. Personnel must take action to protect themselves and the public. Recommended stand-off distances for maintaining radio and cell phone silence if explosives are suspected are shown in Table 10.2.

Standard operating procedures and preplans should dictate what notifications need to be made, because they will differ from one jurisdiction to another. It is important that the first responders and dispatch personnel know who should be notified. When a terrorist incident does occur, it is likely to be well beyond the capabilities of local responders and resources. The incident will be a crime scene, and the FBI and other law enforcement personnel must be alerted. Securing the scene and denying entry to anyone must also be accomplished very soon after arrival.

Just as with any other hazardous materials incident, working or exclusionary zones need to be established. The same terminology can be used for terrorist incidents that is used for hazardous materials incidents when establishing zones for potential chemical or biological releases. The hot zone (exclusionary zone) needs to be identified based upon the hazard(s) of the material(s) involved. This isolation area is established based upon the risk of potential harm to life, critical systems, and property. Decontamination is the primary function of the warm zone, and the cold zone should be a clean (from contamination) and safe area where operations such as staging, support, and the command post are located. Weather conditions, topography, and available resources to implement tactical operations are also important factors for zone identification. The ideal wind speed for agent dispersion is 9–12 mph. Higher speeds will hasten the breakup of vapor clouds. Agent clouds will hold together longer during the night because of inversion factors. Officers in charge must make a determination of whether it is safe for responders to take actions. They must decide if responders have the appropriate protective clothing and equipment to intervene and if decontamination will be necessary.

In addition, perimeters need to be established around the incident scene for security and scene control reasons. The perimeter size is established based upon the perceived hazard on the incident scene. It is always better to overestimate the size of the perimeter than to underestimate. Larger incidents might require outer and inner perimeters to manage incident operations and crime scene activities and to maintain the security of the scene. Outer perimeters are the farthest boundary of the incident for which control points need to be established. Public access is restricted at this point. It might become necessary to map the perimeter area(s) of locations where there are secondary and tertiary events. Control and work zones should also be mapped. Included on the map should be access and egress points, perimeter boundaries, important structures and landmarks, and any important topography. Within the perimeter area it might be necessary to identify clean and dirty areas.

During the bombing in Oklahoma City, the outer perimeter established was 20 square blocks around the Alfred P. Murrah Federal Building. Incident perimeters around the nightclub bombing scene in Atlanta encompassed a 6-block commercial area occupied by nightclubs, restaurants, and businesses. Inner perimeters are used to control hazard or danger areas and restrict movement of response personnel within the perimeter area. There might be hazardous materials such as chemical, biological, radiological, unexploded ordinance, or devices within an inner perimeter. Inner perimeters might also just be an investigation area for the collection of evidence that needs to be preserved. Access points for entering the controlled outer perimeter need to be established, and everyone entering and exiting should be logged in and out.

It is important to establish some form of identification for those who need to enter the secured area. Simply relying on uniforms is not enough. On a large-scale incident, potentially anyone could obtain a uniform that would look official enough to pass through a checkpoint. The same concerns apply for firefighters in turnouts; without official identification, anyone wearing turnouts could pass for a firefighter, especially during the confusion of a major incident. Perimeter areas should be restricted to only those necessary to accomplish the tasks at hand. It is no place for "sightseers." Establishment of perimeters needs to take into account resources available, training level of the resources, self-protection available (PPE), the size and configuration of the incident scene, and the stability of the incident. Those working inside the perimeter should be aware of the crime scene activities and avoid damage to evidence. EMS workers should realize that there might be evidence on victims. Their clothing, if removed, should be saved to be evaluated by law enforcement. In some instances, the clothing might have to be removed for evidence. Staging areas and the command post(s) should be established outside the perimeter. There might be a need for a forward command post within the perimeter area. Any potentially contaminated victims must be kept in the hot zone area or decontaminated and placed in an area of safe refuge until they can be evaluated.

The Murrah Federal Building was a nine-story high-rise constructed of reinforced concrete. When the explosion occurred, the first alarm assignment for the fire department responding to the blast was sent to Harvey and N.W. 5th streets, where firefighters found what looked like a war zone. Not only the Murrah Federal Building but most of the surrounding buildings displayed signs of blast damage. First fire companies, arriving just 2 minutes after the explosion occurred, thought they were dealing with a natural gas explosion. A general alarm was sounded, which brought all of the city's firefighting forces to the scene. Through a prearranged mutual aid plan, other departments responded to cover now-empty fire stations. The fire department in Oklahoma City operates out of 33 fire stations with approximately 1,000 firefighters. Apparatus consists of 33 engine companies, 13 truck companies, and 6 squads. In addition to the personnel from the fire, police, and EMS departments, hundreds of volunteers, including nurses, doctors, and ambulances, were at the scene within minutes of the explosion. Firefighters found many cars on fire, and one of the first priorities was extinguishment. As it turns out, the cars were the only things on fire at the incident scene. Massive amounts of thick black smoke from the car fires actually obscured some of the extensive damage that had occurred to the Murrah Federal Building. Engine companies who responded from the west first saw victims in the windows of the Water Resources Building. Thinking it was the scene of the incident, they entered that building to attend to the victims. Firefighters got their first glimpse of the Murrah Federal Building when they looked out the windows of the Water Resources Building. By the time emergency responders realized what had happened, they were faced with a combined mass-casualty, collapse rescue, hazardous materials, fire, and terrorist bomb scene. Additionally, it was a major crime scene involving a federal facility. The explosion caused a crater 30 feet wide by 8 feet deep and a huge pile of rubble from what used to be the front of the building. Initial rescue efforts were hampered by the instability of the building and concern over additional explosive devices. The south side of the building was covered with $3/4$-inch plate glass. Medical personnel indicated that almost 90% of those injured experienced cuts from flying glass.

Fire Department Chief Gary Marrs realized that while many downtown buildings had been damaged (80 buildings in a 1-mile radius), he wanted to establish just one main command for the entire incident scene, to avoid multiple command posts. Once the magnitude of the situation had been recognized, the task of treating the victims began in earnest. Within the first 60 minutes after the blast, all accessible injured had been removed from the scene to area hospitals. Those most critical were transported within the first 30 minutes. In all, 204 victims were transported in 66 ambulances, 37 from Oklahoma City and 29 from mutual aid departments. Compounding the problems facing responders were large numbers of medical volunteers from the community and nearby hospitals, who arrived at the scene to offer assistance. One civilian volunteer nurse died in the very early stages of the incident trying to rescue people from the debris. It happened while the scene was still in a state of chaos. News media made an announcement early in the incident for all medically trained individuals to report to the scene. This added to the chaos, and there was no accountability for who was there or what they were doing. Managing all of those resources was a significant challenge, creating much confusion and disorganization for a period of time. Because of the complications this caused, procedures were changed for the future. Doctors and nurses now have to report to the hospital and will be called to an incident scene only if needed.

While the fire and EMS responders were trying to treat and transport the victims, the FBI and police were dealing with a massive crime scene and its enormous amount of evidence. The scene needed to be secured and evidence collected. Another logistical nightmare with this and other incidents of this type is accountability of personnel. Because this is such a large incident scene and, in addition, a crime scene, security and accountability are very important. Initially, everyone on scene in Oklahoma City was going to wear FBI badges. Then the problem arose with obtaining clearance for everyone to wear the badges. It was decided that everyone would wear Oklahoma City Fire Department (OKCFD) badges to gain entry to the scene. However, those providing perimeter security were not given the word that those wearing the OKCFD badges were to be allowed in.

A major concern during an operation involving an explosives incident is a secondary device. The scene needs to be evaluated early so that law enforcement bomb technicians can search for and clear secondary devices before rescue operations can safely begin. During all phases of response operations, radio and cell phone communications are vital in responding to and managing the incident. When bombs are involved, radio and cell phone equipment can cause explosive devices to detonate, causing additional problems and danger for personnel. Other forms of communication should be established during suspected explosives incidents to avoid such a situation.

Figure 10.2 Urban Search and Rescue Team from Phoenix, working at the Alfred P. Murrah Federal Building explosion in Oklahoma City. (Source: FEMA.)

At approximately 10:30 AM, just 1 ¹/₂ hours into the incident, it was thought another bomb had been found. Responders and civilians were sent fleeing from the site. Once the site was evacuated, it provided the opportunity to regroup and establish an accountability system and greater scene security. Managing an incident scene will be much easier if some of the problems that were encountered in Oklahoma City could be controlled early on. Because of the collapse of a structure with people trapped inside, the Federal Emergency Management Agency (FEMA) Urban Search & Rescue system was activated. The first Urban Search & Rescue (US&R) Team was mobilized for duty in Oklahoma City at 10:30 AM. Eleven teams consisting of 56 personnel each would see duty over the next 6 days. Rescuers removed the last live person from the rubble at 10:24 PM, before the first US&R team was to arrive on scene. The Phoenix Team (Figure 10.2) was the first of 11 teams to arrive on scene at 10:23 PM at Tinker Air Force Base. They were operational by 1 AM on April 20.

April 30 was when the operation changed from rescue to body recovery. US&R operations would involve over 600 personnel with as many as 4 teams in operation at once. Each team operated for about 5 days on site. Logistics of caring for the needs of large numbers of out-of-town rescue personnel can be very challenging. Not only do their immediate necessities need to be met, but rescuers might require counseling from Critical Incident Stress Teams. At midnight on May 4, the fire department concluded operations at the site. Some of the lessons learned from the Oklahoma City bombing are shown in Table 10.3. Following the incident in Oklahoma City, scene procedures, response of medical personnel to the scene, and many other SOPs were revised to address many of the problems encountered. On May 23, 1995,

Table 10.3   Lessons Learned from the Oklahoma City Bombing

Problems Identified	Positive Points
• First responders were hindered by walking wounded	• All major supervisors had taken a disaster management course together
• Any fire truck, ambulance, or police car became a magnet for walking wounded	• They had pre-established working relationships
• Streets were blocked by wounded and debris	• Stressed that everyone should take the incident command course
• Critically injured could not be reached	• Interagency cooperation, planning, and communications during training exercises proved very valuable
• No common interagency radio frequency for communications	
• Planned on using cell phones, but cells were locked up	• Stressed the involvement of state and federal agencies in local exercises
• Resorted to using runners to communicate and deliver messages	• The chief of police, state director of public safety, and FBI had pre-established working relationships
• Hospital Radio Administrative System fell into disuse; 1/2 of system did not function at hospitals	• Emphasized cross training of team members to allow familiarity with others' expertise
• EMS system had difficulty coping with volume of victims	
• Unable to use triage tags	• Kept updated call lists and added contacts for agencies and vendors
• Could not keep accurate account of victims	• A unified command located in multiagency command center (MACC)
• Unsolicited media request indirectly resulted in one death	• MACC made it easier to find answers
	• Did not micromanage

what remained of the Murrah Federal Building was imploded, at 9:02 AM. A memorial has been built on the site.

US&R teams that operated in Oklahoma City had been trained to search earthquake-damaged buildings for victims. Earthquake-collapsed buildings are honeycombed with void spaces where victims might be located. The explosion at the Murrah Federal Building resulted in few voids. Most of the floors of the building had collapsed tightly and made it difficult to get search cameras into the rubble. Progress was very slow because searchers were unfamiliar with that type of building collapse. Overall, the search and rescue operation was conducted safely. Only 40 rescuers sustained injuries, mostly minor in nature, consisting of cuts, sprains, and debris in the eyes. Much can be learned about managing a terrorist incident by looking at previous incidents. The Oklahoma City explosion was one of the largest nonaircraft mass-casualty incidents to occur at a single location in this country's recent history prior to September 11, 2001, in terms of numbers of deaths, injuries, and rescue requirements.

Although the death and injury counts at the 1993 World Trade Center bombing were small by comparison to Oklahoma City, the logistical problems in terms of number of people in danger encountered by response personnel were much greater. The World Trade Center in New York City consisted of two 110-story high-rise towers. Potential occupancy for the buildings was 150,000 people. That number is larger than the populations of the individual communities protected by over 80% of the nation's emergency responders. The World Trade Center explosion would require the resources of 84 engine companies, 68 aerial trucks, and 31 special units over 11 days. Few locations in this country have those kinds of resources available to them without calling in massive mutual aid.

A firehouse sits right across the street from the World Trade Center and made an average of five responses to the center each day. When firefighters from the station heard the explosion, they responded to the garage area of the complex. They were on scene quickly after the explosion, anticipating a transformer fire. Firefighting crews faced heavy smoke coming from the underground parking garage. Smoke from the garage traveled into Tower One, requiring firefighters to break windows to ventilate, at a cost of $25,000 per window! After working on scene for a few minutes, they realized the scope of the incident, reported a "working fire," and requested a high-rise operation, which brought additional officers and resources to the scene. Firefighters did not know what type of incident had occurred until the large crater caused by the explosion was discovered in the parking garage. Ground zero for the explosion was on a ramp to the B2 parking level, two floors below the Vista Hotel, at the foot of the South Tower. The bomb was placed next to the building's communications and surveillance systems, and knocked them out of service. This location was also next to the building maintenance area; the blast killed several maintenance workers as they ate their lunch. Fifty people were rescued from the rubble in the maintenance area. One firefighter fell four stories while searching for victims. One hundred twenty-three emergency responders were injured during the rescue operations. More than 500 automobiles were on fire in the garage, producing heavy black smoke that was reaching the concourse. Nine hand lines were used to quickly extinguish the fires.

The biggest challenge to responders was the rescue of the people within the high-rise building. Approximately 50,000 people had to be evacuated. Elevator shafts were filled with smoke, and evacuation of the building required using the stairwells. Many handicapped and elderly people had to be carried down 60–70 stories by firefighters and EMS personnel. Communication was difficult because electrical power to the complex was cut and the building's operations center did not have backup power. There was no communication equipment to reach those on the upper floors to tell them to stay in place. Building occupants did not know the fires had been extinguished, and they were safer staying where they were. Thinking the smoke and fire was a threat to them, many occupants broke out windows. The falling glass and debris rained down on evacuees and emergency responders on the ground, cutting many of them. Most of the building's occupants evacuated on their own without notification. Because of this mass exodus, the stairwells were clogged with evacuees, and firefighters had a difficult time reaching the upper floors. One firefighter reported it took 2 hours to reach the top because thousands of people were evacuating down the stairs. Many people were trapped in the 250 elevators throughout the complex when the power failed. Over 500 had to be rescued. One elevator contained a class of 72 school children who were eventually rescued unharmed. More than 174 ambulances were required to treat and transport over 1,042 patients from the incident. EMS personnel established a "mobile army surgical hospital" (MASH) for treatment of victims at the scene. Of the victims caused by the explosion and fires, 400 walked to area hospitals on their own, 15 received traumatic injuries and were transported by ambulance, and 631 were treated at the scene.

Comparing this incident to the Oklahoma City explosion, there are many differences. The explosion in Oklahoma City involved the occupied part of the building. In the World Trade Center, the blast occurred in the largely unoccupied parking garage and maintenance area. Most of the rescue operations in the rest of the building involved a complete high-rise fire evacuation. There was little, if any, structural damage to the occupied towers caused by the explosion. Once again, as in Oklahoma City, the media put out information to the public that was largely inaccurate and complicated the response. The media told occupants to break out windows to prevent smoke inhalation. Also, in stark contrast to the Oklahoma City explosion, in spite of the size and power of the blast, Tower Two of the complex was back in operation within 2 weeks after the incident. As a result of this incident, backup power was provided to the elevators and communications centers of the World Trade Center. A new command center was constructed, which included conference rooms, fax machines, and additional equipment. Because of miscommunication, media policies were also changed by the fire department following the World Trade Center incident.

The World Trade Center in New York City was a complex of seven buildings near the south end of Manhattan in the downtown financial district. Best known for its iconic 110-story Twin Towers, after having survived a bombing on February 26, 1993, all of the original buildings in the complex were destroyed in the September 11, 2001, attacks; two collapsed (1 and 2) and the others (3, 4, 5, 6) were damaged beyond repair. Building 7 of the World Trade Center also collapsed. The September 11, 2001, attacks were a series of suicide attacks upon the U.S. According to the official 9/11 Commission Report, 19 men affiliated with Osama bin Laden and al Qaeda, a loose network of Sunni Islamist operatives, simultaneously hijacked four U.S.

domestic commercial airliners. Two were crashed into the World Trade Center in Manhattan, New York City, one into each of the two tallest towers, about 18 minutes apart, shortly after which both towers collapsed. The official count records 2,986 deaths in the attacks. That does not include the terrorists, but does include passengers of the planes. The 9/11 Commission reported that those attackers turned the hijacked planes into the largest suicide bombs in history in one of the most lethal acts ever carried out in the U.S.. The attacks involved the hijacking of four commercial airliners. With jet fuel capacities of nearly 24,000 U.S. gallons,the aircraft were turned into flying incendiary bombs. American Airlines Flight 11 crashed into the north side of the North Tower of the World Trade Center at 8:46:40 AM local time. At 9:03:11 AM local time United Airlines Flight 175 crashed into the South Tower, covered live on television. The fatalities were in the thousands: 265 on the four planes; 2,595, including 343 New York City firefighters, 23 New York City police officers, and 37 port authority police officers in the WTC; and 125 civilians and military personnel at the Pentagon. In addition to the 110-floor Twin Towers of the World Trade Center itself, five other buildings at the WTC site and four subway stations were destroyed or badly damaged. In total, on Manhattan Island, 25 buildings were damaged. Communications equipment such as broadcast radio, television, and two-way radio antenna towers were damaged beyond repair.

Civil engineers and the official report concluded that the collapse of 1 and 2 WTC occurred because the impact of the aircraft both damaged a large number of the external structural supports of the building and dislocated fireproofing from a large numbers of others. The explosion of the aircraft and the fuel ignited the contents of the floors around impact. This began compromising individual support structures. When enough had failed, this began a chain reaction where the buildings "pancaked" downward, each floor destroying the support of the floor below it. The area surrounding the World Trade Center became the site of the greatest number of casualties and missing and physical destruction. This region became known in the ensuing days as "Ground Zero."

New York City firefighters rushed to the World Trade Center minutes after the first planes truck the North Tower. Chief brass set up a command center in the lobby as firefighters climbed up the stairs. FDNY deployed 200 units to the site. Many firefighters arrived at the World Trade Center without meeting at the command centers. Problems with radio communication caused commanders to lose contact with many of the firefighters who went into the buildings; those firefighters were unable to hear evacuation orders. There was practically no communication with the police, who had helicopters at the scene. When the towers collapsed, hundreds were killed or trapped within. Meanwhile, average response times to fires elsewhere in the city that day only rose by 1 minute, to 5 ¹/₂ minutes. The other firefighters worked alternating 24-hour shifts. Firefighters came from hundreds of miles around New York City, including numerous volunteer units in small-town New York. Doctors, nurses, medical students, paramedics, EMTs, and counselors quickly arrived at the site of the collapse to set up multiple small staging areas and triage centers in the streets surrounding the World Trade Center site. Medical teams from the local neighborhoods, surrounding boroughs, and visiting medical staff worked to set up and staff the multiple triage sites, as guided by FDNY officials. As the afternoon wore on, the triage sites were slowly closed, and the triage efforts were consolidated at the Chelsea Piers. It became evident that there would be few, if any, survivors.

The New York City Fire Department lost 343 members in the attack, but still more firefighters fell ill during the cleanup. An estimated one-quarter of the firefighters and emergency personnel doing cleanup, or about 2,700 people, became sick after doing their duty at Ground Zero, according to the New York City Fire Department's most recent internal survey. Dr. Kerry Kelly, the NYC Fire Department's chief medical officer, told members of Congress that 25% of the department was reporting shortness of breath on exertion. Medical leaves had jumped two-fold, Kelly added, attributing the increase to a rise in respiratory problems and post-traumatic stress.

Identifying the Hazards

Determining what type of hazardous materials have been used by the terrorist can be difficult to accomplish. The usual placards, labels, NFPA 704 marking systems, shipping papers, MSDS sheets, and other identification tools will not likely be available. Protecting responders without identifying the hazards they face means making some tough decisions. The more information response personnel know about chemical and biological agent symptoms and characteristics, the better prepared they will be to make educated decisions to protect personnel. Much of the information available to responders will be in the form of occupancy/location, what they see when they arrive, and what others might have seen. Occupancies with exceptional security — locks, bars on the windows, covered windows, and barbed wire — indicate some type of terrorist or criminal activity might be taking place. Other clues might also be present, such as discarded containers or spray devices. Symptoms of victims and analysis of any damage that has occurred at the incident scene can provide most of the information. Such symptoms could include skin irritation, eye irritation or tearing, and airway irritation. Other indicators could be the presence of hazardous materials, unusual odors or tastes, unexplained vapor clouds, mists, and plumes. Victims with unexplained types of sickness or death, twitching, tightness in the chest, sweating, pinpoint pupils, runny nose, and nausea and vomiting should be evaluated as possible terrorist agent casualties. It is very important that response personnel from all organizations have some awareness-level training for response to terrorist incidents. Without that training, they might be at a loss to determine what has happened.

Public Protection Options

Evaluation of the incident scene might indicate that public protection measures need to be implemented. First on-the-scene personnel should conduct an informal hazard and risk analysis for potentially affected populations. Procedures used for public protection decision making and tactics for terrorist attacks are much the same as for other hazardous materials incidents. Information gathered during the primary size-up must be quickly translated into public protection options. Time is of the essence as the incident might be rapidly escalating. High-risk populations that need to be protected include schools, daycare centers, hospitals, nursing homes, large residential complexes, places of public assembly, and large public events.

Three options are available for response personnel to protect the public during a terrorist event. They are evacuation, protection in place, or a combination of both. Evacuation involves removing the endangered population from harm's way and relocating them to an area of safety. This is often an evacuation center or shelter where they can be fed, clothed, receive medical attention, and have a safe place to sleep. Evacuees' psychological needs should also be addressed. It is traumatic enough to remove people from their homes, but the fact a terrorist event has occurred will instill fear and confusion in the population. Counselors will need to be provided to deal with the psychological needs of the evacuees. If people are going to be evacuated, they first have to be notified. Notification might mean activating the Emergency Action System (EAS), which broadcasts emergency information over radio, television, and local cable networks. Reverse 911 systems are available in some communities to notify residents of emergencies and the need to evacuate or shelter in place. Weather radio systems can be converted to issue the same type of information during a terrorist attack. Siren systems are used in some locations, some of which might have voice capability to transmit emergency information. Responders might have to drive through neighborhoods using loud speakers on their vehicles to alert the citizens of danger. Some situations might require door-to-door evacuation.

Moving people who must be evacuated can be accomplished in a number of ways. Resources and the incident situation will dictate which method is the best. Evacuation can be accomplished by personal vehicle, carpooling with neighbors, buses, light rail, or commuter trains, if available. Each method has its own individual challenges. If people are to use their private vehicles, evacuation routes will need to be identified so that people do not interfere with incoming emergency equipment or drive through a danger or secured area. Community emergency management plans might already address evacuation routes and procedures for establishing shelters. Getting emergency management personnel involved will free fire, law enforcement, and EMS personnel for other functions at the incident scene. Law enforcement personnel should control the evacuation traffic and provide security for the evacuated areas. Security should also be provided at the evacuation center or shelter to help prevent the terrorist from making it another target. Once it is determined that an evacuation is the appropriate action, responders must ensure that the evacuation is conducted at the right time. Law enforcement activities and unstabilized hazards in the form of explosives, bombs, or a chemical release need to be taken into account when issuing the evacuation order. The evacuation might have to be delayed until the appropriate resources have arrived and are in place.

On-scene conditions might require that populations be protected in place. This decision will also be based upon a hazard-risk analysis of the incident scene. If the danger to the public is lessened by having them remain in place, rather than evacuate, then that is what should be done. Until the incident is stabilized, an ongoing hazard-risk analysis needs to be conducted to determine if remaining in place is still the best option under the circumstances. People in the affected areas must receive instructions through many of the same sources that evacuees look to for information.

It would also be helpful if people know what it means to shelter-in-place. During the Gulf War, when Iraq began sending Scud missiles into Tel Aviv, the government of Israel distributed gas masks to the public and provided instructions on how to shelter-in-place. Citizens built "safe rooms" within their homes to aid the shelter-in-place process. Education of the public is necessary to ensure that the shelter-in-place tactic will be successful. Instructions also have to be transmitted to the people who need to shelter-in-place when an attack occurs. Sheltering-in-place is used in hazardous materials emergencies, as well as during acts of terrorism. It might be a good idea to conduct a community awareness campaign to educate the public on how to properly shelter-in-place during an emergency. When instructions are given to shelter in place, doors and windows need to be closed and any cracks filled or taped to reduce the amount of air exchange with the outside. Furnaces, air conditioners, and air handling units should be shut down. People should move to the central portion of the building away from windows. Conditions in certain occupancies might require a combination of evacuation and sheltering-in-place. Moving people from one part of a building to another occurs much like it does in hospitals and nursing homes during fires. Populations might have to be sheltered-in-place until an evacuation can be performed. Some portions of the community might have to be sheltered-in-place while others are evacuated. The decision depends on the hazard-risk analysis of the incident scene, which will determine what protection options will provide the most benefit.

Managing the Incident

According to Presidential Decision Directive 39 (PDD-39), the FBI is identified as the lead federal agency during the crisis management phase of a terrorist event. FEMA is identified as the lead agency for recovery and consequence management. Remember that local responders will still be in charge of all fire, EMS, rescue, and preliminary law enforcement operations at the incident scene. There will be a period of time before any outside resources arrive. The local incident commander will need to implement the incident command system and use it to manage the incident just as any other. When other resources arrive on scene, it will be necessary to switch to a unified command system and begin to coordinate the operation with other agencies. The incident commander (IC) needs to ensure that all responding agencies are able to effectively communicate and participate in the established incident command structure. Planning should involve all agency representatives and be conducted regularly to monitor progress of assigned tasks, incorporate new resources as they arrive, and identify tasks that need to be undertaken. Regardless of who is participating in the incident, it is the responsibility of the IC to manage resources safely, effectively, and efficiently for the purpose of producing a favorable outcome to the incident. The National Fire Academy has developed the "SEE" principle to assist in managing the terrorist incident scene.

S — Safe — No one gets hurt.
E — Effective — Everyone works toward stated objectives.
E — Efficient — All resources are utilized to maximum benefit.

Three factors must be considered to effectively manage the terrorist incident scene. First, establish and update priorities. Life safety is always first and foremost: safety of responders is given top priority, then citizens. Once life safety is addressed, stabilization of the incident scene occurs next, followed by property and environmental preservation. The lives of response personnel should never be placed in jeopardy to save property or the environment. The terrorist incident scene is a crime scene. Investigation into the cause and origin of the terrorist event must be accomplished. This is largely a law enforcement issue, and the other responders will provide a support role.

Second, continual size-up should be conducted, based upon all available information. What has happened up to this point? What is going on right now? Based upon all available information, what is expected to occur? Third, establish and update incident priorities. Part of the incident management process is developing goals and objectives for dealing with the incident. Strategic goals are developed first and involve what needs to be done. Tactical objectives are then established to determine what will be done to accomplish the strategic goals. Task operations are then assigned to designate who will have responsibility for the tasks and when they will be implemented. The incident commander, whether the initial IC or the final IC, has a multitude of responsibilities to successfully manage a terrorist incident. First, and most importantly, command must be established. This is followed by a hazard and risk assessment, notifications, and development of a site safety plan. Responder PPE levels should be established based upon the hazard. Public protection options should be evaluated and implemented. Incident action plans should be developed and implemented. The hazards of the incident should be controlled. Resources necessary to manage the incident should be requested and a system set up to manage the resources. Evaluation of the incident progress should be ongoing, with adjustments to the action plans as needed to meet the changing incident. Logistical support should be established as part of the incident command system. Information concerning the incident should be controlled through the public information officer, with all information approved by the IC for release. Once the emergency is over, proper termination procedures should be implemented and the site, response organizations, and the community returned as near to normal as possible. At the Oklahoma City incident, there were so many agencies represented that a Multi-Agency Coordination Center (MACC) was established on April 22 to coordinate and disseminate information and answer questions. It remained operational until May 2.

National Incident Management System (NIMS)

The National Incident Management System (NIMS) developed by the Department of Homeland Security provides uniform incident management procedures that all responders — federal, state, tribal, and local — can use to effectively respond to WMD incidents. Listed below are the highlights of NIMS from the FEMA Web page. For further information see the following Web site: www.fema.gov.

- **Incident Command System (ICS).** NIMS establishes ICS as a standard incident management organization with five functional areas — command, operations, planning, logistics, and finance/administration — for management of all major incidents. To ensure further coordination, and during incidents involving multiple jurisdictions or agencies, the principle of unified command has been universally incorporated into NIMS. This unified command not only coordinates the efforts of many jurisdictions but provides for and assures joint decisions on objectives, strategies, plans, priorities, and public communications.
- **Communications and Information Management.** Standardized communications during an incident are essential, and NIMS prescribes interoperable communications systems for both incident and information management. Responders and managers across all agencies and jurisdictions must have a common operating picture for a more efficient and effective incident response.
- **Preparedness.** Preparedness incorporates a range of measures, actions, and processes accomplished before an incident happens. NIMS preparedness measures include planning, training, exercises, qualification and certification, equipment acquisition and certification, and publication management. All of these serve to ensure that pre-incident actions are standardized and consistent with mutually agreed doctrine. NIMS further places emphasis on mitigation activities to enhance preparedness. Mitigation includes public education and outreach, structural modifications to lessen the loss of life or destruction of property, code enforcement in support of zoning rules, land management, building codes, and flood insurance and property buy-out for frequently flooded areas.
- **Joint Information System (JIS).** NIMS organizational measures enhance the public communication effort. The Joint Information System provides the public with timely and accurate incident information and unified public messages. This system employs Joint Information Centers (JIC) and brings incident communicators together during an incident to develop, coordinate, and deliver a unified message. This will ensure that federal, state, and local levels of government are releasing the same information during an incident.
- **NIMS Integration Center (NIC).** To ensure that NIMS remains an accurate and effective management tool, the NIMS NIC will be established by the secretary of Homeland Security to assess proposed changes to NIMS, capture and evaluate lessons learned, and employ best practices. The NIC will provide strategic direction and oversight of the NIMS, supporting both routine maintenance and continuous

refinement of the system and its components over the long term. The NIC will develop and facilitate national standards for NIMS education and training, first responder communications and equipment, typing of resources, qualification and credentialing of incident management and responder personnel, and standardization of equipment maintenance and resources. The NIC will continue to use the collaborative process of federal, state, tribal, local, multidiscipline, and private authorities to assess prospective changes and assure continuity and accuracy.

Incident Operations

While overall procedural operations on the scene of a terrorist incident might be similar to other types of emergencies, traditional response tactics might be ineffective, counter-productive, or dangerous. Response to an act of terrorism will present responders with significant challenges. A terrorist event will be like no other emergency you have ever responded to. Concentration on all of the tasks at hand will be difficult. Many things requiring your immediate attention will likely be going on when you are on-scene. Prioritize tasks and realize you can do only so much, and do only what you can carry out effectively. Initial actions taken within the first 30–60 minutes will revolve around scene safety and life safety of the response personnel. Tactics will involve transition from almost total chaos to evaluation and management of what has happened or is happening, and protection of personnel. The incident command system needs to be activated; scene control and security measures should be implemented; public protection actions should be taken; fires should be extinguished; victims rescued or treated; decontamination performed; hazardous materials entry operation; and many other tasks organized. One of the main differences between a terrorist incident and other emergencies will be the potential dangers that chemical, biological, nuclear, and explosive agents present to emergency response personnel. Our inclination to rush in and do something because it needs to be done has to be suppressed. Safety and protection of response personnel has to be carefully evaluated before any actions are considered with terrorist events. Our usual response goal is to make things better when we get there. When we respond to a terrorist incident, that might not be possible. The damage might have already been done; we might not have the ability to protect our personnel from harm or to assist those civilians who might be trapped or injured. Significant risk-benefit analysis will need to be undertaken to ensure that tactical actions will produce desired results. Response personnel must understand which specific risk they are facing. Once identified, the risk is either acceptable or unacceptable.

Response personnel, by nature, rush in to do what is necessary when they arrive on scene. They take risks because "that's the nature of the job." Well, the terrorist is counting on that philosophy. The terrorist wants responders to go rushing in and become victims — part of the problem, not the solution. Vulnerability is being in an exposed position or at a disadvantage. You may, in fact, be in danger and not know it. That is why it is so important that response personnel understand the terrorist mind and dangers presented by chemical, biological, nuclear, explosive, and incendiary agents. First responders to a terrorist incident are vulnerable, meaning that they might become casualties themselves if proper protective actions are not taken. Officers must be able to understand vulnerability to the point where they can make changes in operations to improve your position and decrease the risk. If the appropriate protection procedures are used to sufficiently lower vulnerability, the level of risk will become acceptable.

Make no mistake about it, the dangers to personnel at a terrorist event are great. The purpose of a terrorist attack is to inflict death and injury. Terrorists do not care if the responders are part of the casualties. In fact, responders might themselves be targeted. The National Fire Academy has taken the protective measures of time, distance, and shielding from radioactive materials response and applied the concept to terrorism. Minimizing time spent in an affected area will reduce potential exposure to the hazard. That might mean spending no time at all in the danger area! Techniques such as rapid entry to conduct reconnaissance or rescue might need to be employed. Use the "scoop and run" method of removing victims from the danger area. Once removed to a safe area, triage and treatment can begin. This process is also dependent on the amount of contamination that has occurred. Emergency decontamination might have to be performed before any victims can be removed. Maximize the distance from the hazard area by establishing appropriate zones, perimeters, and downwind distances. Use appropriate shielding for protection from specific hazards. Shielding can be vehicles, buildings, chemical protective clothing, and other personal protective equipment. Be aware of the limitations of shielding for some types of terrorist agents. If officers do not understand or determine how or why personnel are vulnerable, it is quite likely protective measures taken might be inappropriate or inadequate.

Once the issues of risk and vulnerability are addressed, the personnel on scene can begin to determine necessary operational tactics. Lives of the victims or casualties should be the next priority. Difficult decisions might need to be made depending on the numbers and condition of the victims, their proximity to additional harm, and the ability of response personnel to do anything for them. When responding to hazardous materials incidents, the numbers of victims are usually small. Rescue is usually not a tactical option for initial responders because it is generally not an acceptable risk. Terrorist incidents might result in large numbers of victims. It might be necessary for initial response personnel to conduct rescue to save as many as possible. Careful thought will need to be given to rescue tactics to affect the most successful outcome with the greatest numbers of casualties removed. Once the hazardous materials team(s) arrive on scene, they can begin monitoring the atmosphere, and initial distances can be adjusted accordingly. Hazardous materials team functions include reconnaissance, verification of signs and symptoms, agent mitigation (if practical), sampling, and decontamination of victims and responders. Their mission should not involve any extensive rescue of victims.

Triage, Treatment, and Transport

On-Scene Triage

As a result of any natural or human-made disaster, including acts of terrorism, EMS responders will need to act in a swift, effective, and coordinated manner to save lives, preserve health, and minimize injuries. Before any triage or treatment can begin, it must be determined if the scene is safe. Can responders be protected when exposed to a chemically contaminated environment? Inadequate protection will cause the responders to become contaminated and require medical attention themselves. EMS personnel might be among the first to arrive on scene of a mass-casualty terrorist incident. They might also be the first to respond to reports of illness from a biological agent exposure. Bystanders may direct those first arriving crews to the most critically injured persons. When it becomes apparent that there are more victims than medical care personnel can handle, the senior EMS person should take charge of triage operations. EMS responders need to effectively determine which patients should receive immediate care and who can wait without jeopardizing their situation. The on-scene triage officer must be familiar with the signs and symptoms of chemical agent exposures. Understanding the chemical agent symptoms and progression, based upon dose and time exposed, will facilitate appropriate decisions concerning the urgency of treatment. Some victims might require lifesaving treatment during triage. This should be limited, so as not to end up with a treatment area in the middle of triage.

Treatment issues addressed during triage should be limited to the "ABCs" (airway, bleeding, circulation) or "BASIC" (bleeding, airway, shock prevention, immobilize, classify patient) if they can be administered safely without exposing personnel to danger. Triage protocols should be standardized among local response organizations and hospitals, including evacuation policies and procedures and evacuation priorities. It might become necessary for the triage officer to assign a communications officer to relay information to the Emergency Operations Center (EOC), area hospitals, and evacuation agencies. Another person might need to be assigned to record victim identification, status, and patient disposition. This might seem an unnecessary task when so many patients need care, but tracking patients will be very valuable when families and friends start to inquire as to the whereabouts of their loved ones. The triage officer must be aware of his or her resources and the number and types of casualties on the incident scene. Part of knowing the resources is knowledge of the EMS skill level of personnel on scene. The triage officer should also be aware of the availability of medical supplies, patient transport resources, and the census of local hospitals and their ability to accept casualties.

Determining the triage category of victims involves the knowledge of factors affecting the roles that are not directly related to the injured patients. Age can be an indication of the ability of a patient to physically cope with an injury. Elderly victims who have preexisting illnesses affecting the respiratory system or heart might have a less optimistic outlook than a younger person who is healthy. General health and physical condition also play an important role in patient recovery. Victims contaminated with liquid agents will require decontamination, whereas those exposed to vapor might not. When the type of exposure is unknown, decontamination must be done, followed by symptomatic treatment. Depending on the amount of exposure, patient conditions can change and they might get worse. The triage officer must reevaluate the condition of victims once all have been initially screened.

Patients who are triaged will be categorized depending on their condition. Local SOP will dictate what categories are used. For example, one triage system uses a four-stage color-coding system (Table 10.4). Immediate is represented by a red tag; Delayed is represented by a yellow tag; Minimal is represented by a green tag; and Expectant is represented by a black tag. The North American Treaty Organization (NATO) Handbook on Emergency War Surgery identifies treatment that needs to begin right away as Urgent. This definition applies to patients who have conditions requiring the evaluation of the ABCs of emergency care: airway, bleeding, and circulation. Also included would be cases of severe bleeding. Using the medical system triage example, immediate care is much like the NATO Urgent care. It involves advanced life support care, once again addressing the ABCs. Patients may be placed in the Delayed category if postponing treatment will not endanger their recovery. Minimal patients have received only minor injuries that can be treated with first-aid measures and might not require transportation to a medical facility. Patients are placed in the Expectant category when it is unlikely they will survive, regardless of the treatment they receive. Treating them will only use resources that could be used to save other victims.

Table 10.4　Triage by Symptoms

Agents	Red-Immediate	Yellow-Delayed	Green-Minimal	Black-Expectant
Nerve Agent	Unconscious or convulsive	Initial symptoms improving	Walking and talking	No breathing for more than 5 min. No pulse or BP
Vesicant	Moderate to severe pulmonary	2–50% BSA burns by liquid critical areas	<2% BSA burns by liquid in non-life threatening injuries	>50% BSA burns by liquid
Cyanide	Convulsions, apnea, loss of consciousness	Symptoms improving		
Choking Agent	Severe respiratory distress during triage	Symptoms more than 6 hours after exposure		Severe respiratory distress within 6 hours
Radiological	Traumatic injuries and severe burns respiratory tract	Non-life and severe burns, threatening injuries<25% BSA	<10% BSA minimal exposure to radiation	High fever, to face and upper disorientation, bloody diarrhea and vomiting
Bomb Blast	Decrease or loss of hearing, short of breath, change in mental status, penetrating and traumatic injuries		Walk and talk, alert and oriented, intact hearing, absence of trauma	

Note: BSA = Body Surface Area; BP= Blood Pressure.

Treatment

EMS responders might require personnel protective clothing (PPE) (Figure 10.3) to deal with patients who might have been exposed to chemical agents. One of the major problems for medical responders after the Tokyo sarin attack was the lack of PPE being worn by ambulance personnel treating the injured. This resulted in many exposures and injuries to response personnel. Those injured might have to await emergency decontamination before treatment can begin. This could require waiting for the first fire apparatus to arrive on scene to set up emergency decontamination. Minimizing the effects of chemical agent exposure relies heavily on the quick application of emergency decontamination procedures.

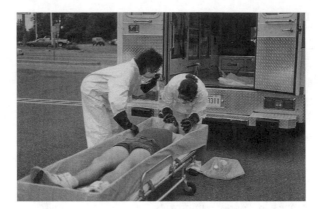

Figure 10.3 Emergency medical personnel will need to wear personal protective equipment for protection against chemical and biological agents.

Injuries encountered from a mass-casualty incident can include thermal burns, multiple trauma, myocardial ischemia or infarction, acute bronchospasm, heat exhaustion, psychiatric illnesses, dermatoses, mild musculoskeletal complaints, embedded foreign objects, and lacerations. While this is not a complete list, it should give response personnel an idea of the spectrum of illnesses and injuries they might encounter during a terrorist incident. When chemical nerve agents are used in a terrorist attack, the most important treatment will be the administration of appropriate antidotes to counter the nerve agent effects. Without antidotes, treatment will be supportive of symptoms and maintenance of ABCs. Triage and treatment will need to be carefully coordinated to ensure that those most needing treatment will get attention as quickly as possible. Some patients will require transportation to hospitals, while others can be treated on the scene. Minimizing the numbers of victims that have to be treated at a hospital will help reduce the burden on emergency rooms. In some cases, field hospitals can be set up to handle treatment of the less seriously injured. Once triage and stabilization treatment have been completed, those who require advanced medical care can be transported to medical facilities for further evaluation and treatment.

Transportation

In addition to triage categories, the military uses evacuation or transport categories. Those victims classified as Urgent require rapid transport. Priority patients are transported within 4 hours and Routine patients are transported within 24 hours. The type of system used to triage and transport victims of terrorist attacks is not important. What is important is that everyone is familiar with the system, it is not complicated, and it remains the same throughout the incident. Transport of victims during a mass-casualty incident will be based on the degree of injury. Those who are in need of critical care will require advance life support transport, while those less seriously injured can be transported by basic life support ambulances. Some circumstances might also require the use of air transportation of victims. There must be close coordination between triage, treatment, and transport of victims. Many of the functions will be occurring simultaneously. During the planning process, care should be taken to prepare for mass-casualty incidents. Both public and private ambulance resources should be identified. Taking appropriate actions on scene for triage, treatment, and transport will make things go more smoothly when patients reach hospitals.

Preparing the Hospitals

It has been reported that should a large-scale biological or chemical attack occur in the U.S., hospitals are poorly prepared to care for victims of such attacks. Hospital staff can be confronted with a mass-casualty incident resulting from natural or human-made disasters. Following a chemical or explosive terrorist incident, emergency room personnel would need to be prepared for a rush of patients, while at the same time working to prevent contamination that might force the shutdown of their facilities. Victims who show up at the hospital emergency room on their own might require decontamination prior to receiving treatment. Emergency room personnel might have no idea what has happened or what hazardous materials are involved. Even if it is known that perhaps a nerve agent caused the exposures, few if any hospitals have antidotes in large enough supplies to deal with such exposures at the present time. Many hospitals do not even have the ability to perform decontamination. Hazardous materials teams might have to respond to a hospital, and set up and perform decontamination operations before treatment can begin. Decontamination of this type should occur outside the hospital.

During the incident in Tokyo (Figure 10.4), over 5,500 people sought medical care. The emergency services transported only 688 of these patients. All of the others went to the hospitals by themselves. You can imagine the chaos at a hospital emergency room if just 10 patients showed up at once in a state of panic, thinking they had been exposed to a nerve agent. Many of those who went to hospitals in Tokyo had not been exposed; they just thought they had. Personnel need to be prepared to deal with mass hysteria along with those victims who are actually injured. Hospitals might also be the ones who are first exposed to victims of a biological incident. If a biological dispersal occurs, those exposed will not start experiencing symptoms until

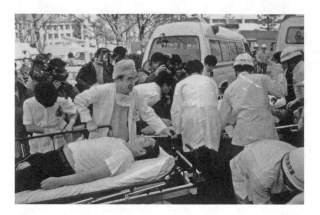

Figure 10.4 Subway passengers affected by sarin nerve agent planted in central Tokyo subways are carried into St. Luke's International Hospital. Twelve people were killed and thousands injured. (Source: AP/Wide World Photos. Used with permission.)

several days after the exposure. People will start showing up at doctors' offices, clinics, and hospitals seeking treatment. They will likely experience similar symptoms. Emergency room personnel should be trained to recognize signs and symptoms of chemical and biological exposure. Hospital personnel should also have access to PPE (Figure 10.5) to provide protection against contamination of themselves.

When large numbers of patients arrive at a medical facility, it will be necessary to triage them to determine which patients will benefit most from immediate treatment. Triage is performed to ensure that limited medical resources will benefit the greatest number of patients. Available resources might not allow every patient to receive treatment in a timely manner. Some

Figure 10.5 Some hospital emergency rooms have specially designed decontamination rooms for contaminated victims.

patients might be so seriously affected by the exposure that there is nothing that can be done to save them. When resources are limited, personnel will need to determine who can be saved and who cannot. Treating patients who are dying takes time that could be used for patients who could benefit and survive from immediate care. Making the decision as to who will get treatment and who will not is a difficult one. This decision process can be further complicated if friends or relatives of the patients arrive at the medical facility. However, when there are large numbers of patients, and medical personnel and supplies are limited, the resources must be used to benefit the majority rather than the individual.

Many different types of incidents can produce mass casualties; those involving chemical and biological agents of terror will certainly be the most challenging. By definition, a mass-casualty incident is one in which the numbers of victims exceed the capability of the healthcare facility or system. Depending on the size of the facility, it might not take many patients to be classified as a mass-casualty incident. What might be routine for one hospital might be a mass-casualty situation for another. Different types of terrorist attacks will provide different types of casualties. Explosions might result in large numbers of trauma patients. A chemical agent attack might cause large numbers of people with severe life–threatening nontrauma symptoms. Biological incidents might provide increasingly large numbers of people experiencing as-yet-unidentified illnesses. Each situation will present its own challenges to the healthcare system. Additional challenges will come from those who are not ill at all, but are experiencing psychological symptoms that might seem very real to them. If emergency room personnel are not aware of the symptoms of chemical and biological agents, their tasks will be more difficult. Professionals in the healthcare system are often overlooked in training programs for hazardous materials and those for chemical and biological terrorism. Several training programs that deal with training of hospital providers for chemical agents are available through the Chemical Stockpile Emergency Preparedness Program (CSEPP).

The person in charge of triage at the hospital will play a key role in a mass-casualty incident. This person should be the most experienced in terms of medical treatment, decontamination, and evaluation. For example, if the situation is a trauma incident, then a trauma surgeon might be the best triage officer. Large numbers of people presenting medical symptoms might be triaged by a physician familiar with medical diagnosis and treatment. When toxic materials such as nerve agents or biological toxins are suspected, the best triage officer might be a toxicologist, or at least someone with a background in treating patients exposed to toxic materials. An experienced triage nurse may also prove effective in conducting the triage operation, freeing doctors for patient treatment. But once again, the importance of providing chemical and biological agent training to hospital personnel cannot be overemphasized.

The majority of victims from mass-casualty incidents arrive at the healthcare facility within the first 90 minutes after the disaster occurs. Many of them have only minor injuries. It is most important that disaster plans for medical centers are implemented quickly. Of equal importance, the hospitals should be notified early on when it appears large numbers of patients will be expected. Not all victims may be transported to the hospital by the EMS system, and their arrival at the hospital might be unexpected and uncoordinated. Ambulatory victims might arrive on foot, as was the case in the World Trade Center bombing, or they might arrive by car, bus, patient transport vehicles, or taxicabs. The vast majority of the victims from the Tokyo Subway System (over 4,800) arrived in this manner. People going to hospitals on their own will generally go to the nearest one. Ambulance personnel may also transport critical patients to the closest hospital. This combination of coordinated and uncoordinated arrival at the medical facility can create chaos and overwhelm emergency room personnel. Because of a lack of coordination, other hospitals might receive few, if any, of the disaster victims.

It is important during an emergency or disaster that some system of communication be established between hospitals. This is not only to reduce overcrowding, but to share information on symptoms and diagnosis. Statistics show that during most disasters, only 15% of those transported to hospitals are actually admitted. Following the sarin release in the Tokyo Subway System, 640 patients exposed to nerve agent were treated at St. Luke's International Hospital. Only 64 of those treated arrived at St. Luke's by ambulance — merely 10%. Of the original 640 patients, 110, or 17%, were admitted. Five of those admitted were classified as critical (requiring ventilatory support). Three of the five experienced cardiac arrest. Only one person was dead on arrival (DOA).

No decontamination was performed beyond removing and bagging patient clothing. Generally, when victims are exposed only to vapors, there is little need for decontamination. However, if it is known that nerve agents were used in a terrorist incident, decontamination might need to be performed, if for no other reason than patient peace of mind. There were no reports of secondary contamination of hospital personnel from the Tokyo incident. Two physicians did develop miosis, and several nurses reported nausea. Most of the patients admitted responded well to the antidote therapy and were discharged the next day. Proper planning, training, and PPE for hospital personnel, including doctors and nurses, will ensure that they are well prepared to deal safely and effectively with the victims of an act of terrorism.

Managing the Deceased

While it might not seem like something that is an emergency response concern, someone needs to be prepared to deal with a large number of fatalities. Most hospitals have limited morgue space and would be quickly overwhelmed. During the planning process, resources should be developed to deal with mass fatalities. Medical examiners should be involved in the planning process as well as local morticians. Find out where there are large refrigerated trucks available along with embalming supplies. These will be needed to store the remains until they can be processed. Determine how to obtain them and get them to the incident scene during an emergency. Determine how long it will take. Personnel will need to be trained to don and use appropriate PPE, respiratory protection, and decontamination procedures. Personnel should also be trained in evidence collection as victim's bodies might contain evidence. Security will need to be provided for the temporary morgue so the chain of evidence can remain intact. When an incident occurs the following steps should be taken:

1. Obtain information from the incident commander (IC).
   - Type of incident and possible hazards
   - Type of chemical or biological agent
   - Estimated number of remains
   - Location of scene and accessibility to remains
   - Location of incident command post
2. Form a team to evaluate the specific incident.
   - Form an evaluation team with the medical examiner (ME/C), hazmat technicians, law enforcement, and other relevant agencies and prepare to enter the scene.
   - Check required level of Personnel Protective Equipment (PPE); ME/C should have two 2-person teams (primary and backup) that can operate in Level A PPE.

During evaluation:

- Determine issues (e.g., fragmentation, difficult excavation).
- Take initial pictures of site.
- Determine total number of remains and their location.
- Determine initial number of cases requiring an autopsy.
- Determine decontamination solvents and safe handling procedures based upon the specific agent.

Fighting Fires Involving Chemical Agents

Most chemical agents have high flashpoints and boiling points and by themselves are not serious flammability hazards. Agents can, however, be involved in a fire, which would effectively aerosolize the agent and carry it downwind. Agents can then fall out as droplets, causing injury to people and contamination of the environment. Decisions to fight fires that might involve chemical agents need to be made carefully. In some cases, applying water to fight a fire might only serve to spread contamination and put firefighters at risk. Under certain circumstances, it might be better to just let the fire burn itself out. Personnel placed in firefighting operations involving chemical agents should be kept to a minimum. They should be wearing full firefighter-protective clothing and SCBA. Skin contact with agents should be avoided at all times. Agent-contaminated runoff should be controlled to avoid environmental contamination. Unmanned monitors and aerial devices should be used as much as possible. All other unnecessary personnel should be evacuated from the danger area.

Fires should be fought using water, water mist, fog, foam, or CO_2. Care should be taken not to splash the liquid or spread it through runoff. Fire might destroy most of the agents; still, care should be taken to avoid contamination of sewers and other areas. Fires involving nerve agent tabun can form hydrogen cyanide (HCN), which is very toxic by inhalation. When nerve agent soman burns, explosive hydrogen can be formed by the corrosive vapors reacting with metals, concrete, and other materials. Nerve agents GB and GD can react with steam or water to create toxic and corrosive vapors.

Investigating the Crime

The primary interest of the FBI and other law enforcement agencies is the protection and investigation of the crime scene. Large explosion scenes such as Oklahoma City's Murrah Federal Building and New York's World Trade Center will be difficult to manage, at best. First the scene needs to be isolated and secured. Conduct an initial walk-through and prioritize evidence collection activities. Document and photograph the scene. Collect, preserve, inventory, package, and transport the evidence. Focusing the investigation on the recovery of physical evidence material, such as the attack delivery system, sample evidence, or biomanufacturing material is key. Recovery of the dissemination device used to carry out the attack should be handled as hazardous material and include analysis for agent residue. Evidence teams must exercise appropriate protection measures and packaging procedures when handling such items. Residual agent can be exploited for detection and iden-

Figure 10.6 Law enforcement personnel in protective clothing and respirators searching for evidence following a mock bombing.

Table 10.5 Evidence Processing Team Components

- Bomb disposal technician
- Evidence custodian
- Forensic specialist
- Logistics specialist
- Medical examiner
- Photographer (still, digital, video, etc.)
- Procurement specialist
- Safety specialist (structural engineer, etc.)
- Searchers/collectors
- Sketch artist

tification purposes and might be the best opportunity for identifying the agent prior to victims becoming ill. Unfortunately, locating sources of residual agent might be next to impossible, and agent analysis is also technologically demanding. The FBI maintains specially trained and equipped Evidence Response Teams (ERT) and a Hazardous Material Response Unit (HMRU) to provide on-scene coordination of the evidence collection effort. Unlike some chemical agents, biological aerosols disseminated outdoors by line source do not leave an agent residue (anthrax spores can be an exception near the line of release). Aerosolized biological agents released inside a building or subway tunnel will ultimately settle out of the air, depositing on surfaces, such as carpet and other flooring, furniture, wall coverings, and window ledges.

When an incident occurs, the entire area needs to be examined for evidence. One primary bit of evidence found in Oklahoma City was the crankshaft of the Ryder truck in which the bomb was hidden. It was found over two blocks from the blast scene. The vehicle identification number stamped on the crankshaft led to the suspects in the bombing. Another difficult incident scene to manage was the World Trade Center in New York City. Initially, poor perimeter security resulted in a lack of understanding of the number of victims, rescuers, or investigators that were on the scene. The explosion left a five-story crater in the basement of the building. How close was the building to collapse? It was originally designed to withstand a 4-inch wind drift; the explosion caused Tower One to drift 4 feet. There were 1,200 vehicles damaged in the underground parking garage from the explosion. This created a large amount of potential evidence. People trying to remove their vehicles from the building made maintaining evidence integrity difficult.

Much like a fire investigation, explosions also leave behind evidence that helps in the reconstruction of the event. Bomb investigators should have a kit so the proper tools will be available to aid in the evidence collection and scene investigation (A list of materials is located in Appendix G). It was pieces of the van used in the World Trade Center bombing that would lead investigators to Jersey City, New Jersey, where the truck was rented and the bomb had been assembled. Maintaining the security of the crime scene is very important, along with preserving the evidence. Not only law enforcement, but all emergency response personnel, share in that responsibility. In the case of the World Trade Center bombing, it was the detailed investigation and examination of the physical evidence that resulted in the fairly quick arrest and prosecution of those responsible. By examining blast waves and the resulting structural damage, FBI agents were able to determine the velocity of the detonation and, thus, the size of the explosive device. Information was passed along to the Bureau of Alcohol, Tobacco and Firearms (ATF) to check for the theft of any large amounts of explosives. Continued investigation resulted in the suspicion of a homemade device, perhaps containing a mixture of ammonium nitrate fertilizer and fuel oil. An identification number on a piece of debris led investigators to another Ryder truck and the eventual arrest of the suspects. Some of the lessons learned from the World Trade Center bombing included the steps of securing the perimeter and safety of the scene before making an entry. The investigation should be conducted by an experienced leader, and those working in the scene should not work longer than 10 days. The large amount of stress involved in this type of incident reduces productivity.

Termination of the Incident

Once the emergency phase of an incident has concluded and the criminal investigation element is complete, the incident scene, emergency forces, and the community have to be returned to as near normal (pre-incident conditions) as possible. Termination of the operations at the incident scene involves debriefing all response resources, formal and informal critiques of response activities, and after-action adjustments to enhance future operations for similar types of incidents. When the incident has resulted from acts of terrorism, debriefing sessions are very important. Leaders of response organizations should realize the need for psychological counseling of personnel. Most emergency personnel are not used to dealing with chemical and biological agents. They might have been targeted with secondary devices or booby traps. There might have been significant numbers of victims and loss of life. All of those issues should raise exposure concerns and might require post-incident stress debriefing. Federal Occupational Safety and Health Administration (OSHA) regulations require that the incident commander provide response personnel with information relating to hazardous exposures. Personnel have a right to know what the agent was, decontamination actions that are appropriate, and any potential symptoms that might develop. This is very important with chemical and biological agents, because some of them have extended periods of time before symptoms will develop. There might be little, if any, evidence at the scene that might indicate an agent, or which agent was used. It might not become apparent until response personnel and citizens start to report symptoms as much as several hours or days later. Incident critiques should cover operational effectiveness, success in carrying out objectives, and if overall incident goals were achieved. Resources should be evaluated to determine if needs were met. All facets of the incident should be thoroughly documented, including personnel exposures to agents, response objectives and actions, resources used, and functions that all personnel performed throughout the incident.

Recovery and restoration of the community will likely involve FEMA through the state and local emergency management agencies, depending on the extent of damage. Evacuees will need to be instructed on how and when to return to their homes. They will need to know what precautions they need to follow, if any. The public should be informed throughout the incident of the progress and after the incident of efforts to restore the community. Some areas might still be restricted for various reasons, and that information should also be conveyed to the residents. As much information as possible should be passed onto the public to restore a "sense of security" and support the transition back to "normalcy." It might also be necessary to establish counseling centers to assist those who need assistance for the mental trauma of the incident.

Developing a Plan

Local response plans need to be developed prior to any incident occurrence. The plan will outline what local actions will be taken until the state and federal response personnel arrive on the scene, and what actions will continue to be the local responsibility. Public protection and the protection of response personnel is a local responsibility. Local government provides all emergency response personnel, whose duties include law enforcement, search and rescue, EMS, hazard isolation, and incident scene control. Once the incident is over, the local government needs to restore critical public systems as needed. The plan should address recovery issues and responsibilities.

Even if federal disaster funds are allocated, the coordination of construction and repairs and spending of the money will take place at the local level. Plans should be developed to process claims and distribute disaster funds. Critical systems that might be disrupted by a terrorist event include electric, gas, water, sewer, and transportation systems and routes. Plans should address reestablishment of those services. Local emergency management personnel assisted by the state emergency management agency will make assessments of local damage, capabilities, and additional resource needs. They will also make application for a disaster declaration, which could result in relief efforts.

A disaster needs to be declared at the local level to start the consequence management process through the state and ending up with FEMA. Once the local resources are exhausted, the state EOC is activated and the state provides necessary resources beyond the local capability. These may include support personnel, equipment, and supplies. National Guard personnel and resources can be activated through the state EOC. A federal program started in 1998 involved 10 strategically located, specially trained National Guard units around the country to assist at the scene of a terrorist incident. They were known as RAID Teams. That designation was later changed to Civil Support Teams. On November 22, 2004, the Department of Defense announced that it had notified Congress of the fielding plan for 11 new Weapons of Mass Destruction-Civil Support Teams (WMD-CSTs). The fielding and certification of these final 11 teams will bring the total number of WMD-CSTs to 55. Only the governor can declare a state of emergency and request federal assistance. Activated by the Federal Response Plan (FRP), the president of the U.S. makes a wide variety of federal agencies and resources available. The FRP is a written document confirming agreements among various federal agencies that would provide disaster aid to the states. Elements of the plan outline coordination of federal resources and activities for disaster response under the direction of the Robert T. Stafford Disaster Relief and Emergency Assistance Act. When the governor of a state declares an emergency or disaster and requests federal assistance, the FRP augments state and local government response efforts. During a terrorist event, the FBI and FEMA would coordinate all federal resources required on the scene. Federal agencies that may provide assistance during a terrorist incident are listed below.

- Department of Justice (FBI)
- Federal Emergency Management Agency (FEMA)
- Treasury Department (ATF)
- Department of Energy (DOE)
- Department of Defense (DOD)
- Army Technical Escort Unit Aberdeen Proving Ground, Maryland
- U.S. Army Medical and Material Command (USAMRMC)
- U.S. Army Medical Research Institute of Chemical Defense (USAMRIC)
- U.S. Army Medical Research Institute of Infectious Diseases (USAM-RIID)

Resources

Resources are generally considered as people and materials that can be accessed during an emergency to help mitigate the incident. They can include personnel, supplies, equipment, information, funding, and anything else that is necessary to handle the emergency and return the community to normal. Once an incident has occurred, it is too late to start seeking locations and availability of resources. That should be taken care of during the planning stage. Detailed information should be included in terrorist response plans to identify locations, quantities, and nature of needed resources. Resources are available from local, state, and federal government agencies and departments. The private sector is also a good source for help. Industry, businesses, trade organizations, public utilities, contractors, and others can provide a vast resource for an emergency.

Figure 10.7 **(See color insert following page 236.)** Sacramento County Fire Department's new hazmat unit with closed circuit television, complete analytical laboratory, light towers and other typical hazmat equipment.

Figure 10.8   Spare air bottle compartments on Chicago Hazmat 512 using usually wasted space over the wheel wells.

Management of resources is also a very important part of response planning. During large-scale emergencies, unsolicited volunteers, equipment, and supplies, including food, will be brought to the scene. A mechanism needs to be established in the planning process to manage these and other resources. Reviewing past incidents such as Oklahoma City, the World Trade Center, and the Tokyo subway can provide insight into what types of resources are needed and what problems are encountered in these types of incident responses.

With little doubt, the Oklahoma City explosion was one of the nation's worst incident scenes in terms of loss of life up to that time. It was also one of the largest in terms of rescue operations and resources that emergency responders have faced in a long time at a single scene until September 11, 2001. Operations involving incidents of the size of Oklahoma City and the World Trade Center bombing and September 11 require enormous amounts of resources. Personnel might be on-scene for many weeks or even months with special needs beyond a "normal" incident response, including food, showers, sleeping areas, communications equipment, shoring materials and tools, construction materials, and equipment, to name a few. During the Oklahoma City incident, Little Caesar's Pizza established several distribution points and served over 9,000 pizzas during the incident. A food fair was going on at the Myraid, sponsored by the Oklahoma Restaurant Association when the explosion occurred. Organizers provided food for the incident during the first 9 days, serving 25,000 meals per day for the first 3 days, 14,000 through most of the operation, and 9,000 over the last few days. What kinds of resources would be available in your community to supply that many meals? While much of the food supplied in Oklahoma City was spontaneous, it is important that sources for serving meals be identified during the planning process. Oklahoma City's convention center was located a few blocks from the scene and became the living quarters for rescue personnel. Facilities were available for showers, lockers, and sleeping areas. Volunteers provided clean linens and kept the area clean. Wal-Mart provided eyeglass examination and replacement. United Parcel Service and Federal Express made their services available for responders. Many companies and volunteers just showed up with food and supplies. Collection, organization, and distribution of donated materials and volunteer workers can be another logistical nightmare. Cellular One and Southwestern Bell arrived on scene to provide assistance with communications in Oklahoma City. Four mobile towers were provided by Cellular One. Over 2,000 phones were provided for the emergency scene, and both Cellular One and Southwestern Bell provided free long distance calls home for out-of-town response personnel. Construction companies provided four cranes within 2 hours, along with other construction materials and tools.

On September 11, 2001, the resources of the New York City were severely taxed with a large loss of emergency responders, mass casualties that turned into a mass body recovery, and massive property damage from fire and structural collapse. Off-duty firefighters responded without being called and many lost their lives. Departments from across the East Coast sent vehicles and personnel. Private companies sent cranes, heavy equipment and people. New York State and the federal government sent massive resources. US&R Teams were activated from across the country and rotated in and out. Body recovery and identification took months, and many were never identified. It was without doubt the largest terrorist attack with the greatest impact to ever occur anywhere in the U.S.

Resources required for chemical, biological, or radiological terrorist incidents would be quite different from a bombing scene. In most cases, hazardous materials and EMS response would revolve around patient rescue, decontamination, treatment, and transport. That type of incident might very well be a mass-casualty event. Large numbers of EMS personnel, ambulances, and treatment supplies would be critical. If the incident were a chemical nerve agent attack, large supplies of antidotes would be required for treatment. Hazardous materials personnel would be heavily involved in providing patient decontamination. Multiple decontamination corridors might be needed, which can require large numbers of technicians and supplies. Monitoring equipment for chemical and radiological releases might be needed to determine what types of agents have been released and which concentrations are still present. Medical and other response personnel will require PPE. Hundreds of chemical suits, respiratory devices, gloves, and boots will be required. All of the resource requirements should be identified during the planning process. Plans should contain detailed information on the location and mobilization procedures for the resources when needed.

Response to Incidents Involving Radioactive Materials

Just as with all hazardous materials and terrorist incidents, approach a scene with potential radioactive materials with caution. Personnel, vehicles, and command post should be positioned at a safe distance upwind and uphill of the site. Responder safety is the number one priority for any incident scene. The following actions should be taken to ensure the safety of response personnel.

- Identify all hazards (TRACEM).
- Identify cargo.
- Obtain information concerning cargo from placards, labels, shipping documents, container shapes, MSDS sheets, and from the driver or shipping company.
- Consult the Department of Transportation (DOT) Emergency Response Guide Book.
- Keep upwind of smoke, fumes, and other hazards.
- Follow usual protocols for respiratory protection, use of protective clothing, and turnout gear.
- Monitor changing conditions that could create hazardous situations.
- Use detection equipment to determine any radioactive materials present.

If victims are present, notify hospitals of a possible radiation incident. Notify organizations in your jurisdiction charged with response to radiation incidents (i.e., state or local department of health, state or local department of the environment, or emergency management agency). Do not allow eating, drinking, smoking, or other activities within contaminated areas that might lead to intake of radioactive material. Avoid direct contact with radioactive materials where possible. Limit time near radioactive materials to the minimum necessary to accomplish required tasks. If the attack occurs inside, ventilation systems should be shut down to prevent the spread of contamination beyond the initial area affected. The most likely scenario would be a dirty bomb — radioactive materials attached to a conventional explosive and decimated by the explosion. It has been estimated by experts that the death rate from radiation caused by a dirty bomb would likely be low with the real danger coming from the contamination caused by the radioactive materials. Anyone in the immediate area would likely be affected by the explosive effects of the conventional explosives, depending on their character.

Nuclear weapons accidents that occur in the U.S. are handled by the Joint Nuclear Accident Coordinating Center (JNACC). They can be contacted at:

JNACC
Albuquerque, NM
505-845-4667
Alexandria, VA
703-325-2102

Many different local, state, and federal agencies have a wide variety of resources available to assist on the scene of a terrorist incident. Procurement of federal resources usually takes place by the governor of a state declaring a state of emergency and requesting aid from the president. Some hazardous materials response resources can be activated by contacting the National Response Center in Washington, D.C. One of the chief complaints of emergency response personnel has been the lack of a federal focal point for training and funds for response to terrorist attacks. To address this need, the Department of Justice, through the FBI, established the National Domestic Preparedness Office (NDPO). Further information can be obtained by contacting the WMD agent at the nearest FBI field office. The following is a listing of some federal resources that might be available during and after an incident involving terrorism. Since September 11, 2001, the president created the Department of Homeland Security to bring all agencies dealing with terrorism outside the Justice Department under one agency. Grant programs, training, and resource allocation all come under the Department of Homeland Security.

Department of Energy Nuclear Emergency Search Team (NEST)

For response to emergencies involving nuclear incidents, the U.S. Department of Energy (DOE) has created a Nuclear Emergency Search Team (NEST).It is headquartered on a remote corner of Nellis Air Force Base near Las Vegas, Nevada. In reality, NEST is the nation's "nuclear fire department," poised to respond to terrorist incidents involving nuclear devices or materials. Its job is to locate the nuclear device or materials, determine what it is, render it safe, and get rid of it. Resources available to the team include satellites, radiation-sensing planes, and helicopters. It is reported they can detect radioactive particles or debris as small as a grain of salt. On-the-ground resources include power generators, secure phone systems, and radiation monitors packed into nondescript vans. These vans can be loaded into a wide-body aircraft and flown anywhere in the country, or the world for that matter, within a moment's notice. The NEST team was organized in 1975, following a threat by an extortionist in Boston to set off a nuclear device. This team is comprised of over 200 searchers and is a joint effort of the FBI, DOD, and DOE. Since NEST's inception, its team has responded to dozens of incidents involving threats or actual use of radiological materials. Some of their responses included stolen plutonium from a Wilmington, North Carolina, plant; recovery of radioactive debris from a fallen Soviet satellite; radioactive monitoring after the Three Mile Island Incident; and nuclear extortion attempts against Union Oil Co. in Los Angeles and Harrah's Club in Reno, Nevada. The team has responded to threats of actual nuclear devices, but has never actually come face-to-face with one.

FEMA's Urban Search & Rescue (US&R) Program

Terrorist incidents such as the Oklahoma City bombing, involving explosions in buildings with trapped victims, will surely result in the activation of one or more of FEMA's US&R teams. The teams are a component of the National Response Plan (NRP). Twenty-seven teams are strategically located in 19 states around the country. US&R teams, or "task forces," are trained to assist with structural collapse as the result of natural or human-made disasters, including acts of terrorism. A complete listing of teams and their locations can be found in Appendix B. FEMA established the US&R Response System in 1989. When a governor requests assistance from the president and the request is approved, task forces are activated or placed on alert for response to a major disaster within a local community. Teams have also been activated and sent to foreign countries to assist at American facilities or to assist the country itself with a disaster. Each task force must be able to have its personnel and equipment mobilized, and at the point of embarkment, within six hours of mobilization. Task forces are composed of 62 specialists and divided into four major areas of expertise: search, rescue, technical, and medical. Task force components are equipped with over 58,000 pounds of specialized search, rescue, and medical equipment, much of which is purchased with grant money provided by the federal government. Individual equipment includes communication, locating, rope, rigging, hauling, and pulling tools. Additionally, they carry with them shoring, structural movement sensing, victim extrication, cutting, and drilling equipment. A medical team, composed of four medical specialists and two physicians, accompanies each taskforce. Medical specialists are usually paramedics and firefighters. The medical team is designed to bring the hospital emergency department into the field. They have all of the advanced life support equipment that would be available in an advanced life support ambulance. The following is a list of capabilities identified by FEMA for each task force within the US&R system:

- Physical search and rescue operations in damaged/collapsed structures
- Emergency medical care for entrapped victims, task force personnel, and search canines
- Reconnaissance to assess damage and needs and provide feedback to local, state, and federal officials
- Assessment/shutoff of utilities to houses and other buildings
- Hazardous materials survey/evaluations
- Structural/hazard evaluations of buildings needed for immediate occupancy to support disaster relief operations
- Stabilizing damaged structures, including shoring and cribbing operations

US&R operations can and do go on for many days or weeks at a time. Teams are often rotated in and out of a disaster scene.

Metropolitan Medical Strike Force Teams (MMST)

Medical strike teams formed to respond to chemical and biological incidents have been created in several U.S. cities. The first team was established in Arlington, Virginia, to cover the metropolitan Washington, D.C. area. These teams are referred to as Metropolitan Medical Strike Force Teams (MMST) and mobile NBC Disaster Medical Assistance Teams (DMATS). The mission of the strike team is to supplement the local hazmat and medical response to terrorist incidents by offering specialized equipment, knowledge, and ongoing training. Arlington's team is divided into three 43-person task forces that rotate through an on-call status system. One team is on duty, while the second is on stand-by, and the third is off. Training for team members may involve up to 125 hours per year. Strike teams in Atlanta, Denver, Philadelphia, Los Angeles County, and other cities are currently in the planning and development stage and will likely be online by the time this book is published. It is projected that there will be teams in the 100 largest cities in the U.S. within the next 5 years.

One of the potential exposures for response personnel at terrorism events is to a nerve agent. There are effective antidotes available for nerve agents if they can be administered soon after exposure. Philadelphia has issued antidote kits to all of the city's fire companies for their personnel, to be carried on their rigs. EMS units also have available to them enough antidotes for 5,000 civilian casualties from nerve agent attacks. According to U.S. Attorney General Janet Reno, studies were conducted into the possibility of purchasing and stockpiling vaccines, antidotes, and antibiotics to deal with the growing chemical and biological terrorism threat to the U.S. These medications would be strategically located throughout the country, with procedures in place to maintain shelf-life and prompt availability if a major chemical or biological incident were to occur. It is quite likely that this stockpile would be connected to the metropolitan strike teams.

FBI Explosives Unit — Bomb Data Center

Many resources are available from the FBI, which will have primary responsibility for the investigation phase of terrorist events, as outlined in PDD-39. One source for explosives investigation is the FBI's Explosives Unit-Bomb Data Center (EU-BDC). They provide training, technical support, and laboratory analysis to support explosives scene investigations. Prior to an incident, EU-BDC oversees the technical training of all public service bomb disposal personnel at the Hazardous Devices School (HDS), located at the Redwood Arsenal in Huntsville, Alabama. Over 5,000 bomb technicians have been trained to date through the program, and another 4,000 have received refresher training. During a special event, such as the Olympics, the unit can provide two bomb disposal trucks with total containment vessels. The trucks are completely equipped to deal with an explosive material or device. They carry a bomb disposal robot, bomb protective suits, screening, and disruption equipment. EU-BDC also conducts research and development operations for new procedures and equipment to safely render explosive devices. They have a publications program to disseminate information to the law enforcement community, including Special Technician Bulletins, Investigator Bulletins, and General Information Bulletins. During the post-blast phase, the EU-BDC provides forensic examination of bombing evidence. Models can be reconstructed of explosive devices to link serial bombers and develop a "bomber's signature," which aids in the identification of a suspect. EU-BDC also maintains the world's largest reference library for identification and comparison examination purposes. This database is called the Explosives Reference and Search System (EXPRESS), and it gives instant access to all of the resources of the unit. EU-BDC can be contacted through the following address:

Federal Bureau of Investigation
Laboratory Division
Explosives Unit-Bomb Data Center
J. Edgar Hoover Building, Room 3918
935 Pennsylvania Avenue, NW
Washington, DC 20535
Phone 202-324-2696
Fax 202-324-3794

Table 10.6   Countries with Potential Chemical and Biological Agent Capability

Country	Biological Weapons	Chemical Weapons
China	Yes	Yes
India	R& D stage	Yes
Iran	Small quantities	Limited scale
Iraq	No	No
Libya	R& D stage	Yes
North Korea	Limited scale	Yes
Pakistan	Limited scale	R& D stage
Syria	R& D stage	Yes

U.S. Army Soldier Systems Command (SBCCOM)*

The U.S. Army Soldier and Biological Chemical Command provides support in three main areas of defense: research, development, and acquisition; emergency preparedness and response; and safe, secure chemical weapons storage, remediation, and demilitarization. From the blackboard to the battlefield, SBCCOM provides defense capabilities by fostering partnerships with communities, industry, and other government agencies in developing and implementing soldier, chemical, and biological defense systems to ensure maximum protection for the U.S. The establishment of the Soldier and Biological Chemical Command (SBCCOM) signaled that the army had embarked on a bold transformation to focus key soldier protection and projection capabilities in one command. SBCCOM is a multifaceted organization that has missions of critical importance to soldiers and citizens. Providing safety, protection, and food for soldiers; supporting their deployments; researching, designing, and acquiring next generation equipment; safely managing America's chemical weapons stockpile; and training for and responding to biological and chemical emergencies worldwide. With SBCCOM in operation, the army is better able to take advantage of new technological gains in all subject matter areas as we seek ways to detect chemical and biological (CB) threats and protect soldiers. SBCCOM is a major subordinate command of the Army Materiel Command (AMC). SBCCOM personnel support soldier missions globally and chemical stockpile and demilitarization functions throughout our nation. The Command includes headquarters facilities and a Chemical and Biological Center (CBC) located

* Effective October 9, 2003, SBCCOM was reorganized into the following divisions: RDE-COM (Research, Development and Engineering Command); CMA (Chemical Materials Agency); GUARDIAN BRIGADE; PM NBC (PM Nuclear, Biological and Chemical Defense); and SSC (Soldiers System Center).

in the Edgewood Area of Aberdeen Proving Ground and the entire Aberdeen Proving Ground (APG) Garrison. Other SBCCOM elements include the Soldier Systems Center (SSC) and the Integrated Material Management Center (IMMC) located in Natick, Massachusetts; a Nuclear Biological Chemical Defense and Smoke portion of the IMMC, which is located in Rock Island, Illinois; IMMC Heraldry and War Reserve facilities located in Philadelphia, Pennsylvania; management and environmental remediation responsibilities for Jefferson Proving Ground, Indiana; War Reserve facilities at Seneca Army Depot, New York; and a component of the Project Manager for Soldier, located at Fort Belvoir, Virginia. In addition SBCCOM manages eight chemical storage sites throughout the U.S. Those eight chemical stockpile sites are located near Edgewood, Maryland; Anniston, Alabama; Blue Grass, Kentucky; Tooele, Utah; Newport, Indiana; Pine Bluff, Arkansas; Pueblo, Colorado; and Hermiston, Oregon. The Research, Development and Acquisition business area provides full life-cycle support from laboratories to chemical and biological protection, detection, and monitoring capabilities for the battlefield. Recognized as the nation's center of chemical and biological expertise, the Edgewood Chemical Biological Center and Project Managers continue research, concept exploration, demonstration, validation and engineering manufacturing development for the production of chemical defense systems, obscuring smoke, aerosol systems, and flame weapons. The Soldier Systems Center at Natick provides total lifecycle management of soldier and related support systems through centralized development, procurement, integration, and management of equipment, clothing, food, and protection for the individual soldier as well as shelters, airdrop, field service, and organizational equipment. The operational capabilities of the command include the safe, secure storage of chemical weapons at the eight U.S. stockpile sites at Anniston, Alabama; Blue Grass, Kentucky; Edgewood, Maryland; Newport, Indiana; Pine Bluff, Arkansas; Pueblo, Colorado; Tooele, Utah; and Umatillla, Oregon. The sites are also involved in Chemical Weapons Convention Treaty compliance, remediation, emergency preparedness, and direct support for the chemical weapons demilitarization.

Capabilities for emergency preparedness and response are present in a variety of command elements. The Army Technical Escort Unit, a globally deployable, highly trained, explosive and chemical/biological response team, has been safely identifying, escorting, rendering-safe, disposing, and mitigating explosive chemical and biological devices for more than 50 years. The command leads the federal Domestic Preparedness Program designed to enhance the capability of federal, state, and local emergency response to incidents involving nuclear, biological, and chemical terrorism. This new interagency effort provides train-the-trainer instructions and emergency response exercises for 120 cities across the U.S., chemical and biological expert assistance, and leadership for the Department of Defense Chemical and Biological Rapid Response Team. The comprehensive remediation of Rocky Mountain Arsenal, cleaning up decades of weapons and chemical production, and the management of a fast-paced DOD program for Assembled Chemical Weapons Assessment to find alternative solutions for destroying chemical weapons are additional missions under SBCCOM management. For more than 75 years, the command and its preceding organizations have led the military in chemical and biological defense and support to the military forces from daily peace activities to preparing and conducting military operations.

SBCCOM Public Affairs Office
Phone 410-436-4345
Fax 410-436-5297

Chemical/Biological Hotline
1-800-424-8802

U.S. Coast Guard Strike Force

Generally thought of as a resource for hazardous materials releases on the nation's waterways, the U.S. Coast Guard Strike Force can also provide expertise during acts of terrorism. They can also respond to incidents that are not associated with waterways to provide assistance. Strike teams are located in coastal areas around the country, along several river systems, and in the Great Lakes region. They are under the direction of the U.S. Department of Homeland Security during peacetime, and often work closely with the U.S. Environmental Protection Agency (EPA) when hazardous materials are released into the environment. The Coast Guard operates the National Response Center (NRC) in Washington, D.C., which is the federal reporting point for releases of certain hazardous materials into the environment. They are also the contact point to activate the Federal Response Plan for hazardous materials emergencies. The federal on-scene coordinator can be activated by NRC and dispatched to incident scenes anywhere in the country. NRC operates on a 24-hour-a-day basis and can provide information on a wide variety of chemicals from their computerized database. Potentially, because of their mobility, the strike teams could be the first federal response to reach the scene of a terrorist incident. Coast Guard Strike Teams can be activated by contacting the NRC. They are also the federal contact point for emergency information concerning WMD incidents. When a terrorist attack occurs in the U.S., the National Response Center should be notified at 1-800-424-8802.

National Guard Civil Support Teams (Formerly Rapid Assessment and Initial Detection [RAID] Teams)

The Defense Department has developed a plan to assist local, state, and federal civil authorities in the event of a terrorist incident. These teams, formed from National Guard components, assist emergency responders upon request by the state or federal government at suspected incidents involving nuclear, biological, or chemical agents. The units have the capability to assess the situation and provide technical assistance to the local incident commander. They also can speed the flow of requested DOD personnel, equipment, and services, to aid in mitigation of a terrorist incident. Rigorous training was conducted during fiscal year 1999 for the men and women selected for the RAID Teams. Each team consisted of 22 members. The training lasted 15 months and was followed by an evaluation to determine operational certification. Team locations were selected to make the most use of existing facilities. Maximum coverage of major metropolitan areas within each of the 10 FEMA regions around the country was also considered. Current plans are to locate teams in Los Alamitos, California; Aurora, Colorado; Marietta, Georgia (Dobbins Air Reserve Base); Peoria, Illinois; Natick, Massachusetts; Fort Leonard Wood, Missouri; Scotia, New York (Stratton Air National Guard Base); Fort Indiantown Gap, Pennsylvania; Austin, Texas; and Tacoma, Washington. The teams will be activated by the governor of a state requesting assistance from the president.

National Guard Civil Support Teams

During an address at the U.S. Naval Academy in May 1998, President Bill Clinton announced the formation of 10 teams in FY 1999 from the DOD to support state and local authorities in the event of a terrorist attack using WMD. Congress directed the expansion of the program to include 27 teams in FY 2000 and an additional 5 teams in FY 2001. At first called RAID teams (Rapid Assessment and Initial Detection Team), National Guard teams are now known as Civil Support Teams. The mission of Weapons of Mass Destruction Civil Support Teams (WMD-CST) is to support local and state authorities at domestic WMD/NBC incident sites by identifying agents and substances, assessing current and projected consequences, advising on response measures, and assisting with requests for additional military support. These unique teams involve a federal-state relationship. They are federally funded, federally trained and evaluated, and they operate under federal doctrine. But they will perform their mission primarily under the command and control of the governors of the states in which they are located unless federalized. The teams were established to rapidly deploy to assist a local incident commander in determining the nature and extent of an attack or

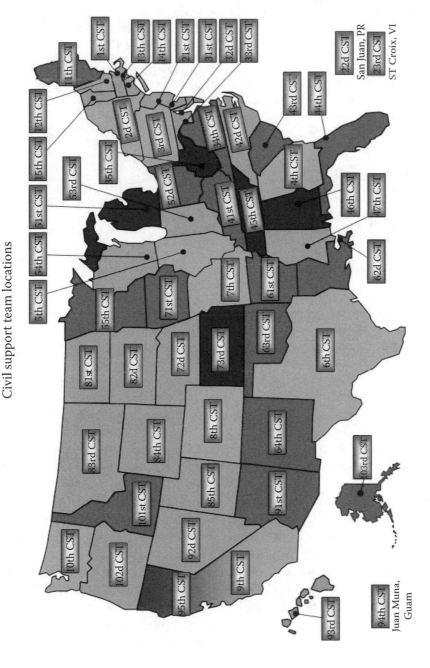

Figure 10.9 Locations of Civil Support Teams Nationwide. (*Source:* U.S. Army)

Table 10.7   National Guard Civil Support Teams

• 1st WMD CST [MA NG] — Natick	• 46th WMD CST [AL NG] — Montgomery
• 2nd WMD CST [NY NG] — Scotia	• 47th WMD CST [MS NG]
• 3rd WMD CST [PA NG] — Annville	• 51st WMD CST [MI NG] — Augusta
• 4th WMD CST [GA DOD DJO]	• 52nd WMD CST [OH NG]
• 5th WMD CST [IL NG] — Bartonville	• 53rd WMD CST [IN NG]
• 6th WMD CST [TX NG]	• 54th WMD CST [WI NG]
• 7th WMD CST [MO NG]	• 55th WMD CST [MN NG] — St Paul
• 8th WMD CST [CO NG]	• 61st WMD CST [AR NG] — Little Rock
• 9th WMD CST [CA NG]	• 62nd WMD CST [LA NG] — Carville
• 10th WMD CST [WA NG] — Tacoma	• 63rd WMD CST [OK NG]
• 11th WMD CST [ME NG]	• 64th WMD CST [NM NG] — Santa Fe
• 13th WMD CST [RI NG]	• 71st WMD CST [IA NG]
• 14th WMD CST [CT NG]	• 72nd WMD CST [NE NG]
• 15th WMD CST [VT NG]	• 73rd WMD CST [KS NG] — Topeka
• 21st WMD CST [NJ NG]	• 81st WMD CST [ND NG]
• 22nd WMD CST [PR NG] — San Juan	• 82nd WMD CST [SD NG] — Rapid City
• 23rd WMD CST [VI NG] — St Croix	• 83rd WMD CST [MT NG]
• 31st WMD CST [DE NG]	• 84th WMD CST [WY NG]
• 32nd WMD CST [MD NG]	• 85th WMD CST [UT NG]
• 33rd WMD CST [DC NG]	• 91st WMD CST [AZ NG] — Phoenix
• 34th WMD CST [VA NG] — Blackstone	• 92nd WMD CST [NV NG]
• 35th WMD CST [WV NG] — St. Albans	• 93rd WMD CST [HI NG] — Honolulu
• 41st WMD CST [KY NG] — Louisville	• 94th WMD CST [Guam] —Juan Muna
• 42nd WMD CST [NC NG]	• 95th WMD CST [CA NG]
• 43rd WMD CST [SC NG] — Eastover	• 101st WMD CST [ID NG] — Boise
• 44th WMD CST [FL NG] — Starke	• 102nd WMD CST [OR NG] — Salem
• 45th WMD CST [TN NG] — Smyrna	• 103rd WMD CST [AK NG]

incident and provide expert technical advice on WMD response operations. Each team consists of 22 highly skilled, full-time members of the army and Air National Guard. Staff members include chemical, biological, and nuclear specialists, medical staff, physician assistants, EOD personnel, firefighters and emergency medical personnel, chemists, physicists, and nuclear technicians. Equipment provided to the teams includes monitoring instruments, protective gear, decontamination supplies, medical supplies, and food and water to be self-contained for 72 hours. Two large pieces of equipment are provided to each team, including a mobile analytical laboratory for field analysis of chemical or biological agents and a unified command suite that has the ability to provide communications interoperability among various response organizations at an incident scene. The Fourier transform infrared (FTIR) and the polymerase chain reaction (PCR) help the teams to be more efficient in their role as the "eyes forward" for state and national public health laboratories. The two pieces of equipment are not based on new science. However, new technology is allowing them to be more mobile than ever before, enabling the WMD-CSTs to perform screening tests in the field. The FTIR uses an infrared laser to identify chemical molecules or rule outbiological molecules in about a minute. Before this was available, lab technicians had to rely on handheld assay tests to try to identify substances. These tests would rule out certain chemicals but not always identify a mystery substance. Now technicians will be able to determine not only what a mystery substance is not but also what it is. The PCR identifies biological warfare agents, such as anthrax, ricin, smallpox, and botulinum, and biological pathogens, including lysteria, E. coli, and salmonella, in about an hour. About the size of a carry-on suitcase, this machine can get results from small or diluted samples. These capabilities help the team assist an incident commander to get a handle on the situation more quickly than might otherwise be possible. The faster you can get the incident commander in control of the situation, the quicker you can provide a sense of relief and support to the community. The first (original) teams are based in Aurora, Colorado; Marietta, Georgia; Peoria, Illinois; Los Alamitos, California; Natick, Massachusetts; Fort Leonard Wood, Missouri; Scotia, New York; Fort Indiantown Gap, Pennsylvania; Austin, Texas; and Tacoma, Washington. DOD plans to field a total of 55 teams when they are through. Team members have been exposed to 800–1,200 hours learning OSHA Standards, National Fire Academy courses, and the Environmental Protection Agency courses. Training has also been provided by the Army Chemical School, the Defense Nuclear Weapons School, the Army Medical Department, U.S. Medical Research Institute for Infectious Diseases, and the Department of Justice Center for Domestic Preparedness. These National Guard Civil Support Teams provide a valuable resource for WMD incidents and other emergencies, which may occur in a state. Response personnel should contact their closest team and invite a representative to a training session or meeting at their department to become familiar with the resources available and the protocol for activation. Training and exercises should also be held with the teams to keep them and local responders ready to respond to acts of terrorism and other emergencies.

Agency for Toxic Substances and Disease Registry (ATSDR)

ATSDR is the lead federal agency for public health involving hazardous materials incidents. The Emergency Response and Consultation Branch, Division of Health Assessment and Consultation provides the services. Assistance is available for health issues surrounding the release or threat of release of hazardous materials and chemical, biological, and radiological materials. By calling their 24-hour emergency response number, the following assistance can be obtained:

- Within 10 minutes: An emergency response coordinator on the phone
- Within 20 minutes: A preliminary assessment team comprised of a toxicologist, a chemist, an environmental health scientist, a physician, and other health personnel as needed, on the phone
- Within 8 hours: An on-site response team

Assistance is available to federal, state, and local agencies, first responders, hospitals, private industry, and the general public. Health consultation and advice cover the following topics.

- First aid/medical treatment protocols/training and implementation
- Decontamination procedures
- Contingency planning
- Health team coordination
- Evacuation/re-entry consultation
- Sampling plans to allow assessment of the health threat
- Worker safety and health
- Other issues as appropriate

ATSDR can be contacted through:

Emergency Response and Consultation Branch
Division of Health Assessment and Consultation
The Agency for Toxic Substances and Disease Registry
1600 Clifton Road, NE (E32)
Atlanta, GA 30333
Phone 404-498-0110
Toll-free 1-888-422-8737
Fax 404-498-0093
24-hour emergency number 404-498-0120

Visual First Responder (VFR)

New technology, called the Visual First Responder (VFR), a wireless camera system that can be carried by emergency responders to a hazardous scene, has potential to give incident commanders and other response personnel a new look. The camera, contained in tough, lightweight, waterproof flashlight housing, sends wireless, real-time video images to incident commanders or other officials as far as 5 miles from a hot zone. The VFR is a unique and powerful wireless camera system. VFR is able to transmit high-quality video in the most difficult environments. The transmission loss problems experienced by other systems have been dramatically reduced in the VFR. This tremendous improvement in steady video is immediately obvious and is due to VFR's patented triple-diversity antenna system. Steady video is achieved in buildings and complex environments.

View Systems, Inc.
1550 Caton Center Drive Suite E
Baltimore, MD 21227
877-VIEW INC (843-9462)

Homeland Security Alert System

Following the September 11, 2001, attacks on the U.S. by al Qaeda terrorists, the White House, through the Homeland Security Office, developed a Homeland Security Advisory System. The system is intended to provide a comprehensive and effective means to disseminate information regarding the risk of terrorist attacks. This system will enable the attorney general in consultation with the director of the Office of Homeland Security to assign threat conditions, which can apply nationally, regionally, by sector, or to a potential target. Some of the factors considered to assess threats include:

- Is the threat credible?
- Is the threat corroborated?
- Is the threat specific or imminent?
- How grave is the threat?

Threat conditions will be represented by a series of color codes and threat level designations. Levels include low-green, guarded-blue, elevated-yellow, high-orange, and severe-red. Just before September 11, 2002, until September 24, 2002, the threat level was raised to orange, or high. It is currently at yellow, or elevated. Figure 10.10 lists protective measures that may be applied as a result of a threat condition.

Trident/One Mass Decontamination Device

The Trident is an expanded shower, low-cost, low-pressure, high-volume water deployment system developed to assist first responders in GROSS MASS DECONTAMINATION on a large volume of people in case of emergency, industrial catastrophe or terrorism (Figure 9.9). The Trident's PATENTED telescoping arms greatly increase the shower area and at the same

Low Condition Green
Low risk of terrorist attack. The following protective measures may be applied: Refining and exercising preplanned protective measures; Ensuring personnel receive training on HSAS, departmental, or agency-specific protective measures; and Regularly assessing facilities for vulnerabilities and taking measures to reduce them

Guarded Condition Blue
General risk of terrorist attack. In addition to the previously outlined protective measures, the following may be applied: Checking communications with designated emergency response or command locations; Reviewing and updating emergency response procedures; and Providing the public with necessary information

Elevated Condition Yellow
Significant risk of terrorist attack. In addition to the previously outlined protective measures, the following may be applied: Increasing surveillance of critical locations; Coordinating emergency plans with nearby jurisdictions; Assessing further refinement of protective measures within the context of the current threat information; and Implementing, as appropriate, contingency and emergency response plans

High Condition Orange
High risk of terrorist attack. In addition to the previously outlined protective measures, the following may be applied: Coordinating necessary security efforts with armed forces or law enforcement agencies; Taking additional precaution at public events; Preparing to work at an alternate site or with a dispersed workforce; and Restricting access to essential personnel only

Severe Condition Red
Severe risk of terrorist attack. In addition to the previously outlined protective measures, the following may be applied: Assigning emergency response personnel and prepositioning specially trained teams; Monitoring, redirecting or constraining transportation systems; Closing public and government facilities; and Increasing or redirecting personnel to address critical emergency needs

Figure 10.10 Protective measures that may be applied as a result of a threat condition.

time minimize the risk of possible contamination to the first responder. The Trident One will connect to any 2.5-foot discharge via the 45 or 90 degree coupling included in kit No. 4, making this device a must-have for any First Responder or Emergency management trailer.

Phone 770-887-0594
1-888-FlowH20 (1-888-356-9420)
Fax 770-887-1949
info@tridentone.com

Terrorism Resources and Response Training

11

Responding to a suspected terrorist attack is much like the response to a hazardous materials incident. Whether the terrorist has used explosives, chemical agents, biological agents, or radioactive materials, they are all considered hazardous materials. If a response agency has the training and resources to respond to a hazardous materials incident, then they can also effectively respond to an act of terrorism with some additional training. If a response agency does not have the capability to respond to a hazardous materials incident, then they will not be able to effectively and safely respond to an act of terrorism. Emergency response personnel must have knowledge of the hazards and symptoms of chemical and biological agents if they are to avoid becoming victims themselves. Those providing training courses and seminars around the country have reported substantial apathy concerning terrorism training. Without a minimum of terrorism awareness training, response personnel will be in great danger responding to a terrorist incident. Many of the clues involving chemical, biological, or radiological materials present for typical hazardous materials incidents will be absent from the terrorist event. Responders will need to rely on the characteristics and symptoms of chemical and biological agents to make a difference in the incident outcome. When first arriving on the scene, actions of responders, or lack of actions, will play an important part in the outcome of the incident. To ensure responders will have the opportunity to learn about chemical and biological agents to protect themselves and the public, various agencies have developed and are providing training programs. It is important that response personnel at all levels take advantage of these training opportunities.

When terrorism was just a new type of response in which little was known about how to respond, the National Fire Protection Association (NFPA) created some temporary interim amendments to its standards relating to hazardous materials response to include issues involving acts of terrorism.

**Table 11.1   OSHA Levels of Training Competencies
Required for Hazardous Materials Responders**

- Awareness
- Operations
- Technician
- Specialist
- Incident Commander

The major standards affected were NFPA 472 Professional Competence of Responders to Hazardous Materials Incidents and NFPA 1991 Standard on Vapor Protective Suits for Hazardous Materials Emergencies. Those temporary standards ultimately were included into the text of each of the aforementioned standards and are considered a part of each of the five levels of hazardous materials training competency classifications listed in NFPA 472 (Table 11.1). Persons who operate at each level of response must have initial training and periodic refresher training to remain certified to respond. Anyone who responds to a hazardous materials incident must be trained as a minimum to the awareness level. The other levels of training are based upon what the employer requires responders to do on the scene of any emergency. They can be trained to the operations level to take certain defensive actions at an incident scene. Technician-level training is required if personnel are required to mitigate hazardous materials releases or to enter the hot zone for other purposes (these are usually hazardous materials team members). Specialists are technicians who have obtained an additional level of training concerning a specialty area, such as tank car specialist, tank truck specialist, chemical specialist, radiation specialist, etc. Those responders who would find themselves required to act as the incident commander (IC) would be required to take training based upon the competencies required of the incident commander found in Occupational Safety and Health Organization (OSHA) 1910.120 and in more detail in NFPA 472. Some of the competency requirements for hazmat responders include knowledge of chemical, biological, radiological, and explosive materials. They should be able to recognize locations that could become targets for terrorist activities. Responders should be able to identify indicators of terrorist activity involving chemical and biological agents. They should know what actions to take when it is determined a terrorist attack has occurred. Technician level personnel should be able to describe identification and detection tools and where they are available for the different classes of terrorist agents. Listed throughout the rest of this chapter are training resources for programs to meet and exceed the training requirements outlined previously. When taking training for hazardous materials or terrorism response, make sure the training covers all of the competencies listed in NFPA 472 and OSHA 1910.120.

Figure 11.1 Baltimore City firefighters use the Emergency Response Guide Book, which now contains information on chemical and biological agents.

Initial training programs available for chemical agent emergencies were developed for the Chemical Stockpile Emergency Preparedness Program (CSEPP) by FEMA during the mid-1990s. Courses included chemical awareness for fire, police, and EMS first responders, and ACT-FAST, a course for EMS providers responding to chemical agent releases. Additional customized courses were developed by the CSEPP states (Figure 11.2) for personal pro-

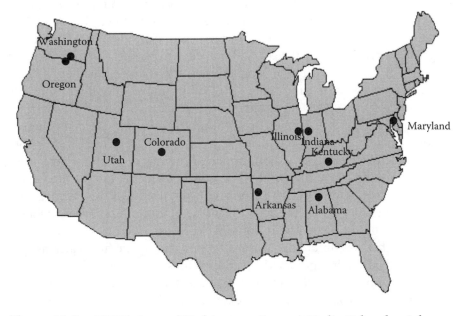

Figure 11.2 CSEPP States (Washington, Oregon, Utah, Colorado, Arkansas, Indiana, Illinois, Kentucky, Alabama, Maryland).

tective equipment (PPE) and decontamination. Some states, including Maryland, developed customized hospital provider courses to train doctors and nurses about decontamination, protective equipment, and treatment for chemical agent exposures. For information about the training courses and to download information for five courses, go to the Oak Ridge National Laboratories Web site. Information about the CSEPP program can be obtained at the following location:

Mr. Robert Norville
Office of Homeland Security/FEMA
Program Manager–CSEPP Training
FEMA HQ
1800 S. Bell Street
Arlington, VA 22202-3546
Phone 703-605-1209
E-mail robert.norville@dhs.gov
Oak Ridge National Laboratories:
Web site http://emc.ornl.gov/CSEPPweb/TRAINDocumentation.html

From September 15–17, 1998, Philadelphia conducted a major terrorism exercise to test its response capabilities. Planners in Philadelphia developed a Terrorism SOP for the city. Training, when it occurs, should be conducted jointly with law enforcement, fire, rescue, EMS, and others who would be working together to mitigate an act of terrorism. Consideration should also be given to training dispatchers and hospital personnel. Agencies should become familiar with each other's capabilities, and training together will help assure operations on the incident scene will go move smoothly. Exercising emergency response plans for dealing with terrorism is almost as important as writing the plan in the first place. Without conducting exercises, there is no way to actually know if the plan will work. During April 1995, New York City conducted an exercise without notice to emergency response personnel. The scenario was very similar to the Tokyo sarin incident, but this time in the New York City subway system. Surprisingly, the results of the exercise were much like the outcome of the actual incident in Tokyo. Response personnel rushed into the subway without donning SCBA or determining the type of emergency that was unfolding. Most of the fire and rescue first alarm assignment team became incapacitated, like the victims they were trying to rescue.

On December 7, 1995, another exercise was conducted, this time in Burbank, California. A simulated release of a nerve gas in a hotel produced much the same results as the New York City subway exercise. The simulated victim count in the hotel was 300 dead and 500 injured. Many of the dead and injured would have been emergency response personnel. Just as it has been difficult to get response personnel to slow down when responding to hazardous materials incidents, it will be difficult to get them to take the time to properly assess a potential terrorist incident scene. After all, they have been trained for many years to get to an incident scene as fast as possible and do something as quickly as possible. When dealing with hazardous materials and acts of terrorism, this has the potential to become a fatal mistake.

National Fire Academy: Emmitsburg, Maryland

The National Fire Academy received funding from the U.S. Department of Justice to develop training courses for emergency responders, particularly firefighters. The following courses were developed as a result of the joint effort.

Emergency Response to Terrorism: Self-Study, a Home-Study Course

This 10-hour self-paced, paper-based course is designed to provide the basic awareness training to prepare first responders to respond to incidents of terrorism safely and effectively. Students who successfully complete the exam will be eligible for a National Fire Academy Certificate of Training. Target Audience: Fire, emergency medical, hazmat, incident command, and law enforcement responders. It can be downloaded from the USFA Web site at: www.usfa.fema.gov/applications/publications. The ERT:SS exam is available online via the NETC Virtual Campus at: www.training.fema.gov. Upon completion of this course, any student wishing to obtain a National Fire Academy certificate will need to complete the online exam successfully and submit a completed FEMA Form 75-5a General Admissions Application Short Form. Other courses are listed below.

Emergency Response to Terrorism: Basic Concepts

The course addresses the special needs of responders to incidents that might have been caused by terrorist action. The Response to Terrorism program builds on the foundation provided by the Hazardous Materials curriculum offered at the Academy and adds specialized information concerning such topics as:

1. Current Department of Justice definitions of terrorism
2. History of terrorism
3. Agents utilized by terrorists
4. Suspicious circumstances
5. Self-protection at potential terrorist scenes

6. Crime scene considerations
7. Specialized incident command issues

The overall goal of the training program is to assist those who respond to the scene of a possible terrorist incident to:

1. Effectively protect themselves from a variety of potential dangers
2. Effectively perform responder tasks in a situation that combines the elements of a hazardous materials incident and a crime scene
3. Notify and respond to appropriate authorities from local, state, and federal jurisdictions

This course was handed off to the states and is no longer taught at the National Fire Academy. You can purchase this course from the National Audiovisual Center (http://www.ntis.gov/index.asp) for $280, which includes 246 slides, one instructor guide, and one student manual master. The **National Audiovisual Center** is a unique centralized resource for federally developed training and educational materials and includes over 9,000 audiovisual and media productions.

Emergency Response to Terrorism: Tactical Considerations: Company Officer

This two-day course is designed to build upon the existing skills of the initial first-responding supervisor from the Emergency Response to Terrorism: Basic Concepts course or Emergency Response to Terrorism: Self-Study guide. The students will be trained in security considerations, identifying signs of terrorism, anticipating unusual response circumstances, assessing information, and initiating self-protection actions.

Target Audience: Anyone who could serve as the first on-the-scene officer in a hazardous materials or emergency medical services incident. Must have a working knowledge of the Incident Command System (ICS). Students will not be taught ICS but will be expected to use ICS during class activities. In the vocational certificate or lower division baccalaureate/associate degree category, one semester hour in fire science, fire protection, emergency management, or emergency medical services.

Emergency Response to Terrorism: Tactical Considerations: EMS

This two-day course is designed for the first on-the-scene responding EMS personnel with the responsibility to render patient care to victims of terrorist incidents. The students will be trained in security considerations, identifying signs of terrorism, anticipating unusual response circumstances, assessing information, and initiating self-protection actions. The students also will

Figure 11.3 ATF Emergency Response Vehicle, Anchorage, Alaska, housed at main fire station.

apply their knowledge about responding to a terrorist event, providing patient care, identifying and preserving evidence, managing site safety, documenting the event, and debriefing personnel. Target Audience: First on-the-scene emergency medical services personnel, who could be career or volunteer firefighters, EMS, industrial contractors, allied health personnel, and members of the military or other government agencies. NOTE: The medical protocols for rendering patient care are at the advanced life support (ALS) level. In the vocational certificate or lower division baccalaureate/associate degree category, one semester hour in fire science or emergency medical services.

Emergency Response to Terrorism: Tactical Considerations: Hazmat

This two-day course was designed to cover the needs of response personnel, who may be career or volunteer. The student will be trained in security considerations, identifying signs of terrorism, anticipating unusual response circumstances, assessing information and taking corrective actions, and most importantly determining strategies for survival. The student will also apply his or her knowledge about response to biological, nuclear, incendiary, chemical, and explosive (B-NICE) events: identifying and preserving evidence, managing site safety, mitigating the incident, documenting the event, and debriefing personnel. It is recommended that they take the ERT:TC Company Officer course to augment this one.

Emergency Response to Terrorism: Strategic Considerations for Command Officers

This two-day course is designed for the senior-level officer(s) who may be responsible for command of incidents involving terrorism. The course is

Figure 11.4 CHEMTREC is an excellent 24-hour toll-free resource for both hazmat and terrorist incidents.

intended to build upon existing skills as an incident commander and knowledge of terrorism from professional experience or from the Emergency Response to Terrorism: Basic Concepts (ERT:BC) or the Emergency Response to Terrorism: Self-Study (ERT:SS). The class will assist the command officer in preparing an effective response to the consequences of terrorism. For the response to be effective, plans must be in place to guide responders in managing the incident. Incident commanders must be prepared to operate as part of a multiagency, multidiscipline, and multijurisdictional response. To address the command and control challenges that likely will confront the incident commander, the class consists of lecture, supported by case studies and practice scenarios. This will enable the students to apply their knowledge of preincident planning, managing emergency incidents, and operating as part of a unified command structure. The primary target audience for this course is individuals (chief officers, emergency managers, shift captains, etc.) who hold command-level positions in their organizations. These people should have command and control responsibilities on incidents involving terrorism and should be familiar with operating in an incident management structure. In the vocational certificate or lower division baccalaureate/associate degree category, one semester hour in fire science, emergency medical services, or hazardous materials.

National Fire Academy
Gordon Sachs
Program Chair Terrorism
gordon.sachs@dhs.gov
Phone 301-447-1594
Web site: http://www.usfa.fema.gov/training/nfa/

Figure 11.5 Students using M-8 papers on VX and sarin in the live agent training facility at the Center for Domestic Preparedness. (Courtesy Center for Domestic Preparedness.)

Center for Domestic Preparedness (CDP): Fort McClellan, Alabama

The U.S. Department of Homeland Security (DHS) has taken over the Center for Domestic Preparedness (CDP), which was established at Fort McClellan, Alabama, by the Department of Justice to prepare emergency first responders, emergency management officials, and other state and local officials to respond to terrorist acts involving weapons of mass destruction (WMD). In November 1997, the CDP was established as a training center for the nation's emergency responders. Their mission is to operate a federal training facility specializing in advanced hands-on training for America's federal, state, local, tribal, and parish emergency responders to prevent, deter, respond to, and recover from terrorist acts, especially those involving WMD or hazardous materials. The center began operations during September 1998. During fiscal year 2003 they presented 960 course iterations and trained over 25,340 fire, police, hazardous material, emergency medical and emergency management personnel to respond to acts of terrorism. It is the only training center in the world to offer live chemical agent training using VX and sarin. This opportunity helps responders build confidence in their equipment and reduces fear of the unknown. Safety is stressed throughout the courses and particularly during the live agent training. Each responder is fit-tested twice for a respirator mask. Over 70,000 people, including 20,000 responders and 50,000 military personnel, have successfully taken part in the live agent training facility without any training-related incident or injury. Instructors are certified to conduct training in the live agent facility. Outside subject matter experts are brought into CDP for training sessions. They come from NYPD; LAFD; Boston FD & PD; Oklahoma City FD; Augusta, Georgia, EMA; Chicago's area fire departments; St. Louis's area fire departments; New Orleans FD; Philadelphia FD; and Atlanta, Georgia, PD. CDP covers training expenses including travel (airfare), lodging (on-site), meals, training costs, and costs incidental to training.

Center for Domestic Preparedness (CDP) Training Programs

Resident Training

WMD Technical Emergency Response Training Course (TERT)*

The WMD Technical Emergency Response Training Course (COBRA) is a 4-day training program designed to provide emergency responders with operational level instruction on responding to and operating in a WMD environment. The course covers chemical, ordnance/explosive, biological, and radiological/nuclear (COBRA) threats; the current domestic and international terrorist threat; managing a WMD scene; determining the breadth of a WMD incident area; and dealing with the media at a WMD incident. In addition, it provides 20 hours of hands-on familiarization training with specialized protective clothing and equipment, chemical detection and identification equipment, decontamination, triage, and ordnance/explosive recognition and response. The course concludes with a multitask, hands-on performance-oriented training in the WMD [Toxic Agent] (COBRA) Training Facility.

Prerequisites: This course is designed for emergency responders who have completed WMD awareness-level training. The target audience for this training is emergency responders in fire service, law enforcement, emergency medical service, emergency management and emergency communications.

WMD Hazardous Material Technician Training Course (HT)

The WMD Hazardous Material Technician Training Course (COBRA) is a three-day in-depth training course in the composition, action, identification, and decontamination of WMD agents that have the potential for use in a terrorist incident. The course also includes training in the preservation of evidence at a crime scene, an overview of the international and domestic terrorist threat, and a series of practical exercises involving WMD detection, identification, and protective equipment and techniques for operating at a WMD terrorist incident. This training course culminates with a multitask, hands-on training exercise in the WMD [Toxic Agent] (COBRA) Training Facility.

---

* This course is not for hazmat technicians.

Prerequisites: Hazardous material technicians attending this training must be certified as having successfully met the competencies outlined in OSHA 29 CFR 1910.120 and NFPA 472 for hazmat technicians.

WMD Incident Command Training Course (IC)

The WMD Incident Command Training Course is three days of in-depth training that take the attendee through the entire spectrum of command of a WMD terrorist event. The course provides instruction on WMD, the incident command system coupled with the federal response, and examines the complexities of operational considerations and actions of command at a WMD event. The course takes the attendee through pre- and post-considerations by incorporating a segment on planning for the response using techniques that allow the commander to determine the correct composition of the planning team, evaluating the threat to the jurisdiction, identifying and prioritizing probable targets, measuring required capabilities, and developing a local incident response plan to a WMD terrorist incident. The course culminates with the attendee participating in an eight-hour real-time tabletop exercise using the materials developed in the previous sessions to plan for and command the emergency response resources at the incident site.

Prerequisites: Emergency responders attending this training must be trained to the competencies outlined in OSHA 29 CFR 1910.120 and NFPA 472 for incident commanders, and they must have a thorough understanding of the incident command system. The target audience for this training includes those command level responders in the fire service, law enforcement, emergency medical service, emergency management and emergency communications, or other emergency response professions.

WMD Hands-On Training Course (HOT)

The Hands-On Training Course consists of a two-day advanced training program providing hands-on training with PPE, advanced sampling and monitoring equipment, mass casualty triage, and explosive/ordnance secondary devices and searches. The course concludes with a multitask, hands-on performance oriented training in the WMD [Toxic Agent] (COBRA) Training Facility.

Prerequisites: The WMD HOT course is for responders who have successfully completed the Center for Domestic Preparedness (CDP) WMD Incident Command Course (after April 1, 2002), a CDP site delivered training program, a CDP Indirect Response Training course, or other DHS-recognized training program as outlined in the Office of Domestic Preparedness (ODP) Training Course Catalog. This course is also a sustainment program for graduates of CDP operations and command courses. Graduates are eligible one year from their initial training date. The HOT course is not for hazmat Technicians. Prerequisite certificate must be sent with application.

WMD Law Enforcement Protective Measures (LEPM)

This 16-hour training program is resident delivered and encompasses WMD-related topics and scenario-driven practical exercises for the in-service training of law enforcement officers. The first eight hours of training presents information on terrorist tactics and targeting, related WMD hazards, indicators of terrorism, and protective measures taken by law enforcement officers responding to a terrorist WMD event. The second eight hours of this training program is a Train-the-Trainer (TtT) session to assist attendees with the skills necessary to present the LEPM training in their home jurisdictions.

Prerequisites: This course is for certified/commissioned state and local law enforcement officers and trainers with more than one year's experience. This course is not an executive-level course.

Instructor Training Certification Course (ITC)

This course is an intensive five-day training course that provides instruction on adult learning theory and practice, job and training task analysis, training risk and hazard analysis, developing learning objectives and lesson plans, communication skills, instruction delivery and delivery media, developing tests and conducting evaluations, and performing after-action reviews. The classroom sections of the training are supported by a series of practical exercises that require the student to perform and teach tasks associated with WMD techniques, procedures, and equipment to support classroom lessons. The evaluation strategy for this training consists of one written test and two performance evaluations. To complete this training and receive a certification from the CDP as a DHS-certified instructor, the student must achieve a minimum score of 70% for each test/evaluation. Students that enroll in this course and fail to achieve the minimum standard for each test/evaluation will receive a certificate of attendance but will not be certified as an instructor.

Prerequisites: Applicants must have successfully completed a WMD operational, technician or command/management level DHS, ODP recognized training program. Prerequisite certificate must be sent with application.

WMD Emergency Medical Services Training (EMS)

The WMD EMS Course is a three-day training program designed to educate paramedic and EMT responders on awareness and operational-level skills needed to respond to a WMD mass-casualty incident. The course instruction includes an overview of WMD materials, including chemical, biological, and radiological agents, and explosive devices. Responders will explore levels of PPE and issues relating to their own safety and wellness during and after a

WMD incident. Methods of victim rescue and treatment will be practiced, including extrication, cutout, triage, decontamination, assessment, and transport. Responders will be encouraged to use routine job skills and experience how they differ in a WMD environment. Responders will be made aware of special crime-scene considerations and the details of working with a multitude of agencies, including the public health department. The training culminates with a multitask hands-on scenario exercise.

Prerequisites: Responders must be state-licensed paramedics, EMT, or emergency care providers (emergency room physicians or nurses).

WMD Emergency Responder Hazardous Materials Technician Training (ER Hazmat)*

The Emergency Responder Hazardous Materials Technician Training course is a five-day training program designed to provide emergency responders with WMD and hazardous materials technical training to satisfy requirements of OSHA 1910.120 (q)(6)(iii). The guidelines of this course target those emergency responders who might respond to the scene of a hazardous materials incident or potential terrorist/criminal use of WMD. This course is a combination of classroom training and several hands-on exercises that culminate in a final day of practical and written evaluations. The training covers WMD-specific material and the Eight-Step Process for Hazmat Incident Management, which includes Site Management and Control, Identifying the Problem, Hazard and Risk Evaluation, Selecting Personal Protective Clothing and Equipment, Information Management and Resource Coordination, Implementing Response Objectives, Decontamination, and Terminating the Incident.

Prerequisites: Hazmat awareness and eight hours of operational level training as identified in OSHA 1910.120 (q)(6)(i) and OSHA 1910.120 (q)(6)(ii)

Center for Domestic Preparedness
P.O. Box 5100
Anniston, AL 36205-5100
Phone 1-866-213-9553
Web site: http://cdp.dhs.gov

Center for Domestic Preparedness Training Update

Homeland Security Director Tom Ridge visited the CDP, located at Fort McClellan outside of Anniston, Alabama. CDP was created in 1998 when the U.S. Army Chemical Corps moved from Fort McClellan to Missouri and left

---

* Course fulfills OSHA requirements for bomb technicians wishing to attend the FBI Hazardous Devices School for delivery of the Hazardous Materials Basic Course [HMBC].

Table 11.2   Graduate Demographics of Center for Domestic Preparedness Anniston, Alabama

Average years experience	15
Average age	40
Trainers	57%
Law enforcement	43%
Firefighter	32%
Hazmat technician	4%
EMS	6%
EMA	2%
Public works	1%
Other	6%

behind a state-of-the-art training facility. He was impressed with the facility's capability, calling it "an impressive national asset." CDP, run by the U.S. Department of Homeland Security, provides the only "live agent" chemical training for first responders in the country. There is a push to consolidate all terrorism preparedness training into one federal agency to ensure that there is consistency in training being taught to emergency responders. President Bush wants the CDP moved from the Department of Justice to the FEMA. FEMA operates the National Emergency Training Center in Emmitsburg, Maryland, which houses the training branches of the U.S. Fire Administration (USFA), which includes the National Fire Academy (NFA) and the Emergency Management Institute (EMI). According to Tom Ridge, "having the center under FEMA's control would give the federal government one agency with the sole purpose of dealing with disasters, including terrorist

Figure 11.6   Anniston, AL, August 29, 2005 — Members of the Massachusetts 2 Disaster Medical Team (DMAT) arrive at the staging area located at the FEMA Noble Training Center. The DMAT teams are poised to move forward to areas affected by Hurricane Katrina to assist in the caring of injured individuals. FEMA/Mark Wolfe. (Source: FEMA.)

attacks." CDP has trained more than 12,000 first responders over the past four years, and Ridge wants to increase that capacity to 20,000 per year. The additional funding to increase the training would come from $3.5 billion proposed for emergency preparedness by the Bush administration. Plane tickets are provided up front and buses transport students from the airport in Atlanta to Fort McClellan. Once on site, students are housed in dormitories and fed at food facilities on campus. There is no cost to the students or their sponsoring agencies for any of the training. To attend the facility, students apply to their state emergency management agency to get on a waiting list. Unfortunately some states are not taking advantage of the training slots made available to them.

L.Z. Johnson Retires as Center for Domestic Preparedness Director

L.Z. Johnson served at the center since its inception in June 1998. It was his brain child, and it would not be the premier training facility it is today without him. When the facility first opened there were five employees; today there are more than 370 people working at the CDP. Funding has increased from an initial $45 million to more than $112.5 million and continues to grow. Since the CPD opened it has trained over 136,000 emergency respond-ers from all 50 states, including 100,000 trained off-site. I grew to know him personally after many trips to the center to take training classes and write articles for *Firehouse Magazine*. He is a professional administrator and a true "southern gentleman." He will be missed by all connected with CDP and the thousands of responders across the country he was responsible for training.

Figure 11.7 L.Z. Johnson, the "father" of the Center for Domestic Prepared-ness, has retired.

Hospital Preparedness for Terrorism

One of the major weak links identified in the terrorism preparedness system is the medical system beyond first responders. Many hospitals are not prepared to deal with patients experiencing symptoms from WMD. During the 2001 anthrax attacks on the East Coast of the U.S., at least one of the victims was treated at a hospital emergency room and sent home. The failure of the medical system to diagnose and provide treatment for anthrax exposure might have contributed to the patient's death. To help combat this lack of knowledge by doctors and nurses, the U.S. Department of Health and Human Services (HHS) has created the Noble Training Center, also located at Fort McClellan, Alabama, near the CDP. The former Noble Army Community Hospital (NACH) at the fort, taken over by HHS in 1999, has been turned into the only hospital facility in the U.S. devoted entirely to medical training for WMD. Noble is used as a mock hospital training facility with 162,000 square feet of space located on 20 acres, including a heliport. Training is conducted using realistic hospital props that include an emergency department and decontamination lanes. Following the creation of the DHS, Noble Training Center has come under the direction of FEMA and the Emergency Management Institute (EMI). Noble's current mission is "to train emergency managers and healthcare professionals in a realistic environment to enable them to manage a mass-casualty event resulting from natural disasters, technological incidents and acts of terrorism." Some of the courses currently offered are listed below.

Radiological Emergency Response Operations (RERO)

This is a $4^{1}/_{2}$-day performance-based course where the participants learn to respond to and manage radiological incidents. The participants, organized as response teams, operate and make decisions in a realistic exercise environment. The course goal is to provide participants with the operational requirements and techniques for proper response and management of incidents involving various radiological hazards through a practical, performance-oriented, team-response approach. Participants are members of organized federal, state, local, or tribal radiological/hazardous materials response teams, or are responsible for responding and possibly managing a radiation incident. Personnel assigned to such teams include fire service, law enforcement, health physicists, industrial hygienists, radiological officers, and other emergency service personnel with similar responsibilities. Federal evaluators of nuclear power plant off-site Radiological Emergency Plan (REP) exercises and state, local, tribal, and utility personnel who are involved in the development of off-site REP plans and exercises also may apply. The course consists of classroom lectures, to teach the concepts of team building and planning, and a series of performance-based field exercises that include on-scene incident assessment, radiological monitoring, radiation exposure and contamination control, and reporting procedures. **Because of the realism of the exercises, the course is physically challenging.**

Advanced Radiological Incident Operations (ARIO)

This is a $4^1/_2$-day advanced-level course for those individuals who need to refresh or improve skills as a radiological responder or manager. This course focuses on response plans and procedures for complex incidents. The performance-based training concentrates on organization and jurisdictional issues and planning considerations, where all levels of government may be involved in responding to an incident such as a terrorism event. The course goal is to provide participants with the operational requirements and techniques for proper response and management of incidents involving various jurisdictional issues and planning considerations, where all levels of government may be involved in responding to a large-scale radiological incident. Individuals who are members of organized federal, state, local, or tribal radiological/hazardous materials response teams, or who are responsible for responding and possibly managing a radiation incident. Federal evaluators of nuclear power plant off-site REP exercises and state, local, tribal, and utility personnel who are involved in the development of off-site REP plans and exercises also may apply. The course consists of classroom lectures and discussions, planning sessions, and a practical exercise. The emergency exercise simulates a large-scale radiological event.

HealthCare Master Exercise Practitioner Program (HCMEPP) Series

The EMI will offer the Master Exercise Practitioner Program (MEPP) Candidates for Health Care to audiences from across the nation at the Noble Training Center in Anniston, Alabama. The new course series, the HC MEPP, will consist of three 1-week resident courses designed to provide healthcare provider candidates the knowledge, skills, and abilities to design, develop, conduct, and evaluate the wide range of exercises in the health and medical community. Eligibility for enrollment in the Health Care Master Exercise Program will be limited to individuals from healthcare audiences with local, tribal, state, territorial, DHS, other federal agency healthcare organizations, and public or private and profit or nonprofit healthcare providers, whose responsibilities include exercise program management or participation in exercise development, conduct, and evaluation of internal or external exercises related to overall emergency preparedness. This training is directed at emergency medical service providers, hospital and other medical facility staff, public and environmental health officers, coroners and medical examiners, medical officers, and emergency managers from related systems. This would include organizations such as the Veterans Administration (VA), Department of Defense (DOD) medical treatment facilities, training and exercise staff from disaster or emergency healthcare providers from Health and Human Services (HHS), National Disaster Medical System (NDMS), Disaster Medical Assistance Teams (DMAT), Disaster Mortuary Assistance Teams (DMORT), Centers for Disease Control (CDC), and community services and volunteer organizations. Individuals with exercise responsibilities from regional health-care emergency systems and providers, such as Metropolitan Medical Response System (MMRS), are eligible to apply.

The following three courses must be completed in this order:

- B132 Health Care Exercise Design and Evaluation Course
- B133 Health Care Exercise Control/Simulation Course
- B136 Health Care Exercise Development Course

Hospital Emergency Response Team Training

The B461 Hospital Emergency Response Training (HERT) for Mass-Casualty Incidents (MCI) Train-the-Trainer Course is designed to provide guidance to hospitals, EMS, healthcare facility personnel and others who might become involved in a mass-casualty incident as a result of a hazardous materials incident or WMD event. The course expands on the incident management system (IMS) used within the hospital during emergencies, addresses chemical protective clothing and equipment (CPC&E) require-ments, and presents guidance for HERT design, development, and training. The course prepares a HERT to conduct a safe and effective emergency response during mass-casualty incidents. It is a hands-on course, and par-ticipants must be physically and psychologically fit to wear CPC&E (Level C ensemble) during the training. Hospital administrators, doctors, nurses, physicians, security personnel, and other hospital staff who would make up or manage their Hospital's Emergency Response Team should attend this course. The course will provide hospitals and healthcare facilities staff with the information and skills they need to go back to their facilities and develop and train their own teams. The HERT/MCI course could be presented as a stand-alone program without the hands-on exercises and the emergency response simulation in a 2^1/$_2$-3-day format.

EMAC TTT

This Emergency Management Assistance Compact (EMAC) TTT is designed to train state EMAC staff and coordinators identified as instructors in the delivery of the new EMAC Field Course. National Open Enrollment System has two open enrollment periods for resident programs at EMI and the Noble

Training Center. During each of the open enrollment periods all potential students from all areas of the country are eligible to apply. To enroll, complete a FEMA Form 75-5 (general admissions application form).

Healthcare Leadership

As a result of the transfer of the operation of the NTC by the Department of Health and Human Services, to the Department of Homeland Security/Federal Emergency Management Agency, the government is instituting a change in the enrollment process for the Healthcare Leadership Course beginning in federal fiscal year 2005. This change will further integrate hospital and public health planning and response into overall community emergency planning and response efforts. Applicants may apply to attend the Healthcare Leadership Course (HCL) or other NTC courses by completing the standard FEMA enrollment form number 75-5, and forwarding it to the appropriate state emergency management office, which will forward it through the respective FEMA regional office to the National Emergency Training Center (NETC) admissions office. The NETC now services both the EMI and the NTC, because NTC is now a part of EMI. The local emergency management officials in your community are familiar with this process and can assist you. In fact, you are encouraged to advise the local emergency management office in your jurisdiction that you plan to participate in this course. A FEMA form 75-5 (application form for enrollment) is available for download on the FEMA Web site. The NETC provides the system of record for all FEMA training and will be processing applications for courses held at Noble as well.

MMRS

The Metropolitan Medical Response System (MMRS) Program began in 1996 and currently is managed by the U.S. DHS. The primary focus of the MMRS program is to develop or enhance existing emergency preparedness systems to achieve an integrated, systematic response to a mass-casualty crisis, especially WMD events. Through preparation and coordination, local law enforcement, fire, hazardous materials, emergency medical services, hospital, public health, and other "first response" personnel plan to more effectively respond with local resources until significant external resources can arrive (typically the first 24 hours). Through FY2003, 125 jurisdictions nationwide participated in the MMRS Program. MMRS jurisdictions throughout the U.S. face unique challenges as they plan and prepare for an integrated response to medical emergencies resulting from terrorists' use of WMD and from other hazards. MMRS requirements center around the following emergency management needs:

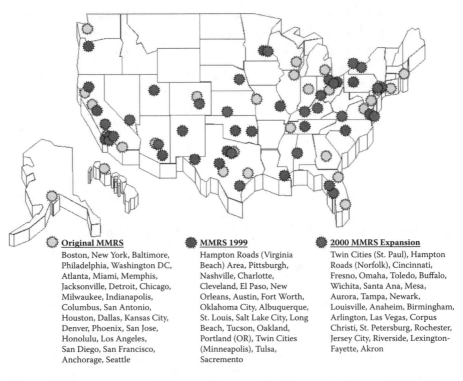

Original MMRS
Boston, New York, Baltimore, Philadelphia, Washington DC, Atlanta, Miami, Memphis, Jacksonville, Detroit, Chicago, Milwaukee, Indianapolis, Columbus, San Antonio, Houston, Dallas, Kansas City, Denver, Phoenix, San Jose, Honolulu, Los Angeles, San Diego, San Francisco, Anchorage, Seattle

MMRS 1999
Hampton Roads (Virginia Beach) Area, Pittsburgh, Nashville, Charlotte, Cleveland, El Paso, New Orleans, Austin, Fort Worth, Oklahoma City, Albuquerque, St. Louis, Salt Lake City, Long Beach, Tucson, Oakland, Portland (OR), Twin Cities (Minneapolis), Tulsa, Sacremento

2000 MMRS Expansion
Twin Cities (St. Paul), Hampton Roads (Norfolk), Cincinnati, Fresno, Omaha, Toledo, Buffalo, Wichita, Santa Ana, Mesa, Aurora, Tampa, Newark, Louisville, Anaheim, Birmingham, Arlington, Las Vegas, Corpus Christi, St. Petersburg, Rochester, Jersey City, Riverside, Lexington-Fayette, Akron

Figure 11.8   Locations of Metropolitan Medical Response Teams (MMRT).

- Development/coordination of response systems
- Development of appropriate MMRS plans
- Acquisition of required pharmaceuticals
- Acquisition of required equipment
- Integration of system organization, plans, pharmaceuticals, and equipment to achieve operational capability for the MMRS
- Planning and resource management coordination with neighboring jurisdictions and state government organizations, including enhanced mutual aid

The key components of the MMRS include the following program elements, all of which can be tested through a typical IEMC program:

- Command and control
- Activation/notifications procedures
- Concept of operations plan
- Bio-terrorism plan coordinated with state
- Public affairs
- **Medical treatment**
- **Medical supplies**

- **Security**
- **Patient tracking**
- **Laboratory support security**
- **Fatality movement**
- **Mental health services**
- **Integration of state and federal systems**
- Agent detection and identification
- Human extraction
- Antidote administration
- Victim decontamination
- Emergency transportation
- Triage and treatment plans

The IEMC is designed to exercise the individual and organizational skills required in responding to and recovering from an emergency. Functional areas addressed by the course include policy making, decision making, communications, coordination of resources, management of personnel, and implementation of procedures — that is, the crisis response system needed for effective emergency response. Since the course participants represent the entire crisis response community, a highly authentic and useful experience is possible. The MMRS IEMC program, conducted for 20 jurisdictions across the nation, began in FY04. **Steps in the application/selection process for the MMRS IEMC Program include:** the chief elected official of the jurisdiction submitting a letter of request, addressing the specified criteria to the director of training. FEMA letters should be sent to:

Mr. Stephen Sharro
Director of Training
Federal Emergency Management Agency
16825 South Seton Avenue
Emmitsburg, MD 21727

A copy of this letter should be sent to the jurisdiction's respective state office of emergency management and appropriate FEMA regional office for review. State and FEMA regional office support of the request is important. FEMA's Training Division will ask our regional offices to prioritize multiple requests from any given region. FEMA's Training Division will accept applications for the MMRS IEMC — immediately! Training Division staff and FEMA program office representatives will review the applications and rank them based on regional priority and information provided in the requests. Communities that were not selected and that want to be reconsidered for the following year must reapply. Applications will not automatically be considered for the following year.

Types of MMRS/IEMC Programs

MMRS IEMC programs will be offered to jurisdictions in two versions: resident and field. Please take a moment to review the differences in the programs. MMRS IEMC Resident Offerings: 12 MMRS IEMC resident offerings will be conducted in FY05 for jurisdictions across the nation. These 12 resident offerings will be conducted in the exercise and simulation lab at the Noble Training Center in Anniston, Alabama. Class size for jurisdictions participating in the resident program will be limited to 75 students. The major advantage to the jurisdiction of participating in a resident offering is that it will give the jurisdiction an opportunity to "get away" from your home environment and focus on emergency management issues without interruption. Hundreds of communities across the nation have taken advantage of IEMC resident offerings over the past 20 years to improve emergency management policies, plans, and procedures. All communities will receive the extra benefit of "teambuilding" while participating in a MMRS IEMC resident offering.

MMRS Field Offerings: eight MMRS IEMC field offerings will be conducted in FY05 for jurisdictions across the nation. These eight offerings will be conducted in or near the jurisdiction requesting the program. Class size for the jurisdictions participating in the field program is limited only by the size of the classroom and exercise facility provided by the community. Past IEMC field offerings have been conducted for 100–125 students. Often times it might be easier to obtain the participation of chief elected or chief appointed officials or key department heads if a program is conducted in the field. However, students during IEMC field offerings can easily be interrupted by daily job-related tasks or emergency-related duties.

Costs Associated with the MMRS/IEMC Program

The majority of the costs associated with the MMRS IEMC programs will be handled by FEMA. Please review the differences in costs associated with the two types of MMRS IEMC programs. MMRS IEMC Resident Offerings: If a jurisdiction is chosen to participate in one of the 12 MMRS IEMC resident offerings to be conducted at the Noble Training Center in Anniston, Alabama, FEMA will be responsible for the following costs associated with the training:

- All costs associated with the actual conduct of the training to include student materials, instructors, and course support
- Transportation costs for all 75 students participating in the training to include coach fare airline tickets, reimbursement of mileage for students choosing to drive, or bus transportation for communities choosing this method of transportation. (Note: FEMA will also be

responsible for the cost of picking up students at the airport and transporting them to/from the Noble Training Center)
- Lodging costs for all 75 students participating in the training
- Meal costs for all 75 students participating in the training

A jurisdiction participating in the program will be responsible for all costs associated with their personnel being "away" from regular duties during the actual conduct of the training.

MMRS Field Offerings: If a jurisdiction is chosen to participate in one of the eight MMRS IEMC field offerings, FEMA will be responsible for the following costs associated with the training:

- All costs associated with the actual conduct of the training to include student materials, instructors, and course support
- All costs associated with the audiovisual equipment required to conduct the classroom portion of the program
- All costs associated with the telephone communication system utilized during the course exercises

A jurisdiction participating in the field version of the program will be responsible for all costs associated with obtaining or renting a suitable training and exercise facility for the field program. The jurisdiction will also be responsible for the lunch meal during the last full day of the program. That is the day of the major exercise, and the program will require the students to eat lunch during the conduct of the exercise. The jurisdiction will also be responsible for all costs associated with their personnel being "away" from regular duties during the actual conduct of the training. A more detailed discussion on costs associated with the MMRS IEMC program will be undertaken with the jurisdiction upon selection.

For additional information about the MMRS IEMC program contact Al Fluman, Branch Chief, Integrated Emergency Management Branch, Training Division, FEMA at al.fluman@dhs.gov.

Classes are designed for physicians, nurses, hospital executives, hospital engineers, EMTs, paramedics, public health officers, pharmacists, and others. Information can be obtained by writing to:

DHS/FEMA
Noble Training Center
490 Care Drive
Ft. McClellan, AL 36205
Phone 256-240-7500
Fax 256-741-3775

National Center for Emergency Preparedness

Training/Exercise

The spectrum of courses, seminars, and curricula available from the NCEP/VUMC addresses the scope of WMD/Mass-Casualty Incident (MCI) preparedness needs. Training is provided in traditional classroom-style formats, distance learning, seminars and workshops, and other learning formats as needed. The goal of the National Center is to develop an integrated and comprehensive curriculum addressing the various needs associated with WMD preparedness and response. The NCEP/VUMC is proud of its tradition of excellence in the quality of the training provided. Comprehensive instructor development and quality improvement programs are integral to these efforts.

Technical Assistance and Planning

The NCEP provides assistance to government, institutions, and other entities in the areas of planning, assessing, exercising, and program development for operational purposes related to MCI. The experience and expertise available through the NCEP staff and faculty is significant in both breadth and depth. Services are provided at all governmental levels (local, state, regional, national, and international levels) and for private as well as public sector entities.

Clinical Training and Education

The School of Nursing has established itself as a prominent leader in distance learning techniques, primarily centered around video-streaming course content to students across the country. In addition, they have been innovators with online testing and evaluation, using the Web-based system Prometheus. Through the work of the International Nursing Coalition for Mass Casualty Education, core competencies have been developed for all nurses that will be reflected in course content. The School of Medicine has the unique experience of developing data mining tools to assess curriculum content and has been examining ways to make specific content more interactive.

Educational and Operational Research

The NCEP/VUMC is engaged in a variety of research projects funded through various grants and contracts. Of significant note is the research being undertaken by the faculty and scientists affiliated with the Learning Sciences Institute (LSI) located within Peabody College. The core goal of the LSI is to transform education by enlarging understanding of the different ways people learn and by designing innovative new teaching practices that meet the diverse needs of learners. The LSI will serve as the lead research and development component of the U.S. Department of Justice's proposal for establishing standardized instructor development and evaluative objective measures for its curricula of courses nationwide.

National Center for Emergency Preparedness
461 21st Avenue South
Godchaux Hall
Nashville, TN 37240-1104
Phone 615-322-7639
Fax 615-322-5828
E-mail NCEP@vanderbilt.edu

National Center for Combating Terrorism (NCCT) (Nevada Test Site)

Located at the remote and secure Nevada Test Site, 65 miles northwest of Las Vegas, the National Center for Combating Terrorism provides an infrastructure that supports an integrated system of facilities. This allows first responders, law enforcement, and military personnel the ability to train together with top science and intelligence professionals in a variety of complex scenarios using the latest state-of-the-art technologies. Mercury, the control center for the NTS, provides WMD training equipment, facility and housing, and food services for 350 personnel. Classrooms equipped with video links to field exercise locations can accommodate up to 200 trainees at once. The Incident Experiment Site (IES) is a unique example of training and exercise location on the NTS because it provides realistic training conditions, such as a plane crash, railroad derailment, helicopter crash, and other scenarios. IES is unique because it is a site where several atmospheric nuclear tests occurred. The soil at the IES provides a realistic training ground for first responders responding to the threat of radiological terrorism.

U.S. Department of Energy
National Nuclear Security Administration
Nevada Site Office
P.O. Box 98518
Las Vegas, NV 89193-8518
Phone 702-295-3521

New Mexico Tech Energetic Materials Research and Training Center (EMRTC)

New Mexico Tech (NMT) is a recognized leader in science and engineering education and is a world class center for research involving energetic materials (explosives and incendiaries) and countermeasures associated with deterring explosives attacks and mitigating the potential destruction associated with such an event. The Energetic Materials Research and Testing Center (EMRTC) is a university-affiliated laboratory dedicated to the research and development of energetic and explosive materials. Under a cooperative agreement with the Office of Justice Programs and the Office of Domestic Preparedness (OJP /ODP), NMT contributes to ODP's First Responder Training Program through the delivery of explosive and incendiary training to first responder personnel. NMT provides both an awareness and an operations-level Incident Response to Terrorist Bombings Course. The awareness-level course is taught at state and local emergency response training centers throughout the U.S., and the operations-level course is taught on site at NMT.

Course Offerings

Incident Response to Terrorist Bombings — Awareness

This 4-hour awareness-level course is designed to provide basic instruction on WMD terrorist incidents, with a focus on explosives and incendiary devices. The course includes classroom presentations that address potential terrorist targets in the U.S., common military and commercial explosives available to terrorists, improvised explosive devices, and response procedures that support safe and effective operations during bomb incidents. The awareness course is designed for law enforcement officers, fire service personnel, bomb technicians, ordnance disposal specialists, hazardous materials responders, emergency medical personnel, and emergency planners.

Incident Response to Terrorist Bombings — Operations

This 32-hour technical-level course is designed to provide participants with the skills and knowledge necessary to evaluate and respond effectively to incidents of terrorism that involve energetic materials and other WMD. The course offers a unique blend of classroom presentations, field laboratories, case studies, and a practical exercise — all designed to familiarize participants with commercial and military explosives, improvised explosive devices, and readily available explosive formulation that have been used or could be used by terrorists. Participants are given an opportunity to visually identify and handle a series of explosive materials and to observe explosives being detonated against witness materials. They are also taught how to identify explosive material and post-blast evidence and response requirements for bombing scenarios. The course will also prepare participants to present awareness-level training to personnel in their departments on procedures for responding to WMD incidents involving energetic materials.

The operations course applicant must be an active member of an emergency response agency and must provide a written justification from their agency to support their selection for training. Participants seeking certification to teach the awareness course must have completed a recognized instructor training program or be certified or designated as a "trainer" by their agency.

The Awareness Course is delivered at a state or local training facility provided by the requesting jurisdiction. The Operations Course is delivered at the New Mexico Institute of Mining and Technology, Energetic Materials Research and Training Center in Socorro, New Mexico. The training and course materials are provided at no cost to the state or local organization or responder. The cost of travel, meals, and lodging are also provided for those attending a course held at the NMT training facility in Soccoro, New Mexico.

EMRTC
New Mexico Tech
1001 South Road
Socorro, NM 87801
Phone 505-835-5312
Fax 505-835-5630

Louisiana State University (LSU) (Academy of Counter-Terrorist Education)

Emergency Response to Domestic Biological Incidents

Operation Level (Direct Delivery)
The U.S. DHS, through the Office of Domestic Preparedness (ODP), is supporting several major initiatives to improve the capability of emergency services agencies to respond to WMD incidents.

Chemical/Biological — Current Courses

Operation Level — 24 Hour

Emergency Response to Domestic Biological Incidents Direct Delivery
E-mail Coordinator
Amanda Millet
Phone 225-578-4528

Technician Level — 24 Hour

- Public Safety WMD Response — Sampling Techniques and Guidelines Direct Delivery

  E-mail Coordinator
  Jermainne Biagas
  Phone 225-578-1133

Law Enforcement — Current Courses

Awareness Level — 16 Hour

- Law Enforcement Prevention and Deterrence of Terrorist Acts Train-the-Trainer

  E-mail Coordinator
  Adale Knabe
  Phone 225-578-0330

Operations Level — 24 Hour

- Utilizing Computer-Aided Management of Emergency Operations (CAMEO) in WMD Train-the-Trainer

  E-mail Coordinator
  Deyvon Cooper
  Phone 225-578-6971

Performance Level — 24 Hour

- Law Enforcement Response to Weapons of Mass Destruction Incidents Train-the-Trainer

  E-mail Coordinator
  Adale Knabe
  Phone 225-578-0330

- Tactical Weapons of Mass Destruction Commanders Course Direct Delivery

  E-mail Coordinator
  Leah Tatum
  Phone 225-578-3367

Technician Level — 40 Hour

* Weapons of Mass Destruction Tactical Operations Direct Delivery

  E-mail Coordinator
  Leah Tatum
  Phone 225-578-3367

Public Health/Medical —Current Courses

Awareness Level — 8 Hour

* WMD Awareness for the Healthcare Professional

  E-mail Coordinator
  Amanda Millet
  Phone 225-578-4528

Operation Level — 24 Hour

* Emergency Response to Domestic Biological Incidents Direct Delivery

  E-mail Coordinator
  Amanda Millet
  Phone 225-578-4528

Operation Level — 32 Hour

* Healthcare Leadership and Administrative Decision-Making in Response to WMD Incidents

  E-mail Coordinator
  Paula Sinclair
  Phone 225-578-1124

Technician Level — 24 Hour

* Public Safety WMD Response — Sampling Techniques and Guidelines Direct Delivery

  E-mail Coordinator
  Jermainne Biagas
  Phone 225-578-1133

National Emergency Response and Rescue Training Center (NERRTC)

The center was established at TEEX in 1998 and funded by the U.S. Congress to improve the capabilities of emergency responders and local officials to respond to acts of terrorism, including those involving WMD. A member of the National Domestic Preparedness Consortium, TEEX provides jurisdictions with hands-on, scenario-driven training and exercises, technical assistance, strategy development and leadership training and development. NERRTC, a member of the National Domestic Preparedness Consortium (NDPC), was established to train local and state officials and emergency responders to prepare for and respond to acts of terrorism, including those involving the use of WMD and other special incidents. The center uses the proven methods of hands-on, performance-oriented training and simulations to enhance a jurisdiction's ability to respond to and manage WMD incidents. The training is conducted under realistic conditions either at the NERRTC in College Station, Texas, or on-site in your jurisdiction. How can NERRTC serve your jurisdiction?

- Hands-on, scenario-driven training and exercises
- Computer-based simulations with state-of-the-art computer-driven human patient simulators
- Internet-based WMD responder training
- Train-the-trainer programs
- Training delivered to your jurisdiction at a time of your choosing

TEEX National Emergency Response and Rescue Training Center
301 Tarrow
College Station, TX 77840-7896
Phone 979-458-1432
Fax 979-845-5726
Toll-free: 877-438-8877
E-mail: nerrtc@TEEXmail.tamu.edu

Training Videos Available from the Department of Justice, Office of Justice Programs (OJP)

Emergency Response to Terrorism Training for Emergency Responders (DVD)

The threat of terrorism is a growing concern throughout the world. While we cannot always stop a terrorist attack, it is important to recognize these situations when they occur and be trained, equipped, and ready to respond. Emergency responders might be confronted with mass casualties, contamination, hazardous materials, trapped victims, a crime scene, and the dreaded secondary device targeted at responders. This DVD contains all six ODP training videos that are designed to increase the awareness and knowledge of emergency responders, enhance their safety, and ultimately help them effectively meet today's challenges involving emergency response to terrorism. When ordering this DVD, the requester should reference the NCJ # 205243.

Managing Terrorism Incidents — Series (Video) The contents of this series were developed in coordination with the Federal Bureau of Investigation, Federal Emergency Management Agency, including the U.S. Fire Administration's National Fire Academy and the Emergency Management Institute, U.S. Department of Energy, U.S. Environmental Protection Agency, and the U.S. Public Health Service Office of Emergency Preparedness.

Using the Incident Command System for WMD Incidents (Video)

This program is part one of the series Managing Terrorism Incidents. It is designed to enhance the knowledge and understanding of the ICS for personnel who might become involved in the response to an act of terrorism. It describes ICS and explains its application in a WMD event and how it evolves during the initial response. It discusses the basic command structure, roles and responsibilities of the incident commander's staff and the functional sections that are established as part of ICS.

Using Unified Command on WMD Incidents (Video)

This program is part two of the series Managing Terrorism Incidents. It is designed for personnel who might become involved in a multiagency or multijurisdictional response to an act of terrorism. This program will build upon the concept of the ICS and show the transition from a single incident commander to a unified command, how the incident is managed under unified command, and the roles and responsibilities of agencies that participate. It will examine the operating facilities that support WMD incident operations and will explain how they work together. In addition, the concepts of crisis and consequence management will be covered.

Responding to a WMD Crime Scene (Video)

Emergency Responders might find themselves responding unknowingly to a criminal incident involving WMD. This is an entirely new and different set of responsibilities for the emergency responder. The purpose of this video is to demonstrate the responsibilities of recognizing, identifying, and preserving potential evidence at a WMD crime scene, thereby affording the best possibility for positive identification of suspects and successful prosecution.

Surviving the Secondary Device — The Rules Have Changed (Video)

Produced in partnership with the Georgia Emergency Management Agency, this video is designed to assist public safety officials in making informed decisions concerning the real potential of secondary explosive devices. These devices, which detonate after the initial explosion, target blast survivors, other individuals who converge on the scene, and, more often, responding public safety personnel. The possibility of secondary devices requires that public safety officials not only look at how to protect the lives of citizens but how to protect the responders. This video discusses policies and procedures for effectively responding to and managing a bomb incident and for better ensuring the safety of the public and the emergency responders.

Surviving Weapons of Mass Destruction (Video)

The threat of terrorist incidents involving chemical or biological agents is very real. This training video is designed to enhance the survival and safety of emergency responders during such incidents. Although protecting the public is the principal mission of all public safety agencies, it is also important that emergency responders do not forget their own safety. This video, produced in partnership with the Georgia Emergency Management Agency, approaches safety from the individual responder and an agency perspective.

Weapons of Mass Destruction — The First Responder (Video)

Being prepared for incidents involving WMD means knowing what to look for and how to react. Preparation means that all emergency response agencies, including law enforcement, fire, emergency medical services, and others at all levels of government work together in responding to such events. This video, produced in partnership with the City of Seattle Fire Department, was prepared to familiarize emergency responders with steps they can take to mitigate the effects of such incidents and to better ensure their safety and the public's safety.

How to Obtain Videos/DVD

Due to public safety concerns, *videos are available to personnel of state and local agencies only*. Individuals wishing copies of videos need to provide a written request on agency letterhead and clearly write **VIDEO REQUEST** on its envelope. Requests should be addressed to:

Director
VIDEO REQUEST
Office for Domestic Preparedness Support
810 Seventh Street, NW
Washington, DC 20531
Please clearly mark on outside envelope: **VIDEO REQUEST**

Conclusion

It is most important that emergency response organizations and responders
come to the realization that a terrorist attack can occur at any time, at any
place, and anywhere. Response organizations must develop an emergency
plan to deal with acts of terrorism that is tailored to each community. Personnel need to be trained at a minimum of the awareness level for terrorism.
Additional levels of training will need to be determined by local needs.
Responders should be able to recognize signs of terrorist events. Terrorist

Figure 11.9 **(See color insert following page 236).** A jet airliner is lined up on
one of the World Trade Center towers in New York, Tuesday, September 11, 2001.
In the most devastating terrorist onslaughts ever waged against the U.S., knife-
wielding hijackers crashed two airliners into the World Trade Center, toppling
its twin 110-story towers. (Source: AP/Wide World Photos. Used with permission.)

training can be integrated into existing hazardous materials training programs. The NFPA has added competencies under Standard 472 to prepare response personnel to deal with terrorist incidents. Target hazards within each community should be evaluated, and vulnerability assessments should be made to determine potential readiness. Assessments should include civil utility systems (water, power, transportation, etc.), financial institutions, population centers, and others. Joint training should take place between law enforcement, firefighters, and EMS personnel. Multijurisdictional incident command structures and systems need to be developed for all communities. Communications procedures should be established to ensure all responders can communicate effectively on the scene of the incident. Information sharing and networking between law enforcement and other emergency response organizations, including state and federal agencies, should also be developed. Up to the present time, many jurisdictions have been slow to recognize or admit the potential threat of terrorism. Appropriate changes to emergency plans and response procedures have not been completed. While planning and preparedness will not prevent a terrorist incident from happening, preparedness will improve emergency response and consequence management when an incident does occur.

DISCLAIMER: Chemical, biological, nuclear, explosive, and incendiary agents; decontamination solutions and procedures; and tactical considerations mentioned in this book are taken from military documents and other response resources that are believed to be accurate. They are not meant to infer this is the best or only way of performing any of the functions or procedures mentioned. The examples are presented here as a sample of how the military and other response organizations conduct standard operating procedures for responses to terrorism, since they are the ones with the most experience with chemical and biological agents. However, local medical treatment protocols and local standard operating procedures should be developed and followed when responding to these types of terrorist incidents. Any products mentioned in this book are presented purely for informational purposes and are not meant as an endorsement of any kind.

Glossary

Absorption The process of an agent being taken in by a surface, much like a sponge and water.

Accelerant A fuel (usually a flammable liquid) that is used to initiate or increase the spread of fire.

Acetylcholine A chemical compound formed from an acid and an alcohol that causes muscles to contract (neurotransmitter). It is rapidly broken down by an enzyme, cholinesterase.

Acetylcholinesterase An enzyme present in nerve tissue, muscles, and red blood cells that catalyzes the hydrolysis of acetylcholine to choline and acetic acid, allowing neural transmission across synapses to occur; true cholinesterase.

ACGIH American Conference of Governmental Industrial Hygienists; establishes exposure limits for workers.

Acidic Sour Having a pH of less than 7.

Acute Exposure An exposure, often intense, over a relatively short period of time.

Acute Toxicity Single or short-term exposure; used to describe brief exposures and effects that appear promptly after exposure.

Adenoma A benign tumor of glandular origin.

Adsorption The process of an agent sticking to or becoming chemically attached to a surface, much like a magnet and metals.

Aerosols A suspension or dispersion of small particles (solids or liquids) in a gaseous medium.

Agent Dosage The concentration of a toxic vapor in the air multiplied by the time that the concentration is present or the time that an individual is exposed (mg-min/m^3).

Alkaline Basic   Having a pH of greater than 7.

Alpha Particle   A specific particle ejected from a radioactive atom. It has low penetrating power and short range. Alpha particles will generally fail to penetrate the skin. Alpha-emitting atoms can cause health effects if introduced into the lungs or wounds — or if ingested.

Alveoli   Microscopic air sac in the lungs where oxygen and carbon dioxide diffusion takes place through the alveolar walls.

Ambient   Environmental or surrounding conditions.

Ammonium Nitrate   Classified as an oxidizer. An oxidizer is a substance that readily yields oxygen or other oxidizing substances to promote the combustion of organic matter or other fuel. Ammonium nitrate alone is not an explosive material. However, federal explosives storage regulations require the separation of explosive magazines from nearby stores of ammonium nitrate by certain minimum distances.

ANFO   An explosive material consisting of ammonium nitrate and fuel oil.

Anticholinergic   An agent or chemical that blocks or impedes the action of acetylcholine, such as the (also cholinolytic) antidote atropine.

Anticholinesterase   A substance that blocks the action of cholinesterase (acetylcholinesterase) such as nerve agents.

Antidote   A substance that neutralizes toxic agents or their effects.

Arsenical   Pertaining to or containing arsenic; a reference to the vesicant lewisite.

Arthralgia   Severe pain in a joint, especially one not inflammatory in character.

Arthropods   Organisms such as insects, arachnids (spiders and mites), and crustaceans, which lack backbones (invertebrates).

Asphyxiation   One of the six types of harm (see TRACEM) that can be encountered at a terrorist incident. Asphyxiants interfere with oxygen flow during normal breathing. There are two types of asphyxiants: simple and chemical.

Asthenia   Weakness or debility.

Ataxia   An inability to coordinate muscle activity during voluntary movement, so the smooth movements occur. Most often due to disorders of the cerebellum or posterior columns of the spinal cord; may involve the limbs, head, or trunk.

Atom   The smallest particle of an element that cannot be divided or broken up by chemical means. It consists of a central core of protons and neutrons, called the nucleus. **Electrons** revolve in orbits in the region surrounding the nucleus.

Atropine   An anticholinergic used as an antidote for nerve agents to counteract excessive amounts of acetylcholine. It also has other medical uses.

Atrophy   The wasting away or reduction in the size of a cell, tissue, or organ(s).

B-NICE   The acronym developed by the National Fire Academy for identifying the five categories of terrorist incidents: biological, nuclear, incendiary, chemical, and explosive.

Backdraft   A deflagrative explosion of gases and smoke from an established fire that has depleted the oxygen content of a structure, most often initiated by introducing oxygen through ventilation or structural failure.

Background Level   Normal environmental concentration of a chemical.

Background Radiation   The radiation in the natural environment, including cosmic rays and radiation from the naturally radioactive elements, both outside and inside the bodies of humans and animals. It is also called natural radiation. Human-made sources of radioactivity contribute to total background radiation levels.

Bacteremia   Presence of viable bacteria in the blood.

Bacteria   Single-celled organisms that multiply by cell division and can cause disease in humans, plants, or animals. Examples include anthrax, cholera, plague, tularemia, and Q fever.

Basic Alkaline   Having a pH of greater than 7.

Becquerel   The SI unit of activity 1 disintegration per second; 37 billion Bq = 1 Curie (see conversion factors in Appendix).

Beta Particle   A small particle ejected from a radioactive atom. It has moderate penetrating power and a range of up to a few meters in air. Beta particles will penetrate only a fraction of an inch of skin tissue.

Bioassay   Test that determines the effect of a chemical on a population of living organisms.

Biodegradation   Decomposition of a substance into more elementary compounds by the action of microorganisms such as bacteria.

Biological Agent   Living organism, or the materials derived from it, that causes disease in or harms humans, animals, or plants, or causes deterioration of material. Biological agents may be found as liquid droplets, aerosols, or dry powders. A biological agent can be adapted and used as a terrorist weapon, such as anthrax, tularemia, cholera, encephalitis, plague, and botulism. There are three different types of biological agents: bacteria, viruses, and toxins.

Black Powder   A deflagrating or low explosive compound of an intimate mixture of sulfur, charcoal, and an alkali nitrate (usually potassium or sodium nitrate). See Low Explosives.

Blast   Air being propelled at tremendous force and speed creates an overpressure wave traveling outward in all directions away from the source for great distances.

Blasting Agent   Any material or mixture consisting of fuel and oxidizer intended for blasting; not otherwise defined as an explosive, provided that the finished product, as mixed for use or shipment, cannot be detonated by means of a No. 8 test blasting cap when unconfined.

Blepharospasm   A twitching or spasmodic contraction of the orbicular oculi muscle around the eye.

Blister Agent   A chemical agent, also called a vesicant, that causes severe blistering and burns to eyes, skin, and tissues of the respiratory tract. Exposure is through liquid or vapor contact. Also referred to as mustard agent; examples include mustard and lewisite.

Blood Agent   A chemical agent that interferes with the ability of blood to transport oxygen and causes asphyxiation. These substances injure a person by interfering with cell respiration (the exchange of oxygen and carbon dioxide between blood and tissues). Common examples are hydrogen cyanide and cyanogen chloride.

Boiling Point   The temperature (pressure-dependent) at which a liquid changes to its gas phase.

Bone Marrow   The soft tissue contained inside the bone.

Bradycardia   Heart rate less than 50.

Bronchiti   Inflammation of the mucous membrane of the bronchial tubes, producing chronic cough.

Bronchoconstriction   Constriction of the bronchial tubes, which tends to trap air in the lungs.

Bronchopneumonia   Inflammation of the terminal bronchioles and alveoli, causing edema and consolidation of alveoli.

BTU   British Thermal Unit. A standardized measure of heat, it is the heat energy required to raise the temperature of 1 pound of water 1 degree Fahrenheit.

Bulk Mix   A mass of explosive material prepared for use in bulk form without packaging.

Cancer   A disease characterized by the rapid and uncontrolled growth of aberrant cells into malignant tumors.

Carcinogen   Any substance capable of producing cancer, or a chemical that causes or induces cancer.

Carcinoma   A malignant tumor of epithelial origin.

Carbuncle   A painful, localized pus-producing infection of the skin and subcutaneous tissue.

Cardiovascular System   The heart and blood vessels.

CAS No.   Chemical Abstracts Service Registry Number. The CAS No. is assigned to a specific compound and is used for cross-referencing chemical names that refer to the same compound.

Cataracts   A clouding of the eye that interferes with light entering the eye.

Ceiling Exposure Value   The maximum airborne concentration of a biological or chemical agent to which a worker may be exposed at any time.

Central Nervous System (CNS)   Portion of the nervous system that consists of the brain and the spinal cord.

Cerebral Edema   Swelling of brain cells which, because of limited space inside the skull, can create brain compression.

Chemical Agent   There are five classes of chemical agents, all of which produce incapacitation, serious injury, or death: (1) nerve agents, (2) blister agents, (3) blood agents, (4) choking agents, and (5) irritating agents. A chemical substance used in military operations is intended to kill, seriously injure, or incapacitate people through its physiological effects.

Chemical Agent Symbol   A code usually consisting of two letters that are used as a designation to identify chemical agents (e.g., GB for the chemical agent sarin).

Chemical Asphyxiant   Referred to as blood poisons, these are compounds that interrupt the flow of oxygen in the blood or the tissues in three ways: (1) They react more readily than oxygen with the blood. Carbon monoxide is the best-known example. (2) They liberate the hemoglobin from red blood cells, resulting in a lack of transport for oxygen. Hydrazine is one such asphyxiant. (3) They cause a malfunction in the oxygen-carrying ability of the red blood cells. Benzene and toluene are two of these.

Chemical Contamination   The presence of a chemical agent on a person, object, or area.

Chemical Harm   One of the six types of harm (see TRACEM) that can be encountered at a terrorist incident. There are two broad types of chemical agents that can cause harm: toxic and corrosive materials.

Chemical Incident   An event in which a chemical agent is used as a terrorist weapon.

Chemical Pneumonitis   Inflammation of the lungs from any one of several sources, such as inhaling chemical vapors or smoke, with injury to the bronchial system as well as the aveoli; may also be caused by infective agents.

Chemical Stockpile Emergency Preparedness Program (CSEPP)   A joint DA/FEMA program to oversee and assist in the development of emergency response plans and capabilities for all jurisdictions that might be affected by a chemical agent release associated with stockpile storage or CSDP activities. The CSEPP is administered by the joint steering committee that is co-chaired by DA and FEMA.

Chemical Warfare Agent   A chemical substance that, because of its physiological, psychological, or pharmacological effects, is intended for use in military operations to kill, seriously injure, or incapacitate humans (or animals) through its toxicological effects. Excluded are riot control agents, chemical herbicides, and smoke and flame agents.

Choking Agent   These agents exert their effects solely on the lungs and result in the irritation of the alveoli of the lungs. Agents cause the alveoli to constantly secrete watery fluid into the air sacs, which is called pulmonary edema. When a lethal amount of a choking agent is received, the air sacs become so flooded that the air cannot enter and the victim dies of anoxia (oxygen deficiency); also known as a dry drowning.

Cholinergic   Resembling acetylcholine, especially in physiological action. Cholinergic symptoms include nausea, vomiting, headache, and sweating.

Cholinesterase (AChe)   Acetylcholinesterase is the enzyme that breaks down the neurotransmitter acetylcholine after it has transmitted a signal from a nerve ending to another nerve, muscle, or gland. Organophosphate pesticides and military nerve agents block the normal activity of Ache, which results in the accumulation of excess acetylcholine at nerve endings.

Chromosome Rodlike structure in the nucleus of a cell that forms during mitosis; composed of DNA and protein; chromosomes contain the genes responsible for heredity.

Chronic An exposure, often mild, over a long period of time.

Ciliary Of or related to cilia; related to the suspension of the lens of the eye. Spasm of the muscles of the eyelids, which are usually painful and can interfere with function.

Commercial Explosives Explosives designed, produced, and used for commercial or industrial applications, rather than for military purposes.

Common Chemicals Any chemical compound or element that, as part of a physical mixture, would be necessary for that mixture to be considered an explosive mixture; or any chemical compound or element that could be classified as an oxidizer or as readily available fuel.

C4 A military plastic/moldable high explosive.

CNS Abbreviation for central nervous system.

Concentration The amount of a chemical agent present in a unit volume of air, usually expressed in milligrams per cubic meter (mg/m^3).

Concentration Time The amount of a chemical agent present in a unit volume of air, multiplied by the time an individual is exposed to that concentration.

Conjunctivitis Inflammation of the mucous membrane that lines the inner surface of the eyelids and forepart of the eyeball.

Consequence Management As described in PDD-39, consequence management is the response to the disaster, and focuses on alleviating damage, loss, hardship, or suffering. The Federal Emergency Management Agency (FEMA) has the lead in consequence management.

Contact Dermatitis Inflammation of the skin, due to either initial acute irritation from short-term contact with a substance, or from chronic sensitization that develops from long-term skin contact with an irritating substance.

Containment The attempt to prevent the spreading of contamination by holding it in, enclosing, encapsulating, or controlling it.

Cornea, Corneal The clear, transparent anterior portion of the eye, comprising about one-sixth of its surface through which light passes to transmit images to the retina. It is continuous at its periphery with the sciera and is composed of five layers.

Corrosive Materials   One type of chemical agent that can cause chemical harm at an incident scene. They are liquids or solids causing visible destruction or irreversible alterations in human skin tissue at the site of contact.

Crisis Management   As described in PDD-39, crisis management is the law enforcement response and focuses on the criminal aspects of the incident. The Federal Bureau of Investigation (FBI) has the lead in crisis management.

Critical Mass   The smallest mass of fissionable material that will support a self-sustaining chain reaction.

Cryogenic   Materials with boiling points below −130°F.

Cumulative Additional Exposure Rather Than Repeated Exposure For example, a 1-hour exposure of HD, followed within a few hours by another exposure of 1-hour, had the same effect as a single exposure lasting for 2 hours.

Curie (Ci)   The basic unit used to describe the intensity of radioactivity in a sample of material. The curie is equal to 37 billion (3.7 × 1010) disintegrations per second.

Cutaneous   Pertaining to the skin.

Cyanosis   A dark-bluish or purplish coloration of the skin and mucous membranes due to deficient oxygenation of the blood, evident when reduced hemoglobin in the blood exceeds 5 g per 100 ml.

Decay, Radioactive   The decrease in the amount of any radioactive material with the passage of time due to the spontaneous emission from the atomic nuclei of either alpha or beta particles, often accompanied by gamma radiation.

Decontamination   The process of neutralizing or removing contaminants that have accumulated on personnel, clothing, and equipment.

Dermal   Of the skin: through or by the skin.

Dermatitis   An inflammation or infection of the skin.

Detonating Cord   A flexible cord containing a center core of high explosives and used to initiate other explosives.

Detonation   An explosive reaction that moves through an explosive material at a velocity greater than the speed of sound (1250 ft per second).

Detonator   Any device containing an initiating or primary explosive that is used for initiating a detonation. A detonator might not contain more than 10 g of total explosives by weight, excluding ignition or delay charges. The term includes, but is not limited to, electric blasting caps or instantaneous and delay types, blasting caps for use with safety fuses, detonating cord delay connectors, and nonelectric instantaneous and delay blasting caps, which use detonating cord, shock tube, or any other replacement for electric leg wires.

Diathesis   The constitutional or inborn state disposing to a disease, group of diseases, and metabolic or structural anomaly.

Diplopia   The condition in which a single object is perceived as two objects.

Distance   One of the three components of the time, distance, and shielding (TDS) response; refers to the recommendation that one maintain distance from a hazard if at all possible. Refer to the North American Emergency Response Guide (NAERG) as an appropriate resource.

DMNB   2,3-Dimethyl-2,3-dintrobutane. One of four high-vapor pressure chemicals approved by the U.N. Council of the International Civil Aviation Organization (ICAO) to be added to plastic explosives as a detection marker.

Dosage   The concentration of a chemical agent in the atmosphere (C) multiplied by the time (t) the concentration remains, expressed as mg-min/m³. The dosage (Ct) received by a person depends upon how long he or she is exposed to the concentration.

Dose   A general term for the quantity of radiation or energy absorbed.

Dosimeter   A small portable instrument (such as a film badge, thermoluminescent, or pocket dosimeter) for measuring and recording the total accumulated personnel dose of ionizing radiation.

Downwind Distance   The distance a toxic agent vapor cloud will travel from its point of origin with the wind.

Dynamite   A high explosive used for blasting, consisting essentially of a mixture of, but not limited to, nitroglycerin, nitrocellulose, ammonium nitrate, sodium nitrate, and carbonaceous materials.

Dysarthria   A disturbance of speech and language due to emotional stress, to brain injury, or to paralysis, incoordination, or spasticity of muscles used for speaking.

Dysphagia, Dysphagy   Difficulty in swallowing.

Dyspnea   Shortness of breath; a subjective difficulty or distress in breathing, usually associated with disease of the heart or lungs; occurs normally during intense physical exertion or at high altitudes.

Edema   Swelling of the tissue.

Electromagnetic Radiation   A traveling wave motion resulting from changing electric or magnetic fields. Familiar electromagnetic radiation ranges from x-rays (and gamma rays) of short wavelength, through the ultraviolet, visible, and infrared regions, to radar and radio waves of relatively long wavelength.

Electron   An elementary particle with a negative charge and a mass 1/1837 that of the proton. Electrons surround the positively charged nucleus and determine the chemical properties of the atom.

Element   One of the 103 known chemical substances that cannot be broken down further without c include hydrogen, nitrogen, gold, lead, and uranium.

Emergency Operation Plan (EOP)   An EOP is a document that (1) assigns responsibility to organizations and individuals for carrying out specific actions at projected times and places in an emergency that exceeds the capability or routine responsibility of any one agency; (2) sets forth lines of authority and organizational relationships and shows how all actions will be coordinated; (3) describes how people and property will be protected in emergencies and disasters; (4) identifies personnel, equipment, facilities, supplies, and other resources available for use during response and recovery operations; and (5) identifies steps to address mitigation concerns during response and recovery activities.

Emphysema   Process of trapping air in the alveoli, associated with loss of elasticity of the lung tissues and resulting in being unable to completely exhale.

Emulsions   An explosive material containing substantial amounts of oxidizers dissolved in water droplets surrounded by an immiscible fuel.

Encephalitis, pl. Encephalitides   Inflammation of the brain.

Endothermic   Absorbing heat during a chemical reaction.

Endotracheal   Placing a device through the lumen of the trachea, such as an endotracheal tube.

Enterotoxin   A cytotoxin specific for the cells of the intestinal mucosa.

Enzyme   A protein, synthesized by a cell that acts as a catalyst in a specific chemical reaction.

Epistaxis   Profuse bleeding from the nose.

ERG   Department of Transportation Emergency Response Guide Book.

Erythema   Red area of the skin, caused by heat or cold injury, trauma, or inflammation.

Etiological Harm   One of the six types of harm (see TRACEM) that can be encountered at a terrorist incident. Involves exposure to a living microorganism or its toxins, which causes (or may cause) human disease. Biological agents are the most obvious examples of etiological agents.

Evaporation Rate The rate at which a liquid changes to vapor at normal room temperature.

Exothermic Generating or giving off heat during a chemical reaction.

Explosive As defined by the U.S. Department of Transportation, "a substance fitting into one of these two categories: (1) any substance or article, including a device, designed to function by explosion; or (2) any substance or article, including a device, which, by chemical reaction within itself, can function in a similar manner even if not designed to function by explosion."

Explosive Incident An event in which an explosive device is used as a terrorist weapon.

Explosive Limits (flammability limits) The lower and upper concentrations of an air/gas-or-vapor mixture in which combustion or deflagration will be supported.

Explosive Materials These include explosives, blasting agents, and detonators. Explosive materials include, but are not limited to, all items in the List of Explosive Materials.

Exposure A quantity used to indicate the amount of ionization in air produced by x- or gamma-ray radiation. The unit is the roentgen (R). For practical purposes, 1 R is comparable to 1 rad or 1 rem for x- and gamma radiation. The SI unit of exposure is the coulomb per kilogram (C/Kg). One $R = 2.58 \times 10^4$ C/kg.

Fasciculation Localized contraction of muscle fibers, usually visible through the skin.

Febrile Denoting or relating to fever.

Federal Response Plan (FRP) Developed to help expedite federal support to disasters. Generally, the FRP is activated when a state's resources are not sufficient to cope with a disaster, and the governor has requested federal assistance.

Filler A type of explosive/incendiary/chemical substance, which, in combination with a fusing or firing system, constitutes an improvised explosive device (e.g. dynamite, match heads, gasoline).

Fissile Material Although sometimes used as a synonym for fissionable material, this term has acquired a more restricted meaning, namely, any material fissionable by thermal (slow) neutrons. The three primary fissile materials are uranium-233, uranium-235, and plutonium-239.

Fission   The splitting of a nucleus into at least two other nuclei and the releaser of a relatively large amount of energy. Two or three neutrons are usually released during this type of transformation.

Flaccid Paralysis   Loss of muscle tone and capability to function. Nerve agents cause this condition.

Flammable Liquid   Combustible. A flammable material is one that is ignited easily and burns readily (i.e., gasoline, charcoal lighter fluid, diesel fuel, and paint thinners).

Flashover   The final stage of the process of fire growth; when all combustible fuels within a compartment are ignited, the room is said to have undergone flashover.

Flashpoint   Temperature at which an ignitable vapor is first produced by a material.

Fragmentation   Any item that is part of or near the bomb when it explodes and becomes a projectile. The larger the explosive charge, the farther the fragments will travel. Fragments normally travel in a straight line but, like a bullet, can also be deflected.

Fuel   Any substance that reacts with the oxygen in the air or with the oxygen yielded by an oxidizer to produce combustion.

Gamma Radiation   Gamma rays are high-energy, ionizing radiation that travel at the speed of light and have great penetrating power. Can cause skin burns, severely injure internal organs, and have long-term physiological effects.

Gastrointestinal Tract (GI tract)   The entire digestive canal from mouth to anus.

Geiger-Mueller Counter   A radiation detection and measuring instrument. It consists of a gas-filled tube containing electrodes, between which there is an electrical voltage but no current flowing. When ionizing radiation passes through the tube, a short, intense pulse of current passes from the negative electrode to the positive electrode and is measured or counted. The number of pulses per second measures the intensity of the radiation field.

Grand Mal   The most pronounced form of epilepsy, usually preceded by an aura, then loss of consciousness and tonic clonic movements.

Gray   The SI unit of absorbed dose; 1 gray = 100 rads.

Ground Shock   The transmission through the ground of the blast wave pressure. This causes problems with gas, water, electricity, sewers, telecommunications, etc., and can also cause structural damage to the foundations of buildings and subway systems.

Half-Life The time in which one-half of the atoms of a particular radioactive substance disintegrates into another nuclear form. Measured half-lives vary from millionths of a second to billions of years. Also called physical or radiological half-life.

Hematemeses Vomiting of blood.

Hemolytic Anemia Anemia caused by increased destruction of red blood cells where the bone marrow is not able to compensate for it.

Hemoptysis The spitting of blood derived from the lungs or bronchial tubes as a result of pulmonary or bronchial hemorrhage.

High Explosives Explosives that are characterized by a very high rate of reaction, high pressure development, and the presence of a detonation wave in the explosive, and which can be caused to detonate by means of a blasting cap when unconfined.

HMDT An abbreviation for the name of the explosive hexamethylene triperoxide diamine.

Hydration The combining of a substance with water.

Hydrolysis The reaction of any chemical substance with water by which decomposition of the substance occurs and one or more new substances are produced.

Hydrolysis Products Those new substances formed when a chemical agent or compound reacts with or is decomposed by water.

Hypotension Subnormal arterial blood pressure.

Hypovolemia A decreased amount of blood in the body.

Hypoxemia Subnormal oxygenation of arterial blood, short of anoxia.

IDLH Immediately Dangerous To Life And Health. An atmospheric concentration of any toxic, corrosive, or asphyxiant substance that poses an immediate threat to life, would cause irreversible or delayed adverse health effects, or would interfere with an individual's ability to escape from a dangerous atmosphere.

Impermeable Protective Clothing Protective clothing that does not allow penetration of gas and liquid or evaporation of perspiration. Designed primarily for protection of personnel engaged in extremely hazardous decontamination or other special operations involving life-threatening danger from liquid or high concentrations of vapor from chemical warfare agents.

Improvised Explosive Devices (IED) Devices placed or fabricated improvisationally, incorporating destructive, lethal, noxious, pyrotechnic, or incendiary chemicals, designed to destroy, disfigure, distract, or harass. They may incorporate military stores, but are normally devised from nonmilitary or commercial components.

Incapacitating Agent An agent that produces physiological or mental effects, or both, that may persist for hours or days after exposure, rendering an individual incapable of performing his or her assigned duties.

Incendiary Device Any mechanical, electrical, or chemical device used intentionally to initiate combustion and start a fire.

Incendiary Incident An event in which an incendiary device is used as a terrorist weapon.

Initial Downwind Vapor Hazard Area Areas initially established to evacuate all unprotected personnel and to prevent other unprotected personnel from entering, thus avoiding agent vapors or any other type of contamination.

Inverse Square Law The relationship that states that electromagnetic radiation intensity is inversely proportional to the square of the distance from a point source.

Ionization The process of adding one or more electrons to, or removing one or more electrons from, atoms or molecules, thereby creating ions. High temperatures, electrical discharges, or nuclear radiation can cause ionization.

Ionizing Radiation Any radiation capable of displacing electrons from atoms or molecules, thereby producing ions. Some examples are alpha, beta, gamma, x-rays, neutrons, and ultraviolet light. High doses of ionizing radiation may produce severe skin or tissue damage.

Iritis Inflammation of the iris, with accompanying pain, photophobia, lacrimation, and diminution of vision. Treated with atropine to dilate pupils, systemic steroids are frequently used.

Irradiation Exposure to ionizing radiation.

Irritating Agent A chemical agent, also known as riot control agent or tear gas, which causes respiratory distress and tearing designed to incapacitate. Common examples include chloropicrin, MACE, tear gas, pepper spray, and dibenzoxazepine.

Isotope One of two or more atoms with the same number of protons but different numbers of neutrons in their nuclei.

Lacrimation Secretion and discharge of tears.

Latent Period   Specifically in the case of mustard, the period between exposure and onset of signs and symptoms; otherwise, an incubation period.

Lethal Chemical Agent   An agent that might be used effectively in a field concentration to produce death.

Liquid Dosage   The weight of a liquid agent received by a person on his or her skin is usually expressed as dosage in milligrams of contaminant per kilogram of body weight (mg/kg). This is equivalent to parts per million (ppm).

Low Explosives   Explosives that are characterized by deflagration (a rapid combustion that moves through an explosive material at a velocity less than the speed of sound) (1250 ft per second).

Lymphandentitis   Inflammation of the lymph nodes.

Mechanical Harm   One of the six types of harm (see TRACEM) that can be encountered at a terrorist incident. Causes trauma from contact with mechanical injury can result from an explosive device. Other types include routine slip, trip, and fall hazards.

Median Incapacitating Dosage (ICT_{50})   The volume of a chemical agent vapor or aerosol inhaled that is sufficient to disable 50% of exposed, unprotected people (expressed as mg- min/m^3).

Median Incapacitating Dosage (ID_{50})   The volume of a liquid chemical agent expected to incapacitate 50% of a group of exposed, unprotected individuals.

Median Lethal Dosage (LCT_{50})   The dosage of a chemical agent vapor or aerosol inhaled that is lethal to 50% of exposed, unprotected people (expressed as mg-min/m^3).

Median Lethal Dosage (LD_{50})   The amount of liquid chemical agent expected to kill 50% of a group of exposed, unprotected individuals.

Method of Dissemination   The way a chemical agent or compound is finally released into the atmosphere.

Microcurie   One millionth (10–6) of a curie.

Millirem   One thousandth of a rem (1 mrem = 10–3 rem).

Milliroentgen   One thousandth of a roentgen, R (1 mR = 10–3 R).

Miosis   A condition where the pupil of the eye becomes contracted (pinpointed), which impairs night vision.

Molecule   A group of atoms held together by chemical forces. A molecule is the smallest unit of a compound that can exist by itself and retain all of its chemical properties.

M8 Chemical Agent Detector Paper   A paper used to detect and identify liquid V- and G-type nerve agents and H-type blister agents. It does not detect chemical agent vapors.

M256 Kit   A kit that detects and identifies vapor concentrations of nerve, blister, and blood agents.

Mutagen   A material that creates a change in the genetic structure, which is capable of being transmitted to the offspring.

Myalgia   Muscular pain.

Mydriasis   Dilation of the pupil.

Nanocurie   One billionth ($10-9$) of a curie.

Narcosis   General and nonspecific reversible depression of neuronal excitability, produced by a number of physical and chemical agents, usually resulting in stupor rather than in anesthesia.

Necrosis   Death of tissue.

Nerve Agent   A substance that interferes with the central nervous system. Exposure is primarily through contact with the liquid (skin and eyes) and secondarily through inhalation of the vapor.

Neutron   An uncharged elementary particle with a mass slightly greater than that of the proton and found in the nucleus of every atom heavier than hydrogen.

Nonpersistent Agent   An agent that remains in the target area(s) for a relatively short period of time. The hazard, predominantly vapor, will exist for minutes or, in exceptional cases, hours after dissemination of the agent. As a general rule, a nonpersistent agent duration will be less than 12 hours.

Nuclear Incident   An event in which a nuclear agent is used as a terrorist weapon. There are two fundamentally different threats in the area of nuclear terrorism: (1) the use, or threatened use, of a nuclear bomb; and (2) the detonation of a conventional explosive incorporating nuclear materials.

Nucleus   The small, central, positively charged region of an atom that carries the atom's nuclei. Except for the nucleus of ordinary (light) hydrogen, which has a single proton, all atomic nuclei contain both protons and neutrons. The number of protons determines the total positive charge, or atomic number. This is the same for all the atomic nuclei of a given chemical element. The total number of neutrons and protons is called the mass number.

Organophosphate   A compound with a specific phosphate group which inhibits acetylcholinesterase. Used in chemical warfare and as an insecticide.

Osteomyelitis   Inflammation of the bone marrow and adjacent bone.

Oxidizer or Oxidizing Material   A substance, such as a nitrate, that readily yields oxygen or other oxidizing substances to stimulate the combustion of organic matter or other fuel.

Oxime   A compound that blocks acetylcholinesterase from combining with organophosphates, formed by the action of hydroxylamine upon an aldehyde or a ketone.

2-PAM CL   Pralidoxime chloride (or Protopam) is an antidote to organophosphate poisoning such as might result from exposure to nerve agents or some insecticides. The drug, which helps restore an enzyme called acetylcholinesterase, must be used in conjunction with atropine to be effective. Restores normal control of skeletal muscle contraction (relieves twitching and paralysis).

Papule   A small, circumscribed, solid elevation on the skin.

Parasitemia   The presence of parasites in the circulating blood; used especially with reference to malarial and other protozoan forms and microfilariae.

Partial Vacuum   Return to normal pressure. At this stage, windows not destroyed by the initial blast can be sucked out.

Parts per Million   Parts (molecules) of a substance contained in a million parts of another substance (or water).

Percutaneous   Through the skin, such as applying an ointment with medication or injection by needle.

Permeation   The process by which a chemical moves through protective clothing.

Permeation Rate   The rate at which the challenge chemical permeates the fabric.

Persistency   An expression of the duration of effectiveness of a chemical agent, dependent on physical and chemical properties of the agent, weather, method of dissemination, and terrain conditions.

Persistent Agent   An agent that remains in the target area for longer periods of time. Hazards from both vapor and liquids may exist for hours, days, or in exceptional cases, weeks or months after dissemination of the agent. As a general rule, persistent agent duration will be greater than 12 hours.

Petechiae, sing   Minute hemorrhage spot of pinpoint-to-pinhead size in the skin, which is not blanched by pressure.

PETN   An abbreviation for the name of the explosive pentaerythritol tetranitrate.

Photophobia   Morbid dread and avoidance of light. Photosensitivity, or pain in the eyes with exposure to light, can be a cause.

Pleura   The delicate sinous membrane lining each half of the thorax of mammals and folded back over the surface of the lung of the same side.

PPE   Personal protective equipment.

Precursor Chemicals   Any chemical compound or element that can be subjected to a chemical reaction or series of reactions in order to synthesize the chemical compound or element into an explosive compound.

Presidential Decision Directive 39 (PDD-39)   Issued in June 1995, PDD-39, U.S. Policy on Counter-Terrorism, directed a number of measures to reduce the nation's vulnerability to terrorism, to deter and respond to terrorist acts, and to strengthen capabilities to prevent and manage the consequences of terrorist use of nuclear, biological, and chemical weapons.

Presynaptic   Pertaining to the area on the proximal side of a synaptic cleft.

Pruritus Syn   Itching.

Ptosis, pl. Ptoses   In reference to the eyes, drooping of the eyelids.

Pustule   A small circumscribed elevation of the skin containing pus and having an inflamed base.

Pyrogenic   Causing fever.

Pyrolysis   The chemical decomposition of substances through the action of heat, in the absence of oxygen.

Pyrophoric   Capable of oxidizing on exposure to atmospheric oxygen at normal temperatures.

Pyrotechnic   A chemical mixture, which, upon burning, produces visible, brilliant displays, bright lights, or sounds.

Quick Mask TM   An emergency respiratory protective device that can reduce the health risks and mortality rates associated with inhalation of toxic air.

Rad   The special unit for radiation absorbed dose, which uses the amount of energy from any type of ionizing radiation (e.g., alpha, beta, gamma, neutrons, etc.) deposited in any medium (e.g., water, tissue, air). A dose of 1 rad means the absorption of 100 ergs (a small but measurable amount of energy) per gram of absorbing tissue (100 rad = 1 gray).

Radiation   There are three types of nuclear radiation: (1) alpha, (2) beta, and (3) gamma. Radiation is the cause of one of the six types of harm (see TRACEM) that can be encountered at a terrorist incident.

Radiation Detection Instrument   A device that detects and displays the characteristics of ionizing radiation.

Radiation Nuclear Particles   (Alpha, beta, neutrons) or photons (gamma) emitted from the nucleus of unstable radioactive atoms as a result of radio-active decay.

Radiation Sickness   The complex of symptoms characterizing the disease known as radiation injury, resulting from excessive exposure (greater than 200 rads or 2 gray) of the whole body (or large part) to ionizing radiation. The earliest of these symptoms are nausea, fatigue, vomiting, and diarrhea, which might be followed by loss of hair (epilation), hemorrhage, inflammation of the mouth and throat, and general loss of energy. In severe cases, where the radiation exposure has been approximately 1000 rad (10 gray) or more, death can occur within 2–4 weeks.

Radioactivity   The spontaneous emission of radiation, generally alpha or beta particles, often accompanied by gamma rays, from the nucleus of an unstable isotope. Also, the rate at which radioactive material emits radiation. Measured in units of becquerels or distintegrations per second.

Radiological   A conventional explosive incorporating nuclear materials.

Rate of Detoxification   The rate at which the body can counteract the effects of a poisonous chemical substance.

Rate of Hydrolysis   The rate at which the various chemical agents or compounds are decomposed by water.

RDX   An abbreviation for the name of the explosive cyclonite, hexogen, T4, cyclo-1,3,5,-trimethylene-2,4,6-trinitramine; hexahydro-1,3,5,-trinitro S-triazine.

Reconnaissance   A primary survey to gather information.

Rem   The special unit of dose equivalent. The dose equivalent equals the absorbed dose multiplied by the quality factor. (100 rem = 1 sievert)

Respiratory Dosage   This is equal to the time in minutes an individual is unmasked in an agent cloud multiplied by the concentration of the cloud.

Retinitis   Inflammation of the retina.

Rhinorrhea   A runny nose.

Roentgen   A unit of exposure to ionizing radiation. It is the amount of gamma or x-rays required to produce ions resulting in a charge of 0.000258 coulombs/kilogram of air under standard conditions.

Saw MINICAD   A pocket-sized instrument that monitors trace levels of chemical agents. It can detect both nerve and blister agents simultaneously.

Sensitize   To become highly responsive or easily receptive to the effects of toxic chemical agents after the initial exposure.

Septic Shock   Shock associated with septicemia caused by gram-negative bacteria.

Shielding   One of the three components of TDS; refers to maintaining significant physical barriers between you and the hazard. Examples include vehicles, buildings, walls, and PPE.

Shigellosis   Bacillary dysentery caused by bacteria of the genus Shigella, often occurring in epidemic patterns.

Short Term Exposure Limit (STEL)   A 15-minute time-weighted average exposure, which should not be exceeded at any time during a work day even if the eight-hour time-weighted average (TWA) is within the threshold limit value (TLV). Exposure at the STEL should not be repeated more than four times a day, and there should be at least 60 minutes between successive exposures at the STEL.

Sievert   The SI unit of dose equivalent; 1 Sv = 100 rem.

SI   International units of measure.

Simple Asphyxiant   Generally, an inert gas that displaces the oxygen necessary for breathing, and dilutes the oxygen concentration below the level that is useful for the human body.

Size-Up   The rapid mental evaluation of the factors that influence an incident. Size-up is the first step in determining a course of action.

Skin Dosage   This is equal to the time of exposure in minutes of an individual's unprotected skin multiplied by the concentration of the agent cloud.

Smokeless Powder   Any of a class of explosive propellants that produce comparatively little smoke on explosion and consist mostly of gelatinized cellulose nitrates.

Solubility   The ability of a material to dissolve in water or another liquid.

Solvent   A material that is capable of dissolving another liquid.

Source Strength   The weight of a chemical agent that is at the chemical accident/incident site and may be released into the environment.

Specific Gravity   The weight of a liquid compared to the weight of an equal volume of water.

Spontaneous Ignition   Chemical or biological process that generates sufficient heat to ignite the reacting materials.

Stafford Act   Robert T. Stafford Disaster Relief and Emergency Assistance Act. Authorizes the federal government to respond to disasters and emergencies in order to help state and local government save lives and to protect public health, safety, and property.

State EOP   The State EOP is the framework within which local EOPs are created and through which the federal government becomes involved. The states play three roles: (1) they assist local jurisdictions whose capabilities are overwhelmed by an emergency; (2) they themselves respond first to certain emergencies; and (3) they work with the federal government when federal assistance is necessary.

Strategic Goals   Strategic goals are broad, general statements of intent.

Stridor   A high-pitched, noisy respiration, like the blowing of the wind; a sign of respiratory obstruction, especially in the trachea or larynx.

Systemic Toxicity   Poisoning of the whole system or organism, rather than poisoning, which affects, for example, a single organ.

Tachycardia   Rapid beating of the heart, conventionally applied to rates over 100 per minute.

TATP   Triacetone Triperoxide-a highly sensitive primary explosive manufactured from common chemicals such as acetone, peroxide, and acid.

Tear Agents   Compounds that cause a large flow of tears, intense eye pain, and irritation of the skin.

Terrorism   As defined by the FBI, "the unlawful use of force against persons or property to intimidate or coerce a government, the civilian population, or any segment thereof, in the furtherance of political or social objectives." This definition includes three elements: (1) Terrorist activities are illegal and involve the use of force. (2) The actions are intended to intimidate or coerce. (3) The actions are committed in support of political or social objectives.

Thermal Harm   One of the six types of harm (see TRACEM) that can be encountered at a terrorist incident. Thermal harm is the result of exposure to extreme heat or cold.

Thermonuclear   An adjunct to the process in which very high temperatures are used to bring about the fusion of light nuclei, such as those of the hydrogen isotopes deuterium and tritium, with the accompanying liberation of energy.

Time   One of the three components of TDS; refers to the amount of time a responder should be exposed to an incident. It is recommended that one spend the shortest amount of time possible in the hazard area.

Time, Distance, and Shielding (TDS)   Three types of protective measures commonly associated with hazardous materials training.

Time-Weighted Average (TWA)   The average concentration for a normal 8-hour work day and a 40-hour work week, to which nearly all workers might be repeatedly exposed without adverse effects.

TNT   An abbreviation for the name of the explosive trinitrotoluene.

Toxemia   A condition in which toxins produced by cells at a local source of infection or derived from the growth of microorganisms are contained in the blood.

Toxic   Harmful, poisonous.

Toxicity   (1) The capacity or property of a substance to cause adverse effects. (2) The specific quantity of a substance, which might be expected, under specific conditions, to do damage to a specific living organism.

Toxic Materials   A type of chemical that can cause chemical harm at an incident scene. They produce harmful effects depending on the concentration of the materials and the length of exposure to them. An individual can have chronic or acute exposures to toxic materials.

Toxins   Toxic substance of natural origin produced by an animal, plant, or microbe. They differ from chemical substances in that they are not human-made. Toxins may include botulism, ricin, and mycotoxins.

TRACEM   The acronym used to identify the six types of harm one might encounter at a terrorist incident: thermal, radioactive, asphyxiation, chemical, etiological, and mechanical.

Upwind   In or toward the direction from which the wind blows. To be upwind of an item, the wind would be blowing from your position to the item.

Uranium   One of the 103 known chemical substances that cannot be broken down further by chemical means. It is a radioactive element.

Urea Ammonium Nitrate (UAN)   UAN solution is a popular liquid fertilizer in the U.S. and other industrialized areas.

Urticant   A chemical agent that produces irritation at the point of contact, resembling a stinging sensation, such as a bee sting. For example, the initial physiological effects of phosgene oxime (CX) upon contact with a person's skin.

Urticaria   A skin condition characterized by intensely itching, red, raised patches.

Vapor Density   The motion of the escaping molecules of a liquid in an enclosed container is confined to the vapor space above the surface of the liquid. As an increasing number of molecules strike and reenter the liquid, a point of equilibrium is eventually reached when the rate of escape of molecules from the liquid equals the rate of return to the liquid. The pressure exerted by the escaping vapor at the point of equilibrium is called vapor pressure.

Variola Syn   Smallpox.

Vesicants   Chemical agents, also called blister agents, which cause severe burns to eyes, skin, and tissues of the respiratory tract. Also referred to as mustard agents. Examples include mustard and lewisite.

Vesicles   Blisters on the skin.

Virus   The simplest type of microorganisms, lacking a system for their own metabolism. They depend on living cells to multiply and cannot live long outside of a host. Types of viruses are smallpox, ebola, marburg, and Lassa fever.

Viscosity   The degree to which a fluid resists flow.

Volatile   Capable of vaporizing or evaporating readily.

Volatility   With chemical agents, it refers to their ability to change from a liquid state into a gaseous state. (The ability of a material to evaporate.)

Vomiting Agent   Compounds that cause irritation of the upper respiratory tract and involuntary vomiting.

Water Gel   An explosive material containing substantial portions of water, oxidizers, and fuel, plus a cross-linking agent that may be a high explosive or blasting agent.

Wheal   An acute swelling of the skin. This condition is common to a bee sting.

Whole-Body Exposure   An exposure of the body to radiation, in which the entire body, rather than an isolated part, is irradiated. Where a radioisotope is uniformly distributed throughout the body tissues, rather than being concentrated in certain parts, the irradiation can be considered as whole-body exposure.

Yellowcake   A solid uranium-oxygen compound (U-3O8) that takes its name from its color and texture. It is a product of the uranium milling process and is the feed material used for fuel enrichment and fuel pellet fabrication.

X-rays   Penetrating electromagnetic radiation (photon) having a wavelength that is much shorter than that of visible light. These rays are usually produced by excitation of the electron field around certain nuclei. In nuclear reactions, it is customary to refer to photons originating in the nucleus as gamma particle.

Zoonosis   An infection or infestation shared in nature by humans and other animals that are the normal host; a disease of humans acquired from an animal source.

References

1. Moultrie, William M., Mass Casualty Decon for Terrorist Incidents, *Fire Engineering*, December 1998.

2. *Hawley's Condensed Chemical Dictionary*, 12th edition, Van Nostrand Reinhold Company, New York, 1993.

3. *National Fire Academy Initial Response to Hazardous Materials Incidents: Basic Concepts, Student Manual*, U.S. Government Printing Office, 1992.

4. *National Fire Academy Initial Response to Hazardous Materials Incidents: Concept Implementation*, U.S. Government Printing Office, 1992.

5. National Fire Protection Association, *NFPA Fire Protection Handbook*, 17th edition, Quincy, MA, 1992.

6. *NIOSH Pocket Guide to Chemical Hazards*, U.S. Government Printing Office, 1990.

7. National Fire Protection Association, *Fire Protection Guide to Hazardous Materials*, 11th edition, Quincy, MA, 1994.

8. National Fire Academy, *Emergency Response to Terrorism: Basic Concepts Student Manual*, 1997.

9. National Fire Academy, *Emergency Response to Terrorism: Tactical Considerations Student Manual*, 1998.

10. *Medical Management of Biological Casualties Handbook, Third Edition*, U.S. Army Medical Research Institute of Infectious Substances, Fort Detrick, MD, July 1998.

11. *Medical Management of Chemical Casualties Handbook, Second Edition*, Chemical Casualty Care Office, Medical Research Institute of Chemical Defense, Aberdeen Proving Ground, MD, 1995.

12. Dehaan, John D., *Brady Fire Investigation, Third Edition*, Brady, Prentice Hall, Englewood Cliffs, NJ, 1993.

13. Roblee, Charles L. and McKechnie, Allen J., *The Investigation of Fires*, Prentice Hall, Englewood Cliffs, NJ, 1981.

14. ATF News, ATF probes largest explosive theft in past years, www.atf.treas.gov/press/fy984.htm, February 20, 1998. © 2000 by CRC Press LLC.

15. Atlanta Bomb Task Force, Statement of FBISAC Jack A. Daulton and Inspector Woody R. Enderson, www.alf.treas.gov/core/explarson/noo97.htm.

16. CNN News, FBI to release "Army of God" bomb letters, www.cnn.com, June 8, 1997.

17. National Abortion Federation, Statement of Vicki Saporta, Executive Director of the National Abortion Federation, www. Pro-choice. Org/media.birmingham.htm, January 29, 1998.

18. FBI, Bombing statistics, December 9, 1996.

19. CNN News, Rudolph to be charged in Birmingham blast, www.cnn.com, February 13, 1998.

20. USA Today, Search is on for abortion clinic bomber, www.usatoday.com, January 30, 1998.

21. MSNBC, Officer killed, counselor loses eye in abortion clinic bombing, www.msnbc.com, January 30, 1998.

22. United States Postal Inspection Service, Mail bombs, www.usps.gov, October 30, 1998.

23. ATF, Explosives statistics, www.atf.treas.gov, October 30, 1998.

24. ATF, ATF detecting suspicious packages and letters. Patterns of global terrorism: 1997, www.atf.treas.gov, January 7, 1997.

25. U.S. Department of State, Chronology of significant terrorist incidents, www.state.gov, June 15,1998.

26. U.S. Army Center for Health Promotion and Preventable Medicine, MSDS Sheets.

27. CNN News, 13th arrest in alleged anti-government plot, www.cnn.com, July 2, 1996.

28. Lukin, Anthony A., Terrorism and weapons of mass destruction: understanding nuclear, biological and chemical weapons, Prepared for the District of Columbia Government Office of Emergency Preparedness, March 1997.

29. Chemical Agent MSDS Sheets, www.cbdcom.apgea.army.mil.

30. NFPA 472 Professional Competence of Responders to Hazardous Materials Incidents, 1997 Edition, Tentative Interim Amendment, 1997.

31. Domestic Preparedness Fact Sheets, 120 Cities for Training, www.apgea.army.mil.

32. The Oklahoma Department of Civil Emergency Management, After Action Report, Alfred P. Murrah Federal Building Bombing, Lessons Learned.

33. Glossary of medical terms, www.nbc-med.org.

34. Belmonte, Richard B., Test Results of Level "A" Suits to Challenge by Chemical and Biological Warfare Agents and Stimulants: Summary Report, SCBRNEN, Aberdeen Proving Ground, MD, June 1998.

35. *NATO Handbook on the Medical Aspects of NBC Defense Operations,* Ameop-Ameop-6 (B) NATO Field Manual FM-8-285. © 2000 by CRC Press LLC.

36. CNN News, Pipe-bombs: low-tech, lethal tools of terror, www.cnn.com, July 27, 1996.

37. NFPA News, August 1998, Volume 2. Number 8 NFPA 1991 Standard on Vapor-Protective Suits for Hazardous Chemical Emergencies, 1994 Edition and proposed 2000 Edition, TIA LOG No 580.

38. FBI, Arizona train wreck, www.fbi.gov.

39. Chemical agent monitors, www.cbdcom.apgea.army.mil, November 9, 1998.

40. NRC, Nuclear site locations, www.nrc.gov, May 6, 1998.

41. Towle, Lisa A., Medical strike teams gather force, *National Fire & Rescue Journal*, 1997.

42. Macko, Steve, ERRI Risk Analyst, Emergency Room Doctors Prepare for Terrorist Chem-Bio Attacks, ERRI Daily Intelligence Report — ERRI Risk Management Services, August 24, 1997.

43. ATF, Bomb threats and physical security planning.

44. Bruno, Hal, Fire politics: a wake-up call for America's firefighters, *Firehouse*, December 1997.

45. Kinerney, Butch, Ed, Maryland Emergency Management Agency (MEMA) Coordinator Newsletter. November, December, January, 1998, 1999.

46. Letter from Battalion Chief Yasuhiro Ohtsu, Special Incidents Section, Fire Suppression Division, Tokyo Fire Department, July 30, 1997.

47. Karter, Michael J., Jr., Report 1997 fire loss in the United States, *NFPA Journal*, September/October 1998.

48. Grant, Rebecca, Khobar Towers, *Air Force*, June 1998.

49. NRC Radiological Glossary, www.nrc.gov.

50. Macy, Robert, Nellis Team ready to respond to nuclear terrorism, Associated Press, *Las Vegas Review Journal*, August 21,1997.

51. SBCCOM press release, Two army commands merge to combine soldier, biological and chemical expertise to protect U.S. troops, www.cbdcom.apgea.army.mil, October 1, 1998.

52. International Association of Firefighters (IAFF), *Training for Hazardous Materials Response, Radiation, Student Text,*1993.

53. CSEPP Chemical Awareness Course, CA101-FEMA.

54. Health Canada, MSDS-Infectious Substances, www.hc-sc.gc.ca, March 12,1998.

55. Scott, David, Facing our worst nightmare, *NFPA Journal*, May/June 1997.

56. Downey, Ray, Chief Rescue Services, The Oklahoma City Terrorist Bombing, FDNY, January 30, 1998.

57. Stube, Peter M., Incidents involving weapons of mass destruction, *Fire Engineering*, November 1998.

58. U.S. Army Program Manager for Chemical Demilitarization, Maryland Hospital Provider Course, CSEPP Program, Student Manual, May 1996. © 2000 by CRC Press LLC.

59. Case Study: Sarin Poisoning of Subway Passengers in Tokyo, Japan, in March 1995, www.nbc-med.org, January 30, 1998.

60. Excite News, Woman held in Los Angeles in alleged cyanide plot, nt.excite.com/news, March 24, 1998.

61. Pennsylvania Fireman, Woman Arrested in Cyanide Scare, by Minerva Canto, Associated Press, September 1998.

62. Massie, Lee, Paper, acetylcholinesterase, and organophosphate poisoning, March 3, 1998.

63. Franz, David R., Defense against toxic weapons, www.nbc-med.org, July 10, 1997.

64. ABC News.com, The prosecution's timeline, www.abcnews.aol.com, January 29, 1998.

65. Landskroner, Lawrence Corporate irresponsibility in the aftermath of Bhopal, www.4you.com, May 19, 1997.

66. Milnet:Mirror, Patterns of global terrorism, www.milnet.com, 1996.

67. The Center for National Security Studies, The FBI Domestic Counter-Terrorism Program, www.interlog.com, April 26, 1995.

68. Treatment of Chemical Agent Casualties and Conventional Military Chemical Injuries, Departments of the Army, Navy, Air Force, and Commandant, Marine Corps, www.nbc-med.org, July 10, 1997.

69. The Ashes of Waco, The Congressional Hearing Statement of Dick J. Reaus to the Congressional Waco Hearing, July 19, 1995.

70. ABC News.com, Right wing rage over Ruby Ridge.

71. Bovard, James, Ruby Ridge: the justice report, *The Wall Street Journal*, June 30, 1995.

72. The Matsumoto Incident, www.capital.net, May 6, 1997.

73. Arizona derailment linked to sabotage: 1 dead, 100 injured. *The Detroit News*, October 10, 1995.

74. National Abortion Federation, 8 butyric acid attacks at abortion clinics in Florida, May 21, 1998.

75. Gay & Lesbian Alliance Against Defamation, Gay bar and abortion clinic bombing attacks linked, June 5, 1997.

76. BBC News, World: America's history of attacks on U.S. personnel, www.BBC.co.uk.

77. Fleeman, Michael, AP headlines, real-life terror scares Hollywood, Yahoo News, August 8, 1998.

78. ABC News.com, Deadly plastic, www.abcnews.com, August 24, 1998.

79. BBC News, World: Africa U.S. embassies hit in Africa blasts, news.bbc.co.uk, August 24, 1998.

80. King, Shelly and King, Charles G., Fire-A terrorist weapon, an analysis of the MOVE confrontation as a terrorist attack, *Fire Engineering,* October 1986. © 2000 by CRC Press LLC.

81. NFPA Fact Sheet on Church Fires in the U.S., www.dps.state.la, September 26, 1998.

82. Lititz Mutual Insurance Companies, Arson Facts in America, United States Fire Administration, FEMA, September 26, 1998.

83. History of biological warfare and current threat, www.nbc-med.org, July 10, 1997.

84. Anthrax: frequently asked questions, www.cdc.gov, February 25, 1998.

85. Neifert, Alex, Case Study: Sverdlousk Anthrax Outbreak of 1979, Camber Corporation.

86. What is plague? www.cdc.gov.

87. Fact sheet plague, www.cdc.gov.

88. Salmonella and food safety, fsissalmonella.Html@ifse.tamu.edu.

89. Presidential Advisory Committee Interim Report, Chemical & Biological Weapons, www.gwvi.gov, March 14, 1997.

90. *BAD BUG BOOK*, Foodborne Pathogenic Microorganisms and Natural Toxins Handbook, Salmonella.SPP.

91. Ebola virus hemorrhagic fever: general information, www.cdc.gov, September 11, 1997.

92. Botulism, food & water borne bacterial diseases, www.cdc.gov, March 9, 1995.

93. The poor man's nukes, *Air Force,* March 1998.

94. Medical Management of Biological Casualties Handbook, U.S. Army Medical Research Institute of Infectious Diseases, Fort Dietrick, Maryland, August 1996, Second Edition, www.nbc-med.org, July 10, 1997.

95. Israelsen, Brent, Sarin spill confined to chemical depot, *Salt Lake Tribune,* September 10, 1998.

96. CNN News, Bomb found at Atlanta nightclub, injures 5; second bomb found near-by, January 30, 1998.

97. Associated Press, Anthrax note evacuates Kansas office, *Pennsylvania Fireman.*

98. Chief Mario H. Trevino, Responder roulette, *Fire Chief,* June 1998.

99. DefenseLink, Weapons of mass destruction response team locations announced, www.defenselink.mil, October 1, 1998.

100. Domestic Preparedness Fact Sheets: M29 Simulator, Detector Tickets Chemical Agent; Blister Agent; M18AZ, Chemical Agent Detector Kit, M8 Paper, Chemical Agent Detector, M9 Chemical Agent Detector Kit, M256A1, Chemical Agent Detector Kit, M34 Sampling Kit, www.cbdcom.apgea.army, April 13, 1998.

101. Conventional and Nuclear Weapons–Energy Production and Atomic Physics. 140.139.42.105.

102. Burke, Robert, *Hazardous Materials Chemistry for Emergency Responders*, CRC/Lewis Publishers, January 1997.

103. Nuclear, Biological, and Chemical Weapons Effects, Field Manual FM8-10-7, www.nbc-med.org.

104. Radioactivity: historical figures, www.gene.com. © 2000 by CRC Press LLC.

105. A, B, C's of Nuclear Science, user88.161.gov.

106. Radiation and Health: Key Facts, www.nei.org, May 6, 1998.

107. Strengthening the Fire and Emergency Response to Terrorism, Presentation Information and Summaries, IAFC/FEMA First Worldwide Conference, November 6–9, 1995.

108. Generation next: CB protective firefighter turnout. www.Firehouse.com.

109. NIOSH emergency response cards, www.bt.cdc.gov.

110. Collapse of the World Trade Center, www.civil.usyd.edu.au.

111. Germ warfare: the hall of shame, http://home.earthlink.net.

112. "Pen" detects peroxide-based explosives, www.rsc.org.

113. Spore kill tests at Dugway Proving Ground, www.deconsolutions.com.

114. Media's initial reports riddled with misinformation, www.usatoday.com.

115. Companies heighten precautions for incoming mail, www.usatoday.com.

116. Anthrax fears close Senate offices, www.msnbc.com.

117. On the trail of anthrax: a detective story, www.usatoday.com.

118. New anthrax exposures in New York, www.cnn.com.

119. Anthrax incidents create growing sense of anxiety, www.usatoday.com.

120. Managing radiation emergencies, www.orau.gov.

121. A white powder incident and the TravelIIR™ HCl. 9/21/02 SensIR Technologies.

122. BioWarfare agent detection devices, Osborn Scientific Group.

123. Science takes on the mother of Satan, www.worldpress.org.

124. FDA issues instructions on nuclear antidote, www.firehouse.com.

125. Detailed description of the synthesis of acetone peroxide, www.totse.com.

126. Pipe bomb incidents casualties and damage 1996–2004, www.atfonline.gov.

127. Smallpox, anthrax: what could happen, www.cnn.com.

128. Early anthrax detection crucial, www.firehouse.com.

129. FBI investigating discovery of ricin in envelope in South Carolina, www.usatoday.com.

130. FBI offers $100,000 reward in ricin case, www.cnn.com.

131. FBI: trace amounts of ricin found in baby food, www.cnn.com.

Appendix A

Terrorism Web Sites

Agency for Toxic Substances and Disease Registry (ATSDR) Home Page: http://www.atsdr.cdc.gov/atsdrhome.html

ATSDR TOXFAQs DATA Sheets: http://www.atsdr.cdc.gov/toxfaq.html

American Chemistry Council: http://www.americanchemistry.com/s_acc/index.asp

Bureau of Alcohol, Tobacco, and Firearms (ATF): http://atf.treas.gov/

Biological and Toxin Weapons Verification Program: http://www.fas.org/main/content.jsp?formAction=325&projectId=4

Centers for Disease Control and Prevention (CDC): http://www.cdc.gov/

CDC Division of Bacterial and Mycotic Diseases: http://www.cdc.gov/ncidod/dbmd/

Central Intelligence Agency (CIA): http://www.cia.gov/

Chemical Abstract Service (CAS): http://info.CAS.org/

Chemical Agents (ASTDR): http://www.bt.cdc.gov/agent/agentlistchem.asp

Chemical and Biological Defense Information (CBIAC): http://www.cbiac.apgea.army.mil/

Chemical Education Foundation: http://www.chemed.org/

U.S. Chemical Safety and Hazard Investigation Board: http://www.chemsafety.gov/

Chemical Manufacturers Association (CMA) (See American Chemistry Council)

CHEMTREC: http://www.chemtrec.org/Chemtrec/

Coast Guard Home Page: http://www.uscg.mil/USCG.shtm

Counter-Terrorism Page: http://www.terrorism.net/index.php

Counter Terrorism Training & Resources for Law Enforcement: http://www.counterterrorismtraining.gov/tta/fr.html

Defense LINK: http://www.defenselink.mil/

Defense Threat Reduction Agency: http://www.dtra.mil/

Department of Energy: http://www.doe.gov/engine/content.do

Department of Energy, Nevada Operations Office: www.nv.doe.gov/

Department of Homeland Security (DHS): http://www.dhs.gov/dhspublic/index.jsp

Diseases Information: http://www.coppettswood.demon.co.uk/diseases.htm

Drager Home Page: www.draeger-usa.com/

Entoxnet Toxicology Network: www.ace.ace.orst.edu/info/extoxnet/

Federal Bureau of Investigation (FBI): http://www.fbi.gov/homepage.htm

Federal Emergency Management Agency (FEMA): www.fema.gov/

Fort Detrick: http://www.detrick.army.mil/

Hazardous Materials Page: www.hazardousmaterialspage.com

International Policy Institute for Counter-Terrorism: http://www.ict.org.il/

Jane's Home Page: www.janes.com/

Military and Emergency Medicine: http://www.usuhs.mil/mim/mim.html

MSDS Sheets for Biological Agents: http://www.phac-aspc.gc.ca/msds-ftss/index.html#menu

National Response Center: www.nrc.uscg.mil/

National Technical Information Service: www.ntis.gov/

Nuclear Energy Institute: www.nei.org/

Occupational Safety and Health Administration (OSHA) Home Page www.osha.gov/

Office of Justice Programs: www.ojp.usdoj.gov/

Postal Inspection Service: www.usps.gov/websites/depart/inspect/

Preempt Medical Counter-Terrorism: home.eznet.net/~kenberry/

Terrorism Group Profiles: www.web.nps.navy.mil/~library/tgp/tgp-ndx.htm

U.S. Army EOD Tech Detachment: https://www.pica.army.mil/orgs/fsac/eod/techdet/counter.cgi

U.S. Department of Justice: www.usdoj.gov/

U.S. Nuclear Regulatory Commission: www.nrc.gov/

U.S. Secret Service: http://www.treas.gov/usss/index.shtml

Urban Search & Rescue National Institute: www.niusr.org/

Appendix B

U.S. Urban Search & Rescue Response System

US&R TASK FORCES

Arizona

    AZ-TF1 Phoenix Fire Dept.

California

    CA-TF1 LA City Fire Dept.
    CA-TF2 LA County Fire Dept.
    CA-TF3 Menlo Park Protection District
    CA-TF4 Oakland Fire Dept.
    CA-TF5 Orange County Fire Authority
    CA-TF6 Riverside Multi-Agency
    CA TF7 Sacramento Fire Dept.
    CA-TF8 San Diego Fire Dept.

Colorado

    CO-TF1 State of Colorado

Florida

    FL-TF1 Metro-Dade Fire Dept.
    FL-TF2 City of Miami Fire Dept.

Indiana

    IN-TF1 Marion County Fire Dept.

Maryland

    MD-TF1 Montgomery County Fire Dept.

New York
NY-TF1 NYC Office of Emergency Mgmt.

Ohio
OH-TF1 Miami Valley Emergency Mgmt.
OH-TF1 Oversight Miami Valley Fire

Pennsylvania
PA-TF1 Commonwealth of Pennsylvania

Tennessee
TN-TF1 Memphis/Shelby Co. EMA

Utah
UT-TF1 State of Utah

Virginia
VA-TF1 Fairfax Co. Fire & Rescue
VA-TF2 Virginia Beach Fire Dept.

Nevada
NV-TF1 Clark County

New Mexico
NM-TF1 State of New Mexico

Washington
WA-TF1 Puget Sound

Appendix C

Conversion Charts

To convert mg/m³ to PPM, use this formula:

$$PPM = \frac{mg/m^3 \times 24.45}{MW}$$

MW is molecular weight.

To convert PPM to mg/m3 use this formula:

$$Mg/m^3 = \frac{PPM \times MW}{24.5}$$

To compute volatility:

$$V = \frac{16020 \times VP \times MW}{^\circ K}$$

VP = Vapor pressure in mm/Hg

°K = degrees Kelvin. To compute Kelvin use 273 + temperature used for the VP. Most use 20°C so the °K would be 273 + 20 = 293.

Temperature Conversions

Standard Temperature and Pressure (STP) is 32°F, 0°C, and 273° D at 760 mm/Hg.

Radiation Term Conversion Factors

To convert from	To	Multiply by
Curies (Ci)	becquerels (Bq)	3.7×10^{10}
millicuries (mCi)	megabecquerels (MBq)	37
microcuries (μCi)	megabecquerels (MBq)	0.037
millirads (mrad)	milligrays (mGy)	0.01
millirems (mrem)	microsieverts (μSv)	10
milliroentgens (mR)	microcoulombs/kilogram (μC/kg)	0.258
becquerels (Bq)	curies (Ci)	2.7×10^{-11}
megabecquerels (MBq)	millicuries (mCi)	0.027
megabecquerels (MBq)	microcuries (μCi)	27
milligrays (mGy)	millirads (mrad)	100
microsieverts (μSv)	millirems (mrem)	0.1
microcoulombs/ kilogram (μC/kg)	milliroentgens (mR)	3.88

Common Conversions

0.30480 m = 1 ft

2.54 cm = 1 in

0.4535924 kg = 1 lb

0.06479891 g = 1 gr

0.9463529 L = 1 qt

3600000 J = 1 kW·hr

Psi = mm of Hg × (1.9339 × 10⁻²)

mm of Hg = psi × 51.71

4.448222 N = lbf

1.355818 J = 1 ft·lbf

0.1129848 N/m = 1 lbf/in

14.59390 N/m = 1 lbf/ft

6894.757 Pa = lbf/in²

1.609344 km/h = 1 mph

Appendix D

Bureau of Alcohol, Tobacco, and Firearms

List of Explosive Materials

Pursuant to the provisions of Section 841(d) of Title 18, U.S. Code, and 27 CFR 55.23, the director, Bureau of Alcohol, Tobacco and Firearms, must publish and revise at least annually in the FEDERAL REGISTER, a list of explosives determined to be within the coverage of 18 U.S.C. Chapter 40, Importation, Manufacture, Distribution, and Storage of Explosive Materials. This chapter covers not only explosives but also blasting agents and detonators, all of which are defined as explosive materials in Section 841(c) of Title 18, U.S. Code. Accordingly, the following is the 1997 List of Explosive Materials subject to regulation under 18 U.S.C. Chapter 40, which includes both the list of explosives (including detonators) required to be published in the FEDERAL REGISTER and blasting agents. The list is intended to also include any and all mixtures containing any of the materials on the list. Materials constituting blasting agents are marked by an asterisk. While the list does not mean that it is not within the coverage of the law if it otherwise meets the statutory definitions in Section 841 of Title 18, U.S. Code. Explosive materials are listed alphabetically by their common names followed by chemical names and synonyms in brackets. This revised list supersedes the List of Explosive Materials dated May 9, 1996, FR, Vol, 61 No. 91, and will be effective as of the date of publication in the Federal Register.

List of Explosive Materials

A

Acetylides of heavy metals
Aluminum-containing polymeric propellant

467

Aluminum ophorite explosive
Amatex
Amatol
Ammonal
Ammonium nitrate explosive mixtures (cap sensitive)
Ammonium nitrate explosive mixtures (noncap sensitive)
Ammonium perchlorate explosive mixtures
Ammonium perchlorate composite propellant
Ammonium picrate [picrate of ammonia, Explosive D]
Ammonium salt lattice with isomorphously substituted inorganic salts
*ANFO [ammonium nitrate-fuel oil]
Aromatic nitro-compound explosive mixtures
Azide explosives

B

Baronol
Baratol
BEAF [1,2-bis (2,2-difluoro-2-nitoracetoxyethane)]
Black powder
Black powder-based explosive mixtures*
Blasting caps
Blasting gelatin
Blasting powder
BTNEC [bis (trinitroethyl) carbonate]
BTNEN [bis (trinitroethyl) nitramine]
BTTN [1,2,4 butanetriol trinitrate]
Bulk salutes
Butyl tetyl

C

Calcium nitrate explosive mixture
Cellulose hexanitrate explosive mixture
Chlorate explosive mixture
Composition A and variations
Composition B and variations
Composition C and variations
Copper acetylide
Cyanuric triazide

* Blasting agents, nitro-carbo-nitrates, including noncap sensitive slurry and water gel explosives.

Cyclotrimethylenetrinitramine [RDX]
Cyclonite [RDX]
Cyclotetramethylenetetranitramine [HMX]

D

DATB [diaminotrinitrobenzene]
DDNP [diazodinitrophenol]
DEGDN [diethyleneglycol dinitrate}
Detonating cord
Detonators
Dimethylol dimethyl methane dinitrate composition
Dinitroethyleneurea
Dinitroglycerine [glycerol dinitrate]
Dinitrophenol
Dinitrophenolates
Dinitrophenyl hydrazine
Dinitroresorcinol
Dinitrotoluene-sodium nitrate explosive mixtures
DIPAM [dipicramide; diaminohexanitrobiphenyl]
Dipicryl sulfone
Dipicrylamine
Display fireworks
DNPA [2,2-dinitropropyl acrylate]
DNPD [dinitropentanol nitrile]
Dynamite

E

EDDN [ethylene diamine dinitrate]
EDNA [ethylenedinitramine]
Ednatol
EDNP [ethyl 4,4-dinitropentanoate]
EGDN [ethylene glycol dinitrate]
Erythritol tetranitrate explosives
Esters of nitro-substituted alcohols
EGDN [ethylene glycol dinitrate]
Ethyl-tetryl
Explosive conitrates
Explosive gelatins
Explosive liquids

Explosive mixtures containing oxygen-releasing inorganic salts and hy-
  drocarbons
Explosive mixtures containing oxygen-releasing inorganic salts and nitro
  bodies
Explosive mixtures containing oxygen-releasing inorganic salts and water
  insoluble fuels
Explosive mixtures containing oxygen-releasing inorganic salts and water
  soluble fuels
Explosive mixtures containing sensitized nitromethane
Explosive mixtures containing tetranitromethane (nitroform)
Explosive nitro compounds of aromatic hydrocarbons
Explosive organic nitrate mixtures
Explosive powders

F

Flash powder
Fulminate of mercury
Fulminate of silver
Fulminating gold
Fulminating mercury
Fulminating platinum
Fulminating silver

G

Gelatinized nitrocellulose
Gem-dinitro aliphatic explosive mixtures
Guanyl nitrosamino guanyl tetrazene
Guanyl nitrosamino guanylidene hydrazine
Guncotton

H

Heavy metal azides
Hexanite
Hexanitrodiphenylamine
Hexanitrostilbene
Hexogen (RDX)
Hexogene or octogene and a nitrated N-methylaniline
Hexolites
HMTD [hexamethylenetriperoxidediamine]

HMX [cyclo-1,3,5,7-tetramethylene 2,4,6,8-tetranitramine; Octogen]
Hydrazinium nitrate/hydrazine/aluminum explosive system
Hydrazoic acid

I

Igniter cord
Igniters
Initiating tube systems

K

KDNBF [potassium dinitrobenzofuroxane]

L

Lead azide
Lead mannite
Lead mononitroresorcinate
Lead picrate
Lead salts, explosive
Lead styphnate [styphnate of lead trinitroresorcinate]
Liquid nitrated polyol and trimethylolethane
Liquid oxygen explosives

M

Magnesium ophorite explosives
Mannitol hexanitrate
MDNP [methyl 4,4-dinitropentanoate]
MEAN [monoethanolamine nitrate]
Mercuric fulminate
Mercury oxalate
Mercury tartrate
Metriol trinitrate
Minol-2 [40% TNT, 40% ammonium nitrate, 20% aluminum]
MMAN [monomethylamine nitrate]; methylamine nitrate
Mononitrotoluene-nitroglycerin mixture
Monopropellants

N

NIBTN [nitroisobutametriol trinitrate]
Nitrate explosive mixtures
Nitrate sensitized with gelled nitroparaffin
Nitrated carbohydrate explosive
Nitrated glucoside explosive
Nitrated polyhydric alcohol explosives
Nitric acid and a nitro aromatic compound explosive
Nitric acid and carboxylic fuel explosive
Nitric acid explosive mixtures
Nitro aromatic explosive mixtures
Nitro compounds of furane explosive mixtures
Nitrocellulose explosive
Nitroderivative of urea explosive mixture
Nitrogelatin explosive
Nitrogen trichloride
Nitrogen tri-iodide
Nitroglycerin [NG,RNG, nitro glyceryltrinitrate, trinitroglycerine]
Nitroglycide
Nitroglycol (ethylene glycol dinitrate, EGDN)
Nitroguanidine explosives
Nitronium perchlorate propellant mixtures
Nitroparaffins Explosive Grade and ammonium nitrate mixtures
Nitrostarch
Nitro-substituted carboxylic acids
Nitrodurea

O

Octogen [HMX]
Octol [75 percent HMX, 25 percent TNT]
Organic amine nitrates
Organic nitramines

P

PBX [RDX and plasticizer]
Pellet powder
Penthrinite composition
Pentolite
Perchlorate explosive mixtures

Peroxide-based explosive mixtures
PETN [nitropentaerythrite, pentaerythrite tetranitrate, pentaerythritol
    tetranitrate]
Picramic acid and its salts
Picramide
Picrate explosives
Picrate of potassium explosive mixtures
Picratol
Picric acid (manufactured as an explosive)
Picryl chloride
Picryl fluoride
PLX [95% nitromethane,5% ethylenediamine]
Polynitro aliphatic compounds
Polyolpolynitrate-nitrocellulose explosive gels
Potassium chlorate and lead sulfocyanate explosive
Potassium nitrate explosive mixtures
Potassium nitroaminotetrazole
Pyrotechnic compositions
PYX (2,6-bis(picrylamino))-3,5-dinitropyridine

R

RDX [cyclonite, hexogen, T4, cyclo-1,3,5,-trimethylene-2,4,6,-trimitra-
    mine; hexahydro-1,3,5-trinitro-S-triazine]

S

Safety fuse
Salts of organic amino sulfonic acid explosive mixture
Salutes, (buld)
Silver acetylide
Silver azide
Silver fulminate
Silver oxalate explosive mixtures
Silver styphnate
Silver tartrate explosive mixtures
Silver tetrazene
Slurried explosive mixtures of water, inorganic salt, gelling agent, fuel
    and sensitizer (cap sensitive)
Smokeless powder
Sodatol
Sodium amatol

Sodium azide explosive mixture
Sodium dinitro-ortho-cresolate
Sodium nitrate-potassium nitrate explosive mixture
Sodium picramate
Special fireworks
Squibs
Styphnic acid explosives

T

Tacot [tetranitro-2,3,5,6-dibenzo-1,3a,4,6a tetrazapentalene]
TATB [triaminotrinitrobenzene]
TATP [triacetonetriperoxide]
TEGDN [triethylene glycol dinitrate]
Tetranitrocarbazole
Tetrazene [tetracene, tetrazine, 1(5-tetrazoly)-4-guanyl tetrazene hydrate]
Tetrazole explosives
Tetryl [2,4,6 tetranitro-N-methylaniline]
Tetrytol
Thickened inorganic oxidizer salt slurried explosive mixture
TMETN [trimethylolethane trinitrate]
TNEF [trinitroethyl formal]
TNEOC [trinitroethylorthocarbonate]
TNEOF [trinitroethylorthoformate]
TNT [trinitrotoluene, trotyl, trilite, trito]
Torpex
Tridite
Trimethylol ethyl methane trinitrate composition
Trimethylolthane trinitrate-nitrocellulose
Trimonite
Trinitroanisole
Trinitrobenzene
Trinitrobenzoric acid
Trinitrocresol
Trinitro-meta-cresol
Trinitronaphthalene
Trinitrophenetol
Trinitrophloroglucinol
Trinitroresorcinol
Tritonal

U

Urea nitrate

W

Water-bearing explosives having salts of oxidizing acids and nitrogen
   bases, sulfates, or sulfamates (cap sensitive)
Water-in-oil emulsion explosive compositions

X

Xanthamonas hydrophilic colloid explosive mixture

FOR FURTHER INFORMATION CONTACT: Wathenia Clark; Program
Manager Firearms and Explosives Operations Branch; Bureau of Alcohol,
Tobacco and Firearms; 650 Massachusetts Avenue, NW; Washington, DC
20226; 202-927-8310.
   This file was last modified on December 3, 2004.

Appendix E

Regulations on the Transfer or Receipt of Select Agents

Effective April 15, 1997, the shipment and receipt of certain microorganisms and toxins (see Appendix A) are regulated as part of the Anti-Terrorism and Effective Death Penalty Act of 1996. The following is a summary of the regulatory requirements.

Registration

The regulation requires facilities that ship or receive these agents to be registered with a registration entity authorized by the secretary of the Department of Health and Human Services. The registration process includes:

- Sufficient information to demonstrate that the facility is capable of handling agents at Biosafety Level (BSL) 2, 3, or 4, depending on the agent
- Inspection of the facility
- Payment of periodic registration fees
- Issuance of a unique registration number
- Follow-up inspections to ensure that the facility continues to meet approved standards and record-keeping requirements

The requirements for BSL-2, 3, and 4 operations are contained in the CDC/NIH publication *Biosafety in Microbiology and Biomedical Laboratories*, Third Edition, May 1993.

CDC Form EA-101

The regulation also requires that CDC Form EA-101 is completed prior to the transfer of these agents. The form contains the following information:

- Name of the requester and requesting facility
- Name of the transferor and transferring facility
- Names of responsible facility officials for both the transferor and requester
- The requesting facility's registration number
- The transferring facility's registration number
- The name of the agent(s) being shipped
- The proposed use of the agent(s)
- The quantity of agent(s) being shipped

The facility receiving the material must acknowledge receipt of the agent telephonically or electronically within 36 hours and provide a completed paper copy or facsimile transmission of receipt within 3 days to the transferring facility.

Disposal

Upon termination of the use of the agent, all cultures and stocks of it must be:

- Securely stored in accordance with prudent laboratory practices,
- Transferred to another registered facility, or
- Destroyed on site by autoclaving, incineration, or another recognized sterilization or neutralization process.

Exemptions

Agents otherwise covered under these regulations are exempt if:

- The agent is part of clinical specimen intended for diagnostic, reference, or verification purposes. The agents must be disposed of in accordance with one of the above methods after diagnostic, reference, or verification procedures have been completed.
- The agent is a toxin having an LD50 for vertebrates of more than 100 nanograms per kilogram of body weight and is used for legitimate medical purpose or biomedical research or is one of the listed toxins and has been inactivated for use as a vaccine or detoxified for use in biomedical research procedures.
- Clinical laboratories certified under the Clinical Laboratory Improvement Amendments (CLIA) of 1988, that utilize agents for diagnostic,

reference, verification, or proficiency testing purposes. Agents must be disposed of as mentioned above.

- The agent is an exempt strain specified in Appendix A and/or on CDC Form EA-101.

Facilities that are not CLIA but are transferring or receiving select agents to or from a CLIA laboratory must be registered with an authorized registration entity, complete CDC EA Form EA-101, properly acknowledge receipt of the agent, and dispose of the agent(s) using one of the methods mentioned above.

Additional exemptions for otherwise covered strains will be considered when CDC reviews and updates the list of agents. Individuals seeking additions to the list of exemptions should submit a request to CDC that specifies the agent or strain to be exempt and explain why such an exemption should be granted. Future changes to the list of exemptions will be published in the Federal Register.

Penalties

Penalties for violation of the regulations are as follows:

- Individuals are subject to a fine of no more than $250,000 or 1 year in jail or both.
- Organizations are subject to a fine of no more than $500,000 per event.
- A false, fictitious, or fraudulent statement or representation on the government forms required to register a facility or to transfer agents is subject to a fine or imprisonment of not more than 5 years, or both for an individual. An organization is subject only to a fine.

Agents covered by the regulation

Viruses

1. Crimean-Congo hemorrhagic fever virus
2. Eastern Equine Encephalitis virus
3. Ebola viruses
4. Equine morbillivirus
5. Lassa fever virus

Transfer of Select Agents

1. Genetically modified microorganisms or genetic elements from organisms in Appendix A, shown to produce or encode for a factor associated with a disease
2. Genetically modified microorganisms or genetic elements that contain nucleic acid sequences coding for any of the toxins listed in this Appendix or their toxic subunits

Other Restrictions

The deliberate transfer of a drug resistance trait to microorganisms listed in this Appendix that are not known to acquire the trait naturally is prohibited by *NIH Guidelines for Research Involving Recombinant DNA Molecules*, if such acquisition could compromise the use of the drug to control these disease agents in humans or veterinary medicine.

Additional Exemptions

1. Products subject to regulation under the Federal Insecticide, Fungicide and Rodenticide Act (7 U.S.C. 136 et seq.) and the Toxic Substances Control Act (15 U.S.C. 2601 et seq.) are exempt.
2. Additional exemptions for otherwise covered strains will be considered when CDC reviews and updates the list of select agents in this Appendix. Individuals seeking an exemption should submit a request to CDC that specifies the agent or strain to be exempted and explains why such an exemption should be granted.

Appendix F

Chronological Listing of UNABOMBER Targets 1978–1995 (Source: FBI Files)

1. Northwestern University, Evanston, Illinois, May 25, 1978. A package was found in the Engineering Department parking lot at the Chicago Circle Campus of the University of Illinois. The package was addressed to an engineering professor at Rensselaer Polytechnic Institute in Troy, New York. The package had a return address of a professor at Northwestern's Technological Institute. The package was returned to the addressor who turned it over to the Northwestern University Police Department because he had not sent the package. On May 26, 1978, the parcel was opened by a police officer, who suffered minor injuries when the bomb detonated.

2. Northwestern University, Evanston, Illinois, May 9, 1979. A disguised explosive device, which had been left in a common area in the University's Technological Institute, slightly injured a graduate student on May 9, 1979, when he attempted to open the box and it exploded.

3. Chicago, Illinois, November 15, 1979. An explosive device disguised as a parcel was mailed from Chicago for delivery to an unknown location. The bomb detonated in the cargo compartment of an airplane, forcing it to make an emergency landing at Dulles Airport. Twelve individuals were treated for smoke inhalation. The explosion destroyed the wrapping to such an extent that the addressee could not be determined.

4. Chicago, Illinois, June 10, 1980. A bomb disguised as a parcel postmarked June 8, 1980, was mailed to an airline executive at his home in Lake Forest, Illinois. The airline executive was injured in the explosion.

5. University of Utah, Salt Lake City, Utah, October 8, 1981. An explosive device was found in the hall of a classroom building and rendered safe by bomb squad personnel.

481

6. Vanderbilt University, Nashville, Tennessee, May 5, 1982. A wooden box containing a pipe bomb detonated on May 5, 1982, when opened by a secretary in the Computer Science Department. The secretary suffered minor injuries. The package was initially mailed from Provo, Utah, on April 23, 1982, to Pennsylvania State University, and then forwarded to Vanderbilt.

7. University of California, Berkeley, July 2, 1982. A small metal pipe bomb was placed in a coffee break room of Cory Hall at the University's Berkeley campus. A professor of electrical engineering and computer science was injured when he picked up the device.

8. Auburn, Washington, May 8, 1985. A parcel bomb was mailed on May 8, 1985, to the Boeing Company, Fabrication Division. On June 13, 1985, the explosive device was discovered when employees opened it. The device was rendered safe by bomb squad personnel without injury.

9. University of California, Berkeley, May 15, 1985. A bomb detonated in a computer room at Cory Hall on the Berkeley campus. A graduate student in electrical engineering lost partial vision in his left eye and four fingers from his right hand. The device was believed to have been placed in the room several days prior to detonation.

10. Ann Arbor, Michigan, November 15, 1985. A textbook-size package was mailed to the home of a University of Michigan professor in Ann Arbor, Michigan, from Salt Lake City. On November 15, 1985, a research assistant suffered injuries when he opened the package. The professor was a few feet away but was not injured.

11. Sacramento, California, December 11, 1985. Hugh Scrutton was killed outside his computer rental store when he picked up a device disguised as a road hazard left near the rear entrance to the building. Metal shrapnel from the blast ripped through Scrutton's chest and penetrated his heart.

12. Salt Lake City, Utah, February 20, 1987. An explosive device disguised as a road hazard was left at the rear entrance to CAAMs, Inc. (computer store). The bomb exploded and injured the owner when he attempted to pick up the device.

13. Tiburon, California, June 22, 1993. A well-known geneticist received a parcel postmarked June 18, 1993, at his residence. The doctor attempted to open the package, at which time it exploded, severely injuring him. It was determined that the parcel was mailed from Sacramento, California.

14. Yale University, New Haven, Connecticut, June 24, 1993. A professor and computer scientist at Yale University attempted to open a parcel, which he had received at his office. This parcel exploded, severely

injuring him. It was determined that the parcel was mailed from Sacramento, California, on June 18, 1993.

15. North Caldwell, New Jersey, December 10, 1994. Thomas Mosser, a New York City advertising executive, was killed in his home when he opened a package addressed to him. The package was mailed from the San Francisco area and bore the return address of a fictitious professor at San Francisco State University.

16. Sacramento, California, April 24, 1995. Gilbert Murray, president of the California Forestry Association, was killed at his office when he opened a package addressed to a person who formerly worked at that location. The package had been mailed apparently at the same time as letters sent by the bomber to the New York Times and to the Yale University professor who received a bomb on June 4, 1993.

Appendix G

Tools Needed for Bomb or Explosives Scene Investigation Safety

Biohazard materials (i.e., bags, tags, labels)
First-aid kit
Footwear, safety (i.e., protective shoes/boots)
Glasses, safety
Gloves, heavy and disposable (e.g., surgical, latex)
Helmets, safety/hard hats
Kneepads
Outerwear, protective (e.g., disposable suits, weather gear)
Personnel support items (e.g., food, water, hygiene items, shelter)
Reflective tape
Respiratory equipment (e.g., particle masks, breathing equipment)

General Crime Scene Tools

Barrier tape/perimeter rope
Batteries
Binoculars
Communications equipment (e.g., telephone, two-way radio)
Evidence collection kits (e.g., latent print, bodily fluid, impression, took mark, trace evidence)
Flares
Flashlights
Generators
Hand knives, utility
Lighting, auxiliary
Hand tools (e.g., screwdrivers, crowbars, hammers)

Tarpstents
Thermometer
Trashcans, large
Tweezers/forceps

Scene Documentation

Computer and computer-aided design (CAD) program
Consent-to-search forms
Drawing equipment (e.g., sketchbooks, pencils)
Logs (e.g., evidence recovery, photo)
Measuring equipment (e.g., forensic mapping station, tape measure, tape
  wheel)
Photographic equipment (e.g., 35mm camera, Polaroid camera, video-
  camera, digital camera, film, lenses, tripods)
Tape recorder and cassettes
Writing equipment (e.g., notebooks, pens, permanent markers).

Evidence Collection

Bags, new (e.g., sealable, nylon)
Boxes, corrugated/fiberboard
Brushes and brooms
Cans, new (e.g., unlined)
Evidence flags/cones
Evidence placards
Evidence tags
Evidence sealing tape
Gloves (i.e., disposable cotton, disposable latex)
Grid markers
Heat sealer
Magnets
Outerwear, protective (e.g., disposable suits, shoe covers)
Rakes, spades, and shovels
Sifters/screens
Swabbing kits
Trowels
Vacuum

Specialized Equipment

Aerial survey/photography equipment (e.g., helicopter)
Chemical test kits and vapor detectors
Construction equipment, heavy
Extrication/recovery equipment
GPS (global positioning system) equipment
Ladders
Trace explosives detectors (e.g., sniffers) or detection canines

Source: FBI.

Appendix H

List of Resource Organizations for Bomb and Explosives Incidents

Bureau of Alcohol, Tobacco and Firearms

Headquarters Enforcement Operations Center
888-ATF-BOMB
202-927-8050
http://www.atf.treas.gov

Arson and Explosives National Repository
800-461-8841
202-927-7930

Arson and Explosives Programs Division
292-927-7930

National Laboratory
301-762-9800

Chemical Transportation Emergency Center (CHEMTREC)

800-262-8200 (24-hour)
http://www.chemtrec.org/Chemtrec/

United States Coast Guard

National Response Center
800-424-8802 (24-hour)
http://www.nrc.uscg.mil/

Federal Bureau of Investigation

Bomb Data Center (pre-blast issues)
202-324-2696
http://www.fbi.gov

Explosives Unit (post-blast issues)
202-324-4341

Federal Emergency Management Agency (FEMA)

U.S. Fire Administration
202-447-1000
http://www.usfa.fema.gov/

Institute of Makers of Explosives

202-429-9280
http://www.ime.org/site/homepage.asp?IdSection=12&memb=1

International Association of Arson Investigators

314-739-4224
http://www.firearson.com/

International Association of Bomb Technicians and Investigators

941-353-6843
http://www.iabti.org/

International Society of Explosives Engineers

440-349-4004
http://www.isee.org

National Center for Forensic Science

407-823-6469
http://www.ncfs.ucf.edu

National Fire Protection Association

617-770-3000
http://www.nfpa.org

National Institute of Standards and Technology

Building and Fire Research Laboratory
310-975-6850
http://www.bfrl.nist.gov

Royal Canadian Mounted Police

Canadian Bomb Data Center
613-993-7889
http://www.rcmp-frc.gc.ca/

U.S. Chemical Safety and Hazard Investigation Board

202-261-7600
http://www.chemsafety.gov

U.S. Postal Inspection Service
Forensic/Technical Services Division
703-406-7100
http://www.usps.gov/websites/depart/inspect/

Index

A

ABC-M18A2 Chemical Agent Detector Kit, 289

Abortion clinic attacks, 1, 42–45, 184, 187, 249

Abrin, 136

ABthrax, for anthrax exposure, 143

AC. *See* Hydrogen cyanide

Academy of Counter-Terrorist Education, Louisiana State University

Acetone, 212–213, 296, 327

Acetylcholinesterase inhibition, 59

Acetylene gas, ignition temperature, 253

AChe. *See* Cholinesterase

Aconitine, 136

Aeromonas, 168

Afghanistan, 25

African Americans, terrorism against, 29

Agency for Toxic Substances and Disease Registry, 391–392, 461

Agent characteristics for monitoring, 287–290

Agent detection, sensitivity, 278

Agent T, 102–103. *See also* Sulfur mustard structure, 103

Agricultural spray planes, 106

AHF. *See* Argentine hemorrhagic fever

Air monitoring during terrorist incidents, 295–296

al Qaeda, 1–6, 11–12, 18, 23, 30–33, 37, 45–50, 53–54, 126–127, 181–182, 190-191, 196, 198, 201, 204, 209, 216, 261, 336–344, 351–356, 374, 378, 393, 429, 489, 491

ALF. *See* Animal Liberation Front

Alfred P. Murrah Federal Building, 1, 26, 36–41, 188, 378
  lessons learned, 351

Alpha-conotoxin, 136

Alpha particle, 226–227, 244
  radiological agents emitting, 314

Alpha-tityustoxin, 136

American Chemistry Council, 461

Ammonia, 327–328

Ammonium nitrate, 32, 204, 209–210

Amtrak Sunset Limited, derailment, 41

Anaheim, California, Disneyland, threat against, 58–59

Anatoxin-A, 136

Anchorage, Alaska, hazmat team members, 334

Animal Liberation Front, 30

Animal research facility attacks, 30, 249

Animal rights movement, 30

Animal venoms, 169–170

Anniston chemical activity, 21–22

Anthrax, 26, 50–51, 131–134, 137–144, 345
  derivation of word, 140

Anthrax field test update, 297–298

Anthrax vaccine, 142

APD 2000 chemical agent monitor, 272–273

Approaching scene, 338–345

Arenaviridae, 162

Argentine hemorrhagic fever, 162–163

Argonne National Laboratories, biochip technology development, 297

Arizona, Urban Search & Rescue Response System Task Force, 463

Army of God, 182, 186

Army Technical Escort Unit Aberdeen Proving Ground, Maryland, 377

3m